Statecraft and Political Economy on the Taiwan Frontier 1600–1800

JOHN ROBERT SHEPHERD

Statecraft and Political Economy on the Taiwan Frontier 1600–1800

STANFORD UNIVERSITY PRESS
STANFORD, CALIFORNIA 1993

Stanford University Press
Stanford, California

CIP data are at the end of the book

Published with the assistance of
the Chiang Ching-kuo Foundation for
International Scholarly Exchange
and Citibank.

For my parents,
Donald E. Shepherd
Joan M. Brown Shepherd

Acknowledgments

IN THE PREPARATION of this study, both in its present form and as a doctoral dissertation, I have enjoyed the help of many persons and institutions and am glad to have the opportunity to acknowledge them here.

My greatest intellectual debt is to my dissertation advisers, who have set such high standards in their own work for the social-scientific study of China. I also thank them for their continuing support. The dissertation benefited not only from G. W. Skinner's critical reading and editorial comments but from his conceptualization of regional systems analysis. Arthur Wolf's pathbreaking work in the household registers and cadastres of Hai-shan has been a continuing source of inspiration. I have enjoyed many conversations with Ramon Myers and appreciate his constant willingness to engage in discussion of the issues of this study.

In preparation of the revision, conversations with or comments from Harry Lamley, Myron Cohen, John Wills, Susan Naquin, David Ownby, and James Lee have helped me refine my arguments. I appreciate their giving generously of their time. At various points over what is now more than a decade, I have also benefited from the help or encouragement of Ch'en Yung-fa, Stevan Harrell, Emily Martin, Steven Sangren, Shih Chin, Shih Li Lin, James L. Watson, Rubie Watson, Bin Wong, and many others.

In 1988 I was an IUP-CSSC Language and Research Fellow at the Inter-University Program in Taipei, and I thank that program, Director James Dew, and Executive Secretary Lyman Van Slyke for their support. During 1989 I was an ACLS-SSRC fellow in Chinese studies, and in 1990–91 an Ahmanson fellow at the California Institute of Technology. Preparation of the maps was underwritten by grants from the California Institute of Technology and the University of Virginia.

During the year of revision in Taipei, I enjoyed the hospitality of the Institute of Ethnology, Academia Sinica, and thank its scholars, staff, and director, Chuang Ying-chang. I also wish to record my gratitude to the Taiwan History Field Research Office and particularly to Weng Chia-yin, Chang Su-chuan, and Li Chi-hua.

Perhaps my greatest debt is to the Chinese, Japanese, and Taiwanese scholars who have preceded me in the study of Taiwan's history. First among these must be the editors of the *T'ai-wan wen hsien ts'ung k'an* series. I am grateful for the assistance of the staffs of the East Asian Collection of the Hoover Institution, the Taiwan Provincial Library, the library of the Institute of Ethnology, Academia Sinica, and the Harvard-Yenching Library.

My warmest thanks go to the community of the Center for East Asian Studies at Stanford during my years as a graduate student. The National Institute of Mental Health sponsored my initial fieldwork in Taiwan and one year of writing. I owe many thanks to Jerome A. Cohen and the East Asian Legal Studies Program at the Harvard Law School, which hosted me while I held an SSRC grant. The assistance of my parents, who have frequently helped out with emergency loans, is greatly appreciated.

In Taiwan in 1975 and 1976, when this study first began to take shape, Huang Ta-chou sponsored my research status. Wang Shih-ch'ing generously provided me with introductions in San-hsia and Shu-lin. Liu Hsiu-yüan provided me with expert fieldwork assistance and the hospitality of herself and her family.

I especially thank Ingrid Ritucci, who entered the manuscript into a word-processing system, and other friends at Lord, Day & Lord for their support. Muriel Bell and John Ziemer have expertly guided me through the editorial process.

J.R.S.

Contents

Tables, Maps, and Figures

TABLES

MAPS

FIGURES

Dates, Measures, and Usages

DATES

Taiwan ruled by:

Dutch, 1624–61
Chengs, 1661–83
Ch'ing, 1683–1895

Ch'ing Reign Periods: Abbreviations and Equivalents

SC	1–18	Shun-chih	1644–61
KH	1–61	K'ang-hsi	1662–1722
YC	1–13	Yung-cheng	1723–35
CL	1–60	Ch'ien-lung	1736–95
CC	1–25	Chia-ch'ing	1796–1820

Dates given according to the Chinese lunar calendar follow the form: year of reign.lunar month.day. An asterisk next to the month indicates an intercalary month. In converting Chinese dates to the Western calendar, I have assumed the equivalence of years given in the Chinese style to Western years, although year-end dates in the lunar calendar fell in the succeeding Western year.

MEASURES

Currency

1,000 cash	=	1 tael (approx.)
1 tael	=	1 *liang*, a Chinese ounce of silver
10 *ch'ien*	=	1 tael
1 *yüan*	=	0.7 *liang* (approx.)
1 real	=	0.72 taels

Weights

16 *liang*	=	1 *chin* or catty
1 *chin*	=	0.597 kg or 1.3 lb (approx.)
100 chin	=	1 *tan* or picul

Capacity

10 *tou*	=	1 *shih*
1 *shih*	=	103.6 liters or 2.94 bushels (approx.)

Rice: Capacity to Weight

1 *shih* of milled rice = 138.75 catties = 82.81 kg = 182.6 lb

Area

1 *chia*	=	0.96992 hectares or 2.396 acres (approx.)
1 *chia*	=	11.3 *mou* (approx.)

Distance

1 *li*	=	0.576 km or one-third mile (approx.)

NOTES ON USAGE

The Chinese terms and names in the text are rendered in Wade-Giles romanization. Manchu names, unless given in Hummel (1943–44), are romanized from the Chinese readings of the characters.

Postal spellings have been employed in some place-names. T'ai-wan-fu, the prefectural capital of Taiwan during most of the Ch'ing, is referred to throughout by its modern name, Tainan. The county that included Tainan for the period under consideration is referred to as T'ai-wan. Dutch Tayouan (Chinese: Ta-yüan), the site of Zeelandia Castle, is modern An-p'ing; Sakam is modern Tainan; Chu-lo is modern Chia-i; Chu-ch'ien is modern Hsin-chu.

Statecraft and Political Economy on the Taiwan Frontier 1600–1800

CHAPTER ONE

Introduction: The Political Economy of the Taiwan Frontier

BETWEEN THE SIXTEENTH and eighteenth centuries, Taiwan was transformed from a little-known and rarely visited island, inhabited by aborigines, into an outpost of China's agrarian civilization. The expansion of seagoing commerce in the sixteenth and seventeenth centuries eroded Taiwan's isolation, and the island became a political pawn contested by the Chinese state, assorted naval warlords and pirates, and European maritime empires. In 1624 the Dutch East India Company established an entrepôt near Tainan and began to colonize the island. The Dutch pushed out rivals, pacified the aborigines, and recruited Chinese labor to work on rice and sugarcane farms. In 1661, as the new Ch'ing dynasty was tightening its hold on south China, the Ming loyalist Cheng Ch'eng-kung (also known in the West as Koxinga) retreated with his forces to Taiwan and expelled the Dutch. Cheng Ch'eng-kung's heirs remained in power in Taiwan until 1683, when they surrendered to the Ch'ing and Taiwan came under the rule of the Chinese empire.

During the succeeding decades of peace and prosperity in the eighteenth century, tremendous population growth stimulated interregional migrations and the expansion of agricultural settlement throughout the empire. Migrants from China's crowded southeast coast flocked to Taiwan and gradually transformed Taiwan's deer fields into rice and sugarcane farms. To preserve its strategic, revenue, and control interests, the Ch'ing state had to manage the process of frontier settlement and arbitrate relations between immigrants and aborigines.

This is a study of the transformation of Taiwan from aboriginal island to trading colony, from refugee outpost to Chinese prefecture, and particularly of the neglected role of Taiwan's plains aborigines in the island's history. Few Chinese frontiers are as richly documented as Taiwan's, thanks to the island's turbulent political history and strategic significance in the seventeenth century. This unusually detailed knowledge of Taiwan's aboriginal situation allows us to chart the expansion of Chinese settlement and to assess how the policies of successive regimes managed that settlement.

Two misconceptions plague the understanding of Taiwan's early history: the "displacement scenario" and the "neglect hypothesis." Students of East Asian history, whether Western, Chinese, or Japanese, generally assume that the seventeenth- and eighteenth-century immigration of Chinese settlers destroyed most of Taiwan's aborigine societies and forced the survivors to retreat to the mountains. Displacement is invoked to explain the presence of tribes in the central mountains and their supposed absence on the plains. Accompanying this scenario is an exaggeration of the size and rate of growth of Taiwan's Chinese population in these centuries.[1] Some historians adopt these arguments even while reporting the continued existence of sinicized, plains aborigines on Taiwan's western coastal plain, where Chinese settled earliest and in greatest numbers. A few even note that Chinese rented land from pacified aborigines.[2] But few histories attempt to resolve the contradiction between the survival of aborigines and aborigine land rights on the plains and the assumption that they were driven into the mountains.

The work of anthropologists and archaeologists casts additional doubt on the displacement scenario. Raleigh Ferrell's survey of Taiwan aboriginal cultures and languages demonstrates the existence of distinct lowland and highland cultures. Archaeological sites document the presence of aboriginal societies in Taiwan's high mountains hundreds of years before the onset of Chinese migrations.[3] If the tribes of the central mountains were not driven there by the expansion of Chinese agricultural settlement, we have yet to explain what happened to the aboriginal inhabitants of the western coastal plains.

This work shows that the indigenous inhabitants of Taiwan's west coast, rather than being pushed into the mountains, remained on the plains to play a critical role in the history of seventeenth- and eighteenth-century Taiwan. Seventeenth-century Taiwan was successively a Dutch colony, the outpost of a rebel Chinese regime, and a prefecture of the Chinese empire, yet a leading economic sector under all these regimes was an export trade in deer products produced by plains aborigine hunters. Only in the eighteenth century, when economic recovery and population growth on China's southeast coast sent migrants to Taiwan, did Chinese agricultural settlement transform the economy of Taiwan's west coast. But even during this transformation, plains aborigine interests had to be accommodated. This history and the role played by plains aborigines in it are easily forgotten from the perspective of later centuries, when plains aborigines were overwhelmed by the large Han population and pushed to the side of the historical stage.

The failure to appreciate the role of the plains aborigines in Taiwan's history points to a larger failure to understand the political economy of Ch'ing frontier administration both generally and in Taiwan. Taiwan was not a neglected frontier of Ch'ing China, as so many histories claim; on the contrary, it was a strategic periphery that frequently commanded central government attention. From the beginning, the Ch'ing government attempted to limit Chinese migration to Taiwan because it feared the growth of a rebel base on the island and because, in its view, Han settlers were intruders disrupting a satisfactory status quo. The economics of controlling the Taiwan frontier convinced many that the government's interest was best served by preserving the livelihoods of the plains aborigines, including their rights to land, and by enlisting plains aborigine braves in pacification campaigns against rebellious Han settlers as well as other aborigines. But to maintain control over an expanding Chinese population and to finance Taiwan's administration, the central government was forced to manage frontier settlement and land reclamation. This work documents and analyzes the processes of conflict and accommodation by which government, settlers, and plains aborigines achieved a modus vivendi in the seventeenth and eighteenth centuries and laid the foundations of Taiwanese society.

The second common theme in the historiography of Taiwan attributes its corrupt administration and frequent outbreaks of rebellion to Ch'ing neglect.[4] Proponents of the neglect hypothesis have generally failed to distinguish fluctuations in government policy approaches from cycles in central government concern. Most histories focus overwhelmingly on the intense communal strife of the nineteenth century and generalize indiscriminately about the seventeenth and eighteenth centuries. These studies fail both to appreciate the calculated nature of the early quarantine policies and to understand the constraints on Ch'ing policy choices, especially fiscal constraints. Equally fundamental is their failure to enunciate a standard of comparison for measuring the quality of government and the degree of civil disorder in Taiwan. Most studies implicitly judge nineteenth-century Taiwan by twentieth-century standards. If, however, neglect by the central government is to be demonstrated, the appropriate comparisons would be of Taiwan (stage by stage, policy phase by policy phase) to other frontiers of the Chinese empire. My own sense is that as knowledge of these other frontiers grows, Taiwan's society, even in the nineteenth century, will not appear to be exceptionally turbulent or its government exceptionally corrupt.[5] Certainly this study demonstrates that the Ch'ing ruled Taiwan with the same repertoire of policies it applied to other regional societies (see also Chapter 12).

The conjunction of two interacting cycles, one broadly economic and the other political, shaped the evolution of Taiwanese society in the seventeenth and eighteenth centuries. Taiwan in these centuries lay in the orbit of the regional economy of China's southeast coast and its international linkages.[6] The expansion and contraction of the southeastern coastal economy and population alternately stimulated and depressed trade and settlement in Taiwan. Opportunities to profit from the commerce of the southeast coast attracted the Japanese and Europeans; the Ming attempt to exclude foreigners from China forced them to trade from Taiwan's ports. The dynastic cycle and the fall of the Ming sent war refugees and conquerors to Taiwan, and Ch'ing armies and bureaucrats eventually incorporated the island frontier into the empire. The Chinese state then arbitrated the interaction of Han frontiersmen and plains aborigines and, in the eighteenth century, oversaw the transformation of Taiwan into a Chinese agricultural society.

The peace and prosperity following the consolidation of Ch'ing rule resulted in the growth of the Chinese population from at most 150 million in 1650 to 270 million by 1776. A population increase of this magnitude required expansion of the cultivated area and large-scale movements of population into frontier regions all over China.[7] Interregional migration and frontier development are therefore salient characteristics of Ch'ing social history and the late imperial state. Among the largest and most sophisticated of premodern agrarian bureaucratic states, the Chinese empire administered and drew taxes from regional societies spread across a subcontinent.[8] The eighteenth-century expansion of population and agricultural settlement challenged the empire's ability to control distant and growing populations and to finance that control. Despite the tremendous growth of population, the eighteenth-century Chinese state (for reasons discussed below) sharply curtailed the growth of its civil and military bureaucracies and its budget, forcing it to concentrate its limited civil and military resources on key problem areas. This resulted in a deliberately uneven distribution of civil and military officers with respect to both population and area and, in the case of a strategic periphery such as Taiwan, a sizable state presence unwarranted by its small population.[9] A detailed local history of Taiwan provides an opportunity to analyze how the Ch'ing state met the challenge of expanding population and settlement on one of its many frontiers.

The late imperial state's mediation of the interaction of Han settlers and Taiwan's plains aborigines cannot be understood apart from this larger political-economic context. More than any other factor, the fiscal limitations of the late imperial state restricted its incorporation of frontier territories and determined the allocation of land rights in the territories it did incorporate. The superiority of Chinese military organization and technology in East Asia made the conquest of new territories militarily feasible, but the high cost of financing permanent military and administrative control over distant and unproductive regions often rendered their incorporation undesirable.[10] When strategy dictated the incorporation of a territory, priority had to be given to minimizing control costs and extracting local revenues to ease the burden on central government finances.

Because of the high cost of collecting revenue, the difficulty of constraining abuse by tax collectors, and the resistance heavy taxation inevitably created, the late imperial state chose to keep taxes as low and as few as possible. This required it to minimize expenditures by keeping the civil and military bureaucracies small (possible only because of its military superiority). To provide governmental services, the state relied increasingly on local elites. These considerations, combined with a Confucian theory of government that assigned a fundamental role to agriculture rather than commerce in fiscal administration and statecraft, led to a state with a limited budget, three-quarters of whose revenues were generated by taxes on privately held agricultural land.[11] To collect this revenue, the allocation of land rights and the determination of land-tax responsibilities had to be made priorities of local government. Clarifying land rights and preventing title disputes were also important for reducing local control costs. The balance between control costs and land-tax revenues in frontier regions determined whether the state backed the land claims of indigenous peoples or favored the expansion of Han Chinese agriculture and taxation of newly reclaimed farmlands. In Taiwan, the experience of the Ch'ing state dictated that considerable efforts be devoted to the accommodation of aboriginal land rights.[12]

Historical studies of Chinese society rarely give due weight to the importance of fiscal considerations in the determination of state policy. An important theme of this study is that the Ch'ing state consistently weighed both the costs of implementing policies and their revenue consequences. Fiscal considerations did not determine policy, but they helped shape it; too many analyses of Chinese history have ignored this important dimension of late imperial administration.[13] For example, comparative studies of Chinese frontiers typically fall back on static geographic distinctions between north and south, Inner Asian and maritime. The argument pursued here sees Ch'ing frontier policies as the product of assessments of each frontier's strategic significance, control costs, and revenue potential. In this argument the only significance accorded the geography of a frontier region is its affect on these assessments; for example, the impact of transport efficiency on control costs, or of agricultural endowment on revenue potential. Foreign threats and important historical trends such as population growth and migrations caused these assessments to shift over time; in response officials proposed new administrative approaches, and the state adjusted (or reaffirmed) its policies. Policies—for example, whether immigration should be encouraged or restricted—fluctuated primarily in response to shifting assessments of strategy, control costs, and revenue potential, not the ebb and flow of Confucian moral resolve in fixed environments.

Comparable to the neglect of the fiscal dimensions of policymaking is a neglect of the military structure of the late imperial state and the role of the military in local government. For too long students of the Chinese state have been satisfied with a description of its military as "widely dispersed," when it was in fact very unevenly distributed about the empire (see Appendix D). It is serious error to neglect the Ch'ing military: its budget consumed half the revenues of the late imperial state and had a substantial economic impact (through both extraction and expenditure of revenues) on the localities in which it was concentrated.[14] As an undeveloped frontier, Taiwan lacked Confucian-educated local elites that could assist in revenue and control functions, and the Ch'ing had to invest in both a large military garrison and a substantial complement of civil magistrates to rule that strategic periphery (see Chapter 7).

As they strive to establish and maintain supremacy in the use of coercive force, state organizations must adapt to changing economic as well as political environments. But states do more than passively adapt; they also transform their environments. Classical political economy recognizes that states, by extracting and expending tax revenues and by defining property rights, are economic actors that powerfully shape societies.[15] As a field of study, political economy properly encompasses the study of economic and demographic cycles that operate independently of and interact with administrative and dynastic cycles. And classical political economy can appreciate that in many historical eras changes in the "mode of destruction" and state predatory strategies outweigh the significance of changes in the "mode of production." Political economy as an approach to the study of history and society rejects both economic reductionism and political and cultural history divorced from social factors.[16] The exploration in this study of issues central to comparative studies of statecraft and political economy enriches the study of both Taiwan and the late imperial state.

The Stage and Major Actors

The isolation (never absolute) of aboriginal Taiwan before the sixteenth century and the near absence of references to Taiwan in the Chinese histories remain a mystery. Taiwan lies only a hundred miles off Fukien. Although Fukien was not incorporated into the Chinese empire until the T'ang dynasty, for the last thousand years merchants from Fukienese ports have conducted an extensive maritime trade with Southeast Asia, the Ryukyus, and Japan. Yet Taiwan is rarely mentioned in early Chinese historical records, and archaeological and ethnographic data confirm that these trade routes largely bypassed Taiwan.[17] Some scholars attribute Taiwan's isolation to the dangerous currents of the Taiwan strait, but fishermen, pirates, merchants, and even Chinese navies frequently overcame this obstacle. The Pescadores, only 25 miles off Taiwan's western coast, were occupied by Chinese fishermen first in the thirteenth century and at least intermittently thereafter. Hsü Wen-hsiung suggests improvement in seafaring skills in the Sung made the Pescadores and Taiwan more accessible to Chinese.[18]

The key to Taiwan's historical isolation appears to lie not in its inaccessibility but in its lack of attractions. Taiwan's natural resources were not of the sort that would have produced valuable trade goods, nor was the island the seat of trading kingdoms or centers of craft production.[19] The hostility of Taiwan's head-hunting inhabitants toward intruders further inhibited the development of trade. Thus for centuries Taiwan remained unattractive to profit-seeking seafarers, and its inhabitants were left largely uncontacted by all but occasional adventurers or fishermen engaging in barter. Taiwan's relative isolation began to decay only with the sixteenth-century expansion of maritime commerce and piracy in East Asia. This sets the stage for our major actors, "aborigines," "Chinese," and the "state."

Aboriginal Taiwan was populated exclusively by Austronesian (Malayo-Polynesian) peoples. We can estimate from the Dutch censuses that in the seventeenth century there were about 100,000 aborigines.[20] Taiwan's aboriginal peoples lived by deer hunting and the swidden cultivation of millet and rice. They resided in semipermanent villages organized politically above the village level only for occasional alliances. Intervillage warfare and head-hunting were universal. This lack of unity facilitated the Dutch and later the Chinese "conquests" of the plains. The Dutch, followed by the Chengs and the Ch'ing, subjected the plains villages to state authority and taxation and suppressed head-hunting. The Chengs and the Ch'ing classified the aborigines as "raw" or "cooked" according to their relation to Chinese authority. The more familiar or "cooked" aborigines (*shu fan*), alternatively referred to as the civilized or plains aborigines, numbered approximately 50,000 and lived in a hundred or so villages or "tribes" (*she*) on the western coastal plain.[21] These plains aborigine villages have been categorized into at least eight ethnolinguistic groupings.[22]

Ten more ethnolinguistic groupings make up the second category, the raw aborigines (*sheng fan*), also referred to as mountain aborigines, who to this day inhabit the central mountains and the east coast. These peoples remained beyond Chinese control and were famous for their head-hunting raids, which were stopped only in the twentieth century. The important effect of incursions of Chinese and trade goods on population movements among the mountain aborigines remains outside the scope of this study.[23] (For a more extensive introduction to the aboriginal cultures of Taiwan, see below and Chapter 2.)

Chinese interaction with Taiwan increased steadily from the sixteenth century.[24] Fukienese fishermen and Chinese and Japanese pirates frequented the coast of Taiwan in the sixteenth century and did some trading, largely iron and salt for deerskins and antlers, with the aborigines. The seventeenth-century dynastic turmoil in China sent refugees to Taiwan to farm under Dutch East India Company auspices and later under an émigré Ming loyalist regime. In the eighteenth century, land-hungry immigrants from China's southeast coast poured into Taiwan. Han Chinese migrants to Taiwan came primarily from two prefectures (Chang-chou and Ch'üan-chou) in Fukien province (Fukienese are also referred to as Hokkien), and from prefectures in northern Kwangtung province; these latter migrants were predominantly Hakka.[25] These migrants tended to adhere in subethnic associations organized by common provenance and dialect (see Chapters 6 and 10).[26]

The repeated references in these pages to the "state," the "government," and the "court" are a necessary shorthand for a center of decision-making power (one that sought to maintain supremacy at least in the use of coercion) whose policies affected social developments in Taiwan. The policymaking process and the apparatus of officials who implemented policies were highly complex and incorporated many actors with disparate interests. We must often refer to them in misleadingly simple collective terms if we are to keep our focus on the policy impact in Taiwan.

Aborigine Land Rights

How these three actors—plains aborigines, Chinese settlers, and the state—learned to deal with one another on the Taiwan frontier is the major subject of this study. The accommodation they achieved in the eighteenth century had its most impressive product in the multi-tiered land rights that still existed in Taiwan at the beginning of the twentieth century. That large areas of Taiwan's west coast were subject to aborigine large-rents (*fan ta tsu*) until the Japanese colonial government abolished the large-rent system around 1900 is striking evidence of the survival of plains aborigine communities on the plains. A brief account of this system in one area of Taiwan will give a concrete illustration.

The traditional system of land tenure in Taiwan was one of split ownership or "two lords to a field" (*i t'ien liang chu*). Split ownership distinguished what were called small-rent and large-rent rights in Taiwan and topsoil and subsoil rights in other parts of China. Large-rents resemble ground rents in Anglo-American law. In Taiwan this dual-ownership system arose through the process of frontier land reclamation. Wealthy and well-connected persons acquired government land patents allowing them to reclaim large tracts of wasteland and obligating them to pay land taxes once the land was reclaimed. Some land-grant holders invested in reclaiming the land, built irrigation canals and terraces, and recruited immigrant settlers as ordinary tenants. In other cases the tenants themselves invested labor and capital in reclaiming the land and thereby acquired a right of permanent tenancy. These reclaiming tenants could not be evicted as long as they paid the patent holder a large-rent fixed in perpetuity; this right of permanent tenancy was called the small-rent right. In many communities, neighboring civilized aborigine tribes, rather than wealthy Chinese, held the land patent rights, and reclaiming tenants were obligated to pay aborigine large-rents. Large-rents, whether Han or aborigine, averaged 6–8 *shih* (18–24 bushels) per *chia* (hectare) per year and constituted 10 percent or less of a farmer's rice harvest.

The cadastral records collected by Arthur Wolf for Shu-lin and San-hsia townships in the southwest corner of the Taipei basin reveal a complex pattern of large-rent rights at the end of the nineteenth century. Han claims predominated in Shu-lin, and aborigine claims in San-hsia. Most small-rent owners in the Shu-lin area paid large-rents to various Han families, among whom the Changs were especially prominent. Patent rights to land in this area derived from a land grant awarded by the government in 1713 to a partnership of four Chinese.[27] One partner was the interpreter of the Tan-shui area tribes, Lai K'o. Through a series of transfers and subdivisions, most of the large-rent rights on these lands had ended up in the hands of the Chang family. Why no aborigine land rights were recognized in this area remains a puzzle, although the participation of the interpreter Lai K'o in the original partnership was no doubt important. Perhaps Shu-lin, being roughly equidistant from the three aborigine villages of Kuei-lun, Pai-chieh, and Wu-lao-wan, fell into the unclaimed interstices of tribal territories (see Maps 1.1 and 1.2). But, as we shall see in the case of San-hsia, a marginal location did not necessarily bar aboriginal claims.

Southwest of Shu-lin, in the hilly areas of Shan-tzu-chiao, Shih-hui-k'eng, and A-nan-k'eng, the Kuei-lun tribe successfully asserted its claim to aborigine large-rents. Indeed, in 1783, after a dispute over the felling of timber in the T'a-liao-k'eng area, the Kuei-lun tribe forced the Chang family to pay 150 dollars (*ta yüan*) in compensation. A contract defining the boundaries of their respective territories was drawn up to prevent further disputes.[28] The cadastres record that to the east of Shu-lin in the Ch'i-chou and Sha-lun areas, the Pai-chieh *she*, just across the river, owned large-rent rights. The presence of Kuei-lun and Pai-chieh large-rent rights on the peripheries of the Shu-lin area suggests that tribal territorial claims, radiating out from aboriginal settlements, were converted into large-rent rights.

The large area south of Shu-lin surrounded by the Ta-han (Tan-shui) river, was originally part of the 1713 Shu-lin land grant. In 1757 one of the partners sold this land to the government. The cadastres record that this

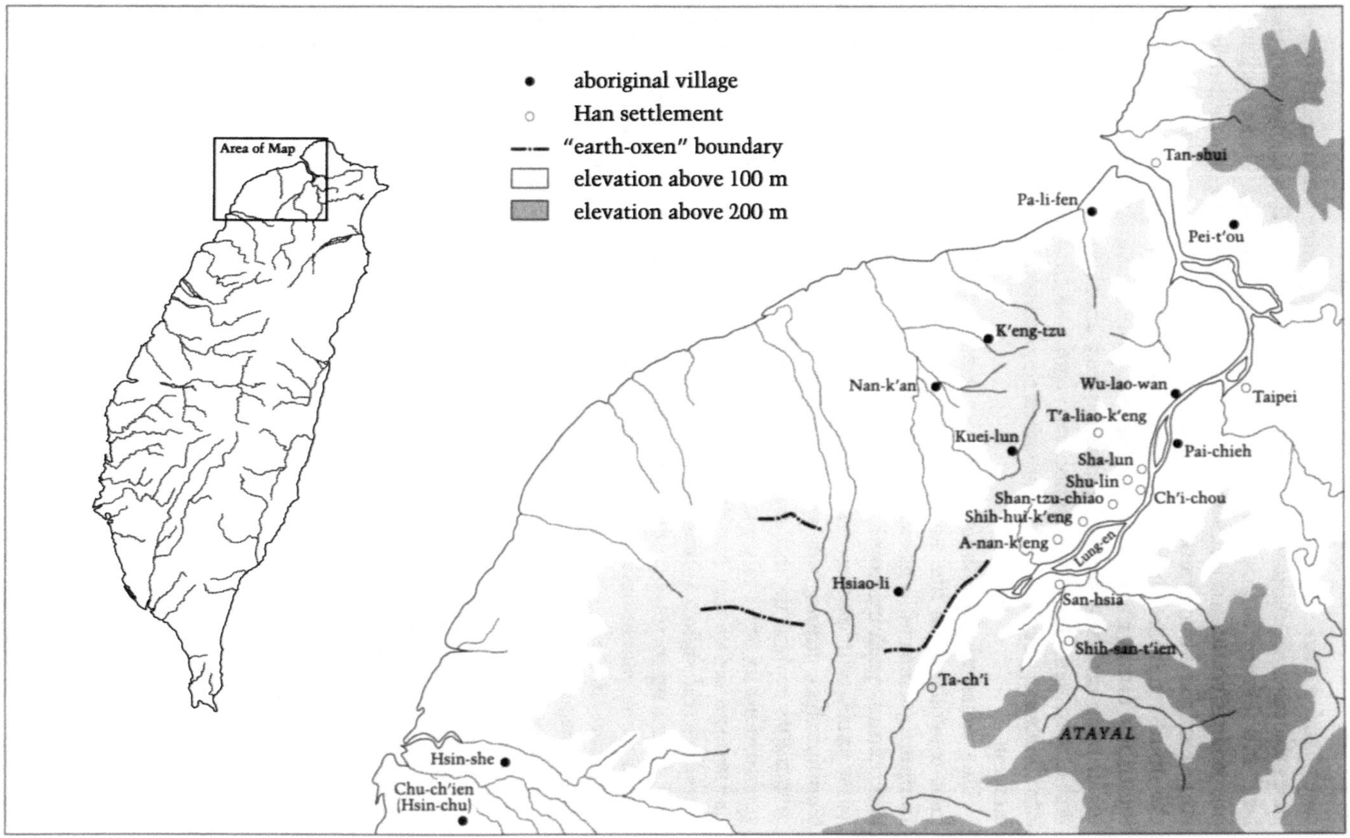

Map 1.1 San-hsia and environs

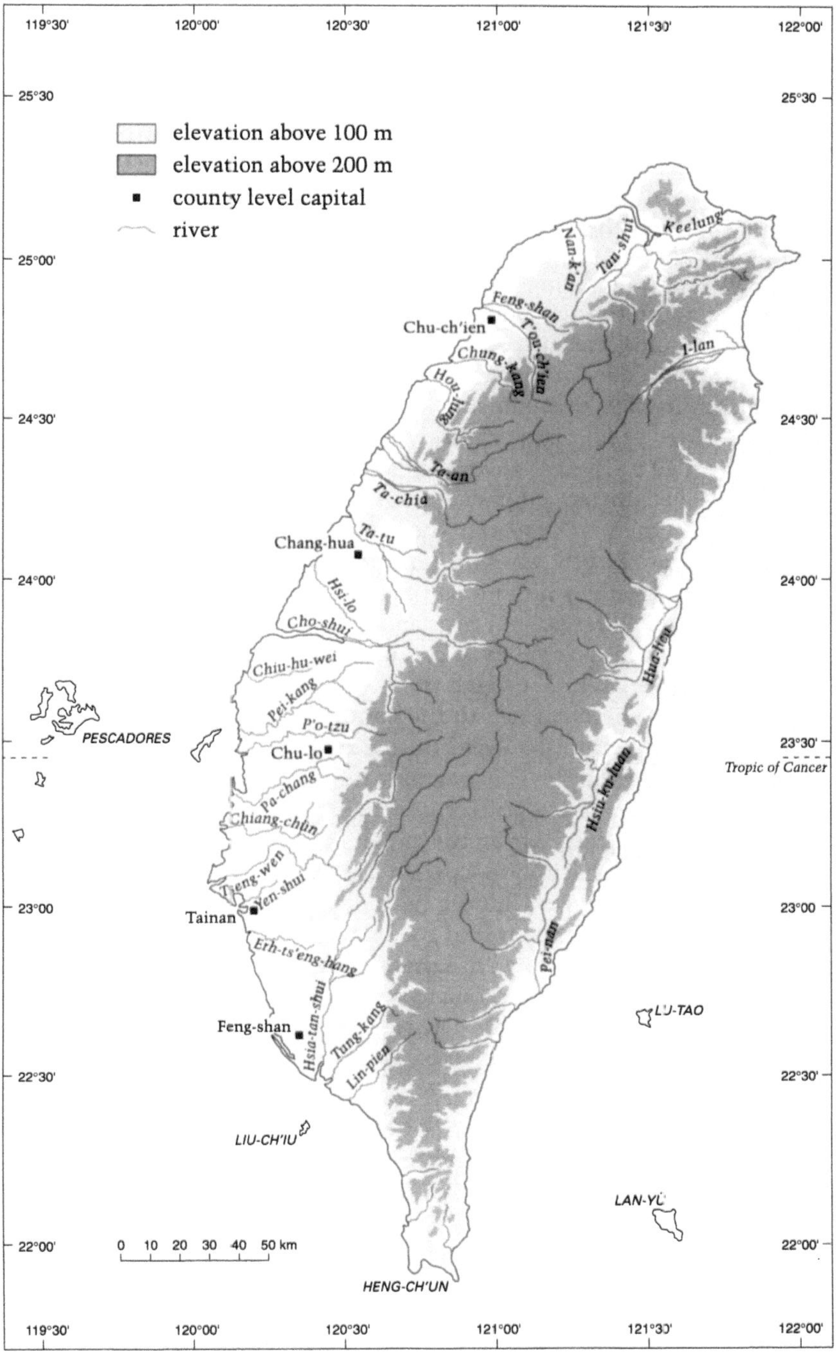

Map 1.2 Taiwan: topography and river systems

land was obligated to pay an official large-rent of the type called *lung en* or bounty rent. These rents went to the local garrisons.[29]

South of San-hsia, in a narrow valley between steep mountains lies Shih-san-t'ien. One corner of this valley was sold in 1778 by two aborigines from the Hsiao-li and Kuei-lun plains tribes, respectively, to a Chinese named Lo. The contract required Mr. Lo to pay the aborigines four dollars (*ta yüan*) for a piece of unreclaimed land the aborigines "had inherited from their ancestors." Large-rent rights to a larger parcel in Shih-san-t'ien were held by three tribes, K'eng-tzu, Nan-k'an, and Kuei-lun. Their claim to this land originated in 1788 when they were ordered to form an aborigine military colony (*fan t'un*) at Shih-san-t'ien. The colony was intended to bolster Ch'ing military strength, especially its defense against the head-hunting Atayal tribesmen in the nearby mountains. In 1816, 53 aborigine military colonists (*t'un ting*) from the three tribes awarded a Chinese the rights to reclaim 57 *chia* of land in Shih-san-t'ien. The contract cited decrees from the early nineteenth century that allowed them to rent out the land rather than found a military colony because the site was far from their home villages.[30]

In the broad valleys around San-hsia, the cadastres record large-rent rights held by a different, yet overlapping set of tribes. The reclamation patent for the San-hsia valley is dated the third month of 1773 and was granted jointly by four aborigine tribes, Kuei-lun, Hsiao-li, Wu-lao-wan, and Pai-chieh. The preamble to the contract states that the four tribes had abandoned a common deer-hunting field in San-hsia because of the decline of the deer herds. The preamble then informs us that the authorities were allowing tribes to recruit tenants to reclaim the land and to distribute rents collected from the tenants as rations to the plains aborigines. The clauses that follow specify the terms of the agreement. The first clause required the Chinese partnership acquiring the right to reclaim the land to make an initial good faith payment of 4,000 *ta yüan* to the tribes. The tribes were to use this sum first to get official approval of the patent agreement, and second to support militia guards to protect the area from Atayal headhunters. The second clause provided that the cost of irrigation works was to be split between the tribes and the tenants on a 40–60 basis and set the yearly large-rent at 8 *shih* per *chia*, after a three-year grace period. If the four tribes could not come up with their 40 percent share of the investment, their large-rent was to be reduced from 8 to 6 *shih* per *chia*. The third clause stipulated that any land taxes levied in the future would be paid by the four tribes. At the time of the contract, aborigine lands were tax-exempt; this clause sought to ensure that a third party's payment of the taxes would not jeopardize the aborigines' title.[31]

Reclamation agreements providing for payment of aborigine large-rents were concluded in many localities all over Taiwan. This is documented by the Japanese colonial surveys of Taiwanese customary law and by the land survey initiated in the late nineteenth century by Governor Liu Ming-ch'uan. As part of the survey, accounts of the corporate (that is, jointly, not individually, held) large-rent income and expenditures of the plains tribes were compiled. The accounts of seventeen tribes of the Taipei area (Tan-shui county) have been preserved; these include all six tribes with holdings in the San-hsia area. Wu-lao-wan's corporate income of 1,759 *shih* is the largest of the seventeen. K'eng-tzu at 314 and Hsiao-li at 320 reported the smallest totals. Kuei-lun, Pai-chieh, and Nan-k'an reported incomes of 1,120, 891, and 916 *shih* respectively.[32] It is likely that Hsiao-li's unexpectedly low income is an artifact of the area surveyed, for most of Hsiao-li's lands lay to the south. Income from those lands would have been reported to Hsin-chu county. Okamatsu Santarō reports that in the area covered by modern Taipei, T'ao-yüan, and Hsin-chu counties, more than half the dry fields were held in common by native tribes.[33]

The descendants of these tribes still live in the area. For example, families surnamed Hsiao and descended from the Hsiao-li *she* that was a party to many of the San-hsia patents live in neighboring townships. The Hsiaos today are organized as a Chinese patrilineage, with ancestral halls, strict patrilineal recruitment, and a professionally printed lineage genealogy. On the altar in the Hsiao lineage hall stands a large ancestral tablet in whose uppermost corners, where native place is usually noted, are the two Chinese characters for Taiwan. This contrasts with the practice of Taiwanese families of Han extraction who record mainland localities as their native places.[34] Also distinctive is the center line of the Hsiao tablet, which identifies the founding ancestor, Hsiao Na-ying, as an interpreter.[35] The office of interpreter was an official post in the Ch'ing administration of the plains aborigine villages. In all other respects, however, the Hsiao tablet resembles that of other Chinese lineages, with the ancestors of succeeding generations arrayed about the center line. The Hsiaos speak Taiwanese, practice Taiwanese customs, and do not differ in any other way from their neighbors. They are highly sinicized and have extensively intermarried.

The San-hsia cadastres confirm that plains aborigines were neither exterminated nor driven into the mountains with the arrival of Chinese settlers. Rather, plains aborigines assumed the role of large-rent holders and rent collectors and were rapidly sinicizing by the mid-Ch'ien-lung era. Frontier land-tenure institutions were made to accommodate the plains aborigines. Why were plains aborigines not simply overrun by the Chinese immigrants, who outnumbered them and looked down on them? Apparently the aborigines were able to rely on the support of the Ch'ing government to defend their claims against the land-hungry settlers. We have seen that the San-hsia reclamation patent of 1773 refers at several points to official regulation of the reclamation of aborigine land. Why did the Ch'ing government consider the defense of aborigine land rights worthwhile? What moral, legal, economic, and political considerations led to the creation of the aborigine large-rent system? In what state did the Ch'ing government find the aboriginal tribes? What balance of power existed between the aboriginal and Chinese communities? What economic and political relations existed between them? To answer these questions, we must reanalyze Taiwan's early history to assess the role of plains aborigines.[36]

Overview

The best estimate of the island's population at the time of Ch'ing acquisition in 1683 suggests that the aborigines numbered somewhat over 100,000 and the Chinese somewhat less. Even at this early date, however, Chinese outnumbered the plains aborigines (about 50,000 people). The Chinese population was concentrated on rice and sugar farms around Tainan. The plains aborigines inhabited the entire western coastal plain, where they lived by horticulture and deer hunting. Despite the succession of regimes, economic relations between Chinese and aborigines remained rooted in the deer trade throughout the Dutch, Cheng, and K'ang-hsi eras.

An extensive international trade in deer pelts was an important component of East Asian commerce in the seventeenth century. Taiwan, along with Thailand, Cambodia, and Luzon, was a major producing area. Deerskins found a ready market in the cooler climate of Japan, where they were used for tabi socks, leggings, and trousers and for ornamentation. Smoked venison provisioned local garrisons and was exported to the China coast. Deer antlers were a valued ingredient in the Chinese pharmacopoeia.

Part I of this study analyzes how the Dutch extended their rule over Taiwan's western coastal plain and organized the deer trade. After establishing political and military control over the plains aborigine villages, the Dutch publicly auctioned village franchises to Chinese traders. Each franchise gave a trader monopoly rights over the deer trade of a village or group of villages for one year. In 1650, for instance, a Chinese trader paid 600 Spanish reals for a monopoly over the deer trade of the Hsiao-li tribe near San-hsia.[37] In exchange for salt, iron, porcelains, cloth, and other trade goods, the monopoly merchant demanded a quota of deerskins and venison from the villagers. The Cheng regime continued the franchise system but replaced the auction with tax farms and fixed aborigine tax quotas. The Ch'ing administration in turn adopted the Cheng system of village tax quotas.[38]

The village monopoly system, in placing the Chinese tax farmer between the state and the weakly organized and unsophisticated aborigines, made him very powerful. Monopoly merchants and their agents exploited their position to make excessive demands on aborigines for taxes, corvée, and sexual favors. Most aborigine revolts against state authority—Dutch, Cheng, or K'ang-hsi-era Ch'ing—can be traced to the tyrannies of these leaseholders and their agents in the villages, the Chinese interpreters and foremen.

Honest Chinese officials sought to remedy these abuses. When tribes had become more sophisticated in Chinese ways, the tax farms were abolished, and the tribes were encouraged to pay their taxes directly and to employ their own people as interpreters. In other cases stricter discipline and an end to official squeeze were prescribed to limit oppressive exactions and the abuse of corvée. Hsiao Na-ying is undoubtedly remembered as the founding ancestor of the Hsiaos because he was the first of his tribe to serve as an interpreter.

The deer-hunting economy and monopoly-merchant form of administration endured into K'ang-hsi-era Taiwan (1683–1722) primarily because of the Ch'ing court's ambivalence toward the colonization of Taiwan. It had waged war against the Chengs to end their rebellion, not to expand the empire. With the restoration of peace, the Cheng troops were repatriated, and many refugees returned home, substantially reducing Taiwan's Chinese population. Only those with both wives and property in Taiwan and hence a stake in the maintenance of law and order were allowed to stay. In the debate among officials in 1683–84 over keeping Taiwan, those who argued Taiwan's strategic location required that it be kept out of the hands of rebels, pirates, and Western barbarians prevailed. Preventing Taiwan from becoming a rebel base was the primary objective; developing trade and agriculture and even increasing tax revenues were secondary. Priority was given to the recovery of the southeast coast from the destruction caused by the coastal evacuation policies adopted to isolate the Cheng regime on Taiwan.

To keep rebels and vagrants out, the Ch'ing strictly regulated communications with Taiwan and imposed the quarantine policies analyzed in Part II. Chinese families were barred from migrating to Taiwan because it was thought they would upset the ethnic status quo. The good behavior of migrant farm laborers crossing to Taiwan was to be ensured by keeping them dependent on the government for access to the mainland and their families there. All shipping was limited to a pair of ports, Tainan in Taiwan and Amoy in Fukien, and ships had to be licensed and inspected for each trip. Despite chronic rice shortages on the Fukien coast, exports of rice were curtailed to ensure a stable food supply within Taiwan. To reduce the expense of governing the sparsely populated and revenue-poor island, Taiwan was garrisoned by Green Standard troops rotated from mainland Fukien garrisons, instead of troops recruited locally, the usual practice in other regions of the empire.

Ch'ing anti-colonization policies had many unintended consequences. Most important, they left the frontier to rowdy gangs of sojourning Chinese laborers that readily participated in rebel movements and communal strife and destabilized frontier society. The quarantine policies, however, reduced the pressure of an expanding Chinese population on the aborigines, and the government discovered that braves recruited from loyal tribes could be used to put down aborigine revolts and apprehend Chinese bandits and rebels.

By the first decades of the eighteenth century, the population and regional economy of the southeast coast had recovered from the devastation of the anti-Cheng campaigns and the policy of coastal removal. Chinese farmers from the crowded coastal prefectures began pouring into Taiwan to take advantage of strong mainland markets for Taiwan rice and sugar. By this time the deer herds, on which aborigine livelihoods and taxpaying depended, had been seriously overhunted. As the expanding Chinese population converted deer fields into farmland, disputes began to arise as Chinese encroached on aborigine lands.[39] This put pressure on Ch'ing officialdom to formulate the policies governing aborigine land rights that are analyzed in Part III.

In 1704 the Taiwan intendant, the highest-ranking resident official, decreed that settlers seeking to contract privately for land with aborigine tribes must also request official permission; such contracts would be approved only after county officials had determined that aborigine claims were respected. Ch'en Pin, Taiwan intendant from 1710 to 1715 and later governor of Fukien province, advocated stronger protections. Ch'en argued that just as the government recognized the ownership claims of Chinese taxpayers, so should the government recognize tribal landownership when the aborigines paid their taxes. This principle should apply not only to farmland but also to deer-hunting grounds. Ch'en complained that local magnates were obtaining land through patents issued by corrupt county officials and thereby stirring up trouble with the aborigines, and he sought to prohibit any further reclamation of aborigine land.[40]

Measures to ensure order and to protect aborigine land rights took a new direction a few years later, in response to a major rebellion by Chinese settlers. In the wake of the Chu I-kuei rebellion of 1721, Governor-general Man-pao ordered the construction of an island-wide set of boundary trenches ("earth-oxen," *t'u niu*) to be built in a north-south direction, ten *li* to the west of the mountain foothills. This cordon was intended (1) to keep robbers and bandits from escaping to the mountains, (2) to keep raw aborigines from coming out of the mountains to take heads, and (3) to keep Han settlers in search of rattan and bamboo from entering the mountains, where they often fell victim to aborigine attack. Reclamation beyond this boundary was forbidden. The quarantine policies were thereby extended to limit expansion of Chinese settlement on the frontier.

Lan Ting-yüan, the most prolific advocate of pro-colonization policies of this era, strongly opposed Man-pao's extension of the protectionist quarantine approach. Lan had gone to Taiwan as a secretary to his cousin, one of the military commanders who led the suppression of the Chu I-kuei rebellion. Lan argued that the rebellion proved the inadequacy of the old anti-colonization policies. The only way to create a stable, law-abiding society was to extend both the civil and the military arms of government to the frontier (to be funded by taxes on newly reclaimed land) and to populate the wastelands. Bandit lairs would be eliminated only when all the land was reclaimed and settled. Lan advocated free migration to Taiwan and the development of the island as a rice supplier to the Fukien coast.

Lan's advocacy of the reclamation of aborigine hunting grounds was the logical consequence of his pro-colonization views. "If we talk of aborigine land, then all Taiwan is aborigine land; the aborigines may want it restored, but it is beyond restoring. The government should decree that each aborigine can reclaim land; all that thereby becomes paddy and garden within the year should be considered theirs; what is left unreclaimed, [Han] settlers should be allowed to open." Lan knew that giving deer hunters one year to convert their holdings to farmland and adopt agriculture would not preserve aborigine livelihoods. His analysis of Taiwan's society required Han settlement, reclamation, and the expansion of taxable acreage, and he gave little thought either to the cost to the aborigines or to the dangers of aborigine revolt. But even Lan approved the common practice whereby settlers paid taxes on behalf of aborigines in return for rights to reclaim land. This practice was an extension of the old village monopoly system and was a forerunner of the aborigine large-rent system. The government did not adopt Lan's proposal to eliminate aborigine titles. In the following years many officials expressed the fear that civilized aborigines pressed too hard and too fast by encroaching Han settlement would revolt and join the raw aborigines in the mountains. Official policy on aborigine land claims, therefore, moved more cautiously than Lan had advocated.

Nevertheless, in the next few years the Yung-cheng emperor (1723–35), who was noted for his aggressive frontier policies and his concern for increasing revenues, adopted many pro-colonization policies. In 1724 and 1725 proclamations allowed tribes to rent (but not to sell) deer fields to Han settlers; once opened, such fields were to be registered for taxation. This measure allowed reclamation to proceed and at the same time protected an aborigine interest in the land and increased local tax revenues. In 1723 two new county-level units were created in north Taiwan, and in 1731 the number of civil officers was increased. Also in 1731 land taxes were drastically reduced to encourage the registration of already reclaimed land; this stimulated further reclamation. It also marked an important shift in the government's fiscal strategy in Taiwan: rather than relying on high taxes on limited acreage, the government sought to increase its revenue by taxing lightly a rapidly expanding acreage. Even a serious aborigine revolt in 1731–32, coupled with another Han uprising, did not slow the pro-colonization trend. On the contrary, this challenge seems only to have strengthened the resolve of the Yung-cheng government to encourage Han settlement. In 1732 the immigration of families to Taiwan was sanctioned for the first time. And the next year many more soldiers were added to Taiwan's garrisons for assignment to frontier posts. Pro-colonization policies in the areas of immigration, taxation, reclamation, extension of the civil and military administrations, and rice exports to the southeast coast all won favor at court in the later years of the Yung-cheng reign.

Concern about the uncontrolled expansion of Han settlement mounted in the early years of the Ch'ien-lung reign (1736–95). Officials reported that many rootless troublemakers were taking advantage of the relaxation of restrictions on migration and posing a threat to local order and that unlicensed reclamation of aborigine land was causing friction between Han and aborigines. In 1738 Governor-general Hao Yü-lin called for clarification of the boundaries between areas cultivated by aborigines and Han. Hao ordered a land survey and required that land contracts between Han and aborigines be presented for official inspection before the land could be registered. Land opened without such contracts was to be returned to aborigine ownership; future encroachment on aborigine land was forbidden. In 1740 Hao Yü-lin convinced the emperor to end the legal migration of families to Taiwan. Thus, the major pro-colonization policies of the late Yung-cheng years were reversed, and the old philosophy of control through quarantine was revived.

The end of legal migration did not, however, mean the end of illegal migration, which continued at a steady pace, much to the consternation of officials deputed to end it. It was too late to turn back the clock. The Chinese population had grown substantially in the years of open migration and now included a large number of females, making possible a rapid rate of growth compounded by continued immigration.[41]

For the next 25 years, this growing settler population exerted continuous pressure on aborigine lands and on Ch'ing policies designed to protect aborigine land rights. Clarifications of the boundaries between Han and aborigine land had to be made repeatedly. Squatters were ordered evicted, but those who had privately contracted with the tribes were often allowed to stay as long as they paid aborigine rents. Because the Ch'ing state was militarily unable to evict large numbers of frontiersmen and financially unable to resettle them, it was forced to acquiesce in most Han reclamation, even though it was technically illegal. The government merely drew new boundary lines, which it declared to be permanent, and tried to enforce the payment of rents to aborigines. These lines were extensions of and additions to Man-pao's original earth-oxen trench.[42] Like Lan Ting-yüan many officials doubted the wisdom of trying to restrict reclamation, both because they were anxious to fill tax quotas, and because they were unimpressed by the threat of strife between settlers and aborigines.

In 1760 Governor-general Yang T'ing-chang ordered the boundary of Han reclamation clarified once again and an earth-oxen trench and stone stelae constructed to mark these boundaries. In addition, Yang ordered that civilized aborigine braves be used to guard strategic passes along the raw aborigine border. These braves were to be paid guard rations out of the rents tribes received from Han tenants. This was an attempt to go beyond simple protection of aborigine land rights and to impose an obligation on the civilized tribes to render service. The first clause of the San-hsia patent of 1773 discussed earlier reflects the terms of this decree.

Another clarification of the boundaries was ordered in 1766 by Governor-general Su Ch'ang, who was upset that tribes were falling into debt to Han creditors and being forced to pledge their land. Su established the Subprefecture for Aborigine Affairs to handle all legal cases and negotiations between Han and civilized aborigines. In the next year, aborigines were allowed to recruit tenants to reclaim tribal lands and to collect rents from them, following the model of Han large-rent holders. This established the legal basis for land grants such as the San-hsia aborigine land patent and put the finishing touches on the aborigine large-rent system in general. Ch'ing authorities finally realized the futility of trying to stop Han reclamation and recognized that the tribes needed the rental income more than they needed land depleted of deer herds that they themselves were unable to reclaim or farm profitably. The aborigine large-rent system accommodated both groups.

After the 1760's the salience of disputes over civilized aborigine land declined markedly. Other problems came to the fore, particularly raw aborigine head-hunting raids and, most threatening to Ch'ing authority, communal strife among Chinese immigrant groups. Because they had a role to play in solving both these problems, plains aborigines were able to maintain their position. Civilized aborigine tribes in the foothills were familiar with the mountain trails and the raw aborigine tribes that lived in the interior. Their knowledge of the mountain areas made them invaluable when the government wanted to punish a tribe for a head-taking raid or to apprehend a Chinese bandit or rebel taking refuge in the mountains. Aborigine skills as archers and marksmen made them an effective fighting force. As a non-Han ethnic group, plains aborigine militia could be counted on to remain loyal to the Ch'ing during the frequent outbreaks of Han communal strife. After the Lin Shuang-wen rebellion of 1786–88, their martial role was institutionalized with the founding of the *fan t'un*, or aborigine military colonies, along the foothills. San-hsia's Shih-san-t'ien was one of these.

Thus, the plains aborigines' utility as a loyal military force (and fear of their potential for revolt), their status as taxpayers, ambivalence toward the immigration of Chinese settlers who disrupted the status quo but contributed to land-tax revenues, and a Confucian concern to preserve the livelihoods of subject peoples motivated the Ch'ing state to arbitrate relations between Chinese immigrant farmers and aborigines. The goal of the Ch'ing state was to keep the competition between settlers and aborigines from disrupting its control of a strategic periphery and imposing additional costs that Taiwan's inadequate revenues did little to defray. Aborigine taxpaying established, in the government's eyes, their claim to rights in land. The government's attempts to restrain the immigrants led it to adapt the institution of split-ownership rights to Taiwan's frontier conditions. Han settlers seeking to reclaim tribal lands were required to respect the tribes' prior claims by paying an aborigine large-rent.

In the chapters in Part I, I reconstruct the history of Taiwan's plains aborigines in the seventeenth century, focusing particularly on the systems of government imposed on them beginning with the Dutch and on the administration and taxation of the trade in deer products. I turn in Part II to the nature of Ch'ing policies toward the newly acquired territory and to their evolution to cope with the constant expansion of Chinese agricultural settlement. In Part III I analyze the interaction of aborigines, settlers, and government on the frontier, paying particular attention to the way competing interests reached an accommodation through the split-ownership system of land tenure.

Chapter 11 concludes the early history of the plains aborigine societies. Income from aborigine large-rents was critical to the survival of the plains tribes. The destruction of the deer herds, caused both by overhunting and the spread of farming, eliminated the hunting sector of the aboriginal economy. Hunters only gradually, and unenthusiastically, adopted intensive agriculture. In this difficult period of adjustment, aborigine large-rents were critical to tribal livelihoods. But the challenge posed by the spread of Chinese settlement was only partially economic. Chapter 11 also explores the problems that intermarriage and cultural change posed for aborigine adjustment.

The conclusion draws out some larger implications of this study. In Chapter 12, I compare the Taiwan frontier with other Chinese frontiers, especially Manchuria and the southwest, where Chinese cultivators competed with aboriginal tribes for rights to land. Comparison enables us to isolate a set of factors—strategy, revenues, and control costs—that explains when the imperial government found it worthwhile to intervene to protect aboriginal claims to land. In Appendix F, I briefly compare the same factors on the North American settler/Indian frontier.

Historians often assert, when pointing to the frequency of Han communal strife and rebellions, that the Ch'ing "neglected" Taiwan. This study should cast doubt on that generalization. The history of Taiwan in the seventeenth and eighteenth centuries reveals a surprising degree of central government interference and surveillance on a strategically important frontier. What appears as neglect to other students of Taiwan history, Part II shows to be a rationally calculated policy of indirect control and quarantine. Chapter 12 reveals that concerns with control costs and revenue generation were central factors in the late imperial state's frontier policies. It was the traditional fiscal system, rather than attitudes of neglect, that seriously limited the policy options open to the government. Even the claim that neglect caused frontier society on Taiwan to be more turbulent than that in other areas can be doubted. Communal feuds and rebellions erupted frequently in the older settled areas of Kwangtung and Fukien, areas that were among the commercially most sophisticated in the empire.[43] The deterioration of social order and government control in nineteenth-century Taiwan does not distinguish it from other parts of the Chinese empire.[44]

Limits and Goals of the Present Study

A study that focuses on two interacting social systems, in this case Chinese and plains aborigine, must explain their independent operation before they begin to interact, as well as their joint evolution thereafter. It is my purpose to show that the Chinese-aborigine accommodation reached in the eighteenth century cannot be understood apart from the complex historical background on both the Chinese and aborigine sides and the encompassing political economy. The great continuity in the economy and administration of the plains aborigines throughout the seventeenth century, despite the presence of three succeeding governments, was a crucial ingredient in this process. The literature on this period obscures this continuity by limiting discussion to one or another regime. Part I is organized to emphasize the continuity.

The seventeenth-century records of the Dutch East India Company make possible an historical anthropology of Taiwan's plains aborigines that begins before Chinese agricultural settlement. The letters of European diplomats and traders often contribute depth and perspective to political histories of China in recent centuries. But only rarely do European records, let alone from the seventeenth century, provide reports of the growth of a local society as detailed as do the reports of Dutch factors and missionaries from Taiwan.

The student of Chinese society in Taiwan has both an embarrassment of riches and the burden of sifting through a massive historical record. Of course, recorded history has its limits. A historical record created by a ruling elite rarely reveals the attitudes and activities of subject peoples in as great a detail as it does those of the governing stratum. Only rarely has a body of data, such as the Taiwan household registers, been created that reveals processes as intimate as those laid bare by Arthur Wolf and Huang Chieh-shan.[45] More commonly, historical records focus on issues of state far removed from the villages and towns, let alone the men and women, of interest to historical anthropologists. But in the case of Taiwan, the development of its frontier society was implicated in the state's strategic concerns for the island. The student of Taiwan history is also fortunate to have available a record beyond central government archives and local gazetteers. Stone inscriptions of local government decrees, Chinese ethnographies and travelers' reports, and, most important, collections of case records and contracts between private citizens, greatly enrich the Taiwanese historical record. These two kinds of data create a rare opportunity to analyze the interaction of the Chinese state and local society.

Despite Taiwan's uniquely rich historical record, its limitations are keenly felt. Too little is known of the growth of Chinese settlements or of internal changes in the plains tribes. Collecting information on individual tribes and localities had to be foregone at this stage in favor of writing a more general local history. This means that the interaction of Chinese settlers and plains aborigines is seen here primarily as reflected in the reports of agents, Dutch or Chinese, charged with governing the frontier. I hope that the detailed outline of the social history of the frontier provided here will be filled in and corrected by later studies of particular localities, tribes, and lineages. These studies should benefit, in turn, from having this analysis of the larger historical context.

The limitations on this study are numerous. Except in the cases of San-hsia and Shu-lin, I have not had access to the earliest Japanese land surveys, which would reveal the actual extent of aborigine large-rent holdings, at least as of the late nineteenth century. The San-hsia and Shu-lin cadastres, the qualitative statement of Okamatsu Santarō cited earlier, and collections of contracts make me confident that such holdings were extensive throughout Taiwan. But any more precise statement or attempts to reconstruct tribal territories must await further research in the land registers. Nor has it been possible for me to do studies of the experiences of individual tribes. Tremendous variation in the success of tribes in asserting their land claims is quite likely. The Hsiao-li *she* and the famous An-li *she* surely represent the more successful end of the continuum.[46] Studies of a number of these groups would add much depth to this present work, which is confined to laying out the institutional and historical background within which such analyses can proceed. Such detailed studies would have to be done in tandem with studies of the spread of Chinese settlement in particular localities.

Nor should this study of the political economy of Han-aborigine interaction be confused for a general history of Taiwan in the centuries studied. The growth of Han communal strife and the causes of the Han rebellions are slighted here. This is not a complete history of the Chinese settlement of Taiwan. Any study of that process should begin where the immigrants did, in the societies and economies of the southeast coast.

There is also a geographical bias in the sources used in this study. The discussion frequently focuses on the colonization of the northern Taiwan frontier. It was the largest and latest settled frontier and thus displays during the Ch'ing period all stages of the colonization process. The Japanese private law studies that provide much of the crucial documentation of land-tenure relations are based primarily, but not exclusively, on contracts and cases collected from the north. I have not hesitated to draw on material from the southern Taiwan frontier when it was available and made for profitable illustration. My impression is that the working of these historical processes was not different in the south, but I cannot document that point at every stage. Certainly the southern tribes were incorporated into the aborigine military colonies at the end of the eighteenth century on the same basis as the northern tribes.

This study concludes with the close of the eighteenth century and the creation of the aborigine military colonies in the wake of the Lin Shuang-wen rebellion. The end of the Ch'ien-lung reign marks the end of the high Ch'ing period, as signs of political decay and economic decline were mounting throughout the empire. In Taiwan the last decades of the eighteenth century are the beginnings of a period of intense communal strife that lasts to the 1860's.[47] The focus of official attention (and the documents left behind) in this era necessarily shifts away from frontier settlement and plains aborigines to the problems of disorder and Han subethnic rivalry.

Not only issues but the nature of the documentary record changes in this period. There was no revision of the prefectural gazetteer in this era, compared to the frequent revisions in the early eighteenth century that enable us to chart changes in settlement, tax revenues, and local government through time. The sources for the nineteenth-century history of Taiwan are both rich and accessible, thanks to the Taiwan Collectanea, and the efforts in recent years to preserve collections of land deeds continue to enrich the documentary base. The importance of sources such as land contracts, genealogies, and memoirs—sources that are rich in patches but not comprehensive—forces a different research strategy on students of local history in the nineteenth century. Island-wide documentation becomes available again at the end of the nineteenth century with the Liu Ming-ch'uan reforms and the Japanese takeover. The prospects for detailed local studies, including studies of plains aborigine villages, in the nineteenth century is therefore excellent. As such studies are completed, they will slowly build up a comprehensive view that will refine our understanding of Taiwan's development not only in the nineteenth century but also in the century that preceded it.

PART I

The Plains Aborigines and the Earliest Stages of Chinese Penetration

CHAPTER TWO

Aboriginal Taiwan in the Early Seventeenth Century

IN THE HISTORY of Taiwan, the Austronesian (Malayo-Polynesian) inhabitants of Taiwan's plains have long been neglected in favor of the Chinese, who began settling Taiwan in the early seventeenth century and soon became the more numerous and powerful group. Yet the role of the aborigines in the expansion of the Taiwan "frontier" was often crucial. The history of Taiwan as a Dutch colony is largely a story of Dutch relations with the aborigines, even as those relations were affected by an increasing Chinese presence. This and the next chapter construct an analytic history of Dutch-period Taiwan that gives full weight to the political, economic, and religious transformation of the aborigines in historical context.[1] This chapter describes aborigine livelihoods, trading patterns, and population, as the Dutch found them in the first half of the seventeenth century. The next chapter narrates the expansion of Dutch rule over the native villages and analyzes the means by which the Dutch governed the villages and Dutch missionaries penetrated aboriginal societies. Finally I focus on the economic policies adopted by the Dutch to increase revenue from their Taiwan colony, including the encouragement of Chinese agricultural settlement, and the problems a growing Chinese population caused for Dutch control.

Prehistory

Before delving into the early recorded history of the Taiwan frontier, I would like by way of introduction to survey some of what is known about the pre- and protohistory of Taiwan's aboriginal cultures down to the sixteenth century. Taiwan's location between the China mainland and island Southeast Asia makes it of great importance for the study of the interaction of these two spheres. Archaeologists hypothesize that Taiwan served as a stepping-stone for the Austronesian peoples in their movement from south China into island Southeast Asia and the Pacific.

The great heterogeneity of the Austronesian languages spoken by Taiwan's aborigine groups suggests to linguists that Taiwan may have been a center of dispersal for the Austronesian family of languages.[2] Linguists constructing the family tree of the Austronesian languages depict the Formosan languages as its earliest and most divergent branches.[3]

Prehistorians have sought to correlate the findings of the comparative linguists with their own from the archaeological record. In an important synthesis, Peter Bellwood hypothesizes that neolithic Austronesian settlers from southeast China had settled in Taiwan by 4000 B.C., displacing or absorbing the pre-ceramic hunting, fishing, and gathering cultures already resident there for thousands of years.[4] These neolithic settlers are distinguished in the archaeological record by their cord-marked pottery and more sophisticated stone tools, such as rectangular adzes. Archaeologists believe these early neolithic settlers introduced an economy based on horticulture and domesticated animals (dog and pig) as well as hunting. By 2500 B.C. the archaeological evidence (e.g., agriculture-related tools such as stone knives) indicates the emergence of cultures practicing grain-growing agriculture (millet and rice). Two contemporary but separate cultural complexes have been distinguished at this stage, the Lungshanoid, with affinities to the neolithic cultures of China's southeast coast, and the more distinctive Yüan-shan, with possible affinities to cultures further south toward northern Vietnam.[5] Archaeologists working in Taiwan have traced the development, over the thousands of years succeeding the initial Austronesian settlement, of numerous regional cultures, each characterized by distinctive pottery traditions and tool industries. These developments represent indigenous processes of ethnogenesis and cultural development, as well as the absorption of influences from outside Taiwan (it is not necessary to postulate that only separate waves of migration could account for these developments). Two late neolithic cultures from Taiwan's east coast are especially intriguing; these are the megalithic Ch'i-lin culture and the Pei-nan culture, characterized by stone cist graves and jewelry made of Taiwan jades but showing stylistic affinities with cultures to the south in the Philippines and northern Vietnam.[6]

Around the beginning of the current era, iron tools began to make their way to Taiwan. We may speculate that the introduction of iron technology, with iron's superior cutting edges, must have transformed aborigine systems of agriculture, hunting, and warfare, and set off numerous realignments within and among the various cultures of the island. Around Taipei in the north of the island, where surface sources of coal and iron ores are present, archaeologists have found evidence of iron smelting. Groups in other parts of the island must have relied on trade with the north and areas beyond the island or on raiding and occasional shipwrecks for their supplies of iron. The continued use of stone tools suggests that supplies of iron remained limited. The privileged access of the coastal groups to sources of iron and other trade goods, such as beads and pottery, must have given them an economic and military advantage in exploiting the plains and competing with highland groups. All the aboriginal cultures of Taiwan that have come to be known historically or ethnographically since the sixteenth century are iron-using cultures.[7]

The introduction of iron and the Indonesian upright bellows demonstrates a continuing interaction between Taiwan and the outside world, including Southeast Asia. Raleigh Ferrell notes that the pottery style, glass bracelets, and harpoon-like iron spearpoints associated with the grouping he designates the "littoral culture," as well as several cultural traits as diverse as pile dwellings and cosmogonic myths, point to Philippine influences among these groups.[8] Recent studies of Philippine boat building and seafaring suggest that Taiwan was within the range of Philippine seamen.[9] Yet the overall impression remains one of a relatively isolated Taiwan, largely bypassed by the busy trade routes around it. Taiwanese aboriginal languages lack the Sanskrit and Malay loanwords found in the Philippines.[10] And archaeologists and ethnographers rarely find in Taiwan the Sung and later porcelain trade wares found in substantial quantities throughout the Philippines.

When contacted in the seventeenth century, the Formosan groups lived in independent villages of widely varying sizes, with populations ranging from a few thousand to less than a hundred. In 1650 the Dutch village censuses reported under 50,000 aborigines in the plains areas under Dutch control; hence population density was low. The universal practice of head-hunting made intervillage relations always suspicious and frequently hostile. But trading and marriages also took place between villages, and villages formed temporary alliances against common enemies. The villages were free both of overarching state authority and of internal stratification, with the exception in the latter case of the Paiwan and Rukai, who distinguished aristocratic founder and commoner households. Villages were organized internally by age grades, cult groups, and other forms of supra-household organization, and never by "lineages" or kinship alone.

The Formosan groups shared largely similar productive technologies: swidden cultivation of millet, rice, taro, yams, and sugarcane, using hoes and digging sticks; rearing of domesticated pigs, dogs, and chickens; hunting of deer and wild boar with bow and arrow, snares, and iron-tipped spears; and fishing along rivers and coasts using basket traps, nets, and derris poison. In many groups pottery had been largely superseded by wooden utensils carved with iron tools. Weaving was done with the backstrap loom, and iron smithing with the Indonesian upright bellows.[11] Draft animals were absent, as was plow agriculture. These basic systems of production were adapted to the many variations of climate and ecology in the island. The broad similarity in technologies was not matched, however, by uniformity in other aspects of culture and social organization. Instead, the Formosan groups displayed great heterogeneity in language and aspects of culture as diverse as house construction, artistic motifs, personal ornamentation, burial customs, kinship and family organization, village size, and religion.[12]

Map 2.1 presents a language-based classification of Taiwan's aboriginal villages. These ethnolinguistic groupings are based on cultural and linguistic similarities among villages as they have been perceived by ethnographers; they were *not* social entities or political units.[13] Language provides a comparatively consistent and systematic basis for the classification of populations (one that also allows us to postulate linkages with groups outside Taiwan), but it must immediately be added that language, while certainly significant, is only one of culture's many facets. Classifications based on language do not always yield groupings that match those based on the distribution of other cultural traits and cannot serve as one's sole guide to prehistory. Indeed, historical interaction between cultural groups should be expected to create new combinations and increase internal heterogeneity so that classifications based on one trait will frequently crosscut classifications based on another. These complexities should not lead us to abandon the exercise of classification, however, for only through classification can we generate systematic observations that lead to hypotheses about the historical interactions of these cultures.

Ferrell's work on the linguistic and cultural classification of the Taiwan aborigines remains the most authoritative synthesis. He has grouped the nearly twenty language groups into six cultural complexes, four upland (Atayalic, Tsouic, Bunun, Paiwanic) and two plains (littoral and lowland) on the basis of broad similarities in material culture and social organization. Ferrell concludes that the Atayalics and Tsouics, linguistically the two most divergent groups, are also distinctive culturally, whereas his other linguistic subgroupings are crosscut or merged by his cultural groupings.[14] For example, the Puyuma fall into the "littoral culture" composed chiefly of the Ami-Kuvalan subgrouping, although linguistically the Puyuma are most closely related to the Paiwan, who are grouped with the Rukai in a "Paiwanic culture." The Bunun, whose culture seems more eclectic than distinctive, are relegated to a separate cultural grouping of their own, and the vaguely defined "lowland culture" includes the highly divergent but poorly known northwest coast groups.[15] The crisscrossing that results from different principles of classification confirms the high degree of historical intermixing among the Taiwan groups. These complexities of language and culture should make us wary of accepting generic descriptions of Taiwan's aboriginal societies and give us some appreciation of the complicated ethnic and political

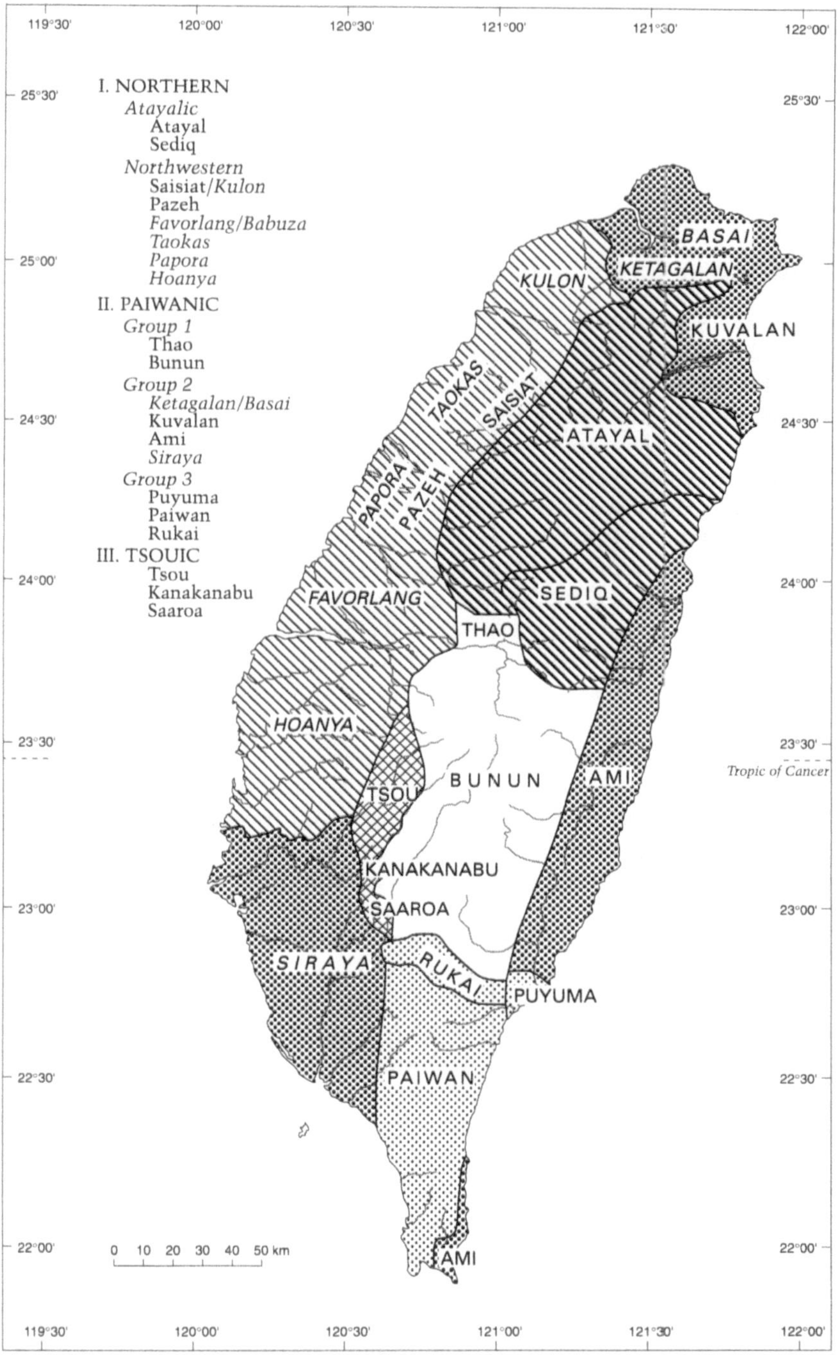

Map 2.1 Aboriginal ethnolinguistic groups of Taiwan. Italics indicate extinct languages.

Adapted from Mabuchi 1953: 4; Ferrell 1969*a*: 26, 1980; Paul Li, 1985, n.d.; and Tsuchida 1985.

situation incoming Dutch and Chinese traders faced in the seventeenth century. It must also be stressed that ethnolinguistic groups were never corporate political actors in aboriginal Taiwan; that role was performed exclusively by independent villages or temporary village alliances. My approach here will be to introduce aspects of the cultures of specific groups only as they become necessary to the narration.

Aborigine Livelihoods

For the seventeenth century, information on the livelihoods of Taiwan's hunter-horticulturalists is best for the southwest core around Tainan, but the evidence points to considerable similarity in crop and tool inventories for the entire western plain.[16] Rice and foxtail millet (glutinous and nonglutinous varieties of both) planted in dry fields were the most widely cultivated grain crops.[17] The first Dutch missionary, Candidius, was surprised to find that although fertile land was abundant, the natives did not cultivate more than "absolutely necessary." His description of the laboriousness of raising a cereal crop and of the abundance of other food sources explains the aborigines' reluctance to invest more labor in agriculture. The natives lacked plows, scythes, and draft animals and had to farm with only hoes, pickaxes, and knives.[18] Aborigine farmers cultivated root crops, vegetables, fruits, and sugarcane in gardens and orchards or collected them from the wild.[19] Rivers and the shoreline were also rich sources of food. Candidius reports that the women collected crabs, shrimps, and oysters and caught and preserved fish, for "next to rice, they consider fish to be their nicest and most important kind of food."[20] Taiwan's teeming deer herds yielded substantial supplies of venison for aborigine diets, as well as hides and dried meat for a thriving trade.[21]

The abundance of fish and game reduced the need to labor long hours in the fields. Among the Siraya only women and old men (age 40 to 60) engaged in agricultural work; the younger men occupied themselves with "hunting and fighting."[22] Rice was valued less as a staple and more for the wine that could be made from it. Candidius asserts that the "greater part" of a year's rice crop went into the manufacture of the native rice beer.[23] The aborigines offered drinks made from fermented rice, millet, and sugarcane to all guests, enjoyed them at all celebrations, and included them in sacrifices offered to the gods. Taboos and rituals focusing on the cultivation of grain emphasized the religious significance of these drinks as much as the importance of grain for subsistence.[24]

What modes of cultivation did the aborigines employ? Ch'en Ti, who visited Taiwan in 1603, asserts that Taiwan's aborigines cleared their fields with fire and did not irrigate them.[25] Ferrell argues: "While it is questionable whether wet-field techniques were known before the arrival of the Chinese, the rice cultivation of the western plains groups in Taiwan may not have been necessarily of the swidden or shifting type, but perhaps was the more extensive type of permanent dry-field cultivation known in Indonesia as *gogo*."[26] In fact, terracing and irrigation techniques, especially for taro cultivation, were widespread in Pacific agriculture.[27] Aborigines could also create wet fields by impounding rainwater or by planting on marshy ground or riverbanks and surely did so in advantageous sites that required little investment of labor.[28] The choice of swidden, dry-permanent, or wet-field techniques is constrained less by technical knowledge than by the economics of land and labor. Where land is abundant, swiddening returns more for labor invested. Seventeenth-century Taiwan was sparsely populated, and aboriginal farmers enjoyed an abundance of land. Plains aborigine population densities, averaging four persons per square kilometer (see below), were well below the maximums supportable by swidden systems of agriculture (estimates range to 50 persons per square kilometer) and are comparable to those reported for swidden groups in the Philippines and Borneo.[29]

Although we do not know the degree to which permanent fields supplemented shifting fields (information on fallowing and rotation periods, techniques for restoring field fertility, and so forth, is unavailable), swidden agriculture did not prevent Taiwan plains groups from living in permanent village sites.[30] The only reported instances of villages abandoning their sites during the Dutch period were due to warfare and not shifting cultivation.[31] Long-term occupation of a village site meant that investment in defense works and homesteads would be repaid. The aborigines protected their villages by impenetrable rings of dense, prickly bamboo.[32] Within the village precincts, each household had a farmstead, with shelter for domestic animals, and patches of garden and orchard.[33] When the Dutch punished rebellious villagers by burning their houses and granaries and cutting down their fruit trees, they were inflicting losses that could not quickly be recouped.[34]

Dutch records contain little about aborigine systems of property ownership or village territories. Households in villages practicing shifting cultivation generally gained exclusive rights to the crops they planted and the fields they cleared only as long as they tilled them; more permanent allocations of land rights were unnecessary so long as uncleared land remained in plentiful supply. Investment of individual effort in hunting or constructing traps or snares also entitled hunters to their game, subject to customary rules ordaining meat distribution to spouses, senior kinsmen, age grades, and village political authorities. Different rules applied to the catch of a group hunt.

We have no reports that village territories were demarcated, but villages undoubtedly had zones of security whose penetration by outsiders they perceived as threatening and treated as such. Villages or component subgroups sometimes claimed exclusive rights to prime hunting territories in their vicinities. There are many reports of aborigines chasing off or beheading trespassing hunters, but these are not specific enough to enable us to distinguish acts of village defense from acts seeking to establish exclusive rights to game.[35] In the twentieth century, when game was much scarcer than in the seventeenth century, Mabuchi Tōichi reports the Bunun of the central mountains recognized a form of ownership over hunting territories that entitled the owners to a portion of any game caught there by non-owners. Non-owners who cleared fields in others' hunting territories were required to offer a feast of millet beer to the owners. The mountain tribes also provide examples of the payment of tribute by one group to another. Weaker groups made gifts of iron, pigs, cloth, and rice wine for the privilege of farming in another group's territory unmolested by head-hunting raids and presented gifts to allay militarily superior neighbors. Similar arrangements among plains groups seem highly likely, but in lieu of concrete information, these examples can only be suggestive.[36]

By the seventeenth century iron and bronze (although in limited supply) had been part of the tool kit of Taiwan's aborigines for a millennium. The superior qualities of sharp metal blades made them most valuable for the weapons employed in hunting and warfare; we have reports of iron-pointed spears, broadswords, and "Japanese hatchets."[37] Metal was also used in agricultural tools for clearing fields and harvesting rice.[38] Iron was scarce and highly valued; the marriage prestations of wealthy families included iron rings, and men stored wealth in the iron hoops and bracelets they wore as ornaments.[39] As mentioned above, aborigines mined and smelted ore in northern Taiwan and also obtained iron and bronze from foreign traders, fishermen, and shipwrecks (quite frequent in the treacherous waters around Taiwan).[40] Their privileged access to sources of metal gave the plains aborigines military and economic advantages over their high mountain neighbors.

An early Chinese report purportedly relating to Taiwan illustrates the value of iron to aboriginal societies like those of Taiwan. Chao Ju-kua records that late in the twelfth century "savages" from P'i-she-ye sailed to Fukien on bamboo rafts and raided the coastal villages for iron:

> They were fond of iron vessels, spoons, and chopsticks; one could get rid of them by closing the entrance door, from which they would only wrench the iron knocker and go away. By throwing away spoons and chopsticks they could be got to stoop down to pick them up. . . .
>
> When attacking the enemy, they are armed with javelins to which are attached ropes of over an hundred feet in length, in order to recover them after each throw; for they put such value on the iron of which these weapons are made, that they cannot bear to lose them.[41]

Whether P'i-she-ye should be identified with Taiwanese Sirayans or Philippine Visayans is a matter of scholarly controversy, but we need not doubt that Taiwanese aborigines were willing to take similar risks to increase their supplies of a metal so important to their livelihoods.[42]

Aborigine Trade

Taiwan was in no sense pristine when the Dutch arrived in the 1620's; a long history of trading contacts preceded them.[43] Chinese records of contacts with Taiwan increase over the sixteenth century when the Chinese and Japanese pirates known as the *wakō* flourished. In the 1560's the pirate Lin Tao-ch'ien took refuge in the Pescadores and Taiwan after being driven from the Fukien coast. Lin reportedly terrorized the aborigines at several points along Taiwan's western coast, forcing many of them to flee inland. In the succeeding year pirates were active in trading (largely for deerskins) and raiding in Taiwan and in nearby Luzon.[44]

In 1603 the Ming admiral Shen Yu-jung led an expedition to the Tayouan area (Chinese: Ta-yüan) to drive out *wakō* pirates. Ch'en Ti, a member of this expedition, wrote a brief description of the aborigines of southwest Taiwan and noted an increasing trade between Chinese (many of whom were fishermen) and Taiwan aborigines that he dated from *wakō* raiding in the late sixteenth century: "[Chinese] from the harbors of Hui-min, Ch'ung-lung and Lieh-yu in Chang-chou and Ch'üan-chou [prefectures] frequently [are able to] translate their language[s], and trade with them. They trade them things like agates, porcelain, cloth, salt, brass [or copper], hairpins, and bracelets, in exchange for their deer meat, skins and horns."[45] Fishermen, who must have had understandings with the pirates (some were occasional pirates), had long anchored in the Pescadores and were active traders along the Taiwan coast well into Dutch times.[46]

By the time the Dutch arrived, Chinese traders were resident in many aborigine settlements; one report estimated as many as 1,500 Chinese traders throughout the island organized the supply of deerskins from the villages to the trading ships at Tayouan. A Dutch visitor to Hsiao-lung (Soulang) in 1623 noted several Chinese traders living in each men's house, who regularly bullied the aborigines by threatening to cut off salt imports.[47] This report implies that the aborigines' lack of interest in agriculture was due, in part, to their ability to trade large amounts of dried venison and skins for rice and salt. Candidius, however, reports the aborigines of the same area trading deer products *and* rice to the Chinese, mainly in exchange for cloth.[48] Although the 1623 report seems to exaggerate the importance of Chinese rice imports, both reports leave no doubt that the aborigines did substantial amounts of trading. In 1624 a single Japanese ship carried off 18,000 deerskins from Tayouan. Numbers like these led the greedy Dutch to (over)estimate the potential exports of their new colony at 200,000 skins a year. The magnitude of the deerskin trade is an indication that the aborigines were part of a commercialized, though not monetarized (deerskins were the medium of exchange) economy, when the Dutch arrived.[49]

To understand this trade, we need to know the value the aborigines put on the goods the trade supplied and the reason for the great demand for Taiwan's deer products among the Chinese and Japanese. Perhaps the most important trade good was iron, for which the aborigines had a large unsatisfied demand. Unworked iron was in great demand for manufacturing the cutting edges of weapons and tools. Imported iron pots, which could be put directly on the fire and were not subject to breakage, were preferred for many uses over wooden, pottery, or gourd vessels. Chinese porcelain containers had similar advantages.[50] Metallic jewelry, quite apart from its aesthetic and status-enhancing functions, was a form of stored wealth and could be traded or converted to practical uses. The aborigines also liked to trade for bronze and copper bells. Candidius reports that bells attached to hunting spears betrayed the location of wounded deer. Aborigines also used bells in ear pendants, headbands, and women's festival dresses. In 1603 Ch'en Ti noted that the aborigines of the Tayouan area were preserving bells as heirlooms.[51]

Imported salt was another important trading commodity. Several aborigine villages made salt and traded it to other villages, but the native product seems to have been deficient in quantity and bitter in taste. Demand for salt was high because the aborigines used it to preserve meat and fish, as well as for seasoning.[52] These commodities were so important to the aborigines that by withholding supplies of salt and iron the Dutch could force rebellious native villages to submit (see the case of Wu-lao-wan discussed in Chapter 3).

The aborigines initially had no "need" for many of the trade goods offered them, and the expansion of trade and aborigine willingness to produce for trade had to await the growth of new needs, fashions, and demands for "creature comforts." One such acquired taste was imported cloth. Demand for cloth was initially depressed by two factors. Native clothing was already available in a wide range of materials: skins (leather and furs), bark cloth, and woven blends of ramie and dogs' hair.[53] But more important, Taiwan enjoys subtropical weather for much of the year, and the natives could wear little if any clothing quite comfortably. Indeed, in the Tayouan area, the wearing of clothing during the grain-growing season was considered offensive to the gods. Village elders forced violators of the taboo to forfeit their clothes and pay a fine. At other times only silk garments were forbidden.[54] Despite these taboos, the natives had begun to acquire colorful cotton cloth (calicoes or cangans) not only for its practical advantages (it was less coarse, more durable, and warmer in winter) but also for its aesthetic and prestige value.[55] Dutch missionary attacks on nudity and native religion further eroded taboos on clothing.

Cloth's economic value and symbolic uses made it a powerful instrument in the hands of the Dutch. The Dutch bought the site of Sakam (Tainan) from the aborigine village of Hsin-kang (Sinkan) for a mere fifteen cangans. They also used cloth to pay for the services of their native auxiliaries.[56] The black capes awarded to representatives to the village delegates assemblies (see Chapter 3) symbolized authority and enhanced their status in their home villages.[57]

Imported textiles not only were of practical value for the natives but also could be used to demand respect and to express cultural allegiances. In 1603 Ch'en Ti noted: "Occasionally [those traders] will give them old clothing, and these they like to store away; should they meet Chinese, they will put them on, and then when [the Chinese] have gone they will take them off again."[58] In 1650 the visitor John Struys noted that most aborigines, when not wearing traditional native attire, dressed in Chinese clothes rather than European (Chinese were more numerous in the colony, and their clothing was undoubtedly cheaper and in greater supply).[59] But it was the Dutch who held wealth and power in the colony and who enjoyed the highest prestige. In 1648 Governor Pieter Overtwater was pleased to report:

> Recently many of the inhabitants of Sinkan came to the schoolmaster and asked him for a list of Dutch names, as they wished to use them in the future for themselves, thus abandoning their own names and adopting ours. Moreover, they decided that hereafter they would dress on Sundays in the Dutch fashion; and that, any one failing to do so, would willingly become liable to a fine of about two pence on each occasion. All this they did of their own free, untrammeled will, without any meddling or interposition on our part; or our holding out any inducement whatever.[60]

By adopting their fashions, the aborigines could lay claim to Dutch prestige and cement alliances with their powerful Dutch overlords.

Foreign trade did not always change native fashions: sometimes it supplied goods to enhance aboriginal styles. This was the case with agate, amber, red coral, and multicolored glass beads, all of which joined shell beads in native jewelry and costumes.[61]

As early as 1623, the Dutch found the natives "surprisingly keen on Chinese tobacco."[62] Tobacco and cheap arrack (molasses) wine, along with cangans, were frequently presented as gifts or used to pay for services of villagers. Tobacco remained an important item in the aborigine trade until it began to be cultivated locally.[63]

Native exports were almost exclusively deer products. In the seventeenth century, forests and tall grasses covered Taiwan's largely uncultivated plains as well as its high mountains.[64] These areas were teeming with herds of deer, "sometimes two or three thousand in a flock together."[65] The most numerous species were the sambar, Formosan sika, and muntjac. The large-antlered sambar and sika could graze in open country on grasses, herbaceous vegetation, and cultivated fields, as well as browse in woodland on trees and shrubs. The smaller muntjacs, with simple, spike-like antlers, preferred to browse selectively in the deeper mountain forests.[66] The aborigines hunted these deer with bows and arrows, spears, and pitfalls and snares and by using dogs or brushfires to drive herds into traps.

In Japan and China, the wide variety of products made of deerskin leather created a substantial demand for pelts and skins. The Japanese civil wars boosted demand for leather for samurai armor, saddle trimmings, and quivers. Deerskin pelts, shorter-haired and much cheaper than sable or fox, were used for jackets, boots, *tabi* (digitated socks), trousers, bags, lacquered leather boxes, blankets, mattresses, tobacco pouches, and wall ornaments.[67] Japan, whose demand for skins per capita must have been greater than China's (due to its colder climate, and perhaps differences in the textile industry and clothing styles), imported huge numbers of deerskins from Thailand, Cambodia, and Luzon as well as Taiwan, giving rise to a large-scale international trade.[68] For skins and pelts, at least, China seems to have relied largely on domestic supplies. But Chinese demand for other deer products was substantial. Dried, smoked, and salted venison was exported to Chinese ports and retained for the rations of Dutch soldiers.[69] Deer antlers and penises were especially valued by Chinese for their medicinal properties.[70]

In addition to exports of deer products, there was a market for rattans and medicinal herbs collected from the forests.[71] In the Tan-shui area, natives traded sulfur, in increasing demand for use in explosives in Chinese dynastic wars. In the Keelung area, the Dutch demanded coal as tribute from the natives.[72]

Aborigine Population: The Puzzle of Village Size

Dutch village censuses provide a unique source of information on the seventeenth-century aborigine population. The Dutch began to compile lists of villages and their populations in 1644; the six extant lists date from 1647, 1648, 1650, 1654, 1655, and 1656. Nakamura Takashi believes the village census lists were compiled from the records of *landdag* meetings at which each delegate reported the number of households and the population of his village (see Chapter 3). In areas where Dutch control was weak, such as the east coast and certain mountain valleys, the reports are clearly estimates.[73] Large areas, especially in the central mountains, lay beyond Dutch control and were not included in the lists. Tables 2.1 and 2.2 are computed from the lists of 1647, 1650, and 1655 and summarize aborigine population by region and ethnic group.[74]

The censuses list villages by small areas and then group these areas together according to their membership in one of the four regional *landdag* councils. Table 2.1 groups the villages into nine geographic subregions. Region 6 is the most diverse and combines villages of the highland ethnic groups from seven mountain valleys from throughout the southwest coastal area. The remaining census regions are geographically compact. The four *landdag* assemblies were held as follows: one in Tainan (Dutch: Sakam) for the area to the north (Regions 3, 4, and part of 6); one in Tainan for the area to the south (Regions 5, 7, and part of 6); one in T'ai-tung (Dutch: Pimaba) for the east coast (Region 9); and one in Tan-shui for the Taipei, northwest coast, and I-lan areas (Regions 1, 2, and 8). The census regions in Table 2.1 correspond therefore to administrative-geographic regions and not to aborigine ethnolinguistic groupings.

The 1650 figures show the Dutch administration at its greatest extent, when 68,657 aborigines in 268 villages were under nominal Dutch control (see Table 2.1). Regions 4 and 5 correspond to the greater southwest core pacified by the Dutch in 1636. The remaining areas were brought under some measure of Dutch control in the early 1640's. Between 1647 and 1650 the increase in enumerated villages indicates expanding Dutch influence in the Taipei area and the southwest mountain villages. The list for 1655 reveals that many villages in the mountains, the I-lan area, and on the east coast had broken away from the Dutch, who by then were too preoccupied with a burgeoning and rebellious Chinese population to reassert control in distant regions. In the southwest coastal areas, where Dutch administration remained strong, the 1655 report of fewer people but not fewer villages appears to be due to an epidemic of "ague and measles" in 1653.[75]

Table 2.2 regroups the plains aborigine villages of the west coast and I-lan by ethnolinguistic affiliation and gives crude territorial estimates as well as population and household figures for 1650, the date of most extensive coverage. The task of identifying the ethnolinguistic affiliation of villages listed in the Dutch censuses presents many difficulties (see Appendix A). Table 2.2 gives population totals for all villages in the 1650 list that Chang Yao-ch'i has identified as belonging to one of the plains aborigine ethnolinguistic groupings. Rough estimates of the extent of the territories occupied by each plains group were obtained by matching the area figures available for Taiwan's modern townships to the broad areas identified as occupied by each ethnolinguistic group in Appendix A.[76]

One big contrast between regions and ethnic groups stands out in

TABLE 2.1

Aborigine Village Population by Census Region, 1647, 1650, 1655

Census region	1647 No. of villages	1647 Pop.	1647 Avg. village pop.	1650 No. of villages	1650 Pop.	1650 Avg. village pop.	1655 No. of villages	1655 Pop.	1655 Avg. village pop.
1. Keelung & Taipei Basin	19	3,800	200	35	6,320	180	38	4,161	109
2. Northwest coast	15	2,594	173	13	3,587	276	18	3,185	177
3. Central coast	33	6,948	211	33 (+13)[a]	8,043	244	33	7,673	233
4. Northern SW coast (Hsin-kang to Chu-lo)	8	8,056	1,007	8	8,096	1,012	8	6,475	809
5. Southern SW coast	9	7,302	811	15	12,247	816	11	9,145	831
6. Mountain valleys of SW coast	51	13,995	274	70	14,510	207	50	6,647	133
7. Heng-ch'un	18	933	52	22	1,779	81	19	1,297	68
8. I-lan	43	9,865	229	45	9,670	215	3	640	213
9. East coast (T'ai-tung)	27	4,086 (est.)	151	27 (+34)[a]	4,405 (est.)	163	43	—	—
TOTAL	223	57,579	258	268	68,657	256	223	39,223	218[b]

SOURCES: Based on the censuses reproduced in Nakamura 1936 (1650), 1937 (1655), 1951 (1647).

[a] Additional villages were listed in 1650 for these areas but not even estimated population figures were given for them.

[b] Average village size computed for 180 villages reporting populations.

TABLE 2.2

Plains Aborigine Population by Ethnic Group, 1650

Ethnic group (census regions in parentheses)	No. of villages	No. of households	Pop.	Area (km^2)	Avg. village pop.	Density (pop./km^2)	Avg. village area (km^2)	Avg. household size
Kuvalan (8)	45	2,272	9,670	739	215	13.1	16	4.3
Ketagalan (1 & 2)	37	1,741	6,972	1,929	188	3.6	52	4.0
Taokas (2)	11	781	2,935	1,315	267	2.2	120	3.8
Papora (3)	4	118	454	196	114	2.3	49	3.8
Pazeh (3)	7	379	1,649	474	236	3.5	68	4.4
Favorlang (Babuza) (3)	11	681	3,171	1,198	288	2.6	109	4.7
Hoanya (3 & 4)	13	1,000	3,940	2,650	303	1.5	204	3.9
Non-Siraya subtotal	128	6,972	28,791	8,501	225	3.4	66	4.1
Siraya (4 & 5)	21	3,866	19,172	3,684	913	5.2	175	5.0
TOTAL	149	10,838	47,963	12,185	322	3.9	82	4.4

NOTE: Plains aborigine villages are assigned to ethnic groups according to Chang Yao-ch'i 1951. See Map 2.1 and Appendix A for the geographic distribution of these groups. Ketagalan includes the recently distinguished Basai and Kulon groups.

Tables 2.1 and 2.2—the large size of the Siraya villages in the southwest core (Regions 4 and 5). The population of these villages ranged from 800 to over 1,000, compared with an average in the 200's (or less) among all other ethnic groups. That such a large difference is obvious in all years of the reports and is consistent with independent sources and ethnographic descriptions suggests that it could not be an artifact of Dutch census-taking methods. What factors can account for this difference?

Ecological factors might explain the difference if we could establish that in the more tropical southwest core, agriculture, as well as hunting and fishing, was more productive and could support higher densities and larger concentrations of people. But there is little evidence that the area around Tainan was richer than other areas or that its resources were so concentrated in space as to foster growth of large villages. One Dutch observer, to the contrary, asserted that "Midag," in the Papora area of the central coast, was Taiwan's "most fruitful region," and the Dutch missionary Junius praised the Hoanya area (modern Chia-i), just north of the Siraya, for its "beautiful and fertile fields, full of stags and hinds." Of course, some areas may have been poorer than the southwest; another Dutchman described the Favorlang area (modern Chang-hua) as "very barren and unproductive."[77] There is no evidence of marked differences in the crop and tool inventories used to exploit the environment that would make the southwest richer than other plains regions.[78] Moreover, if the quality of the ecology were behind the difference, we should expect the immediately neighboring plains region of the Hoanya, which stands between the Siraya and the groups to the north in terms of climate (rainfall and temperature) and ecology, to fall midway along a gradient of population densities and average village sizes. Table 2.2, however, shows a deep divide rather than a gradient between the Siraya and the Hoanya.[79] And where there is most likely the greatest ecological difference, between the mountain valleys (Region 6 in Table 2.1) and the plains, the range of average village sizes is the same as for the other non-Siraya plains areas.

If a richer environment were behind large village size, we would predict a higher overall population density for the southwest core. Using measures of gross plains areas (shown in Table 2.2), we can compare the population densities attained by the various plains ethnolinguistic groups. Table 2.2 shows an overall population density of 5.2 persons per square kilometer for the Siraya, which is indeed higher than the average of 3.4 for the other plains aborigine groups. But whereas Siraya population density was less than twice as great, Siraya villages were on average more than four times as large as the non-Siraya villages. A look at the other groups reveals little correlation between population density and average village size. The Hoanya villages are the second largest, although Hoanya population density is the lowest; the Kuvalan and Ketagalan, who have above-average population densities (greater than the Siraya in the case of the Kuvalan), have below-average village sizes. The difference in densities does not match the difference in village population size: whereas the non-Siraya groups have much smaller village populations, all but the Hoanya have more villages per unit of area than the Siraya. So the differences in village population between the Siraya and non-Siraya are much greater than differences in population density can account for. The factors explaining village size must lie in social organization rather than ecology and population density.

Can a longer history of Dutch trade in the southwest core explain the large average village size? The Dutch commercial presence in Tayouan and that of the Chinese and Japanese before them certainly stimulated a growth in local trade. And with an increase in the division of labor, productivity may have grown. But the same objections to explaining the difference by higher productivity due to ecological variation hold for higher productivity due to commercialization. Population densities do not show sufficient differences between the regions; instead of a gradient in village size between commercialized core and less commercialized peripheral areas, there is a sharp divide. Nor do other regions with a coastal trade, for example, Tan-shui and the central coast, have villages in similar or even intermediate size ranges. The trading hypothesis might also lead us to predict large market centers surrounded by rings of small villages. No such pattern appears: the villages of the southwest core were quite uniform in size. Thus trade and commercialization also fail to explain the large size of Siraya villages.

Did the Dutch impose consolidation on villages under their strongest control? There is only one example of this in the southwest core: three small villages, apparently depopulated by warfare, were urged to unite. The Dutch then set up a school in the consolidated village.[80] The Dutch were more concerned to see that any population movement between villages was done only with their permission than they were to evacuate and regroup villages (surely a politically dangerous task).[81] In any case, the large size of the four main villages in the Tayouan area was noted in Dutch estimates of male combatants in each village in 1625, long before the extension of Dutch administration could have had an impact.[82] If anything, the conquest should have reduced village size, at least temporarily, given the reports of fired villages and fleeing inhabitants (although of course this would be true of other areas as well).[83]

Endemic warfare could lead populations to concentrate in large villages for defense. But intervillage warfare and head-hunting were common throughout the island and thus cannot explain the marked regional difference in average village size. Again, if warfare were the factor, given that the Dutch-imposed peace was of greatest duration in the southwest core, we might expect villages there to have dispersed into smaller units—the opposite of the observed pattern. The absence of intervillage warfare may, however, help explain why villages in Heng-ch'un (Region 7) were extremely small (less than 100): these hamlets were ruled by a single hereditary chief under whom they united to fight against groups in other regions.[84]

Uxorilocal marriage, age grades, and village endogamy best explain why markedly large average village size is observed only among the Siraya. It is common in uxorilocal systems for men to retain important rights and duties in their natal group; among the Siraya this pattern was reinforced by the male age grades that united the village politically and organized its defense. In marrying, Siraya males had to minimize the distance between their natal kin groups and age grade organizations and the residences of their wives and children. By marrying solely within their natal villages, men were able to bridge this distance and retain permanent membership in their age grade sets.[85] The incest taboo (reported to reach to the "fourth generation" among the Siraya),[86] which eliminated close relatives as potential marriage partners, meant that each settlement had to contain a sizable population of non-relatives if men were to find wives within the village. The operation of such a marriage system required that Siraya villages attain a large average village size. By contrast, when marriage is virilocal, the ties between married women and their natal groups are commonly attenuated. Virilocal families give daughters away to partners outside the village and bring wives in, and they have no need for (and may prefer to avoid) contracting marriages with families in the same village. Village exogamy thus results in a smaller average village size.

Do uxorilocal marriage and matrilineal kinship explain the *regional* difference? Reviews of kinship organization for all Taiwan groups report that all non-Siraya groups on the west coast practiced virilocal and ambilocal marriage and reckoned kinship on a variety of patrilineal, ambilineal, and bilateral principles; their small average village size accords with these observations. These same reviews show matrilineal kinship among the Siraya and on the east coast (including I-lan).[87] Why do the east coast regions not show larger average village size on the Dutch lists? There are two possible reasons. Dutch control was both brief and weak on the east coast and in I-lan, and the Dutch census there the least reliable. The east coast census region may also have included villages of non-matrilineal ethnolinguistic groups. Modern studies of the east coast matrilineal groups, Ami and Puyuma, do show a large average village size, in the 600–700 range, and report uxorilocal marriage, male age grades, and village endogamy.[88] But that still leaves the little-known Kuvalan of I-lan. Reports on the Kuvalan describe them as matrilineal and uxorilocal but do not describe age grades. Their villages are on average too small to have made endogamy feasible. The great number of their villages (45 in 1650), however, made village density on the I-lan plain very high (see the village area figures in Table 2.2), reducing considerably the distances between villages. This must have considerably eased the problem men faced in bridging the distance between their natal villages and those of their wives and eased the pressure to find wives within natal villages.

Another factor may explain average village size in a region. Given the endemic state of warfare among the aborigines, once one or two villages succeeded in attaining a large size relative to others in the region, they would enjoy both defensive and offensive advantages. (Groups practicing uxorilocal marriage, because of the special attractions of endogamy for them, have an advantage in forming large villages.) This alone could force competing settlements to regroup into large villages. Because of this escalatory dynamic, large size may itself be a factor causing large size in other villages. Although this dynamic may not fully explain differences between regions, it can explain a suppression of variation in village size within a region.

One more observation can be made from the census: average household size of the four Siraya villages nearest Tainan (Hsin-kang, Mu-chia-liu-wan, Hsiao-lung, Ma-tou) ranges between 5 and 9 and is 5.0 for the Siraya overall; this is markedly larger than that of the other groups, which range from 3 to 6 and average 4.1. I am tempted to see here one more effect of the presence of matrilineal kinship and sororal extended households. Ferrell's comparison of the house styles of the various Taiwan groups found the Siraya house to be much larger than those of the west-central plains. This variation may be due to the fact that Siraya houses were the dwellings of extended kin groups.[89]

Computing average household size from the Dutch figures for population and number of households in a village may compound the healthy margin of error in both numbers. Take, for example, the Siraya village of Hsiao-lung: in 1650 its reported population was 2,093 in 241 households. By 1654 its population had dropped by 600 to 1,490, but the number of households grew by four to 245 (the 1654 average household size, 6.08, is still high).[90] It is hard to imagine a cause for the loss of 600 people (war, epidemic, village fission?) spread so evenly that it would not also reduce the number of households.[91] And this curious discrepancy comes from the figures for a southwest core village where we would expect the intimate knowledge of the Dutch to have produced the most reliable figures. Because of such discrepancies, I do not think the censuses will bear more refined analysis. Nevertheless, I think we can have confidence in the village population figures as estimates so long as we check for major inconsistencies between the years. The finding of large average village size among the Siraya of the southwest core, because it is stable across the years and because the difference is of such great magnitude, remains a firm one.

The large differences in village size imply important contrasts in marriage systems and political organization among the plains aborigine ethnic groupings and suggest the complexity of the aboriginal situation at the time of Dutch colonization. This review of aborigine economies, trade, and population introduces the nature of the societies the Dutch confronted as they sought to expand their control over the aboriginal villages and increase their revenues from them. We turn in Chapter 3 to the Dutch conquest of the plains.

CHAPTER THREE

The Dutch Era, 1624–1661

TAIWAN'S ISOLATION ENDS and its modern history begins in the sixteenth century. Despite Ming attempts to interdict Chinese participation in maritime trade, the sixteenth century saw a general expansion in oceangoing international commerce (and piracy) in East Asian waters. Merchants, pirates, and fishermen from both China and Japan began to make increasing use of harbors in Taiwan and the Pescadores. Ming campaigns against smuggling and piracy in the 1550's and 1560's forced pirates such as Lin Tao-ch'ien to seek refuge in Taiwan, where they sometimes pillaged coastal aborigine villages.[1] After 1567 the Ming relaxed the maritime restrictions for a few decades. Then, in response to continued pirate raids along the Chinese coast and the Japanese invasion of Korea in 1592, the Ming court reimposed its prohibition on direct Chinese trade with Japan. This led to the growth of an indirect and clandestine Sino-Japanese trade channeled through Taiwanese ports. In 1603 a Ming naval force landed briefly in Tayouan on an expedition aimed at eradicating Japanese piracy and smuggling.[2]

New trade linkages established by European merchantmen stimulated the expanding East Asian trade in the sixteenth century. The Portuguese were the first Europeans to establish an important foothold in the China trade, and by the end of the sixteenth century they dominated the Japan trade from their colony of Macao, founded about 1555 near Canton. The Spanish took Manila in 1571 and soon began pouring silver from their New World colonies into a rapidly increasing trade with merchants from the Amoy area of coastal Fukien.[3]

In 1602 the States of Holland awarded its East India Company a monopoly of Dutch trade in the East and gave the company powers to wage war and governmental authority in the colonies it founded. The Dutch were late arrivals to the China coast, and they came determined to break up Portuguese and Spanish monopolies of the China trade.[4] Company fleets launched attacks on shipping lanes and Portuguese and Spanish

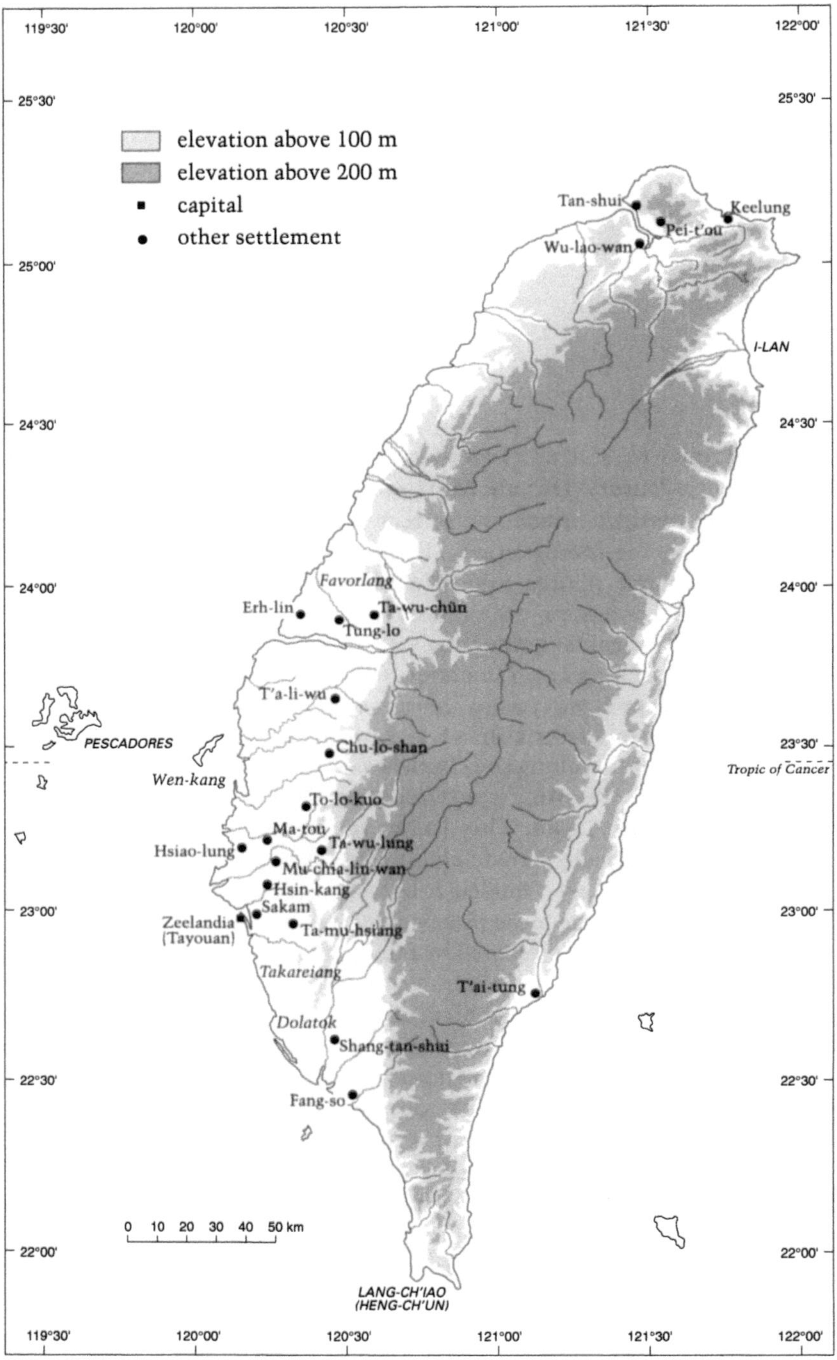

Map 3.1 Taiwan in the Dutch era, selected sites

outposts and searched for a foothold of their own. In 1604 and again in 1607, Dutch fleets anchored in the Pescadores (where they found the only inhabitants to be Chinese fishermen) and sought, unsuccessfully, to induce Chinese merchants from the Fukien coast to come to trade.[5] In 1622 the Dutch East India Company resolved to establish a trading colony either by taking Macao from the Portuguese or by founding a base in the Pescadores. "After having thus spent several years in fruitless expeditions to China, the Company decided, in 1622, to send captain Reyerszoon again to China, either to conquer Macao, or to go to the Fisherman's island [the Pescadores] and see if he could in this way establish a trade with China."[6] When its attack on Macao failed, the Dutch fleet withdrew to the Pescadores in July 1622. There the Dutch erected a small fortress and used the islands as a base for intercepting the Chinese trade with Manila and launching raids on the Fukien coast to "induce the Chinese to trade by force or from fear." The ensuing negotiations between the Dutch and Chinese authorities were protracted by frequent breakdowns and renewed fighting. The Chinese proposed to authorize trade in Taiwan, if the Dutch would abandon the Pescadores. Then, in August 1624, when a Chinese fleet threatened to drive them from the Pescadores, the Dutch withdrew to the harbor of Tayouan (present-day An-p'ing, Tainan; see Map 3.1) in Taiwan, on condition that Chinese trade would be forthcoming.[7]

In Tayouan the Dutch had still to come to terms with Chinese village traders, Japanese merchants, and the aboriginal inhabitants. But at last they had acquired a strategic foothold to challenge the Spanish domination of the Amoy-Manila trade and the Portuguese domination of the Macao-Japan trade.[8] The Dutch planned to seize control of this highly profitable trade by building a fortified trading colony and entrepôt at Tayouan. The Dutch aimed to profit by carrying Chinese silk, the most valuable item in this trade, other textiles, porcelains, sugar, hides, and many other goods to Japan, other countries in Asia, and Europe. Goods produced locally in Taiwan played no role in the Dutch East India Company's commercial strategy at this time. Tayouan's role was to serve as a naval base and transshipment center. Trading factories were established, and a governor and council were appointed to rule the colony and manage its affairs. The Taiwan governor reported to the governor-general in Batavia (in Java), who in turn answered to the company's board of directors (the "Gentlemen Seventeen") in Amsterdam.[9]

The Dutch soon discovered, however, that they could not limit their presence in Taiwan to an entrepôt. First, skirmishes with Chinese and Japanese traders and the aborigines convinced them that they could not be safe in their harbor without some control over its hinterland. The Dutch also feared that if they did not exercise territorial control, then a rival power, such as Japan or Spain, might be tempted to stir up the aborigines against them. Second, relying on imported foodstuffs to supply the garrison of the Dutch fort at Tayouan was risky and expensive. A cheap and reliable local source of supply was needed. Third, the first missionaries, Georgius Candidius and Robertus Junius, who were active in the nearest village, Hsin-kang (Dutch: Sinkan; present-day Hsin-shih *chen*, T'ai-nan county), insisted that extension of Dutch rule was necessary to spread the Gospel (and that spreading the Gospel was necessary to the preservation of Dutch rule).[10] Fourth, large local expenditures (and pacification of the countryside was expensive) increased the pressure to find local sources of revenue, which, in circular fashion, required investment in the extension and maintenance of territorial dominion.

Long-awaited reinforcements arrived in 1635 and were immediately employed in a highly successful campaign to subdue the aborigine villages in the hinterland of Tayouan.[11] In the early 1640's the Dutch pacified villages in central Taiwan and drove the Spanish out of northern Taiwan, where they had arrived in 1626. These campaigns transformed Taiwan from an entrepôt to a full-fledged colony.

To finance the operation of the expanded colony, the Dutch adopted a number of revenue-generating measures. They monopolized and taxed the native export trade in deer products. They licensed Chinese fishermen seeking to exploit the coastal fisheries. And most important for Taiwan's later transformation, they sponsored rice and sugarcane farming by Chinese immigrants. These policies gave rise to a colonial plural society of Europeans, Chinese, and indigenes not unlike those that grew up in Dutch Batavia and the Spanish Philippines.

Once control was established by military means (a task made easy by disunity and endemic warfare among the native head-hunting tribes), the basic plan of Dutch East India Company rule was to use Chinese farmers and village traders to exploit Taiwan's resources and Dutch missionaries to control the native population. This plan created a structure of competing interests from which most of the conflicts in this colonial society derived. Dutch clergy and native deer hunters were united in wanting to limit the exactions of Chinese traders and company agents in the villages. Company agents countered by attacking the excesses of clergymen and native schoolmasters. Chinese farmers and traders resented Dutch taxation and company restrictions on their trade. Company agents and missionaries were united in their interest in maintaining control over what was becoming one of the most profitable of the Dutch East India Company's trading colonies.[12] But the Chinese settlers, who contributed greatly to the colony's commercial success, were also a threat to continued Dutch rule: "The Ch'ing conquest of coastal areas of China caused an increasing flood of immigrants to Taiwan, which was soon recognized as a menace to Dutch control there. Dutch taxation, fixed prices for sugar purchases and efforts to control Chinese exploitation of the aborigines made the Taiwan Chinese receptive to anti-Dutch propaganda, and organization."[13] The Dutch and their native allies easily defeated an abortive revolt of Chinese farmers in 1652. But when Cheng Ch'eng-kung, following defeats in his campaigns against the Manchus, landed an overwhelming force on Taiwan in 1661, the small Dutch garrison could only withdraw to the security of its castle walls. When all hope of outside aid was lost, the Dutch surrendered.

Frederick Coyett, the last Dutch governor, reflected that "it is not always advisable to annex territory when opportunity offers" and that "at the very beginning, the Company should either not have started this work on such a big scale, or afterwards have maintained it by contributing all that was needful for preservation and security, even though this entailed a little loss. The Company would then have preserved its reputation."[14] Tolerance for financial loss, even in the expectation of long-term profit, however, was not a hallmark of the company's history in Taiwan.

The Expansion of Dutch Control over the Aborigines

After their fleet anchored in the Pescadores in 1622, the Dutch sent several ships to investigate harbors and trade in Taiwan. In October 1623 the chief merchant, Jacob Constant, began a stockade on the sandy peninsula called Tayouan, overlooking the harbor of Tainan, already an established entrepôt for Japanese merchants. Relations with the local aborigine villages were cordial until Chinese village traders incited the inhabitants of the village of Mu-chia-liu-wan to attack a Dutch party cutting bamboo for the stockade. The Dutch blamed this on the Chinese fear that the Dutch would interfere with their lucrative trade in deerskins.[15] In 1624, when they retreated to Taiwan from the Pescadores, the Dutch strengthened this stockade and ultimately expanded it into Zeelandia Castle.[16] Early in 1625, the Dutch purchased Sakam (Chinese: Ch'ih-k'an), a site on the mainland side of the harbor, to build a town and locate a trading headquarters. This site eventually became the Chinese city of Tainan. Sakam fell within the territory of the village of Hsin-kang, which received fifteen pieces of trade cloth (cangans) in exchange.[17] Hsin-kang was located inland about seven miles northeast of Sakam.[18] Since the villagers were especially eager to get goods such as cloth and tobacco from the Dutch, relations with the aborigine villages in the vicinity of the harbor (Hsin-kang, Hsiao-lung, Ma-tou, Mu-chia-liu-wan) were at first peaceful.[19]

Dutch intervention in intervillage warfare in these early years won them an ally in Hsin-kang. According to Candidius, "The inhabitants of Mattau [Ma-tou] and Bakloan [Mu-chia-liu-wan] are bitter enemies of the Sinkan [Hsin-kang] village, and would certainly have burnt it to the ground and slaughtered its inhabitants, if the Dutch had not taken pity on them by sending about a hundred musketeers for their deliverance.

The village of Sinkan came under the protection of the Dutch at that time, and without this protection it would not exist for one day."[20] Relations between the Dutch and Hsin-kang soured when they became entangled in Dutch-Japanese rivalry. In 1625, when the Dutch tried to impose duties on the trade at Tayouan, Japanese merchants refused to pay. This was the beginning of a dispute over control of the trade that would boil for several years.[21] In 1627 a Japanese captain transported sixteen friendly Hsin-kang villagers and two Chinese interpreters to Japan, hoping to have them present Taiwan to the Japanese shogun. The scheme failed, and the party returned to Taiwan in 1628, where it immediately came into conflict with the Dutch.[22] The Dutch imprisoned the aborigine representatives. Four managed to escape to Hsin-kang, and the rest were released as part of the concessions the Japanese won after taking Governor Pieter Nuyts (1627–29) hostage.[23] The residents of Hsin-kang were angered by the Dutch treatment, which they contrasted with the generous hospitality of the Japanese. The missionary Candidius, resident in Hsin-kang since 1627, personally observed this change in attitudes toward the Dutch. Candidius's own attempts to "exterminate heathenish malpractice" no doubt helped fuel the antagonism.[24]

After the Japanese ships departed, Governor Nuyts attempted to pacify Hsin-kang by feasting the inhabitants and presenting them with gifts. But, in an abrupt change of strategy in early 1629, he dispatched an armed party to arrest Dika, leader of the Hsin-kang delegation to Japan. Dika eluded capture; when the governor threatened war if Dika were not handed over, the inhabitants evacuated the village. Governor Nuyts then backed down and demanded only fines and the destruction of the houses of those who had gone to Japan. The villagers accepted these terms and warily moved back to Hsin-kang. Their submission to the Dutch demands was due only in part to fear of the Dutch—equally important was their need for the Dutch as allies against their enemies, Ma-tou and Mu-chia-liu-wan.[25]

In July 1629 when the Dutch sent a force of sixty-odd soldiers to chase off Chinese pirates, a war party from Ma-tou ambushed and slaughtered the Dutch and raided Hsin-kang.[26] According to the missionary Junius, "This was looked upon by them as a great unheard of victory and it filled them with pride. Not only Mattau but other villages, [such] as Soulang [Hsiao-lung] and Bakloan, began to rebel against us, and matters took so serious a turn that we hardly ventured to set foot on Formosa. They even went so far as to hint that they would chase us from Tayouan."[27] The Dutch chose to chastise Mu-chia-liu-wan first, because of the three offending villages it had the fewest inhabitants. Its "rebellious spirit was well-nigh crushed" by an expedition launched a few months later. Warriors from Hsin-kang joined the expedition and received a share of the spoils.[28]

It was 1631, however, before the Dutch ventured to mount an expedition against Ma-tou. When adverse winds forced their launches to turn back, the Dutch rerouted the expedition to the southern coastal village of Tampsui with whom Hsin-kang had a dispute. The small victory obtained over Tampsui (only one head was taken) was enough to please the Hsin-kang members of the expedition, and some of them even began to show "an inclination to adopt our religion" as a result.[29] These measures quieted the situation for a time, but by 1633 Ma-tou was demanding tribute from Chinese fishermen at the nearby harbor of Wen-kang (the fishermen were probably already paying a tithe to the Dutch), and its chief was threatening to go to Japan to enlist help against the Dutch. The Dutch tried, to no avail, to win over the Ma-tou leader with gifts and an offer to make him the chief of an expedition. In the next years Ma-tou molested small satellite villages around Hsin-kang.[30]

These events reveal the ambiguity of Dutch relations with the Chinese, as well as with the aborigines. On the one hand, Chinese village traders resident at Ma-tou were suspected of inciting the inhabitants against the Dutch. On the other hand, the Dutch were anxious to protect Chinese fishermen under Dutch license and Chinese farmers suffering aborigine raids on their cattle and sugarcane fields.[31]

In September 1634 Governor Hans Putmans requested that at least 400 soldiers be sent to Taiwan for the purpose of chastising Ma-tou; in August 1635 they arrived. The Dutch party, joined by a force from Hsin-kang, attacked Ma-tou in November and torched the village. This victory had an immediate effect: within days Ma-tou sent representatives to sue for peace.[32] At the end of December 1635, the Dutch sent another expedition south to Takareiang to avenge the murders of both Dutchmen and Hsin-kang villagers. The account of these skirmishes reveals the superiority of Dutch muskets over native spears and shields; Dutch use of military drums and horses in battle also terrorized the aborigines.[33]

In early January 1636, the Dutch marched north again, this time to punish Hsiao-lung. In 1634 Hsiao-lung had temporarily allied itself with Hsin-kang and the Dutch against Ma-tou but then had broken off.[34] Toward Hsiao-lung the Dutch adopted tactics different from those used against Ma-tou. Hsiao-lung had sued for peace and made offers of tribute in December 1635, which the Dutch rejected. Instead, the Dutch demanded that the aborigines themselves hand over those responsible for crimes against the Dutch and that they fire the houses of the guilty so that, reasoned the Reverend Junius, "everyone might know that we were just to the good, but full of wrath against those who were evil-minded." In the face of superior force, Hsiao-lung complied. The Hsiao-lung prisoners were then delivered to Hsin-kang for decapitation, in order "to unite" Hsin-kang to the Dutch and "to turn them from the people of Soulang."[35]

The Dutch victories shattered local power balances. The villagers of Ta-wu-lung (Dutch: Tevorang) to the east were "delighted" by the Dutch victory over their enemies at Ma-tou, and the villagers of Chu-lo-shan (Dutch: Tirosen) and Favorlang to the north began immediately to threaten the newly humbled Ma-tou. The people of Hsin-kang, puffed up by their victories, began spreading rumors and menacing their rivals. Throughout January 1636 the villages of the region sent delegates (they often asked people from Hsin-kang or Chinese to represent them) to beg for peace from the Dutch. Many of these villages had never had direct contact with the Dutch but had "learnt to fear our name."[36]

The Dutch required that submitting villages agree to a short treaty with the following terms:

> 1. That they were to surrender their country and their possessions to the States of Holland; in token whereof they were to bring some small pinang [betel palm] and cocoa-nut trees, planted in the soil of that place, to the Castle.
> 2. That they should no more turn their arms against us.
> 3. That on the day when all our friends and allies appeared before us, they too should appear.
> 4. That in future they should not molest the Chinese.
> 5. That at our desire they should join us in our wars.
> 6. That if the staff of the Prince were sent them they should appear before us.[37]

At the end of February 1636, the Dutch called a meeting of village delegates. In accordance with the terms of the treaties, 28 villages sent representatives; this was apparently all the villages within a two-day journey of Hsin-kang.[38] Thus, within four months in 1635 and 1636, the Dutch had expanded their sphere of influence far beyond what it had been for the ten years since their arrival.

Reverend Junius's account of the delegates assembly or *landdag* stresses the unprecedented nature of the newly established "Pax Hollandia":

> It was delightful to see the friendliness of these people when they met for the first time, to notice how they kissed each other and gazed at one another. Such a thing had never before been witnessed in this country, as one tribe was nearly always waging war against another. . . . Now, however, they were all not only loyal to us, but were friendly towards each other; and if we had not influenced them, they would never have been mutually united; for formerly no one dared to address the other, no one trusted the other, and to practise deception as much as possible was the general rule.[39]

The assembly began with the governor lecturing the delegates on the meaning of the peace and the treaty. Next he presented each delegate his symbols of office: a black velvet robe, a rattan staff headed with a silver

Fig. 3.1 Landdag, ca. 1650: drawing by Caspar Schmalkalden (reproduced by permission of the Forschungs- und Landesbibliothek Gotha, Chart. B533, Blatt 288v/289r; photograph by Eberhard Renno, Weimar).

insignia bearing the Dutch East India Company's coat of arms, and an orange flag.[40] Villages that had not already done so then transferred sovereignty to the Dutch by presenting betel palm and coconut trees. After another round of speeches, the delegates feasted together (see Fig. 3.1).

Before the meeting disbanded, the Dutch informed the delegates that they would visit all the villages represented to lecture the inhabitants on the significance of the symbols of office given the delegates and on the meaning of the Dutch peace.[41] These tours, accompanied by a display of Dutch arms, were conducted in the next few months and served not only to consolidate Dutch influence over pacified villages but also to expand it. News of Dutch military prowess spread rapidly, and distant tribes were soon sending representatives to open relations with the company. By August 1636 an additional 29 villages had sought peace from the Dutch, raising the total to 57. In September 1636, Reverend Junius concluded: "From this you will see the favourable results of the war, and how well it has been that Mattau and Takareiang were burnt for the evil committed against us."[42]

In 1636 and again in 1639 and 1640, Tung-lo (Dutch: Dovale) and Favorlang, two villages just beyond the northern edge of the Dutch sphere of influence, harassed Dutch-licensed deer hunters and killed some Chinese under Dutch protection. The Dutch attempted to chastise these villages in 1637 and 1640, but the small forces mustered proved insufficient to the task. The distance of these villages from Tayouan was cited as an obstacle to effective policing of the area.[43] Finally in late 1641, a war party of 400 Dutch soldiers went north by boat. The Reverend Junius led 1,400 aborigine braves from Hsin-kang and eight allied villages overland and met the soldiers near Tung-lo. There the joint expedition quickly overcame all opposition and torched the village. The aborigine troops then quarreled over possession of the heads of the 30 fallen enemy, and 1,200 of them had to be sent home. But after the initial show of force at Tung-lo, the other villages in the region offered little resistance. In the end this expedition won the submission of eleven northern villages, including Favorlang and Tung-lo.[44]

This northward expansion by the Dutch was also motivated by their rivalry with the Spanish in the Tan-shui–Keelung area. The Dutch feared that the Spanish would try to incite anti-Dutch rebellions among the aborigines and Chinese. A Dutch report of 1636 even claimed that the Spanish had won converts in central Taiwan. The Dutch were also keen to eliminate their Spanish trading rivals and gain control of reserves of sulfur in Tan-shui, coal in Keelung, and gold in I-lan.[45]

The Spanish in the North and the Consolidation of Dutch Rule

In 1626, two years after the Dutch occupied Tayouan in southern Taiwan, the Spanish landed troops at Keelung harbor at the island's northern tip and built the fort San Salvador on an island in the harbor. Northern Taiwan was to serve a dual purpose for the Spanish—as a base from which to protect their Japanese trade from Dutch interference and as a stepping-stone for Catholic missions to China and Japan.[46] Chinese and Japanese traders had long frequented both of Taiwan's northern ports, Tan-shui and Keelung. Li Tan, the famous Captain China, had earlier advised the Dutch to settle in Tayouan in preference to Keelung or Tan-shui, whose "inhabitants were a very murderous people, with whom it was difficult even to speak."[47] The experience of the Spaniards bore him out.

News of the Spanish presence in Keelung soon spread to the aborigine villages at the mouth of the Tan-shui river.[48] In late 1627 one of these villages sought help from the Spanish forces in a local conflict. The Spanish, at the time short on provisions, obligingly dispatched twenty soldiers to the Tan-shui area.[49] After a few months, the Spanish troops apparently outstayed their welcome. The village head secretly came to terms with the rival village and then attacked the Spanish when they were out hunting. In the ensuing battle, eight Spaniards and the village head were killed. The Spanish survivors fled to Keelung by boat. The Keelung garrison, freshly reprovisioned by the arrival of a Spanish ship, dispatched 100 men to punish the treacherous villagers. The natives fled, and the Spanish force raided the native granaries before returning to Keelung.

The Spanish record of this incident reports that the Tan-shui valley was densely populated and produced surpluses of rice. The Spanish decided to gain control of this area and dispatched an army unit to Tan-shui in 1628. This force captured a small fort overlooking the river from either natives or Chinese traders. The Spanish then proceeded to build a new fortification, San Domingo, on the same site.[50]

An industrious Dominican, Jacinto Esquivel, convinced the Senar tribe to return to its settlement one mile from the Spanish fort in Tan-shui (the Senar probably were the people who had clashed with the Spanish in 1627). In honor of their return, Esquivel and the other Spaniards treated the natives to a spectacle that included a castle of fireworks and a sword dance. The Senar followed up this celebration "of the possession taken of this country" by a "disgraceful" eight-hour dance.[51] A church was built in Senar and staffed by the Dominican Francisco Vaez and an assistant. Esquivel soon compiled a *Vocabulary of the Language of the Tamsui Indians*[52] and by 1632 had also founded, apparently in Keelung, a school for native children and the few Chinese and Japanese children (probably born of native mothers) resident as well to prepare these youths for missions in China and Japan.

Esquivel explored the Taipei basin during March 1632, visiting several basin tribes, including the three large villages of Wu-lao-wan (Spanish: Pulauan), near the juncture of the southwest branch of the Tan-shui river.[53] Esquivel noted the arrival in Tan-shui of three Japanese ships to load deer pelts, which a Japanese sailor told him were more profitable to import into Japan than raw silk, which Japan itself produced. He also noted that the natives traded deer pelts, rattans, and sulfur (from the Pei-t'ou deposits) to Chinese for brass bracelets, bells, textiles, and other trade goods.[54]

Meanwhile Father Vaez had had some success in winning converts in Pantao, Senar's rival to the south, and in mediating the feud between the two villages. On January 27, 1633, certain disgruntled Senar tribesmen, whose leader had just been rescued from prison by Vaez, but who were suspicious of the Spaniards' friendly relations with Pantao, waylaid Vaez, took his head and right hand, and fled to the mountains "to celebrate the festival of head-cutting."[55]

In March 1636 the Spanish garrison in Tan-shui again found itself short of provisions. Accompanied by Father Muro, who had arrived in 1635, a party of Spanish soldiers and aborigines went to Pei-t'ou (Spanish: Paktau) to requisition grain and deliver a pardon to the Senar who had fled there after killing Vaez. The Senar ambushed the party. In the ensuing battle, Muro and 24 Spaniards were killed. Spanish attempts to levy taxes on chickens and rice in aborigine households sparked a further revolt.[56]

The Spanish governor in Manila, disappointed in the volume of trade at Keelung with the Chinese and Japanese and unimpressed by the local products, determined to reduce the Spanish presence in Taiwan. When the number of soldiers in the Tan-shui garrison was reduced in 1636, the aborigines took the opportunity to attack missionaries, churches, and outposts.[57] In 1638 the governor ordered a withdrawal of the Tan-shui garrison to Keelung in an attempt to cut financial losses. By 1640 the Keelung garrison numbered only 400 men, consisting of 50 Spanish soldiers, 30 Pampangans, 200 slaves, and 130 Chinese soldiers. The Spanish had also recruited some native archers.[58] The Dutch were quick to capitalize on Spanish weakness.

In September 1640 the Dutch commander M. G. Vries landed in Tan-shui, where he found that the Spanish garrison had already withdrawn. Vries moved on to Keelung but failed to drive out the Spanish before returning to southern Taiwan. From October 1640, the Dutch began to use Chinese agents to trade with the Tan-shui natives for Pei-t'ou sulfur. In April 1641, the Chinese sulfur traders demanded Dutch military protection against the Spanish. The Dutch acceded to this request and sent Vries to reach an accord with the local natives in December of that year.[59] In October 1641 some Tan-shui natives accompanied the Dutchman Thomas Pedel to Dutch headquarters in Tayouan to report on the strength of the Spanish garrison. Certain Tan-shui villages were causing trouble for the Spanish in Keelung at this time.[60]

Appeals for reinforcements from Keelung received only a token response from the Spanish governor in Manila.[61] In August 1642 the Dutch finally succeeded in taking Keelung and ending the Spanish presence in Taiwan. In the years that followed, the task of pacifying the rebellious Tan-shui natives fell to the Dutch.

The Dutch immediately established garrisons at Keelung and Tan-shui. Some of the local tribes submitted at this time; others resisted, and in February 1644 they attacked and killed 70 members of a Dutch party.[62] Late in 1644 a large expeditionary force was raised to consolidate Dutch power over the northern tribes; faced with this superior force, the villages in the Taipei area readily submitted.[63] From Tan-shui, this army moved south by land, crushing all resistance offered by native tribes and clearing the area of Chinese pirates and smugglers. By early 1645, the Dutch had secured a north-south land route along the entire western coast.[64]

In the next years the Dutch extended their dominion to villages on the east coast and even in the mountains. At the height of their influence around 1650, the Dutch could claim sovereignty over nearly 300 villages. After 1650 some remote villages rebelled and broke away.[65] Villages in core areas that revolted against exploitative Dutch policies were forced again into submission.

An example of a village revolt and the reassertion of Dutch control comes from Wu-lao-wan (Pinorouan or Pulauan) in the Taipei basin. In December 1652 the inhabitants of Wu-lao-wan killed and beheaded two Dutch interpreters who had threatened to kill the tribal elders if the natives did not meet their demands for rice, deer pelts, and sexual access to aborigine women. In retaliation for the killings, the Tan-shui commander dispatched 70 soldiers under two sergeants. The inhabitants of Wu-lao-wan had in the meantime thrown up earthwork barricades. In the battle that followed, two Dutchmen and 30 natives were killed. This carnage neither brought Wu-lao-wan to submission nor satisfied the Dutch. The Dutch then withheld salt and iron supplies from Wu-lao-wan. Further military attack was apparently ruled out when the Tayouan garrison, occupied with the suppression of the 1652 revolt of Chinese, reported that it would be unable to send reinforcements to help punish the "rebels." By February 1653 two of the Wu-lao-wan people accused of the murders had been caught and executed and their heads displayed on stakes in front of the Tan-shui blockhouse. Following this, the village sent representatives to Tan-shui to sue for peace. Suffering greatly due to the withholding of salt and iron, they came "with hands folded and on bent knee" promising never to do such deeds again.[66]

The Dutch accomplished their "conquest" of Taiwan with a garrison of less than 700 men.[67] That they were able to do so resulted from the superiority of Dutch weapons, the disunity of the natives and the Dutch ability to enlist them as allies against one another, and the weakened state of the Spanish forces in the north. It was only in the 1650's, as the Chinese population grew and the danger of attack by Cheng Ch'eng-kung was perceived, that the Dutch increased their garrisons to 1,200 and strengthened their fortifications.[68] The distribution of soldiers in 1654 reveals that of a total of 961, well over a third were concentrated at Zeelandia Castle in Tayouan and the immediate vicinity. The rest were spread out in small posts or in major aborigine villages, primarily in the southwest coastal region. The only major exceptions to this were the garrisons at Tan-shui (80 soldiers) and Keelung (50 soldiers). This presence was intended as much to guard the harbors from external threat as to exercise dominion over the northern tribes. Throughout the Dutch period, the center of Dutch influence, where they exercised control the longest and where the missionaries had the greatest impact, remained the southwest coastal area around Tayouan.[69]

Local Administration

The expansion of Dutch dominion first in 1635–36 and then in the early 1640's put the Dutch in control of a large territory that was expensive to administer and defend. Dependent on its trading profits to fund operations (and under pressure to pay dividends to its stockholders in Holland), the Dutch East India Company had to devise means to extract taxes and to develop trade and agriculture that would defray these expenses and increase company revenues. The company had also to devise efficient means of controlling its colonial populations and satisfying the consciences of its missionary employees, on whom it relied to fulfill its Calvinist burden. Dutch taxes on the aborigine and Chinese immigrant economies began contributing substantially to expenses in the early 1640's, and from 1647 the Taiwan colony was regularly profitable. The development of the colonial revenue system, combined with favorable trade, especially with Japan, made Taiwan the Dutch East India Company's second most profitable trading colony from 1649 to 1651.[70] The growing influx of refugees in the 1650's led to further growth in profits from Chinese commercial agriculture.

Affairs in the Siraya villages with which the Dutch had their first contact were traditionally conducted by age-grade councils. These could at most impose fines on wrongdoers, and they lacked the power to inflict corporal punishment.[71] Candidius, writing in 1628, complained that this absence of a "central authority or chief" and the consequent lack of discipline were frustrating his attempts to instruct the inhabitants of Hsin-kang in Christian doctrine. Candidius wanted an officer appointed who could "effectively admonish" his religious opponents and relieve him of the burdens of judicial office. The governor's report of 1631 held that the appointment of a judge would be premature: "We maintain that for the present it is much more expedient that the *takasach* council in the village should, assisted by his [Candidius's] advice, continue to settle all matters till these people become somewhat more civilised and accustomed to our manners."[72]

Dutch strategy attempted to co-opt rather than displace native leaders by requiring them to work with the representatives of the company, who were often missionaries. Some of the tensions in this system of shared authority are revealed in Governor Putmans's 1635 report discussing the clergy's request to be exempted from political duties: "While the clergymen should continue to direct all matters, the elders, or councillors of the village, should execute them . . . to exempt our clergy from the opprobrium which arises when they demand the infliction of punishment, and also because they thought they were always being sorely misrepresented by the village elders in this matter, the fines should henceforth be collected by the sergeant at that time present in the place."[73] After the great expansion of their realm in 1635–36, the Dutch had to accommodate their administration to other ethnic groups, some of which had more powerful councils or headmen than the Siraya.[74] Governor Coyett (1656–62) gives a general description of the system of rule the Dutch imposed on the villages:

> To carry out war or to fight with each other was also forbidden, being now under one ruler, according to whose laws evildoers were punished. Their old form of government remained, however. In each village the governor of Formosa appointed one of the oldest and most capable inhabitants to be captain over his co-villagers. In every village this man, who stayed under the supervision of a Dutch official, had a detachment of twenty-five soldiers. He commanded the villagers, transmitted the orders of the high authorities, and punished lawbreakers with the help of the soldiers. These captains of all villages had to appear before the Dutch governor about the end of April every year to give an account of their activities. On that day those who had ruled well were given a small reward, but those who had misbehaved themselves lost the rattan stick which they held as an emblem of their power and were replaced by others This day was called the Formosan Land Day (Diet).[75]

Coyett's statement has to be modified in some of its particulars. Military rosters make it clear that there were not 25 soldiers in every village; rather, troops were assigned only to large villages or groups of villages in the southwest core area. Nor was there only one delegate per village: in 1638 there were four from Mu-chia-liu-wan and six from Hsiao-lung. When Ma-tou submitted in 1635, its "principal men" were ordered to appear, "of whom the half should be chosen by us to act as elders amongst them."[76] The number appointed reflected a village's population and its internal political divisions. It is possible that the more senior of the several "chiefs" served as "captain," but the sources do not distinguish those offices clearly.[77]

A delegates meeting in March 1647 at Sakam was attended by the governor, other Dutch administrators, soldiers, clergy, schoolmasters, and interpreters in addition to the delegates from the native villages. The governor welcomed the delegates, expressed thanks for the tribute they presented, and reminded them of the importance of maintaining the peace. The yearly evaluation and selection of elders came next in the order of business (the majority were reappointed). Lectures on the duties of elders were followed by admonitions to notify the Dutch of disputes or crimes in the villages. The delegates were asked to help apprehend unlicensed Chinese traders and hunters. Elders were also reminded of their duty to respect the Christian religion and to encourage school and church attendance. The Dutch concluded the meeting with a feast. Nakamura adds that on these occasions the elders renewed their pledges of loyalty to the Dutch and gave reports from which village census lists were compiled.[78]

Such meetings followed the model established by the first delegates assembly held in February 1636, after the submission of the Tayouan area villages. But *landdag* did not become regular annual affairs until the early 1640's. At this time the island was partitioned into four regions (villages north of Sakam, south of Sakam, Tan-shui, and the east coast), and each held meetings separately.[79]

Missionaries serving in the villages were effective enforcers of the Dutch peace. Acting single-handedly in 1638, the catechist Willem Elberts was able to prevent a bloody battle between two southern villages: "He hastened to the scene, and by placing himself between the two parties, happily prevented them from coming to blows. He insisted on their ceasing hostilities if they did not wish to incur the supreme displeasure of the highest authorities, for as unfaithful allies and breakers of the peace, they ran the risk of being punished. They, fearing the consequences of this displeasure, laid down their arms."[80] There were many instances in which clerics, backed by Dutch military force, were able to mediate blood feuds between villages. Of course, peace did not always advance Dutch interests: when their domain might be expanded or access to supplies of gold obtained, the Dutch were quite willing to encourage intervillage warfare.[81]

Missionary Work in the Native Villages

Clergy in the company's employ dominated civilian administration in the aborigine villages of the southwest core area. William Campbell describes the central role the missionaries played:

> Of course, the main object of the Dutch East India Company of that time was to carry on profitable trade in the colonies or factories where they were established; but from want of funds and suitable men they were unable to appoint trading agents familiar with the language, or civil officers for collecting taxes, or police, throughout those regions over which lordship was exercised. Accordingly, clergymen were sent out to Formosa, and their duties soon came to assume a threefold character: (1) by acting as chaplains to the Dutch officials, soldiers, and families who were resident there; (2) as interpreters, civil officers in collecting taxes, selling hunting licenses, or in buying deer-skins and other produce of the country; and (3) as missionaries, in trying to establish and build up Christian congregations amongst the natives.[82]

Dutch East India Company support for the missionary effort was predicated on the belief that native conversion would bring, in addition to "spiritual profit," consolidation of Dutch influence over the villages. The first experiences with the warring and rebellious natives convinced both missionaries and company administrators that conversion to Christianity could not rely on moral example, persuasion, and generosity alone.[83] Only punishment for acts of violence could establish respect for Dutch authority and religion:

> By adopting this course, the people everywhere will be so filled with terror that they will humbly bend their necks and most piteously sue for our friendship. They will afterwards become quite civilised and subject to us; so that, by the grace of God, the Christian religion will make better progress than heretofore. We judge this because past experience shows that mere kindness is thrown away upon this people, and will never bring about the spread of Christianity amongst them.[84]

But coercion alone would not suffice to command the obedience of the aborigines: "the bond of religion is the only tie that can unite this nation to us with any amount of certainty."[85]

The financial costs of mission work were seen as a wise investment. According to Governor Putmans in 1631, "Leaving the matter of the progress of Christianity entirely out of the question, we think that even political reasons . . . should induce us to advance the work; if, indeed, our desire is that peace and order should become permanent among the inhabitants, so that sooner or later we may derive profit therefrom."[86] Nevertheless, the company did not always find missionaries indispensable to administration. When financial and personnel shortages caused company officials to seek in 1657 to eliminate clerical posts in the southern region and leave only civilian officers and schoolmasters in charge "with the object of making its inhabitants merely good civilians," the religious interests rebuked them for adopting a policy that "could not be justified on the great day of judgment."[87] As we shall see below, conflicts between secular and clerical authority escalated in the 1650's.

The pioneers of the missionary enterprise in Taiwan (and the only clergy present until 1636) were Candidius and Junius. Candidius arrived in 1627 and soon took up residence in Hsin-kang, at the time the only, if somewhat unreliable, Dutch ally among the villages. Junius, who had arrived in Taiwan in 1629, joined Candidius in Hsin-kang a year and a half later, as Candidius was preparing to leave upon the completion of his first term. Candidius returned in 1633 for another tour of duty and remained until 1637.[88] Junius remained in Taiwan until 1643. Their study of the language, customs, and politics of the aborigines provided valuable intelligence for the Dutch. Candidius reasoned that the lack of a written creed and the absence of a native state with an official religion would make mission work easier in Formosa than it had been in India. Candidius also believed that the "native religion has been undergoing great decay during the last sixty years."[89]

Candidius, however, underestimated the strength of native "superstition" and the influence of the shamanesses (*inibs*), who were the chief ritual specialists within the villages. The people of Hsin-kang were quite skeptical of Candidius's teachings and proposed experiments to test the consequences of practicing them:

> They have proposed that I should begin by giving Christian instruction in one house only, and that all its inmates should abandon their manners and customs and adopt ours. If their gods still continued to bless that house by giving much rice and other things during the next two or three years, they too would willingly adopt our religion. They also come to me to test my powers, asking me to perform miracles, to give or withhold rain and wind, to foretell future events, or to reveal what is actually occurring elsewhere; and because I cannot do so, they despise me, and say that their priestesses can do all such things.[90]

It was not until the small military victories over Hsin-kang's enemies in 1631 that Candidius made a breakthrough: at that time some of the village notables "cast away their idols" and began to take religious instruction.[91] The first 50 were baptized in March 1631, and by January 1633 reportedly "all" the people of Hsin-kang had converted.[92] Yet there were still many who adhered to the old religion: in the midst of the 1635–36 campaigns, the Dutch "admonished them to serve the only true God, to cast away their idols if they wished to be blessed and obtain the victory over their enemies."[93]

The Dutch military successes made the inhabitants of the subjugated villages much more receptive to the religion of the god who "had so gloriously battled for us in our late wars." Junius in 1636 had other persuasive arguments:

> As to the two large villages of Mattau and Soulang, we do not doubt that it would be an easy task to persuade their inhabitants to renounce idolatry, the more so as they see the prosperity of Sinkan, where the people began many years ago to serve the true God, and whose crops of rice everyone sees to be plentiful, being abundant year after year and promising now to be as plentiful as ever. This test is looked upon as being of great importance by the inhabitants of Formosa. Many old persons in Sinkan, especially among the former priestesses, ventured to prophesy to the people at the time of their conversion that, if they neglected their idols and began to serve the God of the Dutchmen, their fields would no longer yield them their crops of rice. Not only, however, have they seen that the contrary has happened, but that the crops have been even much more abundant than before their conversion. This fact has seriously interfered with the native forms of worship, so much that the people themselves now laugh at their priestesses, whose words were formerly received as oracles, and were believed with the same certainty and conviction which we have as regards the Gospel.[94]

Such arguments were not so impressive, however, as to convince the natives to cast all caution to the wind: "On 21 June the inhabitants of Bakloan accepted our proposal to do away with their idolatry and to cast away their idols, but said they would defer doing so till the rice crop was gathered in."[95] The inhabitants of Ta-mu-hsiang (Dutch: Tavakan), the village nearest Hsin-kang, were more reckless and immediately held meetings at which they burned all their idols. Mu-chia-liu-wan gave up its idols in December 1636, as did Ma-tou and Hsiao-lung in December 1637. This "casting away of idols" in the presence of the Dutch governor and soldiers served as an additional ceremony of submission in which the aborigines renewed their oath of fealty.[96]

Idol destruction was a prerequisite to receiving religious instruction.[97] The natives were then taught prayers and articles of faith and had preached to them sermons condemning lewdness, fornication, nakedness, and idolatry. Although the finer points of Dutch theology may have escaped native attention, the promise of practical results did not: "When they go out hunting they first kneel down and one of the most intelligent among them prays aloud to God to give them success in their hunting expedition; and they are already so sincere in their faith as to feel convinced that, without such prayer, they will not be successful. In the same way they also pray for a plentiful crop, kneeling down in their fields, with much fervour."[98]

Substantial progress in the reform of native customs seems to have been made by 1640, especially in Hsin-kang. Junius reports that the *inib*s were by then "treated with contempt, on account of the many falsehoods they formerly promulgated. They are not allowed to enter any houses except their own, and are thus prevented from practising their former idolatry."[99] Their success in Hsin-kang only made the missionaries more impatient with the opposition of the shamanesses in other villages. About 1641, the Dutch adopted a more radical policy: they banished 250 *inib*s from at least five Sirayan villages of the core area. In Chu-lo-shan, the village to the north where they were resettled, the *inib*s were subjected to intensive religious instruction and promised release once they had reformed. Eleven years later, when only 48 of the old women were still alive, they were allowed to return to their homes. A notice filed two years after their release reported no complaints of misbehavior.[100]

Missionary efforts and Dutch rule had profound effects on the native way of life, especially on the Siraya systems of marriage and age grades. Siraya villages were composed of wards, each with its own men's dormitory and shrine. Many of the idols the missionaries wanted destroyed were from the altars of these wards.[101] Siraya marriage did not create a joint household until the husband reached his forties and retired from age grade service; until that time the husband paid only nocturnal visits to his wife. The *inib*s taught that a married woman should not complete a pregnancy until she was in her thirties. Mandatory abortion by young wives was the counterpart of age grade service by men to age 40: "As long as the men go to war and generate children with their wives, they kill these children up to the time that they do not go to war any more." Only after the husband retired from the age grade ranks and took up uxorilocal residence with his wife did a married couple rear children.[102]

The missionaries attacked both these customs: they outlawed abortion and encouraged couples to live together and rear children jointly.[103] The victories of 1635 and 1636 had demonstrated the power of the Dutch god and discredited the teachings of the *inib*s. Success in war clearly no longer depended on headhunters living apart from their wives in men's houses or on headhunters' wives aborting their pregnancies. By 1636 more than 50 Hsin-kang couples had married according to Dutch rites; by 1639 the total was 119 (the total population was approximately 1,000). Freed from the strictures of the *inib*s, young Hsin-kang couples took up joint residence and began to rear children together. The missionaries assumed the willingness of Siraya youth to marry in the Dutch fashion indicated their acceptance of Christian doctrines and values. A better view of the impact of the missionaries is to see them offering the Siraya not new values but new routes to the achievement of traditional Sirayan values: military alliances that won unprecedented victories in war, and marriages that enabled couples to begin families earlier than ever before.[104]

Villagers were summoned to church services by the firing of muskets or cannon—a symbolism not lost on the natives. Once in church the aborigines heard a sermon preached to them in their native language.[105] Junius's sermons were later criticized because they "chiefly declaimed against the manners and customs of the heathen . . . without properly expounding the principles of Christianity."[106] Failure to attend church might be punished by a fine. Some natives, as well as Dutchmen, looked on the Sabbath as an occasion for intoxication, and the retailing of beer during the sermon had to be prohibited.[107]

The company sought to institutionalize the conversion of the natives through education in a system of church schools. Junius began a school in Hsin-kang in 1636, giving religious instruction to 70 boys and 60 girls, ages 10 to 14. The boys were also taught how to read and write the Sirayan language in roman letters.[108] At first small gifts were awarded the boys to encourage attendance at school; in later years (with the consolidation of Dutch rule over the villages), the incentive structure changed, and fines were levied for failure to attend.[109] The Dutch were eager to identify promising young scholars who might be trained to serve as native ministers and schoolmasters.[110]

People of all ages received religious instruction. Memorization of prayers and a simple catechism was necessary to pass the examination that qualified one for baptism: by 1638 the entire population of Hsin-kang had been baptized.[111] After the expansion of the Dutch sphere in 1635–36, schools were set up in all major villages of the southwest core area. Given the shortage of ordained ministers, a great variety of ecclesiastical ranks—licentiates, catechists, clerks in holy orders—and even soldiers were appointed as schoolmasters.[112]

Prayers, catechisms, and eventually the Gospel of St. Matthew were translated into the Sirayan language of Hsin-kang and its neighbors. After 1636 the Dutch sphere included many language groups, and this placed a burden on the educational work. Additional translations were prepared in the southern dialects and in the northern language of Favorlang.[113] Other strategies were proposed to overcome this linguistic complexity. Young students were "placed in different villages to learn the various dialects," so that they might eventually serve as multilingual teachers. Governor François Caron (1644–46) assumed that "most probably there were two or three well-known native dialects which could be made use of throughout the whole island." The Hsin-kang language was used for instruction for a time in the southern villages. Some argued it would be better to teach Dutch in all the villages and create a lingua franca "as the Portuguese do in their colonies." But as Protestants, the Dutch firmly believed the villagers should have access to Holy Scriptures in their native tongue.[114] Dutch was taught to the young; the adults continued to receive instruction in their native languages.[115]

By 1643 Junius had trained 50 young natives to serve as teachers; they were posted to schools in six core villages with a total of 600 schoolchildren. Because funds were insufficient to pay salaries that would enable them to devote themselves full-time to school work, the number of native teachers was reduced in 1644 to 17. Each village was required to supply its teachers with rice rations, and judicial officers employed the teachers as translators. The initial cohort of native teachers was a disappointment: appointments as schoolmasters led to swollen heads, and many had to be discharged for licentious behavior. But more were trained, and the school system continued to expand, especially in the area north of the southwest core. By 1648, 1,364 men, women, and children were attending schools in these villages.[116]

A 1659 report lists twenty schools in an area stretching from Hsin-kang to Favorlang (the south was not covered in the report), for which the 1656 census lists 41 plains villages. The schools were generally, but not always, located in the larger villages. Adults as well as children were required to receive religious instruction, and to memorize prayers and a catechism. The 1659 report claims that in the twenty villages, with a total population of 10,109, 6,078 men, women, and children could recite the catechism, or at least 47 percent of the total population in every village.[117]

Junius's request to take students to Holland to be trained as clergymen was never accepted by the company. But the advantages of a native clergy were recognized, and by the late 1650's the missionaries were laying plans for a seminary in Taiwan.[118] The most lasting impact of Dutch missionary efforts was in the realm of literacy: native scribes from Hsinkang and neighboring villages produced land contracts in romanized script as late as the first years of the nineteenth century, over 140 years after the departure of the Dutch.[119]

Missionary Authority and the Company

Large-scale village-wide conversions had followed the sudden expansion of Dutch power in 1635–36 over the southwest core villages. In the succeeding decades of Dutch rule, religious progress came at a much slower pace. The early enthusiasm generated by participation in Dutch military victories (at first as victims and later as allies) soon wore off, and the nominal character of the initial conversions became obvious. Deepening the hold of religion over the natives required a much greater investment of resources in religious education and the reform of native customs, yet the advocates of such programs could offer little prospect of dramatic results or immediate advantage to company control or balances. As a result, conflicts between the company and the missionaries erupted over the clergy's privileges, the allocation of resources to the church, and strategies for proselytizing. These disputes reveal much about the way the Dutch wielded influence in the villages.

The judicial duties and privileges of the clergy in the villages were a constant cause of friction. The clergy, beginning with Candidius and Junius, generally wished to be relieved of the onerous responsibilities of the office, but not at the expense of the authority, privileges, and income that came with it. Judges were responsible, in conjunction with the village elders, for settling disputes and imposing fines or punishments. The missionaries objected to these duties because they took valuable time from the work of conversion and because imposing punishments alienated the populace they were trying to win to Christianity.[120] The desire to avoid these duties should not, however, be misunderstood as a desire to withdraw from the political management of the colony: both Candidius and Junius were actively involved in the series of campaigns that led to the expansion of the Dutch sphere in 1635–36, and Junius helped lead the pacification of the Favorlangian villages in 1641.[121]

Not until 1636 was the governor able to appoint a non-cleric to judicial office, but even then it was recognized that any appointee would need several years of language study before taking office: "We cannot judge these people according to our own laws, but must also take their language, customs, and manners into consideration, because, if we did not do so, they would rise and endeavor to expel us from the country."[122] The shortage of qualified personnel and the greater need, after the expansion of Dutch control in 1636, further postponed the day when judicial office could be held by laymen. In 1636 the company began sending additional clergymen to supplement and eventually replace Candidius and Junius. In the next few years, it was possible to appoint company factors or military officers as judges in a few villages; in most, however, clergymen (or their subordinates) continued in judicial office.[123] In early 1643 Governor Paulus Traudenius (1641–43) complained, apparently of Junius, that some clerics had exceeded the bounds of their authority and questioned "the supremacy of our official authority . . . under the promptings of a most improper and worldly ambition."[124] Yet clerical cooperation with secular authority remained high in these years: in 1643 the clergy charged several Dutch schoolmasters with "drunkenness, fornication, and ill-treatment of the inhabitants," and one was even decapitated.[125]

The expansion of the village school system led to an increase in the number of bilingual schoolmasters, both native and Dutch, who could help in judicial matters. But this also led to contests between civil and ecclesiastical officers for schoolmasters' time. These contests were resolved largely in favor of clerical authority by putting strict limits on the services civil officers could command.[126]

In 1644 the Reverend Simon van Breen and a group of two catechists and six soldiers (all of whom were to serve as schoolmasters under him) were dispatched to the recently pacified Favorlang area. Acting as both cleric and judge, van Breen was instrumental in identifying troublesome Chinese and natives and in consolidating Dutch control of the region. In 1645, in gratitude for van Breen's voluntary service, which had saved the company the expense of a separate judicial officer, Governor Caron formally appointed him to judicial office and allotted him "one-third of all fines levied from Chinese living in his district." Serious cases were to be referred to the castle at Tayouan. A few months later the other clergymen received judicial appointments on similar terms, and a superfactor serving as judge in Hsiao-lung was withdrawn.[127]

In 1646 Governor Caron abolished separate judicial offices and placed all judicial responsibilities in the hands of the clergy on the grounds that the workload of judicial office was too light to warrant the expense of separate lay officers. More damaging, he felt, was that the disputes between clerics and judges and the deeply resented claims of the latter to authority over the former were subverting the interests of the company and confusing the natives. This decision left the clergy in unchallenged control in the villages—a control that this time none felt obliged to decline.[128]

The pioneer missionaries Candidius and Junius left Taiwan in 1637 and 1643, respectively, leaving the mission work in the hands of much less experienced churchmen. In 1645 Governor Caron expressed dismay that, despite the large sums allocated to church work and despite the boasting "with so much vainglory, about the progress that the Christian religion has been making here," the native converts were "only Christians in mere name." Caron laid the blame primarily on the undisciplined Dutch schoolmasters (who were often common soldiers). But the next year the formulary or catechism composed by Junius was declared unsuitable and abolished. Attacks on the quality of Junius's work began to increase.[129] Back in Holland Junius had become concerned that the mission was being allowed to decay, and he complained to the responsible ecclesiastical bodies in Amsterdam. But he did so in terms that alienated the clergymen working in Taiwan.[130] In the next years a new cohort of clergymen, whose terms had not overlapped with that of Junius and who were stung by his complaints, found fault with his catechism, translations, sermons, the native teachers he trained, and even the marriages and baptisms he had performed.[131] Even Governor Overtwater joined in, by denying Junius's role in the pacification of a great many villages.[132] This acrimonious feud among the clerics lasted until 1650, when the Amsterdam church managed to quiet it. Kuepers points to the divergence in approach to mission work that underlay this dispute: Junius, who was well acquainted with the customs of the natives, adapted his teachings to their everyday lives; the recently arrived clergy insisted on theological orthodoxy and conformity to Dutch customs.[133]

More feuding among the Dutch sprang up when Nicholas Verburg became governor of the colony (1650–53). At first things ran smoothly; Verburg even approved the appointment of a clergyman to judicial office in Hsiao-lung and granted the income of certain farmlands to clergymen, including Daniel Gravius.[134] But when Gravius, an active detractor of Junius, laid "slanderous" charges against a company factor, Verburg took personal offense and launched a vitriolic campaign against him and against clerical power generally. Verburg's contentiousness hastened the Dutch colony's dissolution into squabbling factions and forced the company to dispatch an investigative commissioner to the island in 1651.[135]

Commissioner Wilhelm Verstegen found both parties much at fault for letting these dissensions get out of hand. Most important, he decided "to discharge the clergymen from their judicial functions" but "to execute this measure in a way that will cause the least possible dissatisfaction, so that the clergymen may not be regarded with contempt by our own people and the natives, or as if they could no longer be trusted." Verstegen noted that what the clerics "really desire is that the income connected with the judicial office, which they received in addition to their salaries as clergymen, should not be withdrawn from them under the altered conditions."[136] Not satisfied by the dismissal of the clergy from judicial office, Verburg continued his attack with a series of substantive structural criticisms of the mission work. Verburg argued that the clergy's income from judicial office was "often so substantial that they enriched themselves in a short time and became homesick," leaving their posts just as their linguistic ability had reached a point that made them most valuable.[137]

The redivision of clerical and judicial offices failed to solve and perhaps aggravated the recurring problem of undisciplined village schoolmasters; each case now became a contest between church and company. According to Governor Verburg, the abuses of the schoolmasters were alienating the natives from the company:

> For, in addition to very many schoolmasters who are of no possible use in converting the heathen, there are also many who make the natives greatly suffer by the illegal means which they often make use of; and as they are controlled by the clergymen—under whose wings they generally take shelter and find protection—it is impossible for the judicial functionaries to reprimand them as they deserve; for they always, under some hypothetical pretext or other, continue to escape punishment.
>
> Hence we see that those harpies are set upon obtaining as much profit as they can, by depriving the poor country folk of the harvest to which they look forward. It is therefore not surprising that the natives feel more hatred than love for us; and that they will one day endeavor in some way or other to cast off from their necks the heavy yoke that presses upon them.
>
> We therefore see no possible remedy against this evil but to place the schoolmasters under immediate supervision of the judicial functionaries; so that, when found transgressing, they may be surrendered into the hands of justice, and meet with their just reward, without the clergymen endeavoring to screen them from the consequences of their misdeeds.[138]

As we saw above, ten years earlier in 1643, the clergy had shown some zeal in chastising wayward schoolmasters, a demonstration of self-discipline that helped convince Governor Traudenius to affirm ecclesiastical authority in the villages. In Verburg's view, putting such complete and unchecked power in the hands of the clergy had given free rein to their "usurpation and covetousness." The decay of ecclesiastical discipline, however, as Verburg's own analysis reveals, was not reversed by his attempt to strip the clergy of secular powers. Verburg's successors, who were also much concerned to discipline the schoolmasters, seem to have realized this, and in their regulations "to prevent all conflicts between the servants of the church and the judicial powers in Formosa . . . precedence was given to the church." Thus, in spite of Verburg's efforts to subordinate the clergy to the company, and perhaps because of his acrimonious and counterproductive way of proceeding, the clergy was able to survive his term of office with the bulk of its authority intact.[139]

Verburg's successors took his call for retrenchment more seriously. As early as 1650, before his dispute with Gravius, and again in 1654, after it, he argued that the clergy, in their ambition to win new converts, had spread themselves thin, to the neglect of the proper instruction of those already converted. Verburg reasoned that "if the inhabitants of the nearer villages are thoroughly imbued with the doctrines of Christianity, the Gospel will, as it were, transplant itself to other places."[140] In 1654 he proposed a solution with a familiar ring: "I think it would be better not to provide the north or the south of the island with any more clergymen at present, but to place all our schools under supervision of the judicial officers, leaving the schoolmasters to do the necessary work till such time as the inhabitants show greater signs of civilisation, and become fitter objects for the higher instruction of the clergymen."[141] Schools in the south were especially difficult to staff due to unhealthy (malarial) conditions.[142]

Despite the talk of geographical retrenchment, the clergy had over the years convinced the company to increase the number of ordained ministers serving in Taiwan. Until 1655 no more than three clergymen competent in a native language were ever concurrently on active service in Taiwan. Due to disease, many more recruits were sent than ever served. These clergymen were supplemented by a large number of catechists and schoolmasters; the ratios of clergymen to catechists to schoolmasters (not including native teachers) ranged from 1:2:6 to 1:5:29.[143] In 1655 five new clergymen were sent to Taiwan, raising the total to eight, plus one clerk in holy orders. One was sent to Tan-shui in the north; the rest were appointed to curacies between Hsin-kang and Favorlang. This gave both the southwest core villages near Tayouan and the more recently pacified Favorlang area villages the most intense supervision they had had to date. The consistory also agreed to supervise the churches and schools in the south on a rotating basis.[144] In 1657 the clergy objected to company policy that would effect retrenchment by requiring the clergymen in the newer mission fields of Favorlang to replace any clergy who died or left posts in the southwest core area. They reported that the schools and churches in the Favorlang area were in "flourishing condition."[145]

The appointment of the first missionary, Marcus Massius, to serve in Tan-shui and Keelung in 1655 came thirteen years after the expulsion of the Spanish and ten years after the pacification of the native villages in that area. Apparently no schools had been established in this interval; the administration was left entirely in the hands of company factors and military officers. Both the company and the clergy had wanted to post a clergyman in Tan-shui, but the shortage of personnel had prevented this. The Spanish had converted "a considerable number" of natives to Catholicism, and the inability to serve these congregations was a matter of some embarrassment to the Dutch, as shown in this 1648 report: "The inhabitants, partly in earnest and partly in jest, have sometimes inquired if we Dutch people really be Christians, seeing that we make no show of Divine service, or try to bring them to the faith and baptize their children—which latter they have, in truth, often and earnestly asked us to do."[146] Perhaps the strategic importance of the northern ports and the need for clerical help in consolidating Dutch control helped exempt Tan-shui from the drive to retrench in 1655. The area north of Favorlang (modern Chang-hua) and south of Tan-shui (all of present-day T'ao-yüan, Hsin-chu, and Miao-li counties) was left untouched by Dutch clerical influence, although the company made its presence felt economically and militarily in these areas.

In their last years in Taiwan, the clergy presided over a much expanded school system and were planning a seminary to train native preachers. Yet the unprecedented strength of the church seems to have heightened the frustration of both clergy and company with the task of reforming native beliefs and customs. In 1658 the following order was made public: "Notwithstanding our repeatedly expressed serious admonitions, the people of Formosa persist in committing the sins of idolatry, adultery, fornication and even of incest. . . . Pursuant to the foregoing, we now declare that idolatry in the first degree shall be punishable by public whipping and banishment, that those who are guilty of incest shall be severely whipped in public and wear chains for six years."[147] Notices of these punishments were to be translated and posted in all public places so that "none may pretend ignorance." The Amsterdam church, when notified of this turn to a coercive strategy, immediately registered its objection to such severe punishments:

> We are quite averse to their being employed; it being our conviction that, if they are used, the people will show more aversion to our rule, and will be led at last to adopt desperate measures. It is our conviction, moreover, that if we cannot influence the inhabitants by our precepts and instruction, they will be much less influenced by such severe punishments. We are also of opinion that Christians should never have recourse to such measures; and it greatly surprises us that the Consistory consented to their being taken.[148]

The consolidation of Dutch control freed both the company and the church to adopt more coercive policies toward the natives, but each Dutch party was motivated to limit the excesses of the other. These conflicts reveal that the clergy did not always act selflessly and the company always selfishly, and that the clergy was sometimes itself a source of abuse in the villages. In the next section we will hear complaints from the clergy about the company's oppression of the natives. The rest of this chapter focuses on the means employed by the Dutch to generate revenue from aborigine systems of production and trade and to encourage the expansion of Chinese agriculture. We will also see how friction with the clergy affected the company's economic policies in the villages.

Dutch Administration of the Aborigine Trade

The Dutch wasted no time devising ways to control, tax, and profit from Taiwan's aborigine trade. On their arrival in Tayouan, they came into conflict with the pre-existing network of Chinese village traders, who quite reasonably feared Dutch interference.[149] To prevent this, the traders incited aborigine attacks on the Dutch. The Dutch did not gain a monopoly over the village trade until they expanded their territorial control in 1635–36.

Dutch naval power, however, enabled the company in the early years to harass shipping in Taiwanese waters not under Dutch license. The first step taken to gain control of the trade was to impose duties on ships trading at Tayouan. This led to a dispute with the Japanese, however, that dampened trade until the dispute was settled in the early 1630's.[150] In 1637 the Dutch imposed a 10 percent export duty on venison and deerskins to help recoup the expense of the previous year's conquests. Dutch efforts to monopolize external access to the trade were not completed until the early 1640's when Chinese "smugglers" of deerskins were finally driven out of the Favorlang area.[151]

The Dutch first attempted to derive income from the internal operation of the trade by issuing hunting licenses to Chinese. Unfortunately, neither the creation of the licensing system nor its exact dates of operation are discussed in available sources. We do not know how the village traders already in place reacted to it, or what the motives of the Dutch in instituting it were. Were Chinese already involved in hunting of deer rather than just the trade in deer products? Did the Dutch think a direct Chinese role in the hunt would increase the supply of deerskins and venison? Was the licensing system an attempt to circumvent the native trade as a mechanism of supply either because the native trade was too expensive or because it produced too little due to lagging aborigine demand for trade goods? Or was the licensing system simply a short-term measure to increase Dutch revenues, created without much thought for its long-term economic consequences? Inferring Dutch strategy is difficult because the deer trade was operating successfully at an early date. In 1634 (*before* the 1635–36 expansion and probably before the institution of the licensing system), the aborigine trade produced over 100,000 deerskins, the second largest number of hides (of the eighteen years for which we have data) to be exported under Dutch rule.[152]

The habit of licensing Chinese hunters to areas not under full Dutch control caused both trouble and embarrassment. On numerous occasions hostile aborigines attacked licensed Chinese deer hunters and chased them from the fields or took their heads. Were these instances of the aborigines acting to defend village or hunting territories, protect deer herds from depletion, or win trophy heads? Probably all these motives and more were in operation.[153] In 1640 Junius counseled the company not to issue licenses in the north because of the embarrassment it would cause to the name of the Dutch among both Chinese and aborigines: "If we allow the Chinese to hunt, our influence and reputation will greatly suffer thereby; for the inhabitants of Dovale [Tung-lo] (perhaps also of

Favorlang) will be constantly coming out of their villages to chase away, to rob, and to murder these hunters—attacks which we shall not be able to prevent, seeing that they will be made at so great a distance from Tayouan."[154] As Junius expected, aborigine attacks on Dutch-licensed Chinese hunters followed, and were cited as a reason for moving against Favorlang in the early 1640's.[155] The earliest references to the hunting license system are dated 1636, and it is possible that it was created in that year. The treaty terms demanded of Ma-tou in December 1635 merely required that the aborigines not molest Chinese engaged in the deerskin trade. But the Dutch claimed that the treaty concluded with Takareiang in February 1636 would leave them free to *hunt* (or license hunters) in a greatly expanded territory.[156]

In 1638 licenses to catch deer by means of snares were being sold for one real per month per hunter and licenses to construct pitfalls were being sold for fifteen reals per month. Missionaries resident in the aborigine villages administered the sale of licenses. The income supported mission work, paid for gifts given schoolchildren, and subsidized clerical salaries.[157]

After the expansion of the Dutch sphere of control in 1635–36 and again in the early 1640's, the need to pay for the campaigns themselves and for an expanded administration and missionary effort in the newly pacified territories made the Dutch anxious to increase their sources of revenue.[158] Yet there was little hope of much revenue from directly taxing the natives. In late 1635 a decision to demand tribute "in pigs and paddy" from newly subjugated Ma-tou was reversed "as being too burdensome for them, and because we were very desirous to make peace with them."[159] In 1636, Governor Putmans argued, "With regard to collecting taxes from these poor people . . . it is quite out of the question; for such a thing would only irritate and estrange them from us, as was the case at Kelang." The reference to Keelung (Kelang) is to the revolt of the aborigines of Tan-shui against the Spanish in the same year.[160] Direct taxation, therefore, because of the resistance it might provoke and because the agricultural sectors of the aborigine economies seemed too unproductive to bear it, was at this time deemed out of the question. Instead, the sale of hunting licenses to Chinese enabled the Dutch to squeeze a cash income from the deer herds by what was in effect an indirect tax on the aborigines' livelihood. The income from the licenses and from fines levied on aborigine lawbreakers helped support the village missions and administration.[161]

Mounting expenses increased the pressure to trim mission expenditures, particularly subsidies given to converts. In the early years, before the Dutch expanded their land base in Taiwan, the missionaries sought to win converts by demonstrations of generosity. Such practices brought these words of caution from the company in 1631:

> You must conduct and further this work by such means as may not burden the Company. Pecuniary assistance should statedly be given by the people of Sinkan to support the poor in that island, and on no account should it be expected that this responsibility will be borne by the Dutch community, who are themselves already sufficiently burdened. . . . Indeed, even as it is, the Company's resources are greatly drained in sending every year about four thousand guilders for salaries and the support of the ecclesiastical staff in Tayouan. Consider, too, that the Company has to think of necessitous widows and orphans who every year look forward to receiving the interest of their capital invested many years ago with just as much anxiety as the people of Sinkan look forward to their harvest of paddy.[162]

In 1637 the company was very pleased to hear that the inhabitants of Ta-mu-hsiang and Mu-chia-liu-wan had, by relying not on company disbursements but on their own enthusiasm (no doubt heightened by fear since the Dutch conquests of 1635–36), built their own churches, schools, and rectories.[163] In the early 1640's the company's expenses continued to grow, but so also did the strength of its military position vis-à-vis the villagers. Governor Traudenius objected in 1642 to the gifts to converts and suggested instead that villagers be required to pay a yearly tribute in exchange for the protection of the company. Junius objected on the grounds that the natives were poor and ignorant. The governor countered that the natives were potentially wealthy in land if only they were not so lazy, and that the threat of Dutch arms could be as effective as generosity in converting them to Christianity. Coercion had recently been effective in retrieving Dutch skulls and in eliminating the influence of the *inib*s.[164] Thenceforth, presentation of tribute was mandated at the yearly delegates meetings. I have no information as to whether the goods presented had more than a symbolic value. At the delegates meeting in March 1647, "thanks were also expressed for the required tribute, not on account of its intrinsic value, for that was of little importance to the Company—since many times that amount was yearly expended for the welfare of the country and maintaining their churches and schools—but because it proved they were willing to fulfill their bounden duty, and felt well inclined towards us."[165] In the Tan-shui area, tribute in deerskins, rice, and coal was demanded. Newly submitting tribes were exempted the first year, but disobedient tribes were required to present a double amount as punishment.[166]

Both the sale of deer-hunting licenses and later the imposition of tribute (though probably of only symbolic value) reflect a shift in the balance of power in favor of the Dutch and a concomitant shift in the economy of compliance. In the early years, the Dutch had to proceed circumspectly, trying to win friends through generosity and offers of protection and extending their influence by playing enemies off against each other. These tactics had only limited success. The increase in the Dutch garrisons and the expansion of Dutch territorial control consolidated their power and permitted greater demands on the aborigines. Villages that began as Dutch allies found themselves becoming Dutch subjects. Changes in taxation and administration as well as in missionary strategies, such as the exile of the *inibs*, fines for failure to attend school, and flogging for idolatry, reflect this fundamental power shift (or at least the Dutch estimation of it).

As early as 1639 Junius had expressed concern that the deer were being overhunted and took steps to limit the number of pitfalls and the number of months they could be used. In 1640 Junius again expressed concern for the effect of depletion of the deerherds on aborigine livelihoods.[167] The meager restraints put on the hunting were, however, insufficient to reverse the decline of the herds: in 1644 the decrease was so great that the Taiwan governor recommended that the company supply the Japanese market entirely from Thailand and Cambodia. In 1645 Governor Caron recommended that hunting be prohibited entirely every third year to prevent extermination of the herds. The deer population seems to have stabilized by the early 1650's.[168]

In 1644 the company decided to extend the system of tax farming to the aborigine villages in order to increase income. Tax farms had been established a few years earlier in Taiwan in sectors of the economy dominated by Chinese settlers (see below). The company decided to sell to the highest bidders (Chinese or Dutchmen not employed by the company) monopolies on trade with aborigine villages. The successful bidder gained a monopoly on all goods traded into the villages and a virtual monopsony on the produce, primarily venison and deerskins, traded out. This system of linking tax farms to monopoly privileges followed the model the Dutch used in their Batavia colony in Java.[169] These monopoly merchants or village leaseholders replaced the licensed deer hunters in the villages. I suspect that the removal of the licensed hunters from the deer fields (the attacks on them suggest the villagers resented their role in the hunting) was one of the advantages recommending the adoption of this system. (The sale of hunting licenses was continued through 1645 but in considerably reduced numbers and was probably restricted to areas not yet part of the monopoly trading system.)[170]

The primary advantage of the leasehold system, however, was that it allowed the Dutch to squeeze revenue out of every aspect of the village trade. The Dutch expressions of concern around 1644 about the depletion of the deer herds no doubt reflect declines in revenues from the sale of hunting licenses. The village trade monopolies squeezed two groups at once: the aborigines, who had to pay more for what they bought from the leaseholder and received less for what they sold to him; and the Chinese leaseholders, who had to extract the expense of monopoly fees from their profits. Nevertheless, in 1644 and 1645, when the Dutch adopted the monopoly system, it does not appear that the company was trying to exploit the aborigines ruthlessly and without regard to the consequences. For in the same years, the company took measures to protect aborigine land rights from encroachment by Chinese farmers (see below).

The burden the trade monopolies put on the natives became one of the issues in the debate between the missionaries and Governor Verburg, who wrote the following defense of the system in 1651:

> You have rightly judged from the way in which the fields are leased that this is not so much to the disadvantage of the Formosans as some persons, chiefly the clergymen, loudly pretend it to be . . . the simple truth being that it is a tax levied upon the natives which they do not find to be burdensome in the least. Surely the present system cannot do anyone harm, when the leases granted under it give natives the right not only to sell their meat and skins to the leaseholders of their own village, or exchange them for other articles, but to sell their wares to leaseholders of other villages, so that they need not be cheated or fined by the Chinese unless they themselves are willing to be cheated or fined. . . .
>
> The crooked ways and pretensions of some clerical persons, who least of all should be guilty of such malpractices, impose upon the Government the very difficult task of endeavoring to prevent all this. They not only intrigue against persons desirous of obtaining leases, but—to the utter shame of the clergymen be it said—they would willingly enrich themselves by the sweat and toil of the poor Formosans, and rob them of their only means of subsistence, namely the income derivable from deer hunting.[171]

Again in 1652, Verburg attacked the clergy on these issues: "The daily complaints of the Chinese leaseholders in the north sufficiently prove how very superficially this Gilbertus [Happart] did his work of converting the heathen. Your Excellency can hardly imagine what measures he adopted in order to rob the leaseholders of their deer's flesh and skins, and what tricks and malpractices he employed to fill his own purse."[172] Verburg no doubt had a point that the clergy were concerned less with advancing the welfare of the natives than with protecting their own status in the villages, which might be undermined if Chinese leaseholders were given too free a rein and if the clerics had no power to keep them in check and prevent their cheating the villagers. It is hard to evaluate Verburg's charges of venality against the clergy. He lodged several such charges, most of which were dismissed, and this one was apparently never pressed.[173]

Verburg's priorities are clear: the company's revenue comes from the fees the leaseholders pay, and it is the leaseholders that he defends. His protests that for the aborigines the leaseholds were not "burdensome in the least" or that the tax was so small that "even very poor people cannot find it to be anything of a hardship" are disingenuous.[174] In 1654, when it served his same anticlerical purpose, Verburg gave a different account of the state of aborigine livelihoods: "I do not consider it at all right to punish the inhabitants more than is absolutely necessary for not attending the schools. At present the fine consists in having to give a deer-skin; and often they have not even rice enough in their dwellings to fill their hungry bellies. Surely, then, this punishment is far too severe."[175]

From the company's point of view, the monopoly system was a great success. From 1645 to 1650, the amounts collected by the company grew steadily—and in 1649 and 1650 astronomically.[176] The revenue increase was due not to increased numbers of deerskins but to the ability of the new tax farms to milk the village trade in general and to the dynamics of the auction process. John Wills points out that the influx of Chinese refugees in the late 1640's intensified the competitive bidding for the trade monopolies and drove prices up. In the amounts bid, 1650 was a year of both boom and bust: "Chinese merchants had paid more for the monopolies of the aboriginal villages than they could earn from them, and the Company had to remit one-fifth of the contracted payments in order to save them from bankruptcy."[177] The amounts bid in the 1650's were deflated but still comfortably above those collected in the early years.

Because the monopoly trade system taxed the trade in general (and because of the competitive bidding), there is no direct correlation between the revenue collected and the numbers of deerskins exported. Nakamura has found figures for deerskin exports (venison and other products are not included) for 18 of the 27 years from 1634 to 1660. In three of these years, the numbers exceeded 100,000 (in rank-order the years were 1638, 1634, 1655); in ten years between 50,000 and 100,000 were exported.[178] The numbers fluctuate considerably, but for the reported years the average number of deerskins exported was 65,525. However, the two years of greatest exports, 1638 and 1634, are also the earliest for which we have figures; this no doubt reflects the situation before the herds suffered greatly from overhunting. Yet it is still ironic that the second largest year of the whole era, 1634, preceded the first Dutch expansion of 1635–36—which suggests that the hunters and village traders were capable of supplying large amounts for export independently of Dutch political control (but not perhaps at prices the Dutch wanted to pay). In later years the depletion of the herds nearest Tayouan was compensated somewhat by exploiting more distant fields made accessible to the Dutch (and less accessible to smugglers) by their territorial expansion. This is confirmed by records of leasehold prices, which were highest for Favorlang and Chu-lo-shan (north of the southwest core) every year from 1648 to 1657.[179]

How important to the Dutch colonial economy was the revenue extracted from the aborigine trade and deer-hunting sector? Throughout the history of company rule in Taiwan, profits from trade (including locally produced sugar) exceeded (usually by large amounts) revenue derived from taxing the local economy.[180] Nevertheless, the sale of hunting licenses and village trade monopolies accounted for the bulk of company revenues from the local economy up through the 1640's. And these figures understate the value of the aborigine trade because they do not include export duties or profits from the sale of deer products to China and Japan, which are in the trade column. Beginning in the 1640's, large numbers of Chinese immigrants and refugees began to arrive in the colony. The resulting expansion of the colony's rice and sugar production meant that company revenue from the Chinese sector of the economy grew rapidly. Thus throughout the 1650's taxes on the Chinese population provided the bulk of the company's domestic income and eclipsed the aborigine sector in value.[181]

The Transformation of Aborigine Agriculture

The Dutch initiated a transformation in aborigine farming practices, especially in the southwest core. In the view of both the Dutch and the Chinese, native agricultural techniques were crude and underproductive, and the abundance of untilled land was striking (both came from densely populated countries practicing intensive agriculture)—witness John Struys's comment in 1650: "Formosa is a very fruitful island, but it lies untilled; as its inhabitants are very lazy, and not unlike the Spaniards in being willing to starve rather than work."[182] (See Chapter 2 for the reasons the natives invested less effort in cereal production than outside observers seemed to think they ought.) Dutch charges of sloth also reflected their disdain for the native sexual division of labor, which offended Calvinist, anti-aristocratic notions of the proper roles for men and women: "The women, who are complete drudges, do most of the farming work"; "While the women work, the men go about doing nothing, especially the strong young men."[183]

To boost aborigine grain production, the Dutch introduced plows and draft oxen (sold to aborigines at cost) in the late 1640's, and by 1650 could report that "the Soulangians have already become fairly well acquainted with the art of ploughing, and are beginning to understand the use of cars or waggons."[184] Unfortunately, the sources give few hints of the motivation behind the effort to reform native agriculture or of its extent. The Dutch were anxious to expand local supplies of grain to their garrisons—and it is indicative of their success among the natives that in 1648 they were able to purchase for cash and cangans a good quantity of grain from Ma-tou and Hsiao-lung.[185] However, the growing colony of Chinese, who were harder-working and more sophisticated farmers, made it unnecessary to rely on less efficient aborigine farmers. Thus, there was little economic rationale for investing in aborigine agriculture. But the missionaries and the company may have had a political rationale. Some expressed concern about the poverty (that is, the inability to pay cash levies) of the aborigines and the need to protect their livelihoods. The sale of licenses and trade monopolies (and overhunting) had adverse effects on aborigine income that some were anxious to curtail, if only to prevent political disaffection in the villages. Encouraging grain production could ameliorate this problem. The aborigines as well were concerned to maintain their incomes (and perhaps to buy more in the way of trade goods), and ox-drawn plows made it easier to produce more grain. There were also direct pressures to boost grain production or change the method of production. For example, villagers were required to supply native schoolmasters with a ration of rice.[186] More important, the expansion of Chinese-operated farms into village territories reduced the area available for traditional extensive agriculture (the Dutch did take some steps to protect aborigine interests in these lands—see below). Plowing allowed the aborigines to farm limited tracts of land more intensively.[187]

We may be sure that in introducing the use of the ox-drawn plow, the missionaries taught the new technique to aborigine men rather than women. Expanding the male role in agriculture may have been a conscious goal of the Dutch. Especially among the matrilineal Siraya of the southwest core, Dutch missionaries were attempting to reform customs of marriage and family by encouraging young married couples to live and rear children together. No doubt the Dutch encouragement to males to participate more in agriculture was intended to persuade them to fill the role of provider to the nuclear, and properly patriarchal, family.

Redefining the male role was not simply the result of a Dutch evangelical desire to impose their culture-bound notions of a proper sexual division of labor, however; they had political and economic reasons as well. The Dutch imposition of peace among warring villages made it crucial in all groups. Opportunities to demonstrate prowess in war and head-hunting were shrinking, and even deer hunting may have been adversely affected, especially in core villages (Hsiao-lung and Hsin-kang) farthest from producing deer fields.[188] (These problems would become especially acute later under Chinese rule.) Plow agriculture was one of the few ways of expanding the male role the new Dutch order could offer. Native schoolteacher was another new male role, open to a few, and may have partly filled the void left by the outlawed *inibs*. But we may doubt that the drudgery of agriculture, traditionally the work of women and old men, proved attractive to young men reared to expect the glories of war and the hunt (missionary education aimed to change that as well). The native gender ideology was a strong point of resistance to change in agriculture, and when denied its traditional expression, demoralization was as likely as innovation.

There was progress, nevertheless, and a good number of natives did buy the oxen. In the early 1660's, native agriculture in the southwest core villages was sufficiently productive for Cheng Ch'eng-kung to purchase grain there for his hungry armies. But in the Favorlang area, the aborigines were still farming in the traditional manner, without plows.[189] The ox-drawn cart was a more successful innovation than the ox-drawn plow. By early Ch'ing times, the use of oxcarts had spread to every aborigine village. The oxcart apparently had none of the liabilities of plow agriculture and may even have appealed to aborigine males (see Chapter 11).

The company encouraged the growth of the Chinese agricultural colony in Taiwan and was anxious to profit from the export of sugarcane produced by the Chinese. But the expansion of Chinese fields inevitably meant encroachment onto lands belonging to aborigine villages. In 1643 the company, apparently at aborigine request, ordered Chinese farmers to abandon lands claimed by five aborigine villages in the southwest core. The Chinese got the Dutch to stay the order until after the harvest in 1644, by which time a compromise had been worked out. The village elders agreed to allow the Chinese to remain, in exchange for the payment each year of two reals per *morgen* (hectare or *chia*). The company reserved the right to evict the tenants in the future on behalf of the aborigines. The total rents to be collected that year were 700 reals (which works out to 350 hectares).[190] The rent was quite low—two reals would not buy two piculs of rice[191]—but the aggregate amount, which could expand with reclamation, and the principle of an aborigine land right were both significant. Dutch support for the aborigine land claim shows they recognized that unlimited exploitation of the aborigine economies would incur political resistance. It may also reveal an early Dutch awareness of a need to court aborigines as allies in the face of a rapidly expanding Chinese colony. This was certainly the case after the Chinese rebellion of 1652. In 1654 the company renewed its commitment to check Chinese encroachment when it "agreed to allow the leasing of some of these fields to Chinese, but not their permanent alienation."[192] Unfortunately, the sources give no further details on the operation or extent of an aborigine leasehold system.

The Dutch were no doubt glad in 1652 that they had given some consideration to the preservation of aborigine livelihoods when Fayet (Kuo Huai-i) led several thousand Chinese farmers in an abortive revolt. A small Dutch force, "supported by two thousand Christian Formosans," quickly suppressed the rebellion, an act reminiscent of the Dutch mobilization of aborigine braves to suppress rebel tribes.[193] Even so, in 1653 the Dutch were suspicious about the loyalty of the aborigines, "seeing that the Chinese have more intercourse with them than we have. . . . Hence those natives may be easily tempted to rise up against us."[194] Efforts to play aborigines off against Chinese apparently had little success, and the company was reluctant to make much financial sacrifice to court the aborigines. When the threat of attack from Cheng Ch'eng-kung grew in 1660, the Dutch took measures to prevent collusion: "Such Chinese farmers who had stirred up fear and bad feeling in the minds of the Formosans, had their houses confiscated, and were expelled from their villages."[195] But when Cheng finally arrived with a vastly superior force in 1661, the aborigines wasted little time in submitting to their new masters (see Chapter 4).

The Growth of the Chinese Colony

The Chinese were no strangers to Taiwan before the arrival of the Dutch. Pirates and fishermen were frequent visitors to the Taiwan coast from the late sixteenth century. In 1603 Ch'en Ti noted the presence in the Tayouan area of traders who had mastered some of the local languages. When the Dutch arrived twenty years later, they confronted a network of Chinese village traders, rumored to number from 1,000 to 1,500. The Dutch were able to communicate with the aborigines through their Chinese interpreters because some aborigines and village traders had learned each other's language.[196]

The village traders were immediately suspicious of the Dutch, rightly fearing that they would interfere with their trade, and they incited aborigine attacks against them.[197] Matters stood largely at a standstill until 1635, when the Dutch garrison was reinforced and the company expanded its territorial base. In the newly subdued village of Ma-tou, for instance, the Dutch victors ordered the Chinese residents to assemble separately. The Dutch upbraided them for encouraging aborigine resistance and threatened them with expulsion, whereupon the Chinese "promised amendment."[198] An indication of the extent and importance of this Chinese network comes from Fang-so (Dutch: Pangsoia), a village far to the south of Tayouan that submitted to the Dutch in 1636. Junius had originally intended to post there a Chinese-language version of the treaty of peace between the Dutch and aborigines. But he feared that "the first article—giving the sovereignty of this land to the states of Holland—might later be explained by some malevolent Chinese in such a way as to cause widespread irritation against us."[199]

Once the Dutch had demonstrated their military prowess, many of the traders proved conciliatory. Their linguistic skills made them valuable to both the aborigines and the Dutch in negotiations. On numerous occasions native villages sent them as emissaries to the Dutch to sue for peace. And the Dutch sent their own Chinese employees to treat with village leaders—some of whom sought counsel in turn from "Chinese advisers," who were undoubtedly resident traders.[200] The village traders, because their middleman role gave them leverage in dealing with the outside world, exercised a high degree of influence in the villages. The

Dutch often accused them of using that influence to bully and deceive the aborigines.[201]

The campaigns of the early 1640's brought the Dutch into contact with Chinese traders operating well beyond the southwest core. In the Favorlang area, the traders had links with pirates and smugglers (some of whom were also fishermen), who evaded Dutch customs patrols on the many rivers.[202] Even on the remote eastern coast, Chinese traders preceded the Dutch and tried to stir up resistance against them. The Dutch managed to expel at least some of these troublemakers from both areas. And under the monopoly merchant system, they encouraged villagers to seize any Chinese seeking to trade without a proper license.[203]

Fishermen, many of whom were also traders, were another group of Chinese present in Taiwan independently of the Dutch.[204] Chinese fished Taiwan's coastal waters in greatest numbers in the winter in search of mullet.[205] The Dutch also imposed a licensing and taxation system on the fishermen and became concerned to protect them from aborigine attack.

The Chinese village traders (as opposed to the immigrant Chinese agriculturalists discussed below) were in constant contact with the missionaries, the major representatives of Dutch authority in the villages. Several factors indicate a rivalry between these two groups for influence among the villagers. A high proportion of the traders apparently took aborigine wives, a reflection of the relatively high status of the traders in village society and the absence of Chinese women in Taiwan. The Chinese imperviousness to the message of salvation rankled the missionaries and embarrassed them in front of the aborigines. In 1644, the Dutch authorities "resolved that all Chinese who cohabit with native Christian women . . . shall be held bound to render . . . a satisfactory account of their Christian faith. In default of this, they must separate themselves from such native Christian women, and in case they have begotten children by them, they will be bound to furnish the necessary means for their support."[206] These missionary efforts to pressure Chinese to convert had little success.

The Chinese traders and missionaries also had overlapping interests. The Chinese were dependent on good relations with the clergy, who sold deer-hunting licenses and in later years oversaw the operation of the leaseholder system. As judicial officers, the clergy were empowered to levy fines and collect taxes from Chinese.[207]

At times, convergent interests made the missionaries anxious to cooperate with the traders. Because many Chinese were too poor to pay for hunting licenses, Junius advanced the money to pay for the licenses on condition that he could buy the skins at the end of the season for a fixed price. The profits went to the support of mission work. Junius gave an additional explanation of the need for such a system: "The Chinese are very desirous of borrowing money from us, as otherwise they must borrow from their countrymen, who show no mercy in their dealings with each other, and charge four or five *per cent.* for monthly interest."[208] Junius was well acquainted with the finances of the Chinese; when the company imposed a head tax on Chinese in 1640, he pointed out to the governor (to no avail) its possible adverse consequences for the aborigines: "Those Chinese, however, who live in the villages are very poor. . . . If they are made to pay a quarter of a *real* monthly, they will certainly attempt to recoup themselves by cheating the poorer class of our people; whom they daily defraud, and who, on that account, can never better their condition."[209] Heavy Dutch taxation contributed to friction among the Chinese, aborigines, and missionaries. Overhunting and the depletion of the deer herds, and the presence of Chinese in the hunting grounds, fueled aborigine resentment.

The village monopoly system, instituted in the early 1640's, did not change this basic pattern. As noted above, Chinese traders could recoup the licensing fees only from the aborigines, since the inflated bidding meant that there were no guarantees of profit, except to the company.[210] The missionaries had an interest in checking exploitation of their native converts, but they also benefited from hunting license fees that helped pay for church expenses. Nor were the missionaries themselves above temptation. Governor Verburg managed to get a conviction against Gravius for extorting 651.5 reals from the Chinese Sakoa, although the sentence was later appealed and overturned in Batavia.[211]

Agricultural colonists eventually constituted the bulk of Taiwan's Chinese population. There were almost no Chinese farmers in Taiwan when the Dutch first arrived (a few of the village traders may have done some part-time farming).[212] Because, as we saw above, the aborigines were not inclined to produce more grain than they required, the Dutch garrisons had to rely on rice imported from Thailand and Japan.[213] To boost the local supply of provisions, the company recruited immigrant farmers through its Chinese trading agents. These farmers came from the same densely populated and rice-deficit areas of the south Fukien coast as did the Chinese village traders, fishermen, and merchants operating in Taiwan.[214] The company's initial limited success in attracting immigrants is reflected in a 1633 estimate that put the Chinese population in company-controlled areas at only 700–800.[215]

During the 1630's the company began to have greater success in attracting Chinese farmers. The promise of profits from the cultivation of rice and sugarcane attracted investment from the wealthy merchant Bencon (Su Ming-kang), the Captain China at the Dutch colony of Batavia, beginning in 1636. With the company's blessing, Bencon recruited Chinese farmers to till the land near Sakam that he and his partners had reclaimed.[216] The Dutch themselves transported immigrants to Taiwan; in

1631 many more wanted to go than their ships could hold.[217] Undoubtedly the greatest number of immigrants took passage on merchant and fishing ships plying the Taiwan strait. During the 1630's the immigration was substantial; proponents of levying a head tax on the Chinese claimed there were as many as 8,000–11,000 Chinese in areas under the company's control in 1638 and 1639.[218]

In 1640 the first levy of the head tax produced an enumeration of 3,568 Chinese, probably reflecting a slightly larger total population. The immigrants were overwhelmingly male sojourners who sent their earnings back to families on the Fukien coast. To encourage permanent settlement, the Dutch offered tax exemptions to women and families; the first few women immigrants appeared in 1646. In October 1650, 10,811 Chinese paid the capitation, and the total population was estimated at around 15,000.[219] In 1656 the capitation was farmed at a rate that presumed at least 13,680 Chinese would pay the tax. At the end of Dutch rule in 1661, the Chinese population is estimated to have included 25,000 able-bodied males. Women and children are unlikely to have added more than a third to that total.[220] Our best estimate, therefore, of total Chinese population circa 1661 is approximately 35,000, and certainly no more than 50,000. Thus, the largest growth in the Chinese population took place in the last decade and a half of Dutch rule, as refugees from the Manchu conquest of China (the new Ch'ing dynasty was proclaimed in 1644) fled to Taiwan.[221]

Immigrants flowed to Taiwan in pulses linked to events on China's southeast coast; occasionally the flow reversed itself. There was a large influx in 1648 of migrants fleeing famine in Fukien (exacerbated if not caused by the dynastic chaos), but once the threat of starvation had subsided, as many as 8,000 returned. Cheng Ch'eng-kung's defeats and retreat to Amoy led to another burst of immigration in 1658–59.[222] Events within Taiwan also caused fluctuation in the Chinese population. The Kuo Huai-i rebellion in 1652 ended with the massacre of as many as 3,000 Chinese rebels.[223] From 1653 to 1655 a series of disasters—epidemics, locusts, and earthquakes—took their toll of the population.[224]

The great bulk of the Chinese immigrants earned their livelihood in agriculture. Farmers in southern Fukien were experienced growers of rice and sugarcane for market. As early as 1636, when the Chinese population was still small, Taiwan exported over 100,000 catties (*chin*) of granulated sugar to Japan. The prospects of a profitable export trade greatly pleased the company, and it reaffirmed its policy of encouraging both agriculture and Chinese immigration. That such an amount was produced in 1636 is even more remarkable when we recall that the Dutch had just pacified the core area.[225] Aborigine harassment of Chinese farmers—cutting off their hair, "injuring" their cattle—was cited as one reason for territorial control: "This enforcement of law and order was also very desirable on account of the Chinese residing here; because the security and prosperity of their sugar plantations required our protection against the natives, who were continually damaging them, as appeared from the many complaints that were made to us."[226] Chinese agriculture began in the immediate vicinity of Sakam, and at its greatest extent under the Dutch it never extended far beyond that city. Conflicts between farmers and natives, therefore, did not figure in later Dutch expansion.[227]

After the Dutch took the Tan-shui–Keelung area from the Spanish in 1642, they were anxious, just as they had been on taking Tayouan, to encourage the local production of fresh foodstuffs for their garrisons. Once again they turned to Chinese farmers, who were accustomed to producing surpluses for both government and market, rather than to the native villagers. Chinese were encouraged to settle in the north, and by 1648 a small colony had begun farming.[228]

Other indicators show a steady growth of agriculture, as well as company attempts to encourage it. Throughout the 1640's and especially in the late 1650's, Taiwan's sugar exports grew steadily, if erratically, as the figures for export to Persia reveal.[229] To encourage the cultivation of rice, which was apparently less lucrative than sugar, the company tried offering cash subsidies in 1637. To facilitate agricultural expansion, the Company imported draft oxen; by 1640 it could report that 1,200–1,300 head were being raised in Taiwan.[230]

The complex system of land tenure and taxation in the Dutch colony is made all the more difficult to understand by the fragmentary nature of the sources. As we saw above, the company did recognize certain native claims to land and saw that rents were paid when Chinese farmed that land. However, it appears that no native claims were recognized on the bulk of the land brought under cultivation.

The Dutch fostered reclamation under a number of different schemes. The company itself is said to have supplied capital for the building of irrigation works and to have provided draft animals and seed to farmers in a "contractor" system. In other cases wealthy Chinese investors (Bencon is the outstanding example) sponsored the reclamation of 20-*morgen* parcels.[231] As an incentive to such investment, reclaimers were promised a tax holiday of five to ten years on new land. In general, the rice harvest on land near Sakam was subject to a 10 percent harvest tax rather than a land tax.[232]

Land devoted to the cultivation of sugarcane, in contrast to rice, was tax free—although a distinction based on who sponsored the land reclamation seems likely. A farmer's income from sugar was taxed, nevertheless, by the company's monopsony on sugar purchases. We can be sure the company did its best to pay less than a free market price.[233]

In addition to taxes, references suggest the company "rented out" land to Chinese farmers and at rental rates much in excess of 10 percent of the harvest; presumably this was on land whose reclamation the company had financed. In some cases the company assigned its income from certain lands to supplement clergymen's salaries.[234] Thus, the terms by which Chinese farmed land in the Dutch colony depended on the kind of crop grown, on who financed the reclamation of the land, on the recognition of aborigine claims, and on the structure of the tax system. To say that all this land was "owned" by the Dutch prince and a uniform rent and tax levied, as later Chinese sources assert (and they may be technically correct as far as title is concerned), is an oversimplification.[235]

The total area under cultivation grew and fluctuated, as did the population of Chinese farmers. Cultivated land was measured for the first time in 1645; this survey revealed a total of 3,000 *morgen*, including 1,713 *morgen* planted to rice and 612 *morgen* planted to sugarcane.[236] In 1655 farmers were cultivating 4,978 *morgen* of rice (of which 3,101 *morgen* were taxed) and 1,443 *morgen* of sugarcane, making a total of 6,421 *morgen*. In 1660 the area of sowed land was reported at 12,252 *morgen*, and sugar culture was said to be at its greatest extent in the history of the colony. The 1660 area is twice that for 1655 and reflects the expansion in response to the heavy immigration of the late 1650's. The rice acreage generally exceeded the sugarcane acreage by a factor of two or three.[237] The comparative price and profitability of each crop was of course an important factor (besides the land and labor requirements) in determining what to grow.

Taiwan sugar was sold on a world market; most of it was sent to Persia or Japan. Profits from sugar and other local products grew in importance to the company in the 1640's when its trade in silk and porcelains was disrupted by the dynastic strife in China. During the 1650's trouble in Brazil disrupted sugar production there and opened the European market to East Asian sugar. Taiwan, which was receiving many immigrants at this time, benefited from these opportunities. When Brazilian production resumed around 1658, sugar prices declined in Taiwan.[238]

In addition to farming, Chinese performed many economic roles in the colony. Besides the deer trade, native commerce, and fishing, Chinese also earned livings in urban retail and service occupations in the markets of Tayouan and Sakam. The Dutch relied on Chinese construction laborers when building forts, warehouses, and residences. Chinese also served as porters and auxiliaries in the Dutch military garrisons and as seamen in the Dutch navy.[239]

Numerous taxes created in the early 1640's were aimed at the Chinese population's various economic activities. All these taxes were let to private tax farmers. Taxes were imposed on butcher shops, fisheries, liquor and distilleries, and market weighmasters. There were also import and export duties on a variety of products. By far the most important tax for the company's domestic revenue was the head tax on Chinese. When first imposed in 1640, it met with protest from the Chinese population, but the Dutch went ahead, both overcoming and ignoring the objections. From 1655 to 1657 the head tax accounted for half the company's domestic revenue (excluding customs revenues), followed by the aborigine trade monopolies (one-fourth) and the rice tax (14 percent). In the 1640's the income from the aborigine trade monopolies had exceeded the head tax in value.[240]

Local tax revenues as opposed to trading revenues began to make a significant contribution to defraying local expenses only in the early 1640's. The aggressive expansion of the tax system in the 1640's meant quick growth in local tax revenues. By 1645 local charges (including customs duties) amounted to more than half of expenses, and they regularly contributed at least that much thereafter. Once the tax system was in place, the rapid growth of the Chinese population in the 1650's meant that local revenues grew substantially. Nevertheless, revenues from trading regularly exceeded the contribution of local tax revenues, an important reminder that the Dutch East India Company operated the Taiwan colony as a commercial venture for profit and not as a local government merely seeking to match revenues against expenditures for government services.[241]

The Chinese population was governed, in the mode usual for East Asian trading colonies, through community headmen. The headmen, or Captains China, were left responsible for the management of most affairs internal to the Chinese community. In Taiwan, each Chinese agricultural settlement had its village chief, and there were a number of headmen rather than a single captain. Other headmen led the mercantile community in the market town of Tayouan. In 1644 a committee of three Chinese and four Dutchmen was created to settle disputes involving the two communities.[242]

Although the rapid growth of the Chinese colony benefited the company economically, it also brought unanticipated political costs. As early as 1646 and again in July 1652, the Dutch heard rumors that Cheng Ch'eng-kung, suffering from defeats at the hands of the Manchus, might seek refuge in Formosa. For these reasons the Dutch garrison was ordered bolstered to 1,200 men in 1650:

> And matters during 1652 fully justified this warning, as Chinese settlers in the island thought themselves too much oppressed by the Company; so that longing for liberty, and having some prospect of assistance from the encouragement of Koxinga, they undertook a dangerous revolt; although the greater number were mere peasants, some of them armed, but the majority with only sticks and bamboos as their weapons. Therefore, with the faithful Formosan natives as allies, the Netherlanders soon subdued them; shooting a few, and easily putting to flight those who were not trained in the art of war.[243]

This rebellion of farmers, in September 1652, was led by Kuo Huai-i or Fayet, headman of Smeerdorp in Amsterdams Polder, two miles north of Sakam, and was apparently instigated by abuses in the collection of the poll tax. The badly outnumbered Dutch survived only because the urban Chinese headmen revealed the plot, giving the Dutch an opportunity to mobilize their forces. One hundred and twenty Dutchmen and 600 "Christian Formosans" went into the field against 4,000–5,000 Chinese rebels; when the skirmishing was over, approximately 3,000 Chinese had been slain. The native troops were rewarded with one piece of cloth for every Chinese head.[244] The Dutch were unable to uncover any proof of a tie to Cheng Ch'eng-kung, but there is no doubt that some of the rebels hoped he would come to their aid.[245]

In 1653 the Dutch built a new fort in Sakam called Provintia, in order to "quell any sudden attack of the peasants and Formosans."[246] Throughout the remainder of Dutch rule, relations with the Chinese remained tense. Rumors of Cheng Ch'eng-kung's designs on the island were widespread, and many of his actions lent them credibility. At various times he cut off trade with Taiwan. Some Chinese traders, fearing an outbreak of war, transported their assets out of Taiwan and made preparations to flee. In 1659 the interpreter Pincqua was discovered to be an agent for Cheng and spreading rumors of his arrival. In 1660 when an attack seemed imminent, Governor Coyett ordered all Chinese farmers evacuated from more distant areas where they could not be kept under surveillance.[247] Chinese were also ordered to vacate native villages because "they were discouraging those friendly to the Company in the Formosan villages by boasting loudly of Koxinga's war forces, stating that his soldiers were protected from head to foot with iron armour, which the Dutch muskets could not penetrate."[248] The Chinese elders, some of whom were suspect, were taken hostage "so that they might not tempt the approaching enemy, or, through their numerous following of tradesmen, farmers, and others, cause any commotion and have themselves proclaimed as leaders."[249] All Dutch schoolmasters were encouraged to arm themselves with rifles and even the Formosans, whose loyalty some questioned, were to provide themselves "with their own kind of arms." After all these preparations had been made, the warning of Cheng Ch'eng-kung's attack turned out to be a false alarm (he changed his plans), and the Chinese settlers were allowed to return to their farms.[250] Although vigilance was maintained within the colony, the Dutch were unable to get the outside reinforcements they thought necessary.

CHAPTER FOUR

The Cheng Era, 1661–1683

Cheng Ch'eng-kung's Conquest

Cheng Ch'eng-kung's northern expedition against the Manchus had crumbled after his defeat at Nanking in September 1659. The area his Ming loyalist regime controlled in southeastern China shrank rapidly as the Manchu armies advanced in the next months, but he repulsed an attack on Amoy in June 1660, and that city remained in Cheng hands until November 1663.[1] On April 30, 1661, Cheng appeared off Tayouan at the head of an expeditionary force of some 25,000 men. Welcomed by the Chinese residents, the Cheng forces quickly gained control of the countryside and besieged the Dutch in their two fortresses. In the city of Sakam, Cheng's army, which was short on provisions, immediately found grain stores that would supply them for half a month. Within Fort Provintia, in Sakam, the well went dry, forcing the besieged Dutch to negotiate for surrender after only a few days. Zeelandia Castle on the Tayouan peninsula, however, withstood Cheng attacks (and remained accessible by sea) until the Dutch negotiated a surrender in February 1662.[2]

Scattered aborigine resistance to the invasion did not last long in the face of such well-armed and overwhelming numbers. On the sixth day after Cheng's arrival, the heads of the plains tribes in the immediate vicinity went to Sakam to offer their respects. These chiefs were feasted and given robes, caps, and boots appropriate to Chinese officials. News of this favorable treatment spread quickly, and elders from more distant villages soon arrived to make peace with the Chengs.[3] Cheng Ch'eng-kung's prompt attention to aborigine affairs is good evidence of the importance to his regime of good relations with the far-flung aborigine villages.

In the aborigine villages, Dutch ecclesiastical authority, robbed of its coercive backing, collapsed:

> These fellows now speak with much disdain of the true Christian faith which we endeavored to implant in their hearts, and are delighted that they are now freed from attending the schools. Everywhere they have destroyed the books and utensils, and have introduced the abominable usages and customs of heathenism. On the report being spread that Koxinga had arrived, they murdered one of our Dutch people, and after having struck off the head they danced around it with great joy and merriment, just as they formerly did with their vanquished enemies.[4]

When a party from Ma-tou returned with three heads taken in an expedition to punish a mountain tribe and discovered that Cheng had defeated the Dutch, they, too, "according to the former heathenish custom when celebrating a triumph . . . began to dance round these heads and to perform other ridiculous antics. Mr. Hambroek [a clergyman] thereupon forbade them, but they were insolent enough openly to contradict and disobey him when he reproved them for acting in their old way."[5] It is unlikely that even when they were in control, the Dutch were able to do more than suppress the open festivals of the head-hunting cult—for the Dutch had relied on bloodthirstiness to motivate their native auxiliaries in battle against other tribes, such as Favorlang, and against the Chinese rebels in 1652. The missionaries' dismay at the resurgence of "heathenish custom" is a bit disingenuous, for the Dutch themselves made quite a show of crueler ceremonies. The second-in-command of the Chinese rebel force in 1652, who had the misfortune to be captured alive by the Dutch, "was roasted alive before a fire in Taiwan, dragged behind a horse through the town, and his head was then stuck on a pole. Two of his chieftains . . . were broken upon the wheel and quartered."[6] In 1636 the Dutch had delivered prisoners from Hsiao-lung to the people of Hsin-kang for decapitation in order "to unite" them to the company. One of Cheng's officials practiced the same style of statecraft: he delivered prisoners taken from a Dutch shipwreck to Hsin-kang and ordered the village chiefs to behead them.[7]

Cheng Ch'eng-kung's troops seem to have been well disciplined: "The Chinese soldiers left the natives perfectly unmolested, but the others often foully abused them."[8] Who the "others" were is unclear, perhaps they were settlers or hangers-on of the army. Tension also increased when Cheng's hungry army requisitioned goods from the natives (see below). At Hsin-kang, "the inhabitants loudly complained of the injustice in taking away from them their very best land, their rice, cattle and wagons. The poor people had to bear this in silence, and even to appear contented. [Meanwhile] the elders amongst them went about in Chinese robes of great value."[9] To maintain good relations with the aborigines, Cheng Ch'eng-kung himself went on a tour of inspection of the major southwest core native villages and distributed cloth and tobacco among the aborigine headmen to win their goodwill.[10]

The Cheng army had landed in the spring, long before any harvests were expected in Taiwan; when bad weather prevented grain ships from crossing to Taiwan, the problem of provisioning the armies became acute. On May 20, 1661, Cheng dispatched subordinates to search for stores of grain in Chinese and aborigine villages. To maintain discipline, Cheng imposed severe punishments on officers found guilty of stealing grain or other goods from commoners. On May 26 he dispersed the brigades not needed for the siege of Zeelandia Castle to suburban areas and ordered them to begin planting. Colonies of soldier-farmers were to be Cheng's long-term solution to the problem of army provisions.[11]

Early in June 1661, Cheng set up a civil administration on the Chinese model, appointing officials to head one prefecture and two counties. Given the regime's pressing need to expand its agricultural base and grain revenues, these magistrates were immediately charged with registering land and collecting taxes. Land registration was also important for preventing conflicts by establishing the title to land farmed by local Chinese and aborigine villagers.[12]

On June 14, 1661, Cheng promulgated regulations governing the opening of new farmlands. Nearly every clause ends with a prohibition on interfering with the already cultivated fields and crops of Chinese commoners and aborigines, a reflection of Cheng's concern to minimize friction between the occupying army and the local populace (early infractions are noted in the Dutch sources).[13] But the main aim of the regulations was to encourage reclamation, to ensure that those who invested labor and capital to convert wasteland into productive farmland would become its legal owners, and to increase revenues. Prospective reclaimers were required to file claims on land before they opened it and were warned not to underreport land subject to taxation.[14]

In July 1661, Cheng dispatched more brigades to set up posts and military colonies at strategic points, but only as far north as Hsin-chu and Hsin-kang-tzu and as far south as Feng-shan and Kuan-yin-shan. The soldiers were given six months' wages to tide them over while they brought land under cultivation. The Dutch garrisons in Tan-shui and Keelung apparently retained control of northernmost Taiwan throughout the summer of 1661.[15]

Two incidents in August 1661 underscored the political importance of the plains aborigines. First, the Chinese uncovered a plot by two captured Dutch schoolmasters to stir up rebellion among the Formosan aborigines. The two were crucified as a warning against similar attempts.[16] Second, the brigade that was stationed (on Cheng's orders of July 1661) in the vicinity of Ta-tu (in north-central Taiwan) apparently mistreated the local aborigines. During August 1661, the villagers killed several officers and put up such a stiff resistance that reinforcements had to be sent twice before the revolt was crushed. Governor Coyett reported that the villagers "killed and dispersed . . . by sudden surprise about two thousand of his [Cheng's] soldiers."[17] Chiang Jih-sheng says that the Ta-tu villagers wanted to aid the besieged Dutch against Cheng. After an investigation of the disturbance, soldiers were warned not to cause trouble in the aborigine villages, and the northern brigades were withdrawn to Nan *she*, south of the Cho-shui river. Aborigine resentment continued to simmer until January 1665 when a second revolt at Ta-tu had to be put down.[18]

In September 1661, Cheng defeated a desperate Dutch land and naval attack on Sakam from Zeelandia.[19] Cheng's troubles in August and September 1661 were aggravated by the failure of his grain ships to arrive. Grain was tightly rationed. Soldiers restricted to two meals per day grumbled openly, and many fell ill from the climate and the lack of food. Cheng sent his officials to purchase whatever grain they could from the four major aborigine villages nearby (Hsin-kang, Mu-chia-liu-wan, Ma-tou, and Hsiao-lung) and even from the central Taiwan villages of Erh-lin and Nan *she*. Although it was harvesttime for the aborigines, this yielded provisions for only another ten days. Because shortages were so acute, severe discipline was needed to maintain order among the troops and to keep the grain officials honest.[20]

In February 1662 the Dutch came to terms with Cheng Ch'eng-kung, surrendered Zeelandia Castle, and sailed away. Shortly thereafter, Cheng, accompanied by numerous officials and over a thousand soldiers, went on a second tour of inspection. Besides the large Siraya villages near Sakam (Hsin-kang, Mu-chia-liu-wan, Hsiao-lung, Ma-tou, and Ta-mu-hsiang), Cheng is said to have visited Ta-wu-lung near the mountains and gone as far north as T'a-li-wu and Pan-hsien (Chang-hua) in central Taiwan. Cheng distributed cloth and tobacco to the aborigines, who greeted him by squatting with folded hands, as was their custom, rather than by kneeling and bowing.[21]

On his return to Sakam, Cheng resolved to carry out his program of military colonization by stationing soldiers on the vast stretches of fertile but unopened land he had seen on his tour. Plows and seed were distributed to the troops, who were expected to catch and tame wild oxen (left behind by the Dutch) on their own. In the first three years, they were to pay 30 percent of the harvest to the public treasury; after that, the land was to be graded and assigned a fixed tax rate. Juan Min-hsi refers to these unopened fields as aborigine lands but makes no mention of compensation to the tribes.[22] Nevertheless, aborigine ownership of land *cultivated* by aborigines was probably respected, as required by the regulations issued several months earlier. There is at least one example, however, of a tribe, Ta-chieh-tien, moving a few miles eastward into the foothills when a Cheng military colony was established near its original village site (south of Tainan).[23] Yang Ying, Cheng's minister of revenue, proposed that tribes that did not already use ox-drawn plows be issued them and given instruction in their use, since larger aborigine harvests would help ease the grain shortage.[24]

Chinese settlers who had welcomed Cheng expecting liberation from oppressive Dutch taxation soon had their hopes dashed.[25] Because the Cheng regime was on a constant war footing, it had to squeeze as much in revenue and provisions as possible out of Taiwan. It confiscated company land, collected the rents, and continued the tax farms and monopolies. Article VII of the treaty of Dutch surrender reads: "The names of all Chinese debtors or lease-holders in Formosa, with particulars of claims against them, shall be copied out from the Company's books, and handed to Lord Koxinga."[26] Armed with this information, Cheng appointed Chinese officials to superintend the tax farms and village trade monopolies, just as the Dutch had appointed leaseholders before him.[27]

Cheng Ch'eng-kung died on June 23, 1662. His generals on Taiwan took his younger brother, Cheng Shih-hsi, as their leader. Cheng Ch'eng-kung's eldest son, Cheng Ching, quickly invaded Taiwan from Amoy and won the succession, but not without alienating some of his father's followers, who defected to the Manchus.[28] Cheng Ching returned to Amoy in 1663, but in November met defeat and was driven from the island-city. In early 1664, Cheng Ching led a force of 6,000–7,000 in a withdrawal to Taiwan.[29]

In Taiwan Cheng Ching had first to contend with naval threats against his island base. The Dutch, now allied with the new Manchu dynasty against the Chengs, reoccupied Keelung in 1664 (and left only in 1668). In 1665, the Ch'ing admiral Shih Lang was threatening an assault on the Pescadores. Cheng mobilized his soldier-farmers, sending some north to guard against the Dutch and a larger force to secure the Pescadores. Shih Lang's planned attack failed when a typhoon dispersed his fleet. Cheng Ching gradually withdrew the large armies sent to the Pescadores and resettled them on military colonies in Taiwan.[30] In 1666 Cheng Ching sent his commander Huang An and a force of over 3,000 men to attack the Dutch fort at Keelung, but they failed to dislodge the Dutch. However, the Cheng forces found favor among the Tan-shui aborigines and induced them to cause trouble for the Dutch. In 1668 the Dutch finally withdrew from Keelung.[31]

The Cheng Administration

In Taiwan, Cheng Ching reorganized his refugee government and took steps to put the economy in order.[32] For nearly a decade, until the outbreak of the rebellion of the Three Feudatories in 1674, Taiwan and the Cheng regime enjoyed comparative peace. Cheng Ching continued the policy of putting soldiers to work on farms to provision his armies. He created additional military colonies and gave them a six-year tax holiday on newly reclaimed land. Trading and fishing were revived. Sugar and deer hides were once again exported to Japan, and an illicit trade along the Chinese coast was organized to circumvent the Manchu quarantine. Confucian academies were founded, and an examination system for the selection of civil officials was established.[33]

The Cheng occupation meant a large increase in Taiwan's population. The best estimate of Taiwan's Chinese population in the Cheng era, by Ch'en Shao-hsing, gives a maximum of 120,000, up 70,000 over the late-Dutch-era Chinese population, generously estimated at 50,000.[34] This is best taken as the highpoint reached during the Cheng era, for the frequent wars meant large fluctuations. Shih Lang offered the following estimates of Taiwan's Chinese population in 1668: 20,000–30,000 under the Dutch, 30,000 (20,000 soldiers) led over by Cheng Ch'eng-kung in 1661, 6,000–7,000 (4,000 soldiers) led over by Cheng Ching in 1664, and more than 6,000 casualties of war and disease since then, putting the Cheng military at less than 20,000 strong, and the total Chinese population at a maximum of 61,000.[35] In 1670, Ellis Crispe of the newly established British East India Company's factory at "Tywan" estimated the Cheng military at 70,000.[36] The renewal of war caused large fluctuations. Beginning in 1674, the military colonists were mobilized and sent to fight on the mainland during the rebellion of the Three Feudatories. In 1680 the Chengs once again withdrew from Amoy and relocated soldiers on military colonies in Taiwan.[37] In 1684, after ten years of war and the final surrender of the Chengs, there were 40,000 soldiers left of the Cheng forces in Taiwan to be demobilized and returned to China.[38] Large numbers of colonists had been sent to fight or lost to disease; only some of them were replaced by new recruits drawn from Taiwan or the mainland.

In addition to the movement of armies, the influx of war refugees was the other important source of migration during the Cheng era. Ch'en Shao-hsing estimates that 30,000 refugees fled Fukien for Taiwan in this period.[39] In 1656 the Ch'ing government imposed severe restrictions on the coastal trade in an attempt to deprive Cheng Ch'eng-kung's armies of provisions. The failure of these restrictions and the expansion of Cheng's realm to include Taiwan in 1661 led the Manchu court to adopt a more radical measure. The entire coastal population was evacuated behind fortified walls several miles from the coast.[40] This harsh policy caused misery for tens of thousands. The Chengs openly recruited these alienated subjects, and a large number fled to Taiwan. After several years of comparative peace, the Ch'ing relaxed the coastal prohibition in 1669.[41] In 1674, with the outbreak of the rebellion of the Three Feudatories, large numbers (no longer under Ch'ing authority) moved back to the coastal regions. But after the collapse of the revolt, the Manchus enforced removal of the coastal population once again from 1677 to 1679, probably driving additional refugees to Taiwan. The coastal prohibitions were not lifted until after the surrender of the Chengs in 1683.[42]

Natural increase contributed little to Taiwan's Chinese population because of the greatly unbalanced sex ratio. In the Dutch era at least two-thirds of the immigrants had been adult males.[43] The Cheng armies brought with them few women and children. In 1668 Shih Lang estimated that 50–60 percent of the Cheng forces were without wives (and lonely); in 1682 he estimated that only one in three was married. The shortage of wives meant that kidnapped women brought a good price in Taiwan. Because of this trade, the number of households on Taiwan "increased daily."[44] Women were not the only ones to be brought to Taiwan against their will. So anxious were the Chengs to increase their agricultural labor force that criminals and prisoners were transported from the mainland to open land in Taiwan. Keelung was one such place of exile and Heng-ch'un (Lang-ch'iao) another.[45]

A comprehensive system of land taxation was the biggest and most immediate innovation in the system of taxation the Chengs inherited from the Dutch. The Dutch had extracted revenues from agriculture by a 10 percent tax on the rice harvest, a monopsony on sugar purchases, and heavy poll taxes. The Chengs, following traditional Chinese fiscal practice, taxed agriculture primarily by assessments on cultivated acreage. Of course, the early Cheng concern to register land for taxation also reflects the regime's pressing need to collect taxes in kind to feed its large and hungry armies. The Chengs continued to collect other Dutch taxes—the village monopoly tax and various commercial taxes—and these yielded important revenues. They eliminated the auctioning of the tax farms, however, which had created large fluctuations in Dutch revenues, and substituted fixed tax quotas. In sum the Chengs replaced the commercially oriented (and market-sensitive) Dutch revenue system with a bureaucratic administration of fixed tax quotas.

Under the Chengs, landownership was divided into three main categories: state, private, and military colonies. (Aborigine claims to cultivated land, though specifically respected by the 1661 proclamation noted above, fall outside this threefold classification.) Ch'ing gazetteers identify state land (*kuan t'ien*) as all land reclaimed under the Dutch, which the Chinese called "king's land" (*wang t'ien*). The Chengs converted the Dutch "king's land" to state ownership and are said to have maintained the Dutch level of taxation, a rather stiff 18 *shih* per *chia* of first-grade paddy.[46] These tax rates were comparable to rental rates. Heavy taxes were necessary to fund the large military expenses incurred by a regime on a constant war footing. I note in Chapter 3 why I think characterizing all land farmed under the Dutch as "king's land" is an oversimplification, but the sources do not provide the detailed information necessary to trace the disposition of each kind of land. A high proportion of the state-

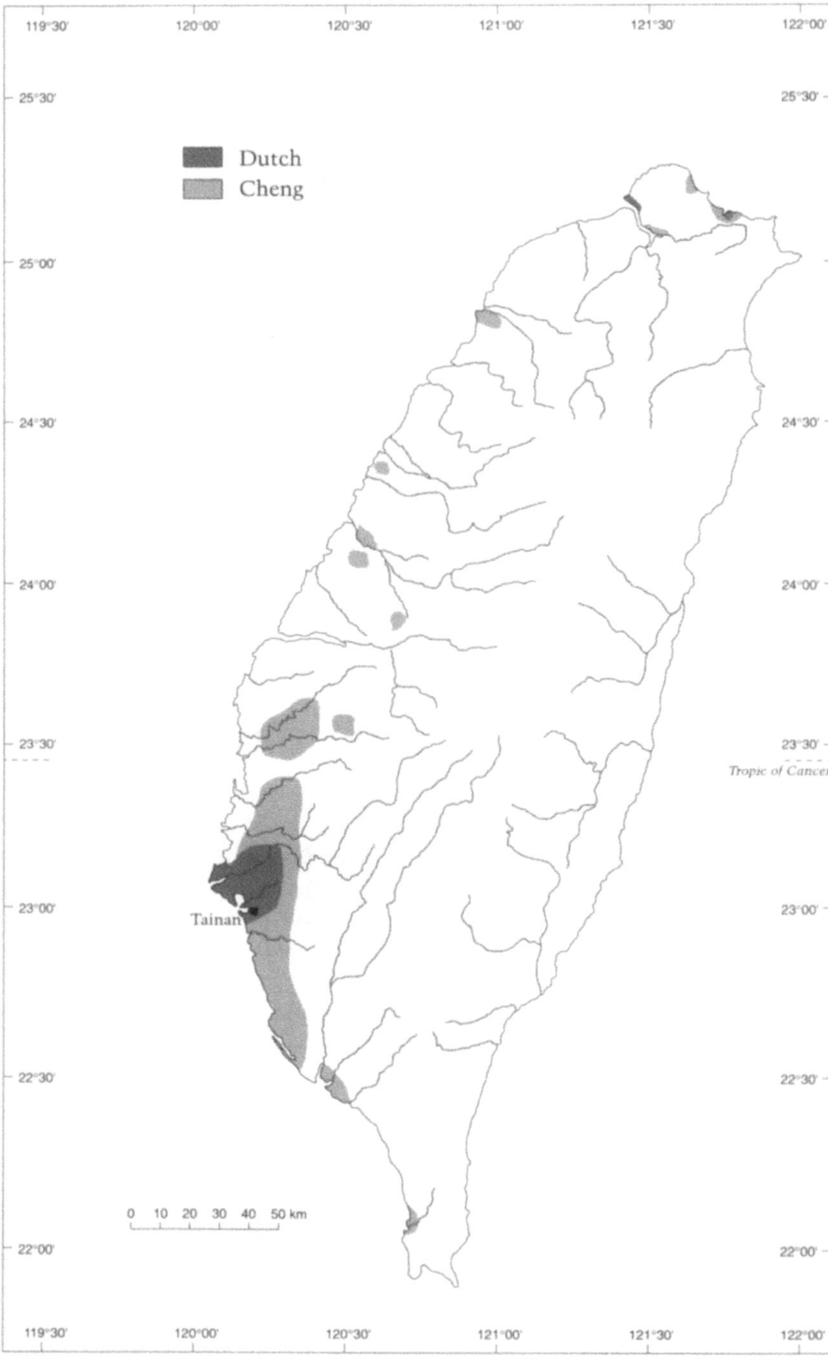

Map 4.1 Military colonization under the Chengs
Based on Ts'ao 1954*a*: 81; and Ch'en Han-kuang 1961*a*: 53.

owned land was irrigated paddy. The Cheng state also encouraged its citizens of means, usually important officials, to recruit refugees and settlers and invest in opening up hitherto uncultivated land (designated *ssu t'ien* or *wen wu kuan t'ien*). This land (most of which was not irrigated) was taxed at much lower rates beginning at 3.6 *shih* per *chia* of first-grade paddy.[47] The third category of land and probably the greatest in area, given the large number of soldiers, was the land opened by military colonies (*t'un* or *ying p'an*). Although said to have been taxed (Cheng Ch'eng-kung charged 30 percent of the harvest for the first three years; Cheng Ching charged taxes only after the first six years), no tax rates for these lands once they were reclaimed are given in the sources.[48]

The area under state ownership late in the Cheng era was 9,783 *chia* and yielded 84,920 *shih* of tax grain. The area reclaimed privately totaled 20,272 *chia* and yielded 41,403 *shih* of tax grain. The total registered area, 30,055 *chia*, was two and a half times the greatest cultivated area reported in the Dutch period (12,252 *morgen* in 1660) and reflects the substantial growth in farm population under the Chengs.[49] The sources give no area figures for military colony land, perhaps because it was land that was periodically abandoned by remobilized troops or land that was not improved but cultivated only by slash-and-burn techniques, or because taxes were levied as a percent of the harvest rather than at a fixed rate per cultivated area.

The bulk of the military colonies were concentrated in southwestern Taiwan, around the city of Tainan (see Map 4.1). The immediate vicinity of Tainan (Sakam) had already been reclaimed under the Dutch, and hence the colonies were at small distances to the north and south. There were also small isolated colonies located at strategic points up and down Taiwan's western coast.[50]

Cheng officials considered the system of military colonies to be well organized by 1665; in 1671 a particularly good harvest was reported.[51] The report on the military colonies given by the British factor resident in Taiwan in 1670 gives a different perspective: "The King's government here is very severe. He has enlisted 70,000 soldiers; for the (first) three years, he pays them money and rice, and gives them a piece of land to live on and also cattle for the manuring of it, and afterwards takes of them money and rice; he will not suffer them to return to China."[52] The hint of disgruntlement is to be taken seriously. Many Cheng soldiers were undoubtedly experienced farmers, but that did not prepare them for the task of clearing land under frontier conditions. Nor was the prospect of life as a pioneer without a family quite what new recruits had expected in the way of wartime adventure.[53]

With the sudden influx of the hungry Cheng armies, the cultivation of sugar was largely abandoned for that of grains. Even in 1672, after several years of comparative peace, the British factor Simon Delboe could report of sugar that "there is not the 1/5 part made now as in the time of the Dutch."[54] Considerable investment in irrigation was necessary to get good yields in the areas of southwest Taiwan settled by Cheng forces. Some canals were built, but large-scale construction demanded excessive amounts of labor and capital. Hence most land, if irrigated at all, was irrigated by small ponds or, most crudely, by impounding rainwater within paddy bunds. The comparative surplus of land allowed cultivators to shift to new, fertile fields every three years.[55] Dry-land rice and sweet potatoes planted on slash-and-burn fields were undoubtedly important in sustaining frontier farmers until they could build irrigation works and terraced fields.

The Cheng government's local revenues were inadequate to support the heavy burden of defense. Trading profits made an important contribution to the Cheng treasury and were maintained through its navy's domination of the coastal trade and its participation in trade with Japan and Southeast Asia.[56] To cut off these sources of revenue and isolate the Chengs, the Manchus evacuated the population of the southeast coast and prohibited maritime trade. At times the Ch'ing embargo did create shortages in Taiwan, despite much smuggling. At other times these measures against mainland Chinese merchants seemed only to strengthen the Cheng trade monopoly and drive up Cheng maritime profits.[57] Despite the success of the military colonies, Taiwan continued to rely in part on imported rice. To encourage its import, it was made duty-free. Cheng ships were sent as far as Thailand and Luzon for rice to feed the armies.[58]

In 1670 the Chengs concluded an agreement allowing the establishment of a British East India Company factory in Taiwan. In accordance with his military priorities, Cheng Ching required that each British ship entering the harbor also bring a quantity of matchlock guns and ammunition and that the company provide two expert gunners "for the King's service."[59]

Within Taiwan the Chengs assumed the Dutch East India Company's monopoly on the major export items, sugar and hides.[60] The shift away from sugar in favor of grains in agriculture greatly reduced sugar's importance in the export trade. But the export of deerskins to Japan was maintained at Dutch levels: English merchants resident in Taiwan estimated the deerskin exports for 1670 and 1672 at 200,000 and 100,000 skins, respectively. Another source puts the amount at 50,000 hides a year.[61]

Because of the large influx of Chinese and the expansion of farmland under the Chengs, revenues from taxes on Chinese grew overall, compared to the Dutch period. Increases in land-tax revenues more than compensated a drop in head-tax assessments due to lower rates. The Dutch had annually charged 3.49 reals per head after 1651 and farmed the poll tax for 39,600 reals in 1655 (this amount assumes at least 11,314 taxed heads).[62] The Chengs charged an average rate of less than one ounce of silver per head and collected only 19,440 ounces of silver (the registered number of taxed heads in the late Cheng era is given as 22,253; Cheng soldiers apparently were not subject to tax). Since the Cheng ounce was equal to 0.7 standard Ch'ing taels and the real generally exchanged for 0.71 to 0.73 taels,[63] reals and Cheng ounces are approximately equal. The Spanish real (rial of eight, Spanish dollar) circulated widely in international trade in East Asia and was used in Taiwan under both the Dutch and the Chengs. The aborigine contribution to domestic tax revenue remained constant, both in proportion to the amount collected from the Chinese and as an absolute amount. Customs duties (we do not know about trading profits) appear to have declined under the Chengs.[64]

Compared with the Dutch East India Company, the Cheng state shifted nearly half of its revenue base to its newly created land taxes levied in grain, but despite the tremendous growth in Han population, overall revenues (not reflecting the military colony sector) grew only marginally. These statements are based on the following assumptions. In 1655, a year for which we have relatively complete information, the Dutch colony of Taiwan had local tax revenues, including customs duties, of 116,513 reals, of which 39,600 reals (34 percent) came from the Han head tax, 20,880 reals (18 percent) from the aborigine trade monopolies, and 12,995 reals (11 percent) from the rice tithe. Most of the balance (37 percent) derived from customs duties. Dutch revenues from agriculture are understated because profits from locally grown sugar were entirely in the trading column rather than under local tax revenues. Trading revenues attributable to Taiwan in 1655 totaled 110,403 reals, nearly as much as local tax revenues.[65] Late Cheng tax revenues (see Table 4.1) came to 65,586 ounces of silver, plus 138,192 *shih* of unhusked grain.[66] If we convert grain to cash (in lieu of a Cheng-era price, I use a low, early Ch'ing price of 0.3 tael per *shih* or 0.4286 Cheng ounces per *shih*), the revenue in grain comes to 59,225 ounces. Added to cash revenues, this yields a total tax revenue worth 124,811 ounces (only 7 percent higher than the Dutch figure). Of this total, 19,440 ounces (16 percent) came from Han head taxes, 21,314 ounces (17 percent) from aborigine taxes in cash and grain, and 54,139 ounces (43 percent) from taxes on arable land paid by Han Chinese. Cheng customs duties of 13,000 ounces (10 percent) are lower than Dutch levels. Cheng trading revenues are estimated to have been substantial, but no figures are available. It is striking that the Cheng fiscal system apparently succeeded in collecting only a marginally greater amount in total revenues in comparison to the Dutch system. This can be attributed to the high rates of extraction tax farming gained for the profit-oriented Dutch and to the agrarian-bureaucratic orientation of the Cheng fiscal system.

TABLE 4.1
Statutory Revenues Under the Chengs, ca. 1680

Revenues in cash (ounces of current silver)		Revenues in kind (*shih* of unhusked grain)	
Han head tax	19,440	Land tax	126,324
Aborigine head tax	16,228	Feng-shan eight	11,868
Mills and carts	2,624	Total revenues in kind	138,192
Shophouses	3,888	Land registered for taxation (in *chia*)	
Misc. land revenues	703	State-owned land	9,783
Fishing	4,249	Privately owned land	20,272
Shipping	1,974	Total registered land	30,055
Salt	3,480		
Import duties	13,000	Population registered for taxation	22,253
Total Revenues in Cash	65,586		

SOURCE: Cheng Hsi-fu 1974*a*: 98–99. For the various categories of revenue, see Table 8.1, which converts Cheng revenues in cash (stated here in ounces of "current silver," or *shih yin*) to taels.

As noted above, the Chengs continued the Dutch system of monopoly merchants in the native villages; but rather than using a competitive bidding system, they assigned fixed cash quotas. The high level of hide exports indicates the continued efficiency of this means of milking the aborigine economies. The total tribal tax of 16,228.08 ounces of silver equaled 67,617 deerskins commuted at 0.24 ounces per skin.[67] Eight plains aborigine villages in the Feng-shan area (the "Feng-shan eight"), apparently because they were more advanced in plow agriculture and less active in deer hunting and trade, paid head taxes in grain rather than cash.[68]

In addition to taxes, the Chengs required the aborigine tribes to render corvée labor service. Plains aborigines were also enlisted in the Cheng military, probably as local auxiliaries. One source refers to aborigines sent to Amoy, in 1674, "to be of service" to the army, which might refer to roles as either porters or soldiers. In 1683, as the Cheng regime entered its last days, both Chinese and "natives" were ordered to defend all strategic points.[69]

The high level of deerskin exports is indicative of a generally peaceful and businesslike relation between the Chengs and the aborigine tribes. Yet, there were also a number of armed clashes between them. The Ta-tu revolts of 1661 and 1665 have already been mentioned. The Cheng general Liu Kuo-hsüan, who was stationed in Pan-hsien (Chang-hua), apparently led several pacification campaigns in central Taiwan. (These must have been before the outbreak of the rebellion of the Three Feudatories in 1674, which took Liu to the mainland.) The aborigines of Sha-lu, near Ta-tu and of the same Papora ethnic grouping, revolted in 1670 (unfortunately no reasons are offered in the sources). The suppression of the revolt severely depopulated the village. Liu is also mentioned as fighting the unpacified raw aborigines of Tou-wei-lung-an (no modern identification has been made for this group) and the An-li tribe (Pazeh group).[70]

The Cheng regime established schools (of an unknown number) in some aborigine villages, but this educational effort is unlikely to have matched that of the Dutch missionaries in intensity. No religious motives required the Chengs to allocate substantial revenues to convert the aborigines. Teaching the Chinese classics to natives who had learned to speak Dutch and to write their own languages in roman script was nevertheless an important step in their sinicization and continued submission to Cheng rule. To encourage Chinese learning, the Cheng government exempted native students from corvée labor. The scholar Shen Kuang-wen, a refugee Ming official, took up residence in the aborigine village of Mu-chia-liu-wan and reportedly taught aborigine students the art of Chinese medicine.[71]

The Last Days of the Chengs

In 1674 Cheng Ching mobilized his soldier-farmers and joined the Three Feudatories (which controlled most of south China) in their revolt against the Ch'ing, ending nearly a decade of relative peace. Amoy once again became his base of operation. Although the rulers of Fukien and Kwangtung had surrendered to the Ch'ing by 1677, Cheng Ching held onto Amoy until April 1680.[72] The loss of Amoy put the Cheng regime under increasing military pressure. Forced to withdraw to Taiwan, Cheng Ching was hard-pressed both for revenue and for provisions for his soldiers, some of whom revolted for want of pay. Military conscription and oppressive taxation alienated the populace.[73]

The strain of the last years of the Cheng regime showed up in a number of conflicts with aborigines. In 1680 reports of a planned Ch'ing naval attack on Keelung led to the destruction of the fort there to deprive the Ch'ing of its use. In 1681, the Chengs decided it would be better to hold the area against attack and ordered the fort rebuilt. Soldiers and corvée aborigine laborers were enlisted for the job. Military colonization had not proceeded far in remote areas such as Tan-shui and Keelung, and it was necessary to ship provisions to the garrisons there. In the third month of 1682, high winds prevented a grain ship from the south from entering the northern ports. It was decided to send the provisions overland by corvée aborigine porters. In the fifth month, tired of suffering under whip-wielding overseers, the aborigine porters in the Hsin-chu area revolted, killed their interpreters, stole the grain, and fled into the mountains. The Chengs sent reinforcements to quell the revolt; when the natives ran out of food in the mountains, they came to terms and were allowed to return to their villages.[74]

The Chengs' desperate need for revenue led them to send expeditions into aborigine territories in search of gold. In 1683, one such expedition ended in the massacre of an aborigine village on the east coast.[75] One aborigine elder in Tan-shui is quoted as prophesying, on the appearance of such an expedition: "When the Japanese came searching for gold, the Dutch seized Taiwan; when the Dutch came searching for gold, the Chengs seized Taiwan; now again they come searching, the dynasty will soon change."[76] A severe grain shortage in 1683 is also said to have caused rumblings of rebellion among several aborigine tribes.[77]

Cheng Ching died in March 1681, less than a year after his second withdrawal to Taiwan. He was succeeded by his young son, Cheng K'o-shuang.[78] Continued food shortages in Taiwan and the proclamation of an amnesty by the Ch'ing governor-general of Fukien, Yao Ch'i-sheng, in 1682 led to numerous defections of Cheng forces eager to return home. In late 1682 a fire destroyed 1,600 homes and shops in Tainan, aggravating the rice shortage.[79] In July 1683 a major naval battle in the Pescadores broke the back of the Cheng resistance. Shih Lang, the victorious Ch'ing admiral, promised there would be no retribution if the Chengs surrendered peacefully. Their surrender was accepted in September, and Shih Lang landed in triumph in Taiwan in October 1683. The surrendering Cheng forces were ordered to shave their heads and adopt the Manchu queue.[80] Representatives of the aborigine tribes attended a ceremony at which they received from their new Ch'ing overlords silver medals of office, robes, hats, and boots, and gifts of tobacco and cloth, just as they had before from the Dutch and the Chengs.[81]

CHAPTER FIVE

Taxation and Administration of the Aborigines in the Early Ch'ing

Establishing Ch'ing Rule

Shih Lang, the victorious Ch'ing admiral, moved quickly to consolidate his control over Taiwan. The peaceful surrender of the Cheng regime meant there was no further organized resistance to Ch'ing rule. The new government did, nevertheless, have to expend considerable effort rounding up unruly remnant soldiers and Cheng deserters.[1] The most serious disturbance came in late 1684 when 3,000–5,000 "bandits" (who I suspect were mostly demobilized Cheng soldiers) gathered at Hsiao-kang-shan, south of Tainan. This was swiftly put down by Commander Wu, who called up aborigine braves from the southwest core villages of Hsin-kang, Mu-chia-liu-wan, Ma-tou, Hsiao-lung, and Ta-wu-lung to join 3,000 government soldiers in the pacification campaign.[2]

Shih Lang's immediate task was to preserve civil order. He disciplined his troops in order to minimize friction between the occupying forces (who considered themselves conquerors) and the local populace (whose recent status as rebels added to their uncertainty about the future). Shih Lang affirmed in his proclamation "On Settling the Livelihood of the People of Taiwan," that all Taiwan's people would be considered loyal subjects who should be protected and pacified. Soldiers were forbidden to occupy homesteads, and petty officers were forbidden to farm the monopolies of villages and tribes. Commerce and agriculture were to continue "at the people's convenience" with no government interference in the local markets. Soldiers were not to interfere with the sugarcane harvest. Burglars were to be apprehended. To avoid overburdening local food supplies, rations for government troops were to be imported, and vegetables were to be bought in the local market at market prices. Shih forbade commandeering supplies at cheaper prices. In addition, he declared a tax holiday to celebrate Taiwan's peaceful return to the empire.[3]

All these measures were intended to ensure a smooth transition to the new order.

Officials in Peking had originally intended, once the rebel Cheng regime was defeated, to abandon Taiwan and evacuate its Chinese population to the mainland. Accordingly, Cheng military forces were either sent back to their home communities or incorporated into Manchu armies. In all, 40,000 soldiers were repatriated.[4] Ho Yu, for instance, the former Cheng commander in Tan-shui, was sent to the Amur river area in Manchuria.[5] Many soldiers and refugees, who had been driven to Taiwan by the civil wars and had had a difficult life under the hard-pressed Cheng regime, eagerly returned to their mainland homes.

The civilian population was also under pressure to leave. The Ch'ing coastal regulations of 1683 decreed that sojourners in Taiwan with neither wife nor livelihood (property or a trade) must return home. Those with wives and property and desiring to remain were required to register with the local officials. However, any otherwise qualified settler who committed a serious crime was to be sent to his mainland home for punishment. By the ninth month of 1684, Shih Lang estimated that nearly half the Chinese population had left the island.[6] Tax quotas for cash and grain were reduced by 49 and 27 percent, respectively (see Chapter 8). Taiwan's Chinese population must have fallen below 80,000 at this time, since its maximum under the Chengs is estimated at only 120,000.[7]

Shih Lang vigorously opposed abandoning Taiwan, a prize he had fought many years to gain. In late 1683 several high officials met at Foochow to debate Ch'ing policy on Taiwan. Shih Lang argued that Taiwan was too important strategically and economically not to be incorporated into the empire and that governing the new territory need not burden the national treasury. Shih pointed out the dangers to coastal security were Taiwan to fall into the hands of a hostile power and argued that a naval station in the Pescadores would be inadequate and could not in any case be held securely without control of Taiwan. Moreover, if Taiwan were under Ch'ing control, the garrisons along the southeast coast (and the attendant expenditures) could be reduced; indeed some of these troops could be used to garrison Taiwan, thereby reducing the expense of administering the new territory. Shih named sulfur (a strategic item) and deer hides as some of the valuable products that made Taiwan worth keeping or at least worth keeping out of other's hands. He also pointed out that the complete evacuation of Taiwan's Chinese population would take years and would create a population of vagrants. Cheng remnants hiding among aborigines in the mountains could never be entirely cleared out—to abandon Taiwan to them would turn it into a pirates' lair.[8]

Shih Lang's arguments in favor of incorporating the island into the empire prevailed, and in the fourth month of 1684 Taiwan was made a prefecture of Fukien province and magistrates and land and marine forces were assigned to Taiwan and the Pescadores. At the same time the anti-Cheng prohibition on maritime trade was lifted, giving Fukien's fishermen and merchants access to the seas, including Taiwan, and allowing farmers and other residents to return to coastal villages. In adopting these policies, the government hoped to foster an economic recovery along the southeast coast that would stabilize social order and generate taxes and customs revenues (from foreign trade) that would ease the court's own fiscal problems. Maritime commerce therefore gravitated back to Amoy as Taiwan lost the entrepôt functions it had under the Dutch and Chengs when maritime trade (e.g., with Japan) had been outlawed by mainland governments.[9]

In Taiwan, however, the court imposed a partial quarantine to prevent the island's again becoming a staging ground for rebellion. Rather than actively foster colonization by Chinese farmers, the government sought to limit the spread of settlement in Taiwan. The court feared Han immigration to Taiwan would create a potentially rebellious population in areas beyond its effective control and upset the ethnic status quo (see Chapter 6). Quarantine policies had the effect of sheltering the indigenous tribes, but the government's priority was to preserve control at the lowest cost, not to defend aborigine societies against the frontiersmen. Disturbances and aborigine revolts in Taiwan were nearly always attributable to the misdeeds of Chinese. Perpetuation of the status quo was seen as the key to maintaining order and effective state control over this strategically important periphery.

The government thought it could achieve control indirectly by regulating immigration, preventing the migration of families (to keep the migrants, mostly males, dependent on access to the mainland), and restricting exports of rice (to guarantee that food shortages would not cause local disturbances). Direct control over the island was to be asserted by a military garrison and a civil administration concentrated in the southwest core around the prefectural capital of Tainan (neither the military nor the civil bureaucracy reached the northern one-third of the western plain, the area above the Ta-chia river). This was all the government presence that the tax revenues of the underpopulated island-prefecture and financially strapped Fukien province could support.

This chapter deals with early Ch'ing taxation and administration of the plains aborigines. Monopoly merchant control of the deer trade continued to structure the interaction of government, Chinese, and aborigines in this period, as it had in the Dutch and Cheng periods. Detailed discussion of Ch'ing policies toward Han agricultural settlers in Taiwan is deferred to Part II.

A sketch of the early Ch'ing civil and military administration of Taiwan will set the stage for discussion of plains aborigine affairs. The highest-ranking civil official in Taiwan was the Taiwan-Amoy military administrative intendant, although between 1722 and 1752 he was outranked by censors sent on annual tours of inspection. The intendant had the power to move troops and oversaw communications between the ports of Tainan and Amoy. Subordinate to him were coastal defense subprefects stationed in each port.

For purposes of territorial administration, Taiwan was organized as a prefecture of Fukien province and headed by a prefect. The Taiwan prefect was subordinate to the intendant, the governor of Fukien, and the governor-general of Chekiang and Fukien. Subordinate to the prefect were three county magistrates. Chu-lo county, in the north, corresponded to the Chengs' T'ien-hsing *chou.* The Chengs' Wan-nien *chou* was divided into T'ai-wan county, covering the Tainan core, and Fengshan county, covering the plains to the south. The Cheng offices of *an fu ssu,* charged with frontier pacification and oversight of the aborigine villages, one in the north and one in the south, were discontinued.[10]

The Ch'ing garrison forces totaled 10,000 land and marine troops, headed by a brigade general. These soldiers were rotated from armies in Fukien every three years. Both the civil and military administrations were concentrated in the Tainan core. A few scattered military outposts reached as far north as Pan-hsien (Chang-hua) but none extended beyond the Ta-chia river (see Chapter 7).

Ch'ing Taxation of the Aborigines

The repatriation of much of the Chinese population at the beginning of Ch'ing rule and the restrictions on new immigration meant that aborigine society and trade were left relatively undisturbed by the accession of the new regime. Indeed, the pressure of expanding Chinese population on aborigine hunting territories diminished. As we saw in the previous chapters, the Dutch and the Chengs had suppressed intervillage warfare and head-hunting (except at the state's behest) among the plains aborigines and imposed overarching systems of administration and taxation. The Ch'ing had no desire to disturb the status quo by creating a new administrative and tax apparatus; it simply assumed the Cheng system of administering the plains aborigine villages and continued the Cheng practice of imposing both a head tax and corvée on the aborigine tribes. The Ch'ing granted across-the-board reductions in the Cheng village tax quotas, but made no effort to adjust the tax burden according to the population or income of the villages. Taiwan's plains aborigines thus remained directly responsible to a Chinese state for the payment of taxes; no system of indirect rule through state-appointed tribal chieftains (on the order of the *t'u ssu* common in southwest China) was ever erected in Taiwan.[11]

The Chinese designated tribes that had submitted to Chinese authority and paid taxes "cooked" or "civilized" aborigines (*shu fan*), in contrast to "raw" aborigines (*sheng fan*).[12] The head tax paid by civilized aborigines was called *fan hsiang* or *she hsiang*, the aborigine or tribal revenue. The Chu-lo county gazetteer of 1717 lists the aborigine head tax as one of the county's five main categories of revenue and as one of its two highest revenue producers.[13] The origin of this tax under the Dutch and Chengs and its nature as a tax on aborigines rather than Han farmers made it necessary to sinicize and justify the institution. Accordingly, the Chu-lo county gazetteer cites a T'ang dynasty precedent: a tax collected from the non-Han peoples of Ling-nan according to the wealth of the native households, wealthier households paying more. The gazetteer then reports that the Dutch had levied such a tax in deer hides. The Chengs had also collected the aborigine tax, but in cash through a tax farmer, and the Ch'ing continued this practice.[14] (For the eight villages of Feng-shan county that paid taxes in grain, see below.)

Although the Ch'ing aborigine revenue was in theory a head tax, no rate schedule was ever published. The gazetteers give only an aggregate number of households and taxable heads and a list giving an amount of tax for each village. The tax was in reality a fixed quota assigned to each village as a whole, and the burden per taxable head varied tremendously among the villages, from one to twenty taels of silver.[15] Whether the quotas had been assessed in proportion to population (or productivity) under the Chengs remains unclear. In any case, the Ch'ing made no effort to readjust the Cheng quotas, other than reducing them across the board. This is not surprising, since taxes stated to be head taxes or land taxes, but in fact fixed quotas, were the norm in late imperial Chinese tax administration.[16]

The state's conception of the aborigine tax and some of the legal consequences for the aborigines can be seen by contrasting the aborigine tax obligation to that of the Chinese. Chinese settlers in Taiwan paid both a head tax and a land tax assessed according to ownership of cultivated acreage. For the Han, payment of the land tax brought recognition of ownership. The discussion of categories of landownership in the Chu-lo gazetteer includes aborigine land, although the gazetteer points out that the aborigines did not pay a land tax on the land they cultivated; instead they paid only a head tax, the tribal revenue tax. Yet, when a holiday on *land* taxes was declared in 1711, the Taiwan prefect argued that the tax holiday should extend by analogy to the aborigine head tax.[17] We shall see later that paying the aborigine tax, though it was not a land tax per se, entitled the aborigines to an ownership right over the lands from which they drew their livelihoods (Chapter 9).

Since the Cheng era, the plains villages had been grouped into 38 taxpaying units, 34 in Chu-lo county to the north, and four in Feng-shan

TABLE 5.1

The Tax Burden of the 38 Aborigine Tax Units Under the Chengs and the Ch'ing[a]

		Cheng quotas				Ch'ing quotas		
						1683–1737	post-1737	
Area	No. of tax units	Households	Taxable heads	Deerskins	Cash in ounces of silver	Cash in taels of silver	Cash in taels of silver	Taxable heads
Chu-lo	34	2,224	4,516	66,093	15,862.32	7,709.5368	880.4	4,402
Feng-shan	4	—	—	1,524	365.76	179.2224	—	—
Total	38			67,617	16,228.08	7,888.7592		

SOURCES: Based on *CLHC*: 96; *TWFC*:Kao: 132, 134; *FCTCTWF*: 166; *TWFC*:Fan: 191–200; and Cheng Hsi-fu 1974*a*: 106. The Ch'ing quotas for 1683–1737 were derived by reducing the Cheng quotas by 30 percent (40 percent in the case of Chu-ch'ien *she*) and converting to taels at the rate of 0.7 taels/ounce of silver (Cheng Hsi-fu 1974*a*: 106).

[a]For the tax quotas of individual villages, see Appendix B.

county to the south, plus the eight villages in Feng-shan that paid taxes in grain.[18] We know little about the four Feng-shan tribes, three of whom broke away from Ch'ing rule (see below).[19] The discussion here will first focus on the tax burdens of the 34 Chu-lo tax units and then move on to the Feng-shan eight.

In Chu-lo a total of 76 aborigine villages were organized into 34 taxpaying units. According to Chi Ch'i-kuang, the first Ch'ing magistrate of Chu-lo county, the Chengs had extracted more from the tribes than had the Dutch. But with the decline in Han population and commerce at the beginning of Ch'ing rule, tax farms became unprofitable, and no village merchants were willing to assume them. Hence the Ch'ing granted a 30 percent (in one case 40 percent) reduction in the Cheng tribal tax quotas (see Table 5.1).[20] Tax reductions for aborigines and Han, despite the concern to garner revenue for the new territory, were aimed at smoothing the Ch'ing accession of power over Taiwan. Once reduced, the aborigine tax quotas remained fixed until 1737.

We can reconstruct one aspect of how the Chengs set their aborigine tax quotas, although this is not spelled out in the sources. The Chu-lo gazetteer reports that six tribes submitting in 1715 had their tax quotas figured in terms of deerskins commuted to silver at the rate of 0.24 *liang* or tael per skin. The Chengs must have used this rate as well, for all the Cheng quotas for the 38 units are round-number multiples of 0.24 (for tax quotas by village, see Appendix B).[21] Thus the 16,228.08 ounces of silver collected by the Chengs from the 38 tribal units equals 67,617 deerskins (see Table 5.1). (This number also fits estimates of yearly deerskin exports during the Cheng period.) The tax quotas in deerskins do not appear to be assigned on the basis of numbers of taxable heads. The 34 Chu-lo aborigine tax units, reported to consist of 4,516 taxed heads in 2,224 households under the Chengs, were paying 29.7+ skins (7.1+ ounces of silver) per household or 14.6+ skins (3.5+ ounces) per taxable head.[22] It is possible that aborigine adults were classified into categories paying different rates, as they were among the eight southern settlements. But it appears most likely that the Chengs assigned quotas to the villages with only partial attention to census figures. Gazetteer commentators noted a great disparity in burden per head among the tribes in the early Ch'ing.[23] The Cheng quotas were undoubtedly set with regard to degree of political control, as well as aborigine population and productivity. Weak extractive capability may explain the especially small quotas of some large composite units in the distant Tan-shui–Hsin-chu areas in the north.

The Cheng figures for Chu-lo's aborigine population, 4,516 taxable heads and 2,224 households, seem extremely low when compared with the Dutch census for the same region, which showed 26,047 persons and 5,785 households in 1650.[24] Since the sources do not account for the

TABLE 5.2

The Tax Burden of the Feng-shan Eight Under the Chengs and the Ch'ing

		Cheng		1683–1725		1726–1737		post-1737	
	Number	Rate in *shih*[a]	Tax	Rate in *shih*[a]	Tax	Rate in *shih*[a]	Tax	Rate in taels	Tax
Scribes	97	1.0	97.0	1.0	97.0	1.0	97.0	0.2	19.4
Adult males	1,395	1.7	2,371.5	1.7	2,371.5	1.7	2,371.5	0.2	279.0
Youths	256	1.3	332.8	1.3	332.8	1.3	332.8	0.2	51.2
Women	1,844	1.3	2,397.2	1.0	1,844.0	—	—	—	—
Old & infirm	753	?	753.3	—	—	—	—	—	—
Total number	4,345								
Total in *shih* of rice			5,933.8[b]		4,645.3		2,801.3		485.6[c]
Total in taels			4,272.3[c]		3,344.6[c]		2,016.9[c]		349.6

SOURCES: Based on *TWFC*:Yü: 247; *FCTCTWF*: 165; Cheng Hsi-fu 1974*a*: 102.

[a]The tax was levied in *shih* of husked rice until 1737 and paid in kind until 1726.

[b]This is the quota; the arithmetic total is 5,951.8.

[c]Calculated equivalent: *shih* of husked rice are commuted to cash at the low price of 0.72 taels per *shih* (*CLHC*: 87; *TWFC*:Yü: 241; Cheng Hsi-fu 1974*a*: 102).

disparity, we do not know whether population decline, the arbitrary assignment of tax quotas, or some other factor explains the low taxable population figures.

With fluctuations in aborigine population and deer herds, the disparity in tax burden among the villages could easily have grown during the Ch'ing. Large inequalities in the tax burdens of the 34 tribes relative to those of other groups remained after the Ch'ing tax reductions. Under the Ch'ing the average burden per taxable head in the 34 tribes, 1.7+ taels, was greater than the heaviest tax rate, 1.2+ taels per adult male head (converting 1.7 *shih* of rice at 0.72 taels per *shih*), levied on the aborigines of the eight southern tribes.[25] Han settlers at this time paid only 0.476 taels per head, but they also paid land taxes. The tax burden of the 34 tribes appears especially heavy compared with the quota set for six newly submitting tribes in 1693. They were required to pay a tax of 98.5 taels for a total population of 487.[26] This works out to less than one deerskin (0.21 taels) per head. Of course, rates were set deliberately low for independent tribes as an inducement to peaceful submission.

We have so far discussed only the official tax quotas and not the substantial amount of squeeze aborigines had to pay tax collectors. In 1722 Chou Chung-hsüan (then magistrate of T'ai-wan county) estimated that in addition to the 7,000-tael tax quota (see Table 5.1), gifts to officials came to 8,000 taels, official requisitions of hemp came to 4,000 taels, compulsory sales of salt (by one of the eight southern tribes) came to 2,000 taels, and that the squeeze of middlemen interpreters more than doubled the burden to the tribes. Chou requested a reform of the administration of the aborigine tax to relieve this burden.[27]

Chou was only one of many officials and scholars who complained about the abuses caused by the monopoly merchant system and the aborigine corvée (see below). After a number of aborigine revolts attributable to these abuses, the tribal tax was reformed in 1737. Before turning to these events, we complete our discussion of aborigine tax burdens by describing the separate system of quotas assigned the eight large aborigine villages of Feng-shan.

Ch'ing Taxation of the Feng-shan Eight

Eight aborigine villages in Feng-shan county depended more on agriculture than on deer hunting for their livelihood. The Chengs had accordingly taxed them in grain in proportion to population (unlike the Han, who paid grain taxes according to cultivated acreage). The Chengs divided the aborigine population into four categories and assessed each a different head-tax rate (see Table 5.2). Adult males were charged the most, 1.7 *shih* of husked rice; youths and women were charged 1.3 *shih*. Scribes were charged only 1.0 *shih* per head. The scribes, *chiao ts'e*, were those aborigines who had learned from the Dutch to write their own languages in roman letters. Their low head-tax rate may reflect their usefulness in local political administration. The Cheng tax on women, though unusual in Chinese fiscal practice, reflects the Chengs' need for revenue and the important contribution of aborigine women to agriculture.[28]

The Ch'ing administration immediately reduced the women's rate from 1.3 to 1.0 *shih* per head. The Ch'ing government also forgave 753.3 *shih* of husked rice levied on 753 people who were either old or infirm.[29] The Feng-shan county gazetteer of 1719 contains an essay decrying the heavy burden of taxation on the eight tribes and advocating a tax reduction and the elimination of the tax on women. In 1725 the court ended collection of the women's quota.[30]

If the eight southern tribes are the eight large southern villages listed in the Dutch records, the 1650 Dutch population figures are two to three times the number of taxed heads listed in the Cheng quotas (see Appendix B). But we can only guess whether the Cheng figures are quotas (in some way proportional to actual population) or reflect a genuine reduction in the aborigine population (even when the large number of children outside the Cheng tax categories is allowed for).[31]

Sometime between 1707 and 1712, five of the eight tribes complained to Prefect Chou Yüan-wen that the Han interpreters in charge of tax collection in each tribe were extorting fees several times the original tax obligation. When an investigation verified the charges, the interpreters were ordered to make restitution. The tax obligations of each tribe were then publicly posted in each village. The temporariness of this solution is shown by the 1722 reports of corruption in the operation of the eight tribal granaries. These granaries, which may have existed since Cheng times, were used to store aborigine tax grain and were built and repaired by aborigine corvée labor. But their Han managers embezzled much of the grain. The women's tax quota forgiven in 1725 was ordered stored in these granaries, to be loaned out in the event of spring shortages.[32] When another investigation in 1726 uncovered continuing corruption in the management of the granaries, the aborigine grain tax was ordered commuted to silver to eliminate the need for granaries.[33] We know because of the Wu Fu-sheng rebellion that the granaries were still in existence, however, in 1732. The importance placed on the security of these granaries in the Han rebellions of 1721 and 1732 indicates that they stored significant amounts of grain.[34]

Abuse and Reform in Aborigine Tax Collection

The official tax quotas described above were only a portion of the aborigines' real tax burden. Corruption in the organization of tax collection added greatly to the economic burden and to social conflict. In Chu-lo county, the Ch'ing state collected its taxes through the Chinese tax farmer or monopoly merchant. The Ch'ing gazetteers trace the origin of the village trade monopolies to the Dutch[35] and document their continued use by the Chengs, who replaced the Dutch auction system with fixed head tax quotas. The Chinese term for this institution was *p'u she*, which means to farm a tribe's aboriginal revenue tax.[36] Under the Manchus, the *p'u she* system retained its dual character. The Chinese middleman as tax farmer paid (in return for the privilege of collecting it) the tribal tax on behalf of an aborigine settlement (*tai shu she hsiang*). And as merchant he acquired a trade monopoly on both buying aborigine produce from that settlement and selling trade goods to it. The holder of these responsibilities and privileges under the *p'u she* system was called a *she shang*, tribal merchant, or *t'ou chia*, master or boss. Later he was designated *t'ung shih*, interpreter, a rank initially subordinate to the tax farmer.[37]

The following quotation from the Chu-lo gazetteer of 1717 makes clear how closely connected the *p'u she* institution was with the continuing trade in deer hides:

> The *p'u she* also originated with the Hollanders. The one who is appointed by the official to contract for payment of revenue is called "village tax farmer" [*she shang*] or "head householder" [*t'ou chia*]. Beginning in the eighth month he collects bands of barbarians whom he supervises in hunting deer, this being called *ch'u ts'ao*. They count up the number of deer legs, and trade them for cloth; the amount of cloth given for the front and rear legs differs. They cut the deer up, and the dried meat, the tendons, the hide and all are turned over to the tax farmer—only the head and the bloody viscera belong to the hunters themselves. By the fourth month of the following year the hunting season comes to a complete halt to enable the deer to bear their young. This off-season is called *san she*.[38]

This description puts the tax farmer in direct control of both the hunting and delivery of the deer products. In some cases tribes exchanged the deer products for silver or salt instead of cloth. Where natives could not rely on deer hunting to pay their taxes, they traded out linseed, hemp, or other substitutes; for example, "laver, *t'ung ts'ao*, and water creepers are gathered and bartered for daily use and are moreover paid as taxes." At Keelung fish and water creepers were collected to pay the tax.[39]

Farming taxes to private merchants was advantageous for the state because it guaranteed payment of the tax quota while eliminating the expense of administering a village tax collection system. The *p'u she* system, however, also concentrated great power in the tax farmer and his subordinates, who mediated between the state and the weakly organized and unsophisticated aborigines. Such power was often abused, as it had been in Dutch and Cheng times. Under the Dutch the aborigines benefited from two sources of competition for power that might check abuse, sources absent under the Chengs and the Ch'ing. These were the competition between the church and the company, and the ethnic competition between the Dutch and Chinese. When abused by one party, the aborigines could find an interested ally in the other. Under the Chinese regimes, the aborigines were at the bottom of a hierarchy of Chinese officials and merchants, both of whom were frequently exploitative; the only route of appeal was to the occasional honest and compassionate official. Yü Yung-ho, who traveled throughout Chu-lo on a trip to obtain sulfur in Tan-shui in 1697 commented:

> The Chengs extracted heavy labor service and taxes from the barbarians, and our dynasty continues this practice. It would seem that it is easy for them to pay grain at the autumn harvest, but difficult to pay taxes. They never understand what money is, so how could they get any to submit as tribute? Hence the system of "contracting out the villages" [*pao she*] is still maintained. In each administrative district a wealthy person is made responsible for the village revenues. These men are called "village tax farmers" [literally village merchants, *she shang*]. The village tax farmer in turn appoints interpreters and foremen who are sent to live in the villages, and who record and check up on every jot and tittle [grown or brought in by hunting] of all the barbarians. All of the flesh of the deer they shoot [the barbarians] make into dried meat, and they also save the hides. Among the Japanese deer hides are in great demand, and there are trading junks which come to buy them; while the dried meat is sold to Chang-chou people. They make a profit from the sale of both of these things after paying their taxes.
>
> But these interpreters and foremen take advantage of the simple-mindedness of the barbarians and never tire of fleecing them, looking on whatever they have as no different from their own property. In connection with the activities of daily life, great and small, all of the barbarians—men, women, and children—have to serve in their homes without a day of respite. Moreover, they take the barbarian women as their wives and concubines. Whatever is demanded of them they must comply; if they make a mistake they must take a flogging. And yet the barbarians do not hate them greatly.[40]

The aborigines' inability to deal with or appeal directly to government officials left them subject to the exactions of predatory middlemen.

Other observers commented that whatever a tribe had that was worth owning soon became the tax farmer's property and that tribes commonly fell into debt to their tax farmers, who charged usurious interest rates.[41] In a few cases the trading profits were small and barely exceeded an aborigine village's tax quota. In such cases no tribal merchant was willing to farm the tribal tax, and government officials had to use Chinese interpreters to collect the quota. This too was often unsatisfactory since the interpreters sought to extort as much profit above the quota as did the tribal merchants.[42]

In 1697 Yü Yung-ho observed how Chinese interpreters and foremen in the aborigine villages abused their position at the expense of both the aborigines and the tax farmer:

> There are also those who secretly obstruct the best efforts of the officials and create disturbances among the barbarians, namely, the village bullies [*she kun*]. This bunch were all criminals on the mainland. Fleeing from death at the hands of the law they hide themselves in distant, out-of-the-way places uninhabited by Chinese, where they scheme to act as foremen and interpreters. With the passage of time they acquire an intimate knowledge of the barbarians and their language. When the father dies the son succeeds him, thus perpetuating the evil endlessly.
>
> The village tax-farmer does nothing but enjoy life in town, demanding revenue and taking in taxes. The affairs of the villages are left to the machinations of the bullies. Therefore the revenues of the village tax farmer are depleted and deficient, while these people simply sit and make a profit. The village tax farmers are changed every year or so, but these fellows [i.e., the bullies] would not leave till they die.
>
> The bullies take advantage of the simplicity of the barbarians, and also want very much for them to be poor. If they are simple then they are completely ignorant, and easy prey; if they are poor then they are easily oppressed, and do not have the strength to resist.
>
> Far from teaching them, the bullies continually get them into trouble. Then, even if there are some who appeal to justice, the judge cannot get at the facts of the case because of the language barrier, and he still has to ask the interpreter to explain. The interpreter turns right into wrong and wrong into right, but it is the barbarian instead who gets a scolding. The interpreter furthermore tells him, "The district magistrate is very angry with you because you have disobeyed the interpreter and foreman." Therefore the barbarian dreads the village bully even more, and serves him like God Himself. They are without redress, and those in charge of them have no way to know about it. In the whole world there are none more deserving of pity than these barbarians.[43]

The interpreters and bullies resident in the villages found the aborigines easy prey. Their abuses could also destroy the leaseholder's ability to profit from his tax farm and trading monopoly. Even after the monopoly merchant system of tax farming was abolished in some villages, the interpreters held on to their position as middlemen in tax collection.

Officials in Taiwan became concerned about corruption in tribal administration because it might cause disturbances and because it interfered with the government's ability to farm the taxes. As early as 1705, Taiwan intendant Wang Min-cheng had attempted to prevent exploitation of aborigines by the leaseholders and to stop the excessive requisition of aborigine oxcarts. In 1710 Ch'en Pin, the Taiwan-Amoy intendant, complained of a chain of extortion: officials demanded bribes from interpreters and interpreters in turn squeezed the aborigines.[44]

Fig. 5.1 Aborigine dress from *Selected Drawings of Ch'ing Tribute Bearers* (*CCKTH*). (*above*) Civilized aborigines of Hsiao-lung *she*, Chu-lo county. (*below*) Raw aborigines of Yu-wu-nai, Tan-shui subprefecture.

Fig. 5.1, cont. (*above*) Civilized aborigines of Chu-ch'ien *she*, Tan-shui subprefecture. (*below*) Civilized aborigines of Ta-tu *she*, Chang-hua county.

To contain abuses by monopoly merchants and interpreters and to eliminate their sometimes costly consequences, some officials advocated abolition of tax farming. The Chu-lo gazetteer reports that the tribal monopoly merchant system was abolished in 1716.[45] Elsewhere the abolition is attributed to Chu-lo magistrate Chou Chung-hsüan. Chou advocated direct payment of the tribal tax to eliminate the monopoly merchants and limit the extortions of interpreters. In 1717 when Intendant Liang Wen-k'o traveled overland as far north as Tan-shui, he attempted to restrict the scope of the interpreters' power by changing the name of their office to "secretary" and holding them responsible for keeping the tribal tax and corvée accounts according to strict regulations.[46] A method of limiting the influence of the interpreters used in Feng-shan was to require them to live in the county seat and allow them to go to the villages only when official business required it.[47] But direct payment was not always feasible, as Chou's essay (discussed below) recognized, for the interpreters were indispensable as tax collectors among remote, less sophisticated tribes.

The Chu-lo gazetteer of 1717 discusses the problems of tax collection among the aborigines and the factors that impeded efforts to correct them:

> The aborigine revenue tax is the responsibility of the interpreter just as among Chinese subjects the land tax is the responsibility of the village chief [*li chia*]. However, Chinese subjects can pay their taxes by the method of "self seal and deposit," but the aborigines are uneducated and can neither write nor figure; so it is not possible to institute the method of "self seal and deposit" among them. Thus, among Chinese subjects the village chief can be eliminated, but among the aborigines the interpreter cannot be eliminated.[48]

In the "self seal and deposit" method, which originated in the single-whip tax reforms begun in the late Ming, "the people themselves wrap up the silver, write on the package their names and addresses and the weight of the silver, and drop it into the chest." Official tax receipts were then issued for the payment.[49] This method of payment enabled individual Chinese taxpayers to pay the state directly (and to be credited for paying) and thereby circumvent easily corruptible village chiefs through whom they had previously to pay their taxes. "Self seal and deposit" was not, however, an entirely appropriate model of reform for an aborigine tax assessed collectively on an entire village. Aborigine lack of sophistication and illiteracy in Chinese, moreover, made it difficult for the government both to dispense with the role of interpreters in collecting aborigine taxes and to prevent interpreters cheating the aborigines.

The same essay reports that in 1715 the Chu-lo magistrate Chou Chung-hsüan (the editor of the Chu-lo gazetteer and probable author of the essay) had investigated conditions among the six tribes in the vicinity of the county seat (the northernmost tribe listed was Chu-lo-shan),[50] "where Han and aborigines lived interspersed." All nominated their own native interpreters. "Every year they pay their interpreter [in produce] only for his toil in keeping accounts and allotting corvée duties. The revenue quota is delivered to the officials by the aborigines themselves, and it does not pass through the interpreters' hands."[51] Three more tribes to the north of Chu-lo-shan (Ta-miao, T'a-li-wu, and Ch'ai-li) were also accustomed to dealing with officials, were nearly as sophisticated as the six tribes to the south, and were nominating their own native interpreters and paying their taxes directly.

> Should not more distant tribes use this method, and although it may not be perfect, can we not see that this is much better than granting trade monopolies to tribal merchants? From Hsi-lo north to Tan-shui, one must go far to exert control. There the aborigines are even more ignorant and suspicious; when they venture more than a few miles out of the mountains, they become awestruck and anxious to retreat. Communicating without an interpreter is impossible; delivering taxes without an interpreter is also impossible; at the end of the year they cannot even arrange the supply of clothing, food, agricultural tools, pots, cloth, and thread without an interpreter to manage it.[52]

Interpreters might remain indispensable to tax collection among the backward tribes of the north, but they were no longer needed among the sophisticated tribes of the southwest core, who lived in close proximity to Han settlers and near the center of Han administration in the county seat.

Magistrate Chou recognized that *official* squeeze remained a potential source of abuse in a system that gave the officials the power to renew interpreters' licenses yearly, but he preached virtue rather than structural reform. Ch'ing officials received only token salaries, and both magistrates and clerks had to rely on customary fees and informal kickbacks to meet expenses as well as to generate the profits expected from office-holding.[53] Officials of course varied widely in rapacity. But for the weak there were few structural checks on official abuse, and they could hope only for the appointment of honest officials with moderate appetites. Chou noted that every year the tribes sent out many deer products and pelts:

> Seeing this, the officials seek to get bribes from the interpreters; interpreters thereby gain the pretext of official squeeze, and every grain and thread of aborigine income and outlay falls into the interpreters' hands. How can we prohibit this? First we must eliminate all corrupt practices and get the interpreters to agree that, excepting compensation for their toil, all kinds of squeeze are forbidden. In this way officials will have no one to take bribes

> from, and we can establish a lawful administration. Those who are just and respect the laws can remain as before; of those who do not reform, we should punish one or two to warn the rest. Though this bunch does not know propriety, they dread the law. They do not dare to do evil openly and will have no pretext to fill their own pockets covertly. Thus both monopoly merchants and squeeze will disappear.[54]

Incredibly Chou seems to be saying that if only interpreters were virtuous, then officials could be too! Chou focused on the middlemen-interpreters, whose bribes were corrupting officials, apparently giving up on reforming the corrupting influence that originated in the official class. A few years later, in 1722, Magistrate Chou estimated that gifts to officials exceeded the tax quota itself. Chou left the task of eliminating corrupt practices to the virtue of officials and interpreters, particularly the latter.[55] But such virtue was not always forthcoming, and as we will see below in the sections on tribal revolts, there were times when the aborigines found the extortions of the village bullies unbearable.

Lan Ting-yüan, writing in 1724, expressed his dissatisfaction with these reform attempts. Lan argued that interpreters, in squeezing the aborigines to recover the bribes they paid to officials, were worse than the tribal merchants they replaced. He noted that Chu-lo magistrate Chou Chung-hsüan had abolished tax farming and ordered the aborigines to nominate their own interpreters, who were to be paid only wages. But bullies and pettifoggers still bribed officials to get licensed as interpreters. Others, who plotted to get licenses and failed, sowed discord among the aborigines and brought calamities to law-abiding people. Some bribed the tribal headmen to get incumbent interpreters removed.[56] Reforms could not succeed as long as official extortion was itself unchecked.

As the essays in the Chu-lo gazetteer acknowledged, the *p'u she* system could not be abolished everywhere at once.[57] The monopoly merchant system was most easily reformed in areas under close official supervision, could only gradually be abolished in intermediate areas, and continued to be useful in remoter areas. The degree of economic, as well as political, penetration in the villages affected the government's ability to reform taxation of the aborigines. Tribes heavily involved in Chinese-dominated trade networks were more likely to have acquired the sophistication necessary to manage their own trade and tax payments. In areas where Chinese penetration was most advanced, competition among Chinese traders may have subverted government attempts to reward exclusive trade monopolies and lessened aborigine dependence on entrenched village bullies. In remote areas taxpaying and the trade that generated the income to pay taxes could best be managed by a tax farmer. Yet, as Lan tells us, even where the reforms were instituted, tribal bullies and corrupt officials could subvert the advantages of the new interpreter system.

In 1727 Governor-general Kao Ch'i-cho called for renewed attempts to reform collection of aborigine taxes. In a memorial Kao called for strictly supervising interpreters, forbidding officials from accepting their gifts, and preventing those without wives, children, farmland, and houses (that is, those without local roots who could not be held accountable) from serving. Kao ordered local officials to forbid both interpreters' squeezing aborigines and yamen runners' squeezing interpreters. He also called for the elimination of the office of interpreter wherever possible.[58] The substantial reduction of the aborigine head-tax quotas in 1737 (see below) should have further reduced the opportunities for extortion by officials and interpreters in the tax collection process. But as we shall see in Chapter 9, the office of interpreter got a new lease on life from the role it played in the opening up of aborigine land to reclamation. Thus, as late as 1758 it was necessary to issue an edict repeating the injunction to appoint native interpreters in place of Han wherever possible.[59] So long as official position held unchallengeable power, both officeholders and their underlings were free to exploit unsophisticated and powerless aborigines, and only constant efforts at reform could prevent excessive exploitation and corruption.

Containing extortion by middlemen in the tax administration is a prominent theme of Ch'ing statecraft, by no means limited to the Taiwan frontier. Attempts to reform the tribal monopoly merchant system by replacing tax farming with direct payment and by reducing interpreters to the role of bookkeepers resemble the pattern common to reform in land-tax collection, where the state also sought to shift from tax farming to bureaucratic tax collection and direct payment.[60] Susan Mann has documented a different path of reform in the Ch'ing taxation of commerce, where the state shifted away from bureaucratic tax collection when it could not limit squeeze by intermediaries; instead it enlisted merchant self-governing bodies ("liturgies") to administer the collection of market taxes.[61] In Taiwan, encouraging the more sophisticated tribes to nominate and use native interpreters resembles this reform strategy. Other strategies of reform targeted the abuses of officials as well as middlemen. Mann points out that curbing the proliferation of taxes and keeping the tax burden light was a Ch'ing strategy to limit abuses of the tax administration by both officials and middlemen.[62] These principles are also illustrated by the Ch'ing reductions in the aborigine tax quotas, especially after 1737. During the Yung-cheng reign, important attempts were made to increase official salaries to reduce the abuses arising from informal fees and official extortion.[63]

Aborigine Corvée

In addition to the tribal revenue tax exacted in kind or silver, the Ch'ing administration required the natives to provide corvée labor service. Like tax farming, corvée reduced the state's administrative expenses, was subject to similar abuses, and was the source of frequent troubles. Aborigines were required to render many different services, including bearing officials in sedan chairs, delivering official documents, and supplying oxcarts to transport lumber for shipbuilding.[64] Aborigines also served as porters for the troops rotated from Fukien every three years.[65] Labor duties were assigned by the tribal merchants and interpreters, who rarely observed any distinction between the levy of government corvée and the extortion of personal service. Some of these abuses are mentioned in the quotations from Yü Yung-ho cited above.

As early as 1695, the intendant Kao Kung-ch'ien ordered the tribal merchants to cease the unauthorized requisition of aborigine oxcarts and drivers. Since the introduction of draft oxen under the Dutch, the number of oxen in Taiwan had grown tremendously, and two-wheeled oxcarts had become the standard means of transport among Han and aborigine alike (see Chapters 6 and 11). Whenever yamen runners and soldiers passed through the villages, they customarily demanded that interpreters supply oxcarts and drivers for every errand. These practices were carried to such an excess that they interfered with aborigine hunting and farming and caused great hardship. Kao complained that local officials were the ultimate source of the abuses. When letting tribal tax farms to the merchants, these officials demanded so much in bribes that the merchants had no alternative but to fleece the aborigines.[66]

Several officials, perhaps recalling the revolt of aborigine porters against the Chengs in 1682, sought to reform the corvée system. In 1710 the intendant Ch'en Pin proposed that porterage fees be paid to ease the burden on the aborigines. All travel over the 2,000 *li* from the prefectural capital to Tan-shui was done in oxcarts supplied by the tribes, and although military postal stations were set up along the route, all documents were transmitted by aborigine runners. Regardless of the weather or terrain, the aborigines were forced to drive the carts and carry the sedan chairs. They were "flogged like slaves," even though they too were "children of the heavenly dynasty." Ch'en ordered that a fee be paid for every ten *li* the oxcarts traveled and that baggage porters be given money for food. He forbade compelling aborigines to carry sedan chairs against their will and had wooden plaques carrying these regulations posted on every important road.[67]

Twelve years later, in 1722, the censor Huang Shu-ching noted that formerly whenever an official or soldier, no matter how petty, went on tour, aborigines carried his sedan chair and bore his luggage. These services so exhausted the aborigines that they had to "flee for their lives." These abuses had then been prohibited. Thus, when Huang himself went on inspection, he rewarded his bearers with money and tobacco. And whenever he stayed in a tribal lodge, he paid for the accommodations with tobacco and cloth.[68] Huang also noted that "the duty of acting as official runners is borne entirely by the *ma ta*," a transliteration of an aborigine word for youth. Huang's notes on the aborigine tribes include an aborigine song entitled "A *Ma Ta* Delivering a Document," whose last line reads: "Should I be late or make a mistake, then I'll be punished by the interpreter."[69]

Writing in 1724, Lan Ting-yüan commented that the aborigines, by supplying carts, relieving troops by doing military service, providing countless labor services, and serving as postal couriers, did ten times more work than the Chinese settlers.[70] Yet the hard-nosed Lan lamented that

> recently the prefect has forbidden the requisition of aborigine carts and will not allow aborigines to render services to the military. This has gone to the point of . . . ordering soldiers to keep accounts and to supply their own rations. This method is absolutely no good. It will make the aborigines dissatisfied with their lot and unwilling to fulfill their service levy; in everything they will compare themselves with Chinese and want to do as they do. The future damage is unthinkable.[71]

The excessive burden of military porterage duties was noted in another official complaint in 1729. Even after the 1737 reform that lowered the aborigine head tax to the same rate as that levied on Han, plains aborigines remained responsible for supplying oxcarts to transport military baggage.[72] In 1752 the heads of various Chu-lo tribes complained of violations of the prohibition on imposing excessive corvée on aborigines. In response, new regulations were formulated and inscribed in stone, an example of which survives at modern-day Kuan-t'ien *hsiang*, T'ai-nan county. This inscription tells us that the most common violations were by the military, and these were again prohibited. Since the Han population was growing, porters for hire were in abundance. Soldiers in need of transport were directed to hire porters on an individual basis. Important officials on tours of inspection were allowed to levy corvée on aborigines, but only within limits. Officials of the rank of intendant, for example, were allowed four carts and 50 porters; the owners of the carts were to be reimbursed 5 cash per *li*, and the porters 3 cash per *li*.[73] Despite the attempts of a few enlightened officials to limit abuses, government functionaries continued to exact excess corvée from the plains aborigines. In 1788 Imperial Commissioner Fu-k'ang-an found it necessary to reassert restrictions on officials' using civilized aborigines as private porters and to ensure that aborigine runners be compensated.[74]

Aborigine Revolts and Official Response

The extortions and abuses of tax farmers and interpreters often reached unbearable levels and in a few instances met with violent resistance. Two plains aborigine revolts occurred in 1699, both in northern Taiwan. Set forth below are the events as recorded in the Chu-lo gazetteer.[75] The first revolt broke out in the second month among the aborigines of the T'un-hsiao tribe in north-central Taiwan. The tax farm for T'un-hsiao was held by the Chinese interpreter Huang Shen. Huang imposed levies so heavy that the aborigines "never had a day of rest." When the tribesmen of T'un-hsiao gathered to begin a deer hunt, Huang demanded that his share be prepaid in cash and rice. This angered two of the tribe's headmen, Cho-ke and Cho-wu, who roused their fellow tribesmen and slew Huang and ten of his fellow gangsters.

The Chinese military authorities called up official troops and a levy of braves from four plains tribes of the southwest core, Hsin-kang, Hsiao-lung, Ma-tou, and Mu-chia-liu-wan,[76] four villages that had supplied auxiliaries to quell disturbances among the Han in 1684 (see above). The Chinese commander ordered the aborigine contingent to lead an attack on T'un-hsiao. The rebels repelled this attack and inflicted heavy casualties. The Chinese commander then changed his strategy. He sent an interpreter to present gifts of sugar, tobacco, silver, and cloth to the chief of the An-li tribes, who lived in the nearby foothills and had not yet submitted to Chinese authority. Pleased with these gifts, the An-li aborigines agreed to help. The An-li force waited to the rear of T'un-hsiao mountain while government troops launched a frontal attack. When the rebels retreated into the mountains, the An-li forces ambushed them and took many captives. These they delivered to the prefectural capital, where they were beheaded and their corpses displayed in the market. The government then sent the heads on exhibit to every tribe. By the time the seven-month-long campaign ended, several hundred government soldiers had died from miasma/malaria.[77]

The second revolt broke out in the fifth month of 1699 in the village of Nei-pei-t'ou in the Tan-shui area of northern Taiwan. The headman, Ma-li-chi-hou, had betrothed his daughter to the tribe's Chinese accountant (a subordinate of the interpreter), Chin Hsien. Chin Hsien was anxious to marry, but Ma-li-chi-hou thought his daughter too young. The dissatisfied Chin bound Ma-li-chi-hou to a tree and flogged him. A weeping Ma-li-chi-hou later told the story to a relative by marriage, Ping-leng. Ping-leng then gathered several tribesmen and shot Chin Hsien and his supporters. At this time T'un-hsiao was also in revolt, and Ping-leng established communications with Cho-ke and Cho-wu. The government dispatched a naval detachment under a sublieutenant to Tan-shui, where unknown to Ping-leng it entered the harbor. The naval commander won over the neighboring tribes by offering them trade goods and then laid a trap and ambushed Ping-leng. His captors had Ping-leng on board ship and had set sail before the Nei-pei-t'ou tribesmen could react. When T'un-hsiao had been pacified and Ping-leng punished, the Nei-pei-t'ou tribesmen sent their interpreter to beg for peace.[78] To instill awe for

Ch'ing authority, Ping-leng's severed head and corpse were displayed to all the Tan-shui tribes, who reportedly feared that the corpse would cause epidemics and dared not approach the head too closely.[79]

Several interesting details emerge from the accounts of these revolts. The establishment of communication between the two rebel forces, separated by over a hundred kilometers, indicates both a substantial degree of intercourse between the tribes, independent of the Chinese administration, and an awareness of shared grievances. We have no record, however, that the communication between the two tribes led to active cooperation. The government had no trouble implementing its strategy of divide and rule, of using barbarians against barbarians. Tribes under considerable Chinese influence and, at the other extreme, those like An-li, beyond government control but eager to obtain Chinese trade goods, were both pliable tools of Chinese strategy. (Despite An-li's willingness to cooperate, it did not formally submit to Chinese authority and consent to pay taxes until 1715 and only as part of an agreement in which the government confirmed its title to agricultural land.)[80]

Ethnic and linguistic divisions among the tribes were not insuperable barriers to cooperation, for example, between T'un-hsiao (Taokas group) and Nei-pei-t'ou (Ketagalan group), but may have aided the Chinese in playing one tribe off against the other, for example, the four tribes of the southwest core (Siraya group) and An-li (Pazeh group) that fought T'un-hsiao. Nor was ethnic unity an obstacle to the Chinese at Tan-shui, where all Nei-pei-t'ou's treacherous neighbors were also Ketagalan.

The Chinese accounts acknowledge that abuses by Chinese interpreters caused these revolts. But the accounts never question that the violent aborigine reaction was an act of rebellion that the government had to suppress and punish. Father de Mailla, who visited Taiwan in 1715, described the revolt of three southern tribes (not part of the Feng-shan eight) against interpreter abuses:

> As regards these tributes, there is in each townlet a Chinese conversant with the language, who serves as interpreter to the mandarins. These interpreters, who ought to assist these poor people, are themselves unworthy harpies who prey upon them pitilessly: indeed they are such petty tyrants that they drive even the patience of the mandarins to the verge of extremity as well as that of the islanders; who, however, have abstained from interfering with them for fear of courting still greater complications. Of twelve townlets which were under Chinese jurisdiction in the south, there now remain but nine; three have rebelled, driven out these interpreters, paid no more tribute to China for three years, and have formed a league with the inhabitants of the eastern portion of the island. It is a very bad example, and will not fail to have its consequences. I mentioned it passingly to the first literary mandarin in Formosa, a Chinese doctor, who had just been made viceroy of the province of Fo-kien [Ch'en Pin]. He replied coldly: it is all the

> worse for these savages, if they insist in remaining in their savage condition; we try to turn them into men, and they do not wish it. All the worse for them. There are malcontents everywhere.[81]

Ch'en Pin's response reflects the haughty attitude of Chinese officials who judged that the benefits of Chinese rule and Chinese civilization far outweighed the inconveniences of occasional corruption and abuse and their surprise that this was not always obvious to others. And Ch'en Pin was far from insensitive to the plight of the plains aborigines. As noted above, he had actively sought to remedy the abuses of interpreters and reduce excessive corvée.

The many proposals for reform of the aborigine taxation and corvée systems were continuously frustrated both by *official* corruption and the ability of Chinese interpreters to exploit their superior access to state authority in dealing with the unsophisticated tribes. The large-scale aborigine revolt of 1731–32 demonstrates that the early reform attempts often made little headway, especially in the area of corvée exactions, where the government was itself the prime source of abuse.

The Ta-chia-hsi Revolt of 1731–1732

The most serious plains aborigine revolt against Ch'ing authority began in the twelfth month of 1731. Taiwan's local gazetteers simply state that a revolt broke out in the plains aborigine village of Ta-chia-hsi, under the leadership of one Lin Wu-li.[82] Ta-chia-hsi was a Taokas settlement located on the coastal plain of present-day T'ai-chung county, north of the Ta-chia river, and the seat of the Peng-shan aborigine tax unit. Palace memorials make clear that excessive corvée and ill-treatment by officials, yamen underlings, and soldiers were basic causes of the revolt, as they had been in several earlier uprisings.

Early in 1731, the government decided to give full fiscal and administrative power to Tan-shui subprefecture, which had been created in 1723, and to establish a number of new subdistrict magistracies.[83] This meant that yamen offices had to be built to house the new officials. The Tan-shui subprefect, Chang Chung-hung, resident in the town of Sha-lu, south of the Ta-chia river, ordered the local tribes to supply labor. The increased official presence meant increased official extortion, and the tribes were soon complaining that yamen runners were sleeping with aborigine women and that government soldiers were commandeering aborigine food supplies. These complaints went unheeded.

Subprefect Chang ordered aborigine laborers from Ta-chia-hsi to supply large logs (for pillars) from forests in the nearby mountains and aborigine women to drive the carts bearing the lumber. When the women refused, the interpreters beat them with rattan strips.[84] Unable to bear this treatment any longer, braves from Ta-chia-hsi and the neighboring village of Ta-chia-tung (also Taokas and part of the Peng-shan tax unit), attacked Subprefect Chang at Sha-lu, where they surrounded his offices, killed some of his subordinates, and set the yamen on fire. Chang fled south to the county seat of Chang-hua. Many settlers in the vicinity were then killed, and their homes burned by the aborigines.[85]

The Taiwan brigade general, Lu Jui-lin, was on patrol in Tan-shui at the time; he promptly headed south, only to be surrounded by rebels at the plains aborigine village of Miao-yü (north of Ta-chia-hsi and also Taokas and a member of the Peng-shan tax unit). After some fighting, Lu and his troops, assisted by loyal aborigine braves from the Taokas tribe of Hou-lung, broke out and reached Chang-hua.[86] In the next weeks Ta-chia-hsi was joined by two neighboring villages, P'u-tzu-li and A-li-shih, from the An-li group of Pazeh villages.[87] Ch'ing troops engaged the aborigines on several occasions but were unable to defeat them.[88]

The government next reinforced its northern garrisons, enlisted the aid of loyal An-li leaders, and pressed the attack. By the third month of 1732, many of the rebel tribes, who had retreated into the mountains, were reported surrendering. And by the fourth month the Ta-chia-hsi tribe itself had expressed its willingness to surrender and was only hesitating over a government demand that it first hand over its leaders for punishment.[89]

The government had responded to its early defeats at the hands of the aborigines by drawing on troops stationed in the south. Taking advantage of the government's difficulty, a group of Han rebels, including some remnants of the Chu I-kuei rebellion (crushed in 1721),[90] raised the flag of rebellion in Feng-shan county in the south. Led by one Wu Fu-sheng, they attacked several government outposts. But within ten days, early in the fourth month of 1732, the Ch'ing commander Wang Chün had crushed the Han rebels.[91]

Things next took a turn for the worse in the north. In the fifth month of 1732, a matrilateral kinsman of Ni Hsiang-k'ai, the Taiwan intendant in charge of suppressing the revolt, had five grain transport laborers from the plains tribes of Ta-tu and Sha-lu killed. Hoping to collect a reward, he and his cohorts presented their heads to the authorities, claiming they were captured Ta-chia-hsi rebels. This failed to deceive Chang-hua county officials, who arrested the culprits. Intendant Ni, however, had them released before a full judicial investigation could be held. This infuriated the remaining, hitherto pacific, civilized tribes of the area, who congregated at Chang-hua to demand justice. Frustrated by official arrogance, aborigines from Ta-tu, Sha-lu, Shui-li, and Niu-ma (all Papora) attacked and burned the house of Intendant Ni and the offices of the Chang-hua county magistrate and jail warden.[92]

The Papora tribes then allied with Ta-chia-hsi and the Peng-shan villages (a group of eight Taokas villages including Ta-chia-hsi and settlements as far north as T'un-hsiao, which had revolted in 1699).[93] The rebels next pressed A-shu and Chai-tzu-k'eng, Babuza villages strategically located between rebel territory and Chang-hua city, into joining the revolt.[94] Within a few days nearly 2,000 aborigines surrounded Chang-hua city, devastated the area around it, and slaughtered the soldiers stationed at two nearby military posts. The rebel tribes seized control of the area between the Ta-tu river (just north of Chang-hua) and the Ta-an river (north of the Ta-chia river), as well as some territory around Chang-hua. "Fleeing settlers flooded the roads."[95] Thus, the misdeeds of Intendant Ni and his subordinates caused the re-escalation of a revolt that had been on the verge of settlement.[96] Chang-hua city only escaped being taken due to the timely arrival of troop reinforcements and several hundred Hakka braves from the south who had proven their effectiveness in the victory over the Han rebel Chu I-kuei in 1721.[97]

In the sixth month of 1732, Governor-general Hao Yü-lin, dissatisfied with the deteriorating situation in the north, transferred Lu Jui-lin away from the front and put Wang Chün in command. Hao had already dispatched 3,000 soldiers from Fukien's garrisons, and Wang requested that he send another 3,000.[98] News that reinforcements were arriving frightened some rebel aborigines into submitting; others prepared for the onslaught by building defensive stockades.[99] In the seventh month Wang moved 5,000–6,000 soldiers north to the port of Lu-kang and began his campaign of suppression. The Hoanya villages southeast of Chang-hua, Mao-lo, Nan-t'ou, and Pei-t'ou, who, along with other plains tribes to the south of Chang-hua, had sympathized with the rebels, sought to make amends by offering their services in suppressing the revolt. Part of the An-li group also remained loyal and helped in the pacification.[100]

Wang gradually swept the rebels from the plain and by the eighth month had the remnants surrounded in the mountains. Surrendering tribes were required to offer up their leaders, who were held for trial or promptly executed. Some of the tribes redeemed their crimes by helping in the pacification. Ta-chia-hsi, Sha-lu, and Niu-ma, the leaders of the revolt, held out the longest and suffered the greatest casualties. By the eleventh month, captive rebel leaders had been executed, those who had been forced to participate in the revolt were pacified, the refugees were resettled, and the troops were withdrawn.[101] Inhabitants of Ta-chia-hsi, Sha-lu, and Niu-ma who took refuge in the mountains were preyed on by head-hunting tribes to whom the government paid rewards for rebel heads. Most had surrendered by the next year.[102]

Governor-general Hao and Commander Wang were duly commended for their successful handling of the campaign. Intendant Ni and Subprefect Chang, on the other hand, were removed from office for incompetence.[103] Two years later, in the twelfth month of 1734, the post-pacification investigations were brought to an official close by a proclamation stating that although "the law concerning rebels provides that all family members should suffer the same punishment with no lenience, the emperor feels ignorant aborigines should not be compared to Han. . . . Since the families of rebels have dispersed to every tribe, now that peace has been restored, arresting them one by one would stir up great alarm. Thus, extraordinary benevolence should be used, and further investigations avoided." This decision was ordered publicly proclaimed, with the appended warning: "If the emperor in this way extends his benevolence and the ignorant aborigines still do not know gratitude, and if some still dare to violate the law, then they are truly dull and stupid and cannot be transformed through benevolence and kindness, and the emperor will be forced to increase the use of severe punishments."[104]

In the 1731–32 revolt, as in the earlier aborigine rebellions, ethnic differences were no barrier to cooperation. At its widest extent, the aborigine alliance included tribes from five different ethnic groupings. The government, as it had in the past, was nevertheless able to exploit ethnic divisions by using certain tribes as auxiliary troops in its pacification campaign. Official mistreatment of the Papora auxiliaries, however, drove them into the rebel camp. All the tribes involved in the revolt were taxpaying civilized tribes and had been so since the Cheng era, with the exception of the An-li group that submitted in 1715.[105]

Three of the rebel tribes, Ta-tu, Sha-lu, and T'un-hsiao, had histories of active resistance against intrusions of state authority. When Cheng soldiers abused Ta-tu in 1661, it revolted and sought to assist the beleaguered Dutch (see Chapter 4). The Chengs suppressed the revolt, but it flared again briefly in 1664–65.[106] Huang Shu-ching, writing in 1722, reports that Sha-lu had nearly been exterminated in a conflict with the Cheng commander, Liu Kuo-hsüan, in 1670.[107] T'un-hsiao had revolted against an oppressive tax farmer in 1699 (see above).

Although official reports make clear that excessive corvée and the petty tyrannies of Chinese officials and their subordinates were the immediate causes of the rebellion, the gradually increasing pressure of Han settlers on aborigine fields and livelihoods must have been an additional grievance. Han immigration to Taiwan was increasing in the Yung-cheng years (see Chapter 6). Huang Shu-ching, writing nine years before the outbreak of the revolt, noted that Sha-lu and the Peng-shan group of eight settlements (which included Ta-chia-hsi) were not allowing Chinese to reclaim fields.[108] Resistance to Han reclamation was no longer possible after the defeat of the 1731 rebellion. In 1733 Governor-general Hao reported that Ta-chia-hsi, Niu-ma, and Sha-lu had 20,000–30,000 *mou* of land set aside as deer-hunting grounds, on which the tribes paid a "deer revenue tax" (*lu hsiang*), and recommended that this "loose reins" policy (appropriate only for distant, unsinicized frontiers) be replaced with a policy favoring land reclamation. Since Taiwan's population was growing, reclamation would ensure not only adequate rice supplies at low cost, but also supplies for the rice-deficit Fukien coast.[109] Large amounts of land were indeed opened to Han settlement in the years after the rebellion. In 1733 Niu-ma *she*, renamed Kan-en *she*, let out land in thirteen villages.[110] In 1734 A-shu *she*, suffering from a food shortage due to the revolt, also let out land to Han settlers.[111] Strikingly, the government continued to recognize the land claims of the defeated tribes. Government control was not so secure that it could afford to ignore the aborigines' claims.

Reconstruction and the Reform of 1737

The dual threat to Ch'ing authority from the revolts of aborigines and Han in 1732 strongly impressed Governor-general Hao. In 1733 he ordered a reorganization of the military in Taiwan, boosting its overall strength by several thousands. Of this number, 1,280 soldiers, the largest of the troop increases, were stationed on the north route, more than doubling the strength of that garrison. Several new military posts were created between Chang-hua and Chu-ch'ien, in the rebel area.[112] This effected a significant shift in the local balance of military power (see Chapter 7).

Lan Ting-yüan was appalled at the extent of the Ta-chia-hsi revolt. He complained that at the time of the revolt Subprefect Chang's headquarters for the Tan-shui subprefecture were still at Sha-lu, in Chang-hua county. Lan advocated building Tan-shui's offices at Chu-ch'ien (modern Hsin-chu) to the north and setting up military farms to increase the administrative presence in the subprefecture.[113] In my opinion, attempting an extension of the civil administration without a concurrent strengthening of the military was one of the fundamental errors of the government's control strategy in 1731.

In addition to making adjustments in the military, administrative, and economic spheres, the government took steps to strengthen the cultural and educational foundations of Ch'ing authority among the civilized aborigines. In 1734 the Taiwan intendant Chang Ssu-ch'ang proposed that instructors be appointed in every county to educate aborigine youth in schools and that county directors of study conduct seasonal examinations in these schools. A total of 47 aborigine schools were founded, the great majority in villages that were also major aborigine taxpaying units (see Appendix A). Seven of the schools were founded among the tribes participating in the Ta-chia-hsi revolt.[114]

In 1740, a decade after the revolt, Liu Liang-pi, the Taiwan intendant, visited Sha-lu. He found it greatly diminished in strength and mentioned that half the women were widows.[115] Liu reports that a benevolent emperor had approved petitions on behalf of the three leading rebel tribes to adopt Confucian maxims as names (the original names had been Chinese transliterations of aborigine names). Sha-lu was renamed Ch'ien-shan "to reform and do good," Niu-ma became Kan-en "grateful for kindness," and Ta-chia-hsi emerged as Te-hua "made virtuous."[116] The Confucianization of place-names was intended to herald the moral transformation and sinicization of the inhabitants.

In late 1736, four years after the Ta-chia-hsi revolt, another revolt broke out on the north route—this time among the civilized Chia-chih-ko aborigines (near Miao-li). Once again, the cause of the trouble was an oppressive interpreter, and after fighting had broken out, a Han troublemaker riled up the tribesmen. The revolt was quickly suppressed, but coming so soon after the major Ta-chia-hsi revolt, it deeply impressed the two Taiwan censors, Pai-ch'i-t'u and Yen Jui-lung, charged with investigating the disturbance. Yen is said to have requested the 1737 reduction of aborigine head taxes (see below), and Pai proposed limits on Han reclamation of aborigine land and on Han marriage to aborigine wives. These policy shifts mark a halt to the aggressive colonization policies of the late Yung-cheng years, reflected in the administrative expansion to the north that led to the Ta-chia-hsi revolt and the increased military presence that followed it (see Part II for further discussion).[117]

In 1737 the tribal tax was changed to a head tax figured at the same rate as for Han Chinese, which had been lowered the year before to 0.2 taels per head.[118] The 1737 reform reduced the official tribal tax quotas by more than 80 percent (see Tables 5.1 and 5.2). The Ch'ien-lung emperor's stated purpose in adopting this reform was to eliminate inequalities in taxation among the tribes and to tax the aborigines at a rate equal to that levied on his Han subjects. He thereby sought to demonstrate that he harbored no prejudice and considered the aborigines, like the Han, his loyal subjects.[119]

The 1737 reform was not applied universally. The An-li group, which had been given a light assessment in 1716 when it submitted, was not included; Shui-sha-lien, which had submitted in 1694 and then revolted in the Yung-cheng years, was given the highest quota. Even after 1737 most newly submitting raw aborigine tribes paid a tax set at a very nominal two deerskins commuted at the rate of 0.24 tael per skin, rather than a head tax based on adult male population.[120]

For the tribes included within its scope, the 1737 reform meant substantial reductions in aborigine tax burdens.[121] This was true for every tribe except the few large northern composite units (Tan-shui, Hou-lung, Peng-shan) whose Cheng-era quotas had been very low, yet whose taxable heads were found to be so numerous in 1737 that their quotas were reduced by only a half or so (see Appendix B). The taxable head quotas used to figure tax burdens in 1737 did not result from a census, however.

In many cases the Ch'ing apparently used the same figures as reported by the Chengs, since the totals for the 34 Chu-lo tax units are so close (4,402 taxable heads in 1737 versus 4,516 under the Chengs).

The Ch'ing in 1737 definitely used Cheng population figures in the case of the eight villages in Feng-shan. The figures show that no new census was taken at the time of this reform: the number of male heads (scribes, adult males, youths) in 1737 was the same number used since the Cheng era.[122] The new rate of taxation, however, substantially lightened the aborigine tax burden (a greater than 80 percent reduction), continuing the general trend during the Ch'ing, as Table 5.2 reveals.

The substantial reduction of aborigine taxes in 1737 was in one sense the ultimate solution to the state's inability to create a tax collection system free of official corruption and interpreter abuse. It also reflects shifts in the fiscal structure of government in Taiwan, as the reclamation of new farms added land to the tax registers and revenues to the treasury. (See Chapter 8 for a discussion of the Ch'ing state's ability to afford substantial reductions in its head-tax revenues in Taiwan.)

The tax reduction of 1737 marks the end of a phase in the history of the plains aborigines of Taiwan's west coast. From the imposition of Dutch rule through the Cheng era down to the early decades of Ch'ing administration, the deerskin trade and the extraction of revenue from that trade, whether by hunting licenses, trading monopolies, or head taxes, structured the relations of plains aborigine hunter-horticulturalists to Chinese traders and governmental authorities. The deer trade produced skins by the thousands, with what seemed only temporary shortages until the final decades. Even after the imposition of Cheng rule, the impact on the plains aborigines of Chinese agricultural settlement remained limited to the southwest core and the sites of Cheng military farms, an area that shrank with the repatriation of Han at the beginning of Ch'ing rule. Thus, the system of trade monopolies and tax farms over plains aborigine villages could remain in place for the first several decades of Ch'ing rule. The system lasted until the growth of the Chinese population and the spread of Chinese farming (which regained momentum by the Yung-cheng reign), combined with overhunting, eroded the plains aborigine economies and transformed the fiscal basis of Ch'ing rule.

PART II

Ch'ing Quarantine Policies and the Spread of Han Settlement

CHAPTER SIX

Immigration and Han Settlement

Colonization Policy Debates

In 1683 the Ch'ing court was impressed more by the burdens of the incorporation of Taiwan into the empire than by its benefits. The court anxiously repatriated the Cheng armies and, afraid that Taiwan might again become a rebel base, imposed a partial quarantine on the island, strictly regulating migration and trade between the island and the mainland, to prevent disruptions of the status quo. To govern the sparsely populated and revenue-poor island, the court concentrated military and civil administrations in the southwest core around Tainan. The court judged that indirect control, exercised by quarantining the island, would be a less expensive and more cost-effective means of preventing disturbance on the frontier, and as Chapter 5 documented, the quarantine served to shelter from change many aspects of the accommodation of the plains aborigine societies to Han traders and Ch'ing rule.

Quarantine and the maintenance of the status quo were the hallmarks of early Ch'ing policy toward Taiwan; the spread of Han settlement and the extension of the government's presence were simply not envisaged. The court's priority was to stimulate the recovery of the southeast coast from the devastation of the coastal evacuation policy and to re-establish a stable society there that would contribute its share to state revenues. By the end of the K'ang-hsi reign, the recovery of the southeast coast—the growth of its population and the expansion of its commerce and foreign trade—was subverting the quarantine of Taiwan.[1] Migrants from the crowded southeast coast began flocking to Taiwan to take advantage of its unopened fields and the high prices Taiwan's sugar and rice fetched on the mainland market. These developments upset the ethnic status quo in Taiwan and tested the government's ability to maintain control.

The government's first response to these developments was to tighten enforcement of the quarantine policies and the restrictions on immigration. Attempts were made to quarantine aborigine territories and limit the spread of Han settlement in Taiwan to areas under effective government control. The Chu I-kuei rebellion in 1721 drew the attention of many high-level officials and scholars to the problems of ruling Taiwan. Several of these statesmen, the most outspoken of whom was Lan Ting-yüan, argued for a reversal of the outmoded quarantine policies and the adoption of a pro-colonization course as the best way to ensure control over Taiwan. In 1723, the Yung-cheng emperor approved a plan to subdivide Chu-lo county by adding Chang-hua county and Tan-shui subprefecture. This increased the presence of the civil administration on Taiwan's northern frontier. However, no expansion of the already large and expensive military presence was ordered at this time.

Throughout the Yung-cheng era (1723–35), the quarantine policies were abandoned one by one in favor of pro-colonization policies. Beginning in 1725, Taiwan rice surpluses were designated for export to Fukien garrisons and for famine relief sales on the rice-deficit southeast coast. Aborigine tribes were encouraged to rent their lands to Han so that "both might benefit and the treasury be filled." Cadastral surveys in 1728 enrolled large amounts of land on the tax registers, especially in newly established Chang-hua county, which badly needed a tax base. In 1731 land-tax rates were lowered to encourage voluntary registration of land; the new policy, unlike that of the K'ang-hsi years, looked to continued reclamation and the expansion of land-tax rolls, rather than high tax rates, to fill the tax quotas. Also in 1731 the court ordered an expansion of the civil administration. But at the end of the year excessive imposition of corvée on civilized aborigines ordered to build yamens in the north brought on the large-scale Ta-chia-hsi tribal revolt. When troops were sent north to quell the disturbance, Wu Fu-sheng took the opportunity to organize a rebellion of Han in southern Taiwan.

This double rebellion, rather than forcing a retreat from expansionism, was taken as proof of the failure of the old policies. The government stiffened its resolve and pressed ahead. In 1732 the immigration of families to Taiwan was approved for the first time. In 1733 large numbers of troops were added to Taiwan's garrisons and new posts sited in weakly patrolled areas. To help pay for the added military presence, continued expansion of reclamation and land-tax revenues was necessary. By the end of the Yung-cheng reign, nearly all the quarantine policies had been abandoned. In their place was a strategy of extending direct control over the frontier through the civil and, belatedly, the military administrations, financed by tax revenues on newly reclaimed land and by subsidies from Fukien.

By the beginning of the Ch'ien-lung reign (1736–95), the costs of the pro-colonization policies were beginning to loom large as the burgeoning Chinese population became increasingly unruly and aborigine disturbances continued. These problems arose despite the expansions in the civil and military presence and the tax base. That many of the pro-colonization policies had been found wanting deflated arguments for continuation of the pro-colonization course and made the new court receptive to proposals to reverse policy. Governor-general Hao Yü-lin ordered a halt to the further reclamation of aborigine land in 1738, and in 1739 he decreed an end, after a one-year grace period, to the legal immigration of families. In 1741 government rice-export quotas were reduced, and in 1744 land-tax rates were raised. But the revived quarantine policies now operated in an environment transformed by a large influx of Chinese farmers and the expansion of frontier settlement. Nor was the government any more successful than it had been in the late K'ang-hsi years at stopping illegal immigration. Thus, in 1746 another survey of aborigine lands had to be ordered, the 1738 ban on their reclamation reasserted, and new punishments set to deal with violations. The revived quarantine policies were repeatedly adapted and compromised to deal with the reality of continued immigration and the spread of Chinese settlement throughout the remainder of the Ch'ien-lung era (for a summary of policy fluctuations, see Table 6.1).

In Part II, I trace the fluctuation in policy for each issue separately and analyze the relation of changes in one set of policies to those in other areas. Many of the debates (and the scholarly articles dealing with this period) are phrased in terms unique to each policy area. This sometimes obscures the significance of the debates for overall trends in colonization policies. But for the Confucian scholars participating in these decisions, the issues unique to each policy seem to have weighed as heavily as the consequences change in one policy area would have for another. Thus, much of the debate on immigration policy was conducted in terms that asked whether bachelors or families would be more law-abiding on the frontier or whether it was ethical to keep families divided, rather than focusing on the desirability of further reclamation or even the economic problems of the southeast coast where the migrants originated. Rice-export policies were discussed less in terms of projected trends in migration and reclamation, or even the fate of aborigine lands, and more in terms of the consequences of harvest fluctuations for local security. And the debate on land-tax rates focused on problems of tax evasion rather than the relation of government revenues (and expenditures) to expanding reclamation.

All the policies debated had pro- or anti-colonization consequences, if not always by conscious and stated intention. And all the policies proposed, whether pro- or anti-colonization, reveal an obsession with control and order. What distinguished the two sides of the debate were the sources of disorder they identified and the methods of control they advocated. For more conservative schools of statecraft, vagrant immi-

TABLE 6.1

Ch'ing Taiwan: Summary of Events and Fluctuations in Quarantine Policies

1683–1790

Major events	Family immigration	Rice exports	Extension of military and civil administration	Land taxes and registration
K'ang-hsi era (1662–1722)				
1683: Ch'ing rule established 1696, 1701: minor Han disturbances 1699: T'un-hsiao *she* and Tan-shui *she* rebellions	1684: forbidden	1684: Limit to 60 *shih* per ship	1684: 3 counties, 1 prefecture, 1 circuit established; army rotated from Fukien 1704: coastal defense strengthened 1710: Tan-shui lieutenancy 1718: Tan-shui battalion	1684: leave land-tax rates high
1721: Chu-I-kuei rebellion			1721: Circuit censors	
Yung-cheng era (1723–35)				
		1725, 1727, 1732: increase allotments of Taiwan rice to Fukien garrisons 1726: liberalize rice export policy	1723: Chang-hua county and Tan-shui subprefecture	1728: large area in Chang-hua registered

1731–32: double revolt of Ta-chia-hsi aborigines and Wu Fu-sheng	1732: allowed		1731: 2 new assistant magistrates and 4 new subdistrict magistrates 1733: military reorganization and troop increases	1731: sharp reduction in land-tax rates
Ch'ien-lung era (1736–95)				
	1740: forbidden 1746: allowed 1748: forbidden	1741: reduce quota for Fukien relief 1743: approve exports of rental grain 1748: raise rice export limit to 200 *shih* per ship		1744: raise land tax rates
1751: Pei-t'ou *she* troubles	1760: allowed 1761: forbidden			
1768: Huang Chiao disturbance 1782: Communal strife 1786–88: Lin Shuang-wen rebellion			1766: aborigine affairs subprefecture 1783: north route coastal defense subprefecture 1790: aborigine military colonies	

NOTE: See Table 9.1 for a summary of changes in policy on aborigine land rights.

grants caused trouble among both Han and aborigines, and the best (and least costly) way to maintain order was to preserve the status quo and to exercise control indirectly by imposing a quarantine. This entailed halting immigration, keeping migrant farmers dependent on access to the mainland, containing Han settlement within areas under government control, and preventing encroachment on aborigine land. The activists, in the ascendant in the Yung-cheng years, countered that control was best maintained directly through an extended civil and military presence that could crush both Han and aborigine disturbances and by filling up open frontier spaces with settlers. To help finance the government, land-tax revenues could be collected from areas newly reclaimed by immigrant Chinese families, who were the allies, not the enemies, of government control. Chapter 9 will show the great difference these two policy regimes implied for the fate of aborigine claims to land.

This chapter focuses on policies toward immigration and rice exports and documents the trends in population growth, agricultural expansion, and Han settlement that transformed the Taiwan frontier in the eighteenth century. Chapter 7 will analyze the state's policies toward the expansion of its administrative infrastructure, and Chapter 8 the state's creation of a fiscal base for its operations in Taiwan.

Restrictions on Immigration

A look at the repeated attempts to prohibit family migration reveals the fluctuating nature of Ch'ing policy toward Taiwan. Between 1684 and 1788, the court on three separate occasions approved family migration and then revoked its approval; during this period family migration was legally permitted for a total of less than twelve years (see Table 6.2). During the long periods of prohibition, the court's enforcement of its regulations fluctuated from strict to lax. This section analyzes the considerations behind these twists and turns in the immigration policy cycle.

The court, persuaded primarily by considerations of maritime security, decided in 1684 to keep Taiwan. But instead of adopting a policy of actively opening the Taiwan frontier, the court imposed a partial quarantine for fear that pirates, Cheng remnants, and rebels might make Taiwan an anti-government base. This led to the numerous restrictions on mainland communications and settlers adopted in 1684. The regulations fell into three major categories. First was the regulation of intercourse between Taiwan and the southeast coast. Those wishing to cross to Taiwan needed travel papers approved by authorities in their native locality and by maritime authorities on both sides of the Taiwan strait. Crossings were allowed only between the ports of Amoy and Tainan. Ship captains were required to compile cargo manifests and crew rolls for

TABLE 6.2
Family Migration to Taiwan: Policy Fluctuations, 1684–1788

Date	Family migration
1684–1732 (KH 23–YC 10)	Forbidden
1732–40 (YC 10–CL 5)	Allowed
1740–46 (CL 5–11)	Forbidden
1746–48 (CL 11–13)	Allowed
1748–60 (CL 13–25)	Forbidden
1760–61 (CL 25–26)	Allowed
1761–88 (CL 26–53)	Forbidden

inspection by the authorities. Rice was not to be exported from Taiwan in excess of 60 *shih* per ship (only enough for the crew's rations). A second set of regulations prohibited those crossing to Taiwan from taking their wives and families; those already settled in Taiwan were not allowed to bring their families across to join them. The third set of regulations prohibited residents of Ch'ao-chou and Hui-chou prefectures of Kwangtung, because they were "pirate refuges," from crossing to Taiwan.[2] These regulations reflected the Ch'ing desire, above all else, to prevent Taiwan's becoming a source of trouble. The development of trade and agriculture and even the expansion of government tax revenues were of secondary importance. Communications were to be strictly regulated and monitored to prevent illicit crossings by marginal and dissident elements. Taiwan's own food supply was to be protected by limiting rice exports.[3]

Discouraging permanent settlement by preventing the migration of families meant that only unaccompanied males could make the crossing to Taiwan. This gave rise to a population of migrant laborers crossing for the spring planting and returning to their mainland homes after the fall harvest. This served Ch'ing policy by creating a population of male laborers dependent on the government for access to families on the mainland. Filial obligations to parents and the duty to maintain ancestral sacrifices reinforced this dependence.[4] The government could avenge wayward behavior on the hard-to-control Taiwan frontier by holding families on the mainland responsible for the migrants' crimes.

These attempts to quarantine the island and to prevent permanent settlement contrast with Ch'ing policies favoring resettlement of depopulated areas already under Han domination but resemble the policies adopted for some non-Han frontier regions. The government rewarded officials who recruited migrants to resettle areas depopulated by the recent dynastic wars, and it provided immigrants with seed, oxen, and special tax exemptions to encourage them to restore land to production and to the tax rolls.[5] In contrast, the government sought to limit Chinese

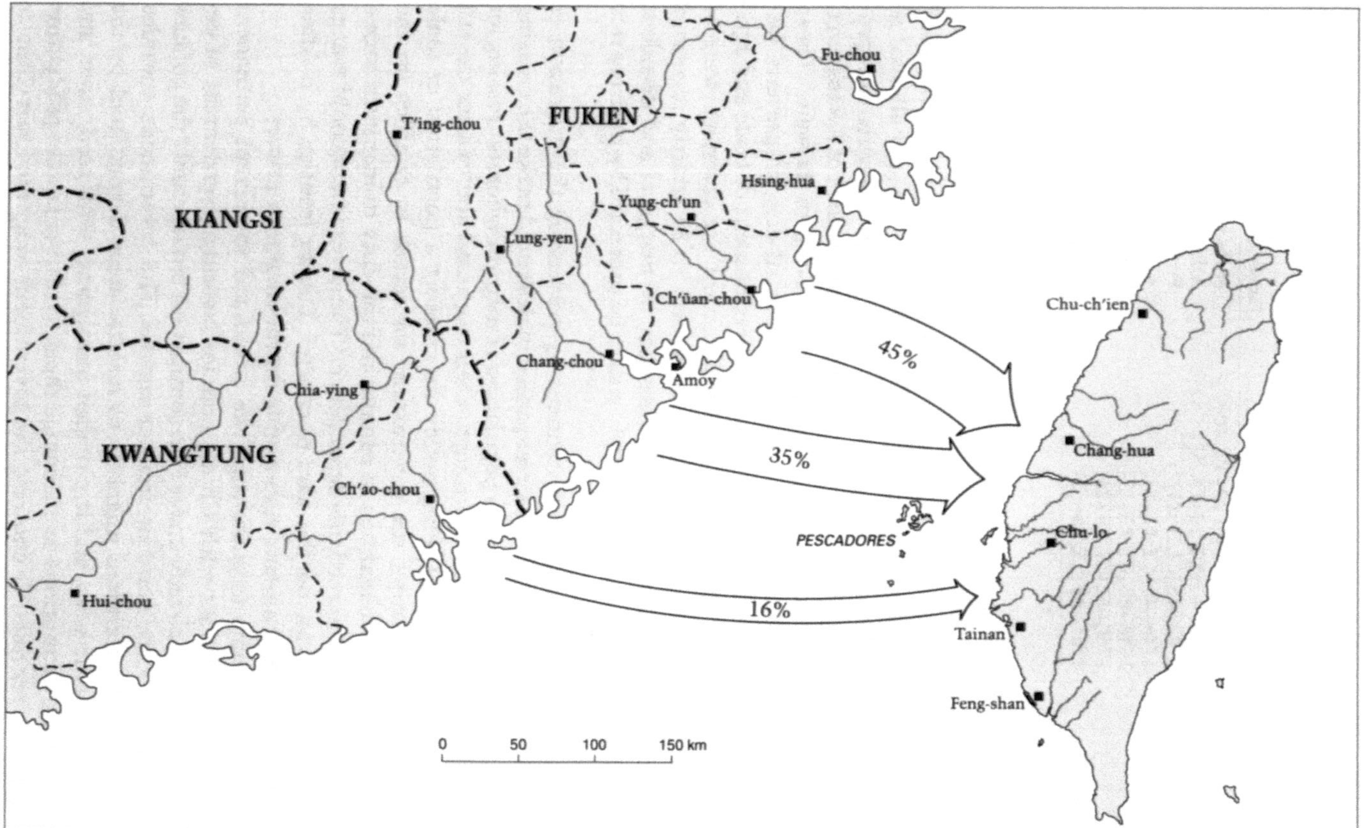

Map 6.1 The southeast coast and migration to Taiwan
Based on Ch'en Cheng-hsiang 1959–61: 1.228.

migration into areas occupied by non-Han peoples where Chinese settlement would upset the ethnic status quo. Thus, in Manchuria and Inner Mongolia, as in Taiwan, the Ch'ing tolerated the seasonal migration of male farm laborers but prohibited the migration of families and women.[6] Quarantine policies, however, were difficult to enforce and, in the Taiwan case, were opposed by many officials who saw them as the source of much of the unrest in Taiwanese society.

The early formulations of immigration policy for Taiwan seldom linked the Ch'ing desire for order with the impact of Chinese immigration on the aborigines; government anxiety in these years focused instead on threats from Ming loyalists and pirates. Taiwan's Chinese population had fallen well below its Cheng-period high in the first years of Ch'ing rule, and it had first to recover before it again pressured the aborigines. Governmental concern about the consequences of Chinese immigration and the expansion of Chinese settlement for the aborigines grew as the Chinese population increased in later years.

Although the regulations were strict in theory, enforcement remained lax, partly because of official complacency. In the early years of Ch'ing rule over Taiwan, there was little need to prohibit migration, for the southeast coast was itself still recovering from the devastation and depopulation that resulted from the forced removal of coastal population during the campaign against the Chengs. But by the end of the K'ang-hsi reign, the pressure of a growing population was undermining the restrictions. Sparsely populated Taiwan lay opposite the southeast coast, one of eighteenth-century China's most densely populated rice-deficit regions (see Map 6.1). Migrants to Taiwan came from the prefectures of Fukien and Kwangtung that had the highest population/land ratios: Chang-chou, Ch'üan-chou, Hui-chou, and Ch'ao-chou.[7] And as we shall see shortly, the heavy demand for rice along the southeast coast meant high prices for Taiwanese grain. Both demographic pressure and economic opportunity subverted Ch'ing attempts to limit migration to Taiwan. Furthermore, the Fukien and the Taiwan coasts provided numerous landing points where immigrants could escape official detection and official squeeze. In 1711 Prefect Chou Yüan-wen noted with alarm that large numbers of migrants were entering Taiwan illegally and requested tighter enforcement of the licensing system and the expulsion of "secret crossers." From 1711, only immigrants whose background passed inspection were to be given passes and allowed to register in Taiwan.[8] Although we lack statistical data from this period, it seems clear that by 1717 Taiwan's population more than exceeded the Cheng-period high and that areas of concentrated Chinese settlement had spread beyond the old Tainan core, both to the north and south (see Tables 6.4 and 6.5 and Map 6.4).

In 1717 the Ch'ing court reimposed the ban on Chinese trading abroad that it had dropped on the surrender of the Chengs. The K'ang-hsi emperor initiated this shift in policy after being informed (erroneously) that shipmasts and rice were being exported to Southeast Asia and sold to pirates.[9] Underlying the shift was a general fear that Chinese trading overseas held rebel sympathies and might collaborate with foreigners. The emperor's decree specifically called for an end to Taiwanese trading with Luzon. This new policy did not prohibit the domestic coastal trade or trade between Taiwan and Fukien, but regulation was tightened to provide greater security.[10]

In accord with these new policies, Governor-general Gioro Man-pao sought to tighten the enforcement of the regulations to prevent illegal crossings to Taiwan. Man-pao also worried that the long years of peace under K'ang-hsi had led to so much carelessness and corruption in the administration of Taiwan that it provided "dangerous opportunities to the ambitious and might result in a great calamity for Taiwan's domestic security."[11] Man-pao proposed that fishing boats as well as merchant ships be required to follow the registration and inspection procedures outlined above and be prohibited from carrying cargo, rice, or passengers. Enforcement was to be tightened. Man-pao's proposal was approved and implemented in 1718. Unlicensed "secret crossings" by single vagrants were henceforth strictly prohibited.[12]

A particularly severe regulation was adopted, apparently at this time, prohibiting migrants from returning to their mainland homes in the agricultural off-season and in effect requiring them to return permanently to the mainland or stay permanently in Taiwan without their families. This is reported only in a memorial of 1760 that reviews the history of Taiwan immigration policies; the regulation is not dated, but it is treated before the authorization of family immigration in 1732. It is likely that this was part of Man-pao's policy, adopted before the Chu I-kuei rebellion of 1721.[13]

The prohibition of the immigration of wives and families led to a volatile, bachelor-dominated society prone to brawling and rebellion. The predominance of unaccompanied males was common on Chinese frontiers and in overseas migration and was not unique to Taiwan.[14] The government ban, even for established property owners, on bringing over wives and relatives impeded the growth of a rooted and more stable population. Tightening enforcement after 1717 may have helped fuel the resentment that burst forth in the Chu I-kuei rebellion.[15]

The Chu I-kuei Rebellion

The disastrous Chu I-kuei rebellion of 1721 demonstrated the fragility of Ch'ing rule in Taiwan and forced the government to re-evaluate its policies toward the island.[16] The harsh tax-collection methods of Feng-shan county magistrate Wang Chen had already alienated the populace when clumsy attempts to arrest outlaws and extort protection money in 1721 heightened popular disaffection. In 1721 Chu I-kuei, who had arrived from Chang-chou prefecture eight years earlier, was a 33-year-old duck breeder. In the third month of 1721, Chu and several confederates met in Feng-shan to plan an uprising. Chu appears to have emerged as the rebel leader in part because he bore the surname of the deposed Ming ruling house. His comrades judged the banner of Ming loyalism would help them win popular support. On the night of the nineteenth day of the fourth month, Chu and some 50 to 80 rebels attacked a military outpost at Kang-shan (south of Tainan) and seized its store of weapons. A raid on another outpost two days later was also successful. Upon hearing news of these exploits, the outlaw leader Tu Chün-ying allied his bandit group with Chu's rebel band.[17]

On the twenty-first, the government mobilized troops and called up plains aborigine porters and auxiliaries from Hsin-kang, Mu-chia-liu-wan, Hsiao-lung, and Ma-tou.[18] Although the outbreak was still small in scale and containable, several government missteps in the following days caused the revolt to spread and escalate. Chief among these was an ill-conceived attempt to incite plains aborigine auxiliaries against the rebels. On the twenty-third, government troops defeated a large concentration of rebels near Hsiao-kang-shan. The rebels dispersed and sought refuge in friendly villages. The next day the victorious Ch'ing commander promised his soldiers and aborigine auxiliaries three taels for every rebel killed and five taels for every rebel chieftain.[19] When the plains aborigines torched houses and killed innocent civilians instead, panic spread among the populace.[20] It was then easy for the rebels to spread fear of the government troops and win support in the villages. Over the next few days, the rebels defeated government troops in several skirmishes, and the government's expeditionary force withdrew from Feng-shan and returned to Tainan. Tu Chün-ying's band then launched attacks on Feng-shan county seat.

News of these defeats panicked officials in Tainan, who put their families aboard ships to flee the island. On the thirtieth, rebel forces approaching Tainan were defeated by government troops. But on the first of the fifth month, rebels "by the ten thousands" congregated outside Tainan, and the forces of Chu I-kuei and Tu Chün-ying led a united attack. The Ch'ing brigade general was assassinated, and ferocious battles resulted in heavy casualties for both sides. The government troops appear to have had superior weapons but were badly outnumbered. Sensing defeat, the military and civil officers commandeered all available shipping and fled to the Pescadores and Fukien.[21] Tu Chün-ying entered the city first, occupying the brigade general's yamen, and Chu I-kuei second, occupying the intendant's yamen. Within a few days, Chu-lo to the north also fell to the rebels, leaving the Tan-shui–Keelung area the only portion of the island under Ch'ing control.[22] On the third, the rebels declared Chu I-kuei king, and he bestowed official ranks and titles on the various rebel leaders. Within two weeks, Ch'ing rule in Taiwan had collapsed. Government bungling had allowed a small outbreak to escalate into a major rebellion.

Rivalry between Chu I-kuei and Tu Chün-ying soon began to undermine rebel unity, however. After a bloody clash in the middle of the fifth month, Tu (who fits the image of a rapacious bandit) led his forces north to prey on Hokkien villages in the Chang-hua area. In the ensuing weeks additional communal clashes polarized Hakka and Hokkien settlers. In Feng-shan, Hakka villages organized a self-defense corps, and a large pitched battled between the Hokkien rebels and the Hakka was in progress in southern Feng-shan when the Ch'ing reconquest began in the sixth month.

By the beginning of the sixth month, the government had assembled an armada of 600 ships, 6,000 sailors, and 12,000 soldiers in Amoy and the Pescadores. The first wave landed outside Tainan on the sixteenth and quickly gained control of the port of An-p'ing; the Ch'ing forces made heavy use of cannon to defeat rebel counterattacks, and within a week the prefectural capital was once again in Ch'ing hands. Chu I-kuei's resistance collapsed, and within a few weeks he was betrayed and taken prisoner. Tu Chün-ying, who had fled to the mountains, surrendered on the tenth day of the ninth month. The large Ch'ing armies dispersed rebel forces and rounded up the remnants with the assistance of the Hakka self-defense corps, now styled "loyalists," in Feng-shan, and by plains aborigines, who guided the troops to bandits in mountain hideaways.[23]

Thus, Ch'ing rule in Taiwan was restored in 1721 almost as quickly as it had been lost, but at a sizable cost in lives and revenues. In the court's eyes, the collapse of Ch'ing control demonstrated the ineffectiveness of Taiwan's civil and military officers. To provide closer supervision, the court decided to send censors on annual tours of inspection. But it rejected a (costly) proposal to garrison more troops in Taiwan on the logic that the sea and land forces were already sufficient to help each other out of difficulties.[24] The sudden collapse of government demonstrated that the administration lacked ties to Taiwan's unstable frontier society that could help impede the spread of outbreaks and shore up government control. To critics like Lan Ting-yüan, Ch'ing immigration policy only exacerbated the problem of creating a stable social order in Taiwan with vested interests in government control.

Immigration Policies After the Rebellion

The Chu I-kuei rebellion's rapid spread among the immigrant Han population reawakened fears that Taiwan might become a rebel base that could threaten the southeast coast. In the wake of the rebellion and on into the Yung-cheng reign, many of the old policies concerning Taiwan were reconsidered and new ones proposed. Lan Ting-yüan, who had come from Fukien to Taiwan in 1721 in the company of imperial forces (under his cousin's command) that helped suppress the Chu I-kuei rebellion, was one of the most prolific participants in these debates and an advocate of an aggressive colonization policy.[25]

Lan argued that Man-pao's immigration policies created rather than prevented disorder. In 1724 Lan advised the Taiwan intendant Wu Ch'ang-tso that tighter restrictions on travel and trade merely provided increased opportunities for officials to extort squeeze.[26] As examples of the disorder resulting from restrictions on family migration, Lan pointed to the settlements of migrant laborers from the Hakka areas of Kwangtung. Within these communities the laborers formed tightly knit gangs that, on the smallest pretext, engaged in murderous brawls. Civil suits abounded, and robbers were so audacious that they even stole branded cattle. The restrictions on bringing wives and families had created a population of rootless vagrants. Lan argued that migrants wishing to farm in Taiwan should be allowed to take families with them and those already in Taiwan should be allowed to bring their families over. It was those *without* families who should be barred from crossing, and the vagrants that should be sent back. Once all settlers had families, the sources of rebellion would be eradicated.[27] As we will see below, Lan was also an active proponent of the reclamation of aborigine lands.

In a 1727 memorial requesting the lifting of the restrictions on family immigration, Governor-general Kao Ch'i-cho continued Lan's argument. Kao found Taiwanese customs unruly, characterized by excessive drinking and gambling. Whereas immigrants in the old settled areas around Tainan had wives and families, those in the newly opened areas to the north and south had none, and the latter, "whose hearts have nothing to remember with affection," were often involved in disturbances. Living in groups of 20 to 40 men, they spent their leisure and their income on gambling and drinking. When drinking and gambling exhausted their earnings, they turned to robbery. "If each had a wife, inner and outer would be distinguished and there would be no confusion and disorder. If each had to support a wife, drinking and gambling would diminish. If each had to protect a household, robberies would decrease."[28]

Kao proposed that certain categories of settlers—property owners and those tenants resident in Taiwan for five years whose landlords were willing to guarantee them—should be allowed to move their families to Taiwan; those without work or property should not. Tied to precedent, the court rejected Kao's request.[29] But despite the tightening of anti-immigration measures, the censors Hsia Chih-fang and Ho-shih-se reported in 1728 that Taiwan's population had grown substantially and much land had been reclaimed during the previous ten years.[30] The policy debates were taking place in an environment where the enforcement of these policies had only limited impact on the migrants themselves.

Both Kao and Lan also lobbied actively for the removal of the ban on maritime trade reimposed in 1717. In 1727 crop failures underlined the economic dependence of the chronically rice-deficit and heavily populated southeast coast on grain imports and foreign trade. Lan and Kao had earlier pointed out the potential of Taiwan's rice exports (see below), and Taiwan rice provided important relief during the 1727 famine. In 1727 the court approved Kao's proposal to lift the ban on maritime trade.[31] Kao and Lan may also have felt that migration to Taiwan would relieve pressures on rice supplies in Fukien. In the following year, Lan wrote another memorial urging repeal of the restrictions against the migration of families; again the advice was not taken.[32] In 1729 the Ch'ing court repeated its prohibition against secret crossings and adopted regulations to tighten enforcement and punish lax officials.[33]

To those like Lan Ting-yüan, the double rebellion of civilized aborigine tribes in the Ta-chia river area and of Han Chinese in Feng-shan in 1731–32 was added proof of the failure of the quarantine policies.[34] Vagrant Han in the south and the near absence of taxpaying Han in the north, they argued, weakened the government's ability to maintain control. When in 1732 Governor Omida of Kwangtung, who had invited Lan to be his secretary,[35] petitioned to allow families to cross to Taiwan, members of the Grand Council (including Ortai, famed for aggressive colonization policies in southwest China) found Omida's arguments sound. Omida proposed that anyone with property and a livelihood in Taiwan could apply to the local authorities for a permit to return to his native locality to apply for a certificate allowing his family to move to Taiwan. This (highly bureaucratic) proposal was adopted by the emperor in 1732.

The period from 1732 to 1740 was the first in which families could legally join settlers in Taiwan, and it appears that many took advantage of the change in policy. In 1743 it was reported that Taiwan's population had increased by several tens of thousands after the lifting of the ban.[36] Kao Shan, who first visited Taiwan as a censor in 1730, was struck by the great increase in population and cultivated area when he returned to Taiwan on an investigation in 1744.[37]

The relaxation of the restrictions on family immigration did not, however, diminish the numbers crossing without permits. In 1733 Governor-general Hao Yü-lin rejected a proposal to restrict those allowed to cross to the wives and children of settlers (thereby excluding parents and siblings), but he adopted a set of regulations requiring visitors to register with the Amoy coastal prefect. Hao's main concern was to exclude troublemakers, and he proposed that secret crossers be dealt with harshly. In 1735 Hao sought stricter enforcement of the regulations against unlicensed crossers by ordering frequent coastal patrols and the cooperation of local fishing stations and constables in inspections.[38]

Hao took his conservative, control-oriented approach a step further in 1739, when he proposed that families no longer be allowed to join settlers in Taiwan. Villains, bullies, and non-family members were taking advantage of the relaxation to cross to Taiwan. Pointing to negligence and corruption in the issuance of permits, Hao proposed that all family immigration be halted after allowing virtuous, gainfully employed subjects one more year to bring over their families. (We will see in Chapter 9 that the previous year Hao had also called a halt to further Han acquisition of aborigine lands.) The Ch'ien-lung court accepted Hao's proposal, and from 1740 to 1746 family migration was prohibited, and the restrictions against secret crossings and the export of rice without licenses were tightened.[39] In 1744 a proposal to reclaim aborigine lands was rejected on the grounds that it would stimulate the illegal migration of vagrants, who were the source of frontier troubles.[40]

Thus, the early years of the Ch'ien-lung reign witnessed a general swing of the policy cycle away from pro-colonization measures and back toward control through quarantine. The reimposition of the strict prohibition of family migration did not go unquestioned. In 1744 Censor Liu-shih-ch'i argued that not allowing parents and wives to join settlers was "to cut off bone and flesh." Parents growing old in Taiwan or on the mainland needed their children and should be able to live with them in Taiwan. Liu argued that immediate family members should be reunited but allowed that collaterals could be excluded. In 1746 Governor-general Ma-erh-t'ai seconded Liu-shih-ch'i's suggestion, and the immigration of families (narrowly defined) who were joining established settlers was again approved.[41] The Board of Revenue, however, warned that Taiwan was a mountainous territory across the seas where it was easy for outlaws to hide; thus, unlicensed crossings were to remain prohibited. The next year, on the recommendation of Governor-general Ho-erh-chi-shan, it was decided that the legal immigration of families should be terminated again in 1748.[42]

During these years the illegal ferrying of unlicensed immigrants and rice from many small unauthorized ports regularly subverted official immigration and quarantine policies. Ship captains contracted to carry illegal immigrants for large fees; the captains then arranged matters with the local authorities. These fees were less bothersome to the immigrants than the troublesome procedures and frequent extortions they had to endure to get official permits, when they were available. For illegal migrants the risks could involve more than apprehension: unscrupulous captains sometimes cheated their passengers and abandoned them on coastal shoals, where many drowned.[43] Nevertheless, illegal crossings to Taiwan far outnumbered licensed migration.

Not until 1760 was permission again granted and legal means provided to allow Taiwan settlers to bring their families from the mainland.[44] In addition to offering the standard arguments against the separation of families, Fukien governor Wu Shih-kung pointed to the exploitation of the illegal immigrants by unscrupulous ship captains and added the objection that the unfavorable sex ratio among Chinese migrants led to their marrying aborigine women (which had been prohibited since 1737) and was thereby disrupting tribal life.[45]

Lifting the prohibition on family migration did not result, however, in an increase in licensed crossings. In a year's time only 48 families, totalling 277 people, requested permits, and the bulk of these were families of yamen runners and clerks serving in Taiwan. In contrast, during a ten-month period in 1758–59, 999 people had been arrested for attempting unlicensed crossings. Those apprehended were known to be only a small fraction of those who had made illegal crossings successfully.[46]

The new policy was quickly reversed. Governor-general Yang T'ing-chang sought and obtained a year's limit on the family migration legalized in 1760. In his memorial Yang explained that open land had formerly been plentiful in Taiwan, but since the approval of family migration in 1732 and 1746 large numbers had moved to Taiwan. And since this burgeoning population was prohibited from reclaiming border lands (Yang himself had ordered the clarification of the aborigine boundary line in 1760), opportunities for new settlers had diminished on the Taiwan frontier. Many had even applied to return to the mainland. Yang concluded that traders preferred not to have their families immigrate and that those illicitly crossing to Taiwan were all villains and bandits. So there was no need to lift restrictions on the immigration of families. Rather, Yang sought to strengthen measures against illegal immigrants, including offering rewards for their apprehension. Those already in Taiwan, however, were to be entered on the population rolls of the *pao chia* mutual-guarantee system.[47]

In 1768 a large-scale disturbance led by the bandit Huang Chiao near Tainan infuriated the court and brought renewed calls for stricter rule. Rootless vagrants who had secretly crossed to Taiwan were "impossible to control; they must be stopped *before* crossing" (my italics). Once again, stricter measures and stronger punishments were adopted.[48] Both changed conditions in Taiwan and a different psychology at court account for the government's reaction. In 1732 the Yung-cheng court concluded that Han and aborigine revolts had discredited the old anti-immigration policies, which it then abandoned. But the revolt in 1768 convinced the Ch'ien-lung court that enforcement was not strict enough.

In 1771 what Chuang Chin-te terms a passive, revisionist period in immigration policy began; restrictions were relaxed either because they were unenforceable or because they had lost their usefulness. In 1771 the requirement that Taiwan settlers apply for permits to return to their native localities was dropped.[49] In 1783 the central Taiwan port of Lu-kang was officially opened to the cross-strait trade. Previously only Tainan's An-p'ing had been open to this trade. Lu-kang had for many years served as an illegal port of entry for immigrants seeking to avoid official entanglements. This opening of Lu-kang was accompanied by a reassertion of the importance of preventing secret crossings to other ports, including Pa-li-fen in Tan-shui.[50] Policy in these years followed the practices, already long established, of the immigrants.

After the calamitous Lin Shuang-wen rebellion of 1786–88, Governor-general Fu-k'ang-an further liberalized immigration policy. He noted that the growing populations of Fukien and Kwangtung produced many migrants seeking to earn livelihoods overseas. Once they settled abroad, they naturally sought to have their families join them. Even though Governor-general Yang had sought in 1760 to end the immigration of families to Taiwan permanently, their immigration had never been cut off. Attempts to prevent migration had resulted only in corruption and secret crossings. Fu-k'ang-an recommended that the families of respectable, settled residents of Taiwan be allowed to join them.[51] Permission to immigrate could also be given to those who had never lived in Taiwan and who wished to immigrate with their families. Vagrants who lacked families and property and who had committed crimes should be expelled and sent back to their native localities.[52]

Fu-k'ang-an also noted the sizable cross-strait shipping at Tan-shui's port of Pa-li-fen, even though it was not an official port. He found that local officials were being bribed to ignore exports of rice from this rice-growing region. He upgraded the military presence in Pa-li-fen and officially opened the port to the cross-strait trade.[53] In addition he created a number of posts to inspect ships in small harbors.

Permission was still officially required to make the crossing, and squeeze and the apprehension of secret crossers continued. Fu-k'ang-an sought to restrict the extortion of bribes and make official crossings more convenient than illegal private crossings.[54] In 1789 several officials were prosecuted for the extortion of bribes in the administration of Taiwan's ports.[55] The sizable amounts they allegedly extorted indicate both the extent of the corruption and the size of the illicit trade in Taiwan's ports. After 1790 the Ch'ing court no longer actively sought to interfere in cross-strait migration, although it reasserted the policy against secret crossings briefly in 1834 and 1838.

The complicated history of fluctuations in immigration policy reveals a Ch'ing government that lacked consistent direction and the ability to enforce its will. Its chief concern was to prevent Taiwan's becoming a rebel base. Yet, prohibitions on the migration of families instituted at the beginning of Ch'ing rule gave rise to an unstable society of migrant laborers. Some officials argued that these settlers could best be kept under control by keeping their families on the mainland. The family could be held responsible for a settler's infractions, and the settler would be dependent on the government for access to the mainland and his family. For officials such as Hao Yü-lin (in 1738–39) and Yang T'ing-chang (1760–61) active in restricting Han reclamation of aborigine lands, an important source of disturbance on the frontier was Han-aborigine conflict, and they pointed to rootless Chinese as the perpetrators. Restrictions on immigration kept down Chinese numbers and made control of the aborigine frontier easier.

Opposed to these conservative and control-oriented policies were officials influenced by Lan Ting-yüan. Lan advocated free, unrestricted migration and the aggressive opening of aborigine lands. For him the sources of Taiwan's troubles were the lack of families for migrants to care for and restrictions on the farming of aborigine wastelands (deer fields), which created vast bandit havens. Restricting family migration only prevented the stabilization of Taiwanese society. Other officials tried to have it both ways. In 1746 Governor-general Ma-erh-t'ai approved both a stringent set of regulations restricting Han reclamation of aborigine lands and Liu-shih-ch'i's proposal to allow the migration of immediate family members.

In these years the Ch'ing court never approved unrestricted migration. Each time migration won approval it was under the guise of the reunification of families of property owners and the "substantial" residents of Taiwan. Whatever its policy, the Ch'ing court had to work through officials whose private goals were as often satisfied by subverting official policy as by carrying it out. And it had to enforce its policy on a populace determined to escape poverty in its overpopulated home prefectures on the southeast coast.[56] Migrants who had immediate interests in earning livelihoods and raising families took little notice of official proclamations and preferred to avoid official contact. The Ch'ing state simply lacked the means to bring their movement to a halt.

Population Growth

In this section I critically evaluate previous estimates of Taiwan's population and develop a best-case reconstruction of population trends in Taiwan. The lack of statistics on immigration to Taiwan make it difficult to gauge the impact of fluctuations in official policies or of changing social conditions (whether on the southeast coast or in Taiwan itself). Several officials serving in Taiwan, such as Kao Shan, noted periods of rapid population growth, in Kao's case between 1730 and 1744. The expansion of registered farmland, the spreading area of colonization in Taiwan itself, and the population figures discussed below indicate substantial increases over the fewer than 80,000 Han who remained in Taiwan after the first year of Ch'ing rule (1683–84). The large population increases, the bulk of which resulted from illegal immigration, testify to the ultimate failure of the quarantine policy.

The growth of Taiwan's population in the eighteenth and early nineteenth centuries is documented by Ch'ing *pao chia* reports preserved in archives and gazetteers. Beginning in 1740, the Ch'ien-lung emperor directed that reports of population be regularly compiled through the *pao chia* organization. Based on a detailed examination of county-level data from annual registers, G. W. Skinner concluded that actual collection of household population information through the *pao chia* system occurred only in response to irregular expressions of imperial concern, after which annual reports were fabricated in yamen offices. Hence, we must evaluate each *pao chia* report according to the specific historical circumstances in which it was made.[57]

In 1756 the year-end memorial on Fukien's population and grain for the first time reports a separate total for Taiwan. This begins a series of Taiwan prefectural reports that continues to 1792. This 1756 memorial reports 84,611 households and 660,147 mouths in Taiwan, giving an average of 7.80 persons per household.[58] The preface to the memorial states that since the *pao chia* has been compiled for Taiwan prefecture, its population should be separately reported. Because previous year-end reports for Fukien did not report Taiwan's population separately, there is an implication that this report represents the first following an actual *pao chia* compilation. This does not appear to be the case, however. The figures reported for all of Fukien for the prior and succeeding years exhibit a regular pattern of increase, and no sudden spurt in 1756, as we might expect if Taiwan's population was being counted anew following a revitalization of its *pao chia* population reporting system. Nor have I identified specific memorials or edicts that would indicate that Taiwan's population-reporting system was being activated in these years, other than the 1756 memorial itself. The memorial appears merely to be recording a change in reporting format and not the addition of new Taiwan figures to the population registers.

The inclusion of migrants (*liu yü*, those who maintained a registration elsewhere) is crucial to the credibility of the 1756 Taiwan report, because Taiwan's population was growing primarily through immigration from the southeast coast. The 1756 report explicitly states that the Taiwan figures include locals (*t'u chu*, those with local registration), migrants (*liu yü*), and plains aborigines (*she fan*); this contrasts with the mainland Fukien figures, which are stated to include only locals. Indeed, the national directives of 1740 and after specifically provided that migrants be excluded from *pao chia* reports (though they were included in the registers) to avoid double counting.[59] But as an immigrant society, Taiwan was for good reason required to report both locals and immigrants. The requirement that migrants (*liu yü*) be enrolled in Taiwan's *pao chia* system dates from at least 1733 when, in the wake of the double revolt of 1731–32 and the opening of family migration, Governor-general Hao Yü-lin ordered the revitalization of the *pao chia* system and the following regulation was added to the Ch'ing Institutes relating to *pao chia*: "Among the residents of Fukien's Taiwan, migrants [*liu yü*] are many; of those who have property and parents, wives, and children, every ten families should have placards for inspection; anyone without a house and property, such as a tenant, laborer or trader, must be guaranteed by the proprietor [he works for], his [residential] landlord, or a neighbor and be added at the end of the [guarantor's] placard."[60] Thus, there can be little doubt that migrants were included as stated in the 1756 report of Taiwan's population.

Wang Yeh-chien's suggestion that the 1756 report understates Taiwan's population because it omits migrants (*liu yü*) must be rejected because it ignores both the explicit wording of the report and the facts of the *pao chia* institution as practiced in Taiwan. Wang's revision of Taiwan's population upward from 660,147 to 900,000–1,000,000 for 1750 is also misguided in its use of outdated and unreliable sources that exaggerate Taiwan's population during the Dutch and Cheng eras and faulty in assuming that Taiwan's percentage of Fukien's population was the same in 1829 (the 1829 figures are themselves highly questionable) as in 1750, when we know that Taiwan's population was growing by immigration from southern Fukien and thus should have been increasing as a percentage of the Fukien total throughout this period.[61]

A population of 1,000,000 by 1750 is implausible on other grounds. First, it conflicts with the report of 839,803 for 1777, which I consider relatively reliable (see below). Second, by estimating reasonable person/land ratios, we can see that a population of 1,000,000 would require a cultivated acreage greatly in excess of what could have been reclaimed by 1750. Third, estimating yields per hectare and total production gives us another means to check the plausibility of population and cultivated acreage data and confirms that Wang's estimate is too high.

Let us begin by estimating reasonable person/land ratios in Taiwan in 1750. By 1903 Taiwan had a Chinese population of approximately 2.9 million and a cultivated area of 534,157 hectares, 52 percent of which was paddy.[62] These figures give a 1903 ratio of 5.43 people per cultivated hectare. Perkins estimates that in 1770 China had a population of 270 million on a cultivated area of 63,333,333 hectares for a ratio of 4.263 persons per cultivated hectare.[63] It is reasonable to assume that Taiwan's frontier agriculture in the eighteenth century was less intensive (i.e., less labor was invested per unit of area) than it was by 1903; there was certainly a smaller proportion of paddy land in the eighteenth century. It is also plausible to assume that it was less intensive than the all-China average for 1770. I propose to estimate Taiwan's person/land ratio at 4.0 people per cultivated hectare in 1750.

We cannot plausibly reduce this figure much further, for traditional agricultural methods required intensive labor inputs, even on dry fields, and too low a ratio would rapidly induce serious labor shortages (although we may reasonably assume that Taiwan in 1750 had a higher proportion of adult males and a higher percentage of its work force in agriculture than it did in 1903, thereby reducing the labor shortage problems). Moreover, land, though perhaps readily available on the Taiwan frontier, was not a free good: it required investment of capital and labor before it could be brought into production.[64] This slowed the expansion of cultivated acreage.

A ratio of 4.0 people per cultivated hectare requires a cultivated area of 250,000 hectares for a population of 1,000,000 and 165,000 hectares for 660,000 people (1756 figure). Taiwan's registered farmland of 63,045 *chia* in 1762 (the close equivalence of *chia* to hectare [0.97] allows us to ignore the problem of converting *chia* to hectares) was generally estimated to reflect no more than half the reclaimed area, which we can thus estimate at at least 126,000 *chia* (see Table 6.5 and Chapter 8 below).[65] (About 27 percent of the registered land was classified as paddy in 1762.) A cultivated area of 250,000 *chia* is implausible on two counts. First, it is twice the estimated reclaimed area in Taiwan. Second, it is nearly half the cultivated area of 534,000 hectares in 1903, when the population was at least three times that of 1750 (even accepting the highest population estimate) and an additional century and a half of reclamation had taken place.[66]

For a population of 660,000, the 4.0 ratio produces a crude estimate of 165,000 hectares, which is much closer to the 1762 estimated reclaimed area of 126,000 hectares. Is this population and cultivated acreage sufficient for Taiwan to have produced the large sugar and rice exports estimated for 1750 as well as subsistence needs? Or would a population of 1,000,000 be necessary to produce these amounts? We can use estimates of yield per hectare and total production to test further the plausibility of the two competing population figures (see Table 6.3).

Taiwan's fields (aggregating dry and paddy lands) produced approximately 1.3 metric tons (MT) of milled rice per hectare circa 1903.[67] I shall assume that the 4.0 ratio could have produced per hectare yields approximating those produced by the higher 5.43 persons/hectare ratio of 1903 because of the higher proportion of adult males in the population in 1750 and the high natural fertility of newly reclaimed land, despite the lower proportion of higher-yield irrigated land in 1750. These are crude assumptions, but using yield estimates that may be high makes higher population estimates more plausible by reducing the area necessary to support them.

Another problem complicates our use of yield estimates from the early twentieth century. Dwight Perkins argues that yields increased substantially during the Ch'ing by assuming that per capita grain output did not change and that rising yields made up for the shrinking cultivated area per person.[68] Perkins's argument suggests that 1903 yields should be higher than those of circa 1750; indeed, this should be the case if only because of a gradually increasing proportion of irrigated area. Because historical data on yields before 1900 are both rare and hard to evaluate, I finesse the problem by using a range of low to high yields, from 1.0 to 1.3 MT of milled rice per hectare, for the aggregated area of paddy and dry farmland circa 1750. My estimates of rice yield closely approximate eighteenth-century reports of yields on Taiwan's low-grade paddy of 1.2 MT of milled rice per hectare,[69] and the 1.2–1.3 MT per hectare yield produced by the 4.263 persons/land ratio estimated by Perkins for China in 1770.[70] As we see below, a population of 1,000,000 by 1750 requires too large a cultivated area whether the higher or lower yield is chosen.

We need next to estimate total amounts of production in order to estimate cultivated acreage. Estimates of annual per capita consumption of milled rice range from a high of 203 kg by Wang Yeh-chien to a low of 133.7 kg by Samuel Ho; I propose to use the average of these estimates, or 168 kg of milled rice per capita per annum.[71] A population of 1,000,000 would consume 168,000 MT of milled rice annually, which, given our assumptions about yield per hectare, would require 129,231 to 168,000 hectares to produce. A population of 660,000 would consume 110,880 MT of milled rice, which would require 85,292 to 110,880 hectares to produce. With respect to rice exports, Wang Yeh-chien and Ng Chin-keong[72] accept as plausible a 1742 estimate that Taiwan was exporting at least 800,000 *shih* of unhulled rice or 400,000 *shih* of milled rice annually.[73] This equals 33,124 MT of milled rice (1 *shih* of milled rice equals 138.75 catties or 82.81 kg).[74] Assuming Taiwan's fields (dry and paddy) produced an average of 1.0 to 1.3 MT of milled rice per hectare, then 25,480 to 33,124 hectares would be needed to produce the amount of rice exported.

Taiwan's substantial sugar exports must also be factored into cultivated area estimates. Ng estimates that Taiwan exported 60–100 million catties of sugar a year by the 1720's. One hundred million catties equals 59,682 MT of sugar.[75] Assuming Taiwan's fields produced 1.5–2.0 MT of sugar per hectare as they did circa 1900 before the Japanese introduced new varieties of cane,[76] then 29,841–39,788 hectares would be needed to produce 100 million catties of sugar for export.[77] Domestic sugar consumption required at most 3,000 hectares to satisfy, an amount too small to affect our cultivated acreage estimates.[78]

Sweet potatoes are Taiwan's third major food crop. Rice, sugarcane, and sweet potatoes accounted for over 80 percent of the total crop area circa 1910, and it is likely that this pattern held for 1750 as well.[79] To

TABLE 6.3

Production, Yield, and Cultivated Area in Taiwan, ca. 1750

	Production (MT)	Yield (MT/ha)	Cultivated area (ha)
Rice consumption			
660,000 pop.	110,880	1.0–1.3	85,292–110,880
1,000,000 pop.	168,000	1.0–1.3	129,231–168,000
Sugar exports	59,682	1.5–2.0	29,841–39,788
Rice exports	33,124	1.0–1.3	25,480–33,124
Sweet potatoes			
660,000 pop.	138,600	6.837	20,272
1,000,000 pop.	210,000	6.837	30,715
Total cultivated area			
660,000 pop.			160,885–204,064
1,000,000 pop.			215,267–271,627

estimate the cultivated area planted to sweet potatoes circa 1750, I use the per capita production and yield figures from 1901–10. Sweet potatoes contributed importantly to both human and animal diets in Taiwan, and production figures (rather than consumption figures) will estimate the contribution to all uses of the sweet potato crop. In 1901–10 sweet potato production averaged 616,078 MT per year, and yields averaged 6.837 MT per hectare.[80] If we divide production by the total Taiwanese population (1905 census) of 2,973,280, average per capita production is 0.21 MT of sweet potatoes. At this rate, a population circa 1750 of 1,000,000 would produce 210,000 MT on 30,715 hectares, and a population of 660,000 would produce 138,600 MT on 20,272 hectares.

The total acreage necessary to produce these production, consumption, and export amounts is shown in Table 6.3. These figures show that a population of 660,000 and an estimated cultivated acreage of 165,000 hectares (based on the 4.0 person/land ratio) could have produced the estimated exports, whereas a population of 1,000,000 requires too great a reclaimed acreage by 1750 to be plausible. Nor do the export estimates put any great strain on the acreage figures for a population of 660,000; these show that only 23 percent of total rice production was needed to meet the amount of rice exported. Thus, because the 1756 *pao chia* report comes from a period of imperial concern about population reporting, because it includes immigrants as well as locals, because it "fits" the cultivated acreage data, and because it is consistent with the reported population of 1777 (see below), I consider the 1756 report of 660,147 to be a reasonable estimate of Taiwan's population at this time.

The years 1775–79 were another period of imperial concern for the reliability of *pao chia* population reports. To improve the accuracy of population reports, in 1775 the Ch'ien-lung emperor ordered that migrant households be included in the reported population nationwide.[81] In response, the provinces produced more comprehensive population reports beginning with the year-end reports for 1775. From 1773 to 1777 Fukien's reported population increased by 41 percent, and Taiwan's reported population increased a considerable, but much smaller, 9.67 percent.[82] Taiwan's gain was much less because, unlike mainland Fukien, migrant households were not being counted for the first time. (The inclusion of immigrants in the 1756 report of Taiwan's population is thus indirectly confirmed by the reports from the late 1770's.) The Fukien provincial regulations include provincial memorials discussing the details of *pao chia* census work in Fukien during 1776, thereby confirming that population reporting was being taken seriously in these years.[83] Thus, the 1777 figure of 839,803 for Taiwan's population can be accepted as comparatively reliable.

No reliable reports of Taiwan's population between 1777 and 1893 have yet been identified. The population undoubtedly declined temporarily after the destruction and slaughter that came with the Lin Shuang-wen rebellion of 1786–88, but these events were not reflected in contemporary population reports. Instead, the reports continued to show regular annual increases, an indication of yamen fabrication. A gap in provincial population reports held by the palace archives for the Chia-ch'ing years is especially crippling to attempts to evaluate the few reports found in the gazetteers. The widely cited report in the *Fu-chien t'ung chih* attributing a population of 1,901,833 to Taiwan in 1811 is demographically implausible on three counts: (1) for its overall size in light of an 1893 population of only 2,545,731, (2) for the enormous average household sizes reported for certain counties, and (3) for the wildly unbalanced distribution of the population between adults and minors in certain counties. The numbers in this report bear all the marks of yamen fabrication rather than an actual *pao chia* count. The *Fu-chien t'ung chih* figure can also be rejected because it is inconsistent with the later figure of 1,786,883 given for Taiwan in the *Chia-ch'ing i t'ung chih*. This number can now be dated to 1824, since the population reported for mainland Fukien in the national registers for 1824 matches that given in the *Chia-ch'ing i t'ung chih*.[84] The lower figure in the *Chia-ch'ing i t'ung chih* suggests that the higher number attributed to Taiwan in 1811 by the *Fu-chien t'ung chih* is anomalous.[85] The 1824 total also appears to be the product of yamen fabrication, however; I know of no independent evidence suggesting that any *pao chia* work was done in Taiwan in these years. Nevertheless, I include the 1824 total in brackets in Table 6.4 because it is somewhat more plausible than the spurious 1811 figure (though still too high) and because it reflects what the reporting system was saying about Taiwan in these years.

The 1893 figure of 2,545,731 is the result of the *pao chia* work initiated by Liu Ming-ch'uan in his efforts to reform Taiwan's fiscal structure.

TABLE 6.4
The Population of Taiwan, 1660–1915
(including plains aborigines and Han, but excluding mountain aborigines)

Year	Population	Annual growth rate[a] (percent)	Interval (years)	Increase during interval
1660[b]	100,000			
		2.33	23	70,000
1683[c]	170,000			
		−23.53	1	−40,000
1684[d]	130,000			
		2.28	72	530,147
1756[e]	660,147			
		1.15	21	179,656
1777[f]	839,803			
		[1.62]	47	947,080
1824[g]	[1,786,883]			
		[0.51]	69	758,848
1893[h]	2,545,731			
		1.30	12	427,549
1905[i]	2,973,280			
		1.12	10	352,475
1915[i]	3,325,755			

[a]Annual rates of growth are calculated using the (compound interest) formula $P_n = P_0(r)^n$, in which P_0 = beginning population at year 0; P_n = population at year n; r = the annual rate of growth (in the formula a 2 percent rate of growth is expressed as 1.02).

[b]This reflects a *maximum* of 50,000 Han and 50,000 plains aborigines at the end of the Dutch period. The true Han population is most likely to have been nearer 35,000 (see Chapter 3). To make the 1660–84 figures comparable to those of later years, plains aborigines have been included (at a constant rate of 50,000; see Chapter 2).

[c]This reflects a *maximum* of 120,000 Han and 50,000 plains aborigines during the Cheng era. Because of warfare and the movement of troops, the Han population in 1683 is likely to have been below this high point (see Chapter 4).

[d]This reflects a *maximum* of 80,000 Han and 50,000 plains aborigines (see Chapter 5 and note c above).

[e]*KCTCL*: 16.102–3 (CL 21.11.16). [f]*KCTCL*: 40.818–19 (CL 42.11.12). [g]*CITCTWF*: 6.

[h]Ch'en Shao-hsing 1964: 161–62.

[i]Barclay 1954: 13. The 1905 figure includes 46,432 plains aborigines, 36,363 mountain aborigines from T'ai-tung (mostly plains dwelling Ami and Puyuma under Japanese control), 2,492,784 Hokkien, 397,195 Hakka, and a small number of Chinese from other localities (*Meiji sanchū hachi nen rinji kokō chōsa: kekkahyo* 1908: 8). In 1935 a comprehensive enumeration of Taiwan's mountain aborigines yielded a total of 150,088 (*KCK* 1935: table 4).

This figure agrees closely with a Japanese survey conducted in 1896 and can be accepted as a reliable indicator of the population.[86] The 1905 and 1915 population figures are the results of modern censuses that give Taiwan some of the best demographic data in the world.[87] The apparent high rate of growth between 1893 and 1905 undoubtedly reflects under-enumeration in 1893, corrected by the exhaustive census work in 1905.

The high rates of population growth in the first half of the eighteenth century reflect heavy immigration into Taiwan and document the failure of the quarantine policies. Assuming that the population grew steadily at the rate computed for the 1684–1756 period in Table 6.4, Taiwan's population would have reached 187,000 circa 1700, 315,000 circa 1723, and

415,000 by the end of the Yung-cheng reign in 1735. In fact, the qualitative evidence cited in the other sections of this chapter suggests a rather slower recovery up to 1710 or so and then an even faster rate of growth, especially during the later Yung-cheng years.

Table 6.4 indicates a slower rate of growth in the last half of the eighteenth century than do previous studies that assumed a count of 1,901,833 by 1811. Similarly, my reconstruction of Taiwan's population growth indicates substantial growth during the nineteenth century, necessary to span the decrease caused by the Lin Shuang-wen rebellion and the 1893 total of 2,545,731. The nineteenth century experienced lower rates of growth than the eighteenth, but since these built on a larger population base, absolute growth was substantial. In the nineteenth century the contribution to population growth of the natural increase of a sexually more balanced population became increasingly more important compared to the contribution made by immigration.

The excessiveness of the 1824 figure is shown by the improbably high rate of growth from 1777 to 1824 of 1.62 percent (which would have to be even higher to make up for the population loss during the Lin Shuang-wen rebellion) and the implausibly low rate of growth of 0.51 percent from 1824 to 1893. If we ignore the unreliable 1824 report, the growth rate during the 116 years from 1777 to 1893, during which time the population of Taiwan more than tripled, is 0.96 percent. This is much more consistent with the rates before and after that period. A more plausible total for 1824 can be constructed by assuming the population grew at the same rate from 1824 to 1905 as it did from 1905 to 1915 (1.12 percent). This yields a backprojected figure of 1,206,248 for 1824, and a growth rate of 0.77 percent for 1777 to 1824. The 1905–15 growth rate is only a rough proxy for nineteenth-century population growth; any increase in this rate due to falling mortality rates resulting from the public health efforts of the Japanese is offset by the termination of migration from Fukien. If we assume a growth rate of only 1.0 percent from 1824 to 1905, the backprojected population for 1824 comes to 1,328,069, and the growth rate for 1777–1824 is 0.98 percent.

The exercise of testing the population and cultivated acreage figures for the mid-eighteenth century has resulted in generally plausible and internally consistent figures. The rapid pace of population growth they show for the eighteenth century is consistent with the pattern of economic development and spreading settlement documented in the following sections.

The Emergence of a Rice and Sugar Export Economy

The substantial depopulation of Taiwan in the first years of Ch'ing rule as Chinese refugees and soldiers returned to their native localities on the mainland caused an economic depression in Taiwan. In a memorial of the ninth month of 1684, Shih Lang expressed concern about Taiwan's declining population, its insufficient tax revenue, and the uncertain future of its trade in sugar and deerskins.[88] A report of 1688 lamented the decline of the cross-strait trade: "Formerly Taiwan was very prosperous and Chinese settlers had to be counted in the tens of thousands, but since the beginning of Ch'ing rule, the settlers have returned to Ch'üan-chou, Chang-chou, and Amoy so that now there are only several thousand. Because of this, the current production of sugar and deer hides does not amount to a tenth of its former level."[89]

Economic recovery was not long in coming. In 1695 the military intendant Kao Kung-ch'ien noted that because sugar fetched higher prices than rice in the cross-strait trade, sugar production had increased three times the year before and ten times in the current year. This was of concern to Kao for two reasons. A glut of sugar would lead to ruinously low prices. But more important, it would have an adverse effect on rice production. Both Taiwan's population and the military units stationed there depended on the locally produced rice. There was only one harvest a year (irrigation and double cropping were not yet well developed), and due to bad weather and locusts only five in ten harvests were good. In years of bountiful harvests sugar could be traded for grain, but in bad years underproduction of rice made famine unavoidable. Kao complained, "For every man sent to the cane fields there is one less man working in the paddy fields; for every additional acre of sugarcane there is one less acre of rice." Kao urged Taiwan's farmers to concentrate on producing rice surpluses to be stored against the possibility of famine. To give force to his arguments, he called for a cadastral survey of the cane fields and their entry on the tax rolls, in an apparent attempt to reduce the profitability of sugarcane production compared to rice production.[90]

Kao's essay shows that Taiwan's colonial agriculture was highly commercialized, dependent on mainland markets, and responsive to price fluctuations there. Kao also expresses the same official concern to protect Taiwan's food supply (so the disorder resulting from shortages could be avoided) that we first saw formulated in the quarantine policies of 1684. Despite Kao's efforts, Yü Yung-ho found the sugar trade still flourishing in 1697.[91] Ng Chin-keong estimates that by the 1720's Taiwan was producing more than 60 million catties of sugar a year, requiring 500–700 junks to carry it to Amoy, where it was transshipped to northern markets such as Soochow.[92]

Taiwan's growing ability to produce rice surpluses, in addition to sugar, near the populous southeast coast with its growing demand for rice posed a serious challenge to Ch'ing quarantine policies. In 1693 a shortage along the Fukien coast caused merchants to "flock" to transport Taiwan's sizable rice harvest to Fukien. Thereafter, whenever shortages led to high prices in Fukien, government patrol boats, in addition to merchants, smuggled rice across the strait.[93] To the government, prevention of food riots and famine on the Fukien coast was preferable to enforcement of the quarantine. From 1702 to 1711, however, Taiwan suffered from a series of bad harvests and high rice prices. Taxes were forgiven in several of these years, and from 1708 to 1710 the government had to make relief sales from its granaries. As a result, in 1711 the government reasserted the prohibition on rice exports and called for stricter enforcement of measures against smuggling (and illegal immigration, see above).[94] Nevertheless, illegal exports continued in years when Taiwan enjoyed bountiful harvests. As early as 1712 Governor-general Gioro Man-pao memorialized in favor of permitting the sale of Taiwan's surplus rice to reduce shortages on the mainland.[95] The prohibition against smuggling Taiwan rice had to be asserted once again as part of the late K'ang-hsi attempts in 1717 to reimpose the ban on maritime trade (motivated in part by a fear that Chinese rice was being exported to Southeast Asia) and to tighten administrative discipline.[96]

As it had in the case of immigration policy, the Chu I-kuei rebellion of 1721 (which reawakened fears that Taiwan might become a rebel base) brought in its wake official debates on rice export policy. Most participants advocated rice export policies consistent with their approaches to immigration policy, lining up in favor of either strict regulation or more laissez-faire, pro-colonization (and pro-export) policies. Censor Huang Shu-ching worried that exports would boost prices in Taiwan and that exported rice would fall into pirates' hands. Impressed, however, by Taiwan's rice surpluses, Huang proposed an exception for famine relief. Thus in 1723 and 1724 Taiwan sent sizable shipments of rice to relieve a famine in Chekiang.[97]

The outlook for Taiwan's rice production was so good that in 1725 it was decided to make regular shipments to mainland Fukien of portions of Taiwan's tax rice, and later officially purchased rice, to provide relief and to provision troops and their dependents (sometimes as part of their salary, sometimes at lower-than-market prices). Previously Taiwan's tax rice had supplied only troops stationed in Taiwan and the Pescadores, and surpluses had been collected in government granaries. Harvests had grown substantially since the days when Shih Lang first arrived and had to import his troops' provisions. These government exports helped relieve pressure on rice-short southern Fukien, where the Ch'ing garrisoned a large military force.[98] These amounts were increased several times in the next years.[99] To ensure rice harvests adequate to these needs, the Yung-cheng government adopted policies that encouraged the reclamation of new farmlands; for example, it approved the renting of aborigine lands and lowered land taxes on newly opened land (see below).

In 1726 Governor-general Kao Ch'i-cho gave four reasons for easing restrictions on *private* exports of Taiwan's rice (restrictions undermined by bribe-taking officials): (1) exports from Taiwan would relieve shortages in Ch'üan-chou and Chang-chou prefectures; (2) Taiwan's populace, rather than suffering from the useless accumulation of a rice surplus, would benefit from its sale, and as a result land under cultivation would increase; (3) people on both sides of the strait could avoid the squeeze extorted by officials on illegally exported rice; and (4) Ch'üan-chou and Chang-chou would not need to import rice from Foochow, thereby easing supply pressures there.[100] Kao proposed that in years when Taiwan's harvests were bountiful, restrictions on rice exports be lifted, but that they be maintained in years of poor harvests and rising prices. Merchant ships seeking to export Taiwan rice were to be licensed, guaranteed, and inspected on both sides of the strait to ensure that none of the shipments went to pirates.

Kao prefaced his argument by claiming great prosperity for Taiwan: "Taiwan's land is broad and its people few, the rice it produces in one bountiful harvest is sufficient to supply its needs for four or five years. The people industriously cultivate the land to supply their own needs and to sell rice for cash."[101] Kao also advocated loosening restrictions on immigration, but he refrained from arguing that a larger population would produce a greater surplus for export. He does, however, link expanded reclamation of land to increased exports. Strong demand and high prices for rice on the southeast coast in these years meant that sugar was no longer Taiwan's most profitable crop; high rice prices were stimulating not only reclamation but also investment (often of profits made in the sugar trade) in the irrigation facilities necessary to produce rice crops reliably.[102] Kao's rhetoric undoubtedly exaggerates the size of Taiwan's rice surplus, but price data make it clear that Taiwan had an abundance of rice available for export.[103] Since Fukien in late 1726 was near famine and Taiwan's rice provided important relief, Kao's opportune proposals were adopted by the court.[104] Kao also won court approval at this time for his proposal to reopen Fukien ports to the import of Southeast Asian rice and allow Fukien merchants to trade in Southeast Asia.[105] Yung-cheng was wary of creating a dependency on imported rice, but this was preferable to excessive exports causing shortages in Taiwan, where his own government needed to maintain control.

Price data compiled by Ng Chin-keong and Wang Yeh-chien show that between 1723 and 1756 rice prices rose generally and that prices in Ch'üan-chou (Taiwan's major market) remained above those in Taiwan. Rising prices and the higher prices in Ch'üan-chou made rice farming and exporting profitable in Taiwan. For the period 1723–34, the low December (post-harvest) market price of rice in Taiwan averaged 1 tael per *shih* of husked rice, compared to an average December price in Ch'üan-chou of 1.13 taels.[106] By the period 1745–56, the average December price in Taiwan had risen to 1.4 taels per *shih* of husked rice, and the average price in Ch'üan-chou to 1.67 taels.[107] Hence, rice farming and exporting received a constant stimulus from rising prices during these years.

Although rice surpluses were growing steadily with expanding colonization and high rice prices were stimulating reclamation, Taiwan itself was not immune to shortages. Natural disasters and undeveloped irrigation and land transportation facilities contributed to fluctuations in grain supplies and prices.[108] A series of bad harvests early in the Ch'ien-lung reign (from 1735 to 1738) saw Taiwan's tax payments fall into arrears; for several years taxes were forgiven. In 1741 Taiwan's rice prices climbed so high the government stepped in to stabilize prices; 60,000 *shih* had to be borrowed from Ch'ao-chou granaries to be sold at an officially set price below market levels (*p'ing t'iao*).[109]

Excessive exports, by both the government and private merchants, appear to have driven prices even higher in 1741. Officials estimated that nearly half the rice Taiwan produced was exported. The censors sent to investigate in 1742 warned that grain movements must be made in accordance with harvest conditions and ordered that Taiwan's reserves be ensured before exports were allowed. The quota of government relief grain sent to Fukien (set in 1731 at 120,000 *shih*) was also reduced by over 40 percent in 1741. The same officials warned that although Taiwan was a rice-producing region, its population was increasing faster than cultivated land.[110] Between 1741 and 1744 various officials wrote memorials emphasizing the importance of stabilizing prices in Taiwan and ensuring sufficient stores in Taiwan's granaries before allowing grain to be purchased for the mainland.[111]

These imbalances in rice supplies and prices seem to have been only temporary, but the cautiousness of the early Ch'ien-lung reign is evident. By the 1750's the government had sharply reduced its Taiwan relief-grain quota. In part this was because of abundant supplies of cheaper Southeast Asian rice.[112] But it is also possible that Taiwan's population had increased so much, as the censors argued, that it was consuming more locally and had less to export.[113] Nevertheless, the absolute size of Taiwan's rice exports in the mid-eighteenth century was substantial.[114]

In 1743, only two years after the crisis of 1741, the court approved giving licenses for the export, to Chang-chou and Ch'üan-chou, of rice collected as rents in Taiwan, apparently in response to the bad harvests in coastal Fukien that year. The granting of export licenses meant that investors in reclamation projects could be ensured of profits by selling their rental income in the lucrative Fukien market. Unauthorized rice shipments by merchants and shipments when Taiwan's harvest was poor or rice prices high continued to be prohibited.[115] In 1748, again in response to shortages and high prices in Fukien, the legal rice-export load of 60 *shih* per ship was raised, eventually, to 200 *shih*. Inspectors overlooked loads above this limit in return for "customary fees" collected on a graduated scale.[116] The Ch'ien-lung government thus facilitated private exports of rice while cutting its own requisitions of relief grain. In Taiwan government requisitioning of relief grain at below-market prices was an irritant best eliminated, especially when the government failed to pay transport costs.[117] Since rice prices remained high on the mainland throughout the rest of the Ch'ien-lung reign, the government generally favored rice imports, especially from Southeast Asia, but also from Taiwan.[118] Despite the competition from cheaper Thai rice, and later sugar as well, Taiwan continued throughout the period to export sizable amounts of both products.[119]

Thus, from the early years of Ch'ing rule, Taiwan developed an important role as grain supplier to the chronically rice-deficient Fukien coast, in addition to its role as outlet for Fukien's burgeoning population.[120] Ng's study of the Amoy trading network shows that Taiwan's rice and sugar exports constituted a large proportion of the Amoy coastal trade and played a critical role in the development of the regional economy of the southeast coast in the early eighteenth century.[121] The emergence of a rice and sugar export economy on Taiwan despite the government's attempts to restrict the cross-strait trade, prohibit family immigration, and limit the reclamation of aborigine lands testifies to the powerful economic stimuli at work in the densely populated but productive southeast coast. No group in the arena of southeast coast policy formation had the interest or the power to enforce the quarantine policies against these economic pressures and opportunities.

The Ch'ing government, acutely aware that rice shortages could lead to disorder, required officials to move quickly to relieve them. The argument that rice surpluses from Taiwan could be used to supply the chronically deficit southeast coast was one of the strongest in the arsenal of advocates of expanded reclamation of aborigine lands in Taiwan. The government itself, by allotting large amounts of Taiwan's tax grain to its Fukien armies, had a vested interest in the maintenance of these surpluses.[122] And local officials, under pressure to fill tax quotas, encouraged (and winked at illegal) reclamation, knowing that increased rice production made filling tax quotas easier.

Taiwan's settler population had a private interest in this export trade as well. The strong demand for Taiwan's surplus rice and sugar meant good prices for farmers. And under these conditions, the small size of the Chinese population meant that labor could demand high wages.[123] These favorable prices and wages were an important factor in making immigration and the hardships of frontier settlement attractive to the land-hungry and commercially oriented people of China's southeast coast. Migrants were "pulled" as well as "pushed" to Taiwan. In the area of producing and exporting rice surpluses, more frequently than in any other policy area we will discuss, the government and the settlers were working toward the same goal rather than at cross-purposes.

The Spread of Han Settlements and Markets

Weak and fluctuating enforcement of restrictions on immigration and the strong economic attractions of the Taiwan frontier led to a growing Chinese population and an expanding area of Chinese settlement. The Chinese monopoly traders, who figured prominently in the early economic penetration of Taiwan's aboriginal societies, were the pioneers of Chinese settlement. Following them closely came land-hungry Chinese farmers. In general, the area of Chinese settlement spread out from the Tainan core, south toward Feng-shan and north toward Chu-lo. Settlement was not continuous, however. Traders and craftsmen concentrated in coastal market towns, and fishermen and salt producers exploited resources along the coast. Farmers clustered in areas that were best suited for agriculture, easily cleared or irrigated, accessible to transport and markets, not subject to prior claims of plains aborigine agriculturalists, and easily defended. Lumbermen and traders in mountain products gravitated toward the hills. In the slack season many farmers went into the hills to cut lumber, which they then transported to Tainan for export. Settlements of Hakka, who brought from their home districts skills in mountain industries, were most numerous in the more remote areas, north of Chu-lo and in Feng-shan beyond the lower Tan-shui river. Only later did farmers fill in the gaps and push east toward the mountains and west toward coastal wastelands.[124] (See Chapter 10 for the spatial segregation of immigrants by provenance and speech group.)

Farmers grew sugarcane in more easily opened dry fields, both in the older area around Tainan and in the newly reclaimed areas of Feng-shan and Chu-lo. Rice became more important when prices rose and irrigation facilities had been constructed. Around Tainan, the natural fertility of the soil was exhausted early, and costly fertilizers had to be applied. Virgin lands, however, were fertile and produced good harvests in the first three years of cultivation even without fertilizer.[125] Much of this land was then left fallow, and new land reclaimed.[126] This shifting pattern of cultivation propelled settlement outward independent of population growth. Dry fields outnumbered irrigated ones, which increased only gradually, since the construction of irrigation works took time and capital. After sugar, the major dry land crops were wheat, barley, and sweet potatoes, all important supplements to rice.[127] The large numbers of domestic animals and the abundance of ox-drawn carts impressed mainland observers[128] and indicate the extensive nature of early frontier settlement and agriculture, compared to the intensive agriculture of the

TABLE 6.5
Land Registered for Taxation in Taiwan by County, 1684–1903
(in *chia*)[a]

Year	Taiwan total	Feng-shan	T'ai-wan	Chu-lo	Chang-hua	Tan-shui
1684[b]	18,454	5,048	8,562	4,844	—	—
	41%	53%	45%	20%	—	—
1693[b]	26,460	7,249	10,345	8,866	—	—
	34%	46%	42%	15%	—	—
1710[c]	30,110	8,731*	10,558	10,821	—	—
	30%	40%	41%	12%	—	—
1735[d]	50,517	10,944	12,244	15,109	11,665	555
	28%	33%	38%	11%	34%	39%
1744[e]	52,851*	10,960	12,004*	15,038	13,030	1,819
	28%	33%	39%	11%	35%	29%
1762[f]	63,045*	12,091	11,994	15,352	18,794	4,814
	27%	34%	37%	10%	22%	51%
1781[g]	—	—	12,146	—	21,405	7,562
	—	—	38%	—	26%	66%
1895[h]	361,417					
1903[i]	534,157					

*Arithmetic total calculated when subtotals do not add to the total reported in the gazetteer.

[a]The percentages below each number give the proportion of land registered as paddy land (*t'ien*). The Pescadores are excluded.

[b]*TWFC*:Kao: 114–26. [c]*TWFC*:Chou: 155–72. [d]*TWFC*:Liu: 138–62. [e]*TWFC*:Fan: 143–67.

[f]*TWFC*:Yü: 191–221.

[g]*HHTWHC*: 75–76 (figures for 1775); *CHHC*: 165–69 (figures for 1781); *TSTC*: 91–93 (figures for 1778).

[h]The cadastral surveys initiated in 1886 by Liu Ming-ch'uan raised the registered area to 290,000 *chia*; by 1895–97 the area had grown to 361,000 *chia* (Ch'en Shao-hsing 1964: 137; Myers 1974: 456).

[i]JCRR: 11; S. C. Hsieh and T. H. Lee 1966: 49; this is the cultivated area, of which 52 percent was paddy (28 percent of the total was irrigated and drained). The increment over 1895 is the result of the Japanese colonial cadastral survey, not reclamation, and shows how much could be concealed from even a large-scale survey.

crowded southeast coast. The abundance of resources per capita on the frontier was soon diminished by continued migration and population growth. Under these circumstances the available agricultural technologies offering the biggest productivity gains were those that were land-saving (e.g., irrigation investment) rather than labor-saving, and agriculture proceeded to intensify.[129]

The increasing amounts of land entered on the tax registers reflect the spread of Han reclamation as well as government tax collectors (see Table 6.5). Registered areas grew fastest outside the southwest core in T'ai-wan county, in the frontier areas. The gains in Chang-hua to the north are especially impressive. (Note that gazetteers report only the area registered for taxation; it is mistaken to imagine that Ch'ing land statistics report "cultivated area.") Despite investment in irrigation and the expansion of irrigated acreage,[130] the statistics on registered area show in this period a decline in the percentage of irrigated area. This reflects only the relative failure of the fiscal system to register land in the higher tax-rate categories.[131]

In 1697 the traveler Yü Yung-ho claimed there were only tribal villages and no Han settlements in Chu-lo. This changed as immigration increased rapidly in the next years.[132] By 1704, when the Chu-lo county yamen was moved from Chia-li-hsing to Chu-lo, settlers were beginning to spread north of Tou-liu-men (in present-day Yün-lin county), the site of the Ch'ai-li tribe. The Chu-lo gazetteer of 1717 reported that deer were disappearing in that region as settlers transformed hunting grounds into cultivated fields.[133]

From 1710 to 1717, the majority of new settlers went to the area around Chang-hua (Pan-hsien); some even penetrated north of the Ta-tu river. But plains aborigines in the Ta-chia area were resisting Chinese reclamation, and the government attempted to restrict the spread of settlement to keep settlers within reach of its control.[134] Increasing numbers were settling north of the Ta-chia area, at points such as Chu-ch'ien (Hsin-chu) and Nan-k'an (near Taipei) where military posts had recently been established.[135] In 1697 Yü Yung-ho recorded that in traveling the 80-odd *li* from Chu-ch'ien to Nan-k'an he had not seen a single person or homestead, Han or aborigine, though he did find many wild oxen. Much the same situation existed twenty years later in 1717 when the Chu-lo county gazetteer reports that travelers were rare along that route, which was "silent, without the smoke of cooking fires," and void of villages.[136] Settlers, in their push northward, were skipping over the dry, windswept T'ao-yüan plain for the more favored hills and valleys around the Taipei basin. Although the Chu-lo gazetteer reports for the Tan-shui area only aborigine tribes (*she*) and no Han settlements (*chuang*), it does mention Han settlers in the area. Chinese agricultural settlement had already begun; Taipei's earliest extant land patent is dated 1709.[137] No mention is made in any of these sources of the Chinese settlements in the Tan-shui area reported for the Dutch and Cheng eras; I suspect they were depleted by the repatriation at the beginning of Ch'ing rule. Substantial Chinese settlement in Taipei would not come until the Yung-cheng and early Ch'ien-lung eras (1723–1768).

The increases in registered land area shown in Table 6.5 reflect both the spread of settlement and government campaigns to register newly reclaimed land for taxation. For Taiwan as a whole, the registered area did not recover the Cheng-era level until 1710 (see also Table 8.3). Registered area increased most dramatically (68 percent) in the interval from 1710 to the end of the Yung-cheng era in 1735, due to the serious effort during the Yung-cheng reign to register newly reclaimed land (see Chapter 8). Before 1710 the great bulk of the increases took place in the frontier counties of Feng-shan and Chu-lo; after 1710 Chu-lo and its progeny, Chang-hua and Tan-shui, accounted for nearly all the increase.

As noted above, officials serving in Taiwan observed large population increases after the eight years of legalized family immigration, 1732–40.

TABLE 6.6
Markets and Population in Taiwan by County, 1694–1768

Year	Feng-shan	T'ai-wan	Chu-lo	Chang-hua	Tan-shui
			No. of markets		
1694[a]	3	17	1	0	0
1740[b]	11	24	16	9	2
1768[c]	16	52	42	19	8
			Population		
1761–64	123,237[d]	—	307,389[e]	—	30,342[f]
			Population/market		
1761–68	7,702	—	7,319	—	3,793

[a]*TWFC*: Kao: 46–48. [b]*TWFC*:Liu: 83–85.
[c]*TWFC*:Yü: 84–90. The Chang-hua county gazetteer (*CHHC*: 39–42) listed over 50 markets in 1830.
[d]*CHFSHC*: 107 (1763 data). [e]*TWFC*:Yü: 251 (1761 data). [f]Ibid.: 252 (1764 data).

The local gazetteers reflect this growth in their listings of village settlements, which show large increases in the frontier regions of Chang-hua and Tan-shui. The number of villages in Chang-hua grew from 1 in 1717 to 110 in 1740 to 132 in 1768.[138] The number of villages in Tan-shui subprefecture went from 0 in 1717 to 35 by 1740 to 132 by 1768.[139] The village lists also give a crude measure of the impact of the spread of Chinese settlement on aborigine villages. In 1717 only 8 of the 76 northern plains aborigine villages were also sites of Han settlements. By 1740 and 1768, respectively, 30 and 45 sites accommodated both aborigines and Han.[140]

Lists of markets can be used to document the spread of both Han settlement and trade (see Table 6.6).[141] The market lists in the prefectural gazetteers are generally comparable both across time and among the counties and show interesting regional trends. Between 1694 and 1740, T'ai-wan county gained 7 markets, whereas the frontier areas to the north and south gained 34. In this period the dominant trend was a rapid outward spread of population. In Chang-hua and Tan-shui, the addition of 10 markets from 1717 to 1740 and another 16 from 1740 to 1768 reflects a substantial northward spread of population to an area previously devoid of Han settlement. However, the much greater increase of 54 markets in T'ai-wan and Chu-lo between 1740 and 1768 indicates that the intensification of settlement and local trade in older areas was the dominant trend in this later period.

Markets proliferate because of commercialization and changing trade patterns as well as population growth.[142] Because frontier settlement in Taiwan was from its beginning highly commercialized and export-oriented, I argue that the increased number of markets in the early years reflects population growth rather than increases in the amount of mar-

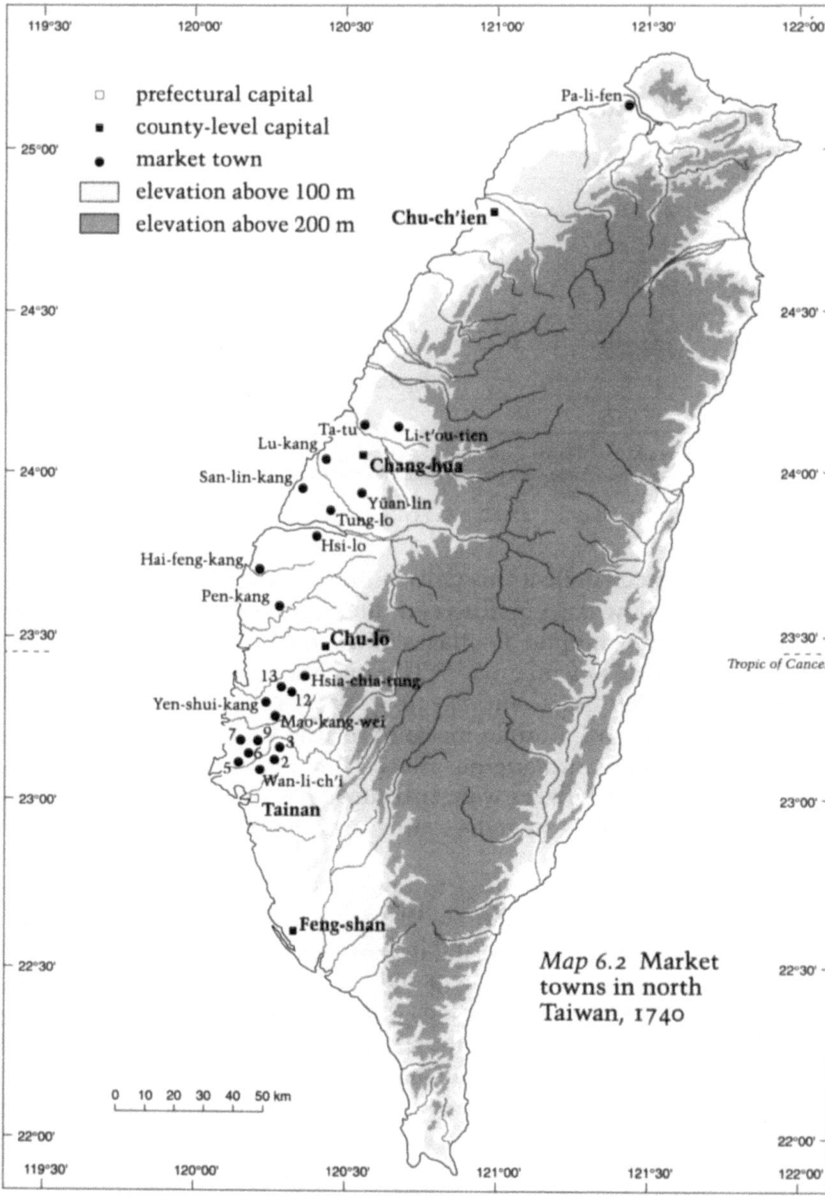

Map 6.2 Market towns in north Taiwan, 1740

	1768 • Market sites	• 1740
	Chu-lo county	
1.	Wan-li-ch'i	x
2.	Mu-chia	x
3.	Wan-li	x
4.	Chiao-pa-nien	
5.	Hsi-kang-tzu	x
6.	Hsiao-lung	x
7.	T'u-shih-tzu (Chia-li-hsing)	x
8.	Fan-tzu-tu-t'ou	
9.	Ma-tou	x
10.	Mao-kang-wei	x
11.	Yen-shui-kang	x
12.	T'ieh-hsien-ch'iao	x
13.	Ching-shui-kang	x
14.	To-ko-kuo	
15.	Pai-fa-kung-t'an	
16.	Ta-ch'iu-t'ien	
17.	Ta-p'ai-ch'u	
18.	Hsia-chia-tung	x
19.	Shui-ch'u-t'ou	
20.	Lu-tzu-ts'ao	
21.	P'u-tzu	
22.	Chu-lo (7)	x
23.	Lu-ma-ch'an	
24.	Ta-miao	
25.	Pen-kang (2)	x
26.	Ta-p'u-lin	
27.	Shih-t'ou-ch'i	
28.	T'a-li-wu	
29.	Tou-liu-men	
30.	Chu-tzu-chiao[a]	
31.	Lien-ch'ih-t'an[a]	x
32.	Chi-shui-ch'i[a]	x
33.	Hsin-pei[a]	
34.	Jung-shu-wang[a]	
35.	Ta-lun-chiao[a]	
36.	———	Hou-shu-kang[a]

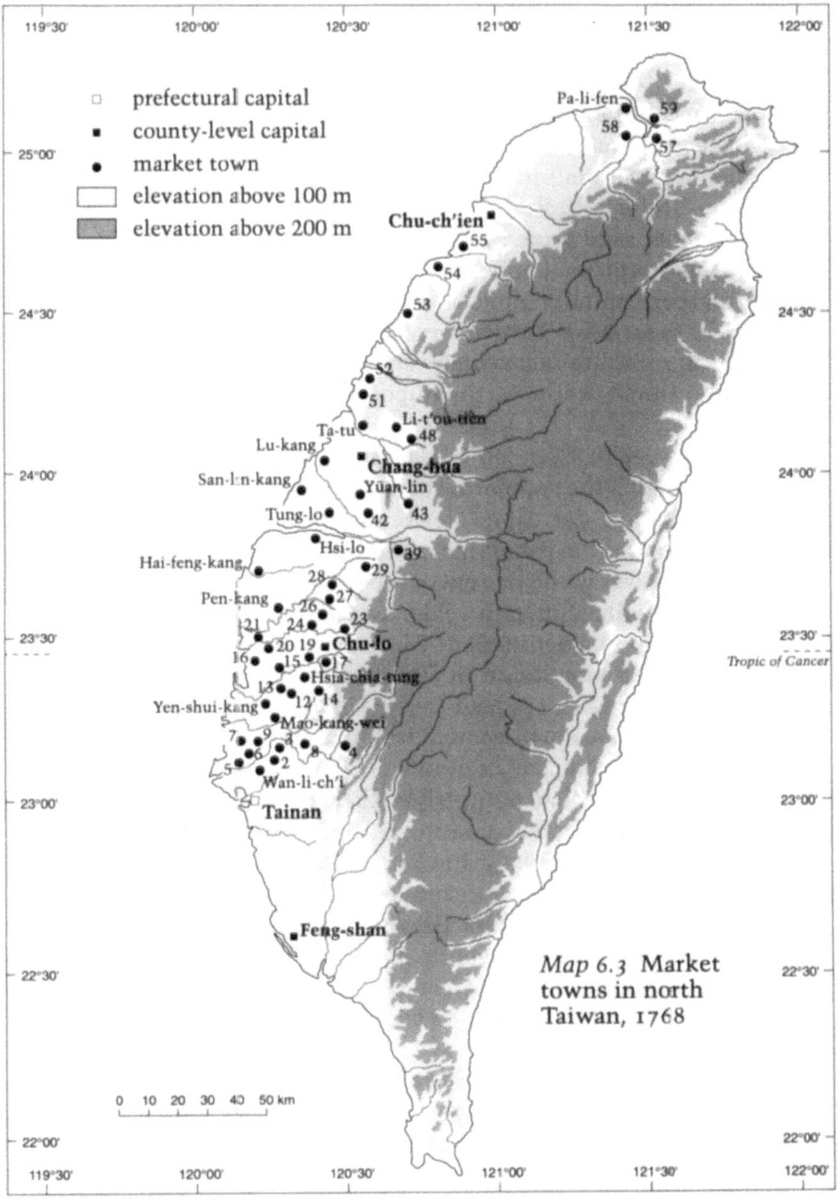

Map 6.3 Market towns in north Taiwan, 1768

1768 • Market sites	• 1740
Chang-hua county	
37. Hai-feng-kang	x
38. Hsi-lo	x
39. Lin-chi-p'u	
40. San-lin-kang	x
41. Tung-lo	x
42. Fan-ch'iao-t'ou	
43. Nan-t'ou	
44. Yüan-lin	x
45. Lu-kang	x
46. Chang-hua (4)	x
47. Hsin-chuang[a]	
48. Ta-tun	
49. Li-t'ou-tien	x

1768 • Market sites	• 1740
50. Ta-tu	x
51. Sha-lu	
52. Niu-ma	
Tan-shui subprefecture	
53. Yüan-li	
54. Hou-lung	
55. Chung-kang	
56. Chu-ch'ien	x
57. Meng-chia	
58. Hsin-chuang	
59. Pa-chih-lan	
60. Pa-li-fen	x

[a]Exact location unknown.

keted surplus by a fixed population. In the newest frontier areas, forest products and lumber were exported before sugar and rice cultivation could begin, and many basic necessities had to be imported. This pattern continued as sugar and rice fields were reclaimed to supply the export trade. Thus, though backward, frontier life was highly commercialized. In older, settled, and more thickly populated areas, more of the agricultural surplus went to supply local demand. Rather than an increase in marketing per capita or rapid population growth, the proliferation of markets in these areas between 1740 and 1768 reflects the intensification of local trade, an increasingly sophisticated local division of labor, and a proportional decline in the importance of the long-distance export trade.

Population per market can be calculated for a few Taiwan counties circa 1768 (though the population data are of low quality).[143] Where there is more marketing per capita, fewer people are required to support a market and population per market should be less. On this theory, frontier Tan-shui's low average of 3,793 people per market in 1768 suggests it was more commercialized than the older areas of Chu-lo (7,319 per market), and Feng-shan (7,702 per market). However, these ratios also reflect the greater density of population in Chu-lo and Feng-shan, and the consequent ability of single markets to serve larger populations. Frontier Tan-shui's sparse population prevented its small markets (even with the aid of oxcarts) from serving larger numbers. Moreover, many of the markets in Chu-lo and Feng-shan were larger than those in Tan-shui and thus were not really comparable. Glaring examples of this noncomparability are the major ports of Lu-kang in Chang-hua and Yen-shui-kang in Chu-lo, which are recorded on the gazetteer lists as large but single markets. Multiple markets are listed for the major centers of Chu-lo, Pen-kang, and Chang-hua, and to the south in Tainan.[144] The differentiation of higher-order market centers such as these indicates that the growth of an interlocking hierarchy of central places was under way in older areas of settlement.

Oxcarts as a means of overland transport and Taiwan's access to waterborne transport along its long coastline had an important impact on the pattern of market growth in Taiwan. Two-wheeled ox-drawn carts were effective on Taiwan's unimproved and muddy roads. Oxcarts could be more cost-effective than river rafts, and both carts and rafts were superior to human porters.[145] The importance of seaports served by river transport and the large supply of ox-drawn carts able to carry bulky loads long distances made it possible for farmers to travel greater distances to market. This was an important factor in the emergence of permanent rather than periodic markets in Taiwan.[146]

Taiwan's western coastal plain is segmented by numerous westward-flowing rivers. This made north-south overland travel difficult, even for

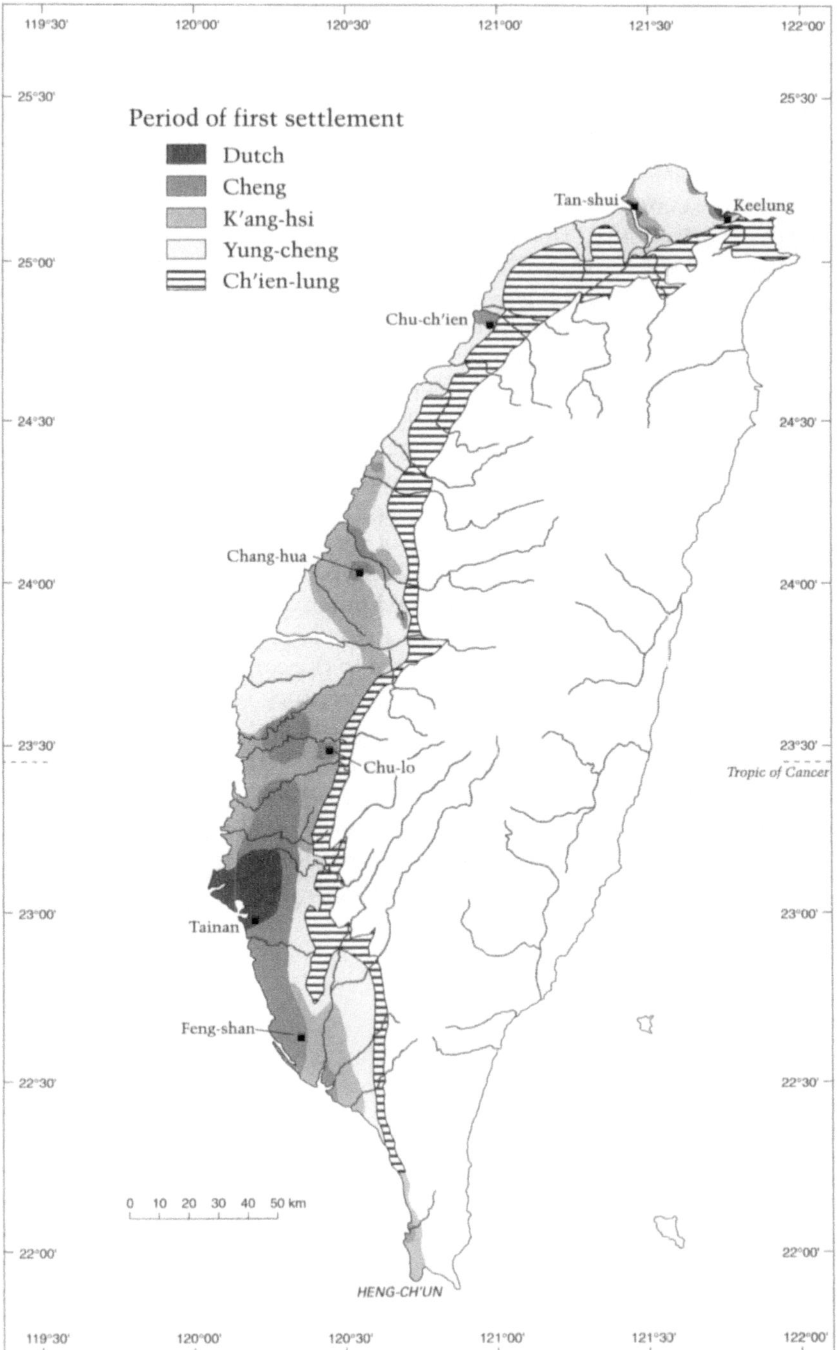

Map 6.4 The expansion of Han agricultural settlement
Based on Ts'ao 1954*a*: 81; Chou Hsien-wen 1957: 15–18; Ch'en Cheng-hsiang 1959–61: 1.31; Ch'en Han-kuang 1961*a*: 53; Chang Ch'i-yün 1962: B43.

oxcarts, and channeled trade toward small coastal ports. In the ports heavy cargoes of rice and sugar were bulked and shipped to Tainan, where they entered the cross-strait trade. These circumstances fostered the growth of a dendritic network of markets spreading inland from coastal seaports. Coastal shipping linked these ports to Tainan, the center of the cross-strait commerce. This coastal network was ideal for serving Taiwan's export-oriented rice and sugar economy.[147]

Maps 6.2 and 6.3 show the proliferation of market towns in Chu-lo, Chang-hua, and Tan-shui between 1740 and 1768. As settlement intensified in later stages, local commerce increased in importance compared to the long-distance export trade. This led to a fleshing out of the marketing system in the interior areas of older settled regions, such as Chu-lo, by 1768.[148] The spread of markets in Chang-hua and Tan-shui in 1768 was still following the coastal-oriented pattern of the early frontier stages. Map 6.4 shows the gradual spread of Han agricultural settlement.[149]

Taiwan's system of regional integration evolved in three stages. First, the extractive role of the capital city of Tainan dominated the economy under the Dutch, Chengs, and early Ch'ing. Next, a dendritic system emerged to service the export-oriented production and wholesale trade in rice and sugar (complemented by a slowly growing hierarchy of administrative centers) that predominated in the early eighteenth century. Finally, in the latter half of the eighteenth century, rural markets proliferated and an interlocking hierarchy of central places evolved to serve a growing retail trade and endogenous demand.[150] The contribution of the extension and intensification of civil and military administrative centers on the frontier to the evolution of regional integration is discussed in Chapter 7, after a look at early government policies that sought to limit the spread of Han settlement within Taiwan.

Scenes of aborigine life from Liu-shih-ch'i's T'ai fan t'u shuo, *ca. 1746 (reprinted with permission of the Fu Ssu-nien Library, Institute of History and Philology, Academia Sinica, Nankang, Taiwan). The legends are translations of the inscriptions on the paintings.*

Map of aborigine villages. [The area shown is roughly the west coast of Taiwan from modern Chang-hua city (center right) to Miao-li. North is on the left.]

Catching fish. Aborigine men from villages of Chu-lo county such as Mu-chia-liu-wan and To-ko-kuo [To-lo-kuo] catch fish by standing on the banks and using spears or bows and arrows.

Monkey plucking. Civilized aborigines from villages of Chu-lo county such as Ma-tou, Hsiao-lung, and Mu-chia-liu-wan climb [betel palms] monkey fashion in the seventh or eighth month; this is called plucking.

Hunting deer. At the end of autumn and the beginning of winter, civilized aborigines from villages of Tan-shui subprefecture such as Ta-chia, Hou-lung, Chung-kang, Chu-ch'ien, and Hsiao-li hunt deer in groups; this is called "going out in the bush."

Cultivating and planting. Civilized aborigines from villages in T'ai-wan county such as Cho-hou, Lo-han-men, and Hsin-kang, both men and women, cultivate rice in paddies, which they harvest in the tenth month.

Cultivating taro. Raw aborigines from the mountains of the Feng-shan area who know nothing of farming plant taro on ridges of land in the mountains. When the rootstocks are ripe, they dig a hole and roast them. They then cover over the pit, and from time to time remove the cooked taro and eat it. In this way they can have long-term provisions.

Husking rice. The women of every aborigine village in Chang-hua county husk rice by using [a hollowed out piece of wood from] a large tree as a mortar and a straight piece of wood as a pestle. All aborigine villages use this method.

Harvesting grain. The men and women of every aborigine village in Chang-hua county harvest millet and rice by hand in the seventh month. They do not use sickles. The villagers of Tan-shui subprefecture use the same method.

Weaving cloth. Aborigine women from villages in Tan-shui subprefecture such as An-li, Ta-chia-tung, and Ta-chia-hsi weave cloth, which is sometimes called *ta ko wen*. The aborigine women of Chang-hua county can also weave. The cloth made by the women of Ta-chia is by far the best.

Sugar mills. The land throughout Taiwan is fertile and suitable for sugarcane. All the inhabitants except for the aborigines grow it. The sugar is processed from the ninth month through the fourth or fifth month of the next year. Merchants sell it everywhere in Kiangsu and Chekiang. It is truly one of Taiwan's most important businesses.

Fording the river. The native interpreters and chieftains of villages in Chu-lo county such as Ma-tou and Mu-chia-liu-wan crossing a rain-swollen river; ordinary aborigines swim across or ride rafts.

Raising a house. The civilized aborigines of Hsin-kang in T'ai-wan county rebuild their houses after a good harvest. All the villages of Chu-lo county do likewise.

Welcoming a bride. In villages of Chang-hua county such as Tung-lo, Hsi-lo, Ta-wu-chün, and Pan-hsien, the husband's relatives welcome the bride. This is called "leading by the hand."

Traveling by oxcart. Throughout Taiwan aborigine men and women use oxcarts for commerce and travel.

Guarding the passes. Throughout Taiwan [civilized] aborigines who live near raw aborigines cut down bamboo to make stockades. Every day the native interpreters and chieftains assign sentries, each of whom carries a spear or a bow and arrows, to guard against raw aborigine marauders.

Village teachers. Villages in the Feng-shan area such as Hsia-tan-shui, Ch'ih-shan, and Chia-t'eng have established village teachers to instruct the aborigine youngsters in reading. T'ai-wan and Chu-lo counties have also established such village teachers.

Hammocks. When the raw aborigine women of villages on Mt. K'uei-lei are raising an infant, they use a large cloth as a swaddling cloth. If they have work—farming or weaving—to do, they tie the cloth to a tree limb [and form a hammock].

Watchtowers. The native interpreters and chieftains of villages in Tan-shui subprefecture such as Chu-ch'ien, Nan-k'an, Chih-pao-li [Chin-pao-li], and Pa-li-fen have set up watchtowers. Every day they send youths on patrol to guard against raw aborigines and to watch over the crops.

CHAPTER SEVEN

Ch'ing Administration of the Han

Taiwan as a Strategic Periphery

The late imperial Chinese state was a highly centralized, agrarian-bureaucratic empire and one of the most sophisticated of premodern states. It ruled over a vast and highly differentiated territory and economy not through semi-independent local fiefdoms but through carefully designed civil and military bureaucracies. The officials and officers who staffed these imperial bureaucracies were selected from candidates who passed civil service examinations and were appointed on the basis of qualifications and experience. Once in office, their performance was reviewed, and they were subject to transfer, promotion, and dismissal.

These bureaucrats staffed civil and military administrative structures that penetrated and encompassed all of China's many regions. Regional systems analysis sees the spatial structure of China as composed of nested hierarchies of functionally integrated regional economies. G. W. Skinner's analysis of the articulation of the Ch'ing bureaucracy to China's regional systems demonstrates how the field administration was designed to give priority to raising revenue in economically developed regional cores and providing defense and ensuring control along regional peripheries.[1] Taiwan joined the Ch'ing empire as an economically undeveloped yet strategically significant periphery of the southeast coast macroregion.

In this chapter I analyze the design of Taiwan's civil and military administrations, as well as the strategies of control used by the Ch'ing state in ruling the strategic periphery of Taiwan. In Chapter 8 I examine the fiscal burden of governmental operations in Taiwan and the state's revenue and tax systems.

The Ch'ing incorporated Taiwan into the empire as a prefecture of Fukien province, with the prefectural capital (and the capital of T'ai-wan county) in Tainan. Taiwan prefecture was subdivided into three counties.[2] The smallest was T'ai-wan county, which covered the central portion of the southwest core and the Pescadores and had the largest Han population.[3] The rest of Taiwan was divided between Chu-lo county in the north and Feng-shan county in the south. A subdistrict magistrate (*hsün chien*) was assigned to assist the magistrate of each county. A higher-ranking assistant county magistrate (*hsien ch'eng*) and an additional subdistrict magistrate in the Pescadores (P'eng-hu) were also assigned to T'ai-wan county.[4] The posting of an assistant magistrate to T'ai-wan, the smallest county in area, and of subdistrict magistrates to all three counties and the Pescadores indicates the strategic significance given to Taiwan prefecture and to T'ai-wan county within the prefecture. In all of China in 1758, assistant magistrates were posted to only one in three counties, and subdistrict magistrates to only two in three counties.[5]

A further indication of the strategic importance accorded Taiwan at court is the provision that Taiwan's county magistrates be selected by the provincial governor and governor-general from a pool of experienced officials rather than appointed by the Board of Civil Office from among those who had recently passed the civil service examinations. Such provincially appointed experienced officials were assigned to only one in four of China's counties.[6] Skinner's analysis of the articulation of Ch'ing field administration to China's regional systems demonstrates that a narrow span of control (of prefectures over counties) characterized Ch'ing administration of strategically important peripheries. Compared with an empire-wide average in 1893 of 6.6 counties per prefecture, Taiwan prefecture had oversight of only three counties. Skinner also points out that a narrow span of control enabled direct supervision of large, sparsely populated counties where friction of distance was high and communication difficult; these conditions characterized Feng-shan and Chu-lo.[7] As documented below, Taiwan's civil administration was stretched thin not in relation to a small population but in relation to the large expanse of wild territory in its jurisdiction.

Yet another indication of Taiwan's role as a strategically important periphery was the posting of the Taiwan–Amoy (Hsia-men) military circuit intendant (T'ai-Hsia *ping pei tao*) as the immediate superior of the Taiwan prefect and the highest-ranking civil official in Taiwan. Only one in four of China's prefectural capitals in 1893 was also a circuit capital.[8] The intendant oversaw communications between the mainland and Taiwan and had the power to move troops. All cross-strait shipping was restricted to the ports of Amoy and Tainan, and he was charged with its supervision. A coastal defense subprefect (*hai fang t'ung chih*) was posted in each of these ports to assist the intendant.[9] The intendant's responsibilities thus were focused on the strategic and external affairs of Taiwan, whereas those of the prefect and magistrates were focused on internal security and revenue collection. The intendant and prefect were in turn subordinates of the governor of Fukien and the governor-general of Chekiang and Fukien, both of whom resided in Foochow.[10]

To provide defense and guarantee local security in Taiwan, the court deployed a garrison force of 8,000 soldiers, 5,000 land and 3,000 marine. An additional marine force of 2,000 was posted in the Pescadores. Although this was not a large force to cover a considerable expanse of land and ocean, it was large compared to Taiwan's small population in 1684 (80,000 Han and 50,000 plains aborigines). It was too large a force to recruit from the local population and too large to provision locally, given the undeveloped state of Taiwan's agriculture and its depopulation in 1684. The court rejected a proposal to establish military colonies of farmer-soldiers, on the Cheng model, as impractical and unlikely to attract recruits to the harsh frontier.[11] Instead, it adopted Shih Lang's proposal that Taiwan be garrisoned by rotating soldiers from the overstaffed Fukien armies every three years. This had the great advantage of requiring no increase in state expenditures and taxation.[12] The rotation of soldiers created a system unique to Taiwan, for the common practice was for Green Standard armies to be recruited and stationed locally.[13] The adoption of the system was accompanied by a prohibition on recruitment of ordinary soldiers in Taiwan.[14] (Taiwanese were entitled to participate in the military examination system that qualified successful candidates for the officer corps; see below.) This reflected the court's distrust of the Taiwanese settlers and the island's rebellious past. Instead, the court put its faith in mainland soldiers, whom it made additionally amenable to government oversight by requiring them to leave their families behind on the mainland.

The highest-ranking military officer in Taiwan was the brigade general (*tsung ping*) posted to Tainan. He was subordinate to the Fukien naval commander-in-chief of the Green Standard forces (*shui shih t'i tu*) in Amoy and to the governor-general of Fukien and Chekiang in Foochow.[15]

The initial distribution of both civil offices and military forces was heavily concentrated in the Tainan area (see Maps 7.2 and 7.4 below). This reflected the concentration of Han population in the southwest core and the region's strategic significance. Military power and civil administration only gradually penetrated the frontiers to the north and south.

The creation of three counties, unwarranted by Taiwan's small population, reflected Taiwan's status as a strategic (maritime) frontier and the importance for defense of government control over territory as well as population. Skinner points out that throughout late imperial Chinese history the number of county-level units in the empire remained relatively constant (around 1,400) despite tremendous growth of population and territory. He argues that problems of organizational control would swamp a traditional agrarian state that expanded the number of basic units in its field administration much beyond this number. Yet, considerations of defense required a greater administrative (and military) presence along frontiers, in terms of both number of county-level units and, due to the narrow span of control desirable along frontiers, number of prefectures, than the population of peripheries might warrant. Given the need to limit the total number of counties, new counties could be created along expanding frontiers only if counties in regional cores were consolidated and reduced in number.[16]

Moreover, because friction of distance limits the territorial range of administrative effectiveness, counties in sparsely populated peripheries tended to have smaller than average populations because such counties could not effectively encompass the area that would contain the average county population. Thus, more counties were created along strategic frontiers than would be predicted if each county contained the average county population, but fewer were created than predicted if each county had been limited to the average area per county (which would be fiscally ruinous; see below).[17] Counties in densely populated cores, on the other hand, tended to have smaller than average areas because they could not effectively control the huge populations that the average county area would contain. Counties in densely populated regional cores, therefore, had higher than average populations and smaller than average territories, whereas counties along sparsely populated peripheries (such as Taiwan) had lower than average populations and larger than average territories.[18] One consequence of these principles of administrative geography is that there was a greater administrative presence per capita (but less per unit of area) in sparsely populated strategic peripheries.

Defending strategically important peripheries and controlling unruly frontiers also required a greater *military* presence, both per capita and per unit of area, in places like Taiwan.[19] In fiscal terms this meant higher government expenses per capita, but because of lower than average county populations, low revenues (revenues being primarily a function of population). Thus, county-level units along sparsely populated peripheries where the state's defense burden was high rarely contributed to the revenue of higher levels of government and usually required defense subsidies from revenue-rich regional cores.[20] Frontiers, as areas of high expenses and low revenues, were therefore areas of fiscal imbalance. To relieve this imbalance, the state sought both to minimize frontier expenditures and increase frontier revenues. Expenditures could be reduced by adopting methods of indirect control (e.g., quarantine), limiting the growth of the frontier administration and defense establishment, and relying on the state's logistic skill to mobilize forces and matériel from regional cores to put down frontier disturbances.[21] Revenues could be increased by fostering reclamation and registering farmland for taxation and by developing non-agricultural sources of revenue. By resisting calls for the expansion of the frontier bureaucracy as long as possible, the state minimized both problems of bureaucratic proliferation and finance. As discussed below, only a growing population and tax base and increasing control problems persuaded the state to gradually expand and extend its military and civil administrations on Taiwan's frontier.

Boundaries and the Quarantine Policy on the Frontier

The Ch'ing did not envisage the expansion of Han settlement in Taiwan when it adopted its quarantine policies in 1684; indeed, these policies were designed to prevent such expansion, primarily by limiting immigration. Thus, the state took few measures to ensure the maintenance of order on an expanding frontier. The state's civil and military presence was concentrated in the Tainan core around the prefectural capital, leaving a vast frontier unoccupied, for its purpose was merely to preserve the status quo and to ensure the capital did not fall into rebel hands. No plans for repopulating the island or even expanding revenue were devised. The court's preoccupation was security and the maintenance of an order that would not jeopardize its security interests. But the revival of the southeast coast economies brought rapid population growth, and by the first decades of the eighteenth century Chinese immigrants pursuing their private goals began undermining the quarantine of Taiwan. Faced with an expanding and unruly frontier population, the government had to choose between two policies: withdrawing and containing the expanding settlement, or tolerating its extension and fostering its control.

Chinese officials posted to Taiwan held ambivalent attitudes toward the expansion of Han settlement. For them the control of unruly settlers, especially on the more remote frontiers, was a major burden. Equally worrisome was the escalation of Han-aborigine conflict as settlers encroached on tribal lands and disrupted aborigine societies. Offsetting the costs of control were the benefits of increasing land-tax revenues as the cultivated area grew. Expanding rice surpluses also made provisioning government troops and filling tax quotas easier. Nor were all settlers villains and vagrants: loyal settlers were allies of the state and aided the government in keeping the peace.

The problems caused by expanding Han settlement necessitated policies aimed at maintaining government control over a volatile society. We have already detailed the fluctuations of immigration policy, which sought to limit the numbers of settlers and to exclude troublemakers, and we have seen how this policy fostered rootlessness among migrant settlers separated from their families. The rice export limitations sought to maintain plentiful food supplies without depriving farmers of a market for their surpluses. The attempts to restrict the abuses of the monopoly merchants and interpreters among the plains aborigines are treated in Chapter 5, and the problems of protecting tribal land rights will be discussed in Chapter 9. Here the focus is on policies aimed at extending direct control over Chinese agricultural settlers on the frontier and the debates on expanding the government presence in conjunction with expanding settlement versus drawing boundaries to circumscribe the permitted area of settlement and keeping settlers within the effective territorial range of the administration already in place.[22]

Essays included in the 1717 Chu-lo gazetteer discuss the dilemma experienced by scholar-officials posted to Taiwan. These essays note that policies keeping settlers behind fixed boundaries had to be adopted as interim measures until administrative and military control in northern Taiwan could be upgraded. The chapter on defense complains of four revolts in the five years between 1696 and 1701, two among Han settlers and two among aborigines, all on the north route. Pirate raids in 1710 had led to the establishment of the Tan-shui subdistrict lieutenancy and seven military post stations, but keeping order remained a problem.

> New settlers increase daily at ever greater distances from the county yamen; they are violent, resist arrest, and steal. Cleverly they seek to open tribal lands, to occupy aborigine homes, and take aborigine wives. The aborigines fear them and suffer patiently, but before long the enmity between settlers and aborigines will bring disaster. The soldiers above Ta-chia are unfamiliar with the terrain; the area is vast; the military posts are few and weak. Having nothing to do, the soldiers can only worry about miasma; when an emergency occurs, they are useless. Hence, the county magistrate, Chou Chung-hsüan, has sought to remove all vagrants from the area above the Ta-chia river, and the lieutenant colonel of the north route, Juan Ts'ai-wen, has requested that the Tan-shui subdistrict lieutenancy and its seven military post stations be withdrawn.
>
> One view holds that the drawing of a boundary at Ta-chia will impede the development of civilization in the 700 *li* [miles] above that line. This is not a place that can be transformed by benign neglect [*wu wei*]; rather, the civil administration should be extended there. Otherwise, hundreds of miles will be abandoned, and there will be no expansive management of the country. Some say that because the northern ports are open and villains can reach the tribes below Keelung through the mountains, a blockade at Ta-chia will not stop their entering that area. Withdrawal from above Ta-chia means government orders will go unenforced and official surveillance will not reach there; the government's only eyes and ears will be three or five interpreters. Is it right to leave 700 miles as a refuge for outlaws? How, with no officials and government soldiers, can the people not do evil, foolish, and criminal things? . . .
>
> Feng-shan is under the jurisdiction of the south route battalion and does not extend over more than 300 *li*, yet the north route covers 1,000 *li* of ever-expanding frontier. One county government and one battalion are inadequate to instill awe there. Things are peaceful now, but what would happen

> if crops failed and Han and aborigine rebels appeared? The 300 *li* behind Tan-shui to the mountains [to the east] is all aborigine and mountainous and insufficient to support a county government. But the 300 *li* from Tan-shui south to Pan-hsien [Chang-hua] is a well-watered and fertile plain. It would be appropriate to establish another county above Pan-hsien and let settlers open it up. And a county should be created in Pan-hsien itself. . . . In addition, a battalion should be located in Pan-hsien and smaller units posted at various points to the north. A subdistrict magistrate should be stationed in Tan-shui and . . . a naval unit in Keelung. A series of military colonies will provide eyes and ears, and government instruction will irrigate the entire region. . . . Nor need stationing more troops in the north require increasing military provisions. The troops can be transferred from the south where they are not needed. . . .
>
> In the past people have risked crossing the Ta-chia boundary even though it was forbidden; if a county is founded, then many farmers can be induced to open the land. Han can reclaim tribal land by paying the aborigine head tax on behalf of the tribes. In this way revenues will increase, and the aborigines will also benefit. And increased tax revenues can pay for soldiers' rations. With an additional county, government officials of both counties can police the area and educate the people; the relations between officials and the people, formerly distant, can grow close; officials can cultivate the people, promulgate imperial edicts, and teach the virtues of filiality and loyalty. Propriety, morality, modesty, and the sense of shame will flourish, and rebellions will cease. The purpose of adding troops and establishing a county is not only to display military might to overawe others but also to spread a refining influence.[23]

This essay advocates the maintenance of frontier control by a simultaneous expansion of the civil and military arms of the government to keep pace with the spread of settlement in contrast to a policy that would withdraw both settlers and government behind artificially set boundaries. The expansion is to be financed through taxes on expanding farmland and need not increase expenditures.[24] The last paragraph especially encapsulates the late imperial model of good government: planted on a stable agricultural revenue base and buttressed by the military, the civilizing influence of scholar-officials spreads Confucian virtues among the populace.[25]

A later passage of the Chu-lo gazetteer takes up the same problems of frontier control and sounds similar themes of statecraft.

> If a military garrison is established but not a county government, then the people will have no champion; if a county is established without a garrison, then the county officials will have no champion. County officials must tame and rein in the people and thereby prevent their rebelling. Military authorities must humble the proud and dilute the audacity of lawbreakers, so that no one will dare to rebel. The north route has two sources of affliction: aborigines and Chinese vagrants. . . . Creating another county government and increasing the number of troops will eradicate these sources of disaster before they grow.[26]

For this author, civil and military power together enhance the government's authority but are ineffective alone. These practitioners of Confucian government understood that normative persuasion needed the threat of coercion to provide effective control (a point commonly lost on intellectual historians). These pleas to upgrade the government's presence in northern Taiwan were soon answered. A battalion of 500 men was set up in 1718 in Tan-shui (see below). The creation of a new county, however, had to wait until after the Chu I-kuei rebellion of 1721, and even then civil offices only moved into the area several years after they were ordered established.

Lan Ting-yüan, whose pro-immigration views we have met before, was an outspoken advocate of colonization and opponent of attempts to quarantine Han settlers behind artificial boundaries on the frontier. In his *History of the Pacification of Taiwan* of 1723, Lan takes up many of the themes addressed in the essays from the Chu-lo gazetteer. Lan commented that "previously Feng-shan to the south and Chu-lo to the north were poisonous and miasmatic areas where county magistrates did not dare to go, yet now settlers are rushing to the 1,500 *li* between Taiwan's southern tip and its northern point like ducks taking to water."[27] Lan argued that reconstruction after the ravages of the Chu I-kuei rebellion required stationing additional troops on the island and the founding of a new county in Chang-hua (Pan-hsien). He noted that although tax revenues were not large in that area, with the aborigine head taxes yearly income would be over 9,000 taels. Although Han settlers had been prohibited from reclaiming much of the area, "once the grasslands are opened to cultivation, revenue will increase, and in a few years it will be an important county."[28] Lan argued that "as historical precedents show, withdrawing the population from an area only turns it into a bandit lair. Where there is land, it should not be left unpopulated. Developing a frontier turns it into a land of taxpayers; left empty, it becomes an area where robbers and thieves cause havoc." Lan warned that an unpopulated Taiwan would attract unwanted attention from Japan and Holland. He also advocated setting up military colonies to spearhead colonization in unsettled areas, such as Chu-ch'ien (Hsin-chu).[29]

Lan continued his arguments for populating the wilderness in an essay written in 1724. Lan noted that raw aborigines on head-hunting raids hid in the thick, uncut forests. Clearing and settling would deprive them of hiding places and end the raids. The court should extend the boundary of permissible settlement and thereby increase both the population and tax revenues. It could attempt to prevent settlers' crossing the boundary into aborigine territory, but "although the court can order the people not to enter, it cannot order the aborigines not to come out. If one foot is marked off, the aborigines will come out another foot; in the end all of Taiwan will be off-limits. Although all the populace cannot sail back to the mainland, both the Japanese and the Dutch can sail there and make of Taiwan a pirates' nest." Lan wrote that he "feared" the aborigines could not single-handedly protect their land from a foreign threat.[30]

The drawing of a boundary limiting Han settlement to the area below the Ta-chia river, as discussed in the Chu-lo gazetteer, and a plan of Magistrate Sung Yung-ch'ing of Feng-shan (1704–12) to withdraw Chinese settlers from Lang-ch'iao (Heng-ch'un) at Taiwan's southern tip[31] were the forerunners of several later attempts to separate aborigines and Chinese and to keep the settlers within the range of control of a Chinese magistrate. Although the troops stationed above Ta-chia were greatly increased in 1718, administrative attempts continued to be made to prohibit settlers from that area. Writing in 1722, the censor Huang Shu-ching noted that several aborigine tribes north of the Ta-chia river refused to allow Han settlers to open tribal lands and that a license from county officials was necessary to gain access to their territory.[32] Lan also claims that parts of Chang-hua had been off-limits to reclaimers.[33] The Ta-chia river's role as a Han-aborigine boundary was short-lived (as were most such boundaries that followed), although it did survive as the line dividing Chang-hua county and Tan-shui subprefecture after 1723.

We saw above how a nervous central government sought to tighten its quarantine of Taiwan in 1717 and how in 1721 the Chu I-kuei rebellion reawakened fears that Taiwan might become a rebel base. In 1722 Governor-general Man-pao responded to these fears by establishing a new, island-wide set of boundaries. These boundaries, unlike the east-west course of the Ta-chia river line, ran north and south, paralleling Taiwan's mountain ranges and dividing the western coastal plains from the mountains. Man-pao decreed that "in the mountainous areas it is easy for villains to hide; thus we order that settlers living within ten *li* of the mountains be removed. From the north route to the south route, we must build a great wall and a deep trench as a permanent boundary; those who cross this boundary will be considered robbers and bandits."[34] Man-pao's reasoning emphasizes the threat of bandits' taking refuge in mountain havens and using them as bases for plotting rebellion (as had happened in the Chu I-kuei rebellion).

Huang Shu-ching's account of the 1722 boundary gives a different but complementary emphasis. Huang saw the boundary as necessary to prevent conflicts between Chinese settlers and raw aborigines (and puts the blame for these on the Han).

> The raw aborigines in the mountains, whose wild nature is hard to tame, burn houses and kill people. In fact, most of the strife is due to the Chinese, who profit by crossing boundaries and encroaching on the land of raw and cooked aborigines; they will not be satisfied until they have snatched it all. They are constantly forming gangs to enter the mountains and put up huts. They watch the aborigines hunt deer and often get killed trying to steal the

> game for themselves. In other cases they go deep into the mountains to cut rattan and timber and meet with harm. In 1722 it was decided to set up stone stelae to mark a boundary ten or more *li* from raw aborigine settlements and to prohibit anyone from crossing it.[35]

Censor Huang appears to have favored the boundary policy, for elsewhere, in discussing the settlement of a newly opened area in the territory of the civilized Ta-chieh-tien *she* at Lo-han-men, he says:

> The Chinese have been gradually increasing, farming and gathering firewood. They are constantly being killed by the spears of the barbarians, or being burned to death and their heads taken. The officials therefore . . . search out and capture these barbarians. But the raw barbarians are all around and about the nearer villages . . . and it is difficult to apprehend them and bring them under control. If a boundary were established to prevent them from going in and coming out [of the newly settled territory], we could prevent these calamities.[36]

The lines set up in 1722 were not a single system of continuous mounds and trenches ("earth-oxen") or stone-marked boundaries. Rather, they were established piecemeal at scattered trouble spots (generally passes that served as corridors connecting mountains and plains) (see Map 7.1). In later years, as we shall see below, the boundaries were abandoned or extended.

Lan Ting-yüan's review of the evacuation order accompanying Man-pao's creation of the boundary gives additional details.

> All settlers living within the mountains have been ordered to move out, mountain passes are to be barricaded by big timbers, and no one is to be allowed to enter or come out. A boundary is to be drawn ten *li* from the mountains and all settlers living between this boundary and the mountains are to move elsewhere. The land is to return to waste. An earthen wall five or six feet high and a deep trench will mark a permanent boundary. Those who cross this boundary will be considered robbers and bandits. . . . Thus, villains will have no refuge and wild aborigines will be unable to come out to cause trouble.[37]

Lan was adamantly opposed to the boundary and evacuation policies. In a letter to Man-pao sent under his cousin's (Commander Lan T'ing-chen) name,[38] he listed "six reckonings" that would have to be made if this policy were to be carried out.

> 1. When moving several tens of thousands of people, there must be a place with several tens of thousand homes that can accommodate them. And since these people must farm and eat, there must be farmland that can support several tens of thousands. Where will this land come from?
>
> 2. The rich can bear the expense of moving: the beams and tiles of their houses can be transported, the loss of the labor and walls amount to only 60 percent. But the poor live in mud huts with thatched roofs that cannot be

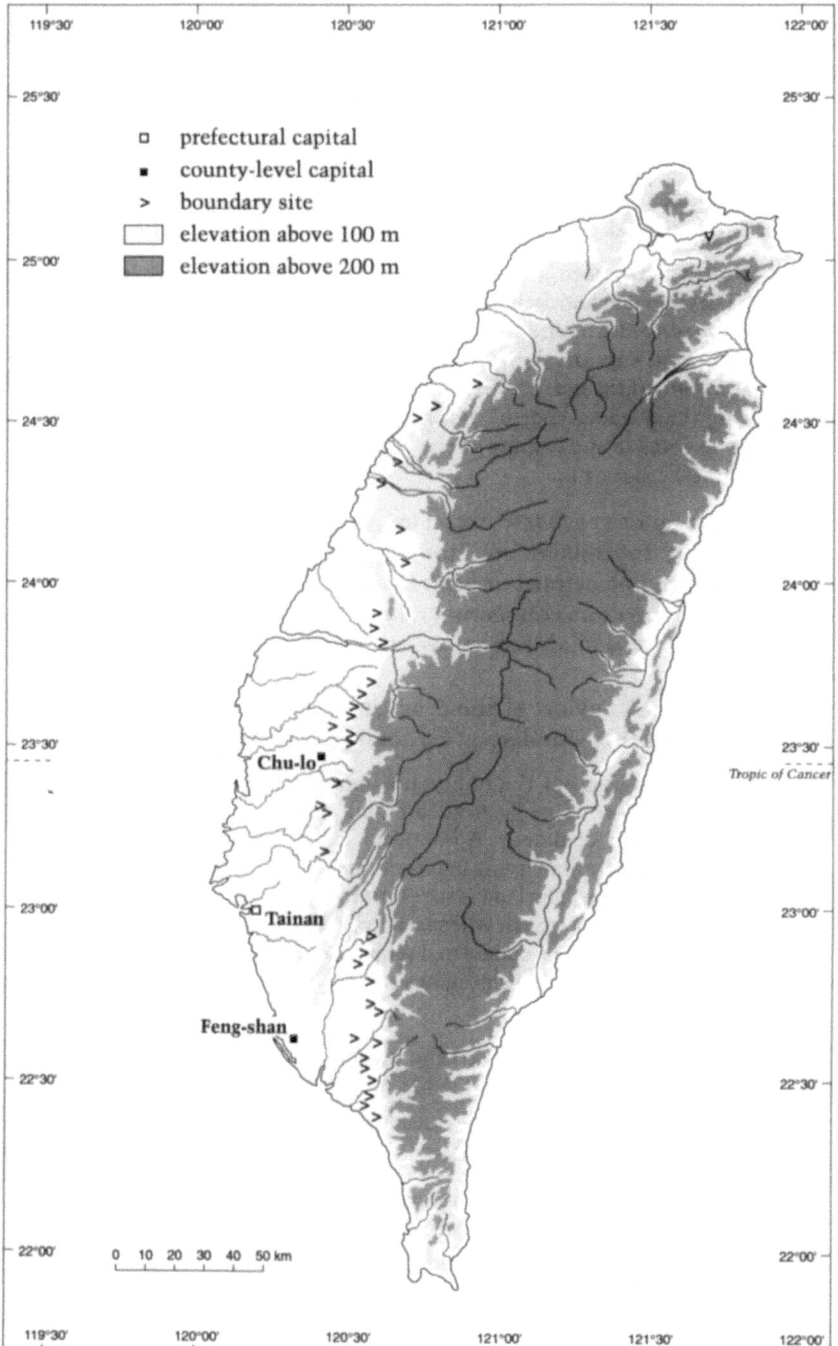

Map 7.1 The raw aborigine boundary of 1722
Based on Huang Shu-ching 1957: 167–68. Of the 54 boundary sites listed by Huang, 36 have been identified.

moved. Thus, the poor must build new houses. How can the survivors after the chaos [of evacuation], bare-armed and barefooted, shoulder the expenses of building new huts? The sound of their wailing will be hard to endure. Relief will have to be provided. At five *ch'ien* each, 5,000–6,000 taels of tax money will be needed. Where will it come from?

3. Every mountain has strategic passes; along 1,500 *li* of mountains there cannot be less than a hundred passes. To cut and transport timbers for each pass will require a hundred laborers for three to five days. Thus, in all, 30,000–50,000 will be needed. Will the officials hire them, or will the people be sent to do it [as corvée]?

4. Building 1,500 *li* of wall and trench is a big task. The cost in tax money will be not less than 100,000 taels. The government does not have that much in funds for such expenses. If the people are required to provide the labor, then there will be discontent on all sides, and there will certainly be an uprising.

5. Land can be provided and houses built, but how many rooms will the charity of only five *ch'ien* build? How much worse when there are no resources to rely on and no room to accommodate refugees. Will the people be willing to give up food and home and be led to any wasteland? If the people consent to move, it will be generous on their part. But if they are stiff-necked, do not comply, and resist, will the government stop in midcourse and let them stay? Or will it use soldiers to threaten them?

6. After giving repeated commands and injunctions and expending much care and effort, can the government allow the people to stay and the authorities not to enforce their orders? That would teach the people arrogance, opposition to the government, and habits of impertinence; this is no way to rule. If troops are used to coerce them to move, and if the people fear they have come to kill them and that they will die whether they resist or not, they will be forced to take up cudgels and oppose the government troops. When matters have gone so far that the people dare to oppose the government, they must be killed. Without cause, our good subjects will be destroyed and our hearts will be difficult to pacify! . . . From ancient times governments have sought to settle the people, not disturb them, to rule them, not remove them.[39]

In Lan's view, not only would any benefit to be derived from the boundary policy be exceeded by the cost of implementing it, it would itself, by disrupting the livelihoods of the settlers, cause disorder on the frontier and thereby impose further control costs on the state. Lan then repeats his argument that empty frontiers only become the havens of bandits and savages. He ends by imploring the government not to carry through its evacuation plans and warns that whoever attempts to carry them out must be prepared to deal with the dangerous consequences outlined in his "six reckonings."

The "borderers" who settled along the raw aborigine frontier had an eloquent spokesman in Lan. His warnings about the disastrous consequences of population removal schemes were well grounded in Chinese historical experience and illustrate the shrewd, practical side of Chinese statecraft. But Lan seems to have exaggerated the number of settlers affected by the 1722 evacuation. The preferred areas of settlement were the river valleys, not the mountains, and the frontier had at that time simply not progressed much further.[40] In any case, Lan's rhetorical skill had some impact on the governor-general, who withdrew his order that certain frontier settlements, including some that had been the homes of Chu I-kuei and his rebel followers, be destroyed.[41] However, Lang-ch'iao (Heng-ch'un) was ordered abandoned and put off-limits to Chinese settlement.[42]

The 1722 "raw aborigine" boundary was established in a piecemeal fashion. In 1750 and 1760 the boundary was redrawn and the prohibition on its transgression reasserted. The later history of the boundary policy becomes entwined with Ch'ing policy concerning tribal land rights, and I shall discuss it at length in that context in Chapter 9.

Wall building and the evacuation of populations have a long history in Chinese approaches to the governance of frontiers (witness the Great Wall), and the Ch'ing dynasty made much use of these traditions. We have already noted the population removal and wall building along the southeast coast that the early Ch'ing adopted to erode the seaborne commercial power of the Chengs. The Manchus also used these policies in the north, for example, along the Amur, where tribal peoples were resettled to quarantine them from contact with the Russians.[43] The Willow Palisade, a barrier of thickly planted trees paralleled by a trench, was intended to keep Chinese settlers out of the Manchu tribal homelands and hunting preserves.[44] The walls dividing Chinese settlers and raw aborigines in Taiwan thus fall into an ongoing tradition (see Chapter 12). These walls were built to aid in the defense of settled areas, to contain the spread of unruly settlers within range of effective state control, and to prevent upsetting the ethnic status quo and the escalation of Han-aborigine conflicts.

Boundaries marked the line beyond which the costs of extending effective administration exceeded any perceived benefits of control, including contributions to government revenues.[45] Opposed to the policy of quarantining the mountains and raw aborigines were literati like Lan, who thought only aggressive colonization could ensure (and finance) government control. The relentless pressure of land-hungry Chinese settlers continually subverted official restrictions on settlement. While government policy fluctuated between withdrawal and advance, the settler population grew continually and steadily moved into aborigine areas. As the costs of pursuing one policy mounted, the benefits of the other looked more attractive. To the advocates of colonization, the mountain aborigines were the enemies of government control, and a growing settler population strengthened the position of the government. The advocates of boundaries and withdrawal saw things differently: the aborigines were the victims of wily, land-grabbing settlers, who might themselves be rebels and bandits.[46] But policy did not simply fluctuate; it evolved as well, as new means of accommodating Han and aborigine interests and new strategies of control were devised, as we shall see in Chapter 9 in the case of aborigine land rights. In many ways, boundary policies were a stopgap adopted until the civil and military administrations could be extended to provide more direct control. Let us turn next to discuss how government organs were extended to the frontier.

The Extension of the Military Presence

Military posts and coastal patrols preceded the presence of civil officials in the frontier areas.[47] In the 1680's the Ch'ing initially concentrated the bulk of its forces around the prefectural capital, assigning only 1,000 mainland soldiers to the north route. Of these, only 340 were posted north of Chia-li-hsing (in southernmost Chu-lo county, just north of Tainan): 85 at Hsia-chia-tung, 85 at Tou-liu-men, and 170 at Pan-hsien (Chang-hua). Pan-hsien's northernmost outpost (*t'ang*) was a station of ten men at Niu-ma far south of the Ta-chia river. A coastal patrol of 55 men was set up at Lu-kang, and another of the same size to the south at Pen-kang (present-day Pei-kang).[48] In the earliest years of Ch'ing rule, the only military, and for that matter official, presence of any kind, in the entire Tan-shui area north of the Ta-chia river was a marine patrol of ten-odd men who sailed from the southern ports to Pa-li-fen (near Tan-shui) and Keelung on the south wind and waited half a year for the north wind to take them back. According to Yü Yung-ho, this patrol merely stayed "two nights" and then returned.[49] This left Chinese in the area unprotected and gave refuge to outlaws. The major purpose of the coastal patrol was to ward off pirates, not to establish control over the local population. Nevertheless, it was the sub-lieutenant (*pa tsung*) in command of this patrol who quashed the Nei-pei-t'ou tribal revolt in 1699. The absence of land forces north of the Ta-chia river was cited as one reason the T'un-hsiao aborigines dared to revolt in 1699.[50] Thus, despite the heavy military presence in Taiwan prefecture compared with that in other jurisdictions, its concentration around Tainan meant that the military presence in the frontier areas of Taiwan was skeletal at best.

The headquarters of the north route battalion moved to Chu-lo in 1704 along with the county magistrate. Also in 1704 southern and central coastal defenses were strengthened by adding more troops (for a total of 380 men in Chu-lo's coastal patrol) and ships and by constructing forts, lookout towers, and furnaces for smoke signals. But the coastal ports north of Lu-kang, including Tan-shui, continued to be visited by only a semiannual patrol.[51] Only the threat from the pirate Cheng Chin-hsin,

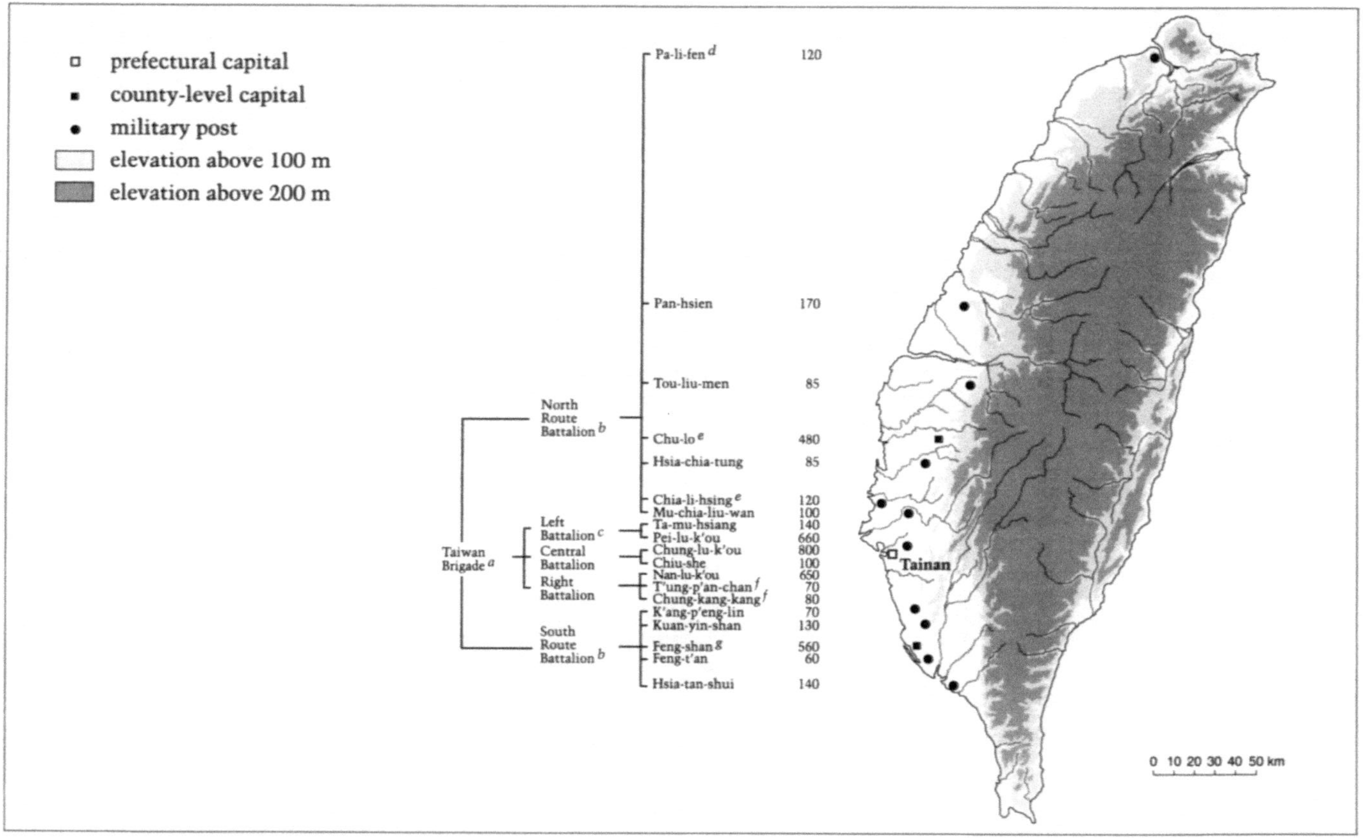

Map 7.2 The military administration of Taiwan, 1711

NOTE: Map 7.2 shows only the distribution of land forces (4,620 strong, see notes *c*, *d*). Marine and naval forces are not shown. Three thousand soldiers in three battalions made up the territorial battalion (*shui shih hsieh ying*) under the command of a naval colonel (*shui shih fu chiang*) headquartered in Tainan's port of An-p'ing. Two thousand soliders in two battalions were stationed in the Pescadores, also under a naval colonel (*TWFC*:Kao: 69–75; *TWFC*:Chou: 85–91). Total theoretical strength was thus 10,000 (5,000 land and 5,000 marine and naval). Troop strength is shown for patrols (*shao*) and posts (*hsün*) headed by lieutenants (*ch'ien tsung*) and sergeants (*pa tsung*). Smaller outposts (*t'ang*) are not shown.

[a]The Taiwan Brigade (*chen piao*) was headed by a brigade general (*tsung ping*). Directly subordinate to the brigade were the Left, Central, and Right battalions (*ying*) each headed by a major (*yu chi*).

[b]The North and South Route battalions were each headed by a lieutenant colonel (*ts'an chiang*).

[c]The theoretical strength of each of these battalions was 1,000; the rest of the soldiers were assigned to a unit under the Taiwan intendant (*tao piao*) (*TWFC*:Chou: 91).

[d]Added in 1711.

[e]The North Route Battalion headquarters moved to Chu lo from Chia-li-hsing in 1704.

[f]Exact location unknown.

[g]Sixty soldiers were assigned to the Manchu general-in-chief (*chiang chün*) at Foochow.

who had been active in the Strait of Taiwan and had temporarily taken refuge in Tan-shui in 1710 or 1711 led to the northward transfer of troops and the establishment of the Tan-shui subdistrict lieutenancy (*fen fang ch'ien tsung*). The creation of a string of seven stations (*t'ang*) linked for the first time the Ta-chia river area to Pa-li-fen. The lieutenant posted at Pa-li-fen had 120 soldiers under his command: 70 distributed among the seven stations and 50 assigned to the patrol headquarters (*hsün*) at Pa-li-fen.[52] The military stations functioned as surveillance points, rather like police stations, and provided courier services. (See Map 7.2 for the distribution of land forces in 1711.)

In 1718 the Pa-li-fen post was raised to the status of a battalion (*ying*) under the command of a second captain (*shou pei*). This was done at the urging of Governor Ch'en Pin, who had served as Taiwan-Amoy intendant during the pirate raids of Cheng Chin-hsin. Governor-general Man-pao's memorial of 1718 calls for a garrison of 500 soldiers (to be culled from the pre-existing Taiwan units) and six warships and for a lieutenant and sub-lieutenant to rotate in defending both Tan-shui and Keelung.[53] Due to these reinforcements, Tan-shui was one of the few areas of the island that did not fall to the rebels three years later during the Chu I-kuei rebellion.[54]

After the Chu I-kuei rebellion, Governor-general Man-pao requested the addition of 3,500 soldiers to Taiwan's garrisons. The court, however, satisfied that the rebellion had been quashed "within seven days" by a force rushed to Taiwan from Amoy (and convinced that the rebellion had broken out because of corrupt civil and military officials and not because of a lack of troops) was uninterested in policies requiring additional expenditures and taxes. In the court's view, the land and naval forces were sufficient to help each other out of difficulties. So the court rejected Man-pao's request, reasserted the policy of using Fukienese troops whose families were left behind, and banned local recruitment once again.[55] Both Huang Shu-ching and Lan Ting-yüan pointed out corrupt practices in the rotation system, such as the hiring of substitutes and embezzlement of salaries. But their proposals for the establishment of colonies of soldier-farmers and for local recruitment brought no response.[56] The court chose instead a plan calling for the annual dispatch of inspecting censors to supervise local officials and identify problems in Taiwan before trouble broke out (see below), and Man-pao adopted a boundary policy quarantining the mountains and attempting to restrict Chinese settlers to areas under effective government control (see above).

In 1730 the brigade general, Wang Chün, requested an increase in the Tan-shui and Keelung forces, but Governor-general Kao Ch'i-cho saw no pressing need for the increase.[57] Kao was proven wrong the next year. The double rebellions of aborigines and Han in 1731 and 1732 revealed the inadequacy of Ch'ing military power, especially in the area north of Ta-chia. This brought the only major military reorganization Taiwan would see until after the Lin Shuang-wen rebellion in the 1780's. Although these rebellions were also suppressed only after mainland troops were dispatched from Amoy, the court approved Governor-general Hao Yü-lin's request to increase Taiwan's garrison to over 12,600 men in 1733.[58] The additional troops were to be rotated from Fukien; local recruitment continued to be forbidden.[59]

Thus, the double rebellion of 1731–32 resulted in a major military reorganization that had not been forthcoming in the wake of the much more threatening Chu I-kuei rebellion of 1721, when even the prefectural capital had fallen into rebel hands. Two differences of timing were important in producing this result. First, the double rebellion demonstrated that the conservative reconstruction policies adopted after the Chu I-kuei rebellion had been inadequate to guarantee order in Taiwan. Second, the double rebellion occurred under the administration of the activist Yung-cheng emperor, who had already set a pro-colonization course in his Taiwan policies. These two factors led to reconstruction efforts of much greater magnitude and aggressiveness.

In the new disposition of its military forces (see Map 7.3), the court continued to concentrate strength around the prefectural capital, the center of government power in Taiwan, where it added 1,000 soldiers and brought the Taiwan brigade to full strength. Sizable increases were made, however, in the frontier garrisons. Five hundred men were added to the south route battalion in Feng-shan. Most significantly, the troop strength of the north route battalion was more than doubled to a total of 2,400 men. Its headquarters were moved north to Chang-hua, and 500 men were posted to a battalion in the subprefectural capital at Chu-ch'ien, which had formerly quartered only 15 soldiers. New posts were created, and the troop contingents of old ones increased.[60]

After 1733 only occasionally would a post be relocated or a new one created. In creating new military posts on the frontier, the Ch'ing government had to proceed with caution, not just because of fiscal considerations or the difficulty of transporting provisions, but also because of the potential of unruly soldiers themselves to be a source of disturbance.[61]

The first non-military institutions (other than tribal interpreters) established by the government in the frontier areas of Tan-shui and Chang-hua were granaries at Tan-shui and Pan-hsien, founded in 1716. The need for granaries points up the dependence of an expanding military presence on the concurrent expansion of agricultural settlement. Before these granaries were established, the military garrisons had to transport their rice from the south at considerable cost. The cost of rice at Tan-shui was 60 percent higher than at Chang-hua, where the garrison could rely at least partly on locally produced supplies. Magistrate Chou Chung-hsüan must have been looking forward to a day when Tan-shui itself could

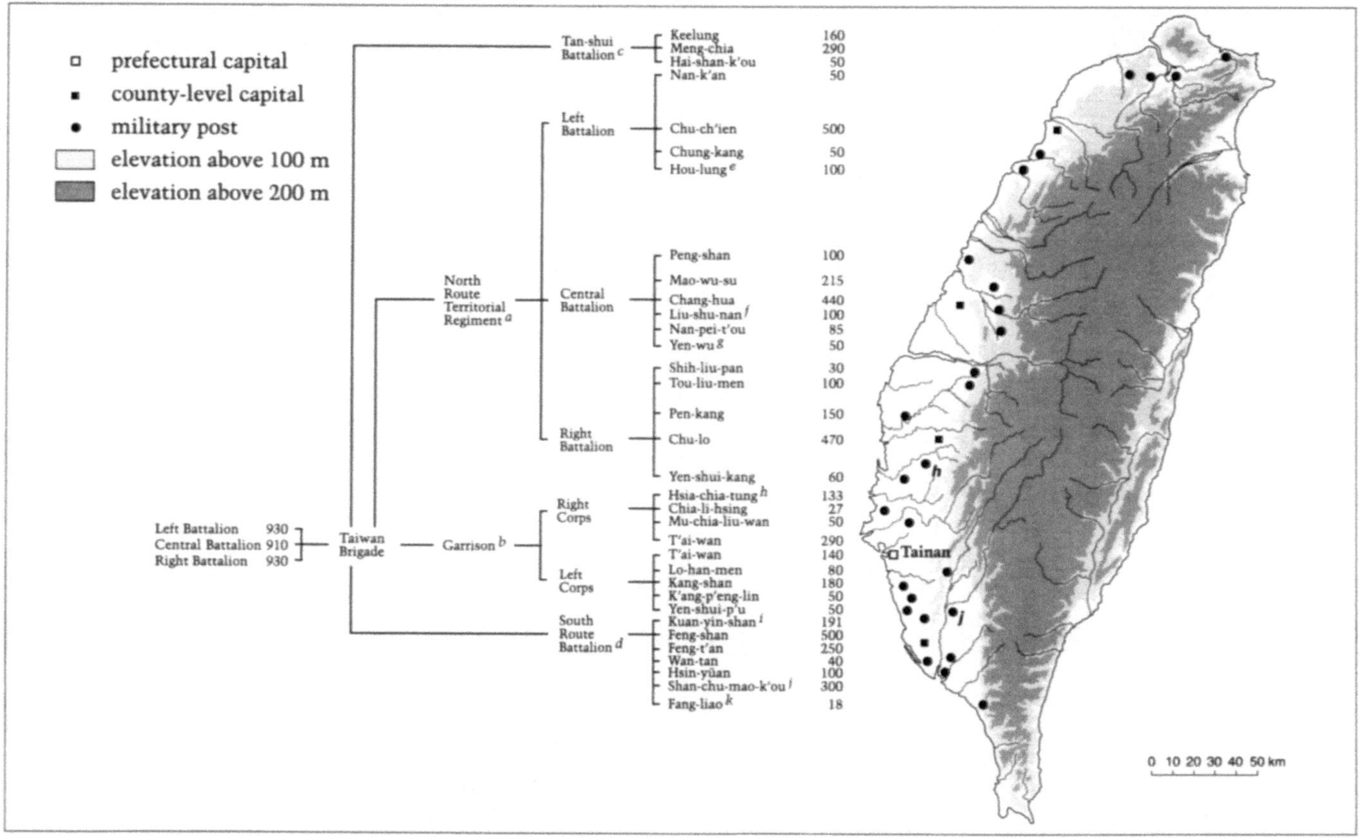

Map 7.3 The military administration of Taiwan, 1733

NOTE: Map 7.3 shows only land forces (see Map 7.2) for a total strength of 8,169. In 1733 the strength of the naval battalions in Taiwan was reduced from 3,000 to 2,500 and naval patrols were stationed in more of the smaller ports to the north and south of Tainan (*TWFC*:Yü: 370–73). Assignments to the intendant were discontinued (see Map 7.2, note *c*). Total strength was theoretically 12,600. The following notes address only changes from the 1711 troop structure (*TWFC*:Liu: 316–25). Troop strength is shown for patrols and posts headed by lieutenants and sergeants, except in the immediate vicinity of Tainan where only larger units are shown. The Left, Central, and Right battalions directly under the brigade general were concentrated in the prefectural capital of Tainan.

[a]The North Route Territorial Regiment (*hsieh piao*) was commanded by a colonel (*fu chiang*). Under him were a first captain over the Central Battalion and second captains over the Left and Right battalions.

[b]The Taiwan Garrison (*ch'eng shou ying*) was headed by a lieutenant colonel (*ts'an chiang*). Under him were the Right and Left corps (*chün*), each headed by a second captain (*shou pei*).

[c]The Tan-shui Battalion was founded in 1718 and was commanded by a first captain (*tu ssu*). The Meng-chia post was moved from Tan-shui port, probably in 1759.

[d]The South Route Battalion continued to be headed by a lieutenant colonel.

[e]Moved inland to Chia-chih-ko in 1766.

[f]Founded in 1738 (*CLSL*: 12).

[g]Exact location unknown.

[h]Hsia-chia-tung is to the northeast of Yen-shui-kang.

[i]Two posts of unknown location are listed with Kuan-yin-shan (73 soldiers), Shih-ching (78), and Pan-kuei-ch'iao (40).

[j]Shan-chu-mao-k'ou also included 28 soldiers at A-li-kang, 30 at Wu-li, and 28 at Hsin-tung-shih (location unknown).

[k]Fang-liao is the southernmost post, but no officer is listed as stationed there.

supply the grain to fill the granary; his arguments in favor of building the granary included the convenience and savings in transport costs to tax-paying farmers of a local granary over a more distant collection point.[62] The spread of military posts on the frontier and the expansion of settlement were thus interrelated. The burden on government revenues of establishing and provisioning garrisons where no local settlers produced rice and paid taxes was a heavy one. Settlers in turn were attracted to areas made more secure by a military presence.[63]

The Extension of the Civil Administration

Military posts sometimes preceded Chinese settlement on the frontier, but the civil bureaucracy almost always lagged far behind settlement, which it periodically tried to contain behind artificial boundaries (see above). Expanding the civil administration on an unsettled frontier increased the strain on local revenues (already burdened by the large military presence). In Taiwan's case, revenue increases depended on land taxes from newly reclaimed lands. Only after settlement had proceeded for a while was it deemed important to register the land and fund an expanded civil administration to control the population.

We now trace the civil bureaucracy's slow penetration of the frontier. In 1683 all of north Taiwan was included in the county of Chu-lo (see Map 7.4), but the magistrate remained far to the south. The county yamen of Chu-lo was first located in the prefectural capital of Tainan, outside the county territory; it later moved a few miles north of Tainan to Chia-li-hsing, also the site of its subdistrict magistracy. Only in 1704 did it move to the outpost of Chu-lo (present-day Chia-i).[64] A series of dispatch stations were all that linked the yamen to the territory north of Chu-lo. At first these reached only to Ta-tu, just north of Pan-hsien, but around 1716 they were extended from Ta-chia to Tan-shui.[65]

Although the court, after the Chu I-kuei rebellion of 1721, refused to add to the Taiwan garrisons, it did initiate important changes in Taiwan's civil administration.[66] To increase surveillance over both frontier bureaucrats and frontier society, the court decided that two censors, one Manchu and one Han, should make annual tours of inspection to Taiwan.[67] In 1722 Huang Shu-ching (Han) and Wu-ta-li (Manchu) became the first censors to tour Taiwan under the new policy. Recognizing that one magistrate could not control all of Chu-lo's vast territory and influenced by arguments in the Chu-lo gazetteer, they recommended that Chu-lo county be subdivided by creating a new county north of the Hu-wei river. Accordingly, in 1723 Chang-hua county was established. In addition, a new Tan-shui coastal defense subprefect was assigned to the north route, from the Hu-wei river to Tan-shui, and ultimately was given administrative responsibility for the territory above the Ta-chia river

(Tan-shui subprefecture). The coastal defense subprefect in Tainan remained responsible for Chu-lo, T'ai-wan, and Feng-shan counties.[68]

The creation of two additional county-level units in 1723 was justified not by the size of the population (estimated at 315,000 in 1723)[69] but by the size of the territory. Although Taiwan's population was growing rapidly in these years, it was far below the level that would have supported five county-level units at the nationwide average population per county. This was especially true in an era when the Yung-cheng emperor was reducing the overall number of counties from 1,509 to 1,360. This raised the average population per county and makes the addition of county-level units in Taiwan all that more remarkable (although, of course, from another point of view, it was not remarkable at all—the consolidation and reduction in number of counties in core areas enabled the state to create new ones along its strategic peripheries).[70] In adding two new county-level units, the state recognized that a single magistrate could not effectively extend control over an area as large as northern Taiwan, especially when a growing population was adding to problems of control. The prospect of increasing local revenue (from taxes on newly reclaimed land) that an expanding population of immigrants from the southeast coast would generate helped overcome opposition to enlarging the Taiwan administration.[71]

In 1727, with the reopening of Amoy to the Southeast Asian trade, Fukien's Hsing-Ch'üan intendant was moved to Amoy. The T'ai-Hsia intendant consequently lost his Amoy jurisdiction and Taiwan became his sole responsibility. As part of these adjustments, a second-class subprefecture with special maritime duties was created in the Pescadores (and the *hsün chien*, subdistrict magistrate, eliminated).[72]

The offices of Chang-hua county (and most likely therefore those of Tan-shui subprefecture) remained in Chu-lo until 1728 when they were finally moved to Chang-hua.[73] Adjustments approved in early 1731 greatly expanded the presence of the civil administration in central and northern Taiwan (see Map 7.5). In the second month of 1731, the Tan-shui subprefecture, created in 1723, was given full jurisdiction in criminal cases and financial independence in the territory north of the Ta-chia river.[74] Four new subdistrict magistracies were created: two in Chang-hua county, one at the port of Lu-kang and one at Mao-wu-su; and two in Tan-shui subprefecture, one at Chu-ch'ien (Hsin-chu) and one at Pa-li-fen (the harbor at Tan-shui in the north). Also at this time it was decided to post an assistant magistrate (*hsien ch'eng*) in Pen-kang town in Chu-lo and to move the Chia-li-hsing subdistrict magistrate (*hsün chien*) to Yen-shui-kang. In posting so many assistant and subdistrict magistrates in central and northern Taiwan, the government acknowledged the growth of market towns and ports and attendant settlement in that region. One assistant magistrate was also added in Feng-shan county in the south.[75]

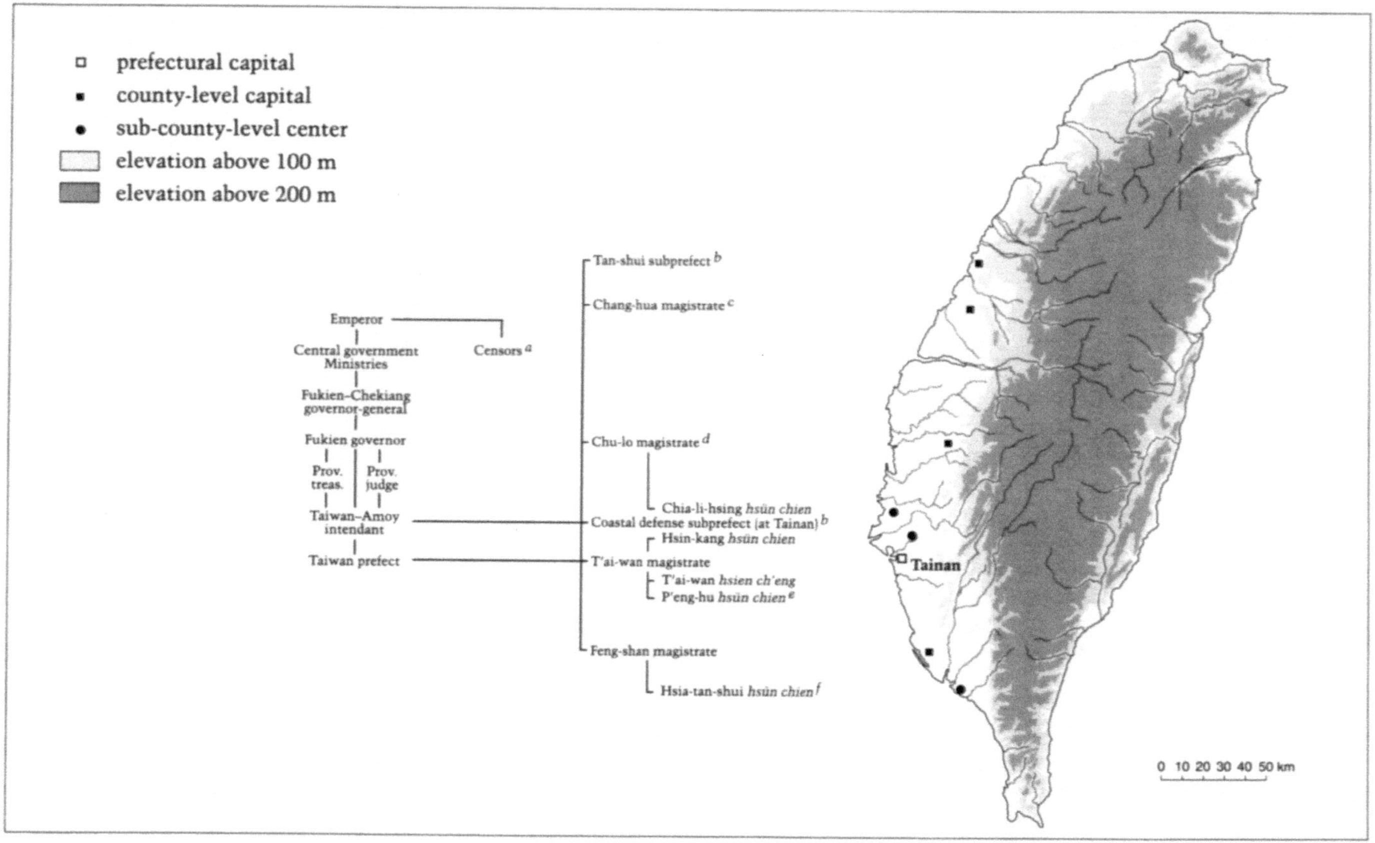

Map 7.4 The civil administration of Taiwan, 1723

NOTE: The chain of command follows Ch'ü 1962: 5. Subprefects were of higher rank than magistrates. A *hsien ch'eng* (assistant magistrate) was of higher rank than a *hsün chien* (subdistrict magistrate).

[a]Censors conducted annual tours of inspection beginning in 1722.

[b]The jurisdiction of the coastal defense subprefect was restricted to the south route (Chu-lo, T'ai-wan, and Feng-shan counties) after 1723, when the Tan-shui subprefect took responsibility for Chang-hua and Tan-shui. The Tan-shui subprefect was still at Sha-lu in 1731 (see text).

[c]Created 1723, moved to Chang-hua from Chu-lo ca. 1728 (see text).

[d]Offices moved to Chu-lo in 1704.

[e]P'eng-hu (the Pescadores) is not shown on the map.

[f]Because eight of the first nine incumbents died in office when this office was located in Tung-kang, it was moved to Ch'ih-shan in 1712.

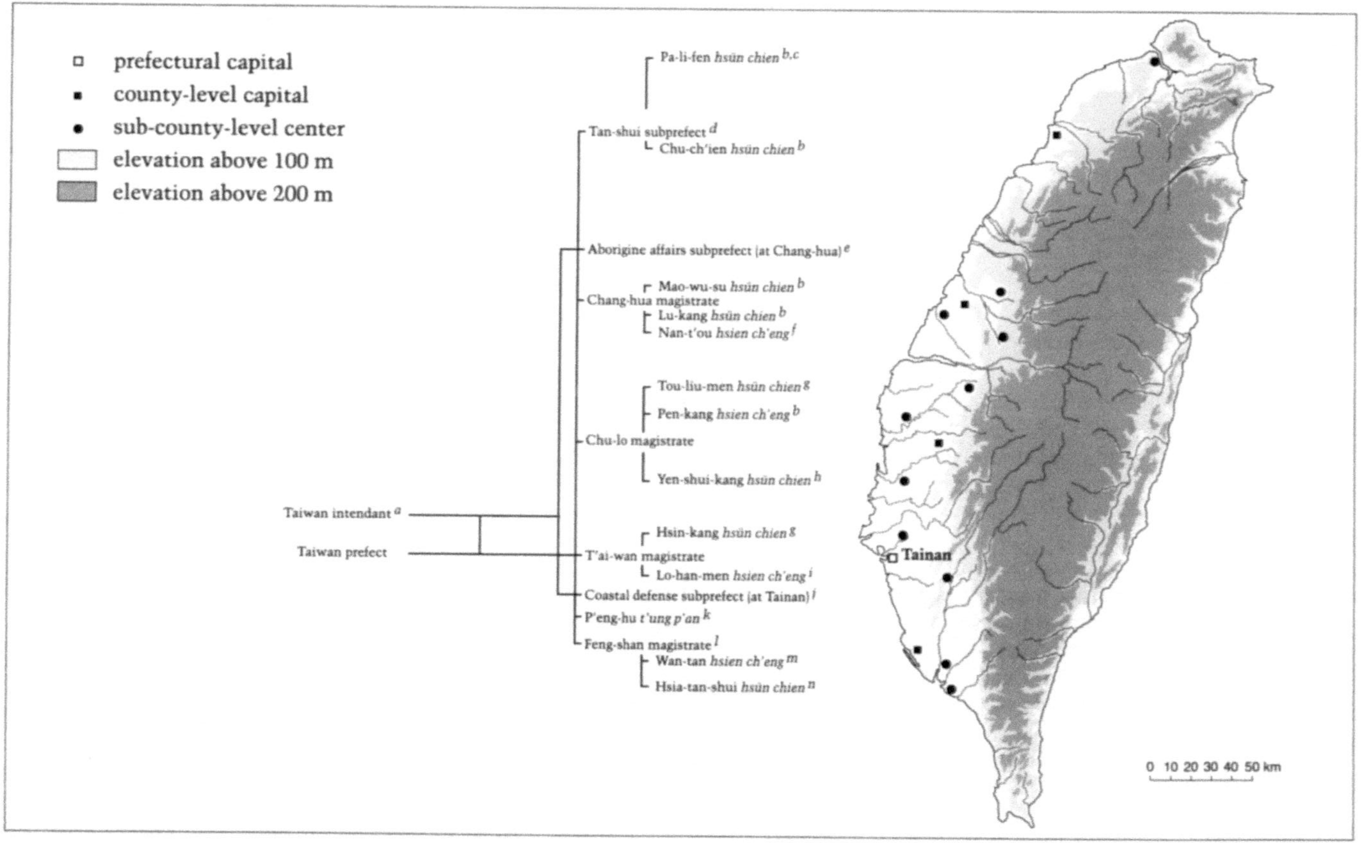

Map 7.5 The civil administration of Taiwan after 1731

[a]After 1727 the Taiwan intendant (*tao t'ai*) resided full-time in Tainan.

[b]Created in 1731.

[c]Moved to Hsin-chuang in 1767, raised to *hsien ch'eng* in 1790.

[d]Given jurisdiction over revenue and criminal cases above the Ta-chia river in 1731.

[e]Created in 1766, given coastal defense duties for the north route in 1783, moved to Lu-kang in 1788. The north route aborigine affairs jurisdiction covered Tan-shui, Chang-hua, and Chu-lo.

[f]Created in 1759.

[g]In 1761 T'ai-wan county's Hsin-kang *hsün chien* was transferred to Chu-lo's Tou-liu-men.

[h]In 1731 the Chia-li-hsing *hsün chien* was moved to Yen-shui-kang; in 1788 it was moved to Ta-wu-lung.

[i]In 1731 the T'ai-wan *hsien ch'eng* was moved to Lo-han-men; in 1789 his status was lowered to *hsün chien*.

[j]After 1766 the south route coastal defense subprefect also had aborigine affairs duties in Feng-shan and T'ai-wan.

[k]In 1727 the P'eng-hu *hsün chien* under T'ai-wan county was raised to the status of a second-class subprefect (*t'ung p'an*) in charge of P'eng-hu subprefecture (the Pescadores are not shown on the map).

[l]The seat of Feng-shan county moved to modern Feng-shan in 1788.

[m]Created in 1731, moved to A-li-kang in 1761, and to Hsia-tan-shui in 1788.

[n]Moved in 1788 to Hsing-lung, the original site of Feng-shan (*chiu ch'eng*).

This sudden expansion in the civil administration without a complementary extension of the military garrisons (there were still only 170 soldiers at Pan-hsien, and five outposts of 5–15 soldiers between Ta-chia and Chu-ch'ien) (see Maps 7.2 and 7.5) had disastrous consequences. The spate of yamen building this expansion required burdened the local civilized aborigines with excessive amounts of corvée. By the end of 1731, the plains aborigines of the Ta-chia area could take no more and revolted, requiring a lengthy campaign and the dispatch of mainland troops to restore order (see Chapter 5).

The expansion in the north planned in 1731 could be implemented only after the suppression of the large aborigine revolt of 1731–32. Lan Ting-yüan sought to persuade Governor-general Hao Yü-lin to move the Tan-shui subprefectural offices north to Chu-ch'ien, where they were originally intended to be sited. Lan thought Chu-ch'ien's location midway between Chang-hua and Tan-shui was ideal for the extension of governmental influence.[76] Finally in 1733 a bamboo thicket was planted and offices were built in Chu-ch'ien, and several bureaus apparently began operation there. However, it seems that the Tan-shui subprefect did not himself take up residence in Chu-ch'ien until 1755.[77]

Most of Taiwan's administrative capitals remained unwalled throughout the eighteenth century. Proper brick and stone walls were expensive to build and, when built, of uncertain strategic value. After the Chu I-kuei rebellion, earthen walls were constructed at Feng-shan in 1722 and Chu-lo in 1723; only a wooden palisade was built for the prefectural capital of Tainan in 1723.[78] After the revolts of the Ta-chia tribes and Wu Fu-sheng in 1731–32, the wall building policies were re-examined. Omida, governor of Kwangtung and Lan Ting-yüan's patron, initiated the debate with a recommendation to build walls. Governor-general Hao Yü-lin, opting for low-cost bamboo thickets rather than walls, pointed out that Taiwan's rebels had been defeated by armies that came by sea from Amoy and not by the static defense of walled cities. Stone walls were not cost-effective. Consequently, the earthen walls and wooden palisades of Taiwan's capitals were merely reinforced by the planting of prickly bamboo in 1733–34 (see Fig. 7.1).[79] The debate on wall building was renewed after the Lin Shuang-wen rebellion (see Chapter 10).

In the decades after the large-scale reorganization of the civil administration in 1731, the court made only marginal adjustments. Repeated instances of corruption and malfeasance caused the Ch'ien-lung emperor to lose faith in the utility of the inspecting censors' annual tours to Taiwan, which, as noted above, were instituted in the wake of the Chu I-kuei rebellion.[80] But rather than heighten surveillance and reform that institution, the emperor reduced its importance. In 1752 the frequency of the censors' tours was reduced to once every three years, and in 1765 it was decided to dispatch censors to Taiwan only under special circum-

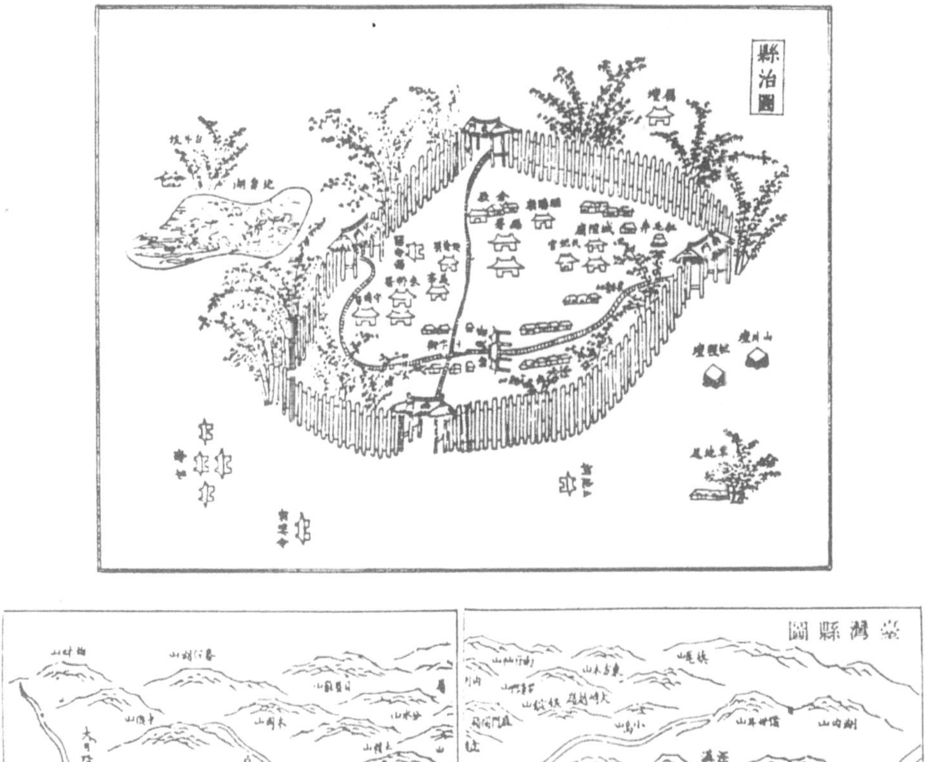

Fig. 7.1 Two frontier capitals. (*above*) Chu-lo, ca. 1717 (SOURCE: *CLHC*). (*below*) Tainan, ca. 1745 (SOURCE: *TWFC*:Fan).

stances at imperial command. In 1785, following the large outbreak of communal strife in 1782 (see Chapter 10), the emperor replaced the system and ordered the governor-general, governor, and land and marine commanders (*t'i tu*) to rotate on annual tours of inspection to increase supervision over Taiwan.[81]

The civil administration on the north route, particularly in areas bordering the hills, was strengthened in the mid-Ch'ien-lung reign by the addition of two officials and relocation of a third. An assistant magistrate was added at Nan-t'ou in Chang-hua in 1759, and a subdistrict magistrate was relocated to Tou-liu-men in Chu-lo from Hsin-kang in T'ai-wan in 1761.[82] In 1766 the government created the post of subprefect for aborigine affairs on the north route with offices at Chang-hua (see Chapter 9), further intensifying its administrative presence in the north. These additions to the civil bureaucracy reflect the spread of population inland toward the hills; the previous increase in 1731 had located new submagistrates primarily in market towns and ports on the coastal plain.

That each of Taiwan's counties had one assistant magistrate (higher ranking than subdistrict magistrates) and (except for T'ai-wan) at least one subdistrict magistrate, whereas only one in three of China's counties had assistant magistrates and two in three subdistrict magistrates,[83] underscores the court's determination to extend effective control over Taiwan's large frontier areas. The requirement that Taiwan's magistrates be appointed by provincial authorities from a pool of experienced officials (i.e., by transfer appointment) appears to have lapsed in the case of the magistrates of Feng-shan, Chu-lo, and Chang-hua counties at least from 1757 to 1763, which are the two earliest Registers of Officials I have seen. By 1773, however, the Register of Officials does designate all of Taiwan's county magistrates as important transfer appointments, an indication the court continued to assign considerable strategic significance to its turbulent and hard-to-control island frontier.[84]

In 1783 the busy port of Lu-kang was officially opened to the cross-strait trade, signaling a significant break with the old quarantine policies. Coastal defense was added to the aborigine affairs subprefect's duties, and his offices were ordered relocated to Lu-kang (a move made only in 1788).[85]

Further intensification of the administrative hierarchy of the north route came after the Lin Shuang-wen rebellion of 1786–88. In central Taiwan, the yamen at Tou-liu-men was raised in rank to that of assistant magistrate, and a new subdistrict magistracy was created at Ta-wu-lung in Chu-lo. In the Tan-shui area, the port of Pa-li-fen was opened at this time to the cross-strait trade, and the subdistrict magistracy at Hsin-chuang (where it had been moved from Pa-li-fen in 1767) was raised to the rank of assistant magistracy in 1790.[86] The Register of Officials for 1794 shows the importance rankings of Taiwan's posts unchanged after the Lin Shuang-wen rebellion. The overall strategic importance of the prefecture had been raised, however: the Taiwan intendant and prefect were now appointed by imperial command. In addition, Taiwan's intendant and brigade general were given the privilege of directly memorializing the throne.[87]

The increasing presence of civil officers on the northern frontier reflects its growing population (and potential for disorder) and its increasing economic importance and revenue potential. The reluctance of civil officials to move to the frontier is notable, however; there was frequently a delay of several years from the establishment of a post to the date offices actually began functioning and the magistrate took up residence in the designated capital.

In the area of Tan-shui subprefecture, the presence of the Ch'ing government was initially very meager indeed; Tan-shui was visited only by a semiannual coastal patrol until 1711. Thus, from 1683 to 1711 the large area north of the Ta-chia river was an administrative void; tribal monopoly merchants and interpreters were the only representatives of the government. Only in 1711 was the Tan-shui subdistrict lieutenancy founded to counter a pirate threat. With the establishment in 1718 of the Tan-shui battalion of 500 men, the Ch'ing military in the Taipei basin became quite formidable. But the stationing of these military garrisons was a reaction not to problems of controlling a growing settler population (minuscule in Tan-shui in 1718) but to the threat of pirate and perhaps foreign intrusion. Nevertheless, such a large contingent did have a substantial impact on the preservation of local order, as shown by its successful resistance in the Chu I-kuei rebellion of 1721. The small forces stationed in the area from Chang-hua to Chu-ch'ien, however, remained weak and vulnerable until the 1731–32 aborigine revolt brought the military reorganization of 1733. The enlargement of old posts and the addition of new ones in 1733 spread and deepened the military presence throughout the area as the guarantee of local order became a major mission. Yet it is ironic that the large military forces posted to Taiwan were still unable to prevent numerous outbreaks of rebellion and communal strife.

In contrast to the military, the civil administration of the north, concentrated in fewer centers and waiting on the expansion of Han settlement, spread more slowly, and seemingly reluctantly. Periodic attempts to restrict settlers to areas under effective government control through boundary policies failed to contain expanding settlement. Briefly, in 1731, direct civil administration expanded ahead of the military in the Chang-hua–Chu-ch'ien area—with disastrous consequences. After the double revolt of 1731–32 the military presence was belatedly enlarged in this area.

The extension of government control through expanding civil and military bureaucracies was always constrained by budgeting and grain supply considerations. A strong aversion to heavy taxes and bureaucratic proliferation guided the court's evaluation of its policy alternatives. We have repeatedly seen that the government's decision making took careful measure of operational costs and limited revenues. The government's control could only be as strong as its fiscal administration and revenue base allowed. As we shall see in Chapter 8, to an advocate of colonization such as Lan Ting-yüan the solution to these problems was simple: fostering reclamation would supply the revenues and grain supplies needed by an expanded administration. But first we turn to consider an important low-cost means of social control, Confucian education and the examination system.

Cultural Policy, Education, and Examinations

The late imperial state ruled its localities through a large repertoire of sophisticated institutions and policies. Elaborate civil and military bureaucracies penetrated and encompassed regional systems and integrated them into the empire. The state pursued social order and local security through the *pao chia* system, which imposed collective responsibility on local communities. A legal code guided the administration of justice, and courts of review and appeal provided a means of supervising its application by local magistrates. State-sponsored granaries provided famine relief and helped stabilize food prices against harvest fluctuations. We have seen in Taiwan how the state restricted immigration and grain exports to control the growth of frontier society. The state recruited ethnic auxiliaries and local militias to supplement its regular military forces. We will analyze in the next chapter state fiscal policies and revenue collection, as well as the allocation of land rights and taxpaying obligations. The state thus operated an elaborate apparatus to maintain and finance control over the localities of the empire.[88]

But the empire's population was huge and its territories were vast. Direct means of exercising social control (through rewards and punishments) made heavy demands on the limited administrative capacity and restricted financial resources of the late imperial state. Less expensive means of social control, creating cultural dominance and enlisting the assistance of local elites in societal management, were necessary complements to effective government. The manipulation of cultural prestige and the channeling of social mobility through the examination system were key mechanisms that enabled a tiny bureaucratic elite to maintain cultural hegemony and control over a vast empire.[89]

Confucian theories of government that emphasized ruling through moral example and education rather than manipulation of rewards and punishments found expression in Ch'ing cultural policies. Multiple assertions of the moral superiority of the Confucian order were necessary to creating its prestige and influence among the populace. The state cult, in which scholar-officials played important symbolic and ritual roles, claimed supernatural sanction for the imperial order. Magistrates officiated at seasonal rituals that portrayed the imperial order as a key link between the supernatural will of heaven and the success of human endeavors. The state used its influence to increase orthodoxy in folk religion and even in popular entertainments, such as operas. Popular religious cults were heavily influenced by bureaucratic models of dealing with the supernatural. The extension of civil administration was accompanied by the extension of a network of government-sponsored shrines and temples.

Ch'ing magistrates were expected to serve as models of virtue for the populace. Magistrates encouraged adoption of elite funerary and other family rites and conferred honors and praise on those who exemplified Confucian virtues. Educational indoctrination and public lectures on the K'ang-hsi emperor's Sacred Edict were intended to convince locals of the moral superiority of the Confucian order and to foster ideological orthodoxy and attitudes of submission to constituted authority. Confucian rituals attempted to create the same effects through impressive performances.[90]

Ch'ing cultural policies in Taiwan resembled those pursued elsewhere in the empire. Confucian cultural messages were familiar to Han immigrants to Taiwan, many of whom had (humble) origins in prefectures of southern Fukien that were among the most culturally advanced in the empire.[91] The Ch'ing state thus had little reason to adjust its standard cultural policies for Taiwan's Han settlers. Although the degree of official attention to the development of local education fluctuated (peaking in the wake of disturbances), there were no reversals in cultural policy toward Han settlers that mirror the vacillations in quarantine and procolonization policies. (See Chapter 11 for a discussion of cultural policies toward the plains aborigines.)

Orthodox social institutions and local elites were weak and undeveloped on Taiwan's newly settled frontier, which had more than its share of outlaws, secret societies, and gangs. The rapid collapse of government control during the Chu I-kuei rebellion in 1721 demonstrated the frail links between state and society. Cultural policies and an educational bureaucracy were important tools of statecraft for creating a culturally orthodox local elite with a vested interest in the social order maintained by the state. The court was aware of Taiwan's status as a culturally undeveloped yet strategic periphery, and in the setting of educational and examination quotas, we find one sphere of cultural policy that was adjusted to encourage the cultural development of Taiwan's frontier society and the growth of an orthodox local elite.

The late imperial Chinese state used its civil and military examination systems to cultivate and co-opt local elites and to channel their strivings for power and status enhancement. The examination system was an ingenious and low-cost method of social control that also helped create an impressive degree of cultural unity across the empire. In Mark Elvin's words, "By making both high office and local privileges accessible almost exclusively to those with official academic degrees, a way was found to absorb the energies and the ambitions of the able and condition them ideologically through the curriculum at their own expense and wish."[92] The late imperial state was able to ensure the indoctrination of local elites in an orthodox curriculum by reserving the posts of civil government only to those who demonstrated mastery of official Confucianism through the examination system. A parallel system recruited officers for the armed forces. Because government office (whether civil or military) offered unrivaled access to power, wealth, and privilege, all aspirants to higher status were channeled into a single avenue of social mobility under the state's control. Thus, through the examination system the imperial state created an impressive degree of ideological uniformity among both local elites and imperial bureaucrats and reinforced this unity by rotating officeholders through the regions of the empire. Through association with overarching imperial power, the same degree- and office-holding elite acquired unrivaled prestige in every locality of the empire.

The system of local schools and educational offices that administered the examinations was a key component of the Ch'ing field administration in every locality. The state's power to set examination quotas further enhanced its control over aspiring elites and the local societies from which they sprang. These quotas were consciously used to ensure broad geographic distribution of the degree-holding elite and to cultivate the growth of a Confucian literati in regions where the state's influence was weak.[93] The following discussion, after sketching the institutional framework established to administer the examinations, seeks to assess the extent to which the Ch'ing state used these quotas as instruments of control in its administration of Taiwan.

The Ch'ing system of examinations awarded three basic academic degrees in a series of increasingly competitive examinations. Twice every three years, county and prefectural qualifying examinations were held to award the *sheng yüan* degree. Once every three years, provincial examinations were held to award the *chü jen* degree, and metropolitan examinations were held to award the highest and most select degree, the *chin shih*.

The scholar-official elite of the empire was composed of holders of the *chin shih* and *chü jen* degrees, along with meritorious holders of the *sheng yüan* degree selected to be *kung sheng*, or tribute students; all holders of these degrees were eligible to hold office in the imperial bureaucracy. Holders of the *sheng yüan* degree, on the other hand, were scholar-commoners; they did not qualify for official appointment and remained subject to supervision by provincial educational commissioners. *Sheng yüan* nevertheless enjoyed substantial prestige and limited legal privileges that made them part of the local elite.[94]

All examination degrees were subject to strict quotas to limit the number of candidates for a fixed number of offices, to prevent the devaluation of status that would result from degree inflation, and to guarantee broad regional representation in the official elite. Quotas assigned to county and prefectural schools set the number of *sheng yüan* degrees to be awarded at each examination and limited eligible candidates to natives of each jurisdiction. The court set provincial quotas to guarantee a broad geographic distribution of *chü jen* degree holders; these quotas therefore reflected only in part the differences in population and academic attainments among the provinces. As a result, *chü jen* quotas favored northern and frontier provinces over the populous, wealthy, and culturally advanced provinces of the southeast; this meant in Fukien's case that competition for its triennial quota of 85 *chü jen* degrees was stiffer than average.[95] Since, however, competition within each province was open to all native *sheng yüan*, candidates from prosperous and academically advanced localities generally dominated the lists of successful provincial graduates.

The metropolitan examinations were also subject to provincial quotas (which largely reflected provincial *chü jen* quotas) set to guarantee a broad geographic distribution of successful *chin shih* candidates. This again operated to the disadvantage of candidates from the culturally advanced southeastern provinces.[96]

The court awarded generous examination quotas to the new island-prefecture of Taiwan with an eye to cultivating a local elite that would foster cultural orthodoxy and social control. The standard educational bureaucracy was created as part of the establishment of civil administration following the surrender of the Cheng regime, and in 1686 the Ch'ing assigned *sheng yüan* quotas to Taiwan. These quotas provided for the admission, following each round of examinations, of twenty *sheng yüan* to the prefectural school, and twelve each to the schools of Feng-shan, T'ai-wan, and Chu-lo counties. In addition, stipends were provided for more qualified *sheng yüan*, termed *lin sheng* (twenty from the prefectural school, and ten from each county school). The schools were also authorized to name *kung sheng*, one every year from the prefectural school and one every two years from each county school. These quotas remained fixed until the early nineteenth century, the only exception being that for the newly created county of Chang-hua, which in 1723 received quotas of eight *sheng yüan* for every examination, stipends for ten *lin sheng*, and authorization to name one *kung sheng* every four years. Only in 1815 did Tan-shui subprefecture receive separate quotas of six *sheng yüan* for each examination.[97]

Given Taiwan's sparse population and undeveloped academic tradition, the 1686 quotas were quite generous. Taiwan's *sheng yüan* quotas compare favorably with the national standard (per examination) of twenty *sheng yüan* per prefectural school, fifteen for a large-county school, and only four to five for a "backward"-county school. The 1686 *kung sheng* quotas also matched the national standard for ordinary counties.[98] The 1686 quotas also appear generous when compared to the much smaller quotas later allowed Chang-hua county and Tan-shui subprefecture. The awarding of such large quotas to an undeveloped frontier prefecture reflects the court's determination to foster the growth of a cultural elite in Taiwan on whom it could rely to strengthen its administrative control over the strategic island.

Taiwan's large *sheng yüan* quotas were a coveted privilege its residents and officials had to defend vigorously. Taiwan's undeveloped academic tradition and small population combined with its generous quota meant the chances of winning a *sheng yüan* degree were greater in Taiwan than in mainland Fukien. Lighter competition attracted a number of interlopers from Fukien's coastal prefectures (where competition was stiff). Examination officials had to be vigilant to prevent this practice from eroding an advantage intended to benefit Taiwan natives.[99] Taiwanese who were natives of Fukien also contested the right of Hakka students to take the *sheng yüan* examination in Taiwan; this issue was especially sensitive given Hakka/Hokkien communal rivalries. Most Hakka, though resident in Taiwan as long as many Hokkien, were natives of the province of Kwangtung. To avoid any adverse impact on a Fukien quota caused by migration from Kwangtung (and perhaps to reward Hakka for their loyalty during Hokkien-led rebellions), the court in 1740 approved a special Hakka quota of eight *sheng yüan* for Taiwan prefecture.[100]

As settlement increased and the island developed economically, academic standards gradually improved. Successive editions of the prefectural gazetteer record the founding of a growing number of academies and community schools and an expanding endowment of school lands.[101] Nevertheless, Taiwan's *sheng yüan* apparently met with little success in the provincial competition for the *chü jen* degree. As mentioned above, Fukien's quota of *chü jen* was lower than its wealth and academic attainments might otherwise have merited. This meant sharp competition for the degree and made success for *sheng yüan* from a culturally undeveloped prefecture such as Taiwan especially unlikely. To overcome this problem, in 1687 the court established a special quota for Taiwan of one *chü jen* degree in each examination. It subsequently abolished this quota

TABLE 7.1
Taiwanese Degree Holders Under the Ch'ing

Reign	No. of exams	Chü jen Civil	Chü jen Military	Chü jen Military/civil ratio	Chin shih Civil	Chin shih Military
K'ang-hsi	13	10	54	5.4	1	6
Yung-cheng	5	6	14	2.3	0	0
Ch'ien-lung	27	66	83	1.3	2	2
Chia-ch'ing	12	37	35	0.9	0	2
Tao-kuang	15	63	55	0.9	7	2
Hsien-feng	5	33	11	0.3	0	0
T'ung-chih	6	48	23	0.5	9	0
Kuang-hsü	11	71	28	0.4	20	0
TOTAL		334	303		39	12

SOURCE: *T'ai-wan sheng t'ung chih kao, chüan ch'i, jen wu chih, ti san ts'e*: 155–218.

in 1697, reinstituted it in 1729, and increased it to two per examination in 1735, where it remained until 1807. Then, during the nineteenth century, in response to Taiwan's increasing population and numbers of examination candidates, and perhaps concern over continued outbreaks of communal strife, the court gradually increased Taiwan's *chü jen* quota, to three in 1807, four in 1828, and seven in 1851. An examination of the number of successful Taiwanese candidates for the *chü jen* degree per examination (see Table 7.1) reveals that only a few Taiwanese scholars attained the degree outside the special quota. Nevertheless, the increasing numbers of prestigious *chü jen* with roots in Taiwan helped foster creation of the literati culture and the loyal elite class desired by the Ch'ing state.[102]

The most striking fact revealed in Table 7.1 is the large preponderance of successful candidates for military degrees, especially in the early reigns. Taiwan's frontier conditions appear to have fostered the acquisition of martial skills more readily than literati skills. This martial disposition could be co-opted, in part, at least, through the military examination system and the development of an official martial culture. The military examination system required only minimal literacy and rewarded expert marksmanship and military skills.[103] Throughout the eighteenth century, Taiwanese were thus much more likely to excel in military than civil careers. But even during the eighteenth century the trend toward an increasing number of the more prestigious civil degrees is clear, and civil degree holders clearly predominate in the nineteenth century.

Taiwanese society, however, remained turbulent and rebellious down through the nineteenth century (see Chapter 10). The Ch'ing state did nevertheless find its degree holders of service in the maintenance of control over the island, if only because of their assistance in recruiting loyalist militia to help put down the worst outbreaks. But frontier society did not provide an ideal environment for the practice of Confucian government by moral influence, and the increasing number of degree holders (or of civil in proportion to military) did not by itself guarantee social order in Taiwan. Instead the central government ruled its strategic periphery on Taiwan through a greater than average density of civil and military officers; thus, Taiwan was not "neglected" by the Ch'ing court. That is not to say, however, that the methods of control (and the means of financing that control) employed by the late imperial state were adequate to create a stable and nonviolent social order on the Taiwan frontier.

CHAPTER EIGHT

The Fiscal Administration of Taiwan

Taxation of the Han and the Structure of Local Finance

After defeating the Chengs, the Ch'ing immediately confronted the problem of financing government operations and a military presence in its newly acquired territory. As a strategic periphery, Taiwan could be expected to require heavy military expenditures and yet contribute little by way of revenues to defraying these expenses. The new rulers had to devise means to minimize expenditures and raise revenues within Taiwan.

In the eighth month of 1683, when Shih Lang assumed control of Taiwan from the surrendering Cheng forces, he declared a tax holiday for the year: all taxes and labor services were forgiven, and the rents on government-owned farms were ordered reduced by 40 percent. Shih Lang announced: "Because Taiwan's land is less productive than mainland land, we will seek to lower taxes. To stay or leave is up to you. . . . Harvest time is near—do not abandon the land."[1] Shih's immediate goal was to keep tranquil a population adjusting to a radically changed political environment. Social peace could be achieved by winning popular goodwill through acts of benevolence and generosity. Such munificence, however politically astute, could not be maintained for long.

In late 1683 Shih met with other high-level officials in Foochow to discuss the fate of Taiwan. One of these was the vice-president of the Board of Works, Subai, who had been in charge of supplying Shih Lang's army in the Taiwan campaign. Subai advocated keeping Taiwan's tax quotas at the high level extracted by the financially pressed Chengs.[2] If Taiwan were to be kept in the empire, it would have to be as fiscally self-sufficient as possible and add little to the fiscal burden of higher levels of government. This required high taxes. Even Shih Lang, in his late 1683 essay advocating Taiwan's retention, expressed some concern about the provisioning of 8,000 troops in Taiwan and 2,000 in the Pescadores. He

TABLE 8.1

Taiwan Prefecture: Statutory Revenues, Cheng-Ch'ing Transition

Revenue source	Cheng	Ch'ing (1684)
Revenues in cash (taels of silver)		
Han head tax[a]	13,608	8,006
Aborigine head tax[b]	11,360	7,889
Mills and carts[c]	1,837	594
Shophouses[d]	2,721	1,266
Misc. land revenues[e]	492	65
Fishing[f]	2,975	2,009
Shipping[g]	1,382	1,172
Salt[h]	2,436	2,436
Import duties[i]	9,100	—
TOTAL	45,911	23,437
Revenues in kind (*shih* of unhusked grain)		
Land tax[j]	126,324	92,128
Feng-shan eight[k]	11,868	9,291
TOTAL	138,192	101,419
Tax base		
Land registered for taxation (area in *chia*)		
State-owned land	9,783	8,391
Privately owned land	20,272	10,063
TOTAL[j]	30,055	18,454
Population registered for taxation[g]	22,253	16,820

SOURCES: Cheng Hsi-fu 1974*a*; *TWFC*:Kao: 115, 117, 127; *FCTCTWF*: 164–65. All Cheng revenues in cash have been converted to Ch'ing taels by multiplying the Cheng figures in Table 4.1 by 0.7.

[a]The Chengs registered 21,320 Han in Taiwan and 933 in the Pescadores; these numbers fell to 16,274 and 546, respectively, under the Ch'ing. The Chengs taxed persons in Taiwan at three different rates (0.38, 0.68, and 0.98 ounces) and in the Pescadores at 1.2 ounces per head. The Ch'ing adopted the medium Taiwan rate of 0.68 ounces (= 0.476 taels) and applied it uniformly to the registered population (Cheng Hsi-fu 1974*a*: 104, 111). The approximately 40,000 soldiers repatriated to the mainland are obviously not included in the head-tax figures (*KHSL*: 135). Chu-lo's first magistrate reported that of the 21,320 registered heads in Taiwan, 8,596 returned to the mainland, and that the Ch'ing enrolled an additional 3,550 to make up the Taiwan total of 16,274. Another 7,717 registered heads had reportedly fled by 1683 (*FCTCTWF*: 165).

[b]For changes in the aborigine head tax, see Chapter 5 and Table 5.1. No values are included for aborigine corvée services.

[c]Taxes on ox-driven mills and sugarcane carts were levied according to head of oxen and number of carts, respectively. The Ch'ing reduced the Cheng quotas (Cheng rates are uncertain) and applied a uniform rate of 5.6 taels per head of oxen and per cart (Cheng Hsi-fu 1974*a*: 110; *TWFC*:Chou: 187).

[d]Taxes on shophouses were assessed per room by type of roofing: a higher rate for tile, a lower rate for thatch. The number of taxed rooms fell from 6,270.5 under the Chengs to 4,705 under the Ch'ing. The Ch'ing also reduced the tax rates per room (Cheng Hsi-fu 1974*a*: 113; *TWFC*:Chou: 181).

[e]Miscellaneous land revenues included a tax on arable land in the Pescadores, and two taxes—a tax on Buddhist monks and Taoist priests, and a tax on salt transported to the Pescadores—that the Ch'ing eliminated. Under the Chengs arable land in the Pescadores was assessed a tax levied in grain commuted to silver; the Ch'ing continued this practice but reduced the Cheng assessment from 212 taels to 65 taels (equal to 154 *shih* of rice) (Cheng Hsi-fu 1974*a*: 111; *TWFC*:Chou: 181).

[f]Taxes on the fishing industry include (1) taxes on local fishermen set as quotas for harbors and fishing ponds (both the number of sites and the individual quotas for the remaining sites were reduced by the Ch'ing); (2) taxes on several categories of fishing nets and traps (only the Pescadores quota was reduced by the Ch'ing); and (3) charges for licenses on fishing boats crossing to Taiwan for the winter catch (quota unchanged by the Ch'ing) (Cheng Hsi-fu 1974*a*: 107–9, 111; *TWFC*:Chou: 184, 186–87).

[g]Taxes on shipping include (1) a tax on boats levied according to carrying capacity (the Ch'ing

proposed that these troops be supplied from overstaffed mainland garrisons to avoid the costs of additional troops and rations. He also advocated that newly reclaimed land in Taiwan be free of taxes for the (customary) first three years of production. With this incentive, Taiwan's grain production and land-tax revenues would eventually increase, and troops stationed there would not need to rely so heavily on mainland subsidies.[3]

In an essay of the ninth month of 1684, Shih attacked Subai's plan for high tax quotas, pointing out that repatriation had reduced Taiwan's population by half and left many fields abandoned. To fill high tax quotas, officials would have to press the settlers for payment; this would lead to rebellion and force military expenses even higher. Imperial benevolence ought to reduce harsh taxes, pacify the people, and win their goodwill. After a few years the population would flourish, all the fields would be cultivated, and tax revenues would be abundant.[4] Shih's arguments point to expanded reclamation rather than higher tax rates to fill government revenue needs (however, we must not attribute strong procolonization views to Shih, who, as we saw above, supported the 1684 restrictions on immigration).

The new Ch'ing administration took over the Cheng tax registers and quotas (much as the Chengs had taken over the Dutch accounts); there was never any suggestion that it create a new fiscal structure, which would certainly have caused popular unrest. Adjustments were made only where necessary to fit changed conditions. A comparison of the Cheng and early Ch'ing tax quotas (Table 8.1) documents how the repatriation of population and the economic depression that came with Ch'ing rule forced the Ch'ing to reduce Cheng tax quotas for almost all categories of revenue. These figures show a 39 percent decline in registered land area, a 27 percent decline in tax grain, a 24 percent decline in taxed heads, a 36 percent decline in miscellaneous revenues (exclusive of import duties), and an overall decline in cash revenues of 49 percent. The tax rates finally adopted were nevertheless quite high by mainland stan-

left the quota unchanged); (2) a tax on smaller boats levied per boat, in the Pescadores (the Ch'ing reduced the quota slightly); and (3) a charge on ferries operating between An-p'ing and Tainan, levied according to carrying capacity (the Ch'ing reduced the quota) (Cheng Hsi-fu 1974*a*: 109, 111, 113–14; *TWFC*:Chou: 184).

[h]The salt revenue derived from charges on salt pans levied by size (the Ch'ing did not modify the quota) (Cheng Hsi-fu 1974*a*: 108; *TWFC*:Chou: 179–80).

[i]The Cheng charges on imports were discontinued by the Ch'ing (Cheng Hsi-fu 1974*a*: 112).

[j]The land area registered for taxation fell considerably under the Ch'ing, especially unirrigated lands subject to lighter tax rates. Under the Chengs, state-owned land yielded 84,920 *shih* of tax grain and privately owned land 41,403 *shih* of tax grain (Cheng Hsi-fu 1974*a*: 101). The figures do not include land in the Pescadores taxed in cash; see note *e* above. The Ch'ing also reduced the Cheng land-tax rates, see Table 8.5. Although the sources mention military colony lands (*t'un t'ien* or *ying p'an t'ien*) in discussions of the Cheng-Ch'ing transition in land tenure (*TWFC*:Fan: 182), they are not included in either the Cheng or Ch'ing figures.

[k]For the changes in the head tax levied in grain paid by the eight plains aborigine villages in Feng-shan, see Chapter 5 and Table 5.2, which gives the figures in *shih* of husked rice.

dards. Because the policy of quarantine did not envisage increases in Han population or cultivated acreage, the numbers already registered had to bear as much as possible of the cost of the new military and civil administration (the extent of Taiwan's deficit is discussed below).

The Ch'ing substantially reduced the Cheng head-tax quota levied on Han. The Cheng government had collected a yearly "labor service" tax on every taxable head "without distinguishing masters and servants and by counting women as men." The medium Cheng rate was 0.68 ounces per taxed head; different rates applied to different categories of the population. The Ch'ing government adopted a uniform rate (it converted the Cheng medium head tax of 0.68 ounces to 0.476 taels per head) and levied it only on adult male members of households; servants, single men, and women were removed from the rolls.[5] After 1684 revenue from the head or "labor service" tax increased as a growing population was entered on updated registers until the quota was frozen in 1711 (see below). Despite the reduction in 1684 of the Han head-tax rate, it remained high by mainland standards, as was recognized in 1737 (see below).

In addition to the major categories of aborigine head tax (see Chapter 5) and the Han head tax, the government's *cash* income was supplemented by a salt tax and a variety of miscellaneous taxes inherited from the Cheng era. Miscellaneous "land revenue" taxes were imposed on shophouses (i.e., a shop with living quarters attached), sugarcane carts, and ox-driven mills.[6] The "water revenue" category (*shui hsiang*) included taxes on shipping and fishing boats, harbors, fish ponds, nets, and traps.[7] The Ch'ing reduced the miscellaneous tax quotas (see the notes to Table 8.1) and eliminated the Cheng customs duties on imports.

The *land*-tax rates adopted by the Ch'ing evened out the large differences in tax rates the Chengs had levied on different kinds of land. The biggest reduction came with the conversion of the Cheng government-owned farmland (*kuan t'ien*) to private ownership. Farmers of this land, who had formerly to pay a rent of 18 *shih* of unhusked rice per *chia* on first-grade paddy, now only had to pay a tax of 8.8 *shih* per *chia*. The tax rate on privately held land of former Cheng officials (*wen wu kuan t'ien*), however, rose from 3.6 *shih* per *chia* for first-grade paddy to 8.8 *shih*.[8]

The Ch'ing land-tax rates for Taiwan were considerably higher than those paid on the mainland. Mainland rates varied widely, but according to the Chu-lo gazetteer, the heaviest rate was 1.22 taels per *chia*. Taiwan's tax rate of 8.8 *shih* of grain per *chia* of first-grade paddy, when converted at the lowest market price (0.3 taels per *shih*), amounted to 2.64 taels, more than twice the mainland rate. The good yields produced by Taiwan's newly opened land eased this burden somewhat,[9] but the most important means landowners had of decreasing taxes was underreporting reclaimed acreage (see below).

TABLE 8.2
Revenue Sources for Chu-lo County, 1684 and 1711–1715

Tax category	1684		1711–15	
	shih	taels	*shih*	taels
Land tax[a]	23,468	[7,040]	41,564	[12,469]
Han head tax		1,998		2,122
Aborigine head tax[b]		7,709		7,820
Miscellaneous taxes		721		737

SOURCE: *CLHC*: 87, 89, 90, 94, 100–102.
[a]*Shih* of unhusked rice are converted at the lowest price of 0.3 taels (see *CLHC*: 87; *TWFC*:Yü: 241).
[b]No figure can be given for the value of aborigine corvée (see Chapter 5).

The Taiwan prefectural gazetteer states that Taiwan's land-tax system differed from mainland systems in three major ways: mainland land taxes were commuted (and thus paid in cash), whereas Taiwan's were paid in kind; mainland taxes were levied only on irrigated fields, whereas Taiwan's were levied on both paddy (*t'ien*) and dry fields (*yüan*); and mainland taxes were calculated in milled rice (*mi*), whereas Taiwan's were calculated in unhusked rice (*ku*).[10] These differences were not in fact unique to Taiwan, but they did distinguish Taiwan's land-tax system from that in commercialized regional cores. Most of these differences can be explained by the fact that local tax grain was needed to supply the rice allowances for Taiwan's substantial military establishment, which could not (in the early years of Ch'ing rule, at least) rely on market purchases in an undeveloped frontier to fill its requirements.[11]

The land tax was Taiwan's major source of revenue growth. A comparison of Chu-lo's tax revenues in 1684 to those of 1711–15 illustrates the changing importance of different revenue sources in the Taiwan county with the largest frontier and plains aborigine population (see Table 8.2). In 1684 Chu-lo's largest single source of revenue was the aborigine head tax. The total value of the land and head taxes borne by Han Chinese did, however, exceed the amount borne by the aborigines, although no value is included for aborigine corvée. Table 8.2 reveals that by 1711 the fiscal importance of the aborigine head tax had declined. As a fixed quota, it could increase only when raw aborigines submitted to Ch'ing authority. Such increases were small, since the few tribes that submitted were wisely asked to pay only token amounts of tax. The leading source of revenue growth was the land tax on newly reclaimed cultivated acreage. Table 8.3 shows that land-tax revenues for all Taiwan in 1768 had nearly doubled over the quota set in 1684 (see also Table 6.5). This substantial increment in revenues nevertheless fell far short of the rate of growth of Taiwan's population, which more than quintupled over the same period (see Table 6.4).

TABLE 8.3
Revenue from Land Taxes in Taiwan, 1661–1768

Year	Registered area in *chia*	Tax grain in *shih*
Cheng era	30,055	126,324
1684	18,454	92,128
1693	26,460	120,098
1710	30,110	129,162
1735	50,517	165,975
1744	52,851	169,541
1762–68	63,045	181,170

SOURCES: *Cheng era—FCTCTWF*: 164; *1684 and 1693—TWFC*:Kao: 115, 117, 127; *1710—TWFC*:Chou: 160, 174; *1735—TWFC*:Liu: 138, 169; *1744—TWFC*:Fan: 145, 169; *1762–68—TWFC*:Yü: 194, 224.

NOTE: See Table 6.5 for a breakdown of registered area by county and percentages of paddy land. P'eng-hu is not included; see Table 8.1 note *e*. The land statistics reported in Tables 6.5 and 8.3 measure only the area registered for taxation, *not* the total cultivated area. Registered area grew faster than tax grain because newly opened land was registered primarily in the lower tax grades. Table 6.5 documents that paddy accounted for a declining proportion of registered area (not cultivated area).

The balance sheet in Table 8.4 illustrates the trends in Taiwan's statutory revenues and expenses between 1710 and 1768. Several caveats are in order. First, all amounts are statutory figures and do not reflect the considerable sums in customary fees and collection surcharges in the case of revenues and non-statutory salaries and expenses in the case of expenditures. Non-statutory civil administrative expenses, for example, commonly reached several times the statutory amounts.[12] Non-statutory revenues were not, however, available to defray statutory expenses. It was the gap between statutory revenues and statutory expenses that the court considered in deciding whether to transfer funds from other levels of government to a deficit jurisdiction.

Second, the balance sheet is constructed to include all identifiable revenues from Taiwan sources, whether or not the revenues were allocated to cover local expenditures, and all expenditures attributable to Taiwan operations, whether or not the expenditures were expected to be met from local sources. Taiwan prefecture was not a single accounting unit, and lateral transfers characterized Taiwan's fiscal structure as they did other jurisdictions of late imperial China. A large part of the income from the official estates, for example, was earmarked for supplemental salary (*yang lien*) payments elsewhere in Fukien, and portions of the salt revenue went to the salt intendant. Similarly, cash salaries paid to troops rotated to Taiwan had largely to be drawn from Fukien sources. Thus, no Ch'ing official ever matched Taiwan revenues against Taiwan expenditures in the way done in Table 8.4.[13] All the numbers presented in the balance sheet, however, with the exception of the cash military salaries, derive from the tax sections of the prefectural gazetteers. Thus, local officials were well aware of imbalances between Taiwan's revenues and expenses. In the wake of the Chu I-kuei rebellion, for example, the court commented on Taiwan's fiscal dependence on Fukien revenues.[14] Hence, the fiscal balance of Taiwan operations was an important consideration for officials making decisions on the administration of Taiwan. The balance sheet confirms that Taiwan's revenue, despite rapid economic growth, remained insufficient to pay for the expense of its sizable military establishment throughout the eighteenth century.

As Table 8.4 reveals, between 1710 and 1768 revenues from head taxes declined substantially, despite Taiwan's dramatic population growth in those same years. First, in 1713 the K'ang-hsi emperor froze the (Han) head tax (labor-service quota) in perpetuity at its 1711 level. Taxable heads registered after that date merely shared a portion of the already existing quota.[15] Then in 1736–37 the Han head tax quota and the equally sizable aborigine head tax (together totaling a substantial 16,293 taels in 1710) were dramatically reduced to a total of 5,377 taels when the Ch'ien-lung emperor approved a low head-tax rate in Taiwan.

In 1736 a memorial to the emperor complained that Taiwan's labor-service tax rate of 0.476 taels plus the meltage fee surcharge exceeded 0.5 taels per tax unit, whereas mainland rates averaged 0.1–0.3 taels. A reduced rate of 0.2 taels was therefore decreed for Taiwan's four counties; the next year the new rate was extended to Tan-shui subprefecture and to the aborigine head tax.[16] This reduction in the head-tax rate substantially reduced Taiwan's local revenues.

In 1747 the government combined the land and labor-service taxes and began collecting the labor-service tax as a surcharge on the land tax. The labor-service tax thereby lost its character as a head tax, and households with no land were exempted.[17] This reform had the effect of distributing the head-tax quotas more evenly among the counties, for until then the newly created districts of Chang-hua and Tan-shui paid totals of only 4.8 and 2.2 taels, respectively (these quotas had been set in 1731 at the pre-1736 rate). The new Chang-hua and Tan-shui quotas were set at 1,160 and 160 taels, respectively.[18]

Between 1710 and 1768, revenues from the miscellaneous land and water taxes and the salt tax grew slowly, if at all, although the numbers of shophouses, mills, and sugarcane carts, and the shipping and fishing industries, which were the object of these taxes, must have grown substantially. The lack of interest in expanding revenue from these sources reflected the traditional state's bias against the proliferation of miscellaneous taxes (which easily led to corruption and abuse) and in favor of the land tax as a source of revenue.[19] The most dramatic addition to the cash revenues generated in Taiwan between 1710 and 1768 was the

TABLE 8.4

Taiwan Prefecture: Statutory Revenues and Expenditures, 1710 and 1768

	1710	1768
Revenues in cash (taels of silver)		
Han head tax[a]	8,306	3,844
Aborigine head tax[b]	7,987	1,533
Mills and carts[c]	728	2,279
Shophouses[d]	1,266	1,467
Misc. land revenues[e]	65	481
Fishing[f]	2,009	2,312
Shipping[g]	1,172	1,576
Salt[h]	2,436	2,436
Official estates[i]	—	30,568
TOTAL[j]	23,969	46,496
Revenues in kind (*shih* of unhusked grain)		
Land tax[k]	129,162	181,170
Feng-shan eight[l]	9,291	—
TOTAL	138,453	181,170
Expenditures in cash (taels of silver)		
Civil administrative expenses[m]	6,722	8,413
Yang lien salaries[n]	—	11,840
Military salaries allocated[m]	[17,247]	[4,758]
Total military salaries[o]	120,000	151,200
TOTAL	126,722	171,453
Expenditures in kind (*shih* of unhusked grain)		
Military grain allowance[p]	72,000	90,720
TOTAL	72,000	90,720
Deficit in cash (taels)	102,753	124,957
Surplus in kind (*shih*)	66,453	90,450

NOTE: The categories of revenue are explained in the notes to Table 8.1; only changes are noted here. In several instances the prefectural gazetteer of 1768 gives county totals that do not sum to the stated prefectural totals; except where noted, I have used the stated prefectural totals.

[a]The 1710 total for Han head taxes given in the prefectural gazetteer (*TWFC*:Chou: 180) reflects increments in taxed heads only through 1691. If the 1710 figure were updated to include all increases through 1711 when the head tax was frozen, it would show an increase of 2,007 heads over the 1684 quota, for a total of 18,827 taxed heads in 1711 and a total revenue of 8,961.7 taels (*TWFC*:Yü: 264). The 1711 quota of 18,827 taxed heads, when taxed at the reduced 1736 rate of 0.2 taels per head, yields 3,765.4 taels. This is slightly less than the sum of county totals for 1768 given in the balance sheet and does not reflect wastage fees and charges (*TWFC*:Yü: 246–64).

[b]The 1710 figure for the aborigine head tax, when compared to the 1684 quotas, reflects a small increment from newly submitting tribes (*TWFC*:Chou: 181; see also Table 5.1). The 1768 figure reflects the reduced tax rate of 1737 (0.2 taels per head), the addition of the Feng-shan eight villages in 1737 (see note *l* below), and increments from newly submitting tribes (*TWFC*:Yü: 247–64; see Tables 5.1 and 5.2). The value of aborigine corvée services is not reflected in these figures (see Chapter 5).

[c]The increase in 1710 over the 1684 quota reflects the addition of 24 carts in 1693. The increase from 1710 to 1768 reflects an addition of 29+ mills and 247+ carts (*TWFC*:Chou: 187; *TWFC*:Yü: 277).

[d]The increase in the shophouse tax from 1710 to 1768 reflects an increase from 4,705 to 5,350 taxed rooms, accounted for by the extension of this tax to Chu-lo county's important port of Pen-kang (*TWFC*:Chou: 181; *TWFC*:Yü: 277, 280).

[e]In 1710 the miscellaneous land revenues included only the tax on arable land in the Pescadores, which increased to 159.6 taels by 1768 (*TWFC*:Chou: 181; *TWFC*:Yü: 221, 224). In 1768 new miscellaneous taxes accounted for the balance of the increase: (1) a tax on betel and mangoes, 136 taels; (2) a tax on tile works, 12.5 taels; (3) a tax on vegetable gardens, 3 taels; and (4) a tax on pawnshops, 170 taels (*TWFC*:Yü: 277–82).

income from 125 official estates. These had been reclaimed with official moneys, but the income was used by officials for local (and private) expenses until the state required an accounting to the public treasury in 1722. In 1729 these funds were assigned to help Fukien fill its supplemental salary quotas.[20]

Taiwan's largest source of revenue, and the one showing the most significant growth, was the land tax. This was assessed and collected in grain, rather than cash, to supply military rice allowances. The process by which the land tax was extended to cover Taiwan's rapidly expanding cultivated acreage is treated in detail in the following sections; here we need note only the obvious fiscal importance of the land tax. When commuted at the low rate of 0.36 taels per *shih* of unhusked grain, the value of the total grain tax in 1768 comes to at least 65,221 taels, more than all cash revenues combined. The market value was twice this amount,[21] and rising prices for grain were increasing the value of the land tax levied in kind. Nevertheless, the market value of the grain tax surplus (0.7 taels per *shih* multiplied by 90,450 *shih*, or 63,315 taels) was still only half of the cash deficit (see Table 8.4).

Expenses attributable to Taiwan's administration and defense were well in excess of local revenues from the beginning of Ch'ing rule in Taiwan; this remained the case in both 1710 and 1768. The moderate

---

[f]The small increase in taxes on fishing reflects increases in taxed fishing ponds and nets (*TWFC*:Chou: 184, 186–187; *TWFC*:Yü: 266–67).

[g]The increase in taxes on shipping reflects increases in taxed carrying capacity and number of boats (*TWFC*:Chou: 184; *TWFC*:Yü: 266–67).

[h]In 1710 the salt revenue was being retained for military expenses in Taiwan by special decree; by 1768 at least part of the salt revenues were allocated to the salt intendant but how they were accounted for remains unreconstructed (*TWFC*:Chou: 179–80; *TWFC*:Yü: 264–65, 283, 289).

[i]Income from official estates became part of statutory revenues beginning in 1722; see text (*TWFC*:Yü: 307; *TWFC*:Liu: 242).

[j]The gazetteers state total cash revenues (exclusive of official estates) as 23,970 and 13,171 taels for 1710 and 1768, respectively (*TWFC*:Chou: 189; *TWFC*:Yü: 283). The stated total for 1710 matches my arithmetic total. The 1768 stated total (exclusive of official estates) of 13,171 is less than my arithmetic total of 15,928 and less than the sum of stated county totals of 17,091 given in the 1768 gazetteer (*TWFC*:Yü: 283–303). I have been unable to determine the source of the discrepancy.

[k]Land-tax revenues, reflecting increases in registered land, grew steadily in this period, see Tables 6.5 and 8.3 (*TWFC*:Chou: 174; *TWFC*:Yü: 224). Changes in land-tax rates are discussed below and in Table 8.5.

[l]The eight plains aborigine villages of Feng-shan paid a head tax in kind until 1737, when it was converted to cash; see note *b* above, Chapter 5, and Table 5.2 (*TWFC*:Chou: 174).

[m]Civil administrative expenses and the allocated contribution to military salaries are the expense items covered by retained revenues (*ts'un liu*) and together match the cash revenue totals given in note *j*. Allocated military salaries are bracketed because they are included in the following line item, total military salaries (*TWFC*:Chou: 189; *TWFC*:Yü: 283).

[n]*TWFC*:Yü: 304–6. On *yang lien* see text below.

[o]Military salaries were estimated using the lowest salary of 1.0 tael per month per soldier (for 10,000 soldiers in 1710 and 12,600 soldiers in 1768) (Hsü Hsüeh-chi 1987: 337; R. Smith 1974: 143; Wade 1851: 414).

[p]Military grain allowances were calculated using an allowance of 0.6 *shih* of grain or unhusked rice (equal to 0.3 *shih* of milled rice) per month per soldier for 10,000 soldiers in 1710 and 12,600 soldiers in 1768. The estimated amounts for 1710 and 1768 match those given in *CHTTWSL*: 62, and *TWFC*:Yü: 242, respectively; see also Hsü Hsüeh-chi 1987: 338, 343–44; R. Smith 1974: 143; Wade 1851: 414.

increase in statutory administrative expenses (primarily local officials' salaries) after 1710 is attributable mainly to the addition of Chang-hua county and Tan-shui subprefecture and the proliferation of assistant (four) and subdistrict (seven) magistrates by 1768. A much larger increase in civil administrative expenses came in the new category of supplemental salaries. These salaries, to "nourish the virtue" of officials, were created as part of nationwide reforms implemented by the Yung-cheng emperor and in place in Fukien by 1730.[22]

The expenses of maintaining Taiwan's military establishment have been conservatively estimated by multiplying the lowest military salary and the standard rice allowance against the number of soldiers garrisoned in Taiwan (10,000 before 1733 and 12,600 after). The actual cash military expenses were certainly much higher (one source estimates 250,000 taels),[23] but my conservative estimates are sufficient to make the point that military expenses greatly exceeded Taiwan's local revenues, even after a half-century of rapid economic growth. The cash amount allocated to military salaries from revenues retained in Taiwan (all cash revenue sources [other than official estates] less statutory civil administrative expenses) supplied only a fraction of the total salary expenses. Moreover, this amount declined from 17,247 taels in 1710 to a stated 4,758 taels in 1768 due primarily to the decline in head-tax revenues. The balance of military salaries was paid from the Fukien provincial treasury.

Only in one category did the revenue Taiwan produced exceed its requirements: in both 1710 and 1768 the revenue in grain from the land tax exceeded the grain allowances paid to Taiwan's garrisons. Still, the cash value of the 90,450 *shih* surplus in tax grain in 1768 (at the 0.7 tael per *shih* rate) is only 63,315 taels, far less than the 151,200 taels in salaries paid to Taiwan's soldiers and the cash deficit of 124,957 taels. The actual allocation of the tax grain in excess of military rations needed in Taiwan varied with government policy. By 1725 Taiwan had accumulated grain reserves sufficient to supply five years of military rations; 100,000 *shih* were shipped to Fukien to be sold as relief grain (*p'ing t'iao*), and 21,000 *shih* were allocated to supply military dependents in Fukien. Additional amounts were allocated to supply Fukien's military in subsequent years (24,000 *shih* in 1727, 15,570 *shih* in 1732, 14,000 *shih* in 1745); by 1745, 74,570 *shih* of tax grain was being shipped yearly to supply military garrisons and military dependents in Fukien. In the nineteenth century these transfers of Taiwan grain were known in Amoy as the Taiwan shipments (*T'ai yün*).[24] Since the grain tax was inadequate to supply relief grain in addition to the military shipments, this was purchased in Taiwan with Fukien tax moneys.[25]

In sum, the government tolerated a large imbalance between revenues and expenses in Taiwan throughout the eighteenth century. While the government eagerly expanded Taiwan's land-tax revenue, it simultaneously reduced its head-tax revenue by a significant amount. These reductions, along with frequent tax remissions, were carried out in the name of equity and benevolence and aimed to win the goodwill of the populace.[26] Taiwan's failure to aggressively expand its revenues beyond the land tax mirrored an empirewide trend. Ch'ing fiscal structure, especially after the Yung-cheng reign, became increasingly rigid. With respect to revenues, Ch'ing statecraft continued to put a high value on low taxes. Because of the economic expansion (and an expanding area of land registered for taxation) in the eighteenth century, the state could count on growing revenues without needing to conduct cadastral surveys or raise taxes. A treasury surplus of 30 million taels in the first years of the Ch'ien-lung reign grew to 70 million taels by 1786. Indeed, the central government enjoyed surpluses down to the end of the Ch'ien-lung reign, despite having to fund the military adventures of the Ch'ien-lung emperor.[27] Government operational expenditures remained low and within a relatively static budget,[28] thanks in part to the absence of a foreign threat and interstate competition.[29] So from both the revenue and expenditure sides, there was little pressure on the government to milk revenues from China's considerable economic growth in the eighteenth century. Taiwan's local finances reflect this institutional pattern, although the rapid growth of its land taxes also reflects its status as a developing area and the need for a tax base that helped pay for the heavy military expenses incurred in its defense.[30]

Taiwan's status as a strategically important periphery made an excess of military expenditures over local revenues and the need for subsidies from higher levels of government expected (see Chapter 7);[31] at the same time it made the proliferation of taxes and the imposition of heavy taxes unwise. Attempts to increase extraction through a predatory bureaucracy often led to taxpayer resistance and heightened control costs, frustrating any attempt to reduce the deficit. How policymakers assessed these risks when devising means to expand land-tax revenues is discussed in detail in the following sections.

The hard facts of Taiwan's fiscal imbalance boded ill for aborigine livelihoods. From the point of view of increasing tax revenues, the government had an unquestioned interest in extending reclamation and plowing up the deer fields. The heavy burden of military expenditures and control costs, however, must have tempered government enthusiasm for expanding settlement. To the extent that colonization spread unruly settlers to distant frontiers, created points of friction with aborigines, and made troops necessary to quell the resulting disturbances, military expenses would go even higher. Thus, from a fiscal point of view, expanding colonization, at least precipitous expansion, carried many risks. Differing calculations of settler loyalty, aborigine resistance, and control costs made the potential increase in land-tax revenue more or less attractive. Our review of the colonization policy debates, especially Lan Ting-yüan's pro-colonization arguments against boundary policies (Chapter 7), indicates how divided opinion could be on these matters. That Taiwan's rice surpluses were deemed sufficient to assign part of its tax grain to supply garrisons in Fukien after 1725 suggests that in the Yung-cheng years policymakers judged that the benefits of expanding reclamation would exceed the costs.

Frontier Land Reclamation

Because the late imperial state looked primarily to taxes on agricultural land for its revenue, allocating rights in land, assigning the tax-paying responsibility, and managing a system for registering newly reclaimed land for taxation were cardinal functions of local government. The organization of reclamation, and the resulting landlord-tenant relations, also affected how and if taxes were paid and the structure of village society. To finance expanded government operations in Taiwan, the state had to create a revenue base by registering newly reclaimed farmland.

In establishing a land administration in Taiwan, the new Ch'ing government had first to deal with the land system inherited from the Chengs. Cheng government estates (*kuan t'ien*) and the private lands of Cheng officials (*wen wu kuan t'ien*) became under the Ch'ing the privately owned lands of those who tilled them. Land opened by the Cheng military colonies (*ying p'an t'ien*) that was not abandoned presumably was transferred to the new government.[32]

The Chu-lo county gazetteer states that four categories of "masters of the land" were distinguished under the Ch'ing. The first category consisted of government estates (*kuan chuang*), which were reclaimed with official moneys.[33] As we saw above, the income from these estates was eventually allocated to pay the supplemental salaries of Fukien officials. The second category, proprietor (*yeh hu*), consisted of gentry and commoners who owned land and paid taxes on it. The third category consisted of managers (*kuan shih*) selected by their villages to oversee payment of the land and labor taxes. A manager's salary was calculated according to the area and numbers he was responsible for; in addition, he and his own land were exempt from taxes.[34] The fourth category consisted of the aborigine tribes (*fan she*), who paid no tax on land they themselves cultivated; instead they paid the aborigine head tax. Each of these categories is distinguished by the nature and method of payment.[35] Rights in land were largely predicated on fulfilling tax obligations due the state.

All the early Ch'ing emperors sought to foster the reclamation of uncultivated land and promulgated a number of decrees to regulate the process. These regulations stated that empty land not already claimed by others could be opened by an applicant if he first applied (*pao k'en*) to the appropriate jurisdiction for a license or patent (*chih chao*) listing the location, boundaries, and area of the site, and the reclaimer's name, locality of origin, and a guarantor. Local magistrates were authorized to issue reclamation patents until 1753, when that power was transferred to provincial treasurers. A procedure established in 1734 provided that if an official investigation and the posting of a public notice for five months turned up no rival claimant, then a patent could be issued. Once the patent was issued with the appropriate official seals (and fees paid), the reclaimer had a specified number of years of tax holiday; at the end of this he was required to submit his claim for a survey and a land-tax assessment (*sheng k'o*). The length of the tax holiday varied in different periods and according to the quality of the land reclaimed: less productive land was given a longer holiday. A distinction was made between paddy restored to cultivation, which was allowed only a short tax holiday, and land brought under cultivation for the first time. The tax holiday (for all China) was originally three years for newly reclaimed paddy land but was extended to ten years in 1673 and then reduced to six years in 1723.[36]

At times the central government or local officials, under pressure to increase the cultivated acreage in their district, gave loans or made available supplies of oxen, tools, and seed to encourage farmers to reclaim land. These government-sponsored colonization schemes occurred primarily in sensitive Central Asian border areas, such as Kansu (where they served government strategic goals), and in areas where devastation from military operations or the number of rootless vagrants made the government anxious to settle the population and restore tax quotas.[37] Taiwan was not the object of such officially subsidized reclamation. Rather the opposite, for as we have seen the government's concern to prevent its island-prefecture's becoming a haven for rebels made for ambivalence toward immigration. In addition, the government feared land reclamation would provoke aborigine revolts. Taiwan, then, is a case where pressure for reclamation came from land-hungry settlers, with the government seeking to limit and control the process.

Reclamation of uncultivated land raised a fundamental question: What constituted a claim in the eyes of the government? The Ch'ing government recognized tribal claims to large amounts of land. How Han settlers acquired rights to cultivate such land is discussed in Chapter 9. The discussion here focuses on the acquisition of rights to farm "waste" land (i.e., land where no aborigine claim was recognized) at the disposal of the government and on the relations between Han farmers and investors in land development.

Acquisition of a patent to reclaim land depended on government officials. Petitioners with influence and the capital necessary to provide "customary fees" to officials were clearly favored in any competition for patents. Small farmers without money, official connections, or sophistication in bureaucratic manipulation were at a distinct disadvantage.

Regulations were necessary to prevent title disputes arising among rival claimants; the requirement, noted above, of public notice and a five-month waiting period adopted in 1734 is an example. Opening land without a government license was termed *ssu k'en* and was treated the same as the criminal infraction of concealing land from taxation. However, a 1688 decree provided that land opened without a license could be entered on the tax rolls, listing the reclaimer as owner, so long as there was no prior claimant. This decree prescribed punishment only for corrupt officials and runners who used this as an opportunity to cheat the original proprietors or for the powerful who forcibly occupied the land. This regulation, as it itself anticipated, proved difficult to enforce. The statutes prescribing punishments in this area were vague and contradictory. Some of these called for confiscation of unregistered cultivated land; others provided that if it were found that the land had only been "omitted" from the registers, registration for taxation was all that the law required. These ambiguities opened the reclamation process to corruption. Occasionally a local magnate would claim land opened by others who lacked licenses or, having licenses, could not defend their rights in ruinously expensive lawsuits. Regulations promulgated in 1734 provided for punishments of both magnates and officials involved in these practices (*lan k'en*).[38] Reclaiming much but reporting little for taxation was especially common in Taiwan (see below). Unreported land was liable to confiscation and, at the least, taxation. In general, an owner could guarantee title to a piece of land by registering and paying taxes on it.

A land developer licensed to open a parcel of land would ordinarily recruit tenants and allocate them subparcels to reclaim and cultivate; patent holders who reclaimed their own land were apparently in the minority. The legal framework and the customary contractual forms used for these arrangements did not differ greatly from those in mainland Fukien; the southeast coast immigrants needed only to adapt the forms to reflect local factor prices. The patent holder and tenant would enter into a reclamation agreement by which the tenant paid a lump-sum fee (*li t'ou yin, p'u ti yin*) for a parcel and thereafter a yearly rent. In the years before the land was fully reclaimed, the rents were share rents or small fixed amounts that increased yearly over the three years until reclamation was considered complete. Then a fixed rent was set in perpetuity, usually at 8 *shih* of grain per *chia* of paddy, less for dry land. The tenant whose labor and capital had actually opened the land to cultivation thereby acquired a right of permanent tenancy, called a small-rent right (*hsiao tsu*), making him exempt from eviction as long as he paid his fixed rent. This tenancy right could be bought and sold, and the land could be sublet at the permanent tenant's discretion. The patent holder, or owner of the large-rent right (*ta tsu*, a ground rent), was responsible for the payment of the land taxes. These agreements gave rise to a dual or split-ownership system of land tenure.[39]

In a discussion of the development of split ownership rights, the Chu-lo county gazetteer reports the common private rental rates: "Newly opened paddy is fertile. A single *chia* of the highest grade yields 60 to 70 *shih* of grain, and the lowest grade yields 30 to 40 *shih*. The tenant gives the property owner 20 to 30 percent of this; the property owner then pays half that amount in taxes."[40] Another passage from the gazetteer notes the problems caused by split ownership:

> From 60 to 70 percent of the owners supply oxen and seed to tenants, who then reclaim the land; only 30–40 percent of owners reclaim the land themselves. When a tenant who has occupied land for a long time fails to pay the rent and taxes go unpaid, the owner seeks to change tenants. But the crowd cries out and rises up, and there emerges the corrupt practice of the long-term tenant becoming the owner. Lawsuits increase, and the cases are increasingly troublesome. . . . Sometimes the tenant pledges the land [a redeemable sale or *tien*] to a third party, creating a right called land bottom [*t'ien ti*], a right transferrable by buying and selling. Or sometimes the owner changes, and the tenant still occupies the land. This leads to the corrupt practice of one field and three masters [*i t'ien san chu*]. When the taxpaying responsibility is transferred and the yamen runners have to chase Mr. Chang to find Mr. Li, the registers grow increasingly confused and the amount of land that pays no taxes grows. This tendency cannot be tolerated for long.[41]

This passage suggests that there was both considerable contention over rights in land and much flexibility in their transfer and that the resulting confusion impeded the ability of the state to collect its revenue. On the one hand, tenants contested the right of owners to evict them and claimed the right to freely transfer their rights of permanent tenancy in land they reclaimed. On the other hand, when owners sold their rights, they commonly left the tenants undisturbed and did not notify the authorities to update the tax rolls.[42]

Split ownership arising from frontier reclamation put a long-term tenant in a strong position: his close connection to the land he farmed derived from his investment in its reclamation and maintenance, from his familiarity with it gained in its everyday management, and from his standing in the local community. All these factors made it difficult for the landlord to interfere in farm operations and remove the tenant. In addition, the high wages, at least of the early Ch'ing years (see above), made tenant labor a commodity dear enough not to be trifled with. Nor, on an unruly frontier, could landlords rely on the state to expend its limited power to enforce their claims.

Neither could the state rely on landlords to control tenants. A passage from the Chu-lo county gazetteer discussing the need to extend simultaneously the civil and military organs of the state to the frontier adds to its list of complaints the following: "Tenants look on their landlords with contempt and dare to resist officials; they are surly and cunning."[43]

Because their tenants did the actual reclamation and farming, most patent holders lived in the prefectural and county capitals. This spatial separation further weakened the ability of absentee patent holders to oversee affairs in the villages and prevent crime.[44] Reclamation contracts included clauses requiring tenants to obey village regulations and warning them not to gamble, harbor criminals, or in other ways violate the law, but such clauses were not easily enforced.[45] Twice in the eighteenth century, once after the Wu Fu-sheng revolt in 1732, and again after a large outbreak of communal feuding in 1782, the government threatened to hold landlords responsible for the criminal behavior of tenants.[46] But few absentees wielded the necessary influence to control their tenants. Thus, the split-ownership system created problems not just of revenue collection but also of law enforcement and social control.

Changing Land-Tax Rates

The rapidly increasing population of immigrants in the late K'ang-hsi and Yung-cheng years meant an equally rapid expansion of reclamation. To finance its expanded operations, the government sought to increase land-tax revenues by taxing the expanding farm acreage. In enrolling this newly reclaimed acreage, the state encountered taxpayer resistance that required substantial administrative effort to overcome. The government ultimately concluded that lower tax rates could reduce resistance to registration and thus expand the local revenue base.

Many commentators, beginning with Chu-lo's first magistrate, Chi Ch'i-kuang, noted that Taiwan's land-tax rates were unusually heavy.[47] These high rates had been adopted in 1684, when the taxable acreage was quite limited, to make Taiwan as fiscally self-sufficient as possible. Lan Ting-yüan, writing in 1724, observed that the tax rate of 8.8 *shih* of grain per *chia* on first-grade paddy, when commuted at the lowest market price of 0.3 taels per *shih*, equaled 2.64 taels per *chia*, which was twice the usual mainland rate. If the price of grain rose, the tax burden rose proportionately. "When newly opened land is fertile," Lan argued,

> it can be surveyed and reported correctly; however, frontier land, if suddenly flooded, can be lost as soon as it is reclaimed, so unregistered land is needed to make up for shortages. Only in this way do the people not suffer greatly. But the Tainan area is small, unlike Feng-shan and Chu-lo [which have much unregistered land]; so the people there have unbearably heavy taxes. *On no account can we heedlessly propose a land survey if the goal is to raise taxes.* The land beyond the seas [Taiwan] is uneven in fertility and because of

> earthquakes, floods, and the convulsions of nature . . . the people fear they will be left with a tax quota and no land; in that case trouble between them and officials will grow. If there is to be a land survey, then the three counties must carefully allocate the tax burden evenly and without bias; only then will it be good. Under no circumstances can the taxes be increased.[48] (my italics)

Once again Lan's sense of realpolitik is striking: land surveys conducted with the intention of raising taxes led only to trouble.[49] Land taxes were already so high and natural catastrophes so frequent that leaving land unregistered was a quite reasonable way of coping with these heavy burdens. Because the Tainan area lacked the surplus unregistered land necessary to help meet the tax burden, the only good a land survey could do, in Lan's view, would be to even out the tax quotas among the counties.

The Yung-cheng emperor's concern with fiscal balance and the pressure he put on local officials to register new land for taxation drew official attention to these problems in Taiwan. In 1726 Governor Mao Wen-ch'üan reported that large amounts of land were hidden from taxation in Taiwan.[50] The next year, the censor So-lin addressed this problem in a lengthy memorial. He noted that Taiwan's plains were unreclaimed grasslands. "Powerful families choose land of higher elevation close to mountain streams, report the boundaries to the county government, request a reclamation permit [*k'en tan*] and call in tenants to open the land. The land tax is levied according to the rent, but taxes are so heavy that the owners have not a grain left after paying them. Hence they cannot but reclaim much and report little [*i to pao shao*] so that they conceal [*ch'i yin*] more than they report."[51] The customary rent of 8 *shih* per *chia* of paddy paid to a patent holder did indeed fall short of the tax of 8.8 *shih* per *chia* paid on first-grade paddy. In addition to concealing newly reclaimed land, landowners coped with high taxes by falsely reporting high-quality land at lower tax grades.[52] So-lin went on to say that he had investigated

> why so much is concealed and no cadastral surveys have corrected the situation; I have found five reasons. First, the land-tax rate, when figured in *mou*, is several times heavier than the mainland rate; so if owners do not reclaim much and report little, they are unable to pay the land tax. Second, every summer and fall heavy rains wash away land and deposit silt, and reclaimed lands become barren; so if one does not reclaim much and report little, the losses cannot be recovered. Third, Taiwan borders the sea, but as there are no dikes, the sea winds blow salty water onto the land; only after several years can the land be cultivated; so unless one reclaims much and reports little, the land tax cannot be paid. Fourth, Taiwan's soil is "hot" and unsuitable for fertilizer; after two or three years the harvests decline and the land must be left fallow for two years before it can be cultivated again. Thus,

> unless much is reclaimed and little is reported, the taxes cannot be met. Fifth, tenants immigrating from Chang-chou, Ch'üan-chou, Ch'ao-chou, and Hui-chou and desiring to open, without licenses [*ssu k'en*], Taiwan's broad land, risk the crossing to Taiwan. If we seek to survey their land and tax it, they will not be able to afford it and will be forced to return to their native places, and the fields will be left barren and tax quotas will go unmet.[53]

After detailing why a cadastral survey would create so many problems, So-lin did not venture to recommend a method of reform.

Nevertheless, in response to an imperial edict of 1727 ordering every province to register new land (and promising that those who registered land would not be punished for tax avoidance), Taiwan's four counties registered 17,170 *chia* by 1729.[54] The prefectural gazetteers' tax sections reveal that the bulk of this land was registered during 1728, primarily in newly created Chang-hua county (over 10,000 of the 12,000 *chia* total for 1728).[55] So-lin and Governor-general Kao Ch'i-cho (see the passages cited below) had considered conducting a land survey for local reasons, independent of the nationwide edict. Chang-hua's new yamen was built in 1728, and the cadastral survey helped create a revenue base for the new county.

So-lin's memorial of 1727 also transmitted (besides a significant proposal concerning tribal land rights; see Chapter 9) an important proposal that the emperor recommended for further study:

> In the newly established Chang-hua county, there is much unopened land suitable for calling in settlers to reclaim. The Tan-shui subprefect, Wang P'ing [the first to hold that office], has found that in recruiting settlers for reclamation there is no need for one person to claim many *li* of land. Rather, the government should let the farmers themselves open the land. One man's allotment should not exceed five *chia*; ten farmers can join together and be mutually responsible for each other. A three-year time limit should be set in which to register the land according to *mainland* [my italics] tax rates.[56]

Wang's proposal, though apparently never adopted, addresses fundamental issues of frontier land administration. In proposing to limit the area that one person could seek to reclaim, he attacks the patent holder system of reclamation.[57] As we saw above, the Chu-lo county gazetteer criticized split ownership as a "corrupt practice" because of the problems it created for both tax collection and the maintenance of order. A 1735 memorial referring to Fukien by Governor-general Hao Yü-lin pointed out the benefits of the existing system. According to Hao, ordinary people were too poor to bear the expenses in oxen, seed, and irrigation construction necessary to bring land into production. To encourage reclamation (and to increase tax revenues), the government should either make it easy for wealthy families to get reclamation patents and privately finance opening the land, or the government itself should subsidize reclamation by commoners.[58] The second alternative held little attraction to a government averse to assuming additional financial burdens, especially when they could be met privately.

Wang's second proposal, to levy the land tax according to the much lower *mainland* rates, is his solution to the corrupt practice of "reclaiming much and reporting little." As we shall see below, other memorialists were calling for a reduction of Taiwan's land-tax rates, and they were eventually lowered in 1731. Criticisms similar to Wang's of the administration of land reclamation in Taiwan are made in memorials dealing with the Lan-Chang-hsing incident of 1725–26 and provide the background for the 1731 tax revision.[59]

In 1726 acting Governor-general I Chao-hsiung and Governor Mao Wen-ch'üan memorialized as follows:

> The Chang-hua county magistrate, Sun Lu, reports that raw aborigines have burned down houses and killed eight [Han] tenants in a village in the Mao-wu-su tribal area. Investigation reveals that this area was originally beyond the raw aborigine boundary, in forbidden territory that included the local natives' deer fields. Naval commander Lan, however, has sought to reclaim this area, and there is no avoiding trouble such as these murders, which have obviously been provoked. . . . Lan has stated that the Mao-wu-su village is his property, that the county has given him a patent, and that he pays the aborigine head tax on the aborigines' behalf. We submit that . . . reclaiming land in a restricted area is contrary to regulations.[60]

The next report of this affair comes in a memorial of Chekiang-Fukien governor-general Kao Ch'i-cho, dated the eleventh month of 1726:

> When the Ch'ing first recovered Taiwan, only the area around Tainan [T'ai-wan county] was settled, paid taxes, and had clearly established rights in land. Chu-lo and Feng-shan were all unreclaimed; so settlers were called in to open those areas. But army officers, from the first commander, Shih Lang, on down, all claimed land, local civil and military officials established official estates [*kuan chuang*], and powerful families arbitrarily reported land for reclamation, called in tenants, and collected rents. Later on, tenants themselves called in tenants, and with transfers back and forth, layer by layer ownership was concealed. The land tax is levied per *chia*, which does not exceed 10-odd mainland *mou*, but each *chia* must pay 8-odd *shih* in tax grain, which is like paying the tax of 10-odd *mou* while farming a single *mou* of paddy. This may seem like "little land and much in taxes" but by transfers and concealment hundreds of *mou* are cultivated but only a few *mou* are reported; so in reality it is "much land and little in taxes." A thorough investigation is needed to clear these matters up. I fear a disturbance on this frontier across the sea; the longer reform is put off, the harder it will be to accomplish. Because the boundaries of landed property are unclear and the names of resident households are in disarray, the mutual-guarantee registration [*pao chia*] is only approximate. Although I desire an immediate reform,

I dare not speak heedlessly. I am now making careful inquiries and pondering alternatives. . . .

In Chang-hua a new county government has been established; yet its land-tax revenue is very limited. Under its jurisdiction is a village called Lan-Chang-hsing. Its land formerly belonged to an aborigine tribe paying 240 taels in aborigine head taxes. The former lieutenant colonel Chang Kuo[61] undertook to reclaim this land, paying the aborigine revenue on the tribe's behalf, calling in settlers, and collecting rents. Several years ago the commander Lan T'ing-chen acquired this village by pledge [*tien*]. There are now over 2,000 settlers there. The local civil and military officials, because of a raw aborigine raid, consider the opening of this land a provocation to the aborigines and want to remove the settlers and return the land to the aborigines.

I, Kao, feel that if reclamation of an area is to be forbidden, it ought to be forbidden from the start. There are now more than 2,000 settlers, and the land has been reclaimed; suddenly removing them would create 2,000 unemployed people, across the seas away from home—Where could they be settled? But letting property owners privately occupy land and tenants seize land in a disorderly fashion rather than managing it well from the start results in the corrupt practices common in Chu-lo and Feng-shan.

Kao proposes to survey all this land and order each settler to register his land and assume the taxes. It will thereby become the settlers' property in perpetuity. There is no need to follow the Chu-lo and Feng-shan precedent of charging 8 *shih* of grain per *chia* in land tax. Rather, the mainland method, which sets the tax by *mou* and productive capacity, should be used; if the tax is set according to the lowest grade, the tax yield would be 1,000–2,000 taels. . . . The aborigine revenue tax of 240 taels can be eliminated, and there is no need to let Lan and Chang monopolize the land. Moreover, we can take the opportunity afforded by a land survey to do a household survey at the same time and put the *pao chia* registration in order. The four boundaries can be set and officials ordered to strictly investigate and not allow settlers to encroach beyond them. In this way by one supreme effort eternal ease can be won.[62]

The Yung-cheng emperor gave Kao a characteristically terse reply: "This is one solution, but why not secretly inform Lan and Chang and order them to do the examining and reporting themselves, and distribute the land-tax burden among the settlers. Would that not save a lot of effort?"[63] The emperor preferred to minimize administrative expenditures rather than maximize revenues.

The attitudes of the responsible officials toward land reclamation and tax abuses are central to our concerns. I and Mao blamed Lan's reclamation of land in a restricted area for the raw aborigine attack that cost several lives, and Kao reported that local officials were recommending removal of the settlers, a view he opposed. Kao's recommendation echoes Lan Ting-yüan's warnings about population removal (see Chapter 7).[64] Kao proposed to give the land to the settlers after a cadastral survey and

TABLE 8.5
Changing Rates of Land Taxation in Taiwan Under the Chengs and the Ch'ing
(in *shih* of unhusked rice per *chia*)

Land grades	Cheng era: Government estates	Cheng era: Officials' estates	Ch'ing era, land opened: before 1729	Ch'ing era, land opened: 1729–1744	Ch'ing era, land opened: after 1744
Paddy					
High	18.0	3.6	8.8		2.740
Middle	15.6	3.12	7.4	1.7583	2.080
Low	10.2	2.04	5.5		1.758
Field					
High	10.2	2.24	5.0		2.080
Middle	8.1	1.62	4.0	1.7166	1.758
Low	5.4	1.08	2.4		1.716

NOTE: The Chu-lo county gazetteer (*CLHC*: 86, 90) and the *Taiwan zeimushi* (*TZ*: 1.50–52) give slightly varying figures for certain categories for the early years. See also Chou Hsien-wen 1957: 97–98 and Okamatsu 1902: 25.

to tax it at a much lower rate. Kao's proposal, which would have eliminated Lan and Chang's land rights, reflects official dislike of split ownership rights. Kao prefaced his proposal with an attack on subletting and complicated transfers that left title unclear and land concealed from taxation.

Kao Ch'i-cho's and Wang P'ing's proposals to adopt lower, mainland tax rates indicate that such a measure was under serious consideration in official circles. Lower tax rates were suggested as a way of coaxing land developers to register more of their land for taxation. Advocating lower tax rates when a growing government bureaucracy was hungry for tax revenues underlines these policymakers' assumption that expanding reclamation would fill the tax coffers by putting more land on the tax registers, as well as their pro-colonization stance.

The decision to reduce Taiwan's land-tax rate was finally handed down in 1731. Unfortunately, I have been unable to locate memorials that would clarify which issues the court considered most significant in ordering this change, although the problem of underreporting must have figured heavily. All land reclaimed and registered for taxation after 1729 was to be taxed according to the tax rates on low-grade tidal lands charged by T'ung-an county (in Ch'üan-chou prefecture, Fukien), which were calculated in silver and charged per *mou* (1 *chia* was set equal to 11.3 *mou*). Taiwan's landowners were to continue to pay the tax in unhusked grain, however; the new rate on paddy land was calculated at 1.7583 *shih* per *chia*, considerably lighter than the old rate of 8.8 *shih* (see Table 8.5).

The considerable tax reduction of 1731 had an impact on many aspects of Ch'ing policy toward Taiwan. Reduced land-tax rates made the unreclaimed fields on Taiwan's frontier even more attractive to immigrants. Consequently the number of unlicensed and therefore illegal "secret crossings" increased, despite the approval in 1732 of family immigration.[65] The growing flood of immigrants put new pressure as well on the Ch'ing boundary policy: increasing numbers of settlers violated the raw aborigine boundary, encroaching on and reclaiming tribal lands.[66] This intensified Han-aborigine conflict and increased the worries of a government whose first priority was the maintenance of order. Thus, the stage was set for another policy reversal.

Opposition to low land-tax rates gained the sympathetic ear of the Ch'ien-lung emperor at a time when many of the other pro-colonization policies of the Yung-cheng period were being replaced with measures to limit Han reclamation of aborigine lands and to quarantine the frontier. The Board of Revenue proposed in 1744 that Taiwan's land tax revert to the high, pre-1729 rates. The emperor, however, reminded the board of the advantages of light taxation. It was decided that land opened before 1729 was to continue at the original rate, and land opened between 1729 and 1744 was to enjoy the light rates decreed in 1731. But land opened after 1744 was to be graded according to fertility and taxed according to the rate schedule in effect in T'ung-an county.[67] The Ch'ien-lung emperor concluded his edict approving the increase by calling for lenience and kindness toward the people of Taiwan.[68] After converting the T'ung-an tax rate from silver and hulled glutinous rice to unhusked rice, the new rate on first-grade paddy was set at 2.740 *shih* per *chia.* The newly decreed rates were nevertheless still considerably lighter than the high, pre-1729 rates. Table 8.5 summarizes the changing tax rates of Taiwan's first century under Ch'ing rule.

One effect of setting rates by year of reclamation was to leave the earliest settled areas around Tainan with much heavier tax burdens. The unwillingness to change old rates even in the interests of equal taxation reflects a peculiar conservatism; it enabled the local governments to avoid revising already established tax registers but almost certainly complicated and confused land-tax collection in later years. (Recall that Lan Ting-yüan had already noted uneven rates of effective taxation between counties due to differing amounts of unregistered land.) Except for the fusing of the land and labor-service tax in 1747 (which by allocating the head tax to registered land had the effect of spreading the burden of the head-tax quota more evenly among the counties), and the change in tax grain measures in 1790 (which effected a 20 percent increase in tax revenue, needed after the destructive Lin Shuang-wen rebellion), there were no further major changes in Taiwan's land taxation until 1843, nearly a century later.

PART III

Accommodation Through the Frontier Land-Tenure System

CHAPTER NINE

The Evolution of Aborigine Land Rights

PART II DOCUMENTED the accelerating immigration of Han settlers in the early eighteenth century. Expanding reclamation and agricultural settlement put tremendous pressure on the plains aborigine hunter-horticulturalists. Yet their villages were not displaced by Han agricultural colonization, nor were they forced to migrate into the mountains. Their ability to remain on the plains and adapt to the transformation of the frontier depended very much on the government's willingness to recognize and enforce their claims to land. This chapter documents the numerous measures the Ch'ing government took to guarantee aborigine livelihoods by managing the allocation of rights in land on the expanding frontier. The government took these measures because of the established status of the plains aborigines as taxpaying subjects and as valued sources of loyalist militia. At first, the government viewed expanding Han settlement as a threat to the ethnic status quo and pursued quarantine policies to limit the disruptive effects of agricultural settlement. When the government found it impossible to impede immigration, it adopted increasingly accommodative policies that sought to reconcile the competing interests of Han settlers and plains aborigines. How these shifts in policy were reflected in specific allocations of rights and duties with respect to the process of frontier land reclamation is the subject of this chapter.

Land policies fluctuated in conjunction with the other pro- and anti-colonization policies discussed in Chapter 6 and throughout Part II. Taiwan's frontier society evolved through the interaction of regional economic cycles and population movements in the southeastern coastal region (including Taiwan) with a government policy cycle that sometimes adapted to, sometimes resisted, developments in Taiwan. In general, pro-colonization advocates supported policies expanding settler access to tribal territories and reducing the extent of aborigine claims;

advocates of quarantine favored limiting Han settlement and recognizing a greater range of aborigine claims over frontier land. The Ch'ing used its authority to allocate rights and duties with respect to land to manage the relations between Han settlers and the plains aborigines and further its own revenue and security goals.

A detailed analytical history of early Ch'ing policies governing the disposition of aborigine lands on the Taiwan frontier follows. The chronological presentation is meant to highlight the broad range of historical factors affecting development of the allocation and administration of rights in land and the flexibility with which Chinese land-tenure arrangements were adapted to the frontier (and thereby correct the rigid topical organization of previous legalistic treatments).[1] Changing government land policies are introduced against the background of a broader historical narrative intended to provide insight into the opportunities and constraints channeling the strategies of the various contending parties—aborigines, settlers, and government.

The state authorities recognized two broad categories of frontier land in Taiwan: tribal land and government-owned wasteland. Under Chinese law all land not under cultivation was generally considered subject to government "ownership" and control.[2] In Taiwan, however, the Ch'ing state recognized tribal ownership of large amounts of uncultivated land. How aborigine settlements initially won (and lost) government recognition of tribal claims to uncultivated land such as hunting grounds is, as we shall see below, only murkily revealed in the sources. Surveying of tribal areas before Han settlement (e.g., the case of An-li in 1715; see below) occurred only rarely and locally, never comprehensively. Rather, the allocation of land between the two categories of ownership appears often to have become fixed only in the process of opening the land and resolving (and negotiating compromises in) disputes over title. We can be sure that the areas of both waste and tribal land were extensive.[3]

At the government's (and settlers') disposal was land that fell between tribal claims (the sparse settlement of the aborigines ensured that this category was a large one) and land on which an aborigine claim had been extinguished. To reclaim government wasteland, settlers and land developers could petition the government for patents according to an established procedure (see Chapter 8). Because the Ch'ing recognized tribal ownership of uncultivated land, a large amount of the land Han immigrants desired to open was subject to prior ownership claims. This chapter provides a history of the means by which settlers obtained the right to reclaim tribal lands.

Aborigine practice recognized a variety of claims to land. We know little about the specifics of the plains aborigine systems of land tenure, although the sources occasionally reveal some details in the course of discussing disputes over tribal claims. Aided by twentieth-century accounts of other aboriginal groups in Taiwan,[4] we can draw a general picture that is unlikely to diverge much from the historical reality.

Plains aborigines generally lived in nucleated villages on permanent sites. Groves of prickly bamboo and wooden palisades enclosed the villages and defended them from attack. Housesites within these villages, including small patches of garden, fruit and betel nut trees, and space for a granary and domestic animals, were allocated among small groups of kin (variously defined). These housesites were owned semipermanently and were transmitted within kin groups through rules of inheritance. Within the village, sources of water, shrines, men's houses (where they existed), and plazas were publicly owned.

We can visualize the territory outside aborigine villages as divided into concentric rings, distinguished by the productive activities conducted in each ring and by the exclusivity of tribal territorial claims. Village farmland was located in the nearest ring, and exclusive sites for hunting, fishing, and gathering were located in the next ring. Outside these two rings were more distant hunting grounds the village was forced to share with other tribes, wastelands, and the territories of neighboring villages.

Fields for rice, millet, and miscellaneous crops were located in the innermost ring around the village. Some of these were permanent fields, garden, and orchard owned and transmitted in the same fashion as housesites. A larger area of shifting fields rotated around the village according to a fallowing cycle. At the beginning of a new rotation, the men of the village would mark off a large sector and do the preliminary clearing. Then each kin group/domestic unit would delineate, physically and ritually, a smaller plot within the cleared sector, do more intensive preparation of the land, and plant crops. This joint clearing of land meant that the village fields, though constantly rotating, were concentrated in space; people working in the fields could thus come to one another's defense in case of attack, assist in crop watching, and cooperate to prevent the invasion of the fields by deer and other wild animals. A kin group's investment of labor in a set of fields was recognized as giving it exclusive rights of usufruct for the duration of each cropping rotation. Since the fields were not permanent, concepts of permanent ownership and inheritance did not apply. But the lack of permanent ownership did not mean that land within the agricultural ring was open to anyone; the right to such land was predicated upon recognized membership in the village.

In the next outlying ring were the territories exclusively reserved to village members for hunting, fishing, and gathering. Some groups recognized certain hunting grounds as the property of clans, and nonclan members were expected to request permission to hunt from clan members and to distribute a portion of the game to them. But such claims did not affect all hunting grounds; nor was this a universal practice, even among those aborigine groups to whom clan organization was important. Among plains groups such as the Siraya, who had village-wide age sets, clan membership was much less significant. Thus, a large portion, if not all, of this second band of territory was a public commons, and village members were free to exploit the game and other resources found there. Attempts by non-village members to enter and exploit this territory were perceived as threats to be met with force. Beyond this outer ring, villagers might claim exclusive rights to certain hunting grounds but were unable to enforce such claims except by catching trespassers in the act; they had in effect to share this land with hunters from other tribes.

Thus within two bands surrounding each village, non-village members were excluded from farming and hunting, and the village was able to enforce an exclusive territorial claim. As Chinese settlement expanded onto the frontier and the aborigine economies themselves changed, these arrangements came under increasing pressure. Later, the tribal system of land tenure eroded from within as the area of permanent fields expanded because the plains aborigines were adopting intensive agriculture (as the hunting sector of their economies declined) and plowing up the territory formerly reserved for shifting horticulture. Since the native systems of tenure recognized ownership claims established by the investment of labor in reclaiming land, permanent fields reclaimed by plains aborigines were recognized as the private property of plains aborigine families. Such fields might in turn be alienated to Chinese. Pressure on village land tenure also came from without. Throughout this period villages and clans claimed large areas as their collective farmland and hunting grounds. As Chinese settlers began to eye fields in the vicinity of aborigine villages, they encountered exclusive claims to tribal lands. Much of this chapter discusses how the government sought to accommodate the groups competing for this tribal land.

To reclaim tribal land, settlers had to come to terms with the aborigine claimants. Outsiders might obtain village membership and thus acquire access to tribal land by establishing friendships within the village or by marrying a village woman. And village monopoly merchants and interpreters, taking advantage of their economic and political position, no doubt could override native custom and reclaim, or recruit settlers to reclaim, village land. The monopoly merchant might also broker "sales" of land between Chinese and aborigines, who probably did not understand the concept of permanent alienation of land. And some settlers simply squatted on land, defying both tribe and government (though sometimes aided by colluding officials) to remove them. In later years we have reports from certain localities where settlers outnumbered plains aborigines that harassment by Han (e.g., brawling, stealing water buffalo, setting fire to houses) caused plains aborigines to abandon their land and migrate to new villages.[5] None of these methods received official sanction. Some of them the government explicitly condemned and sought to prohibit, for fear that abuses would lead to Han-aborigine conflict and frontier disorder.

Two methods by which Han acquired aborigine land—renting by "assuming the tribal tax" (*tai fan shu hsiang*) and renting by payment of a tribal ground rent (*fan ta tsu*, "aborigine large-rent")—preserved an aborigine ownership right and guaranteed the tribes a source of income. Arrangements of these kinds between tribes and settlers did at times receive government sanction. The evolution of these arrangements, in the context of government attempts to regulate the reclamation of tribal land, is the subject of this chapter.

The recognition and protection of aborigine land rights and the accommodation of settler and tribal interests through the frontier land-tenure system were significant products of the balance of forces in Taiwan's frontier society as it evolved within the parameters set by the political economy of Ch'ing China. These arrangements enabled the plains aborigines to survive into later centuries on the plains. As the deer-hunting economy declined and Han settlers advanced, plains aborigine livelihoods declined disastrously. Aborigine hunters only gradually and with little enthusiasm became farmers (see Chapter 11). An income from lands let to Han settlers often provided the tribes with a crucial margin during this difficult period of adjustment.

Government Recognition of Tribal Land Claims

The flow of land-hungry immigrant farmers into Taiwan's broad open spaces put pressure on aborigine livelihoods. What looked like wasteland ready to be transformed into rice paddy or cane field to the Chinese was an active component of aborigine production systems as deer-hunting grounds (and buffer between hostile settlements). Eventually, excessive exploitation of the deer herds along with the encroaching transformation of hunting grounds into paddy led to the disruption of the deer-hunting sector of the aborigine economies and seriously disrupted aborigine livelihoods.[6] This dislocation made the protection of tribal land rights a matter crucial both to a government seeking to maintain peace on the frontier and to aborigines seeking new strategies of survival. This section is devoted to detailing the earliest steps of the accommodation worked out by three actors: the tribes, the settlers, and the government.

In southern Taiwan land in the core of Chinese settlement around the city of Tainan had been reclaimed under the Dutch and Cheng regimes. The Dutch required Chinese farming tribal land to pay rents (see Chapter 3), and the Chengs honored aborigine claims to land aborigines farmed themselves, but probably not to lands farmed by Cheng armies and by Chinese farmers, from whom they extracted heavy taxes (Chapter 4). By

Ch'ing times, it is likely that much (but by no means all) of the flat land in this core area had either been bought outright or taken over with no recognition given to tribal claims.[7] Nevertheless, at least two of the four large core-area tribes, Ma-tou and Hsiao-lung, still had aborigine large-rent rights at the end of the nineteenth century, and many contracts demonstrate continued landownership by members of all four tribes.[8]

With the fall of Taiwan to the Ch'ing in 1683, the repatriation of Chinese to the mainland depopulated the southwest core and created a surplus of cultivable land. Thus, pressure to reclaim land beyond the core was delayed until the Chinese population recovered and began growing again with the heavy immigration of the late K'ang-hsi years (see Chapter 6). The amount of land registered for taxation under the Chengs in 1683 was not matched again until 1710 (see Tables 6.5 and 8.3). Moreover, the aborigine deer trade was still prospering. Hence, there was no pressure from expanding settlement that required the Ch'ing to formulate a policy governing aborigine land rights in the earliest years of its rule.

The first notice of government concern for tribal lands dates from around 1704, a full twenty years after the Ch'ing conquest.[9] The Taiwan-Amoy intendant, Wang Min-cheng (served 1704–9), decreed that settlers must first obtain government permission before opening aborigine land. Unfortunately, we do not have a complete text of this decree. Inō Yoshinori (who gives no citation) tells us that the decree required Han (privately) contracting to reclaim aborigine land to petition for *official* approval. Local officials were then to investigate the costs and benefits for Han and aborigines before deciding whether to approve the request. Land whose reclamation was sanctioned was to be reported for taxation. The procedure established by this decree enabled a government worried that Han encroachment would provoke conflict to ensure that any land reclamation agreements between Chinese settlers and aborigine tribes were voluntary. A government kept fully informed of the process of reclaiming tribal land could require the reclaimer to fulfill the terms of his agreement with the aborigines and thereby "prevent villains from making trouble."[10] A fundamental question remains, however: What lands did the government consider to be "aborigine lands" as opposed to unreclaimed and unclaimed land to which the government held ultimate rights?

Chinese law supported the position that uncultivated tribal territories and hunting grounds should be considered ownerless wasteland, open to reclamation. Such a denial of tribal land claims was rejected, however, by Ch'en Pin, who succeeded Wang Min-cheng as Taiwan-Amoy intendant from 1710 to 1715.[11] Ch'en Pin presents his position in favor of recognizing aborigine land claims in the essay "Forbid Encroaching Reclamation in Order to Protect Aborigine Property":

> Mainland subjects pay taxes on land and thereby acquire an ownership right that can be passed down through the generations; aboriginal tribes, since the present dynasty took control, also pay yearly tax quotas; therefore, the land of such tribes should be [recognized as] aborigine property. The tribes themselves should be allowed to decide whether to plant their land in seed, use it as pasture, or leave it as deer field. Moreover, every tribe has boundaries with its neighbors, and the aborigines do not allow these boundaries to be violated. How can Chinese coming from outside be allowed to occupy the land [and violate these boundaries]?[12]

Ch'en's essay makes clear his concern that influential Chinese rushing to claim reclamation rights to fertile tribal lands and county officials "deceptively" issuing patents were stirring up trouble. Ch'en argued that Han reclamation of aborigine land ought to be permanently prohibited. "All aborigines must be protected in their property so they need not fear losing their livelihood."[13] Ch'en thus was a strong advocate of the position that paying the tribal taxes, which in theory were head taxes and not taxes on land, entitled the aborigines to rights over their land regardless of how they chose to use it. However, his reference to tribally recognized boundaries left open the possibility that some lands lay outside tribal territorial claims.[14] Ch'en's comments indicate that the current practice, which he criticized, had been to issue patents without regard to aborigine territorial claims. In the exceptional case of the An-li tribes that submitted in 1715, the government issued a proclamation that ensured their rights to a large and clearly demarcated tribal territory.[15] But for plains tribes whose submission dated from before Ch'ing rule, there were no such formal guarantees.

In 1715 Ch'en Pin, in Peking (from Hunan where he was serving as governor) for a special audience with the K'ang-hsi emperor, took an even stronger position on tribal land rights:

> [Emperor] What is the situation concerning uncultivated land in Taiwan? [Ch'en] There is no uncultivated farmland in Taiwan. Although there is much uncultivated land along the south and north routes, that is all deer-hunting land for the native barbarians; they pay taxes and support their families from these lands, so that if the lands were opened up for cultivation, they would lose their hunting lands and in turn they would have no way to support themselves. This is why the Governor of Fukien has repeatedly issued notices strictly forbidding any local villains from annoying them along these routes under the pretext of opening uncultivated lands. This is why these barbarians have been able to live peacefully together with the common people without any disturbances.[16]

Ch'en's argument emphasizes two points in support of recognizing tribal claims: the taxpaying that establishes the status of the aborigines as loyal subjects and the government's duty to protect aborigine livelihoods. This latter point reflects the Mencian philosophy that characterized Ch'ing administrative theory: governments should nurture their subjects and foster their economic well-being to ensure their submission and prepare the way for moral cultivation.[17] A few days after his audience, Ch'en Pin was appointed governor of Fukien,[18] from which post he was no doubt influential in enforcing his views. That his concluding comment about the peaceful coexistence of settlers and aborigines was overly optimistic will be seen below.

In 1711 Prefect Chou Yüan-wen took a position identical to Ch'en Pin's when he argued that a holiday on Han land taxes should be extended to the aborigine head tax since it was analogous to a tax on aborigine deer fields. He added that "because the aborigines are not good cultivators, deer-hunting grounds have been allotted to them."[19] Huang Shu-ching reported in 1722 that Han Chinese could be arrested for hunting deer in aborigine fields, on the grounds that they were interfering with payment of the aborigine head tax.[20] Both Chou and Huang assume that the payment of taxes should establish, in the eyes of the government, the aborigines' claim to tribal territories and entitle them to government protection of their property rights.

The 1717 Chu-lo county gazetteer takes a slightly different position. The gazetteer includes aborigine tribes in its classification of landowners and comments that aborigines are not obligated to pay a land tax on land they themselves cultivate because they pay a head tax.[21] The gazetteer thereby recognizes that taxpaying established aborigine land rights, but it mentions only land farmed by the aborigines and not hunting grounds. This suggests the lack of a consistent definition of what was and what was not "aborigine land." It is clear, nevertheless, that aborigine land rights of some kind were widely recognized. The exact nature of these rights only came to be defined in practice as tribes and the government were forced to assert these claims against expanding Han settlement.

Policy and Practice on the K'ang-hsi Era Frontier

What was practice in regard to tribal lands in the K'ang-hsi era? The property rights the government recognized by inclusion in the land-tax registers or authorized by issuance of a patent did not necessarily coincide with those negotiated between a reclaimer and a tribe. The triangular relationship among the government, settlers, and tribes allowed many permutations. Let us look first at the government side.

Intendant Wang Min-cheng's decree (ca. 1704–9) provides for the reclamation of aborigine land only with government permission. However, this decree does not define aborigine land. Wang's requirement of government permission implies that the government investigated the local situation and the terms of the agreements between reclaimers and tribes before issuing patents, but it is doubtful that Wang's regulations were universally enforced. Ch'en Pin complained that officials "deceptively" issued patents, apparently without regard to aborigine desires or tribal territorial claims, and were thereby stirring up trouble with the aborigines.

In certain areas, however, the local government apparently enforced a moratorium on the issuance of patents during this period (probably during and after Ch'en Pin's terms in office). Lan Ting-yüan noted in 1724 that the Chang-hua area had formerly been aborigine land that Han were prohibited from "encroaching" (*ch'in*) on to cultivate.[22] Ch'en Pin's comment to the K'ang-hsi emperor suggests that an absolute prohibition of reclamation had been in effect in 1715. Ch'en Pin himself, in the essay cited above, had advocated such a prohibition. But Lan, who says literally that only "encroaching" was prohibited, leaves open the possibility that private agreements between reclaimers and tribes (with appropriate official sanction) were not outlawed and that only squatting was prohibited. Although we lack texts of the decrees they refer to, Lan and Ch'en clearly indicate that some degree of prohibition was in force in certain areas, at least after Ch'en Pin's term as intendant. That an imperial decree was necessary to sanction Han renting of aborigine land in 1724 (see below) supports this interpretation. Government policy against Han encroachment into aborigine territories apparently tightened in the years before the Chu I-kuei rebellion of 1721. Chu-lo county magistrate Chou Chung-hsüan's proposal to prevent Han crossing the Ta-chia river (see Chapter 7) was part of this trend toward tighter restrictions imposed in response to a quickening influx of settlers.

Reclaimers and tribes in this period came to a wide variety of private arrangements. In some instances squatters simply occupied land and defended their claims, with force if necessary. Huang Shu-ching reported several instances of tribes' suffering from the encroachment of squatters and cited squatters and their provocation of tribal attack as a reason for drawing the Han-aborigine boundary in 1722.[23] The Chu-lo county gazetteer lamented the trouble caused by "vagrants casting lustful eyes on aborigine land."[24] And Magistrate Chou Chung-hsüan records the daily increase in immigrant trespass: "What was formerly aborigine deer-hunting ground and hemp field is today land that developers request to reclaim or land that vagrants occupy and cultivate. . . . Before long there will not be a hundredth left of the aborigines' ancestral property." Chou prefaced these remarks by saying that "the powerful cheat the aborigines and treat them as oppressively as meat on a platter, and the weak flatter the aborigines and lead them on like monkeys up a tree."[25] Although Chou distinguishes patent holders from squatters, some of these squatters probably managed to obtain patents or register the land as theirs after the fact. Thus, with official collusion they could acquire a government-recognized title, as Ch'en Pin had noted.

Private agreements between settlers and the tribes concerning land rights were of various kinds. A sale (probably of dubious legal status) was possible when a reclaimer convinced a tribe to accept suitable compensation. The earliest examples of clear and outright sales in the contract collections are dated 1726, 1734, and 1738; there is also an example of a conditional (redeemable) sale (*tien*) from 1726.[26] These examples include both sales by tribes as corporate bodies and sales by individual aborigines of private plots. I have seen no regulation from this early era that explicitly forbade aborigine sale of land to Han. But there are indications that outright sales were, in theory, prohibited. Most important is the negative evidence that an imperial decree in 1724 approved only the renting out of land by tribes. Sales (a more complete form of alienation of land rights) were not approved or even mentioned.[27] Sales may have been prohibited because they permanently reduced the ability of the tribes to pay their taxes in a way that the leases and rental agreements discussed in the next sections did not.

Paying the Tribal Tax in Exchange for Land

The one early method of acquiring aborigine land that received explicit official sanction (because it guaranteed state revenues) required a settler to assume the aborigine head-tax burden of a tribe in return for rights in land.[28] This method derives directly from the *p'u she* system (see Chapter 5). To collect aborigine head taxes, the state generally awarded a Chinese tax farmer a monopoly over a tribe's trade from whose profits he derived the cash to pay the tax. The *p'u she* system was originally invented to facilitate exploitation of the trade in deerskins and venison. As the herds were depleted and as land-hungry Chinese immigrants pushed the agricultural frontier outward (one or the other came first in different localities), tribal livelihoods based on deer-hunting were disrupted, but tribal tax obligations remained the same. By paying aborigine taxes, Han could acquire land rights in tribal territories.

It was hard for the government to fault an arrangement that guaranteed tribal tax payments. Some tribes may have willingly made the transition from deer hunting to landlording. Others may have been in arrears in tax payments or in debt to their monopoly merchant and pressed by him to let out land. In some cases the merchant or interpreter himself acquired the land. I also suspect that official corruption sometimes allowed an impatient land developer to pay the tax (and establish his rights) contrary to a tribe's wishes.

This method of acquiring rights in aborigine land was called *tai fan shu hsiang* by the Chu-lo gazetteer and *t'ieh fan na hsiang* by Lan Ting-yüan; both phrases mean to pay taxes on behalf of the tribe. The same meaning is conveyed in descriptions of the tax-farming aspect of the *p'u she* system by the terms *tai shu she hsiang* and *tai fan na hsiang*.[29] We have in fact already discussed one instance of this relationship in the investigation of Commander Lan T'ing-chen's claim over Lan-Chang-hsing village (see Chapter 8). In Kao Ch'i-cho's memorial, Lan's land claim is stated to have derived from Chang's assuming the aborigine revenue tax (*tai fan na hsiang*) on behalf of the Mao-wu-su tribe.[30]

The earliest land grant in the Taipei area, issued in 1709, also derives from this relationship and clarifies for this period the government's attitude toward these agreements.

> Magistrate Sung [Yung-ch'ing] of Feng-shan county, acting on behalf of Chu-lo county, for the purpose of opening wasteland and enriching the tax revenues, issues a patent on the basis of a petition presented by [partners] Ch'en, Lai, and Chang in accordance with Taiwan's regulations encouraging reclamation. Ch'en has discovered in Tan-shui's Ta-chia-la [located along the Tan-shui riverbank area of present-day Taipei city] a tract of wasteland whose four boundaries . . . do not violate the line between people [Han] and aborigines [*ping wu fang ai min fan ti chieh*]. Ch'en is now recruiting tenants to reclaim the land; thus, he has applied for approval of a patent to facilitate reporting the land for tax registration, etc. [The magistrate] has ordered the tribal merchant, interpreter, and chief to make a field investigation and report back. The tribal merchant Yang, the foremen Hsü and Lin, and the chief Wei-chih-tou-chin, et al., have assumed this responsibility and report that the tribal merchant, having complied with the order and working together with the foremen and chief, has measured the area that Ch'en, Lai, and Chang have applied to reclaim and found that it covers 50-plus *chia* of land and that the boundaries do not violate [the line of demarcation, *ping wu fang ai*]. According to these facts, we report to the county.
>
> On the basis of this report, the county hereby issues this patent for reclamation to Ch'en, Lai, and Chang, who may immediately recruit tenants and go forth to Ta-chia-la to reclaim and cultivate within these boundaries and register the land for taxation. Tribal bullies [*she kun*] and idlers are not to be allowed to stir up trouble and make claims. Should this sort of willful offense occur, the reclaimer [Ch'en] is allowed to report them and petition the county authorities, who on this basis will arrest them. The reclaimer must now by all means earnestly recruit tenants to open the land and must not "open much and report little." Everyone must conscientiously obey this order and not be negligent. Especially posted. Issued: 1709.
>
> This patent is to be posted publicly in Ta-chia-la of Tan-shui *she*.[31]

This patent raises a number of points. In accordance with the regulations decreed by Wang Min-cheng, who was in his last year as intendant when the patent was issued, the text mentions twice that there is no violation of the boundary between Han and aborigine. The patent could not be referring to the line that the government first established in 1722 as an official boundary to separate Han and raw aborigines. Thus, this reference must be read to mean a local demarcation of land between Han and the plains aborigines participating in the agreement. Unfortunately, I do not know how this line originated; it may have been a local convention separating aborigine village territory from an area open to Han settlement, or it may have existed only on paper to satisfy official requirements that these agreements not provoke trouble with the aborigines. This clause cannot, however, be taken to imply that the land on the Han side of the boundary was ownerless, for we shall see below that the reclaimer was required to pay a rent to the aborigines. Similar clauses occur in all the patents extant from this era from Chu-lo county.[32]

The process of consulting with tribal officers and reporting for taxation outlined in the patent matches that detailed in a 1708 patent issued for land of the Ta-miao *she* just north of the town of Chu-lo.[33] There were three main steps. First, the Ch'en, Lai, and Chang partnership,[34] as reclaimer, petitioned the magistrate for a patent; second, the magistrate ordered the tribe whose land was affected to conduct an investigation; and, third, on the basis of the tribal report, the magistrate issued the patent. Inō argues that this patent exemplifies Wang Min-cheng's decree requiring government permission to open aborigine land.[35] The tribal investigation, it can be argued, gave the tribe a veto over the petition. This step in the process seems to assume prior agreement between the tribe and the reclaimer. Indeed, as we know from other sources, it is of great significance that the patent was issued on the basis of agreements between the petitioner and the tribal officials, which the patent does not mention.

By issuing the patent, the government indirectly approved and gave force to the otherwise private agreement between reclaimer and tribe. Unfortunately, no copy of this agreement is available, but because of a legal suit in 1735 over boundaries involving this land we know more about the agreement. The documents submitted in the 1735 case state that Ch'en, Lai, and Chang had leased (*p'u*) land in Ta-chia-la in an agreement to assume the yearly aborigine head tax (*tai na hsiang k'o*) on behalf of Pai-chieh *she*. Other documents in the case argue that the disputed land was the common property of two tribes (Pai-chieh and Wu-lao-wan), not just one; another document asks which tribe had the right to "sell" the land. One litigant held that the land should be considered ownerless and open to anyone holding a reclamation patent for it.[36] This dispute reveals the problems in defining tribal land rights. The patent itself, while naming particular tribal officials, does not identify them by tribe.[37] In any case, it is clear that the land was granted by the tribe(s) in return for the reclaimers' assuming the tribal tax obligation. The dispute, though occurring several years after the patent was issued and thus perhaps affected by a different set of official policies, reveals that tribal boundaries and land claims were by no means simple and fixed. In the ambiguities of the situation, one litigant even sought to have the land categorized as ownerless, which, as we saw above, was in accord with Chinese customary law, especially as interpreted by land-hungry settlers.

What was the nature of the land rights turned over to the reclaimer by the 1709 patent? Again the available documents are vague. The reclaimer at minimum acquired use rights and managerial rights over the land covered by the patent. The documents from the legal case of 1735 call the agreement a *p'u mai*, or lease-purchase.[38] But Ch'en, Lai, and Chang did not acquire a simple ownership title; their rights to the land depended on fulfilling their private agreement with the tribe. This meant paying the yearly aborigine head tax.

The clause calling for assuming the aborigine head tax is unqualified, implying the reclaimer assumed all of it; but we may wonder whether the reclaimer did assume all the tax quota or just a portion. The 1709 patent covered only 50 *chia* of land, a mere fraction of any tribal territory. It seems unlikely that a tribe or its agents would let a parcel in return for the reclaimer's assuming its entire quota and then make no further claims on its remaining land. The tribes had a livelihood to rebuild in addition to a tax obligation to meet. If letting out tribally claimed land was to provide such an income, then the tribe must have demanded more than its tax quota even while continuing for legal purposes to use the tax label. In the case of Lan T'ing-chen's Lan-Chang-hsing village, the obligation to the tribes (240 taels) far exceeded the tax quota recorded for the Mao-wu-su tribe (29.6352 taels).[39] But the amounts paid some tribes (presumably for a proportionally small amount of land) were only a fraction of their tax burden.[40] The size of the payment clearly was open to negotiation. Although the legal rationale was that the payment covered the aborigine head tax, it need not have been identical to the quota.[41] Amounts in excess of the official tax quota (plus surcharges and squeeze) should have been paid to the tribes and not to the government. The payments were labeled "aborigine head tax" to ensure government approval of the arrangement.

A number of extant tribal agreements with Han impose obligations to make payments under the rubric "aborigine head tax" in return for access to land.[42] One contract dated 1723 for the Ta-wu-chün *she* revealingly states, "since there are no deer to hunt, the taxes go unpaid."[43] Some of these agreements require payments in cash; while others require payment in grain or in both cash and grain. A 1737 contract requires payment in grain because "the tribal head tax quota is already being paid in full by previous reclaimers."[44] Agreements of this nature are also mentioned in the gazetteers for the Ta-chieh-tien *she* and the To-lo-kuo *she*.[45]

Interestingly, in two early sales of aborigine land (dated 1726 and 1738), Han purchasers aimed to eliminate their obligation to pay the yearly aborigine head tax by offering the tribes a large lump-sum cash settlement.[46] The drastic reduction in aborigine tax quotas in 1737 should have meant that amounts formerly paid to the government were redirected to the tribes. Failure by a Han reclaimer to make this adjustment was a part of the Han-aborigine dispute that led to the Pei-t'ou incident of 1751 (see below).[47] A 1774 contract, however, shows that some pre-1737 agreements continued completely unaffected by the change in tax quotas.[48]

In addition to the aborigine head tax, the Han reclaimer was required to pay a land tax to the state: the 1709 patent mentions twice the requirement that the land, once opened, be registered for taxation (*sheng k'o*). Thus, the reclaimer's land rights were doubly burdened, once to the tribes and once to the state. This problem of double taxation received some official attention in later years (see below). Land cultivated by the tribes was not subject to a land tax because the tribes paid a separate head tax. Ch'en Pin argued that tribal landownership and nonliability to land taxation extended as well to hunting grounds and pasture land. But once land was let to Han settlers, the exemption from the land tax ended. According to the Chu-lo county gazetteer, "When Han settlers reclaim aborigine land and assume the aborigine head-tax obligation of the tribe, both the revenue from *land* taxes increases and the aborigines benefit greatly" (my italics).[49] Examination of patents and contracts from this era confirms this conclusion.

The formula by which aborigine villages gave Han reclaimers access to tribal land in exchange for their assuming tribal tax obligations made most sense when tribal tax quotas were high. But after the substantial reduction in aborigine taxes in 1737, this formula was increasingly replaced by a competing arrangement, the aborigine large-rent model, that could provide more income to the tribes.

The Emergence of the Aborigine Large-Rent Model

The earliest known example of an aborigine large-rent (*fan ta tsu*) arrangement that reflects the terms of a standard Han reclamation agreement comes from a court-imposed settlement spelled out in a 1721 contract from the Hsia-tan-shui tribe in Feng-shan county (see Fig. 9.1). This contract is one of several bilingual contracts preserved from Siraya villages.[50] It is written in Chinese and the aborigine language, as transliterated by the tribal scribe according to the romanization system introduced by the Dutch. The locale of the land involved is Tun-wu *chuang* in present-day Chu-t'ien *hsiang*, P'ing-tung county.[51] According to the con-

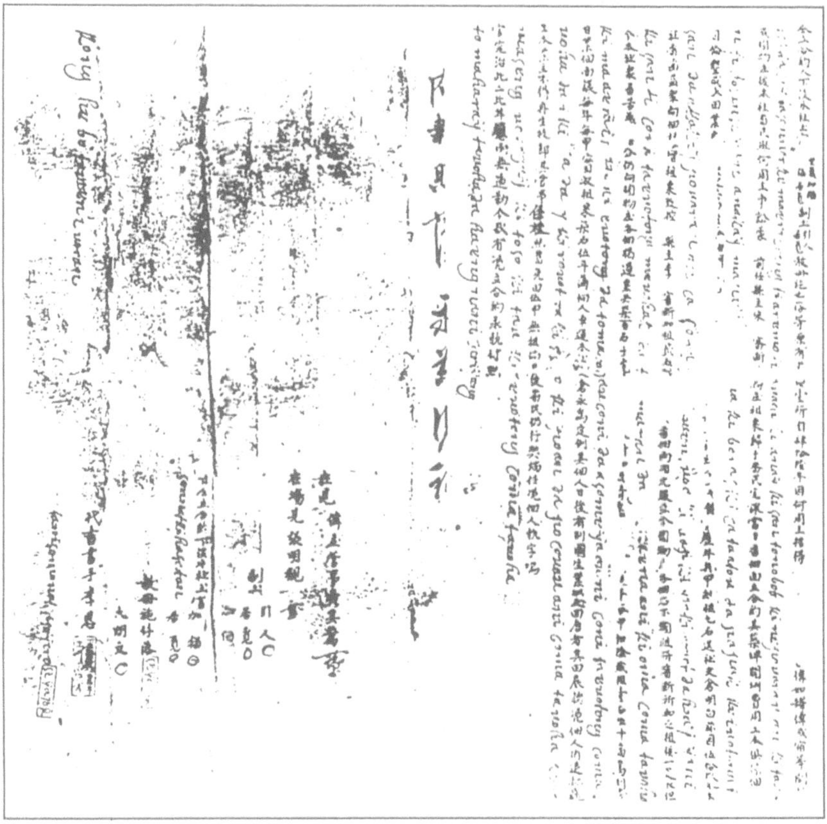

Fig. 9.1 The bilingual contract of Hsia-tan-shui *she*, 1721 (SOURCE: Murakami 1933: pl. XII).

tract, in 1707 a group of Chinese had reclaimed fields belonging to the Hsia-tan-shui tribe. The tribe then complained to Feng-shan magistrate Sung Yung-ch'ing, who allowed the Han farmers, in recognition of their investment of labor and capital in converting the land to irrigated paddy, to remain on the land. Sung required the settlers, however, to pay a yearly rent of 7 *shih* of grain per *chia* to the tribe, which in turn was to cover the payment of any taxes (*k'o*). In 1720 the tribe, arguing that its increasing population required a larger income, sought to increase the rent. It took its case to the magistrate, now Li P'i-yu,[52] who awarded them an increase of 2 *shih* per *chia*. In 1721 the tribe borrowed 700 *shih* from its tenants in return for a permanent rent reduction of 1.5 *shih*, making their yearly rent 7.5 *shih* per *chia* in perpetuity, and it is this arrangement the contract is confirming in writing. The contract also confirmed that the tribe recognized the right of the farmers to a permanent tenancy and the right to sell their interest in the land should they decide to return to the mainland. The tribe also agreed never to seek rental increases again.

This contract creates a set of tribal rights in land similar to those a Han developer would retain when subletting to reclaiming tenants, according to the customary large-rent/split-ownership model familiar to the Han immigrants (Chapter 8). The major difference is that the tribe's rights had to be established after the fact in court, on the basis of a tribal land claim. Another difference is the tribe's success in 1720 in getting a rent increase on the basis of need only, without even the pretext of having to pay a tax increase. This reflects the magistrate's Mencian/paternalistic concern for the preservation of aborigine livelihoods. But the awarding of a permanent rental right to the tenants follows the usual large-rent precedent. The settlement imposed by Magistrate Sung in 1707 is the one eventually followed in private agreements between tribes and settlers all over Taiwan. That this model appeared so early in Feng-shan may be related to the different nature of the aborigine tax assessed the eight south-route tribes (see Chapter 5). A settlement in terms of grain assessed by the *chia* rather than in terms of the aborigine tax quota makes sense for the south-route plains aborigines, since they, like the Han, paid taxes in grain (although as a head tax and not according to cultivated area), unlike the Chu-lo tribes who paid taxes in deerskins commuted to cash.

The 1721 contract gives no evidence of the care we saw in the 1709 Tan-shui patent over respect for boundaries. In part, this may be due to the special circumstances involved (the reclamation having already taken place), but the earlier agreements (including a county-approved patent?) mentioned in the contract but which are no longer extant may have dealt with boundary questions. Interestingly, both documents mentioned decisions made by Magistrate Sung, who granted the 1709 Tan-shui patent. On that basis, we would expect similar care to conform to official regulations.

One important difference with the 1709 Tan-shui patent does stand out: both documents mention that taxes are to be paid on the land involved, but the Hsia-tan-shui contract, in a difficult-to-interpret passage, holds the tribe responsible for land taxes, whereas the Tan-shui patent holds the Han reclaimers responsible. The Hsia-tan-shui contract thereby follows the usual reclamation agreement, in which the large-rent holder remained responsible for payment of land taxes. By arrangement, however, that responsibility could be assigned the reclaiming tenant. An example can be found in the reclamation agreement (*p'u te*) (also bilingual) entered into in 1727 by the Chia-t'eng tribe, also one of the Feng-shan eight. This agreement guaranteed the tribe a rent of 7 *shih* of grain per *chia* of paddy and granted the Han tenants permanent tenancy rights but imposed on them the duty to pay the land taxes.[53]

Reclamation agreements by which *Han* patent holders let land in perpetuity to reclaiming settlers in return for the yearly payment of 8 *shih* per *chia* of paddy (the usual customary figure, less for dry land) were common in the Yung-cheng era in Chu-lo county.[54] Setting a permanent, fixed rent according to the area actually reclaimed guaranteed these Han patent holders the largest income they could expect from their grants of unopened land (without funding the reclamation themselves).

By contrast, in agreements calling for payments under the label "aborigine head tax," the aborigine tribes in Chu-lo were letting to Han developers large, often unmeasured, parcels for fixed amounts that were not adjusted according to the area actually reclaimed. That the aborigines were forgoing potential future income (often unwittingly) is shown by the fact that Han who acquired such tribal patents could themselves profitably divide and sublet such land to Han farmers for reclamation. The Han developers could collect the customary 8 *shih* per *chia* rate from their tenants, pay the tribal rents out of that income, and still have large profits left over.[55] Such arrangements created three tiers of owners: tribe, Han developer, and reclaiming tenant. In the case of the Lan-Chang-hsing lands acquired from the Mao-wu-su *she* for 240 taels per year, 491 *chia* were reclaimed. This works out to less than 1.4 *shih* per *chia* for the tribe (converting at the rate of 0.36 taels per *shih* of grain). Lan T'ing-chen, the patent holder, collected rents from the Han tenants of 6 *shih* per *chia*, for a total income greater than 1,000 taels, more than four times the amount paid in tribal rent.[56] Because they lacked official connections and influence, the plains tribes were not yet able to use the standard large-rent reclamation agreement when opening their land to Han farmers. They thus were failing to capture a large portion of the income generated by their lands, especially in the early years of the eighteenth century.

The earliest example in the contract collections of a north Taiwan aborigine tribe's letting land at a fixed rate per area reclaimed (also at the 8 *shih* per *chia* customary rate) is dated 1737. After this date examples of aborigine villages granting standard reclamation agreements become increasingly common and supersede the old formula of letting land in exchange for Han payment of the aborigine tax.[57] Important differences in the allocation of the land tax–paying responsibility (usually to the Han tenant, and later exempting tribal land entirely) distinguish aborigine from Han large-rent arrangements.

A number of factors contributed to the shift to a standard reclamation agreement calling for tribal large-rents of 8 *shih* per *chia*. In part the shift reflects increasing aborigine sophistication in dealing with the legalities of land patents and the economics of ground rents. The increasing numbers of Han reclaimers and tenants competing for a declining supply of open land made it easier for the tribes to obtain the full large-rent amount. Important legal changes also facilitated the shift to the aborigine large-rent model. The 1724 decree (discussed below) that permitted Han rental of tribal lands removed legal impediments to the use of a standard reclamation formula; in earlier years legal restrictions on Han reclamation dictated the use of the *tai fan shu hsiang* formula that justified renting aborigine land by promising the payment of aborigine taxes. The elimination of heavy tribal tax quotas in favor of much smaller head taxes in 1737 also reduced the need to let land under the rubric of "assuming the aborigine head tax." Continued ability to use the aborigine large-rent formula depended on continued recognition of tribal land claims and decisions about the allocation of land-tax obligations, the subjects of the policy debates discussed in the next section.

Tribal Land Claims in the Yung-cheng Era

The increased scrutiny of Taiwan in the wake of the Chu I-kuei rebellion brought debates among high-ranking officials and literati on tribal land policy. These officials acknowledged the accelerating migration of settlers to Taiwan and the expanding reclamation of tribal lands. The conservative policies seeking to quarantine the mountain foothills adopted by Governor-general Man-pao in 1722 especially provoked Lan Ting-yüan. Lan denounced the new boundary policy, arguing that removing settlers behind the boundary would further disrupt an already unsettled society, that an artificial boundary could not prevent trouble from arising in the quarantined areas, and that instead unreclaimed land should be opened and tax revenue thereby increased. Lan had similar procolonization views on tribal land rights. In 1724 he argued:

> In northern Taiwan's Chang-hua county the land is plentiful and empty. The government should let settlers open it up, rather than leave it as waste. Previously all this land was aborigine land, which settlers were prohibited from encroaching on to cultivate, but now a county government has been established and there is no reason to leave it abandoned. If we talk of aborigine land, then all Taiwan is aborigine land; the aborigines may want it restored, but it is beyond restoring. The government should decree that each aborigine can himself open land; all that thereby becomes paddy and garden within the year should be considered theirs; what is left unreclaimed, [Han] settlers should be allowed to open. And according to the regulations, the reclaimers should become the owners. Or let settlers pay the aborigine head tax on the tribes' behalf in return for land to open; in this way both sides can benefit.[58]

Lan's proposal to give the aborigines a year to reclaim land, after which they would lose all rights to land left unopened, was made in the knowledge, as Lan states elsewhere, that the aborigines were not good farmers. This proposal can be interpreted as evidence either of Lan's complete lack of sympathy for the plains aborigines or of his rhetorical skills. Allowing settlers to assume the aborigine head tax in return for land, although clearly a second preference for Lan, was still preferable to prohibiting reclamation altogether.

In 1724 the Yung-cheng emperor, some say in response to Lan's advocacy,[59] had the following regulation entered into the Ch'ing Institutes (*hui tien*): "Order the local officials to investigate all aborigine deer fields left as waste that are reclaimable. Each tribe may rent [*tsu*] these fields to settlers for cultivation. Enter them on the tax registers."[60] The 1724 decree both acknowledges tribal title in unopened deer fields and permits the tribes to rent these fields to settlers. It thus falls far short of Lan Ting-yüan's extreme proposal to abrogate aborigine land rights. This new regulation gives official approval to private rental agreements between tribes and settlers, thereby reducing the need to use the rubric of "assuming the aborigine head tax" to justify these arrangements and opening the way for greater use of the aborigine large-rent model. That the 1724 proclamation was necessary to authorize leases is further evidence that policy in the late K'ang-hsi years, as the number of immigrants increased uncontrollably, had tightened up against Han rental and reclamation of aborigine land. The new regulation is also significant for its vagueness: it offers no guidelines for determining tribal land claims. The 1724 decree approves rental agreements only; sales are not given official sanction.

The Veritable Records for 1725 repeat nearly verbatim the above regulation and comment: "With time the land will be reported for taxation [*sheng k'o*]; thus, aborigines and settlers will enjoy profit and mutual trust, and the land taxes will be paid and not deficient."[61] The government's intention to tax the tribal lands whose lease to settlers it was now approving is clear. By taxing these lands, the government could raise the revenues to pay for its expanded administration (Chang-hua county and Tan-shui subprefecture were created in 1723) and fulfill the military grain export quotas set the same year.

In sum, the thrust of the 1724 decree was to give Han settlers access to tribal land on the condition that they pay rents to aborigine tribes and land taxes to the state.[62] My investigation of the extant patents and contracts between tribes and settlers from the K'ang-hsi and Yung-cheng eras (noted above) reveals no immediate change in the form or substance of these agreements. Aborigine tax quotas remained high until reduced in 1737, and some post-1724 contracts still use the *tai fan shu hsiang* formula. The shift to the aborigine large-rent model occurred gradually as the tribes became more sophisticated and land became more valuable. The most immediate change was the ability to get reclamation agreements between Han and tribes formally approved by county magistrates.

Continued use of the aborigine large-rent model in frontier reclamation depended, however, on continued recognition of tribal land claims.

Pro-colonization advocates in the Yung-cheng era proposed important limits on tribal claims. In 1727 the Tan-shui subprefect, Wang P'ing, proposed to restrict aborigine land rights to small but permanent tribal reserves, and the censor So-lin included his proposal in a memorial to the emperor.[63] Wang was the first Tan-shui subprefect and had therefore to deal constantly with problems arising from frontier reclamation and aborigine affairs. In 1724 he had led a force of civilized aborigines and Han militia as part of a campaign to pacify the Shui-sha-lien tribe of the present-day Sun Moon Lake area.[64] Wang thus had direct personal experience of revolt by aborigines that had submitted and of applying the policy of using aborigines to control aborigines.

Subprefect Wang's 1727 land proposals had two parts: restricting the scale of Han reclamation and delimiting tribal territories. Wang advocated limiting Han reclamation to 5-*chia* parcels available only to reclaiming farmers. Wang thus opposed allowing influential land developers to gain control of larger areas (see Chapter 8). He also called for organizing the farmers into *pao chia* groups to guarantee local security.

The second part of Wang's proposal addresses the issue of aborigine lands. Wang reports that in the past, villains and bullies had contracted to reclaim civilized aborigine fields by assuming the aborigine head tax (*jen hsiang pao k'en*). "Land given out is never returned. If this gradual encroachment is allowed to continue, the aborigine masses will soon have no property or livelihood to rely on. This will certainly result in their retreating to the mountains and becoming raw aborigines." To prevent this, Wang advocated that tracts of paddy and dry fields (500 *chia* for large tribes, 400 *chia* for medium-sized tribes, and 300 *chia* for small tribes), referred to as tribal farmlands (*she t'ien*), be reserved for aborigine farming and hunting. Boundary markers would be set up, and the area and four boundaries would be recorded in the land registers to forestall land-grabbing reclaimers. The remaining grasslands would be opened to Han reclamation, subject to a three-year limit to report the land for taxation. Wang's proposal appears to take protection of aborigine livelihoods seriously, but its central thrust is to limit tribal claims and facilitate Han reclamation and settlement.

At this point in the memorial, So-lin adds that detailed investigations had been made and that Wang's recommendations ought to be carried out. "Farmers should be called in to reclaim land according to the methods stated in memorials previously submitted and the settlers should be ordered to live in villages and form *chia* [decimal] units; it is essential that bandits and villains have no toehold and that the lairs of robbers be cleared out." This is a standard pro-colonization argument. The Yung-cheng emperor found that although the matter was in its initial stages, Wang's proposals were worth further investigation. There is no further record of debate, but other sources tell us that Wang's proposals were not adopted.[65]

The proposals of Wang and So-lin reflect the pro-colonization views of Lan Ting-yüan. They advocate expanded reclamation, and So-lin suggests that further settlement will eliminate places of refuge for bandits. But Wang sees the importance of protecting at least some of the tribal lands if only to prevent civilized aborigines from going wild. He recognizes that the advancing Han agricultural frontier has disrupted their livelihood and that they are at the mercy of encroaching settlers. Yet the amount of land he reserves to the aborigines is pitifully small for a livelihood based on herding and hunting as well as farming. Curiously, Wang makes no mention of the tribes' right to rent out unreclaimed land to settlers, recognized in the emperor's 1724 decree. His hostility to large land grants (and the large-rent model) in favor of owner-cultivators suggests Wang would deny aborigine claims to a rental income from the grasslands (outside the tribal allotments) he wants to open to Han reclamation and government taxation. We may also infer from Wang's background in the Shui-sha-lien campaign that he saw the protection of some civilized aborigine land rights as facilitating yet another goal: making a civilized aborigine military force available for government purposes. Certainly this consideration was to become more salient in later years, as we will see below. Wang, interestingly, makes no mention of the aborigine boundary line in his proposals. Apparently the civilized aborigine lands he discusses were all within the area under effective government jurisdiction and open to Han settlement.

In a 1729 essay, Shen Ch'i-yüan, the acting Taiwan prefect, took a position on aborigine land rights similar to Wang's. Shen's proposals take a pro-colonization stance, advocating open immigration (while emphasizing the need to exclude criminal elements from Taiwan) and reclamation, both of which will in his view relieve the poverty of the populace of southern Fukien and increase state revenue.[66] Shen also advocated redeploying government troops to the frontier (a reversal of the preoccupation with maritime security that led to their overconcentration near the prefectural capital) to prevent trouble caused by raw aborigines and bandits in the vast mountain expanses. Out of sympathy for the aborigines, Shen notes, the government had so limited reclaimable areas that [nearly] all the land was considered aborigine land (*fan ti*). Yet, since the aborigines were few in number and unable to farm such a large area, much land was left waste, and Han had been able to purchase large acreages for little. "Now that the plains aborigines have learned to farm, they have no land left to farm. If the government does not take care, the aborigines will be reduced to poverty, and a calamity will result." Shen argues that in administering the reclamation of wasteland, areas must be reserved for the aborigines, either for farming or collecting rents: "Those that can farm can be allocated land and taught to farm; those that cannot farm can be paid rations [*hsiang*] according to the area cultivated."[67] Shen thus recognizes the importance to frontier security of preserving an aborigine income from land, while advocating that reclamation be allowed to proceed.

The Taiwan intendant, Liu Fan-chang, submitted a memorial in 1730 discussing the disposition of aborigine land rights from a tax viewpoint.[68] Liu begins by asserting that the Chengs had imposed a tax (*she hsiang*, the aborigine head tax) on aborigine hunters assessed according to the size of tribal territories (Liu is mistaken here; the aborigine tax was in theory a head tax). Since then, many Han had rented aborigine land by paying the aborigine tax on behalf of the tribes, but they had not registered the land for taxation. As a result of the edict of 1727 (see Chapter 8) providing that those who enrolled land and began paying taxes would not be punished for previous tax avoidance, 17,170 *chia* of land had been entered on Taiwan's tax registers. The portion of this newly registered land rented from aborigines was thereby being doubly taxed, for both settlers and aborigines were separately paying taxes on the same land. Liu suggests that Han discontinue paying the aborigine rentals on land they have registered for taxation and that the tribes be forgiven the aborigine taxes he (wrongly) assumes were levied on tribal land. The aborigines need only pay the tax (proportionately reduced) on their remaining unreclaimed land. Moreover, as the aborigines learn to farm, land they reclaim should also be reported for taxation in the same manner as Han, and the separate aborigine head tax can be eliminated. "In this way there will be no uncultivated land and no untaxed land." The emperor's rescript calls for further deliberation and implementation by the governor-general and governor; the available evidence indicates this proposal was never implemented.

Ch'en Pin and others had drawn an analogy between the aborigine tax and the land tax to establish aborigine rights to unreclaimed land and to defend those lands against Han encroachment. Liu drew the same analogy but reached the opposite conclusion. He used the analogy to advocate eliminating the special tax status of aborigine land as it was reclaimed; apparently Liu would also eliminate the aborigine right to a rental from land on which Han pay land taxes. In Liu's hands the analogy works to the benefit of taxpaying Han farmers and appeals to a state hungry for land-tax revenues. Liu is unconcerned with the problems of aborigine livelihood as the aborigines adjust to the loss of their hunting economy and adopt farming; he assumes they can reclaim land and pay taxes the same as Han.

The proposals of Lan, Wang, Shen, and Liu and the 1724 decree aim at allocations of rights and duties with respect to land that balance the government's goals of regulating Han competition for land, preserving aborigine livelihoods, increasing revenues from land taxes, and maintaining peace on the frontier. The 1724 decree gave Han settlers access to tribal land on condition that they pay rents to the aborigines and taxes to the government. The other proposals were much more strongly pro-colonization and generally favored eliminating aborigine claims over large amounts of land, reclaimed or not, and leaving only small tribal reserves.

Boundary Policy and Practice in the Yung-cheng Era

The Yung-cheng government adopted pro-colonization policies across a broad range of policy spheres: in 1723 it began to expand the civil administration, in 1724 it sanctioned the renting and reclaiming of tribal land, in 1731 it lowered land-tax rates, in 1732 it legalized family migration, and in 1733 it increased its military presence. These were years of accelerating Han immigration and settlement. The pro-colonization and pro-reclamation policies had their costs in increasing conflict between settlers and aborigines and repeated violation of the raw aborigine frontier. Aborigine land disputes and enforcement of the boundary policy demanded the constant attention of officials.

Despite the pro-reclamation policies of the Yung-cheng era (and the hostile rhetoric of Lan Ting-yüan), the 1722 boundary policy prohibiting Han entry into the mountains was never abandoned, nor could it be, given the hostile reception raw aborigines gave intruding settlers. The proscription of Han settlement in the mountain foothills (see Chapter 7) added another factor to be considered in categorizing land as legally reclaimable or not. Settlers were ordered to withdraw from areas beyond the boundary.

The land-tax section of the prefectural gazetteer records that in 1722 only 21 *chia* of land were removed from the tax registers because they were in a prohibited raw aborigine area.[69] One explanation for the removal of such a small area from the registers is that the boundary policy was not seriously enforced. But only land already registered for taxation could be removed from the tax rolls. Thus, greater amounts of unregistered land may have been affected by the prohibition; this appears to have been the case in Lang-ch'iao at Taiwan's southern tip, which was ordered evacuated.[70] Also, in 1722 Han settlement had yet to fill the plains, and few settlers had reclaimed land in the foothills marked off by the boundary.

The 1722 boundary was intended, according to Huang Shu-ching, to protect Han settlers from raw aborigine attack. The boundary was therefore drawn to defend lowland settlements against attacks from the mountains. The boundary thus did not mark off territories claimed by the civilized aborigine tribes; rather, it cut through those territories that bordered the mountains. This created two sub-categories of plains aborigine land—tribal land within the raw aborigine boundary and tribal land outside the boundary—that will complicate the interpretation of subsequent land regulations.

A particularly important theme arising for the first time in reports from the Yung-cheng era is that civilized aborigines, dissatisfied with their lot under the Ch'ing, especially as settlers pressed into their territories, might "go wild." In 1727 Governor-general Kao Ch'i-cho reported several reasons why aborigines (both raw and civilized) burn and kill: "(1) Because settlers, in reclaiming land, encroach beyond the boundary, cut rattan and hunt deer, aborigines kill them. (2) Because interpreters exploit the tribes, the aborigines become enraged and kill recklessly, even to the point of attacking neighboring settlers. (3) Because, once aborigines have killed a few Han, their audacity grows and they do it repeatedly; when they kill a man, they take his head, show it off, and claim to be heroes."[71] Kao recommended that the boundary be clarified and marked by stone stelae in order to prevent contact and segregate Han from aborigine. "Should an instance of burning and killing occur, then the officials should go forth to investigate. If Han have crossed the boundary to farm, cut rattan, or hunt deer and are killed, then punish the landowner and the village heads whose negligence let the Han enter the area. If Han have not crossed the boundary and still the aborigines have killed settlers, then the aborigines must be severely punished." Kao ordered officials in Taiwan to survey the location of the line and to set up inscribed stone markers along it. At this point in the memorial the Yung-cheng emperor noted that Kao's report was vague because he had failed to distinguish the civilized aborigines and the raw aborigines; he warned that their respective affairs and properties should not be confused. Kao's memorial continues: "Once the line is set, moving across it by only an inch will not be allowed. Once the boundary is clear, then if there is trouble, whether it is due to aborigines or to settlers, there will be grounds for an investigation and appropriate punishments can be administered."

In addition to tightening the boundary, Kao ordered all local officials to investigate the tribal interpreters and prohibit bribery and the holding of that office by men who lacked wives, property, or administrative competence. Each county was ordered to prohibit yamen runners' extorting bribes from interpreters and interpreters' exploiting aborigines. Kao reported that he was also investigating which tribes no longer needed interpreters so that those that were dispensable could be removed.[72] Interpreters were a chronic source of trouble in plains aborigine affairs during the K'ang-hsi and Yung-cheng eras (see Chapter 5). In that period, aborigine revolts, such as those of 1699, were usually attributed to the cruelty and tyranny of the interpreters. Kao's analysis and proposals for reform of the institution are much the same as those that preceded his.

What is new in Kao's memorial of 1727 is his identification of encroaching Han agricultural settlement, in addition to exploitative interpreters, as provoking aborigine revolts. In 1721 Huang Shu-ching had also blamed trespassing for much of the strife between Han and aborigines.[73] Kao, although a leading advocate of expanding reclamation and freer immigration, was also determined to maintain control over the frontier by enforcing the boundary restrictions (although he was willing to bend them where settlers were already established as at Lan-Chang-hsing) and eliminating troublemakers from tribes. Lan Ting-yüan, by contrast, advocated abolishing the boundary restrictions, as well as lifting restrictions on immigration and reclamation.

Like the emperor, we can fault Kao for not distinguishing the effect of Han settlement on civilized and on raw aborigines. Reclamation most affected the civilized aborigines in the more easily reclaimed plains, and Han penetration of the mountains in search of mountain products most affected the raw aborigines. But this is overly simplistic, because streams and springs in the foothills provided irrigation water, which made the foothills very attractive to Han settlers. Moreover, mountain products were important to the civilized aborigines as well, and civilized tribes' territorial claims went beyond the government-established boundaries along the foothills. The three-way competition of raw aborigines from the mountains, plains aborigines, and Han settlers for access to foothill resources made the government's enforcement of its boundary policy particularly difficult.

Various forms of aborigine resistance to Han encroachment continued to trouble the government as Han settlement spread throughout the Yung-cheng and Ch'ien-lung eras (indeed, resistance continued into the twentieth century). The possibility that civilized aborigines might go wild as a result of this encroachment was particularly worrisome to the government. In a review of Taiwan's military defenses in 1728, Governor Ch'ang Lai noted: "The civilized aborigine character is weak, and they are easily cheated by the settlers; when this becomes excessive, they unite with the raw aborigines and cause trouble."[74] Formulation and reformulation of regulations governing tribal property rights was an important part of the government's response to this potential threat from civilized aborigines.

The case of Lan-Chang-hsing village reveals much about actual practice in the administration of border policy and aborigine land rights (see also Chapter 8). The case came to official attention because of a murderous raw aborigine attack on a Han village in the tribal territory of the Mao-wu-su civilized aborigines.[75] Investigation revealed that the area was being reclaimed under the auspices of the naval commander Lan

T'ing-chen. He had acquired rights to the land by pledge or redeemable sale (*tien*) from the military officer Chang Kuo, who had himself acquired them by assuming the aborigine tax burden of the Mao-wu-su tribe. Moreover, Lan claimed that the county had issued a patent confirming his rights. In these respects, this case complies with all the regulations observed in the 1709 Taipei basin patent issued to the Ch'en, Lai, and Chang partnership.

What complicated the case of Lan-Chang-hsing was that it lay beyond the 1722 boundary. Indeed, Huang Shu-ching, writing in 1722, lists Mao-wu-su as one point on that line.[76] Accordingly, some local officials saw reclamation of this land as a provocation and sought to remove the settlers. Governor-general Kao Ch'i-cho, perhaps recalling Lan Ting-yüan's warning against such removals, proposed to allow the over 2,000 settlers to remain, to give them title to the land, and hold them responsible for the land taxes. In doing so, Kao would have eliminated the claims of the owners cum tax middlemen, Chang and Lan, and the rights of the Mao-wu-su tribe.[77] The emperor rejected Kao's proposed reforms in favor of the status quo. This guaranteed compensation to the tribe, as had the decree on rental of tribal lands in 1724. However, in 1727 Lan donated this land to the state, and there is no evidence that aborigine claims were honored after that.[78]

For both Kao and the Yung-cheng emperor, when it came to a choice between enforcing the raw aborigine boundary and removing encroaching settlers, it was the boundary that had to be compromised. This was to be a common pattern in the years to come. Another significant point in this case is that a civilized tribe continued to exercise rights over land after it had been classified as "beyond the boundary." Mao-wu-su's territorial claim preceded the 1722 demarcation (Chang Kuo, the original patentee, served in Taiwan in 1705–9). The local officials who sought removal of the settlers were attempting to follow the regulations. It took the governor-general and the emperor to permit the settlers to stay. Hence, one portion at least of civilized aborigine territorial claims was left ambiguous: the government recognized tribal claims to lands beyond the boundary while forbidding (in theory at least) Han from crossing the line to farm such land. Han reclamation on such land was seen as a provocation to raw aborigine attack, even though civilized aborigines claimed ownership of the land. Its proximity to the mountains and undoubtedly the dubious status, in raw aborigine eyes at least, of such territorial claims made its reclamation dangerous and a potential source of trouble.[79]

Once presented with a situation where reclamation was under way, the government was not anxious, in this case at least, to enforce the boundary. But to pre-empt further violations, Governor Mao in 1725[80] and Kao himself in 1727 sought to clarify the boundary and tighten the regulations against trespass. Fluctuating enforcement of the boundary policy in response to encroaching Han reclamation and raw aborigine counterattack characterizes at least the next 60 years of Han-aborigine relations.

In the next few years, other steps were taken to tighten enforcement of the boundary policy. In early 1729 Commander Wang Chün reported that raw aborigines had killed a group of twelve settlers from Feng-shan who had crossed the boundary to construct an irrigation canal in the foothills. Wang called for stricter enforcement of the boundary.[81] Probably in response to Wang's report, a statute was promulgated in 1729 providing that in the area beyond the boundary raw aborigines should be left unmolested and allowed to hunt deer; if settlers crossed the boundary to open land, build huts, cut rattan, hunt deer, or smuggle goods, then for his carelessness the responsible official was to be reduced one degree (within a rank) and transferred, and his superior was to be docked one year's salary. If bribery was involved, the official was to be removed and punished. If for three years the settlers and the aborigines were peaceful and there was no trouble, it was to be noted on the official's record and the governor was to reward the tribal braves and settlers' headmen.[82] In practice, it can be argued, this decree allowed, by default, Han settlement beyond the boundary as long as no trouble arose because of it.[83] But the next year, 1730, the government decreed that those who occupied land in raw aborigine territory were to be punished and sent back to the mainland.[84] Once again the government was ordering the boundary enforced, especially if a threat to order grew out of its transgression.

In the late Yung-cheng years, policy decisions in other spheres undermined enforcement of the boundary policy. The drastic lowering of the land-tax rate in 1731 and the legalization of family immigration to Taiwan from 1732 to 1740 increased the flow of settlers and consequently pressure on the boundary line. Cycles of lenience toward settlers, aborigine resistance, and then a retightening of policies on the boundary and tribal land rights emerged as a pattern in the Yung-cheng era and continued in the Ch'ien-lung reign. The relentless advance of Han encroachment, which underlay these policy fluctuations, was only marginally affected by government attempts to slow its pace or regulate its direction.

The bulk of reclamation of tribal land during the Yung-cheng years occurred in areas outside the raw aborigine boundary. Evidence for both aborigine large-rents and the sale of aborigine land in these years comes from a proclamation issued by the Chang-hua county magistrate in 1730.[85] The Tung-lo *she* had called in tenants to reclaim 99.5 *chia* of land, on which the tribe collected rents and paid taxes at the lowest rate for dry fields, 2.4 *shih* of grain per *chia*. In 1730 the tribe sold its rights to this land to a Han *chü jen* for 110 taels. The magistrate countenanced the sale and, at the request of the Han purchaser, issued a proclamation notifying the tenants of the change of ownership, warning them to pay their rents, and authorizing the new owner to file complaints against defaulters. Another sale of aborigine land, by Chu-ch'ien *she* in Hsin-chu, is recorded in a contract of 1733.[86] Thus, sales of aborigine land (we cannot be certain these were *absolute* sales, but the contracts give no hint of rental arrangements), though given no explicit statutory approval, were taking place with the cooperation of local officials.

Perhaps the most striking development in these years, and one not related to boundary policy, is the survival of tribal claims to land rights following the large-scale Ta-chia-hsi aborigine revolt of 1731–32 (see Chapter 5). After pacification of the revolt, the government took the lead in pressing for the opening of land to reclamation. Large tracts of unreclaimed deer-hunting grounds, on which the plains tribes of Ta-chia-hsi, Niu-ma and Sha-lu were described as paying a "deer revenue tax" (i.e., the aborigine head tax), were ordered opened to reclamation (this land appears not to have been restricted land beyond the raw aborigine boundary). Governor-general Hao Yü-lin advocated this measure to ensure the rice supply not only for Taiwan's growing population but also for the rice-deficient Fukien coast;[87] it is likely that Hao believed that Han settlement in these areas would facilitate government control over the aborigines. Hao did not propose dispossessing the aborigines of their land, however, even though confiscation of rebel estates was standard practice. Rather, aborigine rights to a rental income from reclaimed land were preserved. In the case of Niu-ma *she* (renamed Kan-en), the reclamation began in 1733 under contractual terms that gave the aborigines a large rent at the standard amount of 8 *shih* per *chia*.[88] In 1734 the A-shu *she*, who had joined the second stage of the 1731–32 rebellion, entered into a variant of the large-rent model. Suffering from food shortages following the rebellion, A-shu "sold" a parcel of unreclaimed land (of unknown area) for 100 taels and a fixed annual rent of 40 taels to a Mr. Ch'en; the contract also conferred on Ch'en, should he later build an irrigation canal, a right-of-way over aborigine lands.[89]

In 1732 and 1733 the An-li tribes entered into an interesting variation on the usual reclamation agreement. When the An-li tribes submitted in 1715, the government recognized their ownership of a large territory.[90] Beginning in 1732, the tribe, led by its entrepreneurial interpreter, Chang Ta-ching, let parcels to Han land-development partnerships, including one organized by Chang himself.[91] Besides fixed sums of rental grain to be paid yearly to the tribe, the Han investors, who were building irrigation canals, were required to guarantee the supply of water to tracts of land reserved for aborigine farming (two of fourteen shares in one case and two of ten shares in the other). The contracts refer to these arrangements as "exchanges of land for water."[92] These arrangements reflect a growing aborigine understanding of the economic value of land in the rapidly changing economy of the frontier.

Restricting Reclamation of Aborigine Land, 1737–1746

Continued Han-aborigine friction in the early years of the Ch'ien-lung reign brought revisions and ultimately reversals of many pro-colonization policies. A late 1736 revolt among the civilized aborigines of the Chia-chih-ko tribe (see Chapter 5) disturbed the Taiwan censors, Pai-ch'i-t'u and Yen Jui-lung, who were charged with investigating the outbreak, and they made numerous proposals for reforming the administration of the plains tribes. In 1737, "to prevent agitation and deception," Pai proposed a set of punishments aimed at stopping government soldiers from entering aborigine settlements, extorting goods, and causing trouble and a prohibition on Han taking aborigine wives.[93] Yen recommended that the aborigine head tax (*fan hsiang*) be replaced with much smaller head-tax quotas (*ting yin*) set at the newly reduced Han rate.[94]

In 1737 the government (perhaps also at the instigation of Pai and Yen) adopted a number of statutes aimed at tightening control over settlers on the frontier. Punishments were prescribed not only for frontiersmen who violated the raw aborigine boundary but also for lax officials who failed to stop such crossings, and rewards were established for officials according to the number of trespassers they apprehended.[95] The manufacture of fowling pieces in Taiwan was also prohibited.[96] The 1737 measures exhibit a stern attitude toward unruly settlers and a more protective stance toward the aborigines.

Most important for our discussion of rights over tribal lands is Pai's contribution to what must have been an ongoing policy debate (of which we have only partial documentation) on the return to aborigines of aborigine land illegally reclaimed by Han. Pai's 1737 memorial marks the beginning of a dramatic reversal of the Yung-cheng pro-reclamation policies in favor of limiting the reclamation of tribal lands. Pai argued that

> in carrying out the policy of returning aborigine lands [*fan ti*] to aborigines, care must be taken to keep the [Han] peoples' livelihood settled. Order the local officials to prevent Han illicitly acquiring [*ssu mai*; the implication is that such purchases would be unlicensed and without government sanction] aborigine land and clearly draw the boundary along aborigine lands to prevent trouble. All aborigine land illicitly occupied [*ssu chan*, i.e., by squatters] is ordered returned to the aborigines. Land acquired by contract [*ch'i mai*] and already reclaimed and paying taxes should have its four boundaries clarified and be registered.[97]

The prefectural gazetteer of 1746 reprints an order from Governor-general Hao Yü-lin dated 1738, which must have been the final formulation of Pai-ch'i-t'u's proposal:

> Clarify the boundary between civilized aborigines and the areas cultivated by Han; for those who have the proof of contracts and have already long been paying land taxes, draw the line according to the contractually specified boundaries. Where Han have not yet reclaimed the land within areas already leased [*p'u*], let them reclaim such land and report it for taxation. Have them present their lease-purchase [*p'u mai*] contracts for official sealing. Each county should set up land registers to record ownership changes, boundaries, and taxes. . . .
>
> Once there are land registers to refer to, there will be no squatting [*ch'in chan*] on aborigine property [*fan yeh*]. If beyond the contractually specified boundaries [*ch'i wai*], there is any encroaching reclamation [*yüeh k'en*] or forcible occupation [*ch'iang chan*] by local bullies, the local officials are ordered to investigate and return all such areas to the aborigines. In the future, Han are forbidden, in perpetuity, to encroach beyond tribal boundaries [*ch'in ju fan chieh*] to lease-purchase aborigine property. Local officials, in cooperation with tribal officers, are to set up boundary markers and compile a register of locales on the boundary.[98]

Both Pai's and Hao's versions of the decree create three categories of tribal land. Squatter land is ordered returned to the aborigines (presumably the Han squatters are to be evicted).[99] However, settlers' rights in land already the subject of lease contracts (the only contracts ever officially sanctioned) between tribes and settlers are not to be disturbed. Such land is to be registered with the government, and taxes are to be paid on it.[100] The decrees create a third category of land, aborigine land that Han are forbidden in the future to acquire, even by lease. Tribal territories are to be demarcated and registered to prevent further Han encroachment.[101]

These decrees mark a sharp reversal of the Yung-cheng pro-reclamation policies. Only where settlers had already concluded contracts with the tribes were they allowed to remain within tribal territories. (Hao is more lenient than Pai in allowing settlers to retain rights to land already contracted for but not yet reclaimed.) This is the limit of the government's willingness to accommodate the settlers. Squatters are ordered to return the land to the tribes, although the government could have adopted the less onerous alternative of ordering the squatters to legitimize their land claims by concluding contracts with the tribes (as reported in the 1721 Hsia-tan-shui contract; see above). Most significantly, the decree reimposes a quarantine on frontier settlement by calling a halt to *future* Han acquisitions of tribal lands. All future lease-purchases (*p'u mai*) of tribal land are forbidden. This is tantamount to revoking, without explicitly acknowledging it, the 1724 decree sanctioning Han rental (*tsu*) of unreclaimed aborigine land.[102]

These 1737–38 decrees mark a return to the position of Ch'en Pin, who opposed reclamation within tribal territories in the K'ang-hsi era. In the Yung-cheng years the government encouraged reclamation (in part at least to increase land-tax revenues) and focused on the problems that arose from settlers' crossing the raw aborigine boundary. These early Ch'ien-lung decrees reveal a shift in concern to the consequences of the expansion of settlement for the civilized tribes living on the plains. This reflects concern over the problems expanding reclamation was posing for the plains aborigines, as their deer-hunting economies collapsed and they struggled to adopt intensive agriculture, as well as the problems of disorder and ethnic conflict.

To ensure that the prohibitions on the reclamation of aborigine land would be enforceable, the decrees called for clarifying the boundaries of aborigine land and registering them with the government. This created another set of boundaries, distinct from the raw aborigine boundary paralleling the mountains, which for the first time demarcated tribal territories on the plains.

A contract dated 1738 that may represent an early and unintended consequence of the 1737–38 decrees—the sale of aborigine lands—illustrates how the changing legal and tax status of aborigine land affected accommodations between settlers and tribes. Aborigines of the Ta-wu-chün tribe (located in present day She-t'ou *chen*, Chang-hua county) had "ancestral lands" in Nan-kang-hsi village. Their chief "sold" (*mai*) (the original agreement of 1725 is not extant) a part of these lands to a Mr. Ting, who built irrigation works and called in tenants to reclaim the land. The terms of the "sale" contract provided for annual payment of 110 *shih* of grain to help the tribe meet its yearly aborigine tax.[103] In 1727 Mr. Ting sold his rights in the lands to Messrs. Wu and Lin, and the chief affixed his seal and signature to the contract. Wu and Lin were then ordered to report the land for taxation according to official regulations (Ting had avoided such taxes). They began to make excuses and not pay the grain rent to the tribe. The tribe asked a Mr. Cheng to mediate. In 1738 Wu and Lin agreed to pay the tribe 40 taels to cancel the 1725 contract's provision calling for payment of grain to the aborigines.

> When this sum is paid, the previous contract with Mr. Ting will be annulled, and the land will forever be free of such payments, and the tribe will not dare in the future to say otherwise. . . . So now this area has no relation to aborigine land, nor does it transgress aborigine property boundaries. There is no unpaid price or revenue that is owed that involves others. This tribe is not in the future to propose redeeming its ownership or collecting rents. If certain aborigines seek to instigate a dispute and regretting (the sale) cause

trouble, the tribal chief and others who sign this contract will make efforts to ward them off and will not interfere in Wu and Lin's affairs.[104]

The land covered by the new 1738 contract thus went through several phases of obligation to the tribe within whose ancestral territory the land lay. The 1727 contract between Ting and Wu and Lin, which is also extant, confirms the history. When the land was first let, the tribe retained the right to a yearly rent, paid under the rubric of the aborigine head tax. The original 1725 contract between Ting and the tribe (which is not extant) was not an absolute sale, for rentals were due.[105] The 1727 contract shows that Wu and Lin did indeed agree to continue to pay the aborigine tax amount and the tribal chief did cosign the sale.[106] Yet after Wu and Lin were ordered to pay taxes, they sought to avoid any rental obligation to the tribe.

Then in 1738 (perhaps with reference to the decrees of 1737 and 1738, which gave official approval to previous acquisitions of tribal land but not to any future ones and required that such land be registered for taxation), an agreement was worked out by which the tribe, in return for a lump-sum compensation, gave up all further claims to an income from the land. This was tantamount to an absolute sale of tribal land, a kind of transaction that had never been officially sanctioned. Technically, the tribe had long ago bargained away its right to farm the land, and in 1738 it was selling not the land but its right to a rental income from it. By renegotiating the original reclamation agreement into an absolute sale, Wu and Lin seem to have succeeded in exploiting the ambiguity of the 1737–38 decrees' confirmation of previous acquisitions of aborigine land to win a secure and absolute title.

Hao Yü-lin's 1738 decree dramatically shifted government policy away from the pro-colonization trend of the Yung-cheng years by attempting to halt further reclamation. Hao followed up this decree the next year when he successfully petitioned for an end to the legal migration of families (see Chapter 6). Taken together, these two early Ch'ien-lung decrees mark a reversal of expansionist policies and a return to the quarantine strategy of control. But on a frontier that had been transformed by the rapid influx of immigrants and fast pace of settlement in the Yung-cheng years, the old quarantine policies could not be readopted. They had to be adapted to deal with a much greater Chinese presence (one that continued to grow despite government attempts to stop immigration).

This early Ch'ien-lung policy reversal came at a time when many of the goals of pro-colonization advocates had in fact been reached. Both the military and civil administrations had greatly expanded on the frontier, and reclamation had proceeded far enough to provide a sufficient tax base to help pay for the governmental presence, even at the newly reduced land-tax rates. Rice exports from Taiwan were relieving shortages on the southeast coast, and many settlers had already been joined by their families.

The costs of controlling the larger and still volatile Han population and the dangers of tension with civilized and raw aborigines now loomed large in policymakers' thinking. In the many decrees and regulations dealing with aborigine land rights issued over the next years, the status-quo-oriented quarantine policies had to be adapted and compromised to deal with the steady (and uncontrollable) advance of Chinese settlement. This adaptation brought attempts to return Han-reclaimed land to aborigine control, to guarantee aborigines a rental income from their lands, to prevent illegal and fraudulent sales and usurious lending, to regulate rents, to adjust taxes and to exempt land from taxes, and to assign aborigines border guard functions. All these policies were tested in the following years as the government sought to implement conservative policies designed to preserve order on the frontier and to protect, neutralize, and even utilize the civilized aborigines.

In 1744 an edict was promulgated forbidding the acquisition of property, especially aborigine property, by military officials stationed in Taiwan.[107] These practices violated regulations that forbade officials from acquiring land in areas under their jurisdiction because it encouraged abuse of their positions for private gain.[108] This decree called for land reclaimed by officers but encroaching on the aborigine boundary to be returned to aborigines. It thus affirmed the government's commitment to continue to honor tribal boundaries as they were frozen by the order of 1738.

Later in 1744 the Taiwan censor Hsiung Hsüeh-p'eng proposed that "Taiwan's wastelands [*huang ti*] be opened to reclamation by poor commoners seeking a livelihood." Governor-general Na-su-t'u rejected the proposal on the grounds that "the source of trouble in Taiwan is neither the raw nor the cooked aborigines but the immigrants who are tramps and vagrants. The rebels Chu I-kuei and Wu Fu-sheng are clear examples. Although there is much open land that could be cultivated, it has been restricted for a long time and would be very difficult to reclaim. Even if reliable people were allowed to reclaim it, I [Na] fear many troublemakers would secretly cross over and the benefit would be small and the harm great."[109] This brief debate demonstrates that pro-reclamation policies continued to find advocates among certain officials. The government's doubts about its ability to maintain order among the immigrants, let alone among aborigines, led it to reject such proposals. The emphasis on the long-term preservation of order meant continued restrictions on Chinese settlement in Taiwan. Guided by its paradigm of control and quarantine, the government saw the source of frontier disorder not in unpopulated wasteland, as Lan Ting-yüan would have argued, but in the presence of vagrant immigrants.

The continued expansion of Han settlement, unimpeded by ineffective attempts to stem migration, meant increased pressure not just on plains aborigine lands but also on the raw aborigine boundary. In 1745 concern over raw aborigine attacks brought forth an unusual proposal from Kao Shan, then serving as Fukien provincial treasurer. He proposed creating a *t'u ssu* jurisdiction, following Szechwan and Hukuang precedents regarding the Miao, by selecting a plains aborigine native chieftain who would be given authority over all civilized and raw aborigines. This proposal was quickly rejected when the inappropriateness of the Miao analogy was pointed out: the great differences in Taiwan between civilized and raw aborigines could not be bridged by such an office, and there were no pre-existing, large-scale hereditary native chieftains who could be co-opted for such an enterprise. Defense against raw aborigine attack could not be left solely to civilized aborigines.[110] The discussion concluded that the only way to handle the raw aborigines was to keep settlers and (civilized) aborigines from trespassing across the raw aborigine boundary and causing trouble. The memorial called for establishing blockades at strategic points to prevent raids by raw aborigines.[111]

This memorial is clearer than most in putting civilized aborigines along with Han on one side of the boundary and raw aborigines on the other, and it clearly refers to the boundary itself as the "raw aborigine boundary." Yet the next month a memorial reported an incident of civilized aborigines, disguised as raw aborigines, burning and looting.[112] Tighter enforcement of the raw aborigine boundary could not solve the problem of civilized aborigines "going wild" as a result of Han encroachment on their land. However, restrictions on Han reclamation, such as those in the 1737–38 decrees, could ease this potential sore point.

In 1746 the court promulgated another decree to protect tribal land rights, primarily by setting punishments that would put "teeth" in the enforcement of the 1737–38 decrees (which must have been lax until then, for the contract collections preserve numerous examples of early Ch'ien-lung leases of aborigine land).[113] The memorial, submitted by Governor-general Ma-erh-t'ai, began by noting:

> Han are reclaiming aborigine land [*fan ti*] even though it has long been prohibited; because punishments have not been set, commoners do not fear the law. Henceforth let all aborigines cultivate their own aborigine land. If villains again lease [*p'u*] it, return the land to the aborigines; punish people who illicitly lease land [*ssu p'u*] according to the statutes against the illegal cultivating [*tao keng*] of another's land and according to the area of said land; the punishment should be reduced one grade if it is wasteland and increased one grade if the land was taken by force. If villains have crossed the raw aborigine boundary to open land illicitly, punish them according to laws governing the trespassing of strategic borders.[114]

To aid in the enforcement of the restrictions on reclamation, Ma-erh-t'ai ordered a land survey.

> Formerly, local officials restricted access to tribal territories [*fan she ti chieh*], but bandits recklessly killed and coveted to encroach. Petty officials were not enough to suppress them. The local officials should be ordered to make surveys in person in the agricultural slack season and inform the chiefs, interpreters, local headmen, and proprietors to set up boundaries and within one year to complete registration of the land.[115]

This decree instituted punishments for the protection of aborigine lands and established procedures for clarifying and registering the boundaries of tribal territories where aborigines were, apparently, to be left to cultivate the land themselves. The language of the order specifically provides punishment for "illicit" and "unlicensed" leasing of land (*ssu p'u*) (the Chinese does not imply by default, as does the English translation, that licensed leasing might be approved) and refers to an unqualified prohibition on the opening of aborigine land like that in Hao Yü-lin's 1738 decree. Opening land beyond the raw aborigine boundary is also clearly distinguished from opening tribal land within that boundary by the different punishments for the two infractions.

This 1746 decree reaffirms the Ch'ien-lung court's determination to enforce the policy it first adopted in 1737–38 by prescribing punishments for its violation. A quarantine of the frontier is to be effected by prohibiting further reclamation of aborigine lands, although there is still no explicit revocation of the 1724 decree allowing Han to rent tribal lands. The government's forbidding of tribal leases implies that the aborigines themselves were willing to conclude leases that brought them income. The government, out of paternalistic or security motivations, sought to prevent the practice.

In the 1746 decree Ma-erh-t'ai also proposed solutions to the continuing *raw* aborigine threat.

> In the 2,000 *li* of Taiwan along the mountains, raw aborigines are everywhere; there are not enough soldiers to post along [the foothills], and there is danger of trouble. Order each locale's military personnel and [tribal] chiefs and interpreters to be more careful in their patrols. To defend against raw aborigines who penetrate the forests and cross the boundary to make attacks, order scattered settlements of Han in the area near the aborigines to move out in the fall and winter seasons to larger villages nearby. However, because it is feared that the settlers will find this burdensome, local officials should be ordered to persuade them; it is not necessary to establish regulations. In places where defenses are established, lookout towers should be built near raw aborigine villages and guard posts established. For each tower assign five men to guard through the night. For those near [civilized] aborigine tribes, assign *aborigines*; for those near villages, assign Han. Rotate these men every ten days, and in this way provide for self-defense. If a

> neighboring village is threatened, there should be mutual aid; those who sit by and only watch and do not come to their aid should be investigated and punished.[116] (my italics)

This decree provides for self-defense measures along a troubled boundary that the military's limited resources could not adequately defend. One of its more interesting aspects is that it calls for the participation of civilized aborigines as well as Han in these efforts. We have seen several earlier instances of the government's using civilized aborigines in military campaigns, especially against other rebellious aborigines. This decree is evidence that the government continued to value the military potential of the civilized tribes. We will see below how the government in 1760 and 1790 sought to expand the military role of the plains aborigines.

Policy and Practice on the Frontier, 1747–1756

Despite official restrictions on family migration, Taiwan's Han population grew rapidly in the mid-eighteenth century, as reflected in the rapid increase in the number of villages and markets and in the acreage registered for taxation. Of the 76 plains aborigine villages in northern Taiwan, 30 by 1740 and 45 by 1768 were also the site of a Han village (see Chapter 6). The year 1747 brought more reports of increased immigration, reclamation, and rice production.[117] Other reports tell of the effects on the plains aborigine villages:

> Han settlers, clever and perverse, are forcibly seizing aborigine interests; aborigine livelihoods are becoming more difficult by the day, and Han cheat them endlessly. Soldiers and runners use them arbitrarily and treat them cruelly. And local officials, for their own convenience, let matters drift and do not correct the situation. They look on their offices as transitory posts . . . and wait for promotion and transfer. Not a few seek private profit in the name of the public good.[118]

This memorial advocated the appointment of capable men to the posts of Taiwan intendant and prefect to correct this situation and guarantee the livelihood of both Han and aborigines.[119]

This report and one later that year also refer, for the first time, to the civilized tribes as impoverished aborigines (*ch'iung fan*). These developments give reason to doubt the effectiveness of the punishments instituted in 1746 to prevent Han encroachment or to protect aborigine livelihoods. Lax enforcement meant that the new decrees were no obstacle to spreading Han settlement. In some instances impeding Han leasing of aborigine land simply reduced the tribes' rental income rather than preserving their livelihood. The reports also suggest that the civilized aborigines were having trouble becoming farmers. In 1747 a drought is reported endangering the livelihood of aborigines (but not Han) throughout Taiwan. The plains aborigines apparently had fewer irrigated fields and smaller grain reserves than the Han. In response, the government specifically ordered that relief grain be distributed to the plains aborigines. The government planned to create a revolving loan fund modeled on the granaries established earlier among the eight tribes of the south route.[120]

In the wake of the drought, new proposals to stimulate construction of irrigation works were put forth in 1748. However, the building of embankments and canals required entering mountain watersheds, which were generally beyond the forbidden raw aborigine boundary. Previously, the government had sought to enforce the boundary despite the irrigation needs of farmers,[121] but this quarantine of difficult-to-control territory created problems for farmers seeking to irrigate land, a task that required cutting across the raw aborigine boundary to gain access to the foothill watersheds.

A memorial of 1748 listed several proposed canals that could be built with landlord capital, tenant labor, and official management. The construction, it was recognized, required drawing water from raw aborigine territory, but it was not to be allowed to obstruct aborigine lands. The decree required the settlers to follow the precedent of tenants in southern Feng-shan who purchased water from aborigines. "Order the chiefs and interpreters to notify the local aborigine tribes and ensure that every year the landlords and tenants benefiting from the irrigation give salt, cloth, tobacco, and sugar to the aborigines so that strife can be avoided."[122] Thus, the drought led to relaxation of the aborigine boundary policy to construct badly needed irrigation works. Given the state's willingness to loosen enforcement of the raw aborigine boundary, where the presence of hostile tribes was a direct threat to the security interests of the state, we may wonder if there was not an even greater willingness to allow Han encroachment into civilized tribal territories, where the state's security interest was less immediate.[123]

In 1750 the court ordered clarification of both the raw and the civilized aborigine boundaries. The relevant memorial reported that most of the old markers along the raw aborigine boundary could be left in place but called for the placement of additional boundary stones at a variety of locales, some natural features such as rivers or the feet of mountains, some the artificial "earth-oxen" trenches. In some instances the boundary lines were pulled back from the foothills. Local officials were ordered to investigate unlicensed reclamation by Han that violated the boundary restrictions. The decree repeats the order of 1746 to persuade scattered settlers to move into large villages in the fall and winter and to establish lookout towers and guard posts to aid in defense against raw aborigines. Soldiers and clerks whose extortions or laxness led to raw aborigine attacks were to be severely punished.

Most important for plains aborigine rights in land is a clause in the 1750 decree that states "where Han settlers and civilized aborigines have contested lands, sanction is to be given to court judgments already handed down, but after this let the civilized aborigines cultivate the remaining aborigine land and do not allow Han to interfere. Violators should be punished."[124] The 1750 decree reasserts both the raw aborigine boundary defense policy and the policy to protect civilized aborigine land from Han encroachment, first decreed in 1738. The 1750 decree thus illustrates the government's conservative strategy of control: eliminate ethnic friction on the frontier by freezing the advance of Han settlement, whether into civilized or raw aborigine domains, for Han encroachment is the force most disruptive of the established order.

A number of stone markers erected following the 1750 decree (and still standing at the beginning of this century) give solid evidence that the government enforced the ban on Han reclamation of civilized aborigine land. One stela set up in 1752 at Ch'i-li-an (present-day Pei-t'ou in the Taipei basin) clearly stated that it marked the boundary of land "returned to aborigine ownership."[125] A bilingual stela (in Chinese and romanized Sirayan) erected in 1752 at Fan-tzu-t'ien (in Lung-t'ien *ts'un*, Kuan-t'ien *hsiang*, T'ai-nan county) forbade Han encroachment on aborigine lands.[126] A stone boundary marker erected in 1755 at Liu-chang-li in Fan-shu-liao in the Ta-chieh-tien tribal territory (present-day Ch'i-shan *chen*, Kao-hsiung county)[127] is specifically mentioned in the 1750 decree. The inscription carefully listed sites beyond the raw aborigine boundary where unlicensed reclamation by either Han or civilized aborigines was prohibited; within that boundary, however, the remaining land was open to civilized aborigine reclamation but not to Han seeking to lease land illicitly (*ssu p'u*). This accords fully with the policy of protecting plains aborigine land from further Han reclamation reasserted in the 1750 decree.[128]

An incident in late 1751 shows the limits of the trust aborigines could place in court enforcement of their land rights.[129] In 1729 the Chinese Chien Ching had contracted to open land of the Pei-t'ou tribe at Nei-yao village (present-day Ts'ao-t'un *chen*, Nan-t'ou county) in exchange for a rent of 500 *shih* and payment of the tribe's aborigine tax of 207.5 taels. After the 1737 reduction of aborigine taxes, large amounts that reclaimers of tribal lands formerly paid to the government were now theoretically available to be paid directly to the tribes. In 1735 Chien Ching had also forcibly occupied an additional parcel for which he agreed to pay another 90 *shih* in rent. By 1747 Chien had fallen more than 6,000 *shih* behind in rents and owed the tribe over a thousand taels in unpaid tax moneys.[130]

San-chia, the son of a Chinese man and probably an aborigine woman and the interpreter of the Nan-t'ou and Pei-t'ou tribes, sued Chien Ching to recover the arrears.[131] In 1749 the prefect ordered Chien to return 40 *chia* of paddy to tribal management and to pay 2,000 *shih* in back rents; however, he forgave Chien the unpaid aborigine taxes. Chien Ching was willing to pay only 1,000 *shih* in back rents, and he turned the land over to his tenants instead of to the tribe. Dissatisfied with Chien's partial compliance, San-chia complained to the brother of Chien's aborigine wife, a fellow member of the Pei-t'ou *she*. This had no effect on Chien, and San-chia gave up hope of further recourse to the courts or to family pressure. He thereupon decided to induce raw aborigines to kill Chien Ching.

Through a local raw aborigine intermediary, San-chia contacted four inner-mountain tribes: Miao-mei, Mei-chia-la, To-ko-kuo, and Fu-ku. In 1722 Huang Shu-ching listed these four as part of the "extremely intransigent" Pei-kang river group. However, sometime after 1737 they became part of the Shui-sha-lien tribal taxpaying unit and thus were considered at least partly civilized.[132] On the appointed day, San-chia and a few co-conspirators met with the raw aborigine braves in the mountains and pointed out Chien's house. The attacking band of 70 tribesmen then went down the mountain to assassinate Chien Ching. They were unable to penetrate to the center of Nei-yao village where Chien lived, however, and instead killed 22 members of the Lai and Pai families who lived at the village entrance. San-chia, fearing that the link between the attack and his feud with Chien might be discovered, then ordered the raiders to attack the military post at Liu-shu-nan.[133] In this way he hoped the attacks would confuse witnesses and appear to be genuine pillaging by raw aborigines. Three days later the raiders took the heads of seven soldiers and burned the village.

On the same day as the attack on Liu-shu-nan, the Chang-hua magistrate was at Nei-yao investigating the first murders. The villagers claimed to recognize two of the magistrate's sedan chair carriers (who were members of the Pei-t'ou *she*) as perpetrators of the attack, and a crowd attacked and killed them.[134] The magistrate concealed this, however, and reported that raw aborigines had perpetrated the Nei-yao attack. The north-route captain investigating the events at Liu-shu-nan then submitted a false report saying that the soldiers had been killed while on patrol. The Chang-hua magistrate ordered the interpreters Chang (of An-li *she*) and Lin (of Ta-chia *she*) and Yeh Fu (San-chia's half-brother and, unknown to the magistrate, his co-conspirator) to organize a party of civilized aborigines to go into the mountains to recover the lost heads.

By the second and third months of 1752, separate investigations had turned up information linking the attacks to the dispute over Chien Ching's land and revealing the murder of the sedan chair bearers. This led some officials to suspect that the civilized aborigines were trying to place the blame on raw aborigines. By the end of the year, the officials who filed false reports had been impeached, and the case had been solved.[135] However, provincial legal review of the case and the determination of punishments dragged on until 1754.[136]

San-chia and his co-conspirators were sentenced to be executed. The raw aborigine participants in the attack and the Han murderers of the sedan chair carriers were to be apprehended. Chien Ching was to pay both the grain rent and the aborigine taxes he owed the Pei-t'ou tribe (thereby modifying the earlier judgment), and the 40 *chia* of land Chien had refused to return to the tribe and the parcel he had forcibly occupied were to be returned to tribal control.[137] Chien Ching himself, "whose forcible occupance of aborigine land, and failure to pay aborigine rents and aborigine taxes made him the source of all the trouble," was ordered punished according to the statute forbidding "taking of possession by force of public or private mountain fields."[138] The punishment stipulated was 100 lashes and permanent exile at a distance of 3,000 *li*.

These disputes and the resulting legal cases illustrate the complex interplay of interests on the frontier and the difficulty the Ch'ing court had in using its officials to contain conflict. Many disparate groups—settlers, interpreters, civilized aborigines, and raw aborigines on the one hand, and civil and military authorities on the other—were jockeying for advantage and trying to shift blame or responsibility onto another party. The Nei-yao incident points up the dangers inherent in land agreements contracted between aborigines and Han. When settlers scornfully disregarded their contractual obligations to the tribes and legal means were ineffective, the aborigines readily turned to violent solutions. The nature of the case—a dispute with Han over land in which civilized aborigines induced a raw aborigine attack to get revenge—is also significant for what it reveals of the brutal and turbulent nature of frontier society. Both settlers and the government feared revolts by civilized aborigines, who lived among the Han and were often in government service. Perhaps even more frightening was the ability of civilized aborigines living along the raw aborigine boundary to turn their knowledge (often used by the government in pacification campaigns) of raw aborigine tribes into a threat to government control. And Chien Ching's disregard of the court's decision suggests that many Han settlers were unimpressed by the government's power to enforce its will and restrict reclamation of aborigine land.

Reports of a number of other incidents in these years reveal both the volatility of frontier society and the degree of the government's resolve to enforce its strict policies against Han reclamation of aborigine lands. Interpreters, by abusing their advantageous positions, often caused trouble.[139] The office of tribal interpreter was well worth holding in this era of rapid reclamation, for the interpreter was in a position to take advantage of the tribes' privilege of approving land grants and collecting rents. This remained true despite the restrictions on Han reclamation imposed after 1737. The post of interpreter had been sufficiently desirable to induce rivalry among competing claimants in the deer-hunting era of the plains aborigine economies. The government's decrees protecting aborigine land rights ensured that the post of interpreter remained lucrative in the period of agricultural colonization.[140]

The continued pressure of expanding Han settlement in these years also tested the government's resolve to enforce the raw aborigine boundary. In 1751 investigations of a land dispute among Han revealed that 24 villages and 1,571 *chia* of land had been opened in the Shui-sha-lien area in modern Nan-t'ou county,[141] apparently beyond the raw aborigine boundary. This reveals that the redrawing of the raw aborigine boundary the preceding year had been done without thorough field investigation. Significantly, in this case the government, rather than enforce the boundary restrictions, chose to avoid risking the trouble that eviction might cause. The land in question was confiscated, the tenants were left in place and ordered to pay rents to the government, and the raw aborigine line was redrawn.[142]

In 1755 an order forbidding Han settlement in Ch'üan-t'ou-mu-shan (in the Taipei basin) and an additional Shui-sha-lien area was countermanded because these areas were found to be "30 *li* distant from the nearest raw aborigines." Instead, the court ordered the land to be registered for taxation and self-defense guards (*ai*) established.[143] Several years earlier, in 1749, bandits had been reported operating in Ch'üan-t'ou-mu-shan. Apparently the area was also made a government estate at that time.[144] This 1755 order indicates increased government confidence in its ability to handle raw aborigine and settler conflicts and a preference for maintaining the status quo even if based on previous violations of the boundary.[145] In compromising the boundary restrictions, policymakers seem to be heeding Lan Ting-yüan's warnings against disturbing settlers already in place.

The Shift to Accommodation, 1757–1761

Beginning in 1759, a series of decrees reformed government policies toward aborigines and their lands. Policy shifted to an approach that attempted to accommodate the interests of both Han settlers and plains aborigines. Intendant Yang Ching-su (in office 1758–61), a proponent of boundary clarification, reform of government treatment of civilized aborigines, and their sinification, played an important role in these reforms.[146] Let us look briefly at the shifts in cultural and administrative policies before turning to the details of the land policies.

In 1758 civilized aborigines were ordered to conform to Han and Manchu customs and to adopt the queue.[147] This was the first overt attempt to dictate plains aborigine behavior in these spheres (up to this time Ch'ing cultural policy had sought merely to lead by example) and marks a significant heightening of official expectations with respect to the cultural conformity of the plains aborigines. I have seen no reports of resistance to these orders; indeed, aborigines (in several places at least, see Chapter 11) had already voluntarily adopted the dress and customs and learned the language of the dominant Han.

An additional reform to aid in protecting clearly demarcated aborigine lands from Han encroachment was also initiated in 1758. The governor-general ordered tribes who had recently learned Chinese to choose their own interpreters so as to eliminate the trouble caused by the "vagrants" who usually filled that post (this continues earlier reform attempts; see Chapter 5). For distant tribes who did not speak Chinese, suitable Han candidates were to be chosen.[148] These new cultural and administrative policies toward plains aborigines were adopted in a period of renewed concern over the fate of aborigine lands.

A campaign in 1757 to register land for taxation in Chang-hua county and Tan-shui subprefecture, whose revenue bases were still inadequate,[149] drew the attention of officials to the situation with regard to the reclamation of aborigine land. Finding that Han farmers often encroached onto civilized aborigine lands (*shu fan ti chieh*), the governor-general in 1758 ordered field investigations.[150] In 1759, apparently in response to this decree, 282 *chia* of land in Tan-shui subprefecture registered for taxation in 1757 were declared "beyond the boundary" and removed from the tax rolls.[151] In 1758 the governor-general also ordered that ditches be dug to mark a clear boundary around aborigine lands. Creating a cordon by digging a trench and piling the earth along one side (earth-oxen) had been ordered before in 1722 and 1750, sometimes to demarcate tribal from Han property, sometimes to mark the line of defense against raw aborigine attack.[152] As we will see below, the attempt to draw a permanent boundary between Han and aborigine lands was renewed in 1760.

A 1759 decree modified the thrust of the 1758 boundary clarification and sought to protect aborigine rights to an *income* from tribal land (rather than to the land itself). This decree, most likely a response to the 1758 effort at boundary clarification and the resulting discovery that much aborigine land had already been leased to Han, stated that all holders of "land lease-purchased [*p'u mai*] by Han settlers for reclamation and registered for taxation, regardless of whether the land was acquired before or after the promulgation of this decree, must pay a rent to the aborigines [*t'ieh na fan tsu*]."[153] The thrust of this decree was to enforce the rent-paying obligation of Han settlers on aborigine land, rather than to remove them from aborigine lands. The decree thus seeks to accommodate aborigine interests in an income from the land and settler interests in the land they have reclaimed, in accord with the large-rent model. The 1759 decree also preserves government revenues by requiring that the land be registered for taxation.

Much tribal land had been leased to Han before the 1737–38 restrictions on reclamation, and, as we have seen, these restrictions were not always strictly enforced. It is interesting that this 1759 decree makes no allusion to leases made in violation of the 1737–38 and 1746 decrees (which should be designated *ssu p'u* or *ssu mai*), to the punishment prescribed in 1746 for Han concluding such leases, or to the remedy, also prescribed in 1746, that such land be returned to aborigine ownership. In its reference to land acquired "after the promulgation of this decree," the 1759 decree seems to assume continuing Han reclamation. The decree also assumes settlers had no problems registering land for taxation despite the local government's duty under the 1738 and 1746 decrees to maintain records of aborigine territorial boundaries. In its accommodative approach to the expansion of Han settlement, the 1759 decree diverges from attempts to freeze the boundaries of aborigine land and bar further Han reclamation; it thus represents an acceptance by the government, or one group of officials at least, of its inability to limit Han settlement and to enforce a quarantine of aborigine land. With the 1759 decree the government shifted its attempts to preserve frontier peace to ensuring that Han settlers lived up to the terms of the agreements, legal or not, by which they obtained access to tribal land for farming.

A contract of 1759 illustrates how the tribes adapted to these decrees in practice. In 1759 the Lei-lang *she* (an amalgam of Lei-li *she* and Hsiu-lang *she* in the Taipei basin) let a plot of aborigine land that had been encroached on by one Liu Yu-jen and returned to aborigine control by official order. The tribe rented the 2.2 *chia* to another Han tenant for the customary large-rent of 8 *shih* per *chia* of paddy; the rental grain was to be distributed as aborigine rations. This land may well have been returned to the tribe in accord with the 1758 boundary clarification and then rented out again under the 1759 decree.[154]

In 1760 aborigine land policy was significantly modified, and the policy of accommodating plains aborigines and settlers continued. Governor-general Yang T'ing-chang called for a clarification of the raw aborigine boundary and the regulations governing it in Chang-hua county and Tan-shui subprefecture, "because the encroaching reclamation of settlers grows nearer the inner mountains and raw aborigines come out and attack."[155] This clarification continued that begun in 1758, although as we shall see the ultimate disposition of the land marked off would be different. Yang ordered that obstacles such as streambeds, canals, and the bases of mountain ranges be used to define the boundary. If none existed, a trench was to be dug and an earth-oxen mound paralleling it was to be built to define the boundary. In Tan-shui several places had been designated as boundary sites, but stone markers had been set up only in strategic passes likely to be used by raw aborigines; many places had still not been demarcated.

> So we must weigh the strategic importance of different areas and use mountains and streams for boundaries. Where there are no mountains and streams, dig a trench and build mounds to draw the line. In Chang-hua in each of the twenty places where encroaching reclamation [*yüeh k'en*] has taken place between the new and the old boundaries, Han-aborigine relations are peaceful. This is so whether it is [civilized] aborigine tribes who themselves have reclaimed the land or whether they have leased it out [*p'u kei*] to Han to reclaim in return for a rent. If we establish official estates [in these locales], then all the land will belong to the government, and both the aborigines and settlers will lose their property.[156] We ought rather to follow the 1746 precedent and return the land to aborigine management. Make the interpreters and chiefs of each tribe managers, and make the reclaimers into tenants who should pay rent. Order each interpreter and chief to keep accounts, open to public investigation, of the amounts of yearly rental grain received and of taxes paid out [*wan na k'o yin*].
>
> Beyond the *newly* drawn boundaries in Tan-shui and Chang-hua, all the paddy, gardens, and fields must be abandoned and returned to aborigine management. Han are not allowed to conclude leases for reclamation [*p'u k'en*] there. As for places such as Ch'üan-t'ou-mu-shan in Tan-shui, which are located near raw aborigines who sometimes come out and cause trouble, and where tenants have fled and left land uncultivated, take such circumstances into account when the tax grain is being collected. As for unreclaimed fields, inform landlords and tenants that there is a three-year limit on the time to reclaim before registering for taxation.
>
> Send aborigine braves to guard strategic places along the border. After resetting the boundary in Chang-hua, guardhouses should be set up in ten places in the new border area, and 217 civilized aborigines should be posted to them. In Tan-shui, set up eighteen guardhouses and depute 720 civilized aborigines to increase defenses. In Chang-hua aborigine braves rations [*fan ting k'ou liang*] should be disbursed out of the tribes' rental grain income. In Tan-shui there is still no rental grain. Investigations reveal that each tribe still has vast fields that are not yet reclaimed; each tribe ought to survey and petition for reclamation to provide the braves [*ai ting*] rations. Continue to order subdistrict magistrates and those in the nearby military posts to patrol the boundary areas.[157]

This significant decree (apparently unknown to the compilers of the Taiwan private law studies) called for redrawing the raw aborigine boundary, which in some cases was moved closer to the mountains, reflecting the encroachment of Han reclamation beyond the old boundary. This adjustment of the boundary created a new category of land between the new and the old boundaries. The decree considered the land beyond the old boundary to be the property of the civilized aborigine tribes, which the tribes were themselves already either cultivating or letting out to Han. This is shown by its rejection of government confiscation of such land and its explicit appeal to the precedent of 1746 returning land to aborigine control. This decree recognized tribal land claims beyond the newly redrawn boundary as well, even as it prohibited Han reclamation there. The 1760 decree thus specifically recognized plains aborigine land claims on both sides of the raw aborigine boundaries.[158]

The 1760 decree continued the policy of accommodation first manifested in the decree of 1759 that required Han to pay tribal rents on all lands acquired from civilized aborigines. Rather than driving off the Han squatters and illicit lessees and returning the land to the tribes as called for by the 1737–38 and 1746 decrees, the decree ordered land to be returned only to aborigine "management" and rent collection; it left rent-paying Han tenants in place.

The 1737–38 and 1746 decrees had sought to ensure peace by restricting the advance of Han settlement into tribal territories. But enforcing a policy prohibiting reclamation demanded more in determination and resources than the government could muster. Removing settlers might provoke Han revolts (as Lan Ting-yüan had warned), and enforcing the boundary could require removing land from taxation (as we saw in 1722 and 1759), causing a loss of revenue. The 1760 decree provided for taxation of aborigine land rented to Han, as assumed in the 1737–38 and 1759 decrees. But in those decrees the Han farmers were to pay the taxes. The 1760 decree made tribal officers responsible for keeping the accounts, implying that the tribes would pay the land tax (for the significance of this shift, see below). In either case, taxation of Han-reclaimed tribal lands meant that the state, too, would share in the benefits of reclamation.

The 1760 decree took one more significant step in allocating rights and duties along the hostile raw aborigine border where the government had a direct interest in defense. In return for requiring Han settlers to pay rent to the tribes on this border land, the government imposed an obligation: the civilized aborigine tribes were to organize militia to guard against raw aborigine attack.[159] A portion of the rents to be collected were especially designated as "aborigine braves rations" to cement this connection. In Tan-shui subprefecture, where land of this category had not already been opened, the government called for its early reclamation so that the aborigine braves rations could be supplied. San-hsia's lands east of the Tan-shui river were opened under these terms thirteen years later in 1773 (see Chapter 1). This also clearly reveals the government's role as final arbiter of aborigine land claims. Unfortunately, the decree does not enumerate the sites where the boundary adjustments were made.

The linkage of tribal rents to militia service continues the government's policy of using civilized aborigines in its pacification campaigns and anti–raw aborigine defense strategy. Earlier the 1746 decree had also called on civilized tribes to cooperate in guarding against raw aborigine attacks. The proponents of this policy apparently concluded that assigning the aborigines a positive role in the newly Han-dominated frontier society and providing them rental incomes and rations would create a loyal military force out of tribes whose traditional means of livelihood and modes of social relations were crumbling under the impact of encroaching Han settlement. After the Lin Shuang-wen rebellion in the late 1780's, the government set up aborigine military colonies on border lands along much the same lines as laid out in this 1760 decree (see Chapter 10).

Concrete evidence of the enforcement of the 1760 decree comes from the inscription on a stone boundary marker erected in 1761 at P'u-tzu-li, one of the An-li settlements (Shih-kang *hsiang*, T'ai-chung county), giving the dimensions of the earth-oxen line (marking the new raw aborigine line) and "permanently" prohibiting "crossing the line for unlicensed reclamation."[160] A 1762 reclamation contract by the Hou-lung tribe (in Tan-shui subprefecture) is one of the earliest I have seen that refers to aborigine guards rations.[161]

In 1761 Governor-general Yang T'ing-chang halted the immigration of families that had been legalized briefly from 1760 (see Chapter 6). Yang pointed out that the ban on reclaiming lands along the newly redrawn raw aborigine border (ordered again as part of his 1760 decree) meant there was no more room for new settlers. Yang also sought to stop the flow of "secret crossers," all of whom were "villains and bandits." Yang's policy recommendations thus fall within the paradigm of quarantine and freezing the ethnic status quo, even while he advocated accommodation between settlers and aborigines with regard to rights on land already reclaimed.[162]

The Subprefecture for Aborigine Affairs, 1766

In 1766 more frontier trouble drew high-level official attention and led to the creation of the Subprefecture for Aborigine Affairs. A raw aborigine attack took the lives of several Chinese villagers in the eighth month of 1766. The report filed by Governor-general Su Ch'ang states that the area of Tan-shui subprefecture involved (San-hu, in modern Hsi-hu *hsiang*, Miao-li county, near the Hou-lung *she*) had at one time been within the boundary and had been reclaimed and settled. Later, due to aborigine attacks, the raw aborigine line had been redrawn so that the reclaimed land lay beyond the boundary. But the "covetous" settlers were unwilling to give up the land and secretly crossed the boundary to cultivate it. The attack in question was precipitated by settlers searching for an oxen that had wandered across the boundary; raw aborigines chased them back into the village, burned their houses, and killed many of them. The previous winter the villagers had shot some raw aborigines who had crossed the boundary in pursuit of deer. Since then the raw aborigines had "nourished a grievance."

The governor-general ordered the reporting provincial judge, Yü Wen-i (the editor of the Taiwan prefectural gazetteer of 1768), to send neighboring civilized aborigines to investigate and find a way to attack the perpetrators (who were discovered to hail from the aborigine settlement of Yu-wu-nai).[163] An attack force of government soldiers accompanied by plains aborigine guides and interpreters was organized and entered the mountains to punish the culprits. The government contacted other raw aborigine tribes, but attempts to enlist them in the campaign failed. But after seeing government soldiers march through and attack their neighbor at Yu-wu-nai, these raw aborigine tribes agreed to submit and pay a yearly tribute of four deerskins and 4 *shih* of grain.[164]

Although the governor-general's reports cite the Chinese settlers' violation of the government-drawn boundary, local officials chose to blame and make an example of the raw aborigines. The government's use of the civilized aborigines as guides and the attempt to enlist the aid of raw aborigines against the guilty tribe reveal a discerning divide-and-conquer strategy. The incident also shows that the government could muster a technologically, numerically, and organizationally superior military force to harass and even subdue (at least periodically) raw aborigines in their mountain refuges.

In the midst of this campaign, Governor-general Su Ch'ang clarified and reasserted the boundary policy in the Hou-lung area of Tan-shui subprefecture.

> Most of the land declared to be beyond the boundary is land that has been reclaimed and cultivated for a long time. Poor people build scattered huts in these border areas and seek to reclaim land illicitly [*ssu k'en*] and surreptitiously cultivate it [*t'ou chung*]. When they see how sparsely settled the farmers are, the raw aborigines take advantage to attack. Hence all border area settlers are hereby ordered to move to neighboring large villages.[165]

Su also gave orders to establish military posts in two villages[166] near the border and quite far from the nearest military post in Hou-lung. The soldiers to staff them were to be transferred from Hou-lung, which had already become part of the "interior" secure areas and thus could spare them.

> Although guardhouses [*ai*] have been established at strategic passes, the raw aborigines are good at slipping by and can appear anywhere; so the settlers all suffer from their burning and killing. According to the decree of 1745 [apparently a mistake for 1746], lookout towers and patrols were to be set up

for mutual defense. But since the aborigines took advantage to attack, building bamboo lookout towers was difficult. Every village should build a fired-brick lookout tower on its mountain side; order four villagers to rotate on guard in each tower every night. If raw aborigines approach, they should fire shots and beat a gong so the villagers can hear and respond.

In the border areas poor people building huts and reclaiming land without a license cross over the boundary and secretly cultivate aborigine land; when they are surprised by raw aborigines, not a few lose their lives. Henceforth . . . no unlicensed cultivation is allowed beyond the boundary, and [reclaiming] empty fields near the boundary is prohibited. Each subdistrict magistrate and neighboring military post must patrol these restricted areas every month.[167]

Once again boundaries are to be clarified, cultivating beyond the raw aborigine line is again prohibited, and monthly patrols are ordered out to ensure enforcement. Anti–raw aborigine defenses are to be strengthened by consolidating settlers in large villages and by building a system of lookout towers at strategic points. This reasserts the border defense plans of 1746 and 1750. No notice is taken, however, of the role of the civilized tribes in anti–raw aborigine defense, first mentioned in the 1746 decree and institutionalized more recently in 1760, despite the prominent role being played by the civilized tribes in the Yu-wu-nai campaign.

Coupled with this call for vigilant enforcement of the raw aborigine boundary came Su's order to evict settlers from civilized aborigine lands. The heightened concern for security along the border is evident throughout the memorial. Su's instructions mark a return to the strategy of prohibiting Han reclamation and turn away from the willingness of the 1760 decree to accommodate Han settlement by ensuring only rental payments to aborigines:

In 1738 and 1746 Han-aborigine boundaries were clarified and put in order, but there is no one more stupid than the aborigines. Han villains beguile them with money and then, pressing for repayment of debts, demand land leases [*chai p'u*]. In this way the boundaries are eroded, and settlers gradually encroach. Every year civilized aborigine numbers increase, and the problems of their livelihood grow more urgent. If these problems are not solved now, they will seek refuge in the mountains and go "wild."

The precedents must be reviewed. Wherever boundaries were set up previously and there are registers that can be checked, things must be clarified and the boundary re-established. If there has been encroachment, [the settlers] must be chased off and the land returned to the aborigines to cultivate. Henceforth all land acquired through unlicensed leasing [*ssu p'u*] and debt-fleecing [*chai po*] must be returned to the aborigines, and these culprits must be expelled across the water [back to the mainland] to prevent lawsuits.

But the character of the aborigines is inconstant, and I still fear they will again be misled and cheated by the villains and will again make unlicensed

> sales. Thus, we must clarify and make registers of the area and boundaries of the fields of each tribe and all land that was lease-sold [*p'u mai*] and returned; and the registers must be put on file. Local officials who do not expend effort to carry out these orders will be punished. Each tribe should have wooden boards on which are written the sites of all tribal lands. If any land is again illicitly leased or sold [*ssu p'u, ssu mai*], it will be confiscated by the government and punishments determined by the area of the land involved.[168]

Su's 1766 memorial thus calls for clarification of the territorial boundaries of the civilized tribes, as well as raw aborigine domains. The strong measures Su proposes would punish not only Han but also aborigines who engage in such illegal sales and leases by confiscating their land. Su's policies against Han reclamation (reinstating the policy of the 1738 and 1746 decrees) probably were enforced most strictly where the state's security interest was greatest: where reclamation violated the raw aborigine boundary. As for reclamation of civilized tribal lands, Su's policy of prohibition and eviction seems to have been short-lived. Decrees issued in 1767 and 1768 (discussed below) again approved aborigine rentals to Han of land returned to the tribes.

Several sources reveal that in 1767 surveys were carried out and land returned to tribal control in accordance with Su's policies. A 1772 contract of the Lei-lang *she* in the Taipei basin, far from the raw aborigine boundary, reports that 247 *chia* had been "returned to the tribe according to official decree in 1767."[169] A decree of 1772 (discussed below) specifically mentions the role of Tan-shui subprefect Tuan Chieh in the 1767 reforms.[170] In 1767 Tuan had surveyed 191 *chia* of Wu-lao-wan tribal lands but registered them for taxation under a Han name, which led to a dispute (discussed below).[171] A 1767 survey is also mentioned in contracts with the Pei-t'ou *she* in Chang-hua county.[172]

The month after Governor-general Su submitted the memorial discussed above, his proposal to establish a special office to oversee aborigine-Han affairs was approved. Su had memorialized that a subprefect of aborigine affairs (*li fan t'ung chih*) should be appointed to oversee the large civilized aborigine population of Tan-shui subprefecture and Chang-hua and Chu-lo counties and to manage all negotiations between Han and aborigines. Su argued that the new office would require a minimum of new expenditures. Since a garrison was now posted in an area of Ch'üan-chou where large lineages had formerly engaged in constant feuding, it was no longer necessary to station a subprefect there. That office could be abolished and transformed into the Taiwan prefecture's Subprefecture for Aborigine Affairs on the north route. The new subprefect could occupy the abandoned yamen of the Tan-shui subprefect in Chang-hua city. In the south, in Feng-shan and T'ai-wan counties, the tribal populations were smaller, and the subprefect for coastal defense (resident in the south) could serve simultaneously as the subprefect for aborigine affairs of the south route.[173] Obviously, Su was being careful to minimize the financial costs and any unmanageable bureaucratic proliferation that the establishment of this new office might entail.[174]

In the first part of the memorial (as reprinted in the Chang-hua county gazetteer of 1830), Su justifies in detail the establishment of this new office. Echoing the concerns about border security and aborigine land rights expressed in his 1766 memorial, Su argues that a new post for managing aborigine affairs is needed to calm the frontier.

> Taiwan is surrounded by the ocean and is important to the [maritime] defense of seven provinces. It is a place where Han and aborigines live interspersed. Defense must be tight against raw aborigines who hide in the high mountains and at the slightest relaxation of vigilance come out and cause trouble.
>
> The civilized aborigines live in villages interspersed among the Han; several tens of years ago they learned to dread the law and to be obedient. But in these many years abuses have sprung up; Han villains have illegally entered the tribal settlements and have usurped the "fat of the fish" to the point that tribal lands are occupied by Han. The aborigines do not know where to turn; they find it difficult to avoid fleeing to the mountains and becoming raw aborigines. This is Taiwan's latent affliction; we must prepare against such a calamity.
>
> The Yao of Kwangtung are no different from Taiwan's civilized aborigines; the former have a subprefect for Yao affairs to oversee them. Today Taiwan's civilized aborigine population is large, the same as the Yao of eastern Kwangtung. We ought to establish a subprefecture for aboriginal affairs in Tan-shui, Chang-hua, and Chu-lo to manage all negotiations between Han and aborigines. When bullies are overbearing and purchase [*kou tien*, a redeemable purchase] aborigine land, the subprefect can correct the situation and return the land to the aborigines. If there are any who seduce aborigine women and live in the tribal settlements, he should arrest these villains and expel them. He should investigate and punish excessive corvée and the extortion of supplies from aborigines by worthless officials and clerks and punish those who still dare to connive at these things. He should charge officials and clerks with clarification of the aborigine boundary and defense against raw aborigines. This will be of great benefit in our frontier across the sea.[175]

The causal links are quite clear. By encroaching on tribal lands, Han settlers were forcing civilized aborigines to turn to the mountains; a subprefect for aborigine affairs could help prevent this disaster. The memorial is more explicit than any previous one about the mistreatment of the aborigines at the hands of wily Chinese bullies and arrogant officials. The subprefect's duties were to include overseeing all land negotiations between Han and aborigines to protect aborigine claims against Han encroachment. Eventually reform of customs, instruction in farming techniques, appointment of chiefs and interpreters, and aborigine population registration were also to come under the new subprefect's administration. The account books of the tribes, already public as required by the decree of 1760, were to be under the subprefect's scrutiny. However, the collection of land taxes and aborigine head taxes remained within the jurisdiction of the regular county and subprefectural administrations. Administratively, the aborigine affairs subprefecture (*li fan t'ing*) was an independent, functionally specific (rather than territorial) unit (*chih li t'ing*), not subordinate to the Taiwan prefect. The subprefect could hear suits brought by aborigines against Han and between aborigines. Thus, not only Han-aborigine affairs but internal tribal affairs came under the subprefect's jurisdiction.[176]

Although this new office was rarely administered vigorously in later years, it probably had some success in retarding or limiting the effects of Han encroachment. Subprefects for aborigine affairs, for example, were involved in administering the policy changes discussed in the next section. But in 1783, after less than seventeen years as an independent office, the subprefect for aborigine affairs was given additional responsibilities in coastal defense on the north route, and his duties in the area of aborigine affairs were inevitably downgraded. Then, in 1786 the office was ordered moved to the port of Lu-kang (the move did not occur until 1788, after the Lin Shuang-wen rebellion).[177] The new office facilitated routinization of government oversight of aborigine land management. But, as we shall see below, its failures (as in the case of the aborigine migrations of the early nineteenth century) were as striking as its achievements.[178]

Exempting Aborigine Lands from Taxation, 1767–1768 and 1788

An important set of decrees handed down in 1767–68 and in 1788 modified government policy requiring taxation of tribal land let to Han and ultimately exempted such land from taxation. K'ang-hsi-era land policy and the 1724 order allowing the rental of aborigine land to Han settlers exempted aborigine land cultivated by the aborigines themselves from land taxes but not aborigine land cultivated by Han. In most instances, the settlers had to pay both the tax and tribal rent. Early Ch'ien-lung decrees continued this distinction with regard to the taxation of aborigine lands and continued to see aborigine head taxes as analogous to land taxes. In 1738, in response to a series of droughts, the government forgave Han farmers their land taxes (see Chapter 6). In the tenth month of 1738, when the government for the same reason ordered that the current year's aborigine head tax be forgiven, it also ordered that the rents paid by Han in return for tribal land (*p'u fan ti t'ieh hsiang yin*) be reduced by half.[179] The government's assumption of the power to reduce such rents, in theory set by private negotiation, was in accord with a provision, readopted in 1735, that required local officials to urge that 30 percent of any land taxes forgiven a landlord go to a reduction in rent paid by tenants.[180] In the state's eyes, taxpaying bore a direct relation to ownership of rights in land. Because aborigines paid taxes, the state recognized tribal ownership and the right to collect rents from tribal land. When the state reduced landowners' taxes to ease the burden of the drought in 1738, it saw that tenants shared in the relief by ordering rents reduced as well.

In 1747 when land and labor service taxes were combined in Taiwan, aborigine fields were excluded from the process. This was because "land farmed by aborigines does not pay the land tax; instead, aborigines pay a head tax, and the old practice is to be continued."[181] This passage from the Ch'ing Institutes confirms that the land-tax immunity of tribal land cultivated by aborigines, first reported in the Chu-lo gazetteer of 1717, continued in force.[182]

Tribal land reclaimed by Han was expected to be registered for taxation. The 1759 decree that inaugurated a more accommodative approach to reclamation (discussed above) reaffirmed that Han settlers on tribal lands were to pay both taxes and aborigine rents. The 1760 decree redrawing the raw aborigine line also allowed Han to rent tribal lands in the area newly demarcated between the new and old lines. But in a shift of policy, the 1760 decree required the tribes to keep accounts of rents received and land taxes paid, implying that the tribes, rather than the Han settlers, were to pay taxes on such land. This is the first indication of a shift away from the traditional policies in which aborigines paid a head tax and only Han paid land taxes.

A contract dated 1764 reveals how far practice could deviate from the traditional policy and suggests that local governments' revenue needs made them unwilling to let all tribal land escape taxation. This contract between an aborigine landowner (of the Ta-lang-tun tribe of the Taipei basin) and an aborigine tenant makes clear that the landowner had to pay the land tax. Indeed, officials came to survey the land and register it for taxation.[183] This contract resembles in all respects contracts between two Han parties. That it was between aborigines was of no apparent interest to the tax collectors. In this case aborigine land not self-cultivated but rented out, even though to another aborigine, was subject to taxation.

An order dated 1767 modified the rent-paying obligations of Han tenants paying taxes on tribal lands they had reclaimed. The portion of this decree that has survived reads:

> It has been decided that settlers should be allowed to [continue to] cultivate land that aborigines cannot cultivate themselves but are willing to let out.

The settlers should pay according to Taiwanese custom a large-rent of 8 *shih* of grain per *chia* of paddy, and 4 *shih* per *chia* of dry field. Moreover, the precedent has been set that henceforth land found already reclaimed and registered to pay taxes, but which is not yet paying [aborigine rent] ought, according to its area in *chia* and according to Taiwan precedent, pay such rent, but reduced 60 percent so that each *chia* of paddy pays aborigine rents of 3.2 *shih* and each *chia* of dry field pays 1.6 *shih*, to assist the aborigines and supply them with rations.[184]

This regulation sets aborigine rents on returned aborigine land let to Han at the customary large-rent rate. But the second section (overruled the next year) provides for reducing these rents in cases where the land is already registered and paying taxes. This makes sense only if the land taxes were paid by the Han who had (illegally) registered the plots. Since this made reclaiming tenants in such cases doubly obligated—once for a tax and once for a rent—the decree approved reducing the rents they had to pay to aborigine tribes (the wording implies this was already the usual practice).

The standard practice between Han large-rent and small-rent holders was for the large-rent holder to pay the land tax. A small-rent holder who paid the land tax paid a reduced amount of large-rent. The 1767 decree applies this same principle to aborigine lands on which Han tenants were paying the land tax.

It is aborigine land, illegally reclaimed and registered to pay taxes by Han settlers and ordered returned to aborigine ownership under large-rent arrangements (pursuant to the decrees of 1737–38, 1746, 1759, 1760, and 1766) that fits the conditions of the section of the 1767 decree providing for reduced aborigine rents. Significantly, this 1767 decree and the 1768 decree considered next clearly approve Han renting of aborigine land and thereby reverse Su Ch'ang's extreme policy of 1766 that forbade further leasing and called for the eviction of Han settlers from aborigine lands illegally reclaimed along the border.

The decree of 1768 was issued under the name of the intendant Chang T'ing. Chang declared:

In Taiwan there is no precedent for levying a land tax on aborigine land [*fan ti*] or for allowing Han tenants to purchase irrevocably or pledge-lease [*tu mai, tien p'u*] such land. When investigations revealed such land and it was returned to the aborigines, the Tan-shui subprefecture, not knowing that such regulations had been set, registered these lands for taxation according to the regulations governing Han-owned land. Since the tax has already entered the quota, it is difficult to remove.

According to regulations adopted in 1765 [not extant], a distinction was made: land self-cultivated by aborigines was not to be reported for taxation, but aborigine land cultivated by Han tenants was to be registered for taxation according to the precedents. This refers especially to land not returned to the aborigines.

Now, in regard to aborigine property in Taiwan, a directive has been received that the situation is to be thoroughly clarified. Wherever Han by pledge-lease [*tien p'u*] have encroached on land, it is to be returned to aborigines to manage and cultivate. But land within this category that the aborigines cannot cultivate themselves should be let to tenants who will pay a rent according to the area cultivated, and the rent will be distributed equally to the aborigines as rations. This demonstrates imperial virtue, benevolence, and compassion toward the aborigines. . . . This intendant, because he is aware that civilized aborigine numbers are increasing, and that their livelihoods are so precarious it is difficult for them to survive, is seeing to it that the counties diligently investigate and clarify these matters.

Any land taken by fraud by Han villains is to be returned to aborigine management. Give excess land the aborigines cannot cultivate themselves to the original tenant to cultivate, and, according to precedent, let the aborigines collect a rent of 8 *shih* on each *chia* of paddy and 4 *shih* on each *chia* of dry field and distribute it as rations.

If we order [the aborigines] to pay the land tax, the land is returned to aborigines in name only, and they may fear that in the future they will suffer by being pressed for payment of taxes. Henceforth all land returned to aborigine management that settlers farm and pay rents on to aborigines need not report for taxation. This will make effective our compassion for the aborigines. The intendant has received notification that this policy has passed the provincial treasurer's review and received the approval of the governor-general and the governor.

In addition to ordering implementation by the counties, announce this order so that all Taiwan's property owners, tenants, and aborigines will be informed and thankful for the greatness of imperial benevolence. The local authorities' kindness is expansive; each must attend to his duty and exert himself in administering the land and seeing that rents are paid according to precedent. Settlers and aborigines will thereby live in harmony together as of old and collectively enjoy a peaceful fortune.[185]

The 1768 decree broadened the land-tax exemption on aborigine lands to include land returned to aborigine ownership and rented to Han settlers. The exemption was extended because of the increasing precariousness of aborigine livelihoods (now to be relieved by rents distributed as rations to the tribes). The decree stated that it was overturning a Tan-shui subprefectural regulation and regulations adopted in 1765, which had erred in taxing lands returned to aborigines and leased by Han. It also set the rent paid on aborigine land leased to Han at 8 *shih* per *chia* of paddy, the customary Taiwanese rate for large-rents (though Han large-rent holders had to pay land taxes out of their rent). The 1768 decree thus overrode (though there is no specific reference) the decree of 1767 calling for taxing tenants of such land and reducing aborigine rents in compensation. The 1768 decree did, however, continue the policy embodied in the 1767 decree of reducing the double burden on Han tenants of land taxes and tribal rents but did so by eliminating the taxes rather than by reducing the tribal rents. The exemption of Han-cultivated aborigine land from taxation was to apply only to two categories of land: land that following boundary surveys was "returned to aborigine ownership" and aborigine land let to reclaiming Han tenants in the future.

As we saw in the case of the land-tax adjustments in 1731 and 1744 (see Chapter 8), changes in the tax status of land were rarely given retroactive effect, so as not to disturb the government's revenue base (or its tax registers). The 1768 decree nevertheless substantially reduced the potential for future revenue growth by eliminating taxes on a large category of land—an unusual move, but one we saw earlier in 1722 and 1759 when land was declared beyond the raw aborigine boundary and removed from the tax registers. Granting such a broad land-tax exemption may have been made easier by the substantial tax base in place by 1768, although we know that Taiwan operations overall remained in substantial deficit. The government's willingness to forgo substantial revenues from aborigine lands must also have been conditioned by the general prosperity of the late eighteenth century and the central treasury's substantial surplus.

This government paternalism may have had several unintended effects. In some instances it may have weakened the aborigines' ability to enforce their claims to land. Making aborigine land tax-exempt made it less likely that tribal ownership claims would be recorded in the all-important tax registers (even though this had been ordered in 1738 and 1746). Local officials had less incentive to enforce regulations protecting the rights of tribal landowners who did not pay the taxes necessary to filling tax quotas (and official pockets). In other instances, however, tax-avoidance schemes by Han tenants (discussed below) mitigated the negative effects on aborigine land claims.

The rental burden this decree imposed on Han tenants surely did not make its initial enforcement an easy task. The expenses of Han tenants on aborigine land turned into paddy under the 1767 decree would have included a land tax of 2.74 *shih* (the 1744 land-tax rate) and a reduced aborigine rent of 3.2 *shih*, for a total of only 5.94 *shih* (tax surcharges not included) compared to the 8 *shih* aborigine large-rent required by the 1768 decree. However, some Han tenants may have concluded that paying an aborigine rent was better than having to deal directly with voracious tax collectors. This was true especially if the aborigine large-rent were reduced to compensate for irrigation investments by tenants (see below).

But there was yet another opportunity open to Han tenants. The tax exemption created an incentive for Han reclaimers to reduce their aborigine rents to a minimum by paying large deposits or pledge-purchasing (*tien mai*) aborigine rights. Complete ownership acquired through an absolute sale (which the government presumably would not sanction anyway) became undesirable because it would eliminate all aborigine title and with it all claim to a land-tax exemption. Negotiating a minimal rent but preserving aborigine title and the tax exemption gave the Han tenant the best of both worlds. This gave the Han tenants a material interest in preserving at least minimal aborigine land title.[186]

In 1788 after the Lin Shuang-wen rebellion, Governor-general Fu-k'ang-an modified tax policy for border lands returned to aborigine control in an attempt to eliminate this abuse and increase the state's revenue. He distinguished two types of land. Land the aborigines merely rented (*tsu p'u*) to Han for a yearly rent and a small deposit was properly considered aborigine land and was to remain tax-exempt, the same as aborigine self-cultivated land. However, land that aborigines had "sold" to Han for a yearly rent and a large deposit (Fu-k'ang-an uses *mai tuan*, irrevocable sale, and *tien mai*, pledge sale) was to be taxed, but at the lowest rate (1.7583 *shih* per *chia* instead of 2.74 *shih*). Fu-k'ang-an says "such land is no longer aborigine land," despite the rent paid to aborigines.[187] His purpose in reducing the tax-avoidance advantages of these arrangements was not to return rights to aborigines but to impose taxes that would generate state revenue.

On tribal land simply rented (*tsu p'u*) by Han, the rental arrangement had to be renewed every two or three years, and the amount was open to renegotiation.[188] On land under *tien mai* or *mai tuan*, the Han settler paid a fixed aborigine large-rent and had a right of permanent tenancy. *Mai tuan* ordinarily means an unconditional and absolute sale, but in these cases aborigine rents were still paid and aborigine title and tax exemptions preserved.[189]

The decree of 1768 gave explicit recognition and government backing to the leasing of aborigine land on the aborigine large-rent model (see below). Despite Fu-k'ang-an's attempt to reduce the tax exemption of aborigine border land, lands under aborigine large-rent generally remained tax-exempt until the Liu Ming-ch'uan reforms of the late nineteenth century.[190] Liu ordered all small-rent holders to pay land taxes and in exchange reduced the large-rents, whether paid to aborigines or Han. He compensated the Han large-rent holders by relieving them of their tax-paying obligation. But the blow to plains aborigine income from the reductions in tribal large-rents could not be offset in this way because the tribal land had been tax-exempt.[191]

Maturation of the Aborigine Large-Rent System, 1768–1785

Numerous examples of court decisions and contracts (many reflecting the negotiated resolution of disputes) illustrate the operation of the aborigine large-rent system in its fully institutionalized form. These cases show how the government in mediating between tribes and settlers recognized and gave force to aborigine large-rent rights and shaped the land-tenure arrangements negotiated between settlers and aborigines.

In the twelfth month of 1772, a local court decision resolved a dispute between the tribes of Ta-chia and Te-hua (Ta-chia-hsi, leader of the 1731–32 revolt) and settler tenants. The decision imposed an aborigine large-rent of 8 *shih* per *chia* despite the terms of the reclamation contract between the tribe and the settlers and evidence that the settlers had invested in irrigation.

> This decree is issued in the name of the subprefect for aborigine affairs of the north route, Li Pen-nan,[192] with the approval of the intendant.
>
> This case was brought by the interpreter et al. of the Ta-chia and Te-hua tribes against their tenants, Liu et al., for having made insufficient rental payments. What was once barren land was leased out by the Han tribal interpreter Lin to Han tenants for reclamation at a time "when land was plentiful and people few." The tenancy contract provided that once the land was reclaimed, a rent of 6 *shih* per *chia* would be paid. But the decree of 1767 declared that henceforth rents should be paid according to Taiwanese custom at the 8 *shih* rate for large-rents on paddy (4 on dry land) and that tenants could not use the excuse of having invested in irrigation works to pay a lighter rent or to delay payment.
>
> When the tribal proprietors took the nonpaying tenants to court, the Tan-shui subprefect ordered that the 8 *shih* rate be paid (if the fields were damaged by flood, then less could be paid), and the tenants supplied written guarantees that they would obey and pay. But later the tenants went to the former intendant Chiang[193] and reopened the case; Chiang got an order from a superior restoring the old 6 *shih* rent rate. All the tenants were informed that they could pay less as they desired. Accordingly the aborigine tribesmen had no rations paid to them. Because of this they conferred with the local proprietors, and the tribal clerk wrote out a complaint and brought suit. . . . So now the decision must be made whether these tribes can collect an 8 *shih* rent as decreed by the authorities or a 6 *shih* rent according to Chiang's previous decision. . . .
>
> This office has found that the Taiwanese custom is that large-rents are 8 *shih* on paddy and 4 on dry land. During the reform of 1767, the Tan-shui subprefect Tuan[194] decided that the amount invested and spent in repairs by tenants was not substantial, and hence he did not reduce the rents in such cases. Tuan feared that if he allowed exceptions, villains would take advantage. A fixed rent was set on all land returned to aborigines so that all rents would be uniform.
>
> Now the tenant Liu has petitioned to restore the old 6 *shih* rate and reduce the rent to compensate him for investments in irrigation. The various officials have rejected this because the "land is broad and the rents light." Liu and the tenants use their investment in irrigation as an excuse to litigate and pay a lower rent. The intendant has ordered us to compare past practice and the present policy and make a detailed report. I have obeyed and found

> that the intendant's original order did not refer to tenants' expending labor and capital [on irrigation], and there is no written order approving reduced rents [in such cases]. Thus, regardless of whether the original tenant or subtenant has expended labor and capital or not, we order all those who lease aborigine land to pay rent according to the Han precedent [8 *shih* rate]. Since there is no provision for reduction in compensation for irrigation expenses, there is no excuse for tenants' bringing suit for a reduction. This has confused the regulations and led to landlord-tenant disputes. On all aborigine land, rents are to be collected according to the promulgated quota; there is to be no reduction so that all rents will be uniform. Thus, the tenants Liu et al. must pay the promulgated rate, and no reduction is to be allowed. Notify all the tribal tenants that the land of the two tribes must [be let] in conformity with the original regulations, at the Taiwan customary rent of 8 *shih*. Tenants are not to use the pretext of having expended labor and capital to pay too little in rents or to delay payment. If some still dare to disobey, the owners may submit petitions naming them. Orders will be given to runners to arrest them, bring them to trial, and severely punish them. There will be no lenience.[195]

This decision reveals again the government's resolve to protect aborigine rights and prevent their erosion by legal maneuvers and nonpayment of rents. Both parties to the dispute had official decrees to back their claims, and this discrepancy in official policy must have been an embarrassment to the government. The tenants' case for a lower rent rate (though not their record of nonpayment) had considerable merit: the original contract provided for a 6 *shih* rental rate. Moreover, the tenants had invested in irrigation facilities, and according to Taiwanese custom (see below), that bolstered their claim to a reduced large-rent. But the subprefect for aborigine affairs, fearing that any exceptions made would be exploited by conniving Han tenants to the detriment of aborigine livelihoods, decided in favor of preserving a uniform aborigine rental rate.

This decision affirms the 8 *shih* rental rate on aborigine land first decreed in the order of 1767. The requirement that settlers pay an 8 *shih* rate was further bolstered by the 1768 decree, which eliminated the provision in the 1767 decree lowering rents when settlers paid taxes and made aborigine lands, even though rented to Han, tax-exempt. The portion of the 1767 decree available to us certainly makes no provision for rental reduction due to tenant investment in irrigation facilities, and this agrees with the local court's interpretation of the 1767 decree in its 1772 decision. The 1767 decree, however, was much more sympathetic to the settlers, in that it sought to lighten settler rents when they also paid taxes.[196] In 1772 the government preferred the uniform 8 *shih* rate because it combined administrative convenience and a larger income to aborigines.

To add weight to their arguments, the officials denigrated the amount invested in irrigation by the tenants and claimed that "the land is broad and the rents light," apparently to imply that paying the customary 8 *shih* instead of 6 *shih* was not a heavy burden. Interestingly, this partially contradicts the description of the person/land ratio that the aborigines had offered to justify raising the rent from 6 to 8 *shih.* The tribe had claimed that the original low contractual rate of 6 *shih* was set at some past time "when land was plentiful and people few" in order to imply that now, at a later stage of settlement when land was scarce, population was greater, and land values were higher, revising rental rates upward was reasonable. The plenitude of land obviously depended on the perspective of the party making the argument. It is interesting that here two of the parties, the aborigines and the government, are arguing toward the same goal, an 8 *shih* rate, but their respective social positions lead them to appeal to different principles that require the situation to be described in diametrically opposite ways. The government officials, in the name of the good of the society as a whole, need to justify their conclusion by minimizing the cost it imposes on any one party; hence the claim that the land is plentiful and that rents are light.[197] The aborigines, however, facing a situation where open land is no longer plentiful, are anxious to increase their income from reclaimed land that has risen in value by raising rents (which does not necessarily make the rents heavy in any absolute sense).[198]

Among other points of interest raised by this case is the subprefect's immediate reaction to the aborigines' suit, which was to suspect pettifoggery by Han tribal bullies. After an interrogation, he found that the case did indeed have merit. This decision is one of the first instances we have of the new office of aborigine affairs intervening on behalf of the aborigines. Nevertheless, the subprefect's decision is written in such "officialese" that practically no responsibility can be placed directly on him. Rather, all is attributed to precedents and the instructions of superiors; the subprefect himself does not offer an opinion. This was a skill that magistrates valued highly in their legal secretaries.[199] Nor was intendant Chiang, whose decision to restore the 6 *shih* rate was overturned, criticized; Chiang, too, had acted on the basis of instructions from superiors.

In his 1772 decision the subprefect for aborigine affairs seemed determined to allow no exceptions to an aborigine large-rent rate of 8 *shih* per *chia.* Much evidence reveals that this was an extreme position that violated precedent and was not followed in policy or practice. Despite the language of the 1772 decision, reclamation contracts calling for reduced large-rents to compensate builders of irrigation works were common both between Han and between aborigines and Han. One of the earliest contracts containing such terms between aborigines (of Houlung *she* and Hsin-kang-tzu *she*) and a Han settler is dated 1747.[200] This contract confers a right of permanent tenancy and reduces a 6 *shih* per *chia* large-rent by 2 *shih* to compensate a tenant who paid for irrigation construction.

By a 1772 contract, the Lei-lang *she* in the Taipei basin rented a plot to a Han tenant from the excess of "247 *chia* returned to the tribe according to the official decree of 1767." These fields had been let on a landlord-tenant 30/70 share rent until 1766–67. Since they had gradually been converted to paddy, it was decided in 1767 that they were to pay, according to contract and village custom (*chuang li*), a large-rent of 6 *shih* per *chia*. The tribe agreed to collect 3 *shih* as "dry-land rent" (*yüan tsu*) and forgo the remaining 3 *shih* to be paid as water rent to compensate the household that built the irrigation works.[201] The reference to the large-rent paid to the tribe as "dry-land rent" emphasizes that the aborigine large-rent was paid only for the unimproved land and that the land's conversion to paddy was the result of the investment of others. The reduction from 6 to 3 *shih* is even more extreme than the reduction from 8 to 6 *shih* that provoked the 1772 suit by Ta-chia and Te-hua.

It was not unusual for local custom, in these cases setting the large-rent at 6 *shih*, to diverge from the wider Taiwanese custom of 8 *shih*. But there might not even be consistency within a locality. A contract issued in 1759 by the same tribal proprietor (Lei-lang *she*) concerning land in the same area (modern Chung-ho in the Taipei basin) as the 1772 contract cites the Taiwanese precedent of 8 *shih*. Which precedent to cite was clearly subject to some negotiation.[202] A contract of the Hsiu-lang *she* relating to land in the same area dated 1782 cites the 6 *shih* precedent.[203]

The 1773 San-hsia reclamation contract (mentioned in Chapter 1) also follows custom rather than the 1772 decree. This contract provides that the aborigine proprietors and the Han tenants pay respectively 40 percent and 60 percent of the costs of building irrigation canals in accordance with Taiwanese custom.[204] After three years, the reclaimed paddy and dry fields were to be surveyed and rents assessed. Each *chia* of irrigated field was to pay 8 *shih* of grain as "large-rent rations." If, however, the four tribes could not pay their share of irrigation construction, the tenant would be responsible for raising the necessary capital: "It is agreed in this case that the tribes will collect 2 *shih* less to cover a water rent, and the tenants will pay 6 *shih* of grain as large-rent rations on irrigated paddy."[205] Only a year after the uniform 8 *shih* rate was proclaimed, "regardless of investment in irrigation facilities," this contract reverts to the proscribed customary practice. The contract appeals to another version of Taiwanese custom, which requires joint landlord-tenant investment in irrigation for the full 8 *shih* rent to be paid.

The San-hsia contract's clause on taxation reads: "In the future if a decree is received that the land ought to be reported for taxation, it will be the business of the four tribes and will not concern the tenants." The 1768 decree exempted aborigine border lands from taxation. The contract, however, envisions the possibility of a future order to pay taxes, and it takes a precaution to protect the tribes' title—taxes are to be their duty alone. The Han tenants are not to interfere. The implication is that the Han tenants are not to use taxpaying to subvert the tribes' title.[206]

Even local officials intervening in disputes between tribes and their Han tenants in the years following 1772 did not seek to enforce the 8 *shih* per *chia* rent. However, several cases from these years do reveal an officialdom actively protecting the land rights of the aborigine tribes through the accommodation of settler and tribal interests.

In the late 1770's it took several officials to resolve a land dispute between the Wu-lao-wan *she* of the Taipei basin and the Liu family. Two contracts recite the history of the dispute and the settlement imposed by the government.[207] In the Yung-cheng era, Liu Ho-lin "bought" (*mai*) from Wu-lao-wan 50 *chia* of wasteland (between modern Hsin-chuang and Wu-ku *hsiang*) and in exchange agreed to pay annually 30 taels of the aborigine head-tax money (labeled *she fan hsiang yin*) and a rent of 50 *shih* of grain. Liu also reported the land for taxation. All these terms fit the *tai fan shu hsiang* model discussed earlier.

In 1761 the Lius began building a canal to irrigate a large area.[208] In 1767 Tan-shui subprefect Tuan Chieh surveyed the newly irrigated land and registered 191 *chia* for taxation. Because no aborigine ownership rights were recognized in this survey, the Wu-lao-wan *she* brought suit. Ultimately the tribe appealed to Taiwan prefect Chou Ying-yüan.[209] Chou overruled the subprefect and ordered the 191 *chia* returned to aborigine ownership, but left the Lius in control of the original 50 *chia*. On a further appeal, the intendant Chi Lung-ko[210] set the rentals on the various categories of land. On the original 50 *chia* registered for taxation, the Lius were entitled to collect from their tenants 8 *shih* per *chia*, 4 *shih* each for the large-rent and the water rent. There is no repetition of the terms of the Yung-cheng-era agreement, but it seems likely they were to remain in force (see the discussion of the riverbank land below). On the 191 *chia* returned to aborigine ownership (and apparently removed from the tax registers), the tribe was to collect 4 *shih* per *chia* as "dry rent" (*han tsu*), and the Lius were to collect the water rent. But on a portion of this land that was poorly irrigated (the "water tail"), the tribe and the Lius were to get only 3 *shih* each.

Because, in carrying out these decrees, Tan-shui subprefect Sung Hsüeh-hao[211] failed to distinguish clearly which category of land each tenant occupied, thereby confusing rental obligations, the tribe had again to petition local officials for relief. In 1778 Ch'eng Li-t'ai, acting as both the subprefect for aborigine affairs and as Tan-shui subprefect,[212] erected boundary markers and made lists of the tenants on the 191 *chia* of returned aborigine land (*kuei fan t'ien*) and on the Lius' 50 *chia* of taxed land (*k'o t'ien*).[213] At that time Ch'eng resolved yet another dispute. The Lius had built a dike to protect some riverbank land let to tenants for growing sweet potatoes. Ch'eng agreed that this land was within the boundaries of the Lius' original (Yung-cheng-era) contract, but since it was subject to flooding, he did not require that it be registered for taxation. He ordered the Lius to pay yearly an additional aborigine rent fixed at 40 *shih* of grain for this unmeasured area.[214]

In all, more than ten years were required to resolve these disputes. We can see in the decisions of these officials a determination not only to protect aborigine land rights but also to follow standard practices, which required that rents be adjusted to circumstances, rather than to impose the uniform rate adopted in the 1772 decision. The same policies are evident in two other disputes resolved by subprefects for aborigine affairs, one in 1777 involving the Ma-tou *she* of the Tainan area,[215] and one in 1779 involving the To-lo-kuo and Ta-wu-lung *she.*[216] In these cases the subprefects, seeking to prevent further confusion or litigation, had their decrees carved on stones and placed in the disputed areas.

The creation of the Subprefecture for Aborigine Affairs, coupled with the decrees of the late 1760's that regulated the taxation and rental of aborigine lands, mark the maturation of the aborigine large-rent system.[217] From then until the creation of the aborigine military colonies after the Lin Shuang-wen rebellion in the late 1780's, problems in administering aborigine lands were dealt with routinely. The government's energies were consumed by other problems in these years, primarily raw aborigine raiding and the growth of Han communal strife (see Chapter 10).

The organization of border guards to counter raw aborigine raids met with only limited success. Settlers continued to cross the border in search of mountain products, and they often lost their heads to aborigine raiders.[218] In several instances the unruly guards (Han in these cases) became involved in disputes with the settlers they were deputed to protect (and who were supposed to pay them rations). One official commented that recruiting guards locally was the same as "distributing weapons to the unemployed."[219] In one of these incidents, the Hsiao-li *she*, as the tribal owner, sided with one settler against another in a dispute over payment of guard fees. Because of this, the investigating official recommended, "despite the precedent [I assume the reference is to the decree of 1760] by which tribes having land beyond the boundary may call in tenants to reclaim it to provide a livelihood," confiscating the land beyond the boundary at issue in the disturbance. He barred both Han and aborigines from further reclamation in the area. The state's first interest was in security and the preservation of order; aborigine claims to land received protection only when they furthered these goals.[220]

These incidents and the communal strife of 1782 led to another resurvey and clarification of the raw aborigine boundary line in 1784. This revealed over 11,000 *chia* of land reclaimed beyond the boundaries set in 1750 and 1760.[221] This survey was incomplete at the time of the Lin Shuang-wen rebellion, and the disposal of most of these lands was not decided until after the rebellion (see Chapter 10).[222]

Conclusions

Before summarizing Ch'ing management of the frontier land-tenure system and the evolution of aborigine land rights, let us take a critical view of the sources. A much richer body of data on land tenure, in terms of central government decrees, local court decisions, and land contracts, is available for Taiwan than for most other parts of the Chinese empire. These describe in detail land arrangements at specific times and places and enable us to identify recurring issues and patterns of development, which we can relate to data from other sources about the evolution of frontier society in Taiwan. But the sources on land tenure are probably not so comprehensive as to capture all significant variations in time and space; the reconstruction presented here may need to be modified by intensive studies on specific localities. Nor can we make quantitative statements about how much land fell into the many categories of property created by these decrees.

A number of problems remain in interpreting the eighteenth-century decrees on the disposition of aborigine lands. Perhaps most fundamental is the constant vagueness about what the government recognized as aborigine land. The decrees refer repeatedly to self-cultivated land, land beyond the boundary, and grasslands and hunting fields. Yet what constitutes a proper tribal territorial claim is never defined; the government apparently preferred to recognize land claims on a case-by-case basis, waiting to resolve disputes and conduct surveys (sometimes in response to petitions to reclaim land, sometimes in response to boundary problems) before delimiting tribal land claims in specific localities.

Late K'ang-hsi reports complained that reclamation patents were being issued without regard to tribal claims, in violation of regulations adopted to protect aborigine lands. Large areas must have been lost to the aborigines in the ensuing years of accelerating Han migration and settlement. The most authoritative Japanese study, the Taiwan Private Law project (*TWSH*), fails to document its claim that before 1738 the government demarcated land to be let by the tribes from land to be let by the government.[223] Several Yung-cheng-era proposals advocated reserving small areas for the tribes and opening all remaining land to Han reclamation, but they were never adopted by the court. Continued violation of tribal territories prompted the decree of 1737–38 that attempted to

TABLE 9.1

Summary of Major Decrees Defining Aborigine Land Rights, 1704–1790

1704–9[a]	Require county inspection of boundaries before approving land grants relating to aborigine land.
1710–15[a]	Payment of the aborigine head tax entitles tribes to unreclaimed land.
1722	Establish the raw aborigine boundary.
1724	Allow Han to rent aborigine lands; register such land for taxation.
1737–38	Forbid future leasing of aborigine lands.
	Return squatter land to tribes.
	Do not disturb settler land leased from tribes and registered for taxation.
	Draw boundaries and set up registers dividing settler and tribal land.
1744	Forbid military officers from reclaiming aborigine lands.
1746	Punish illicit leasing and squatting on aborigine land, return this land to the aborigines.
	Draw boundaries and set up registers of aborigine lands.
	Punish crossing the raw aborigine boundary to open land.
	Enlist plains aborigines in defense against raw aborigine attack.
1750	Redraw the raw aborigine boundary.
	Reassert the ban on Han reclaiming tribal land.
1758	Dig earth-oxen trenches to mark off aborigine land.
1759	Han settlers who have lease-purchased tribal lands must pay an aborigine rent.
1760	Redraw the raw aborigine boundary.
	Return the land between the new and old boundaries to tribal management and let the aborigines collect rent on this land from the Han settlers.
	Post aborigine guards along the boundary to be supported by these rents.
1766	Enforce the ban on farming beyond the raw aborigine boundary.
	Return illicitly leased land to aborigines and evict Han settlers, update the land registers, and clarify the boundaries of tribal lands.
	Forbid Han leasing tribal lands.
1767	Allow settlers to remain on tribal lands that aborigines cannot cultivate themselves.
	On these lands settlers must pay aborigine rents of 8 *shih* of grain per *chia*.
	Settlers already paying land taxes may reduce their aborigine rents 60 percent.
1768	Return illegally acquired land to aborigines, but where aborigines cannot cultivate it themselves, allow the settlers to remain as tenants.
	Exempt this land from taxes and require Han settlers to pay aborigine rents of 8 *shih* per *chia*.
1788	Tax lightly aborigine border land pledge-sold to Han but not land rented to Han.
1790	Allot unreclaimed land beyond the boundaries of 1750 and 1760 to aborigine military colonies.
	Order Han settlers on land reclaimed beyond the boundaries to pay rents to the aborigine military colonies.

[a] These are the dates Wang Min-cheng and Ch'en Pin, respectively, served as intendant.

freeze Han reclamation of aborigine land. Not until 1738 and 1746 did decrees call for the clarification of tribal boundaries and the inclusion of aborigine lands, both reclaimed and waste, in the land registers. These were the earliest systematic attempts to define and register tribal territories (see Table 9.1), and they came only after a considerable acceleration of Han settlement.

Another problem lies in determining how the decrees were intended to relate to one another and whether they applied to the same or to different categories of land. Only three decrees, those of 1766, 1768, and 1772, refer explicitly to previous decrees and make clear how they relate to previous policy (several land contracts also make references to decrees or court settlements). Several boundary-redrawing decrees void the terms under which aborigine land was opened and require Han tenants to abandon the land or to pay aborigine rents on the terms promulgated. Yet it is not always clear if the decrees are to apply only to land involved in the boundary redrawing or to some broader category of aborigine land. The 1760 decree clearly creates a new category of land, that between the newly redrawn boundary and the old one, and promulgates special terms for its disposition. Similarly, it seems likely that several of the decrees phrased in generic terms were in fact meant to apply only to specific categories of land (for example, "land returned to aborigine management," "land beyond the boundary," or land reclaimed within certain time periods or under certain terms). Perhaps access to land registers (first mentioned in regard to aborigine land in 1738 and again in 1746 and 1766), which may have listed land, even though unreclaimed, as belonging to certain categories of aborigine ownership, made the decrees much easier to interpret for officials as well as for the tribes and settlers competing for rights in land. The process of boundary clarification resembles the process by which land-tax rates were reformed, in which the new rates applied only to land opened after certain dates. This created wide differences in the rate of taxation (see Chapter 8). Similarly, wide differences emerged over time in the degree of recognition of aborigine rental rights and the tax status of aborigine land leased to Han.

The most important dimensions along which the decrees categorized land were (1) whether the land was under tribal ownership; (2) whether tribal land was in an area that could be rented to Han or whether it was in a restricted area (e.g., limited to aborigine self-cultivation or beyond the raw aborigine boundary); (3) the nature of the rents that could be collected; (4) whether the land was to be registered to pay land taxes and who would pay the taxes; and (5) whether there was an obligation to provide guard duty. In some instances the tribe held the right to collect rent, but the obligation to pay taxes fell on the Han tenant. Aborigine land let to Han after 1768 was tax-exempt, except for the border lands affected by Fu-k'ang-an's 1788 decree. These decrees thus created a complex series of subcategories of land subject to different regulations and different rent and taxpaying obligations. We have seen throughout this chapter how the state used these dimensions to allocate rights and duties with respect to land on the frontier, to accommodate Han settlers and plains tribes, and to further its own revenue and security goals.

It is striking that none of the decrees distinguished individually owned from corporately owned aborigine lands.[224] That aborigines made such distinctions is clear in some contracts.[225] The decree of 1760, by allotting land beyond the old boundary, allowing such land to be let to Han, and requiring tribal officers to keep rental accounts and pay out rations to aborigine border guards, created a separate corporately owned body of tribal lands.

This chapter has traced the evolution of aborigine land rights out of the system of taxing the deer trade established by the Dutch and continued by the Chengs and the Ch'ing. In the K'ang-hsi and Yung-cheng reigns, tribes' claims to the hunting territories from which they drew their income and paid their taxes were recognized. Han seeking to reclaim these lands could contract with a tribe to assume part of its tax burden, apply for a government patent, and receive in return the right to farm the land.

In the Yung-cheng reign, when the government was hungry for additional revenues to pay for its extended civil and military presence and when pro-colonization arguments gained influence, measures were adopted that sanctioned Han "rental" of aborigine land to speed up the pace of reclamation and the registration of land for taxation. Han settlers and the tribes frequently adopted the large-rent model, which conferred rights to income on tribal owners and usufruct on reclaiming tenants (who also were made responsible for paying land taxes), but Han tenants also sought to lessen their rental obligations through modified purchases of aborigine land. Although these lease-purchases meant a reduced rental income stream in the future, plains aborigines in straitened circumstances willingly sacrificed long-term benefit for the short-term benefit of a larger initial payment. In the early years when unopened land was abundant, these payments might be set at amounts equal to very low rates per unit of area. Years later, large tracts of increasingly valuable land were subject to very light rental obligations to the tribes.

The early Ch'ien-lung reign witnessed increasing concern about declining plains aborigine livelihoods and the government's ability to control large frontier populations. In a dramatic shift of policy to a conservative and control-oriented strategy, the government in 1738 halted Han settlement by drawing boundaries around the areas already reclaimed and forbidding further acquisition of aborigine land. But government resources and resolve were rarely sufficient to enforce such a radical policy against the steady influx of land-hungry immigrants, and the government had repeatedly to redraw the boundaries. Ultimately the state retreated from a total prohibition on Han reclamation to the guarantee of a rental income from these lands to the tribes, primarily on the large-rent model. General prosperity and treasury surpluses helped make the late eighteenth-century state willing to forgo additional land-tax revenues and to exempt reclaimed tribal land from taxation, despite continuing deficits in its operations in Taiwan. By the late 1760's, government policy toward reclamation and taxation of aborigine territories had led to the mature system of aborigine large-rents (*fan ta tsu*) that would endure through the nineteenth century.

Government land policy on the frontier was guided by two primary security considerations: (1) to prevent conflict between Han and civilized aborigines in order to minimize the danger that aborigines would revolt and "go wild," and (2) to keep Han settlers on the plains side of the raw aborigine boundary to prevent trouble arising between Han and raw aborigines. The first objective required protecting the livelihood of the civilized, taxpaying tribes by limiting Han encroachment or by guaranteeing a rental income to the tribes. Because the pressure of Han settlement was continuous, the raw aborigine boundaries and the boundaries demarcating civilized aborigine territories from areas of Han settlement were frequently transgressed. The government thus had to intervene repeatedly either to correct the violation and return the land to the aborigines or to redraw the boundary and register the land in a way that would protect aborigine rights to an income from it. Because of the high costs of returning land to aborigines—displacing settlers, risking their disaffection, and reducing both government tax revenues and grain surpluses—the government gradually sanctioned the extension of the aborigine large-rent system.

The government also used its ability to allocate land rights to further its second objective of security against raw aborigine raiding. In 1746 and again in 1760, it designed a system of guard posts along the raw aborigine boundary, to be staffed by civilized aborigines, and assigned rental income to pay for the guards' rations. This continued a tradition of using aborigine braves to suppress anti-government disturbances by aborigines and Han. An important extension of this policy came with the establishment of aborigine military colonies in the wake of the Lin Shuang-wen rebellion (see Chapter 10).

Important changes in aborigine land policies were coordinated with changes in other spheres of government policy toward Taiwan: sometimes changes in land policy were made in conjunction with other policy shifts; sometimes land policies responded to problems created by these other policies (compare Tables 6.1 and 9.1). The initial recognition of aborigine rights to unreclaimed land and government efforts to limit Han encroachment were part of the quarantine policies of the K'ang-hsi era.

The 1724 decree approving Han rental of aborigine lands was the first of a series of pro-colonization policies in the Yung-cheng years. These included reductions in land taxes, expansion of the civil and military presence, family migration, and allocation of Taiwan grain to the southeastern coastal garrisons. The early Ch'ien-lung court reversed many of these policies, seeking to limit Han reclamation of aborigine land in 1737–38, ending family migration in 1740, and raising land taxes after 1744. In later years, the policies of the Ch'ien-lung court fluctuated, mostly in retreat from extreme quarantine policies. An unstoppable influx of Han settlers and the continuing need for Taiwan's surplus grain on the southeast coast forced the court to adopt policies more accommodating to the spread of agricultural settlement. Hence, the frequent adjustments made in the raw aborigine boundary and the extension of the aborigine large-rent system.

Protection of tribal land claims was an expression more of a central government policy of keeping order on the frontier than a recognition of aborigine "rights" or interests.[226] Restricting Han reclamation of tribal land, and later guaranteeing rental incomes to the tribes, was seen as a low-cost means of minimizing disruption of the ethnic status quo on the frontier. The tribes were in most cases too weak to defend their claims to such lands from Han encroachment, although they were feared as a source of disturbances and were of use to the government as a countervailing source of military power. Distrust of the unruly Han settlers heightened the strategic value of the plains aborigines in the government's eyes, and aborigine braves repeatedly demonstrated their utility as a loyalist force against aborigines, raw or cooked, and rebellious Han.

Certain fundamental orientations of Chinese statecraft also favored plains aborigine claims to land. The Mencian strand of Chinese statecraft practiced by the Ch'ing emphasized that the economic well-being of the empire's subjects had to precede moral cultivation, and livelihoods had to be ensured if order was to be maintained, civilization spread, and submission won.[227] Non-Han ethnicity did not disqualify plains aborigines, as taxpaying subjects, from these considerations. Of course, procolonization advocates could argue that the livelihoods of Han immigrants should be given consideration, if not priority. Thus, Shen Ch'i-yüan in 1729 wrote that the prohibition of migration not only did not benefit the state treasury (*kuo chi*) but harmed the people's livelihood (*min sheng*).[228] The late imperial state had a large repertoire of social control policies, including protection of rights in land. This history of aborigine land rights illustrates how the Ch'ing state used its ability to allocate rights and duties with respect to land to accommodate the competing interests of Han settlers and aborigine tribes and to achieve government revenue and security goals.

The government's special interest in the security problems along the raw aborigine border made lands there the most frequent object of its reform attempts. Civilized tribal claims to land in the border areas were probably protected more strictly against Han encroachment by the local governments than claims to land on the coastal plains.[229] Government regulation could serve the double purpose on the border of ensuring tribal livelihoods and border security either by restricting Han access or by providing for aborigine guards rations. We will see in the next chapter how the Ch'ing state pursued this strategy by creating aborigine military colonies. In the succeeding chapter, we will assess how the plains aborigines adapted to the disruption of their traditional livelihoods caused by the spread of Han settlement.

CHAPTER TEN

Han Communal Strife and Aborigine Military Colonies

THE ESTABLISHMENT OF the aborigine military colonies and the related land survey and reform of 1788–90 were the culmination of more than a century of interaction among the Ch'ing state, Han settlers, and plains aborigines.[1] By the end of the eighteenth century, Taiwan had moved beyond the early pioneering stage of frontier development. A stage of secondary development marked by increasing density of settlement had begun. Population growth and reclamation intensified in the plains areas, where a basic accommodation between civilized aborigines and Han settlers had already been achieved. Harry Lamley has noted, and we shall see below, that this second stage of development was marked by increasingly severe communal strife within the Han population.

In this new stage the historical role of the plains aborigines became increasingly marginal. First, as an increasingly small minority in almost every locality surrounded by expanding Han agriculturalists, plains aborigine communities faced severe problems of adjustment. The next chapter analyzes the plains aborigine adaptations to this new environment. Second, the continued expansion of Han settlement led to increasing friction with head-hunting raw aborigines in the mountains, who resisted both incorporation in the Chinese state and Han exploitation of foothill resources such as timber, mountain products, water supplies, and land. The state, as we saw in Chapter 9, had already enlisted plains aborigine braves to patrol the foothill margins of settlement and to mediate relations with the raw tribes. The creation of the aborigine military colonies in 1788 further institutionalized this role for the plains aborigines. But raw aborigine troubles would rarely match the significance that issues concerning reclamation of plains aborigine lands or Han revolts and communal strife had for the state's security and revenue goals.

In 1786 the largest and most destructive rebellion in Taiwan's history broke out. The role of the plains aborigines in the campaign to suppress the rebellion and in the reconstruction plans formulated in its aftermath mark a significant stage in their history. The creation of aborigine military colonies was the last major Ch'ing effort to mobilize the aborigines and to see in protecting aborigine interests a means of minimizing control costs. This chapter begins by reviewing the history of Ch'ing use of aborigine auxiliaries in Taiwan and then analyzes developments leading up to the rebellion and the aborigine role in pacification and post-rebellion reconstruction.

Civilized aborigines were frequently called to render military aid under the Ch'ing (as they had been under the Dutch). In Chapter 5, we saw plains aborigine militia used to help suppress a revolt of Cheng remnants south of Tainan in the first year of Ch'ing rule, quash the 1699 revolts of plains villages in northern Taiwan, and pacify the rebel tribes around Ta-chia in 1732. The government also enlisted plains aborigines as guides and interpreters on campaigns launched to punish raw aborigines in the mountains (for example, the Shui-sha-lien campaign in 1724 and the Yu-wu-nai campaign in 1766; see Chapter 9). The decrees of 1746 and 1760 institutionalized their role in raw aborigine border defense by stationing plains aborigine braves at guardposts along the border and requiring that the guards' rations be paid from rents on the border lands allotted to the civilized tribes.[2]

The state used civilized aborigine troops not only against other aborigines, raw and cooked, but also against rebellious Han. We saw that early in the Chu I-kuei rebellion of 1721, a military commander mobilized civilized aborigine braves from villages near Tainan (Hsin-kang, Mu-chia-liu-wan, Ma-tou, and Hsiao-lung; the same four had been mobilized in 1684 and 1699) and offered them a bounty for each rebel killed. When the aborigines proved overenthusiastic and started killing innocent Chinese and looting commoners' homes, they drove large numbers of Chinese into the rebel camp.[3] However, other aborigines served well as guides and interpreters in expeditions to apprehend rebels who fled into the mountains.[4] By the end of the Ch'ien-lung reign, the Ch'ing had used plains aborigine auxiliaries in at least twelve campaigns, four each against Han, raw aborigine, and other plains aborigine rebels.[5] The large-scale outbreaks of communal strife among Han settlers in the last half of the Ch'ien-lung reign, along with continual raw aborigine raiding, turned the government's attention once again to the military utility of the civilized tribes.

Hunting gave plains aborigine braves the skills needed in warfare, and their heroic culture, which celebrated successful warriors, motivated valor in battle. Plains aborigine men were strong, fast runners, skilled archers and marksmen, and expert trackers familiar with the mountain hideouts of bandits and raw aborigines; these traits earned them the praise of Imperial Commissioner Fu-k'ang-an for their role in the Lin

Shuang-wen rebellion.[6] Muskets did not give government troops technological superiority over Han and aborigine opponents, for as Mark Elvin points out, the eighteenth-century musket was not always a "match for the expertly handled bow": "The musket had greater penetrating power than the composite bow at pointblank range to set against its lower rate of fire and shorter range; but the quality of archery depended to a far greater extent on continuous training than did that of musketry."[7] Hunting gave plains aborigines constant training in the use of bows as well as muskets. Their skill as archers and marksmen was superior to that of the Green Standard garrisons, who were poorly trained and suffered from low morale.[8] By the 1780's, plains aborigine braves had on numerous occasions demonstrated their value as military auxiliaries to the Ch'ing.

Immigrant Social Organization and Communal Strife

As settlement intensified, instances of large-scale subethnic strife became more frequent. These affrays, sometimes induced and sometimes merely exploited by opportunistic elements in the population, and unchecked by ineffective government peacekeeping, polarized society into hostile blocks of settlers united primarily by common provenance. For example, in 1768 local officials attempted to apprehend a Mr. Huang Chiao who had cut off the ears and nose of an opponent in a lawsuit. Huang, the head of a gang selling oxen protection to local farmers, met his pursuers with armed resistance. In the tenth month, he and his followers raised the flag of rebellion at Kang-shan (located midway between Tainan and Feng-shan in southern Taiwan). Huang's cause found considerable sympathy among certain elements of the populace. Helped along by an initially inadequate official response, his band held out well into the next year until suppressed with the help of plains aborigine auxiliaries.[9] In the unstable situation created by Huang's revolt, armed feuding broke out between Hakka and Hokkien (Fukienese) settlers.[10] Huang, himself a Hokkien, tried to stir up communal strife by attacking several Hakka villages, thereby adding to the burden of officials seeking to re-establish law and order.[11]

On first hearing of Huang's rebellion, the central government ordered civil and military officials to tighten defenses at the aborigine boundary and along the coast to prevent the rebels' escaping and the rebellion's spreading. Local officials were directed to offer rewards to raw aborigines who handed over bandits fleeing into their territory.[12] Government troops who entered raw aborigine territory to give chase were to notify the aborigines that they were only pursuing rebels and not seeking to disturb aborigine lands. In the end, the government pronounced itself pleased by the cooperation it received from the aborigines, both raw and civilized, and few rebels dared to flee into the mountains.[13] For their failure to end quickly what should have been a small matter, several civil and military officials were removed from office.[14]

Official dissatisfaction with the handling of the Huang Chiao incident led to calls in 1768 for tighter enforcement of immigration restrictions (see Chapter 6). Huang's revolt was taken as proof that rootless vagrants and discontented elements were making their way to Taiwan; controlling them in Taiwan was considered much more difficult than weeding them out before they arrived. These lawless elements were styled *lo han chiao* and likened to the troublesome *kuo lu tzu* bandits of Szechwan province.[15] The pattern of the Huang Chiao revolt fits many of the local disturbances in Taiwan during the Ch'ing period. Government police actions against gangsters sparked conflicts that escalated into communal strife when one subethnic group gave refuge to its outlaw compatriots and the other subethnic group took the side of the government.

To understand the patterns of Han frontier community organization, we need to consider the migration and settlement process and how it contributed to the emergence of a society easily polarized into hostile subethnic blocks. The process of migration from China's southeast coast and settlement in Taiwan was characterized by six salient factors.

First, most migration began as a sojourning strategy and only evolved over time into a permanent relocation to Taiwan. When male family members (traveling in groups of friends and kin) left home in search of economic opportunity, they retained important rights in and obligations to their natal families. A married man left behind a wife to serve his parents and care for his children. This minimized travel and living expenses and gave the sojourners great flexibility in pursuing opportunities. The sojourner's definition of success was to *return* wealthy to family and native place. The stay in Taiwan was intended, therefore, to be only temporary; indeed some, especially the Hakka, initially went to Taiwan as seasonal laborers and returned home in the off-season. Only gradually, as they realized the limits of their success and assessed their opportunities, did sojourners decide whether to make their stay permanent. Those who decided to relocate initiated chains of migration from their native places, recruiting close kinsmen and neighbors to join them in their pioneering enterprise and gradually bringing over wives and dependent parents and children. The initial movement to Taiwan was rarely intended to be a permanent relocation, therefore, and permanent residence usually grew out of a sojourning strategy.[16]

Second, the vanguard of the movement was overwhelmingly male. Most of the initial migrants were young men; most were unmarried. Because of Chinese families' strong preference for sons, coupled with female infanticide and daughter neglect, males commonly outnumbered females at marriageable ages throughout late imperial Chinese society. This already unbalanced sex ratio was made worse in Taiwan by the overwhelmingly male composition of arriving migrants. Only later were women, children, parents, and ancestral remains brought over to join male kin. Government restrictions on family migration, however ineffectively enforced (see Chapter 6), merely aggravated and did not singlehandedly create this preponderance of males. The many unattached males, with limited marriage prospects and fond of gambling and brawling, helped destabilize frontier society.[17]

Third, Han migrants to Taiwan exhibited great diversity in class and occupational backgrounds. Most migrants were, of course, poor agriculturalists, but many were not. Wealthy investors brought capital with which they acquired reclamation patents over large parcels and financed clearing and irrigation construction. Others set up mills and granaries and participated in the export trade in sugar and rice. Small shopkeepers, itinerant peddlers, and craftsmen serviced civil bureaucrats and the military, as well as the agricultural population. Fishermen, salt producers, food stall operators, yamen clerks, prostitutes, lumbermen, market gardeners, seasonal laborers, and medicine hawkers alike found opportunities to employ their skills on this highly commercialized frontier. Class and occupational differences did not emerge slowly from a purely agricultural economy within Taiwan; rather, they were brought from the southeast coast by migrants who then adapted their various resources and skills to local conditions.[18]

Fourth, the occupational differences just noted tended to align with differences in place of origin and location of settlement within Taiwan and thereby created subethnic enclaves. Most Hokkien migrants to Taiwan came from Ch'üan-chou and Chang-chou prefectures in Fukien, and most Hakka migrants came from the prefectures of northern Kwangtung (see Table 10.1 and Map 6.1). At least for parts of Taiwan, Ch'üan-chou settlers predominated along the coast, Chang-chou settlers on the inland plains, and Hakka settlers in hilly areas and along the foothills (see Map 10.1).[19] The conventional explanation for this pattern has been temporal priority of settlement: Ch'üan-chou settlers were the first to colonize Taiwan (Cheng Ch'eng-kung was from Ch'üan-chou) and hence settled on the coast; the Chang-chou settlers arriving in the next wave pushed inland, the late-arriving Hakka were relegated to the hilly regions. The three bands of ethnic settlement are assumed to reflect three successive waves of migration. We have long known that this explanation is at least partially false; in many localities Hakka were among the first settlers (not the last) and were later driven out during communal conflicts. In at least some cases, the three-band pattern of settlement reflects the outcome of communal strife rather than timing of settlement.[20]

Research by Shih T'ien-fu has contributed an important explanation for the three-band pattern of ethnically segregated settlement. Shih argues that the occupations of migrants in their native prefectures were

TABLE 10.1
Mainland Origins of Taiwanese, 1926

Place of origin		Percentage of population
Fukien province		
Ch'üan-chou prefecture		45
San-i counties[a]	18	
An-ch'i county	12	
T'ung-an county	15	
Chang-chou prefecture		35
Other prefectures		3
Kwangtung province		16
Ch'ao-chou prefecture	4	
Hui-chou prefecture	4	
Chia-ying *chou*	8	
Other provinces		1
TOTAL		100

SOURCE: Ch'en Cheng-hsiang 1959–61: 1.237; Ch'en Han-kuang 1972. Note that the 1926 survey reports only locale of ancestral origin, not dialect, and that complete identity between the two cannot be assumed. A small proportion of Hakka speakers migrated from Fukien prefectures and some Hokkien speakers migrated from Ch'ao-chou in Kwangtung. It remains true, nevertheless, that an overwhelming majority of Taiwanese Hakka hail from Kwangtung prefectures and that the majority of Kwangtung migrants were Hakka.

[a]The three counties of Chin-chiang, Nan-an, and Hui-an.

the key determinants of their choice of habitat on the Taiwan frontier. Ch'üan-chou had the least agricultural land, and its population, crowded onto a long, jagged coast, supplemented agriculture with handicraft production, trade, fishing, aquaculture, salt production, and overseas commerce. Thus, Ch'üan-chou migrants were attracted to the coastal cities and markets that organized Taiwan's commerce, where they could pursue trade and handicrafts, and to the coastlands, where they could pursue fishing, aquaculture, and salt production, as well as agriculture. Chang-chou prefecture has a broad arable plain and is much more agricultural than Ch'üan-chou; accordingly, Chang-chou's skilled farmers settled Taiwan's fertile inland plains.[21] The Hakka came from the poor interior highlands of the southeast coast, where they had become expert at clearing, terracing, and irrigating hillsides, and supplemented their meager incomes by exporting male laborers. Many Hakka came to Taiwan as early as migrants from Ch'üan-chou and Chang-chou, but as seasonal laborers they often lost any opportunity to become permanent tenants on the fields they helped clear. Hakka who stayed found their comparative advantage lay in exploiting the hills.[22]

Shih thus explains the three-band pattern of subethnic settlement as

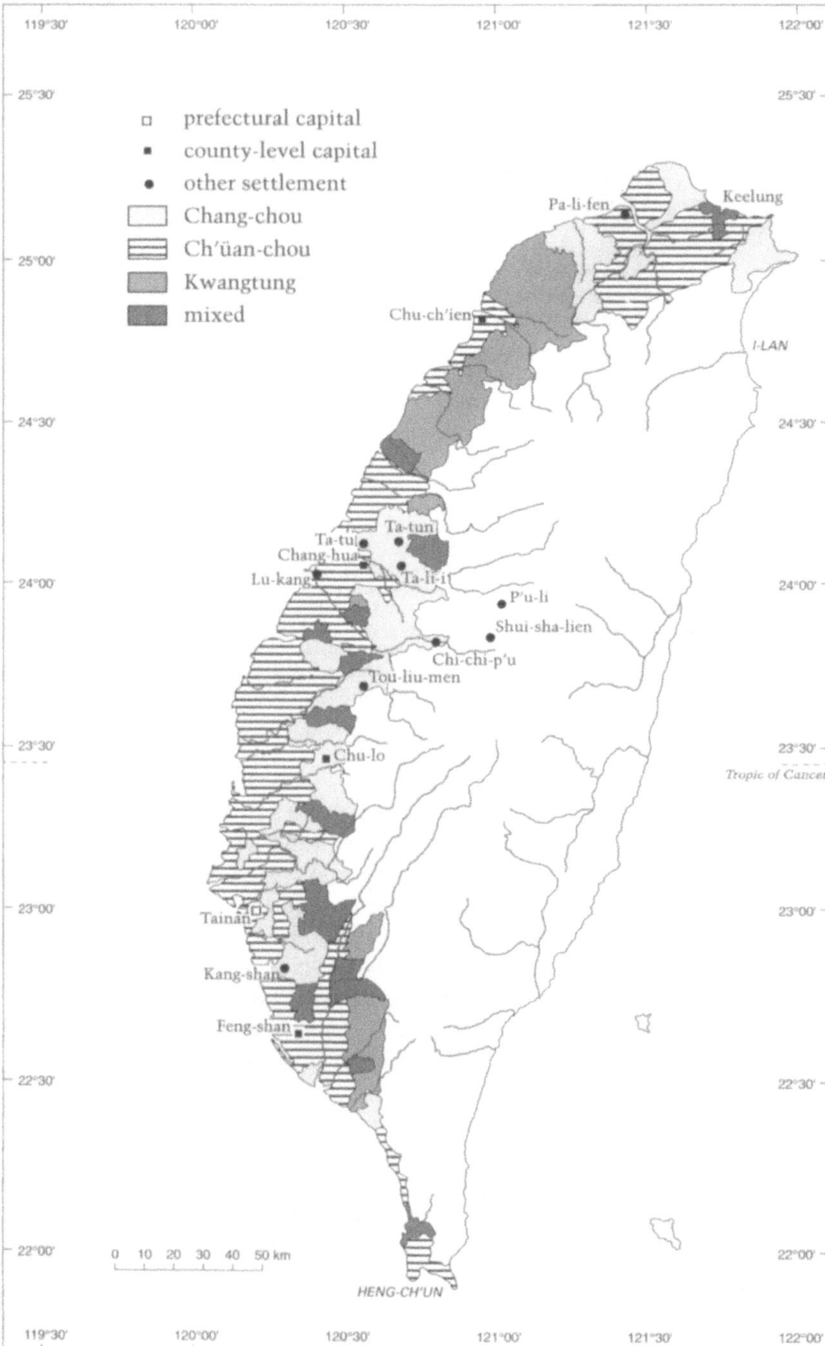

Map 10.1 Distribution of population by locale of origin, Taiwan, 1926
Based on Table 10.2.

TABLE 10.2
Segregation by Provenance Among 222 West Coast Districts, Taiwan, 1926

Percentage of district population	Provenance (number of districts)			Total	
	Ch'üan-chou	Chang-chou	Kwangtung	Number	Percent
90–99	33	20	23	76	34
80–89	20	11	4	35	16
70–79	19	7	4	30	14
60–69	18	17	3	38	17
50–59	11	9	3	23	10
<50[a]	—	—	—	20	9
TOTAL				222	100

SOURCE: Ch'en Han-kuang 1972. Included in the 222 districts are 217 townships and 5 cities.
[a]Of the 20 districts where no single origin group constituted 50 percent or more of the population, 12 had Chang-chou–Ch'üan-chou pluralities, 6 had Chang-chou–Kwangtung pluralities, 1 had a Ch'üan-chou–Kwangtung plurality, and 1 had a Chang-chou–aborigine plurality.

the product of migrants pursuing the modes of livelihood they brought with them from the southeast coast in the niches in Taiwan most suited to their specialties.[23] This pattern emerged before the intensification of communal strife in the late eighteenth century. Shih argues that subethnic conflict served only to reinforce the three-band pattern, not to create it. Occupationally specialized migration, targeted at foci of opportunity in Taiwan, thereby created the spatial segregation of subethnic groups on the frontier.[24] Table 10.2 illustrates the striking degree of spatial segregation by provenance. In 1926, in 50 percent of Taiwan's west coast districts 80 percent of the population originated from a single group; in 81 percent of the districts, solid majorities of 60 percent or more derived from a single group. Data from 1926 cannot, of course, shed light on which historical processes (e.g., selective migration and settlement, communal strife) generated the pattern, but they do document the high degree of spatial segregation by provenance these processes must explain.

Fifth, social ties reinforced, rather than crosscut, native-place ties and subethnicity. In Taiwan migrants tended to locate among and associate with other migrants from home—kin and fellow villagers. Chain migration reinforced this pattern. Fellow migrants formed associations such as brotherhoods and worship groups that rendered mutual aid and provided companionship and security.[25] These voluntary associations (some endowed with estates purchased through share subscriptions) remained important and even influenced how groups later organized on the basis of agnatic ties and common surname (*within* communities based on common native place). Corporate lineages, on the other hand, were not transplanted wholesale to Taiwan, rarely achieved more than shallow depth, and remained of minor significance.[26] Larger communities coalesced around temples dedicated to patron gods identified with the settlers' native place.[27] Social networks therefore followed primarily lines of common origin, and migrants relied on common provenance to identify which strangers could be trusted. Settlers were suspicious of neighbors who were immigrants from other locales, and misunderstandings were frequent between groups speaking different dialects and worshipping different patron deities. Social relations did form and could be quite cordial across the lines of common provenance and speech group, but the tendency was for such crosscutting ties to be more casual, superficial, and contextually specific.[28]

Sixth, the migrants brought with them traditions of violence and self-defense. The communities of China's southeast coast are famous for their feuding clans and lineages, and the turbulence of the dynastic interregnum on the coast in the seventeenth century no doubt reinforced local traditions of violence.[29] Migrants knew how to defend themselves if required and how to employ violence to obtain advantage. Combine this with large numbers of unattached males, fond of gambling and brawling, and the presence of criminals and vagrants, and it is not hard to explain the frequency of violence on the frontier.[30]

The outcome of these six characteristics was a society easily polarized into hostile subethnic blocks. Taiwan's frontier society was constructed along lines of common provenance, in groups that were often spatially segregated. Only weak ties linked groups not united by common provenance. Within each group the large number of unattached males with a high propensity for violence made the situation volatile.

Lamley notes that Taiwan entered a severe phase of subethnic strife in the late eighteenth century, a phase that lasted from 1782 to 1862.[31] He speculates that growing population and intensifying competition for land and other resources helped fuel this strife. Whether or not population pressure is the key (population also grew *after* 1862), increasing population and declining opportunities to reclaim new land seem at least to have led to frictions that sparked frequent outbreaks of communal strife, and they certainly contributed to the "magnitude" of the conflicts (see below). I would argue that equally important to the intensification of subethnic strife in the 1782–1862 period is the overall decline in the effectiveness of government social control and the militarization of the social structure taking place throughout China.[32] When the government and local leadership proved incapable of containing the outbreaks, they turned into epidemics.[33]

Proof of the importance of common provenance to immigrant social organization, legal and extralegal, and of the mutual suspicion between competing groups is the frequency of communal feuds in the eighteenth century.[34] The government often turned subethnic divisions among the settlers to its advantage. Loyalist militia recruited from the Hakka villages of Feng-shan were crucial to its victories over Chu I-kuei (a native of Chang-chou)[35] in 1721 and over the dual revolts of Wu Fu-sheng (also a Chang-chou native)[36] and the Ta-chia-hsi aborigines in 1731–32.[37] After the Chu I-kuei rebellion, the grateful commander, Lan T'ing-chen, requested that all restrictions on Hakka immigration be lifted (see Chapter 6). Hakka and Ch'üan-chou loyalists played important roles in the defeat of the Lin Shuang-wen rebellion, and an adjustment of immigration regulations (to prevent officials extorting bribes from Hakka seeking to visit their mainland homes) was again part of the Hakkas' reward.[38]

The government had to find means to manage and contain, as well as exploit, communal divisions, if social order was to be maintained. The appearance of official impartiality was important to winning the trust of competing groups. In 1771 Governor-general Ts'ui Ying-chieh initiated a discussion of how the "law of avoidance" should be applied to Taiwan. (The law of avoidance prohibited an official from holding office in his native province on the grounds that claims by his lineage and hometown loyalties would make impartial administration an impossibility. Thus, Fukien natives were barred from civil office in Taiwan.) Ts'ui argued that since "half" of Taiwan's villages were populated by settlers (largely Hakka) from Kwangtung province, officials from Kwangtung would be unduly lenient to their compatriots. "Even if they acted fairly, resentments would easily arise and lead to trouble, thus, their handling matters would create problems." Ts'ui proposed that all Kwangtung candidates be barred from civil office in Taiwan.

The Chin-men brigade general Kung Hsüan countered that in the fighting between Hakka and Fukienese of the previous year civil and military officials of both Kwangtung and Fukien were instrumental in gaining the trust of their respective compatriots to end the fighting (Fukien natives were not barred from serving in military posts in Taiwan): "If a disturbance breaks out between the two groups and only Fukienese military officers are sent out, Hakka villagers cannot but suspect them of prejudice, and the officers will be unable to gain their confidence." The government needed officials who could avoid any semblance of either prejudice against or favoritism toward subgroups of the populations under their jurisdiction. And yet a basic trust between officials and people and a reputation for impartiality were difficult to achieve in a volatile environment ridden by subethnic rivalry and suspicion. In the end a compromise was agreed on. Only candidates from the Kwangtung prefectures that sent large numbers of migrants to Taiwan (Hui-chou, Ch'ao-chou, and Chia-ying) would be barred; candidates from other Kwangtung areas could serve in Taiwan.[39]

Two years later, in 1773, the issue of avoidance was raised again, this time in regard to a high military post, when Lan Yüan-mei, a descendant of Lan T'ing-chen and a native of Chang-p'u county in Chang-chou, was named Taiwan brigade general.[40] To counter any objections, it was quickly pointed out that Huang Shih-chien, the current Fukien naval commander-in-chief, was also a Fukien native. That a military commander's provenance was made an issue at this time, since many previous officers had also been Fukien natives, reveals a heightened sensitivity to this problem. When a Taiwanese native had been appointed commander in Taiwan in 1752, mainland troops dissatisfied with his alleged favoritism toward the locals attempted to assassinate him.[41] As a precaution in Lan's case, the court ordered a report a few months after Lan took office to ensure that his performance was honest and impartial.[42] Huang's origins became an issue in the communal strife of 1782, but during the Lin Shuang-wen rebellion the imperial commanders saw Lan's provenance not as a liability but as a resource (see below).

In 1781 an unprecedented series of impeachments, both of officials serving in Taiwan and their superiors, began. In the eighth month of 1781, the Chu-lo county magistrate was impeached and removed from office for his failure to capture a local bandit chief. In the tenth month, the Feng-shan magistrate was impeached after important criminals being sent to the provincial capital managed to escape. These cases of malfeasance were cited as reason to investigate the diligence of a former provincial governor who had recently been transferred and promoted.[43] On the sixth day of the eleventh month, the subprefect for aborigine affairs on the north route was impeached for attempting to quash an aborigine's suit against a yamen runner for extortion. And for their failure to investigate the case, in part due to bribery, both the intendant and the prefect were also removed from office. On the twelfth day of the eleventh month, the governor-general called for the impeachment of the Tan-shui subprefect because of a raw aborigine attack that left 28 dead.[44] And in the twelfth month of 1781, after receiving from the Taiwan censors a superficial report that contradicted his other sources of information, the emperor had them impeached.

To the court the impeachment of eight high officials in four months necessitated a full investigation of what appeared to be a corrupt and extremely lax administration.[45] The Veritable Records report little of what such investigations revealed; nor were any new regulations adopted. But in the ninth month of the next year, Governor-general Ch'en Hui-tsu, who had memorialized for the impeachment of five of the six officials listed above, was himself removed from office.[46] Ch'en was charged with "conducting his office for personal gain with no consideration for the public welfare." He was later blamed for the sorry state of Taiwan's military preparedness revealed when a serious feud between natives of Chang-chou and Ch'üan-chou broke out the next month.[47] This accusation of corruption raises the question whether the impeachments Ch'en prosecuted the year before were motivated more by a desire for personal gain than by fervor for honest administration. Ch'en's case, pressed by the scheming courtier Ho-shen, ended in his being ordered to commit suicide.[48] This series of impeachments and the uncontained outbreak of communal strife in 1782 mark a low point in administrative effectiveness.

There are a number of indications that social order was breaking down in central Taiwan in the early months of 1782. Bandits were going unapprehended,[49] and in the third and fourth months local officials issued several decrees prohibiting criminal practices and banditry and admonishing the populace. Some of these were issued in response to requests from local notables. Four of these decrees were inscribed on stone plaques and placed in temples or market squares.[50] Also in the fourth month, the island was raked by a severe typhoon that destroyed housing and crops, further disrupting normal social life.[51]

Prelude to Rebellion, 1782–1786

In the eighth month of 1782, armed affrays broke out between Chang-chou and Ch'üan-chou settlers in Chang-hua county, and "rootless hooligans took advantage of the situation to rob and plunder." The fighting quickly spread southward to Chu-lo county and was serious enough to require the dispatch of troops from the mainland under the command of Huang Shih-chien.[52] Matters were reported under control by the end of the eleventh month, although several important instigators were still at large.[53] The feuding arose from a dispute between Chang-chou and Ch'üan-chou gamblers over gaming losses. The fighting quickly escalated because large numbers of people had gathered for a festival and opera performance.[54] Gambling dens attracted many underworld figures and were always suspected by Chinese officialdom of harboring outlaws. Investigations in the aftermath of the fighting revealed some evidence of secret society activity, in particular the Small Knives Society, among the Lins of Ta-li-i, a Chang-chou stronghold.[55] But once under way, the fighting was not limited to troublemakers. One leader of the Chang-chou faction was identified as a military *chü jen* from the Chang-chou stronghold of Tou-liu-men.[56] And a very wealthy and prominent Chu-lo landlord of Chang-chou extraction lent aid to the Chang-chou side, for which his entire estate was confiscated.[57]

One incident in particular during the 1782 feuding revealed the sensitivity of the government to the strength of the antagonism between settlers from different localities. It had been reported that Ch'üan-chou villagers, knowing a certain sub-lieutenant to be of Chang-chou origin, had waylaid and killed him. The emperor knew that Commander Huang Shih-chien[58] was also a Chang-chou native and feared that any suspicions by Ch'üan-chou settlers of prejudice on Huang's part would make his job of pacification even more difficult. The emperor ordered Huang to proclaim his Chang-chou origin and to investigate the Chang-chou villages first. "Only after apprehending troublemakers there should he seek to punish Ch'üan-chou lawbreakers. This will demonstrate his impartiality."[59]

Dissatisfaction with the tardy response to the feuding by local officials brought another round of impeachments, this time of the Taiwan prefect, the Taiwan brigade general, and six lesser officials.[60] Despite, or perhaps because of, the severe suppression campaign, two more incidents of feuding occurred the next year. These events convinced the emperor that, in spite of the stiff punishments administered the year before, Taiwan's population had become incorrigible, and years of lax rule could be corrected only with great effort.[61] The next month the Tan-shui subprefect and the north-route colonel were impeached and the Taiwan intendant demoted and transferred for their inept handling of a violent feud between Hakka and Hokkien settlers over the payment of border guard (*ai*) defense fees.[62] The governor-general ordered Taiwan's officials to exert themselves in investigating and responding to all such outbreaks. For their part in these disorders, 289 people were either executed or exiled to the far western reaches of China (over twenty of them Lins from Ta-li-i).[63]

In late 1783 Governor-general Furgun (Fu-le-yün) outlined a six-point plan for Taiwan's reconstruction after the feuding of the previous year.[64] Three of the points sought to enlist on the government's side local landlords and community leaders and to impose on them responsibility for social order and welfare. The remaining three points sought to prevent abuses by tightening discipline over low-level state agents.

1. During the strife the wealthy carried off their goods to secure areas, leaving their tenants behind to suffer the effects of the devastation caused by the feuding. Government officials were to encourage wealthy landlords to provide seed and other aid to their tenants and to request the expulsion of idle tenants to the mainland.

2. Local officials were to select village and lineage heads with care and hold them responsible for reporting troublemakers and preventing outbreaks of communal strife.[65]

3. Because landlords collected rents through bailiffs, they were out of touch with village affairs. Landlords and bailiffs were ordered to cooperate with village and lineage heads in investigating troublemakers among tenants and getting them deported if necessary. Landlords who failed to report such troublemakers were to be held responsible for any crimes these people perpetrated.[66]

4. Because many land contracts and deeds had been lost in the fighting, landowners and creditors were encouraged to apply for certificates proving ownership that could be verified and guaranteed.[67] The government was concerned to prevent runners and clerks from taking advantage of the situation and causing a great many title disputes.

5. Runners and soldiers who caused trouble under the guise of apprehending criminals were to be punished.

6. Lists of the criminals involved in the feuding and the punishments they received were to be published. The system of border guards along the aborigine boundary was to be reformed.[68]

In 1784 a resurvey of lands illegally opened beyond the raw aborigine boundary was conducted.[69] The events of the following years, however, undermined and overwhelmed these and other attempts to achieve order.

The unending disturbances and, we may suspect, dismay over the constant impeachment and removal of officials prompted the government to change its personnel policies as part of its effort to re-establish order in Taiwan. In late 1783 the terms of office of the Taiwan brigade general, intendant, and prefect were lengthened from three to five years. In addition, their tenure was staggered, so that experienced officials familiar with the local situation would always be in office.[70] In the meantime, the newly appointed intendant was impeached for misconduct in his previous office before he could assume his duties in Taiwan.[71] The previous intendant (who had been demoted) was ordered to stay on and help out during the transition. Leadership at higher levels was no more stable. In 1786 the Governor-general Ya-te was removed from office in connection with the impeachment case of his predecessor, Furgun, who was initially accused of allowing his retainers to abuse their positions and extort large sums of money. Ya-te, who had served as Fukien governor under Furgun, was soon implicated in one of Furgun's irregular financial transactions. Ya-te attempted to impeach a military officer for lax leadership "as a way of redeeming himself." The officer turned out to be highly regarded by the provincial commander, and the government proceeded to impeach Ya-te instead. He was later accused of extorting a huge sum from salt merchants under his jurisdiction.[72]

From 1781 to 1786, an unprecedented number of officials from county magistrates to governors and governors-general had their careers destroyed or at least damaged as a result of serving in Fukien and Taiwan. Rampant corruption and recurrent local disturbances (one feeding on the other) did them in. Although many of these officials were undoubtedly corrupt, cowardly, or incompetent, their replacements were rarely any better and were themselves frequently impeached. Repeated use of impeachment may well have aggravated the administrative malaise by making effective supervision of subordinates impossible and creating further opportunities for corruption. Fear of impeachment may also have encouraged local officials to cover up and minimize local sore spots rather than risk the use of stern measures, which would certainly draw the attention of superiors and perhaps stir up more trouble. No structural reforms (besides the lengthening of terms of office, which impeachments made a dead letter) were instituted to correct the abuses; nor did any vigorous reformers appear.

The recurrent impeachments were not, however, unique to Taiwan. They were certainly related to the corrupting influence of Ho-shen, who had gained the emperor's unquestioning favor and was at this time making his influence felt throughout the empire. In these years the entire bureaucracy was "rocked by case after case of official malfeasance. Vast sums were embezzled by officials under constant pressure to secure themselves by gifts and bribes to Ho-shen."[73] Ho-shen's use of his control over promotions and demotions to accumulate a fortune created a chain of extortion that reached from the capital to the countryside. He and his associates used impeachment and military campaigns to expand their power and their fortunes. When the Lin rebellion revealed the degeneration of Taiwan's military garrisons as well as its civil administration, blame would be heaped on the long series of impeached officials and their successors responsible for Taiwan's affairs.[74] Even more corruption was uncovered during and after the rebellion.[75]

During 1784 and 1785 no major incidents of strife between Chang-chou and Ch'üan-chou settlers are recorded. In 1786 wild aborigines surprised and killed the Tan-shui subprefect and more than ten aides, who were on their way to conduct an investigation in Miao-li. There was some fear at the time that discontented Chinese may have instigated the murders, but no evidence was turned up. The Tan-shui subprefecture gazetteer reports a dispute between the settlers and the aborigines at the time.[76] The local subdistrict magistrate and captain were impeached for their failure to maintain a vigilant defense on the aborigine boundary, and the border guardposts were reorganized. To avenge the murders, a campaign guided by civilized aborigines was carried into the mountains to punish the raw aborigines.[77]

But these were years of peace only on the surface and were in hindsight merely a prelude to the Lin rebellion. In 1783, while investigations of the previous year's feuding were being held and punishments meted out, one Yen Yen, "in the guise of a cloth seller," crossed to Taiwan "preaching" the message of the Heaven and Earth Society. In an environment fractured by subethnic antagonism, Yen Yen found ready recruits among his compatriots from Chang-chou, and a network of society members quickly extended from Tan-shui to Feng-shan.[78] United by common provenance, men from all walks of life were attracted to the secret society. Landowners and men of great wealth, along with disaffected former army officers, gamblers, and vagabonds, joined.[79] The Lins of the Chang-chou stronghold at Ta-li-i readily enlisted. In the seventh month of 1786, the society was forced into the open by an incident in Chu-lo county.

When Chu-lo officials got wind of the society, they arrested several adherents. The succeeding investigation led to the arrest of the wealthy Yang Wen-lin. Yang's two sons (one was adopted), both of whom held purchased degrees,[80] were engaged in a bitter property dispute. The adopted son found allies in the Increase Younger Brothers/Heaven and Earth Society, and the other organized a society of his own, the Lei Kung Society.[81] The adopted son's son, who had been arrested with Yang Wen-lin, bribed his jailer and escaped. He proceeded to gather together a band of fellow society members to attack a government force that had detained a comrade at Tou-liu-men. In the process they killed the sublieutenant instrumental in the arrests. At this point government forces were mobilized, and they apprehended many of those involved. The officials in charge now sought to minimize the gravity of the situation, and their reports attributed all the trouble to the dispute between the two brothers of the Yang family. It was later alleged that the cover-up invented a spurious name for the Heaven and Earth Society, the "Increase Younger Brothers" society (in Chinese both names are read "*t'ien ti*").[82] When eighteen prisoners were beheaded, a provincial judge was sent to investigate, but he did nothing. By this time many society members had fled to Ta-li-i to take refuge with Lin Shuang-wen. Yamen runners in Chang-hua were now pressing the investigation, or at least extorting bribes from suspected society members, and threats of military action were made. These events pushed Lin's group into open rebellion in the eleventh month of 1786. When the Taiwan commander failed to respond, the revolt quickly grew. Society members persuaded large numbers to join them by warning villagers that government troops in search of rebels would spare no one. The fighting spread rapidly, and society chapters in the north and south joined in the revolt. Soon all of Taiwan was embroiled.[83]

That the rebels were nearly all Chang-chou men was immediately apparent both to the government and to other settler groups. The government wasted no time in dispatching Ch'üan-chou and Hakka degree holders to recruit loyalist braves among their compatriots. Before long Taiwan was once again divided into subethnic camps, feuding on a scale much larger than that of 1782.[84] The subethnic nature of the strife shaped the Ch'ing government's strategy of suppression and its plans for reconstruction and determined the role played by the aborigines, both raw and cooked.

The Role of Aborigines in the Lin Shuang-wen Campaigns

A detailed history of the Lin Shuang-wen revolt and its suppression lies beyond the scope of this study. The focus here is on particular imperial policies and local responses that reveal an awareness of the depths of communal antagonism and the role that aborigines might play to keep them in check.

For background, a brief chronology of the rebellion and campaign of suppression is in order.[85] Lin Shuang-wen and his Heaven and Earth Society comrades went into open rebellion in the eleventh month (December 1786). After a successful attack on government troops at nearby Ta-tun (present-day Taichung), the rebels quickly overran the county capital of Chang-hua on the twenty-eighth (16 January 1787). After an unsuccessful thrust at the key port city (and Ch'üan-chou stronghold) of Lu-kang, Lin's forces marched south, taking Tou-liu-men and the county capital of Chu-lo by the end of the first week of the twelfth month. Concurrent society-led uprisings in Tan-shui subprefecture were initially successful, but were then thwarted by loyalist Hakka and Ch'üan-chou forces, who kept the port of Tan-shui in government hands. More successful was the uprising in the south led by society member Chuang Ta-t'ien, who captured the county capital of Feng-shan by the end of the second week of the twelfth month. Lin's forces parried attacks by Brigade General Ch'ai Ta-chi's army based in the prefectural capital at Tainan, and on the twenty-fourth linked up with Chuang Ta-t'ien.

At the end of the month, the two leaders launched a joint attack on Tainan, but met stiff government resistance bolstered by loyalist militia. On hearing that the attack on Tan-shui had failed, that Chang-hua was retaken, and that Commander Huang Shih-chien would soon arrive from Fukien at the head of a force of Green Standard troops, the rebels abandoned the assault on Tainan. Lin withdrew to the north, and Chuang to the south. With the key ports of Lu-kang and Tan-shui and the prefectural capital still in the hands of a government aided by significant loyalist forces, it was now clear that Ch'ing rule would not collapse as it had during the Chu I-kuei rebellion in 1721. But as events were soon to prove, neither would rebel forces disperse in a matter of weeks. The rebellion would drag out for another year, require the dispatch of nearly 50,000 mainland troops, and cost eight million taels to suppress.[86]

Huang Shih-chien and his reinforcements arrived in Tainan the first week of the first month in 1787. Troops sent against Chuang Ta-t'ien in the south and Lin in the north made slow progress, and the cities of Feng-shan and Chu-lo were not retaken until late in the second month. (Feng-shan fell into rebel hands again the next month.) Dissatisfied with the pace of the suppression, the Ch'ien-lung emperor put Governor-general Ch'ang Ch'ing in charge of the campaign. Ch'ang Ch'ing arrived in Tainan on the ninth day of the third month. A plan to attack rebel strongholds simultaneously from Lu-kang and Chu-lo was formulated but never successfully prosecuted. Lin's forces in the north and Chuang's forces in the south engaged the Ch'ing armies in numerous skirmishes and remained strong and mobile. Government forces repulsed a joint attack on Tainan on the twenty-fifth day of the fourth month and a separate attack on Lu-kang on the fifth day of the sixth month. On the twentieth of the sixth month, Lin attacked Chu-lo, trapping Brigade Commander Ch'ai Ta-chi and the populace inside for five months. During this period the stalemate allowed Lin to consolidate his strongholds along an axis stretching from Chu-lo north through Tou-liu-men to Ta-li-i, an area of solid Chang-chou settlement (see Map 10.1).

Ch'ang Ch'ing's failure to conclude the war frustrated the emperor. On the second day of the eighth month, he gave an imperial commission to the governor-general of Shensi and Kansu, Fu-k'ang-an, and put him in charge of the campaign. Fu-k'ang-an assembled a force of veteran troops from Hupei, Hunan, and Kweichow and aborigine military colonists from Szechwan, all of whom were experienced in mountain fighting. After a delayed crossing, Fu-k'ang-an landed in Lu-kang on the second day of the eleventh month. This army lifted the siege of Chu-lo on the eighth and retook Tou-liu-men on the twenty-first. A fierce battle at Ta-li-i followed on the twenty-fourth; aided by the use of cannon, the army destroyed much of Lin's forces. The Lin remnants fled to Chi-chi-p'u, far upstream on the Cho-shui river and neighboring raw aborigine territory. The Ch'ing army pursued the rebels and defeated them at Chi-chi-p'u. Lin Shuang-wen then fled with the remainder of his forces into the mountains, where they fell easy prey to aborigine headhunters and pursuing troops. Lin surrendered early in 1788. Fu-k'ang-an's army then went south to mop up Chuang Ta-t'ien's forces; Chuang surrendered a month later after being pursued to the Heng-ch'un area.

As early as the first month of 1787, the government had formulated a rather full analysis of the potential dangers of rebels taking refuge among the wild aborigines of the mountainous areas.

> After [Commander] Huang Shih-chien arrived in Taiwan, his cannon killed over 2,000 rebels; the survivors scattered and fled into the mountains. The mountains are the haven of the raw aborigines, who kill any Han who happen to enter. Government troops are now on the offensive and pursuing the rebels, who know that once the soldiers capture them they will have no future. So they either bribe the raw aborigines with their plunder to let them go into hiding, or they rely on force of numbers to intimidate the raw aborigines, who respect their threats and let them take refuge. We fear that when the troops withdraw, the rebels will incite surprise attacks by the raw aborigines. This requires special consideration. We must make arrangements in advance to wipe out this seed of rebellion. The land and naval commanders-in-chief are presently leading large numbers of troops to destroy the rebels in Taiwan; we must take advantage of this military strength to completely exterminate them. We cannot allow the rebels to take refuge in the mountains. . . . [The troops must] clear them out and extirpate them root and branch. But we cannot allow the pursuit of the rebels to antagonize the raw aborigines. . . . We hear that formerly when Yang Ching-su was

> intendant [1758–61], he established an earth-oxen boundary marking off the interior. Has it been managed satisfactorily?[87]

A few weeks later a report that the rebels were seeking to stir up the raw aborigines prompted a bullish government response: "Our military force is now at its greatest strength; it would not be difficult to wipe out the raw aborigines who are in league with the rebels. Last year trouble-making aborigines killed [Tan-shui] Subprefect P'an; if we could take advantage of our present troop strength to clear them out, we could transform the mountains into a civilized aborigine area."[88] A captured rebel revealed that Lin Shuang-wen, in league with an aborigine interpreter, Tu Mei, was befriending raw aborigines and preparing a possible refuge in the mountains. Apprehending Tu Mei thereby became a high priority.[89] But nothing so drastic as large-scale campaigns in treacherous mountain territory against a combination of rebels and raw aborigines was ever required. Instead, ways were found to procure the cooperation of the raw aborigines against the rebels. Interpreters were dispatched to inform raw aborigine chiefs to guard against fleeing rebels and to offer them big rewards for cooperating.[90] Under the supervision of the subprefect for aborigine affairs, interpreters were ordered to enlist civilized aborigines familiar with the mountain trails to lead them to raw aborigine villages.[91] Plains aborigine villages along the raw aborigine boundary were also warned to be on their guard. Reports soon followed that the raw aborigines had no use for silver money but cared only for gifts and cloth. Other reports record that silver medallions, along with tobacco, tea, and salt were highly prized.[92]

But the Ch'ing strategy did not rely on material inducements alone: "The raw aborigines' nature is like that of wild animals. One cannot reason with them, but they will respond according to profit and loss. . . . Let them know that if thousands of rebels hide in their territory, they will encroach on their lands and steal their game. . . . But if the raw aborigines capture the rebels and hand them over, we will reward them with gifts and cloth, and they will thus avoid destruction at the hands of the rebels."[93] Wanton killing of raw aborigines by the rebels helped convince the tribes of the validity of the government's warning.[94] Raw aborigine cooperation was no doubt prompted by a desire to keep out pursuing government troops as much as fleeing rebels. In the end, no major raw aborigine attacks were incited, and no clashes with government troops occurred. Certain raw aborigine villages were instrumental in rounding up the last remnants of the rebel leadership.[95] Two of these villages, Shih-tzu and Wu-ao, had come under suspicion for an attack on Han settlers back in 1766.[96] In 1788, with the conclusion of the pacification campaign, many of these villages submitted to Ch'ing authority, and their chiefs were granted an imperial audience and banqueted in Peking in an attempt to awe and impress them with the power of civilization.[97]

These episodes show that the government valued the civilized aborigine groups for their knowledge of the mountain tribes and their ability to carry the government's message to the raw aborigines. The plains aborigines also took part in the fighting against the rebels. In the very first days of the revolt, government officials had mobilized civilized aborigine braves along with Han loyalists to help defend Chang-hua city.[98] The Tan-shui magistrate's first news of the revolt and the fall of Chang-hua came in a letter carried by an aborigine runner (of the Ta-tu *she*) from the interpreter of the Ta-chia *she*.[99] The foothill area between the Ta-tu and Ta-chia rivers (just north of Chang-hua city) was dominated by Chang-chou settlers, most of whom joined in (or were forced to lend aid to) the revolt.[100] Ta-tu *she*, however, remained loyal to the Ch'ing, and its leaders were duly rewarded. Ta-chia and Niu-ma *she* of this same area also fought against the rebels.[101] Allegiances had changed greatly in the 50-odd years since 1731 when the plains aborigine villages of this area revolted against the government. In one sense, both revolts pitted the plains aborigines of this particular region against their Han neighbors. But anti-Han antagonism did not lead plains aborigines to join the rebels when their neighbors were Ch'üan-chou or Hakka. Instead, the aborigines cooperated with local Han loyalists.[102] The overwhelming loyalty (from whatever motive) of the plains aborigines and the speed of its manifestation throughout the island stand out.

Many reports testify to the military aid rendered by the plains aborigines. One hundred aborigines, led by their interpreter, served as archers in an attack against a rebel stronghold in southern Feng-shan in the second month of 1787.[103] An-li *she* figures prominently in the reports due both to the size of its population (over 3,000) and to its strategic location near the main rebel stronghold. An-li earned the gratitude of the government for refusing to join the rebels, who actively sought to enlist its support. An-li's leaders were also among those active in carrying the government's warning to the raw aborigine tribes.[104] This was especially important in the nearby Shui-sha-lien (Sun Moon Lake) area, where large numbers of rebels and Chang-chou refugees had fled.[105] An-li's leadership ranks included at least two holders of *kung sheng* degrees.[106] Their loyalty demonstrated the success of the government's education policies. Both were graduates of the schools the government had set up in aborigine villages, including An-li, in 1734 following the Ta-chia-hsi revolt.[107] In the sixth month of 1787, the imperial commanders planned to use An-li braves as part of a force to attack the rebel stronghold at Ta-li-i from the north, while government troops pressed in from the south.[108] For this purpose the Tan-shui subprefect organized a combined force of Han loyalists and civilized aborigine braves recruited from his district.[109] Late in the campaign, the civilized aborigines of the Pei-t'ou area (present-day Nan-t'ou county) helped lead government forces into the P'u-li area where Lin Shuang-wen had fled.[110] Further to the south, a Chu-lo licentiate familiar with aborigine matters had success in gaining the cooperation of the civilized Nei-yu tribes in the Ta-wu-lung area (eastern T'ai-wan county).[111] In Feng-shan the civilized Chia-t'eng *she* and the "submitted raw" tribe of K'uei-lei were cited for rendering valuable assistance.[112]

Government Policies to Contain Communal Strife

The government's considerable success in gaining the cooperation of the aborigines, both civilized and raw, seems even greater when contrasted with its frequent difficulties in controlling Taiwan's feuding, unruly, and rebellious Chinese inhabitants. The government had to take many precautions to prevent subethnic tensions from subverting the loyalty and discipline of both the Taiwanese loyalist forces and its own troops from the mainland.

Government suspicion of Chang-chou people was not limited to Taiwan. When the first rebels were captured in 1787, questioning revealed that they had close family members still living in Chang-chou. Regular procedure and collective responsibility required a thorough investigation and apprehension of the rebels' mainland relatives. However, such investigations were ordered indefinitely postponed to avoid alarming the people of Chang-chou.[113] At the outbreak of the rebellion, Fukien garrisons had been quickly dispatched to Taiwan, "but the 4,000-strong Chang-chou garrison had not been sent because Lin Shuang-wen and his party were predominantly Chang-chou men."[114] Later, when reinforcements were badly needed, it was decided to select 2,000 married Chang-chou soldiers and put them under the command of Lan Yüan-mei, also of Chang-chou. The government thought only a compatriot could command the Chang-chou troops effectively. Married soldiers, leaving their families behind, were deemed more likely to remain loyal.[115] Later in the campaign, the government needed recruits, and the two prefectures of Chang-chou and Ch'üan-chou, closest to Taiwan, were obvious sources. But the governor-general demurred.

> Investigation has revealed that Chang-chou men cannot be trusted. Chang-chou and Ch'üan-chou have long been separate communities. The rebels Lin Shuang-wen and Chuang Ta-t'ien are both Chang-chou men, and in Taiwan most of the Chang-chou settlers have been seduced by the rebels, whereas all those resisting the rebels are from Ch'üan-chou. On the mainland news travels well; when Ch'üan-chou people hear that soldiers are being recruited to kill Chang-chou people, they are enthusiastic; if we

> recruited Chang-chou men for the campaign, we would not get much out of them. Moreover, if Chang-chou men were recruited, we could not guarantee that [secret] society bandits would not be among them.[116]

In the end it was decided to recruit fewer soldiers from Chang-chou and more from Ch'üan-chou and other areas. Two months later Chang-chou troops dispatched to Taiwan were ordered dispersed among all battalions and regiments, where tight discipline and security were to be maintained.[117] These policies suggest that rivalry and even communal hostility between these prefectures may have existed in Fukien before their emigrants came into contact in Taiwan; certainly sojourners carried subethnic prejudices and hostility acquired in Taiwan back to their home communities.

At times the suppression campaign sparked uncontrolled vendettas, as the following report from the Taipei area reveals:

> The refugees are overwhelmingly from Chang-chou. The Ch'üan-chou and Hakka settlers attacked them indiscriminately, because they were compatriots of the rebels, and forced them to flee to Pai-shih-hu. . . . Now they are being resettled, and the local officials have warned the Ch'üan-chou and Hakka people that they are not to attack them again.[118]

Even among the loyalist forces precautions had to be taken.

> Investigate the loyalist militia; whether they come from Chang-chou, Ch'üan-chou, or eastern Kwangtung, they stand apart from each other and are mutually suspicious. Even the Chin-chiang and T'ung-an people, who both come from Ch'üan-chou, cannot get along. . . . Each village of people hailing from the same locality has been ordered to guard its own frontiers against the rebels. Thus, the loyalists are not congregated all in one place, and trouble is avoided.[119]

Careful investigations also had to be made to guarantee that rebels did not infiltrate the loyalist forces. For while the rebels were predominantly Chang-chou people, there were also Hakka and Ch'üan-chou men among them.[120] The rebel Chuang Hsi-she and his band, for instance, hailed from Ch'üan-chou, but their early defection to the government illustrates the general inability to create mutual trust between subethnic groups on either side of the law.[121] Thus, subethnic diversity did not necessarily strengthen the rebel movement. Neither did all Chang-chou settlers join the rebel cause. Chang-chou degree holders and others helped the government convince Chang-chou villagers to remain peacefully in their homes; a few even recruited and led Chang-chou loyalist forces.[122] The T'ung-an community in particular seems to have been split by the revolt. Although T'ung-an county is in Ch'üan-chou prefecture, its dialect is nearer that of Chang-chou, with which it shares a common border. We noted above the enmity between T'ung-an and other Ch'üan-chou loyalists. Both leading rebels and degree-holding loyalist leaders were drawn from the T'ung-an settlers.[123]

The disastrous rebellion caused the court to examine its policies concerning Taiwan and evaluate their utility in post-rebellion reconstruction. In mid-1787 the emperor turned for guidance to the writings of Lan Ting-yüan. In Lan's account of the suppression of the Chu I-kuei rebellion, *P'ing T'ai chi lüeh*, the emperor found hints on military strategy and, from the swift success of that campaign, an exacting standard for measuring his own commanders.[124] But the emperor seemed most impressed by Lan's collection of essays, *Tung cheng chi*, which he recommended to his governor-general and field commander. Lan's advocacy of an increased civil and military presence on the frontier seemed particularly sound in light of the present rebellion. Lan had questioned the utility of limiting Han cultivation by setting up an aborigine boundary and lamented the withdrawal of such land from production and the inevitable encroachment and boundary disputes that would result. His advice seemed wise, given the results observed since Yang Ching-su had supported redrawing the raw aborigine boundary in 1760.[125] Yang Ching-su, who served as Taiwan intendant in 1758–61 and as governor-general from 1778, was among those officials later blamed for maladministration in the years before the Lin rebellion.[126]

The court frequently directed letters to its officials in the field proposing bold, simplistic solutions it thought would yield permanent reform. Time and again, we find Fu-k'ang-an formulating replies that first explain the many conditions that make such single-stroke solutions unfeasible and then proposing more moderate alternatives. In the tenth month of 1787, for example, the emperor reviewed the history of restrictions on immigration to Taiwan. At their strictest these had limited migration to unaccompanied men. The emperor exclaimed that if the wives and families of Lin Shuang-wen and other rebel leaders had been required to stay on the mainland (within the reach of the law), "they would have to think twice and would not dare to revolt." He then ordered Governor-general Li Shih-yao and Fu-k'ang-an to investigate and make recommendations on immigration policy.[127] Fu-k'ang-an pointed out that the time had long since passed when the prohibition on immigration of families made sense: "In every village I visit, the settlers have families, and among the refugees women and children are especially numerous. These people have already lived in Taiwan for several generations; they could not be ordered back to the mainland. If the prohibition were reinstituted now, single men arriving in Taiwan could still [find wives and] establish families here; so, no matter how strictly enforced, it would be a prohibition in name only."[128] Moreover, Fu-k'ang-an realized, as had Lan Ting-yüan and others before him, that those without families and property were the most likely to be vagrants and troublemakers. It was natural that settlers should want their relatives to join them; attempts to prohibit this would merely lead to evasion of the law. The only effective policy for the government would be to require licenses of immigrants and then enter them in the local *pao chia* registers. This would weed out any troublemakers.[129] Nevertheless, over the next few years several incidents testify that, as they had in the past, many migrants continued to prefer the risk of "secret crossings" to the extortions of license-issuing yamen underlings.[130]

Disgust with unending communal strife led the court to seek long-term solutions. Relocating settlers into spatially segregated subethnic territories seemed like a promising way to end subethnic friction. An edict of the tenth month of 1787 reads:

> Scoundrels are constantly forming bands and feuding in Taiwan. This is due to Chang-chou, Ch'üan-chou, and Kwangtung people living there, to the traditional ill-will between Chang-chou and Ch'üan-chou, and their common hostility to the Kwangtung people. Their settlements and lands are interspersed, and they are constantly quarreling and taking up arms in feud. Local officials do not fully investigate but only wish to make the best of it and close the cases. Thus, the scoundrels have no respect for them, and trouble arises. Now Lin Shuang-wen leads riots, breaks the law, plunders yamen, kills officials, forms bands, organizes a society, and rises in revolt. Fu-k'ang-an is leading a large force, and by inspiring the braves to attack and destroy the rebels, he will be able to subdue them before long and finish the matter.
>
> But what of the rabble in this place whose evil ways have already persisted so long? If in the future the troops are withdrawn, then unavoidably old ways will re-emerge, and managing them will not be easy. This time we must deal severely; we cannot but deliberate carefully, manage it properly, and in one great effort gain lasting ease.
>
> We think that the Hakka, Chang-chou, and Ch'üan-chou [settlers] will always be quarreling among themselves. It would be best if we could order them separated into distinct areas, so that one group has no involvement with the other. But they have lived in their present areas many years and have property there; to order them suddenly to leave would be very difficult. When the rebel bandits have been suppressed, Fu-k'ang-an must gauge the situation and devise ways to handle it properly.
>
> Consider the case of the righteous Hakka braves of Shan-chu-mao [in Feng-shan county] who have already received official plaques celebrating their loyalty and are most courageous in their zeal for the public good. Naturally, they should be left to live peacefully as before, as should loyalists of other areas who follow the armies into battle against the rebels and put forth great efforts. How could we order them relocated and cause them to lose their ancestral property?
>
> If rebel villages and properties are, in accordance with precedent, confiscated, law-abiding people from other areas will be recruited to live there. What about people from the neighboring villages? Although there is no clear

proof that they followed the rebels, yet they lived together with them in the same district; those whose hearts are divided cannot be trusted. We could take advantage of our military forces to order the inhabitants of such villages moved away. Separate those whose native place is Kwangtung, Chang-chou, and Ch'üan-chou, and order them to form distinct villages distant from each other to prevent disputes. . . .

Many of Taiwan's villages, north and south, have been burned or destroyed by the rebels, and the inhabitants killed. The land and homes left by the rebel leaders and the masses forced to follow them cannot be conveniently redistributed to Chang-chou and Ch'üan-chou people. We cannot allow them to profit from the labor of others. Moreover, we fear that rootless vagrants might congregate in the devastated areas and cause trouble; so naturally we must take such properties, confiscate them, and dispose of them in another way.

We note that the "cooked" aborigines of the area long ago became civilized. When the rebels caused trouble, the civilized aborigines not only did not follow them, but in Tan-shui and other areas many aborigine braves enlisted. We cannot do better than to take this confiscated property, on the model of the Szechwan *t'un lien* [military agricultural colonies], and give it to the civilized aborigines to cultivate, pay taxes on, settle down on, and defend. By doing this, we can demonstrate that peace has been restored, and we may even pacify raw aborigines and thereby accomplish two things with one stroke.[131]

The court saw in the creation of separate districts for Taiwan's feuding subethnic groups an effective (and time-honored) means of preventing future strife.[132] The court recognized that the forced relocation of settlers was fraught with danger (recall Lan Ting-yüan's warnings about such schemes in regard to aborigine boundary policy). But the existence of large areas of devastated and confiscated property was an opportunity to further the goal of ethnic peace through ethnic segregation. Where Han were allowed to resettle, they were to be segregated by subethnic affiliation. But another possibility also intrigued the court. The support rendered by a non-Han ethnic group had impressed it: civilized aborigines in military colonies would make loyal settlers. How Fu-k'ang-an, who was charged with planning for post-rebellion reconstruction, modified the court's plans is the subject of the following section.

Fu-k'ang-an's Plan for Aborigine Military Colonies

In the context of worsening Han subethnic strife, the court began to see the possibility of an expanded role for the plains aborigines. As one more ethnic group it could play off against the others, plains aborigines could facilitate the court's strategy of divide and rule. From the beginning, the Ch'ing had used plains aborigine braves, primarily against other tribes and raw aborigines but also against Han rebels. Later, civilized aborigines were enlisted to guard the raw aborigine boundaries. Now, as military colonists, their role could expand to aid the government in preventing the escalation of Han subethnic feuds into rebellions.

The large-scale redistribution of confiscated rebel land to civilized aborigines envisaged by the edict of 1787, however, never took place. Instead, aborigine military colonies were founded along the raw aborigine boundary, continuing the policy of using plains aborigines as border guards. A number of factors led to this modified result. Early in 1788 Fu-k'ang-an argued against any large-scale relocation of the population, including any plan of retribution against settlers who had followed the rebels.

> The villages are constituted of people of common provenance only, but because these villages are interspersed and their fields border one another, there are often disputes. If we could relocate the Chang-chou, Ch'üan-chou, and Hakka villages, clarify their borders and keep them separate, we could prevent these quarrels. But the north and south routes are vast. Surveying the land to exchange houses and fields fairly when the houses vary in size and the fields vary in fertility would be very difficult. And the surveyors put in charge could not but rely on the help of [corrupt] yamen clerks, which would hardly be satisfactory; [in that case] we could expect trouble. Distinguishing loyalists who are to remain on their ancestral lands from those who lived in the same villages as the rebels and are to be resettled will be difficult. . . . There were both Chang-chou loyalists and Ch'üan-chou and Hakka rebels. Besides a few villages that solidly opposed the rebels from the start, there are villages where even families split over which side to support. When Chu-lo was under siege, there were those among the rebels that secretly sold grain to relieve the inhabitants, and loyalists captured by rebels have gone over to them. . . . Those who have surrendered are glad to get a second chance; they return to their villages and lead contented lives.[133]

Fu-k'ang-an strengthens his argument that relocation is not feasible by denying that the line between loyalists and rebels can be clearly drawn. His first priority is to resettle refugees, regardless of past loyalty, and return land to production to prevent grain shortages and further outbreaks.[134] Relocating ethnic groups in a society already so unsettled would add tremendously to the problem of maintaining order. Communal strife could be prevented in the future only by officials who were honest and vigilant. Fu-k'ang-an advised reducing the amount of land to be confiscated and proposed different purposes for its use. One was to allot the income from such land to the regular army.[135]

In the meantime, however, proposals were being shaped for the founding of aborigine military colonies. In the third month of 1788, Fu-k'ang-an was ordered to investigate the feasibility of organizing a civilized aborigine detachment, on the model of the Szechwan *t'un lien* or the Hupei Miao.[136] The Szechwan *t'un lien* system was no vague abstraction to Fu-k'ang-an or his superiors. A-kuei, who advised the emperor on the Taiwan campaign, had been Fu-k'ang-an's commander in the fighting against the rebel tribes of Chin-ch'uan in western Szechwan. When this campaign was brought to a successful close in 1776, plans for reconstruction included the reform and extension of the local *t'u t'un* system.[137] Submitting aborigines were enrolled in a military detachment and given allotments of land. Under the supervision of an independent subprefect, they were to play the dual role of soldier-farmers.[138] The founding of military colonies among aborigines was one means by which the Ch'ing sought to break the power of rebellious aborigine chiefs and can be seen as a step toward incorporation of aborigine areas into the regular field administration.[139]

In 1784 both A-kuei and Fu-k'ang-an were sent to Kansu in northwest China to crush a Moslem rebellion.[140] A corps of Szechwan aborigine military colonists served with distinction under their command. When Fu-k'ang-an was chosen to lead mainland forces against the rebellion in Taiwan in 1787, it was a matter of course that 2,000 of the same Szechwan aborigine military colonists were selected to join the expedition.[141] Their performance in the Taiwan campaigns brought them further praise.[142]

Thus, from the point of view of both aborigine frontier control and military recruitment, the Szechwan *t'un lien* constituted a highly successful model for the Ch'ing court. But there was an obvious difference between Taiwan and Szechwan. The Szechwan military colonies were established as a means of settling recently pacified rebellious aborigines. In Taiwan, plains aborigines had long been incorporated in the regular system of administration and had supplied loyal troops to a government besieged by rebellious Chinese. The fiscal advantages of military colonies were no less appealing. If they could be made largely self-sufficient through the allotment of farmland, there would be no added burden on tax revenues. Military colonies had a utopian appeal to Confucian scholars and were attractive to a state that preferred light taxes and limited spending.[143]

In the first month of 1788, Fu-k'ang-an proposed a number of reforms of Taiwan's military system, including plans for aborigine military colonies. Once again we find the government formulating a role for the civilized aborigines in the context of controlling Han subethnic strife. Fu-k'ang-an began by arguing against an earlier proposal to recruit half the soldiers posted in Taiwan from among both Han and civilized aborigines. Such a plan had obvious merit in reducing the expense of rotating soldiers from mainland Fukien. But the loyalty of mainland troops, who left their families behind, would be easier to guarantee.[144] Taiwan was unique in that no garrison troops were recruited locally.[145] Fu-k'ang-an objected that the loyalist militias, the obvious source of local recruits, lacked training. Moreover, recruiting in Taiwan would bring more troops of Chang-chou and Ch'üan-chou origin into an army that was already heavily recruited from those same mainland areas. Taiwan was full of vagrants who, if recruited into the army, would be sure to cause trouble. Those with families would not want to be separated from them. Yet if they were stationed near their families, petty differences might lead to friction. Mainland troops were better trained. Chang-chou and Ch'üan-chou troops need not constitute the majority in any one place, and soldiers could be assigned to guard villages whose inhabitants were of different provenance.[146] Fu-k'ang-an's arguments on training and stationing seem especially weak (all troops have to be trained, and all troops are separated from their families at times). This underlines the importance of communal tensions and the untrustworthiness of Han Taiwanese in Fu-k'ang-an's thinking.

One memorialist proposed that Chang-chou troops should stand guard over Ch'üan-chou villages and Ch'üan-chou troops should watch over Chang-chou settlements, thereby guaranteeing mutual surveillance.[147] What this memorialist failed to note was that such a control strategy would play on subethnic antagonism, rather than defuse it. Troops stationed in such a fashion would find it hard to maintain neutrality once subethnic feuding broke out and might even initiate it. In nineteenth-century Taiwan there were instances in which communal feuding originated in fights between Chang-chou and Ch'üan-chou soldiers and then spread to the community.[148] Later memorials seem to have realized the dangers of this strategy and sought less risky ways to repress subethnic feuds.

Although aware that the Lin rebellion had originated in Chang-chou and Ch'üan-chou feuding, the government also realized that not all Chang-chou settlers were rebels and that not all Ch'üan-chou settlers were loyalists. This precluded the use of troops recruited exclusively from one locality. Because the government feared that the stationing of Chang-chou and Ch'üan-chou troops in Taiwan might provoke trouble, it advocated dispersing such troops among garrisons recruited from other areas of Fukien.[149] Later it ordered that the 1,200 soldiers added to bolster the post-rebellion Taiwan garrisons not be recruited from Chang-chou or Ch'üan-chou. Nor were soldiers to be stationed near areas settled by their compatriots. This last policy would help prevent illegal collusion between soldiers and villagers of the same provenance.[150] Taiwan was to remain garrisoned by mainland troops.

One locally recruited military force could, however, be trusted to remain loyal—the civilized aborigine military colony. Fu-k'ang-an's memorial of 1788 reasons:

> The "cooked" aborigines of Taiwan have long been civilized. In the recent rebellion, An-li *she*, Chia-t'eng *she*, and Hsiao-lung *she* put forth great effort

> in fighting the rebels. All these civilized aborigines live along the mountains. Hitherto garrisons have been widely dispersed for local defense, but the foothills area is vast, aborigine tribes are interspersed there, and surveillance is difficult. If civilized aborigines were recruited as military colonists, even if they were unable to go far from their own villages, they could aid local garrisons in the patrol of the immediate vicinity. Since army rations are already set, it would not be desirable to recruit aborigines beyond the quota and thereby increase expenses. Taiwan's foothills are all wasteland. . . . During the pacification campaign, I led troops into these areas and on both the north and south routes discovered many good fields already reclaimed and much land that remains to be opened. From this land we should make allotments for the aborigines to farm; so there will be no need to give them rations. On the model of military colonies, we can select civilized aborigines as soldier-farmers. There is enough land for allotments to 4,000–5,000 men; even more [could be supported] as more land is reclaimed. The aborigines are by nature simple and strong and can be trained into military talent. When there is no trouble, they can farm their fields and guard the passes. If troublemakers cross the boundary or bandits seek hiding places, the aborigines can be sent to apprehend them. We can order the aborigines to reclaim the land allotted to them, and in accord with Taiwan precedent they need not pay land tax on aborigine fields.[151]

In this memorial Fu-k'ang-an prescribes a role for civilized aborigines quite unlike that originally envisioned by the court in the tenth month of 1787, but much closer to that recently played by them. Rather than site aborigine colonies between antagonistic Han subethnic groups, Fu-k'ang-an advocates locating the colonies between the Han-dominated plains and the raw aborigine territories in the mountains. This institutionalizes the roles assigned to civilized aborigines as *ai* guards, begun by the decrees of 1746 and 1760 (see Chapter 9), and as channels of communication between Han and raw aborigines, demonstrated in the recent campaigns. So the colonies, rather than being founded on confiscated rebel farmland, were to be allotted unopened foothills land that the braves would themselves have to reclaim.

Fu-k'ang-an made much of the fiscal advantages of military colonies. Not even rations would have to be provided, and the aborigine land-tax exemption was to be extended—to land never before taxed. But his plan diverges from reality when it refers only to tribes that live along the mountainous frontier. Many civilized aborigine tribes living in the plains (e.g., the Ta-chia and Ta-tu valley tribes in Chang-hua noted above) had also aided the government against the rebels. They could settle distant foothill military colonies only with some difficulty.

Two weeks later Fu-k'ang-an presented more detailed plans for the construction of the colonies.[152] The first two sections of the six-part memorial lay out the basic organizational framework of the colonies. Four thousand braves from 93 plains aborigine villages were to be organized into twelve colonies: four large colonies of 400 men each and eight smaller colonies of 300 men each. Fu-k'ang-an's investigations revealed that in Tan-shui posting civilized aborigine braves to guard strategic passes (*ai k'ou*) had been ineffective because the units were too dispersed. The positioning of the military colonies was to be made with reference to natural topography, local concentrations of civilized aborigine population, and the location of the garrison troops with which the colonies were to coordinate. Colony officers were to be selected for six-year terms from among well-respected aborigine chiefs (not interpreters) with military skills. The colonies were to be under the joint supervision of the subprefect for aborigine affairs, the Taiwan intendant, and the local military hierarchy.[153] The third and fourth sections, dealing with land allotments, I treat separately below. The fifth section argued that the aborigines could best use their own weapons, for example, deer-hunting spears and fowling pieces, and thus no weapons needed to be issued to them. All weapons in the aborigine colonists' hands were to be marked and registered.[154] The sixth section exempted military colonists from corvée as post runners, laborers, or porters. Civilized aborigines not serving in the military colonies were to be liable only for duty as runners and were to be compensated. Officials abusing their position by ordering aborigines to act as private porters were to be punished.[155]

Surveying and Distributing Lands Beyond the Boundary

The third and fourth sections of Fu-k'ang-an's 1788 memorial deal with the allotment of land to the colonies and the clarification of aborigine land rights beyond the raw aborigine boundary. This was no simple task and would require a cadastral survey to clarify ownership and boundaries. Fu-k'ang-an noted that surveys of the foothills areas had been conducted in 1750 and 1758 (and 1760)[156] and an earth-oxen boundary drawn to prevent Han encroachment into aborigine preserves. But these measures had not succeeded in stopping Han reclamation in these areas. In 1784, before the Lin rebellion, Governor-general Furgun had ordered another survey, but the rebellion had prevented its completion.

Fu-k'ang-an estimated (apparently on the basis of the 1784 survey results) that beyond the aborigine line were 12,000 *chia* of reclaimed land and over 8,800 *chia* of unreclaimed land. Of the latter, 3,380 *chia* had been confiscated because of communal feuds, and 5,441 *chia* were apparently claimed by no one. These 8,800 *chia* would allow an allotment of 2 *chia* per military colonist (more for officers) to be reclaimed through their own efforts. Use of the land was to be a privilege of those actively serving as military colonists and pledge-sales were forbidden. However, Fu-k'ang-an's provision that brothers or sons could succeed to a relative's

TABLE 10.3

The 1790 Disposition of Lands Beyond the 1750 and 1760 Boundaries

Land category	Area (*chia*)	Disposition
Reclaimed land		
Revealed in the survey begun 1784	11,204[a]	1,961 *chia*[b] Cultivated by aborigines or rented to Han (*tsu p'u*) Must pay aborigine rent but no land taxes 8,780 *chia*[b] Pledge-sold to Han (*tien mai* or *mai tuan*) Must pay aborigine rent and low land tax
Revealed in the survey completed 1790	3,735	Encroaching reclamation, paying no aborigine rent Han farmers ordered to pay rent to aborigine military colonies of 22 *shih* per *chia*
Unreclaimed land		
Revealed in the survey begun 1784	3,380	Land confiscated because of feuds Allotted to rental fund of regular garrison troops
Revealed in the survey begun 1784; total revised in the survey completed 1790	5,441[c]	No Han claims Allotted to the aborigine military colonies

[a]Some sources give 12,000 *chia*.

[b]These area figures can only be tentatively identified with these categories for reasons elaborated in note 158 to this chapter (*TACC*: 8–9).

[c]This figure was revised to 5,691 *chia* by the 1790 survey.

vacated post added an element of private inheritance. Just as Taiwan precedent and the payment of the tribal head tax exempted aborigine-owned and -farmed land from taxation, so were colony lands to be exempt. Therefore, no rations needed to be paid.[157]

Aborigine rights over the 12,000 (usually said to be 11,204) *chia* of reclaimed land also had to be clarified (see Table 10.3). Fu-k'ang-an's exposition of the various terms by which Han acquired aborigine land is linked to the problems of land-tax evasion discussed in Chapter 9. He distinguishes two types: the rental-lease (*tsu p'u*), in which a use-right in land was acquired in exchange for a small deposit, and the pledge-sale (*tien mai*), in which an ownership right in land was acquired in exchange for a larger deposit. The latter form was apparently a pledge in name only, for there was no possibility of redemption. Fu-k'ang-an notes that now that the civilized aborigines were becoming good farmers, all their land was in Han hands. He pointed out that all over Taiwan the earth-oxen boundary was without effect and that to avoid confusion and disputes the land had to be surveyed and registered.

Fu-k'ang-an then divided the land into three categories for the purpose of taxation. First is the land that Han lease (*tsu p'u*) from aborigines, on which the Han farmer is an ordinary tenant and the aborigine a landlord. This is identical to the first category Fu-k'ang-an defined earlier. This category of land, he said, is not large and is the same as simple aborigine land; like it, it should be exempt from the land tax.

The second category contains land that aborigines have "unconditionally" sold to Han farmers (*mai tuan*). "Such land is no longer aborigine land and should be registered for taxation." But, Fu-k'ang-an added, although Han have "bought" such land and invested much to reclaim it, they are still obligated to pay yearly aborigine rent (*fan tsu*). This category thus most closely corresponds to land aborigines have pledge-sold (*tien mai*). Fu-k'ang-an recommended that the land tax on such land be set at the T'ung-an lower sand-land rate (1.7583 *shih* per *chia* compared to 2.740 *shih*, the standard post-1744 rate on first-grade paddy). This would prove a lighter burden to a farmer already paying an aborigine rent, especially if the tax were commuted to cash (commutation, by reducing transport costs and because of a good official rate, was considered favorable to the farmer).[158]

Fu-k'ang-an added a third category of land. In a number of locales bordering raw aborigine areas, Han settlers had reclaimed land. Although this kind of encroachment "should be punished according to precedent," Fu-k'ang-an found that the settlers had had peaceful relations with the raw aborigines and no trouble had broken out.[159] He argued that removing these admittedly illegal settlements would only turn productive land into wasteland and create homeless vagrants. The government should, "according to the new regulations on Han buying aborigine land" (he seems to be referring to the second category of land he had just defined), simply require that the land be registered for taxation (whether the land is to be taxed at the regular 1744 rate or at the specially proclaimed lower rate is left unspecified). The memorial makes no mention of whether the settlers in these areas paid, or should be required to pay, an aborigine rent.

All three of Fu-k'ang-an's land-tax categories amounted to official acquiescence in Han violation of the government-drawn aborigine line. Thus, Fu-k'ang-an was following in the footsteps of many previous officials confronted with the same situation. Faced with massive violation over a long period, he could only seek to salvage rental rights for the aborigines and thereby "make content" both Han and aborigines.[160] He did not discuss instances where Han had occupied aborigine land without rental agreements. Can we conclude that if such land was to be eligible for the light T'ung-an tax rates, the settlers would have to conclude agreements and pay aborigine rents? Also, like his predecessors, Fu-k'ang-an asserted that once the present area had been surveyed and registered, a new and clearer boundary could be drawn. Henceforth all encroachers beyond this new boundary, along with careless officials, should be punished severely.[161]

To implement Fu-k'ang-an's plans, a detailed land survey had to be carried out, and officials deputed to conduct it. By the end of 1788, the proposal to allot the land confiscated due to feuds (3,380 *chia*) to the aborigine military colonies was dropped. That land was instead added to the confiscated rebel land to create a fund paying cash supplements to regular garrison soldiers (see Table 10.3).[162] This reduced the area available to the colonists to 5,000-odd *chia* or approximately one *chia* per colonist. Governor Hsü Ssu-tseng termed this generous enough, considering that both layers of ownership (and a tax exemption) were going to the aborigines, who thus might expect to obtain 30–40 *shih* of grain per *chia*.[163] The importance attributed to the military potential of the colonists in comparison to regular garrison troops was gradually being diminished, as Fu-k'ang-an's recommendations on weapons and the allotment of unreclaimed land had indicated earlier. The reports of those charged with the land survey revealed more doubts about the feasibility of establishing aborigine military colonies and, once established, their utility.

Hsü Meng-lin and Huang Chia-shun, the two officials in charge of the survey, were both experienced in Taiwan affairs. They were first sent there early in 1787 to replace officials killed by the rebels. Hsü, as Tan-shui subprefect, had earned the high regard of Fu-k'ang-an as an able leader of Han and aborigine loyalists and manager of raw aborigine affairs.[164] In 1788 his rank was raised to full prefect, and he served for a while as acting Taiwan prefect. Later he was promoted to prefect of Ch'üan-chou, and it was while on special assignment from that office that he headed the Taiwan land surveys.[165] Huang served from 1787 to 1790 as subprefect for aborigine affairs on the north route.[166] So both Huang and Hsü had knowledge of the civilized aborigines in Taiwan when given this assignment. Hsü surveyed first Tan-shui and then the counties of T'ai-wan and Feng-shan; Huang surveyed first Chang-hua and then Chu-lo (renamed Chia-i for its loyalty in the rebellion). The planning and surveying took two years. Thus, Governor-general Wu-la-na could not present a final proposal for the establishment of the colonies until the ninth month of 1790.[167]

Once the survey was completed, there remained the task of matching colonists with available land. This presented formidable difficulties. It was at this point that Hsü Meng-lin posed fundamental questions concerning the organization of the colonies to his superiors.[168] All that remains of these discussions is a long letter written on behalf of Governor Hsü Ssu-tseng (a co-author of Fu-k'ang-an's original plan) in response to Hsü Meng-lin's query. Hsü Meng-lin reported that the survey of wastelands beyond the boundary had revealed both fertile and infertile, reclaimed and unreclaimed, tracts of land that would be difficult to distribute equally. He accordingly proposed that the land be given to Han tenants to cultivate and that *rents* be collected to provision the colonists. The governor replied that what distinguished a military colony from ordinary garrisons was the allotment of *land* to soldier-farmers (not the collection of rents). By cultivating his own land, a colonist could support a family of eight. "Moreover, most aborigine land in Taiwan has been occupied by wily Chinese. The imperial benevolence commanded that military colonies be established not just to strengthen the military forces but also to preserve the frontier out of generosity to and sympathy for the aborigines." On this strongly moral and Mencian/paternalistic note emphasizing the need for a settled agricultural livelihood, the governor reaffirmed the plan to allot land to the colonists.[169]

Hsü Meng-lin listed in detail several of the problems he had encountered in planning for the colonies. Although colonies were to be established all over Taiwan, much more land was available in Tan-shui and Chang-hua than in the counties to the south. But colonists could not be expected to go far from their villages to farm. The land also varied greatly in fertility and accessibility, and in some areas the land was in large tracts, and in others in dispersed plots. It would thus be very difficult to allot equal shares. Sizable investments in irrigation would be needed to make unreclaimed land productive, yet the aborigines lacked capital. It would be difficult to remove Han landlords and tenants from land already reclaimed and would impose on them great losses. Given these obstacles, collecting rents and dispersing rations would be much easier. The governor countered that colonies, though difficult to establish, would cause few problems thereafter, whereas a rent-collecting system, though simple to set up, would in time be easily corrupted. A rent-collecting system would require a schedule of rents set according to land grades, and adjustments would have to be made when conditions changed. Once the land was rented, checks would still have to be made on boundaries, changes of tenants, and illegal sales. Tenants would cause problems by paying less than was due and by falling in arrears. Those put in charge of rent collecting would surely seek to embezzle the rents. The income received from renting out the land would be less than that gotten from directly farming it.[170] Each alternative had advantages and disadvantages.

The governor suggested a compromise. A comparison of the number of colonists with the area of land available in each county suggested that in Tan-shui and Chang-hua, where land was plentiful, allotment to the aborigines was most appropriate, whereas in the southern counties, where the land area fell far short of what would be required, renting out the land would be easiest.[171] In the northern districts, the colonies could be established on tracts of one *chia* per colonist, adjacent to aborigine villages.

Where there was not enough such land, large tracts could be assembled by trading plots for confiscated rebel property or with willing settlers. The land could then be divided up on the well-field (*ching t'ien*) method, distributed by drawing lots, and registered. On poor-quality land, the allotments could be enlarged to allow for fallowing. Colonists from tribes in the three southern colonies could be provisioned with rents from the small amount of land available in their own areas plus rents from the sizable surplus still available in the north. A schedule of rents and a set of regulations to guard against embezzlement could be established. Funds could be supplied to construct irrigation works, and surplus rents could be spent on military supplies. Hsü Meng-lin had apparently also proposed that aborigines who already had land within the boundary not be given allotments beyond the boundary. The governor replied that colony lands should be assigned to accompany an office, regardless of the holdings of any particular incumbent.[172]

That many of Hsü Meng-lin's suggested "solutions" would in effect have eliminated the colonies as localized military units betrays his serious doubts about their potential value. Wu-la-na's final plan adopted elements of the governor's suggested compromise between allotment and renting out, but the sharp distinction between north and south was eliminated, as considerably more land became available for colonies in Feng-shan. The final plan thus made important modifications to Fu-k'ang-an's proposal.

Wu-la-na's memorial of 1790 deals explicitly with several of the problems raised by Hsü. An examination of the actual land and colony locations (see below) will enable us to answer whether the most fundamental problems were solved. First, we complete our discussion of Wu-la-na's plans for the aborigine military colonies in the context of the land surveys. How the government disposed of land depended on how it was categorized in the survey. The survey begun in 1784 uncovered 11,204 reclaimed *chia* and over 8,800 unreclaimed *chia* beyond the boundaries established in 1750 and 1758–60 (see Table 10.3).[173] We have already discussed the disposition of the 11,204 *chia* of reclaimed land and 3,380 *chia* of the unreclaimed land; only 5,441 *chia* of unreclaimed land remained available for the colonies. The resurvey conducted after the rebellion revealed that an additional 3,735 *chia* had been reclaimed beyond the boundary (or at least discovered not to have been included in the 1784 registers).[174] Since Fu-k'ang-an's plan was based on 1784 estimates, this additional 3,735 *chia* provided the basis for a compromise. It could be rented to provide an income for the colonies, thereby leaving intact the 5,441 unreclaimed *chia* for allotment to colonists (and making Governor Hsü's revision of the plan unnecessary).

Wu-la-na's memorial makes clear the reasoning behind the disposition of this newfound category of land. These 3,735 *chia* were beyond the boundary; encroaching Han settlers had not rented (*p'u*) them from aborigines and did not pay an aborigine rent (*fan tsu*). Thus, in theory, because they were reclaimed illegally, the government "ought to combine these areas with those in the unreclaimed category and distribute all of them to the colonists."[175] But for a number of reasons the government sought an alternative solution. The land had been reclaimed in widely dispersed small plots; to cultivate them, the colonists would have to be dispersed. Farming plots interspersed with those owned by Han would easily lead to disputes. Moreover, variations in fertility made distributing equal shares of land more difficult than collecting and distributing rents. But perhaps the most important obstacle to redistribution was posed by the settlers whose investment of labor and capital had opened the land. Imposing a rent would eliminate any need to relocate settlers; in this way both Han and civilized aborigines could benefit.[176] So it was decided to rent out this category of land for the benefit of the colonies.

A rent schedule adjusted rents according to the productivity of the land. In all, six grades of paddy and dry land were distinguished. In a few cases, exceptions to these rates were allowed. The highest-grade land was to pay to the colonies a rent of 22 *shih* of unhusked grain per *chia*, considerably higher than the usual aborigine large-rent of 6–8 *shih* per *chia*. It was also much higher than the rent and taxes paid by those settlers who had acquired by pledge aborigine land uncovered in the 1784 survey. Fu-k'ang-an's memorial of 1788 had ordered them to pay the usual aborigine large-rent and the low T'ung-an tax rate of 1.7583 *shih* per *chia*. So the new rent schedule disadvantaged the settlers on the 3,735 *chia* who had not rented their land from the tribes. Yet the colony rent of 22 *shih* was substantially lower than the official rent of 32 *shih* imposed on first-grade paddy confiscated from rebel estates.[177] The discrepancy in this case, I would argue, is to be explained as government recognition of the reclamation investment made by the settlers now being required to pay the colony rent. Moreover, no provision was made for taxing land on which colony rents were to be paid. Based on Governor Hsü's estimate that first-grade paddy would produce 80 *shih* a year, the colony rent equals 27.5 percent, the official rent on confiscated lands equals 40 percent, and the aborigine large-rent equals 10 percent or less. The colony rents were commuted into cash, which would save transport expenses. The rate was fixed not in treasury silver but in foreign silver, the currency in common use in Taiwan, to prevent yamen clerks' charging meltage and exchange fees.[178]

Rents were to be collected by head tenants or interpreters selected from respected and well-off families. Their salaries (fixed at 60 *shih* each) were to be paid from the amount collected, and they were not to make extra demands on the tenants. Rent books and receipts were to be kept in proper order, under the supervision of the county, which was to receive the rents for later disbursement. Corruption was to be dealt with severely. All contracts transferring tenancy rights were required to record the amount of colony rent to be paid. Tenants failing to pay rents or otherwise causing disputes would be evicted.[179]

In addition to the lands required to pay colony rents at the established rates, the colonies acquired a variety of rights over additional parcels of land. Most important were the large-rent rights on parcels in Tan-shui where *ai* guards had previously been established. The government's policy was to maintain this system as part of the defense against raw aborigines. These guards were paid by contributions from the settlers, usually 40 percent from property owners and 60 percent from the tenants. The colonies, as the new proprietors, were therefore required to assume the 40 percent obligation.[180]

The yearly income from colony rents totaled 41,341 *yüan*. Of this amount, 450 *yüan* was allocated to the salaries of rent collectors,[181] and 1,680 *yüan* was to be paid to *ai* guards in Tan-shui. The largest sum, 33,240 *yüan*, was to be paid out to the colonists at a rate of 8 *yüan* each annually, more for officers. This amount was paid to subsidize the colonists in recognition of the fact that the colony lands allotted them were as yet unreclaimed. Thus, Fu-k'ang-an's plan for totally self-supporting colonies was significantly modified. A substantial amount, the remaining 5,971 *yüan*, was to be kept as a surplus against contingencies; small amounts might even go toward construction of irrigation works or for gifts at weddings and funerals.[182] Nearly half the colony rent was collected in Tan-shui, and another fourth in Chang-hua. These two areas also had the largest contingents of colonists and therefore the largest expenses. Small amounts were assigned to subsidize the deficit southern counties. Local officials were to disburse the rents to the colonists twice yearly. Graft would be reduced, if not eliminated, if yamen clerks were bypassed. Each colonist was issued a name board or waist plaque that he had to present to receive his rations. Accurate account books and rosters of colonists were to be kept.[183]

All the lands covered in the survey were to be registered, and deeds (*i chih chang tan*) issued to each household. Two copies were to be made of each land register, one to be kept by the county and one to be kept by the prefecture. Rent collectors and interpreters were to be given copies of deeds specifying rental obligations to facilitate the collection of rents.[184]

Thus, the final disposition of the great bulk of the land found lying beyond the boundaries of 1750 and 1760 was to impose on it *rents* to be paid to aborigine tribes, military colonies, and regular garrison troops (see Table 10.3). Only 5,441 *chia* of unreclaimed land was reserved for actual allotment to the plains aborigine colonists.

Organizing the Colonies

More important for the organization of the aborigine military colonies was the disposition of the 5,441 *chia* of unreclaimed, beyond-the-boundary land surveyed in 1784. Wu-la-na kept Fu-k'ang-an's original plan for twelve colonies of 4,000 men drawn from 93 aborigine settlements and assigned specific quotas and groupings.[185] The major problem was matching concentrations of colonists to available tracts of land. Fu-k'ang-an had included in the area to be allotted 3,380 *chia* of land that had been confiscated because of communal feuds. This would have enabled allotments of approximately 2 *chia* per colonist and eliminated the need to disburse rations to the colonists. Instead, as we noted earlier, this 3,380 *chia* area was added to the confiscated rebel land to provide subsidies to the regular garrison troops.[186] Compensating for this loss to the colonies, another 3,735 *chia* had been "found," not to be allotted to the colonists to farm but to provide a rental income (see Table 10.3). In many ways, this compromise of Fu-k'ang-an's plan suited the needs of colonists given only unreclaimed land, the reality that settlers were already farming the newly found lands, and the difficulty of distributing scattered parcels of land.

But the problem of serving the government's security goals by matching colonists to colonies remained. The resurvey—after correcting inaccurate records and eliminating eroded land and land too rocky to reclaim—came up with a revised total of 5,691 *chia* of reclaimable land. Wu-la-na hit upon a simple solution to the problem of distributing dispersed pieces of land: "Of land that is located near the colony headquarters, allot 1 to 1.2 *chia* per colonist; of land that is more distant, because labor and expenses will be greater, allot 1.3 to 1.6 *chia*."[187] So the problem was construed as one of treating colonists equitably; a larger share would compensate for a disadvantageous location. But more than equity was involved. Fu-k'ang-an had attributed the ineffectiveness of the *ai* guard system to the excessive dispersal of its forces.[188] Wu-la-na's memorial glosses over the need to avoid this pitfall. Governor Hsü's reply to Hsü Meng-lin's hard questions, as we saw above, suggested that plots of land be traded so that colony holdings could be consolidated in large tracts.[189] However, an earlier draft of the 1790 plan rejected such plot exchanges as difficult to carry out and likely to stir up trouble; renting out the more distant plots was even considered.[190] Wu-la-na's version of the plan ignores this problem altogether. An examination of the colony registers that accompany Wu-la-na's plan will enable us to determine how serious the problem was.

The challenge to the planners was to organize colonists recruited from 93 civilized aborigine villages into 12 units and then to disperse these

TABLE 10.4
The Organization of the Twelve Military Colonies

County from which colonists recruited[a]	Number of colonists[b]	Number of locales dispersed to[b]	Number of villages recruited from[b]	Aborigine linguistic group(s) recruited from	
				Number	Name(s)[c]
1. Feng-shan	400	3	5	1	Siraya
2. Feng-shan	300	4	4	1	Siraya
3. T'ai-wan	300	3	3	1	Siraya
4. Chia-i	300	6	12	3	Siraya, Hoanya, Tsou
5. Chia-i	300	6	8	4	Hoanya, Tsou, Babuza, Thao[d]
6. Chang-hua	400	4	8	2	Hoanya, Babuza
7. Chang-hua	300	4	7	3	Hoanya, Babuza, Papora
8. Chang-hua	300	2	7	2	Papora, Pazeh
9. Tan-shui	400	3	8	1	Pazeh
10. Tan-shui	300	4	5	1	Taokas
11. Tan-shui	400	4 (+1)[e]	11	2	Taokas, Ketagalan[f]
12. Tan-shui	300	7	19	1	Ketagalan
TOTAL	4,000	50[g]	97[h]		

[a]Numbers of the colony organizational units assigned from south to north by author.
[b]Computed from *TWSHF*: 1.381–96 and Cheng Hsi-fu 1976.
[c]Chang Yao-ch'i 1965: 531–32. Taivoan are included in Siraya, and Saaroa are included in Tsou (see Appendix E).
[d]The proper ethnic identification of the historical Shui-sha-lien tribe is a matter of dispute: Inō (1904: 575) gives Bunun; Mabuchi (1953: 4) gives Thao.
[e]One very small locale of only 8 *chia* is included in the roster assigning land to villages, but is not listed in the roster listing land alone.
[f]The Ketagalan group should, following Ogawa 1944 and Tsuchida 1985, be divided at least between Basai, Ketagalan, and Kulon; unfortunately so little information is available on these languages that it is not possible to assign most tribes to one or the other.
[g]The locales column totals 50, though only 35 (+1; see note *e*) locales were allotted because some locales were shared by more than one organization ($24 \times 1 + 8 \times 2 + 2 \times 3 + 1 \times 4 = 50$).
[h]Because three villages were split between two organizations, we can reduce 97 to 94, which is still one more than the stated total of 93. Tribes split between north and south or east and west settlements were often counted by the government as separate units; miscounting one of these may account for the discrepancy.

units over land available at 40 (I count 41) separate locales (see Table 10.4). Because there were so few units compared to the number of aborigine villages, each unit was formed by consolidating colonists from several neighboring villages. The number of villages per colony organization ranged from 3 to an extreme of 19 in the greater Taipei basin. The average was 8; the median 7.5. In three instances recruits from a single village were split into two units. But in two of these instances, the smaller unit was assigned land in the same locale as the larger subgroup, thereby reuniting the tribe's braves on the ground.

Of the twelve colonies, six were recruited from one linguistic group only, and two more were heavily dominated by a single group (95 percent and 80 percent, respectively). This follows naturally from the geographical concentration of the groups involved. Thus, the Siraya dominated Colonies 1–4 in the far south, and in the north, the Pazeh dominated Colony 9, the Taokas Colonies 10 and 11, and the Ketagalan Colony 12.[191] Colony 8 was split evenly between Pazeh and Papora, which might be explained as simple overlapping. But the assignment of land dispersed its members in a way that placed them with three more language groups (land assignments are discussed in detail below). The linguistic situation seems most complex in Colonies 5–7. Babuza and Hoanya occurred in all three colonies, and in two of them they were joined by additional groups. Although Babuza and Hoanya settlements occupied spatially discrete territories, the colony recruitment system intermixed them thoroughly.

The intermixing does not appear to follow from a government policy of ethnic divide and rule. These villages were being organized into colonies, after all, because they had "long ago turned toward civilization," which meant not only that they paid taxes and lived in peace with their Chinese rulers, but also that they were sinicizing (see Chapter 11). By the late Ch'ien-lung reign, plains aborigine men, at least, had a working command of the Chinese dialect spoken by neighboring settlers (either Minnan [Hokkien] or Hakka), and Chinese served as a lingua franca between plains aborigines of different linguistic background. Nevertheless, the impression that the organization of the central Taiwan colonies was more complex is confirmed by analysis of the allotment of land (see Appendix E).

Of the 40 locales where colony land was made available, it was decided that five, three in Tan-shui and two in Feng-shan, were not needed for defense purposes. Instead, they were rented out to provide additional income to the colonies. So there remained 35 locales on which to consolidate colonists from 93 villages, or, from another viewpoint, on which to disperse twelve colony units.

Although there were many more villages than locales, recruits from six villages were split between two locales, and two villages were split between three locales. This might be expected due to the wide variation in size of both village recruit quotas and locales, which made it difficult to match recruits to nearby locales. Recruit quotas varied from 4 to 201 per village and averaged 43. Locales varied from 10 *chia* (8 *chia* in an additional locale not included in the official count of 35 locales) to 597 *chia*, and averaged 145 *chia*. It is interesting that of the eight instances of splitting recruits from the same village, only one occurred in the central colonies (nos. 4–8). The central colonies were quite successful in locating all recruits from a given village in only one place. Nor does a high number of locales per colony distinguish all the central colonies. Colony 12 with seven locales and Colonies 4 and 5 with six each were on the high side. The average number of locales per colony was 4.5. If each locale were allotted to a single colony, we would expect an average of 2.7.

Far more complex was the allocation of locales to colony organizational units in the central colonies. Of the 35 locales, 24 were assigned exclusively to a single colony. The bulk of these were in the north, where nearly half of the total, seventeen (plus the additional uncounted one) locales, were assigned to only four colonies (nos. 9–12); only one of these was split between two units. Eleven locales were split between two or more colony units. What was the logic behind splitting the colonists in one place between two or more organizations? Conceivably, this could enhance coordination among a series of dispersed units. Such an argument can best be made for three cases (including both of the locales split between three organizations) because colony officers were also stationed there. These officers were no doubt essential to coordinating across colony lines, and in the locales split among three units they were of superior rank. The locale split four ways was the largest of them all, with 597 *chia* and 557 colonists. But it benefited from the presence of only one sergeant, who had direct control of less than half of the men (252), those from Colony 8. I suspect that the recruits from the other three units were allocated land there, not to enhance coordination, but simply because land was available. I suspect this because 557 men was much more than the strategic value of any single location could justify and because the three additional contingents came from widely dispersed units, two in three additional locations (including one where they co-occur again), and the third (Colony 5) in *five* additional locations. Colonies 4 and 5 were assigned to six locations each; of these they occurred together in three locations, and Colony 5 occurred twice with two other colonies, nos. 6 and 7. Colony 12 was dispersed over seven locations, but it shared only one.

Thus, there was a marked pattern in the central colonies of excessive dispersal (five colonies and twelve locales versus 22 separate land assignments) and excessive overlapping of units (Colonies 4 and 5 co-occurred three times, nos. 5 and 6 twice, nos. 5 and 7 twice, and nos. 6 and 7 twice). Coordination should require only one overlap between adjacent units. (In the south, the pairings 1–2 and 2–3 each co-occurred twice.) In two cases a locale was shared between two colonies that were not even adjacent (nos. 10 and 12, and 4 and 8), which would make coordination exceedingly difficult. This adds up to a pattern that enhances confusion, not coordination, and leads me to think that land was allocated with little real thought to creating functioning military units.

A look at the distances between tribal settlements and allotments of colony land confirms this view. Colony 3 provides a striking example. Fu-k'ang-an's original memorial had noted that although T'ai-wan county had few civilized tribes, its territory was narrow and its prefectural city was already garrisoned "heavily enough to maintain order."[192] Nevertheless, Wu-la-na's memorial states that the colony recruited from T'ai-wan (no. 3, Hsin-kang *she*) should be located in T'ai-wan county near the *northern* border with Chia-i.[193] The colony registers tell a different story. Since T'ai-wan county had no land of the proper category to be allotted to colonies and Feng-shan had a surplus, Colony 3 was assigned land in three locales in Feng-shan, beyond T'ai-wan county's *southern* border.[194] Because Chia-i had only 66 *chia* available for allotment, its two colonies were assigned land to the north in Chang-hua. The southernmost Tan-shui colony (no. 9, which included An-li) was also assigned land in Chang-hua, but in this case the land was located near the tribal settlements. Thus, land was being allotted to units simply on the basis of availability, with little regard for colony organization and strategy.

The distance tribal recruits had to travel to their colony lands varied greatly. Many colonies were obviously too far from home settlements to be farmed without permanently relocating. This fundamental flaw was built into Fu-k'ang-an's proposal from the start. Fu-k'ang-an, while emphasizing the importance of defense along the boundary and therefore the allocation of colony land there, had glossed over the fact that many of the 93 civilized villages were located on the plains, some even on the coast,[195] far from the mountain foothills. This conflicted with another of his principles: aborigine villagers should be able to patrol in the vicinity of their home settlements.[196] The exchange between Governor Hsü Ssu-tseng and Prefect Hsü Meng-lin during the survey had reaffirmed the goal of allotting farms near the aborigine settlements. The final plan did not resolve this contradiction; it only sought to compensate farmers given distant land by increasing their allotted area.[197]

It is hard to know if the planners of the military colony system really thought the aborigines would farm their allotments. Fu-k'ang-an implied that the civilized aborigines would welcome the additional land when he lamented that they were finally becoming good farmers but only after all their land had been pledge-sold to Han.[198] Wu-la-na stated bluntly that the civilized aborigines were poor farmers, and he stipulated that colony officers should have more skilled aborigines teach the rest.[199] Perhaps the greater obstacle was the difficulty in reclaiming and irrigating uncleared land that was often far from home.

The skewed distribution of the amounts of land allotted is another indication that the military functions of the colonies were not taken seriously. Ten locales exceeded 200 *chia* (at 1.3 *chia* per brave, 200 *chia* would accommodate 150 colonists). This was larger than any one locale's strategic importance for defending against small-scale and intermittent raw aborigine raids could justify. Twelve locales were too small, at 50 *chia* or less, leaving only a third of the locales in the moderate size range.

Aggravating the irregular sizes of the locales was the truncated command structure. Providing only one sergeant for every 300–400 colonists, who were dispersed in a number of locales (from two to seven), further reduced the possibilities of coordination and command. Fu-k'ang-an had argued that the Taiwan colonies would not need as many officers as the Szechwan *t'un lien* (over 100 for 2,000 mobilized men) and recommended only one sergeant per colony (*t'un*), giving an extremely low ratio of twelve (eighteen if superior officers are included) for 4,000 recruits.[200] The regular garrisons often had one sergeant for as few as twenty garrison soldiers.[201]

On close examination, Wu-la-na's plan reveals a mechanical adherence to certain guidelines. The rigid symmetry of Fu-k'ang-an's plan, 4,000 braves organized into twelve colonies, four large and eight small, is preserved undeviatingly without regard for the actual distribution of either strategic locales or aborigine settlements. The colonists were drawn from all 93 villages, ignoring any distinction between those located on the plains and those located along the border and near the colony sites. It is interesting in this regard to note that three villages that had aided the government against the rebels, and whose leaders were banqueted in Peking, K'uei-lei, Shih-tzu, and Wu-ao, were not incorporated into the colony system.[202] Although they were located in the border regions, their short history of submission and sinification apparently barred them from consideration.

All the land allotted came from the survey category "unreclaimed land beyond the boundary." Admittedly, such land was bound to be located near raw aborigine territories. But that strategic considerations were rarely considered is revealed in the failures to consolidate extremely small locales by trading or even eliminating less important ones, to consider renting out parts of oversized locales, and conversely, to consider allotment of parts of the locales declared surplus and rented out in toto. Two of these rented locales in Tan-shui, Yang-mei-p'u and Ta-ku-k'an (modern Yang-mei and Ta-ch'i in T'ao-yüan county), were of sufficient size and strategic importance to warrant consideration as colony sites. Surely smaller but better-organized and better-situated colonies could have served the purpose.

Adherence to these rigidities in organization, numbers, and locales forces us to conclude that equitable distribution rather than military function was the guiding operational principle in the creation of the colonies. Several scholars emphasize that the colonies constituted more a *reward* to the civilized aborigines for loyal service in the Lin Shuang-wen campaigns than part of a serious defense plan.[203] This seems also to have been the opinion of the late nineteenth-century governor, Liu Ming-ch'uan.[204] The overall role in the suppression of the Lin rebellion played by plains aborigine braves, so few in number, had after all been minor compared with that of the loyalist militias.

Wu-la-na's memorial concludes with a call to reset the aborigine boundary (set previously in 1750 and 1760). Aided by the newly revised land registers, officials could patrol this boundary to prevent Han encroachment. Encroachment is once again "permanently prohibited," though Wu-la-na is fully aware of the failure of the past attempts and the constant disruptive pressure of new settlers: "Taiwan's land is fertile, and it is easy to make a living there. Homeless commoners gather in increasing numbers, penetrate the inner mountains, reclaim land, and cause disturbances."[205]

Not two years passed after the adoption of Wu-la-na's plan before the Taiwan prefect approved a serious departure from one of its major tenets. He allowed Feng-shan county to turn over its duties of collecting and dispersing colony rental funds to the officers of the colonies themselves.[206] Governor Hsü had debated the dangers of corruption in a rental system compared with those in land allotment, and Wu-la-na's plan therefore provided for strict accounting procedures and direct official management of collection. This 1792 deviation had the predictable results: tenants refused to pay, and colony officers embezzled most of what was paid. Direct official management was not restored until 1811, but many problems remained.[207] This was only the beginning of a long process of degeneration, punctuated by attempts at reform, in the nineteenth century. In fact, history reveals that many colonies were never even established as territorial units.

Although the nineteenth century lies beyond the scope of this study, a brief review of certain major points that reflect flaws in the original plan for the colonies is in order. Colony lands were frequently leased to reclaiming Han settlers as well as encroached on by squatters. A contract dated 1794 reveals that Chang-hua magistrate Sung Hsüeh-hao (1788–92)[208] had approved an arrangement by which An-li *she* leased colony land to Han settlers for reclamation rather than establish a colony on the land. In return An-li's colony unit received the 8 *shih* per *chia* large-rent.

In later years such permission was frequently given, but officials carefully made clear the reasons for granting "exceptions." These included aborigine lack of agricultural skill and capital and, most frequently, the great distance of the colony lands from aborigine settlements.[209] This is what makes a contract as early as An-li's even more remarkable: not only were no excuses made, but the land involved was in the immediate vicinity of the tribe.[210] There were other indications that the civilized aborigine braves were not becoming resident soldier-farmers as envisioned. Although we lack real figures, we may speculate whether the civilized aborigine population could spare the workers to open such a large area. So much of the unreclaimed colony land had been appropriated by Han or pledge-sold to Han settlers by 1810 (just twenty years after the founding of the colonies) that the governor-general had to order another resurvey. A statement signed by several tribes in 1823 argued that the "aborigine colonists do their duty though their stomachs are empty" and complained about nonpayment of aborigine rents and nondelivery of colony rations.[211] For the rest of the century, the colony lands experienced the same pattern the plains aborigine lands had the century before: Han encroachment, government intervention (but only to ensure payment of rent), and a resolution to enforce redrawn boundaries.

Despite these problems, the aborigine colonies did survive as organizational units (if not as border colonies of soldier-farmers) and were called up at various times for military service in both the mountains against raw aborigines and the plains against rebellious Han (see below).[212] Thus, the colonies came to serve not just in patrols against raw aborigines and outlaws in the border areas but also in support of the government in the plains, as the earliest plans had proposed.

We turn next to Fu-k'ang-an's other plans for post-rebellion reconstruction and a brief look at developments in the nineteenth century.

Taiwan Pacified?

Chapter 10 brings this analytic history of Ch'ing administration of the Taiwan frontier and the land-tenure institutions created to accommodate the plains aborigines down to the end of the eighteenth century. Chapter 11 assesses the effects of these developments on the plains aborigine societies, and Chapter 12 attempts to put the Taiwan frontier in comparative perspective. This section reviews reform measures adopted in the wake of the Lin rebellion, in addition to the aborigine military colonies discussed above, and looks briefly at events down through the end of the Ch'ien-lung reign and the beginning of the new century to assess the efficacy of the post-rebellion reconstruction. The next section surveys the major events of the nineteenth century affecting the plains aborigines.

Fu-k'ang-an's plans for reconstruction called for strengthening the official civil and military presence on the island. Changes on the civil side were relatively minor. No new counties were created, as happened following the Chu I-kuei rebellion. The biggest change in the south was the relocation of Feng-shan's county seat, which had been destroyed in the rebellion, to a nearby town.[213] In the north, one subdistrict magistrate (*hsün chien*) was added to a settled border area (Ta-wu-lung nei-shan, one of Chuang Ta-t'ien's strongholds), and the post of subdistrict magistrate of Tou-liu-men of Chia-i county was raised in rank to assistant district magistrate (*hsien ch'eng*).[214] A year later the *hsün chien* of Hsin-chuang (in the Taipei basin) was also raised to assistant district magistracy status, and then, to keep the bureaucracy and the budget in balance, a *hsien ch'eng* in T'ai-wan county was correspondingly lowered by the same degree.[215]

The court also took steps to reduce corruption among Taiwan's bureaucrats and improve their supervision. At this time the court made some revealing comments on Taiwan's highest civil office, the post of Taiwan intendant, whose incumbent was appointed on the recommendation of the governor and governor-general. Rather than viewing appointment to the island as a hardship, prospective officials saw in Taiwan a rich center of commerce that afforded opportunities to profit. Bribery and favoritism figured heavily in selecting candidates for the lucrative post (*mei ch'üeh*) of intendant. This venality had had unfortunate consequences for effective administration and the maintenance of local order. With reconstruction, such corrupt practices in awarding appointments were to be eliminated. Henceforth, appointments of both the Taiwan intendant and prefect required special imperial edicts. Additional steps were taken to increase court surveillance of the island. To improve communications in times of crises, the intendant and the brigade general were given the privilege of directly memorializing the throne.[216] In 1785 the emperor discontinued the practice of triennially dispatching inspecting censors to Taiwan. To increase the quality of surveillance, he ordered his highest-ranking provincial officials, the governor-general, governor, and Fukien's land and marine commanders, to rotate on annual tours of inspection to Taiwan.[217] Bureaucratic recognition of Taiwan's importance as a strategic periphery had never been higher.

It was on the military side that the greatest changes on the ground were ordered, the largest since 1733 when garrisons were added in the wake of the civilized aborigine and Han revolts. In general, Fu-k'ang-an found Taiwan's garrisons in an extremely sorry state. Many soldiers had taken sideline jobs to boost their income. Others were involved with criminal elements in gambling and prostitution. Discipline and morale were nonexistent. He was critical of both the lax military commanders and the civil administrators and saw their impeachments in the years preceding the Lin rebellion as justified.[218] He also blamed Brigade General Ch'ai Ta-chi personally for letting the rebellion get out of control (see below).[219]

Fu-k'ang-an planned a substantial increase in Taiwan's garrisons, including cavalry, if the horses could adjust to Taiwan's climate. We have already discussed the debate over the subethnic identity of the 1,200 additional recruits to be stationed in Taiwan (see above). The allocation of rents from confiscated rebel lands was meant to supplement troop income and make outside employment unnecessary.[220] What, if anything, was done to tighten discipline and boost morale except to threaten punishment is unclear.

Let us examine now the spatial distribution of the new troops proposed in Fu-k'ang-an's memorial of 1788.[221] Nearly half the 1,200 new soldiers went to strengthen the garrisons in the three county seats of Chang-hua, Chia-i (formerly Chu-lo), and Feng-shan and in two assistant district magistracies. Since the prefectural garrisons around Tainan were sufficient, most of the remainder went to strengthen other established garrisons on the settled plains. Four additions stand out for their size and/or location. In Chang-hua, 130 soldiers were stationed for the first time at two points guarding the Shui-sha-lien (Sun Moon Lake) area, which had been a refuge for many Lin rebels and whose proximity to wild aborigines made it a continuing source of trouble.[222] In addition, 120 soldiers were posted at Wai-hsiao-lung in T'ai-wan county (further inland from the new subdistrict magistracy at Ta-wu-lung) to guard an important entrance to the mountain areas, 150 soldiers were posted at Shui-ti-liao, in the "far southern" reaches of Feng-shan, and 50 soldiers were posted at Ta-li-i, Lin Shuang-wen's base.

Notable in this new distribution of troops is the minimal movement toward the foothills compared with the advance of population and the boundary line over the previous 50 years. Two factors contributed to this outcome. First, the aborigine military colonies were charged with patrolling the border areas, in coordination with the regular garrisons. Second, preservation of order on the plains among the Han was an obvious priority in the wake of the rebellion. The low priority assigned to patrolling the foothills is most graphically demonstrated in Tan-shui subprefecture, which suffered less than other areas from the Lin rebellion but whose mountainous territory was highly vulnerable to raw aborigine attack. Tan-shui's total increment consisted of only two posts of 30 men each, neither located near the mountains. One was at Shih-men and charged with patrolling the sulfur deposits coveted by smugglers; the other at the port of Pa-li-fen.[223]

Another policy change reflecting the government's preoccupation with lowland security was the decision to strengthen the fortifications of the capital cities. Early in the rebellion when Taiwan's county seats were falling one after the other to the rebels, the court had been surprised to learn that Taiwan's capitals were protected only by rings of bamboo thickets, or at most earthen walls, on the theory that "what was easily lost could be easily regained" (besides saving considerably on construction expenses, see Chapter 7). The court thereupon resolved that since Taiwan had long been incorporated into the empire, its capitals, like those on the mainland, should have walls of brick and stone, on the theory that walled cities "can be defended and need not be lost."[224] Since Lin Shuang-wen's defeat had taken more than a year, some argued that this disproved the easy recapture theory. Others argued that the rebels fled the unwalled cities on the appearance of government troops, making them easy to recapture. In the end a compromise was reached: only the prefectural city of Tainan would be walled (for the first time) and Chia-i's walls would be reinforced. Budgetary considerations also limited the amount of construction finally undertaken, and inexpensive earthen walls were chosen over brick or stone.[225] But there was enough construction to create a labor shortage, and government construction funds (some collected locally) did double service as a form of relief to refugees.[226]

As noted above, Fu-k'ang-an's policy toward immigration was quite lenient, requiring only registration to gain a permit. He also favored relaxing restrictions on merchants in the Taiwan trade. Recognizing the importance of Taiwan rice to coastal Fukien, he doubled the maximum load that ships could legally carry. This benefited trade and eliminated an opportunity for official extortion.[227] For the same reasons he ordered the port of Pa-li-fen opened to the cross-strait trade (Lu-kang had been opened in 1784). Marine defenses were also bolstered.[228]

The suppression of the rebellion was quickly followed by a series of impeachments of lax officials and a trial of Brigade General Ch'ai Ta-chi. However, the unprecedented number of allegations of malfeasance and corruption and the large number of impeachments, both before and after the rebellion, cannot be taken as an indication of a resolve to reform the administration. Rather, officials were using impeachments to extort wealth and destroy the careers of rivals. Fu-k'ang-an's leading role in the trial of Ch'ai Ta-chi fits this pattern. Rather than signaling a cure, impeachments were thus the symptom of a deepening corruption extending to the highest levels of the government. This situation did not change with the suppression of the rebellion. Ho-shen was still the emperor's favorite and would remain in power until 1799, and Fu-k'ang-an, well-known for his venality, was an important collaborator of Ho-shen.[229]

Events of the last six years of the Ch'ien-lung reign, and into the nineteenth century, demonstrate the marginal efficacy of Fu-k'ang-an's reconstruction measures in pacifying Taiwan's turbulent population. Three cases of banditry from different areas of Taiwan came to the court's attention in the tenth month of 1790, but they were quickly cleared up.

At the end of the year, a more ominous development came to light. Chang-chou settlers in the Nan-t'ou area of Chang-hua county, disgruntled at their treatment by Ch'üan-chou settlers, had revived the Heaven and Earth Society. This, of course, was abhorrent to the court, and severe punishments were quickly meted out.[230] In 1791 there were two small incidents. A band of pirates was rounded up in Tan-shui, and in the Taipei area a Hakka settler, disgruntled with his Ch'üan-chou neighbors, sought to incite a raw aborigine attack against them.[231]

The Fukien naval commander resolved in 1791 to do his annual patrol of Taiwan in the fall, for it was after bad harvests that criminals caused the most trouble. Concern over piracy grew in 1792, and the government continued to round up followers of Lin Shuang-wen. The same year saw a bloody clash between soldiers and raw aborigines hunting deer on the civilized side of the boundary.[232] In the eighth month of 1792, over a hundred people were arrested in Ch'üan-chou following disturbing reports that a T'ung-an group was seeking to revive the Heaven and Earth Society and trying to recruit new members. Further investigations revealed that the instigators had been involved in the Lin rebellion and escaped to the mainland. At the end of the year, some of these secret society members had still not been apprehended.[233] The next year passed quietly enough. Only some routine cases involving "secret crossings" and the adoption of new measures against pirates were entered in the Veritable Records. In early 1794 another case involving an attempt to revive the Heaven and Earth Society came to light.[234]

Early in 1795 it became apparent that some of those who had escaped the roundup of society members in late 1792 on the mainland had fled to southern Taiwan. In the second month, a society-organized attack on a government military post in Feng-shan failed, resulting in the arrest of some and the flight of others to Chang-hua. At the time rice prices were high, and riots had occurred in Chang-hua. So Ch'en Chou-ch'üan, a leading society member, found that he had fled into fertile territory. Ch'en himself hailed from T'ung-an (whose swing role between Chang-chou and Ch'üan-chou was mentioned above); in Chang-hua he quickly organized a group recruited from all three major subethnic groups, Chang-chou, Ch'üan-chou, and Hakka, an unprecedented feat. On the tenth of the third month they took an oath to rebel.[235] The uprising met with quick initial success: Lu-kang fell by a ruse, and shortly thereafter Chang-hua city was taken. But once mobilized, the government troops easily crushed the rebellion. They were aided once again by loyalists, some of whom had also served against Lin Shuang-wen. Even braves of Chang-chou origin joined the government side, apparently eager to do in Ch'üan-chou rebels.[236] Ch'en Chou-ch'üan was unable to turn the subethnic diversity of his group to advantage.

In addition to the uprising in Taiwan, there were other signs of deterioration in the provincial government. An upsurge in piracy threatened coastal security.[237] A 1795 investigation of high rice prices revealed shortfalls in the stores of government granaries, which should have been sold to lower the market price. It was asserted that high prices were forcing poor people into criminal pursuits, including piracy. The laxness and corruption were declared more serious than in the days of Furgun and Yate. Governor-general Wu-la-na, along with the Fukien governor and treasurer, was duly impeached.[238] Also implicated in the granary shortages and impeached were two officials who had gained high praise for their service against the Lin Shuang-wen rebels and had been active in the planning of the aborigine military colonies: Yang T'ing-li and Hsü Meng-lin.[239] Wu-la-na's accuser and ultimate successor as governor-general was acting governor K'uei-lun, who was himself later reported for obstructing the work of a "righteous" subordinate official.[240] Ho-shen was still influential in these years, and his influence was probably at work in this series of appointments and impeachments.

The turbulence caused by banditry, secret society rebellions, and subethnic feuds in the next half-century of Taiwan's history casts doubt on the adequacy of the measures adopted to create an orderly society on Taiwan in the wake of the Lin Shuang-wen rebellion. The Ch'ien-lung emperor's desire that the post-rebellion reconstruction of Taiwan be so thorough that "by one great effort eternal ease could be gained" was frustrated by settlers, aborigines, and officials alike.[241]

Nineteenth-Century Developments

During the nineteenth century, rebellions throughout China and growing foreign aggression sapped the energy of the central government and frustrated attempts to maintain, let alone deepen, social control. In Taiwan subethnic strife and the inability of the government to contain it effectively continued through the 1860's, although the building of city walls and the growth of a gentry elite point to the maturation of Taiwan's Chinese society.[242] Disorder within Taiwan had many effects on plains aborigines, including the use to which the military colonists were put. According to Huang Huan-yao, the colonists were mobilized eighteen times in the nineteenth century.[243] All nine mobilizations from 1804 to 1862 were against Han bandits or to aid in putting down Han communal strife. Only the nine mobilizations in the final decades of the nineteenth century were against raw aborigines (see below).

The steady encroachment of Han settlers became too oppressive for many civilized aborigines early in the nineteenth century; this is most dramatically indicated by migrations to plains areas beyond Han domination on the east coast and in the P'u-li basin. In 1804 a group of over 1,000, drawn from ten settlements in Chang-hua and southern Tan-shui, crossed the steep central mountain range to settle in the I-lan plain on the east coast. That ten bands from as many as five ethnolinguistic groups joined together for this migration is good evidence of the diminished significance of linguistic divisions among plains aborigines. Shortage of agricultural land was not the cause of the migration, since colony lands allotted to these aborigines were going unreclaimed. The immediate cause was a clash between Han and civilized aborigines involving the incitement of raw aborigine attacks.[244] That only subgroups joined the migrations is demonstrated by the fact that six of the villages also contributed settlers to the later migration to the P'u-li basin. This includes both A-li-shih *she* and A-shu *she,* which contributed the largest contingents to the 1804 migration. In 1823 the migration to the P'u-li basin began and ultimately involved 30 villages, also from Chang-hua and southern Tan-shui. Once again only subgroups and not entire villages joined the migration. In southern Taiwan Siraya migrated to the southeast coast and rift valley; again only a small part of the population of these plains aborigine villages took part in the migrations.[245] Since rents were declining due to weak government enforcement against Han nonpayment and increasing alienation of land rights to get cash, and since these rights were increasingly concentrated in the hands of a few families in each tribe, the most disadvantaged families joined the migrations (see Chapter 11).

It is these nineteenth-century migrations that have given rise to the common misperception that Chinese settlers pushed Taiwan's plains aborigines into the mountains or, in a different version, that the ancestors of all present-day mountain aborigines lived on the plains. Both versions are incorrect. Many plains groups never participated in the migrations, and those that did, did not do so in toto. Rather, many plains aborigine villagers remained and became increasingly sinicized. Moreover, those that resettled migrated not into the mountains but to plains areas free of Han domination (the east coast and the P'u-li basin). In these areas, plains aborigine crop inventories and agricultural skills were superior to those of the native inhabitants, who had not yet learned Han farming techniques. By contrast, plains aborigines were ill-adapted to mountain life. The presence of distinct ethnolinguistic groups in the mountains predates and is not explained by either the Chinese occupation of Taiwan or the nineteenth-century migrations of the plains aborigines.[246] What is striking about these migrations is their selective character and that they took place only after more than a century of intensive Han settlement and repeated government attempts to manage the frontier.

The fate of the aboriginal Kuvalan of the I-lan plain on Taiwan's northeast coast provides a sharp contrast to that of the plains aborigines on the western coastal plain. Government administration was not extended to the I-lan plain before the nineteenth century, and the Kuvalan were not taxpaying subjects of the Ch'ing, which therefore did not recognize Kuvalan title to unreclaimed land. Han migration into the isolated I-lan plain in the early nineteenth century began suddenly and on a large scale. Thus, the Kuvalan did not have an opportunity to adapt gradually to the consequences of Han settlement, as had the plains aborigines on the west coast. Nor had the Kuvalan participated in the land-tenure institutions that protected the west coast groups or the military colonies that gave the west coast groups a role in the Ch'ing administration. The Kuvalan were totally unprepared for the onslaught of Chinese settlers that saw the Han population of I-lan grow to nearly 40,000 by 1810.[247] The colonization of the I-lan plain had proceeded beyond the reach of government control and was far along when the Ch'ing created a subprefecture to govern the territory in 1810.

The threat of pirate raids on Taiwan's coasts and the fear that rebels and bandits would find a haven in I-lan stimulated this sudden extension of the administration. To finance the high administrative and defense costs incurred in ruling this rude frontier region, the first prefect, Yang T'ing-li, "demanded that the entire large-rentholder yield be remitted as land-tax revenue to the Ko-ma-lan [I-lan] government."[248] The split-ownership system of land tenure was thereby abolished in I-lan; this foreclosed the possibility that aborigine large-rents could provide for the accommodation of Han agricultural settlers and the Kuvalan, whose hunting economy was rapidly being destroyed. Thus, the balance of strategy, control costs, and revenue needs that had benefited plains aborigines on the west coast worked against restriction of Han immigration and aggressive protection of Kuvalan livelihoods in I-lan.

Yang T'ing-li did adopt policies barring Han from acquiring land in the immediate vicinity of Kuvalan villages, where land was reserved for aborigine use and made tax-exempt, following Taiwan precedent. Yang's stated purposes were to ensure aborigine livelihoods and avoid aborigine-settler conflict.[249] In 1813 the aborigine reserve land was surveyed and registered, and Han were barred. Yang also provided for an allotment of land reclaimed by Han to pay a rent to the aborigines of 4 *shih* per *chia*.[250] But it was too little too late, for the Kuvalan were unable to adapt to such rapid change. They lacked the sophistication and institutional position necessary to see their rights enforced against unscrupulous Han. Impoverished Kuvalan, who were poor farmers, alienated their lands for ready cash. By the end of the nineteenth century, the Kuvalan population had declined by approximately 70 percent, and many were migrating to Hua-lien.[251]

As Han subethnic strife subsided after the 1860's and self-strengtheners reformed Taiwan's local administration, a more stable gentry-led society emerged.[252] All nine mobilizations of the plains aborigine military colonists from 1875 to 1892 were to fight raw aborigines in the mountains rather than to suppress communal fighting.[253] This late-nineteenth century pattern reflects the aggressive attempts to extend government control over (rather than quarantine) raw aborigines through the new *k'ai shan fu fan* policies. The court endorsed these policies of "opening the mountains and pacifying the aborigines" after the Japanese sent a naval expedition in 1874 to punish raw aborigines in Heng-ch'un, at Taiwan's southern tip.

The foreign powers held the Chinese court responsible for protecting foreign sailors, who frequently shipwrecked on Taiwan's wild coasts and fell victim to head-hunting aborigines. Also, during the Sino-French war of 1884–85, the French navy attacked the island and blockaded its ports.[254] These repeated threats of foreign aggression made increased control over the strategically important island an imperative. Each of these acts of aggression, the Japanese in 1874–75 and the French in 1884–85, brought attempts to tighten control over the island by posting more, higher-ranking officials. In 1875, the island was divided between two prefectures (presiding over eight counties and four subprefectures), with the new T'ai-pei prefecture having jurisdiction over the north. In 1887 the court divided the island among three prefectures, north, center, and south, having jurisdiction over eleven counties and four subprefectures, and created an autonomous *chou* on the east coast.[255] The court also raised the island to provincial status under an aggressive governor with a military background, Liu Ming-ch'uan.

Governor Liu's campaigns in the late 1880's against the mountain aborigines were intended to end head-hunting and open the mountains to allow tea planters and camphor workers to take advantage of booming international markets for Taiwan's tea and camphor.[256] These aggressive colonization policies reflect the changed political economy of Taiwan in the last half of the nineteenth century forced on the court by the strategic challenge posed by foreign imperialism. Criticized for the expensive mountain campaigns, Governor Liu sought to reduce his control costs by following an old Taiwan pattern: he offered to accommodate the raw aborigines of the mountains with allocations of land and rights to collect rents from Chinese settlers.[257] At the same time he sought to increase his revenues through an island-wide cadastral survey to enroll "hidden" land on the tax registers.[258] Liu's goal was to create a fiscal base that would generate the tax revenues needed to finance military and infrastructural modernization, as well as the campaigns against the mountain aborigines. As part of the survey, Liu made small-rent holders directly responsible for the land tax (thinking they would be less successful at tax avoidance) and reduced proportionally the rents all small-rent holders paid to large-rent holders. For the Han large-rent holders, the reduction in rents was offset by the shift to small-rent holders of the tax burden, and their net income was unaffected. But because lands under aborigine large-rent had not previously been liable to taxation, there was no offsetting shift in the tax burden, and the reduction in the aborigine large-rent meant a direct reduction in plains aborigine incomes. Liu's reforms thereby dealt a serious blow to plains aborigine livelihoods.[259]

The magnitude of the changes in Taiwan's fiscal structure envisioned in Liu's program is reflected in tax figures. When Liu Ming-ch'uan started his survey in 1886, approximately 70,000 *chia* of agricultural land was registered for taxation, only a little more than the area registered in the 1760's, despite a tripling of the population since that time (see Tables 6.4, 6.5, and 8.3). Liu's survey quadrupled the taxed area to 290,000 *chia* and more than tripled Taiwan's annual land-tax revenues, from 183,366 taels to 674,468 taels.[260] But this substantial increase in land-tax revenues could fund only a portion of Liu's expenditures on modernization and defense. The magnitude of these expenses is indicated by the size of the subsidies the court granted to Liu to help finance his program: a subsidy from Fukien of 440,000 taels annually for five years as well as the Imperial Maritime Customs receipts collected in Taiwan, totaling 1.4 million taels annually.[261] Combined with Taiwan's pre–land survey revenues, operations under Liu therefore required an annual minimum expenditure of two million taels. This amount is roughly eight times my estimate of statutory expenditures (generously converting each *shih* of unhusked grain to one tael) in 1768 of only 262,173 taels.[262] These huge increases in taxes and expenditures suggest not only the expense of responding to the challenges of the late nineteenth century but also the degree of stagnation in Taiwan's local finances since the late eighteenth century, a topic students of nineteenth-century Taiwan must pursue in greater detail.

Thus, in the nineteenth century strategic threats from pirates and foreign powers (absent in the eighteenth century) forced the state to increase expenditures for Taiwan's defense and administration. The state turned to the land tax to supply substantial portions of these revenues, and in doing so, it redefined land rights and reallocated land tax–paying responsibilities. In I-lan under Yang T'ing-li and throughout Taiwan's western coast under Liu Ming-ch'uan, the state's need to maximize its land-tax revenues meant reduced tolerance for plains aborigine large-rents and tax exemptions. After 1895 a revenue-hungry Japanese colonial government completed this process by expropriating all large-rent rights and ending the aborigine large-rent system.[263]

CHAPTER ELEVEN

The Transformation of Plains Aborigine Cultures

THIS CHAPTER DESCRIBES changes in Taiwan's plains aborigine societies and economies due to the influx of Chinese during the eighteenth century. Previous chapters have noted many such changes primarily in the context of Dutch, Cheng, and Ch'ing attempts to regulate and control Han-aborigine interaction, at first through the deer trade, monopoly merchants, interpreters, and tax farms, and later by the management of frontier land reclamation. The discussion here focuses (to the extent the sources allow) on the adaptations improvised by the plains aborigine populations. The analysis begins with the economic transformations brought about by the deer trade and its decline. Next, we consider traditional Chinese attitudes toward sinicization of non-Han groups, as reflected in the Ch'ing ethnographic accounts that provide much of the material analyzed here. Then, we look at the differential adoption by the plains aborigines of elements of Chinese culture, differential not only by the gender, age, and rank of those doing the adopting, but also by the customs and status characteristics adopted.[1] In particular, we examine changes in material culture, education, religion, and kinship, as well as the impact of intermarriage. In conclusion, we note political changes within aborigine villages and offer an explanation for village fission and the migration of sub-groups to the foothills and the plains of the east coast.

In analyzing cultural change, I emphasize historical process and see the direction of change as guided by political, economic, and prestige considerations. In particular, I reject current approaches to the interaction of cultural groups that reify concepts of ethnicity and enshrine questions of ethnic identity while ignoring cultural transformations and borrowings that cannot be interpreted as signaling changes in ethnic consciousness or a reassertion of it.[2] Studies of ethnicity narrowly conceived are crippled by the failure to distinguish "acculturation" (the adoption of the customs and ways of life of another group) and "assimilation" (an individual's identification with another group). Two groups may have similar lifeways and be highly acculturated one to another, yet insist they have separate ethnic identities, for example, Irish Protestants and Irish Catholics or Manchus and Han in the twentieth century. Other groups may display tremendous internal cultural diversity yet claim a shared ethnic identity, for example, Chinese or Americans. Thus, a high degree of acculturation does not ensure the shared identity implied by assimilation, nor does a shared identity require cultural homogeneity resulting from acculturation. Used in this way, "acculturation" implies an external, objective standard for the measurement of changes in cultural similarity and difference over time, and "assimilation" requires an assessment of shared identity from an actor's subjective point of view.

Only in specific circumstances is the adoption of elements from another culture seen as compromising an ethnic identity or signaling a desire to join another group. Paradoxically, it is frequently only after a group has already become highly acculturated to another that members discover an advantage (psychic, political, or economic) in maintaining a separate group identity. They then begin to raise ethnic boundaries by reinventing group traditions, often using as symbolic markers of group membership traits that have acquired contrastive significance only in the present and that their unacculturated ancestors would have been surprised to learn represented unique group characteristics.[3]

In general, when cultural interaction leads to competition on a group basis, perhaps in periods of diminishing opportunity, then we can predict erection of ethnic group boundaries as rival groups seek to exclude one another from the competition for prestige and advantage. When opportunities are expanding and open to members of different groups, and competition proceeds on an individual basis, we can predict permeable ethnic boundaries and unimpeded acculturation to the high-prestige group.[4] Thus, the salience of ethnic identity and the maintenance of group boundaries to processes of cultural change depend greatly on the structure of group interaction and competition. Understanding how group competition comes to be structured requires that analysis begin not with group self-definitions but with the historical circumstances shaping group interaction. Group self-definitions are constructed in the process of interaction and are thus a transitory product of group history, to be deployed, modified, and discarded according to circumstance. Only a thoroughgoing historical approach encompassing the operation of a wide range of historical factors can account both for the direction of cultural change and for the varying significance of ethnicity within the process of change. Questions of ethnic identity and assimilation arise, then, only under certain (often politicized) circumstances and are themselves a product of the processes of cultural change and interaction.[5]

As known to ethnographers in the twentieth century, Taiwan's plains aborigine groups are highly acculturated to Han ways of life and, except for a few words and songs remembered by the senior generation, speak only Chinese dialects. Despite a uniformly high degree of acculturation, plains aborigine attitudes toward their separate cultural heritage and identity vary greatly both among villages and among individuals. These attitudes range from a denial of non-Han origins (often involving radical reinterpretations of group history) to ambivalence to pride in their aboriginal heritage and its celebration in an aboriginal religious cult.[6] Plains aborigines thus present a range of cases that illustrate both the convergence and the divergence of assimilation and acculturation. This chapter analyzes the beginning of plains aborigine acculturation to Han Chinese cultural patterns in the eighteenth century, a process appropriately labeled "sinicization," in the full context of plains aborigine adaptation to Chinese political domination and the intrusion of Han agricultural settlers.

As discussed in Chapters 1 and 2, there were at least eight separate ethnolinguistic groupings within the historical-geographic category "plains aborigine." Because of this ethnic diversity, there were many starting points and subsequent reactions to increasing contact with the culture of the Chinese state and the Han settlers (themselves a diverse lot). Because none of these individual groups has yet been intensively studied for the period under review, this chapter necessarily presents a preliminary, and overly homogenized, view of the adaptations improvised by many separate groups and individuals. I hope the historical outline sketched in this book will provide a framework to help guide future, more intensive studies as well as present hypotheses about the nature of the acculturation process that these studies can test and refine.[7]

Economic Adaptations to the Declining Deer Trade

During the eighteenth century, expanding agricultural exploitation of the frontier gradually undermined plains aborigine hunting economies, dislocating aborigine social arrangements and forcing new modes of livelihood. But Han migration to Taiwan had its greatest impact (especially for groups outside the southwest core) in the middle decades of the century. The first stages of Han-aborigine interaction revolved around the deer trade. Although the trade in deerskins and venison peaked under the Dutch and the Chengs, it remained central to Han-aborigine economic exchange throughout the K'ang-hsi years. This is confirmed, though without quantitative estimates, by the descriptions of the trade by Yü Yung-ho in 1697[8] and Huang Shu-ching in 1722[9] (see also Chapter 5). The degree of continuity in the trade pattern between the Dutch and Cheng eras and the early Ch'ing is striking. This continuity was made possible by the repatriation of the Cheng forces, the quarantine policies of the early Ch'ing, and the slow pace of the early immigration, which reduced and then limited the growth of Taiwan's population of Han agricultural settlers.

The Chinese manufactures and the native produce exchanged in the trade remained largely the same as they had been under the Dutch (see Chapter 2). This pattern endured longest in the frontier areas of Chang-hua and areas to the north, remote from the southwest core centers of settlement.[10] Thus, as late as 1722 Huang Shu-ching could still describe the trade of Ta-chia and the aborigine villages of the north with the Chinese core in the south as primarily the exchange of deer products for Chinese manufactures: "Each [of these villages] has interpreters, who go back and forth, to and from the capital. The goods that [are taken] from the south to the north include salt, sugar, tobacco, cloth, and thread. [The goods taken] from the north to the south include dried deer meat, deer sinews, deer horns, deer skins, sesamum, 'water creepers,' laver, and *t'ung ts'ao.*"[11] The aborigines were especially eager to trade for iron goods such as tools, weapons, and cooking pots; the increased supply of metal tools significantly enhanced the efficiency of aborigine systems of production. Trade was necessary to acquire the shot and powder needed for aborigine hunting guns, as well as the textiles and ornaments that satisfied an expanding need for creature comforts. To acquire these goods and to meet the demands of the state and interpreters for revenue and squeeze, the plains aborigines overhunted the deer herds.[12]

Both overhunting and the destruction of habitat caused by the spread of Chinese farming precipitated a decline in the deer herds, first in the southwest core and then ultimately throughout the coastal plains and foothills. The prefectural gazetteer of 1740 reported that overhunting had led to the disappearance of deer with more than seven growth rings on their antlers (each growth ring indicates a year of life). Another gazetteer commented that although the absence of tigers in Taiwan would ordinarily make for a large population of deer, herds could be found only in the inner mountains and no longer on the plains.[13] Other gazetteers reported that the destruction of grazing land by the conversion of deer fields to paddy was causing deer herds to disappear.[14] The destruction of the deer herds caused the collapse of the deer trade and eliminated an important source of aborigine income. This forced aborigine hunters to search for new modes of livelihood.[15]

Agriculture was an obvious alternative for aborigines who had an abundance of arable land at their disposal. Huang Shu-ching found that the southern plains groups were using agricultural implements (plows and harrows, for example) comparable to those used by Chinese. Some groups were even transplanting rice seedlings in irrigated paddies.[16] Groups in the foothills and in the north, however, continued to use hoes instead of plows and to plant millet rather than rice.[17] The easy availability of land and access to Chinese agricultural techniques were insufficient to make rice cultivation attractive to displaced aborigine hunters. For them farming had two major drawbacks: first, according to the traditional sexual division of labor, it was women's work;[18] second, it was labor-intensive drudgery. Although Lin Ch'ien-kuang's 1685 description of plains aborigine farming asserts that "all of the tilling is done by the wife,"[19] the later descriptions of Yü Yung-ho and Huang Shu-ching do not identify agriculture as a predominantly female task. The introduction of the ox-drawn plow as a male agricultural technique under the Dutch contributed to acceptance of an expanded role for men in agriculture, and increased exposure to the example of male Chinese farmers reinforced the changing gender identity of farming after Dutch times.[20]

But even if gender ideology was diminishing as an obstacle by Ch'ing times, intensive farming's burdensome labor requirements remained a deterrent to its adoption. For example, several gazetteers praise a special variety of fragrant rice grown in dry fields by the aborigines. Mixing a small amount with ordinary varieties could flavor an entire pot. The gazetteers suggest that Han purchases could easily multiply.[21] Huang Shu-ching added his endorsement: once cooked, this variety would remain fresh, without souring, for two or three days. But, Huang noted, "each year [the aborigines] plant only enough of this for their own consumption during the year. They do not market it; even though its value is several times higher [than that of ordinary rice], they will not sell it."[22] The opportunity to profit was insufficient to entice the aborigines into investing more labor in cultivation of this variety. Unpredictable demands for corvée and guard duty also disrupted the ability of aborigine males to invest labor in agriculture.[23] Aborigine farmers remained less commercially oriented than Chinese farmers who planted rice and sugar for export. Some aborigines no doubt preferred to leave farming to the Han and take the cash and grain payments from Han that plains aborigines could obtain from sales and leases of a seemingly endless supply of land. The bulk of plains tribes therefore maintained their reputation as poorly skilled, subsistence-oriented farmers throughout this period. Only Hsin-kang *she*, in the heart of the southwest core, earned praise for the improved quality of its farmers in a 1752 gazetteer.[24]

As an occupational alternative and source of cash income, displaced aborigine hunters found that ox herding and cart driving not only lacked the drawbacks of agriculture but were positively appealing. Oxen (and horses) were unknown to the aborigines until introduced under the Dutch for drawing plows and carts.[25] By the time of the Ch'ing conquest, oxcarts were used in every aborigine village. In 1697 Yü Yung-ho traveled the length of the island by changing cart and driver in each aborigine village en route. The large number of oxen and the abundance of domesticated animals in Taiwan impressed Chinese observers accustomed to dense settlement and human-labor-intensive agriculture.[26] Excessive corvée of oxcarts was often a sore point and was one cause of the large 1731 aborigine revolt (see Chapter 5). That aborigines might lose their oxen and carts by defaulting on high-interest loans obtained from Han was also a matter of official concern.[27]

The degree to which the plains aborigines incorporated the recently introduced oxen into their cultures was striking. Oxen were slaughtered for marriage feasts in many villages, although some Papora villages seem to have followed Chinese custom in their aversion to eating oxen.[28] Dutch-period observers had recorded that plains aborigine villages assessed compensations for adultery and fines for infractions of village customs in deerskins. By Huang Shu-ching's time in the 1720's, villages assessed compensations and fines in terms of oxen and carts, reflecting the changes in aborigine economies.[29]

Demand for oxen was high because they performed a wide range of economic functions on the Taiwan frontier. Two-wheeled oxcarts were a highly efficient mode of transporting bulky loads of sugarcane, grain, and lumber over Taiwan's crude roads (see Chapter 6). Oxen also pulled plows, turned the stones that crushed sugarcane and milled grain, and propelled the wheels that lifted water to rice paddies.[30] This variety of uses made oxen indispensable to Han settlers.

Oxen were in plentiful supply in eighteenth-century Taiwan. Since Dutch times, oxen had been allowed to run wild and multiply in the foothills, where they could be recaptured when needed. Wild oxen replaced the depleted deer herds in the foothills and on fields not yet reclaimed by Han farmers.[31] The presence of wild oxen in the hills continued to be noted throughout the nineteenth century, and one southern plains village is reported to have had a herd of over 2,000 head.[32]

Both Yü Yung-ho and Huang Shu-ching describe aborigines capturing wild oxen, taming them, and trading them to Han. Huang notes: "In these mountains there are wild cattle. When there is a Chinese buyer, a posse of barbarians chases after them on horseback and captures them. The selling price is one-half that of a domesticated ox."[33] The flavor of a "cowboy" economy is even stronger in the following passage from Huang: "North of Tung- and Hsi-lo the barbarians like to raise horses. They ride bareback. When they are after crafty animals or intercepting darting birds, they can twist and turn at will in the thick grass or among the tall trees. They pick out the best mares and trade them at several times their value so as to breed from them."[34] Herding livestock thus preserved some of the excitement of the hunt. Deer hunters found it easier to adapt to the role of herder than to the drudgery of farm labor, and in villages bordering the foothills or located on the plains remote from areas of Han settlement, the plains aborigines developed a pastoral economy to compensate for the declining deer trade.

Fig. 11.1 Aborigine scenes from Chu-lo, ca. 1717 (SOURCE: *CLHC*).

舂米

乘屋

登場

插秧

Tribesmen in areas of Han agricultural settlement were less fortunate. They had either to migrate to the foothills to take advantage of the wild herds, to turn to agriculture, or to find other alternatives. The Chu-lo gazetteer of 1717 reported poor aborigines from Hsin-kang *she* begging in nearby Tainan. Conditions seem to have improved by 1752 when another gazetteer reported that the corvée had been reduced and that the farmers of Hsin-kang *she* were well off.[35] In the early Ch'ien-lung years, several franchises on the ferry business at river crossings in the southwest core were awarded to plains aborigine tribes as a means of poor relief.[36] Relief grain was also distributed to poor aborigines in 1747 and 1756.[37] These welfare measures indicate that not all plains aborigines enjoyed sufficient income from rents on Han-reclaimed tribal lands to enable them to adjust comfortably to economic dislocation. The several examples noted in the gazetteers of cooperation between Han and plains aborigines in the construction of irrigation works are a bright spot in the pattern of aborigine adjustment to the expansion of Han agriculture.[38]

Civilization and Sinicization

The aborigines were also the object of cultural influences and policies emanating from a growing Han population and the Chinese civil and military administrations. The "civilizing" of the plains aborigines was an important means by which the Chinese state sought to extend effective control over the plains groups. Confident of the superiority of Chinese culture, most officials assumed that civilization and even sinicization would come naturally with time, as aborigines came to understand the self-evident superiority of Confucian morality. Until then, cultural conformity need not be actively enforced so long as cultural differences did not directly challenge government control.

The Chinese world order was a sinocentric one that defined the Middle Kingdom as the single center of civilization and culture; all who stood outside its bounds were barbarians who lacked culture and civilization. The defining characteristics of civilization were the principles of Confucian social hierarchy, the five cardinal relationships, and the forms of ritual propriety (*li*) that embodied and expressed these principles. Confucianism thereby defined the superiority of Chinese civilization in moral rather than economic, political, or technological terms. "A random perusal of discussions of barbarians in the various encyclopedias and other sources reveals again and again the degree of emphasis on the five relationships, the 'three bonds' (*san kang*) and the whole body of *li* as providing the absolute criteria dividing barbarians from the men of the Middle Kingdom."[39] China was defined as " 'the land of ritual and right behavior' (*li i chih pang*)," and barbarians exposed to Chinese culture were expected to be impressed by its moral prestige. Over time the barbarians would feel a natural attraction to Chinese culture that would result in their moral transformation. The histories praised barbarians who "'admired right behavior and turned toward Chinese civilization' (*mu i hsiang hua*)."[40] To incorporate non-Han groups within the empire (a complicated process of political-economic calculation; see Chapter 12) and effectively subject them to the limited means of social control available to the imperial state required extending the reach of Confucian civilization and making non-Han groups amenable to social control through prestige processes.[41] In theory this did not require assimilation of non-Han groups to Han.

Sinicization (*han hua*, the adoption of specifically Han customs) must be distinguished from more inclusive concepts in Chinese political thought that emphasize the adoption of elements of Confucian civil culture (*chiao hua, shang wen*) or at the very least submission to imperial authority (*wang hua*) but do not entail the adoption of narrowly Han customs and the loss of a separate ethnic identity.[42] This distinction is particularly important for a conquest dynasty like the Ch'ing, for the ruling Manchus were themselves actively resisting sinicization and seeking to preserve their separate traditions and ethnic identity. The Manchus could reject many Han customs, for example, footbinding, without sacrificing their claim to head a Confucian state.

Much of Confucian political theory is encapsulated in the phrase *wen chih chiao hua*, to govern by refinement and to transform through education. Good government meant ruling by moral persuasion and example (at least in theory), not by military force.[43] Belief in the universal validity of Confucian morality as the only form of "civilization" and the ability of peoples of all ethnic backgrounds to acquire the essential attributes of civilization through education is commonly referred to as Confucian "culturalism." The emperor and his officials embodied the highest moral learning, and it was their duty as moral superiors to instruct an ignorant and morally inferior populace.[44] Ch'ing administrative theory adapted this philosophy (along with a Mencian emphasis on the ensurance of livelihoods) in its approach to local cultures. Magistrates were expected to serve as models of Confucian virtue that the populace could emulate and to reward and praise commoners who exemplified Confucian virtues.[45]

The civilizing mission of local magistrates (toward Han and non-Han alike) was to propagate Confucian civic culture and attitudes of submission to constituted authority rather than wholesale sinicization, although it was not always a simple matter for Chinese officials to distinguish Confucian attitudes from Han customs. To the extent the plains aborigine hunter-warrior culture led to the training of braves that could be enlisted by the state and a separate plains aborigine ethnic identity facilitated Ch'ing policies of divide and rule and the containment of Han communal strife (see Chapter 10), it was in the state's interest to oppose wholesale sinicization (which might erase ethnic divisions) while fostering the loyalty that came with "civilization" and "Confucianization."[46]

Pro-colonization advocates sometimes advanced bolder visions of the transformation of aborigine cultures. Shen Ch'i-yüan, the acting Taiwan prefect in 1729 (see Chapter 9), argued that good government would transform Han immigrants (*liu min*) into rooted locals (*t'u chu*), cooked aborigines into Han (*hua shu fan wei han jen*), and raw aborigines into cooked.[47] In Shen's view, then, the ultimate product of Confucian governance was not just that aborigines would become civilized, law-abiding subjects, but that they would be transformed into Han. As Han, their social customs and mores would correspond to the expectations embedded in the state's routine methods of administrative control. Pro-colonization advocates sometimes exaggerated the ease by which indigenes could be culturally transformed (thereby minimizing the costs of extending government control) to overcome the objections of more conservative officials opposed to the aggressive expansion of Han settlement.[48] Conservative officials expected only limited cultural transformations at a gradual pace, spearheaded by youths educated in the classics.[49]

Education Policy

The Ch'ing state saw education of aborigine youths in the Confucian classics as the premier means of turning the plains aborigines toward civilization and creating a loyal elite among them. Education was the state's most direct (noncoercive) means of fostering cultural change. Through education in the classics, aborigine youths were taught to revere Confucian civilization and the imperial state. (See Chapter 7 for the importance Confucian statecraft placed on inculcating its moral values as a means of controlling and co-opting local elites, both Han and non-Han.) To achieve these goals, officials in Taiwan initiated a variety of schemes to institute formal instruction of aborigine youths and set up tribal schools.

The curriculum in the tribal schools did not differ from that in Chinese village schools. As was customary, it began with the Trimetrical Classic and the Thousand-Character Classic and then proceeded to the Sacred Edict and the Four Books. Emphasis was at first on character recognition and calligraphy and then on recitation and memorization of texts. Instruction in reading Chinese was supplemented with illustrated glossaries and reading primers and strengthened the linguistic competence of aborigine youths who learned Chinese (primarily the Minnan dialect) as a second language.[50]

The content of traditional education centered on inculcation of Confucian morality. Both teacher and text spoke of notions of social hierarchy, duty, obligations to parents, and the subordination of women. Rudimentary cosmological notions rooted the imperial state and Confucian morality in the natural order of heaven, earth, and man.[51] Students were taught the duties appropriate to each of the five cardinal relationships of ruler-minister, father-son, husband-wife, older-younger brother, and friend-friend (the first three are the Three Bonds), as well as the key virtues of loyalty and filial piety. They were introduced to history through the names of benevolent emperors and sages and the succession of dynasties. The primers also taught students values of self-discipline and emotional self-control and the importance of educational achievement, diligence, and hard work to social advancement. Study of the Sacred Edict was intended to discourage unlawful behavior.[52]

Despite the importance the Ch'ing state assigned to the education, moral transformation, and civilization of the plains aborigines, it did not allocate scarce tax revenues to mount a sustained educational effort. Rather, periodic campaigns to set up schools were launched either by the few vigorous reforming officials or in reconstruction efforts following major disturbances when lack of education was always identified as contributing to social disorder. Financial and organizational responsibility for schooling generally remained with or quickly devolved to the tribes and low-level officials, who had only occasional interest in sustaining broad-based education. Without institutionalized financial support, many schools disappeared shortly after being founded. Initiative in village-level education remained (as in the case of the Han) with leading families that recognized the opportunities and advantages education could provide their sons.[53]

Nevertheless, the frequency with which the gazetteers record efforts to foster education among the plains aborigines does suggest that Confucian officialdom took its educational and civilizing mission seriously. In 1686, shortly after Ch'ing rule was established, the magistrate of Chu-lo county founded schools in each of the four major Siraya villages near Tainan.[54] Unfortunately none of the sources reveals anything about the staffing, funding, or operation of these schools. Several officials are reported fostering education among Taiwan's aborigines in the later years of the K'ang-hsi reign. Chin Chih-yang, prefect during the aborigine revolts on the north route in 1699 (see Chapter 5), is credited with expanding education in aborigine villages.[55] Ch'en Pin, while serving as Taiwan intendant in 1710, a post which in those years combined the duties of director of studies and examiner, reportedly established schools and engaged teachers to teach aborigines writing and Confucian propriety.[56] In 1713 Ch'en lamented that in the previous three years no aborigine students had competed in the local examinations, perhaps because of official neglect; he therefore ordered that announcements commanding aborigine students to sit for the current year's examinations be made in every aborigine village. To encourage aborigine educational attainment, the prefecture and every county were ordered to register several of the better candidates as official students.[57] During his tour of the north route in 1715, Lieutenant-colonel Juan Ts'ai-wen summoned aborigine students from neighboring villages and gave small rewards to those who successfully recited the classics.[58]

The lists of aborigine schools in the county gazetteers compiled in 1717–20 give a more limited picture of the spread of aborigine education. The Chu-lo county gazetteer of 1717 reports a total of eight aborigine schools in the county, the four established in 1686 and four more to the north established in 1715 (in Chu-lo-shan, Ta-miao, To-lo-kuo, and Ta-wu-chün, all south of Chang-hua). The gazetteers for the counties of T'ai-wan and Feng-shan fail to report any aborigine schools.[59] The expansion of schools in the aborigine villages seems thus to have proceeded rather slowly and unevenly, and no commitment of government funds to speed the process is reported in the gazetteer sections on local revenues and expenditures. Nevertheless, the expansion of education and the hiring of teachers seems to have been greater than the lists of schools suggest. Huang Shu-ching's account of his 1722 tour of inspection cites cases of aborigine students capable of reciting the classics from villages in the Chang-hua area (Mao-erh-kan, Tung-lo, A-shu, and Pan-hsien) and in four of the eight villages of the south route in Feng-shan county.[60]

Reconstruction following the Chu I-kuei rebellion of 1721 included official programs for the encouragement of aborigine education. In 1723 Prefect Kao To rewarded aborigine students in every village with wine and a gift of the Four Books. Huang Shu-ching also reports that Intendant and Director of Studies Ch'en Ta-nien (1722–24), who had been active in the pacification following the Chu I-kuei rebellion, awarded the more proficient aborigine students roles as musicians and performers in the Confucian rituals sponsored by the prefecture and counties.[61] From this time it became customary to include among the *i sheng* (ritualists) aborigine students who failed to obtain the *sheng yüan* degree. The *i sheng* served as musicians and performers in the solemn ceremonies school temples conducted each spring and autumn to honor Confucius; among their privileges was exemption from labor service.[62] These Confucian sacrifices and the roles played by each ritual participant are described in precise detail in the prefectural gazetteers, which include diagrams specifying the position of each actor.[63] Participation in these elaborate performances, attended and presided over by local officeholders, must have been awe-inspiring for aborigine students and helped instill in them the desired respect for Confucian governance.

Following the Ta-chia-hsi aborigine rebellion (see Chapter 5), the intendant Chang Ssu-ch'ang acted in 1734 to establish an unprecedented number of community schools in aborigine villages (*t'u fan she hsüeh*).

Forty-seven schools were created, one in every important aborigine village: five in T'ai-wan county, eight in Feng-shan, eleven in Chu-lo, seventeen in Chang-hua, and six in Tan-shui.[64] The list of school sites corresponds closely to the list of tribal tax units as subsequently reorganized in 1737 (see Chapter 5 and Appendix A). Each school was to have an instructor, and the students were to be examined at regular intervals. The censor Liu-shih-ch'i's tour of inspection in 1744 found many aborigine students who could recite the classics without error and produce excellent calligraphy. Liu-shih-ch'i noted, however, that though dressed and wearing the queue like Han, these students retained aborigine names and lacked Han surnames. Although no item appears in the prefectural and county budgets for these schools, Liu-shih-ch'i asserted that official grain was provided to the instructors of the aborigine schools.[65] Nevertheless, we may question how long and at what level of quality as many as 47 schools could be maintained, teachers provided and paid, and student attendance kept up, especially when this had to be done largely at aborigine expense. This was a large number of schools for the small aborigine population to sustain, especially when the prefectural gazetteer of 1768 reports the much larger Han population, numbering in the hundreds of thousands, as supporting only twelve community schools and five academies.[66]

We do not know how many aborigine students passed the *sheng yüan* examination before the late nineteenth century. As was standard practice nationally, the Taiwan gazetteers include lists only of successful candidates for the *kung sheng*, *chü jen*, and *chin shih* degrees, and not of the lowly *sheng yüan*.[67] We do know of a few plains aborigine degree holders in the eighteenth century, most prominently the *kung sheng* from the An-li tribe who aided the government during the Lin Shuang-wen rebellion.[68] To learn of others, we must await the results of studies in local history and genealogy.

There appears to have been no proposal to establish a special aborigine *sheng yüan* quota before 1870, although such quotas, including quotas for aborigine *chü jen*, were not uncommon in other areas of the empire.[69] In proposing such a quota in 1870, the Taiwan intendant spoke of the need to stimulate the education of the sons of aborigine headmen and military colony officers and ensure their mastery of the classics, including the Sacred Edict. The proposal cited a Kweichow Miao precedent. A number of plains aborigines benefited from the new quota, although the number of candidates in the early years was disappointingly few.[70]

Educated youths could hope to act as political leaders within their communities, to mediate tribe-state relations, and to manage relations with military officers, yamen underlings, and bureaucrats. Youths educated in ways Chinese could use their skills in negotiating arrangements for the reclamation of aborigine lands and expect to fare better in commercial dealings with Han. Students who excelled could even hope to win a literary degree and qualify for lucrative government office. Both state and society honored those who mastered Confucian learning and might one day achieve political office. Because of these rewards, youths from prosperous and astute families were encouraged and motivated to do well in school. And it seems to have been these leading families who took responsibility for the provision of schooling in the villages.

Differential Sinicization

Outside the sphere of education, the state rarely expended its scarce resources to mandate cultural conformity. Rather, it relied on its prestige as the center of political and economic power and of high culture to impress and instill awe and respect in its subject populations. Manipulation of cultural prestige was the state's most cost-effective means of maintaining social control. By cultivating its claim to civilizational prestige through ceremony, by conferring honors and rewards, and by opening up opportunities for advancement to those who excelled in the performances it valued, the state could stimulate efforts by its subject populations to conform to its values. And by claiming highest prestige for its own values, the state could deny respect and esteem to nonconforming values and thereby discourage behavior it deemed undesirable.[71]

The Ch'ing state's ability to impress the plains aborigines with its high culture was limited in at least two important ways. First, plains aborigines learned much more of Chinese culture from Chinese settlers than from the remoter organs of the state. Acculturation among the plains aborigines was in large part a reaction to the popular culture carried by the Chinese immigrants, who increasingly dominated Taiwanese society. Second, not all elements of the intrusive culture, whether propagated by the state or by the immigrants, were attractive to the plains aborigines. Some they simply found more advantageous for their lives (even at the cost of abandoning or suppressing aspects of their own traditions). Other Chinese cultural elements, for example, female footbinding, plains aborigines rejected despite their high prestige in Chinese eyes. From the aborigine point of view, we should expect that the adoption of Chinese ways would be highly selective and would follow a cost-benefit calculus independent of Confucian cultural priorities. The benefits of some Chinese ways clearly outweighed their cost. For example, the plains aborigines quickly perceived the utility of Chinese muskets and unhesitatingly adopted them. Learning a Chinese language in a political and trade environment dominated by Chinese speakers had immediate advantages, at least for men operating in these spheres. In other cases the costs were perceived to outweigh the benefits, for example, the aversion to certain Chinese agricultural practices that made excessive demands for male labor inputs. In still other cases the benefits of Chinese ways were only gradually perceived. Chinese claims about the efficacy of Chinese medicines and Chinese gods eventually convinced many plains aborigines that they had at least instrumental value and were worth a try. In yet other spheres, where the practical advantages of adopting Chinese ways were less straightforward, considerations of social status weighed more heavily in the calculation. In these cases plains aborigines adopted Chinese ways when adopting them increased plains aborigine prestige.

Acculturation is never a linear function of the intensity of contact between cultural groups.[72] Rather, the direction and speed of acculturation depends heavily on the structure of the interaction between the groups and the prestige orders that emerge as a result. If one group acknowledges (or is forced to acknowledge) another group's claims to be wealthier, more powerful, and the bearer of a "higher" culture, then a clear prestige hierarchy emerges. Members of the low-prestige group will be motivated to adopt the status characteristics of the high-prestige group *if* they have the means to acquire them and the acquisition of such characteristics can be expected to raise the status of the individual or group. By thus raising their status, members of the low-prestige group can expect both increased self-esteem and greater respect and courtesy when interacting with members of the high-prestige group. Where these conditions—an unambiguous prestige hierarchy and open channels of status mobility—obtain, adoption of the higher-status characteristics should be rapid and across a broad front. Where the prestige hierarchy contains ambiguities or channels of mobility are blocked, then acculturation will be slower and uneven, competing ethnic cultures will endure, and countercultures may even emerge.[73]

The increasing dominance (political, economic, demographic) of Chinese immigrants over the plains aborigines on the Taiwan frontier resulted in prestige hierarchies across a large number of spheres that awarded higher prestige to Chinese status characteristics. Chinese officials and immigrants alike were confident of the superiority of their own culture and the inferiority of aborigine cultures. Pride and arrogance on the part of the powerful coupled with contempt and ridicule from the immigrants eventually convinced the plains aborigines (facing economic decline and increasing numbers of Chinese) of the inferiority of many aspects of their own cultures and the desirability of elements of Chinese culture.[74] The following gleanings from the historical record give instances of plains aborigine adoption or rejection of Chinese customs that illustrate the variety of spheres in which change occurred and the complexity of motivations for acculturation. (The following sections discuss changes in kinship and the growth of internal stratification.)

The eighteenth-century Chinese literati who provide us with descriptions of aborigine cultures and society used their own values as a reference point and standard of judgment. They unapologetically assumed Chinese ways were superior, but there is little missionary zeal in their writings. Their tone is objective, though sometimes tinged with ridicule. They pay considerable attention to exotic costumes, hairstyles, and nakedness, to the eating of unusual foods (especially raw flesh), and to violent behavior. They assume that clothing and cooking divide humans from animals, and emotional self-control distinguishes the cultured man from the uncouth. The most damning remarks—that groups were "hair-eating and blood-drinking" and that "they do not know how to become civilized; they are really no more than beasts"—referred to the head-hunting raw aborigines of the mountains, who had yet to submit to Chinese authority, rather than to the plains aborigines.[75]

Each writer, in quite predictably Confucian fashion, mentions that the aborigines lack surnames, proper coffin burials, mortuary rituals, and ancestral sacrifices and that aborigine parents do not arrange the marriages of children, who thus enjoy sexual license. Chinese observers were thus quick to notice the absence of practices central to the Chinese family, which they considered necessary to reinforce the proper generational and gender hierarchies of parents over married sons and men over women and to instill the key virtue of Confucian morality, filial piety. But such prejudices could also lead to insights, for example, that aborigine families are happier at the birth of a girl than a boy because daughters are responsible for the continuity of the family and marry uxorilocally.[76]

Yü Yung-ho and Huang Shu-ching, the authors of two of the most valuable accounts (dating from 1697 and 1722, respectively), convey an impression of a very slow rate of cultural change by the early eighteenth century. Yü traveled in Taiwan well before the upsurge in Chinese migration restored Taiwan's Han population to its Cheng-period highpoint. The persistence of customs that were exotic to Chinese eyes—tattoos, extraction of incisors, tooth blackening, perforated earlobes, elaborate jewelry for both men and women, feathers used to decorate coiffures, tribal costumes, as well as aboriginal marriage and kinship practices—dominate Yü's descriptions.[77] Yü had been told that the four large aborigine villages of the southwest core, because of their proximity to the prefectural capital, had gradually adopted the ways of civilization: "But when I saw the men and women of the four villages, with their hair hanging unkempt down their backs and trouserless, still keeping to their old ways, they really did seem rather crude."[78] Despite the barbarity of aborigine customs, both Yü and Huang (in accordance with "culturalism" and the primacy Confucianism assigns to education) rejected racial explanations of the aborigines' lack of sophistication and denied any fundamental difference in their "heaven-conferred nature." Yü says that only plains aborigines' round eyes made them different in appearance from Chinese.[79] The Chinese perceived no racial divide between Han and aborigines that would impede the ability of aborigines to acquire Chinese status characteristics or deny legitimacy to mixed marriages and their offspring.

New prestige orderings among plains aborigines were signaled first by superficial changes in material culture and fashion. These aborigines easily effected by purchasing a trade good, and it is in these areas that Huang Shu-ching in 1722 most consistently noted change. In the seventeenth century, the aborigines held Dutch culture in high esteem, and the cultural influence of the Chinese settlers was limited, though they far outnumbered the Dutch, by their low status in the Dutch order. It was not until the eighteenth century, after Chinese had dominated as holders of wealth and power for several decades, that Chinese goods came to enjoy growing prestige among the plains aborigines. Several K'ang-hsi-era writers noted the persistence of Dutch influence on aborigine fashions, despite the intervening years under the Chengs.[80] An elaborate sash worn at the waist of the black (not Chinese-style white) mourning clothes used by some aborigines was said to be a borrowing from the Dutch. Dutch coins were used in jewelry and on costumes. Some central Taiwan groups decorated the doors of their houses with pictures of Dutchmen.[81] The alphabet the Dutch missionaries taught the aborigines provided a favorite motif for body tattoos.[82] Aborigine scribes wrote official documents and kept tribal accounts in the Dutch writing, and, as we saw earlier (Chapters 3, 9), the southwest core groups used this writing system to the end of the eighteenth century.[83] The Chu-lo gazetteer's sense of unease over the persistence of Dutch writing is evident in its haste to add that schools have been set up to teach aborigines Chinese. The 1740 prefectural gazetteer, with a premature sense of relief, reported the disappearance of the Dutch writing and claimed that all aborigine accounts were being kept in Chinese.[84]

With the advent of Ch'ing rule and the growing dominance of Chinese settlers, things Chinese became increasingly fashionable during the eighteenth century. Huang Shu-ching reported that aborigine men had begun dressing "half like Chinese," wearing trousers, and "copying the Chinese by wearing hats and boots."[85] The "dragon-embroidered robes of actors," modeled on the attire of the all-powerful mandarins, were especially popular among village headmen at formal occasions. A portrait of the An-li chief in the robes of a Ch'ing official shows his traditionally perforated earlobes but with the earplugs removed.[86] Many tribesmen adopted the Manchu queue long before the 1758 order requiring all aborigine men to shave their foreheads and braid their hair. For the plains aborigines adopting the queue was a matter of high style rather than a sign of submission. Boys attending Chinese schools in the 1730's wore Chinese clothes and the queue but lacked surnames.[87]

That many cultural items were acquired in order to make claims to increased status and respect becomes most obvious when these items were not put to their accustomed use. Huang Shu-ching reports that well-to-do aborigines had begun to furnish their homes with Chinese-style beds, but continued to sleep on deerskins laid out on the floor. Tables, chairs, and multichrome pottery were also acquired, primarily for ostentation rather than use. In one village, however, serving meals on tables was beginning to replace the custom of squatting to eat.[88] More auspiciously for Confucian morality and the veneration of ancestors, groups that traditionally buried their dead wrapped in deerskins began using coffins.[89]

Reforming aborigine attitudes toward production was more difficult than influencing their patterns of consumption. Although aware that aborigines stored grain in granaries,[90] observers such as Yü Yung-ho considered the aborigines to be lacking in the diligence, future orientation, and the ability to defer consumption that they valued in Chinese:

> They do not prepare the grain and keep it in advance for their meals. They rise at dawn to pound and cook it. . . . When they go out they don't worry about wind or rain; when they are going they don't plan where they will stay for the night; when they are happy they laugh, and when they are in pain they grimace. They do not know the seasons of the year, nor do they know how many years have gone by as they grow old and die. Only after it gets cold do they seek [warm] clothing; only after they get hungry do they look for food; they do not plan in advance. . . . They have no market places for the trading of goods. If they have money, it is of no use to them, so they know nothing of saving. . . . The new grain for the coming year having been planted, they likewise use all the leftovers for brewing liquor . . . even if they go hungry they do not regret [having thus used it].[91]

The aborigine failure to adopt intensive commercialized agriculture was seen as a moral failure reflecting both laziness and irresponsibility toward family obligations. "Knowing to lay up savings" was considered a sign of advancement, and the spread of civilization required teaching the aborigines "the way to save against want." The aborigines' lack of sophistication in the use of money was cited as necessitating the continuation of the monopoly merchant (*p'u she*) system of taxing the deer trade.[92] As we saw in earlier chapters, officials were frequently concerned that unwary aborigines would fall prey to shrewd Chinese traders and, either through trickery or reckless spending, contract loans at exorbitant rates of interest and lose their property.

Chinese medicine was another sphere of Han cultural influence. The settlers considered Chinese medicine superior and convinced the aborigines of its efficacy. Chinese observers report gifts of Chinese medicine as acts of benevolence that earned the gratitude and admiration of the aborigines.[93] A timely gift of medicine to a tribe suffering an epidemic in the Taipei basin reportedly ended its opposition to Han land reclamation within its territory.[94] Missionary doctors working among sinicized Siraya in the late nineteenth century were frustrated by aborigine adherence to Chinese remedies.[95]

The settlers also boasted of the superior efficacy of Chinese gods. Two very early reports mention plains aborigine participation, together with Han, in temple building and dedication ceremonies.[96] Tribes even donated land to Chinese temples. In 1763 Fang-so *she* gave 30 *chia* to the city god temple at Feng-shan. Ma-tou *she* gave land to a temple and then decided it wanted rents as well, causing a dispute in 1777. Also in 1777, Nan-t'ou *she* helped endow a temple.[97] The tolerant syncretism of Chinese popular religion encouraged pragmatic experimenting with approaches to the Chinese supernatural and erected few barriers to aborigine learning about Chinese rituals and religious beliefs. But there was push as well as pull. Neighboring Han also pressured plains aborigines to contribute money and participate in temple festivals conceived to benefit entire communities.

Nineteenth-century Westerners described the plains aborigine religions as minglings of Chinese and aborigine observances. The aborigines often celebrated Chinese holidays without knowing the legends behind them and without resorting to Chinese religious specialists.[98] Native gods were in some instances assimilated to Chinese supernatural counterparts and worshipped in accordance with the Chinese religious calendar.[99] Other native gods have maintained distinct non-Han identities. An example is the goddess A-li-tsu, whose worship remains widespread among sinicized Siraya in T'ai-nan county. Siraya rituals preserve aboriginal forms described during the Dutch period, while incorporating many Chinese usages.[100] Many plains aborigine families eventually adopted Chinese-style ancestral sacrifices and mortuary customs.[101]

Religious influences traveled in both directions, however. An aborigine sorceress is reported to have cast a spell on two Chinese geomancers in 1699. When they fell ill, they sought a cure from the aborigine wife of a Chinese neighbor. Even in the twentieth century, Chinese villagers in P'u-li feared the black magic of the neighboring plains aborigines.[102] The worship of A-li-tsu has also spread to Han.

Confident in the superiority of Confucian culture, both Yü Yung-ho and Huang Shu-ching saw the cultural refinement of the aborigines as coming gradually through good government and education: "It is only a matter of those who are their superiors urging them on, and guiding them to change for the better."[103] Yü Yung-ho encapsulates what the aborigines should learn of Confucian civilization:

> If they could be civilized by the code of proper social behavior, influenced by literature, taught the way to save against want, regulated by the protocol of

> clothing, eating, capping at manhood, marriage, mourning, and ancestral sacrifice; if they were caused completely to understand to love their parents, respect their elders, honor their sovereign, and be friendly to their superiors . . . then within from thirty to one hundred years, we would see their customs change. If they were [thus] to follow the code of civilization wherein would they be different from the people of China?[104]

Yü expresses no anxiety about the slow rate of acculturation. From the government's point of view, plains aborigine cultural nonconformity could be tolerated because, unlike some heterodoxies, it did not challenge the dominant cultural order, because it reinforced a separate ethnic identity for plains aborigine braves that served Ch'ing divide-and-rule methods of control, and because gradual acculturation was, in any case, eroding the customs that most offended Confucian and Han sensibilities.

With time more and more plains aborigines became increasingly proficient at speaking a Chinese language (and spoke that language to their children), used a Chinese name, adopted Chinese hair and clothing styles, built and furnished houses in the Chinese manner, and began worshipping in Chinese temples. They abandoned wholesale the clothing styles, jewelry, and body ornamentation that fascinated Yü Yung-ho in 1697 and brought ridicule from Chinese. Plains aborigines acquired at least the external trappings that facilitated their interaction with the dominant culture of the Han settlers. Racial or other boundaries did not bar plains aborigines from acquiring Han culture, and official policy encouraged its adoption. Plains aborigine desire to acquire the status attributes valued by Chinese and to escape the contempt shown for aboriginal culture by Han settlers motivated the adoption of much of Han culture, and a high degree of acculturation was the predictable result.[105]

But acculturation is not the same as assimilation, and plains aborigines have held on to their separate identity and ethnic history longer than they have held on to many aboriginal customs. Two examples from the nineteenth century reveal that many plains aborigines had not adopted a Han identity: the 1823 compact that led to the founding of a plains aborigine colony in the P'u-li basin, and the collective conversion to Christianity of many plains aborigine villages in the 1870's. The 1823 compact underlines once again the important distinction between Confucianization and sinicization during the Ch'ing. In the compact the plains aborigines emphasize in Confucian terms their loyalty to the Confucian state, complain bitterly of their treatment by Han settlers, and resolve to found a colony that excludes Han. The aborigines appeal to the Ch'ing state to mediate between competing ethnic groups in a society in which the Han are described as less than exemplary Confucians. The compact displays plains aborigine mastery of Ch'ing Confucian political rhetoric and its availability to criticize the Han populace. (See below for more on the compact.)

Separate plains aborigine identities were revived when the political economy of prestige changed radically in the latter half of the nineteenth century. European military victories had already tarnished the prestige of Chinese officialdom when the representatives of Western power arrived in Taiwan in the guise of Christian missionaries. The missionaries made few converts among the Han, who saw no advantage in adhering to a foreign religion. Plains aborigines, on the other hand, hoped that conversion would bring European protection against oppressive Han, and in an attempt to define a set of values that gave plains aborigines greater prestige vis-à-vis their Han neighbors, several increasingly impoverished, but acculturated, plains aborigine villages converted to Christianity in mass movements during the 1870's. We know many of the converts were highly acculturated because they kept Chinese-style ancestor tablets and god statues that the missionaries ordered burned before granting admission to the church.[106] These instances of conversion to a foreign religion remind us that the use of prestige as a means of social control was most effective when the state monopolized key avenues to advancement and its claims to represent the highest civilization went unchallenged. When the state was weak, its hegemony fractured, and competing groups (e.g., cultural minorities, Western imperialists) challenged the official definition of civilization, the state's ability to enforce cultural conformity through prestige processes declined.

Today there are Taiwanese of plains aborigine descent who actively deny non-Han origins (and have invented genealogies to prove it),[107] as well as those who celebrate their plains aborigine heritage (e.g., by adopting aborigine costume at festivals). There are many more between these two extremes who display considerable ambivalence toward their ancestry. Yet all these groups are highly acculturated and intermarried and move unrecognized in the social environments of Taiwan's modern cities. What these groups choose to make of their plains aborigine heritage is very much a political decision that is and will continue to be affected by the mobility strategies they adopt and the changing valuations of ethnicity (especially aborigine ethnicity) and Taiwanese identity adopted by the larger society in which they live.

Kinship Change, Gender, and Intermarriage

Aboriginal societies appear to have adopted Chinese customs most slowly in the sphere of kinship relations. These were usually insulated the longest from direct Chinese scrutiny, and their private nature reduced the pressure to seek status by conforming to Han patterns. Intermarriage with Han men, however, threatened the survival of aborigine societies perhaps more than did the demise of the deer trade.

Aboriginal family and kinship systems contrasted sharply with the extreme patrilineal and patriarchal organization of Chinese families, which subordinated the conjugal bond to parent-son ties. Many of the plains groups married uxorilocally, with one daughter, or sometimes the oldest or youngest child, bringing in a spouse. They did not share the Chinese ideal of "all the generations living together" in patriarchal, multi-generational households. "By their custom the birth of a girl is welcomed rather than the birth of a boy. A boy will leave and become a son-in-law in some other family, while a girl will bring a son-in-law into her family."[108] Since the "woman's side of the house" extended aborigine families, aborigines lacked the patrilineally transmitted surnames Chinese considered a hallmark of a well-ordered kinship system.

To Chinese, the adoption and proper transmission of surnames were necessary for defining the patrilineal group, recognizing obligations between the generations, fulfilling duties in the ancestral cult, and avoiding incestuous marriages. Surname groups were also important units of collective responsibility in late imperial law and administration. The adoption of Han surnames by aborigines was therefore an important goal of official Confucianization policies.[109] The earliest Chinese names adopted by the aborigines were transliterations of their native names. Following the sinicization policies announced in 1758, family units adopted a wide variety of Han surnames. Some were chosen for their meaning; others for sound resemblances to aboriginal names. In practice, many plains aborigines retained an aboriginal name and used a Chinese surname only in transactions involving the government or Chinese. But over time multisyllabic aborigine names were simplified and approached the three-character names typical of Chinese.[110] The most commonly adopted surname was P'an, which is the Chinese character for barbarian (*fan*) written with a water radical added. Plains aborigine adoption of Han surnames generally did not reflect a sinicization of family and clan organizations. So many families adopted the P'an surname in some villages that the Chinese practice of surname exogamy was impossible. Other groups transmitted their Han surnames matrilineally or changed them at will.[111]

Aborigine marriages were not arranged exclusively by parents, without the participation of either bride or groom, as Chinese custom dictated and Confucian generational hierarchy required. Plains aborigine youths chose their own marriage partners through courtship, without the use of go-betweens, and premarital sexual liaisons were condoned and even celebrated.[112] Aborigine marriage customs thus fostered the growth of conjugal attachments that Chinese considered incompatible with continued parental authority over married children. The parental arrangement of marriages in two aborigine villages gave credence (in Chinese eyes) to their claim to descent from shipwrecked Chinese.[113] Among the aborigines, divorce was easy, and widows commonly remarried, in contrast to Chinese ideals of a permanent marital bond and widow chastity.

The 1740 prefectural gazetteer reports some progress in the sinicization of aborigine kinship relations. Tribes close to the prefectural capital are reported using matchmakers to arrange proper marriages that brought in daughters-in-law and sent daughters out.[114] One aborigine woman even won a place of honor in the gazetteer, where the chaste mothers of the literati editors usually predominate. Ta Nan-man's husband died and left her a widow at age 20. Reflecting the importance Ch'ing Confucians placed on widow chastity, Huang Shu-ching's 1722 account of plains aborigine customs reports for each group (under the heading of mourning and burial) not only that aborigine widows were free to remarry, but that they were allowed to do so after shockingly brief periods of mourning.[115] Ta Nan-man, in contrast, chose not to remarry, a sign of Confucian virtue, and endured tremendous hardship while singlehandedly raising her son. When she reached 56, the magistrate of Chu-lo county honored her with a testimonial.[116]

The marking of burial sites of parents with gravestones in the Chinese style is another indication of the penetration of Chinese values. The earliest reported examples are the graves of prominent tribal leaders from 1806 and later. These stones mark the graves of military (probably *t'un*, military colony) leaders and their wives who had received from the state honorific titles of the fifth and sixth rank. The stones indicate a tribal name as the place of origin, where Han would cite a hall name or native place on the mainland.[117]

Confucian attitudes toward the proper roles of women were severe, requiring chastity, the subordination of women to parents, husbands, and in-laws, the arrangement of marriages by parents without any participation by the bride (or groom), segregation of women from men, and clothing that fully covered the female body. Nor were proper Chinese women allowed to work outside the home or travel unaccompanied.[118] Aborigine women, on the other hand, expected to court and marry a man of their own choosing (and be free to divorce him), to make significant economic contributions to their families by farming and to have such contributions acknowledged, to sit as an equal among the men at family meals, to occupy positions of authority in the family (often bolstered by uxorilocal residence, which puts mothers, daughters, and sisters at the core of the household) and to participate in important family decisions.

This considerable gap between Chinese practice and aborigine norms meant that the Chinese model of family organization held little attraction for aborigine women. Moreover, two of the three practices that most appalled the aborigines and seriously undermined Chinese claims to moral superiority in aborigine eyes were female infanticide and footbinding (the third was the Chinese use of nightsoil). Plains aborigines never adopted footbinding, despite its prevalence among their Hokkien neighbors.[119] And plains aborigine women retained traditional hairstyles, headdresses, and costumes longer than did plains aborigine men, who had to operate much more in Han-dominated contexts.[120]

Aboriginal marriage and family relations changed only slowly. Land contracts provide many eighteenth-century examples of matrilineal inheritance of land among plains aborigines.[121] Ancestor worship and lineage organization remained weak.[122] Only reports from the twentieth century generally reveal a Chinese-style family organization, including the practice of little daughter-in-law marriage in one area (the adopted daughters may have been from Chinese families).[123]

The greatest challenge to plains aborigine families and society came from the loss of aborigine women who married Han immigrants. The social patterning of Chinese migration from the southeast coast, aggravated by government restrictions on family migration, led to a predominance of bachelors and a severe shortage of Chinese women on the frontier (see Chapter 10). Lan Ting-yüan, for example, reports visiting a settlement of 257 men and finding that only one had a wife.[124] This sexual imbalance destabilized frontier society and led to a number of social problems. Han interpreters and traders sometimes provoked aborigine revolts by coercing sexual favors from aborigine women.[125] Under such circumstances, the demand for aborigine wives among Han frontiersmen was high.

In a seller's marriage market, aborigine women found themselves highly valued. Chinese settlers began to outbid aborigine men in the competition for wives. Both aborigine women and their enterprising parents saw potential advantages in the greater wealth and higher status a Chinese man would bring to a marriage. A Chinese husband would also expect less field work from his wife, and since his mother was unlikely to have crossed over to Taiwan, the aborigine bride need not fear a domineering Chinese mother-in-law. A Han son-in-law might also provide Chinese business and political connections for his wife's kin and cooperate with them in economic enterprises. At the same time that aboriginal male roles were being devalued and eroded by the spread of agricultural settlement and the decline of hunting and warfare, aborigine women found their domestic and child-bearing roles valued as never before.[126]

When marriage was virilocal, intermarriage meant the loss of aborigine women to Han communities. But when marriage was uxorilocal, with industrious Chinese recruited in as sons-in-law, the gain in aborigine family incomes was eventually paid for by a loss in land. A Chinese laborer who, by giving gifts or through labor service, married an aborigine bride uxorilocally could eventually gain control of the land inherited by his wife.[127] These in-marrying Chinese males might adopt aborigine customs, dress, and speech, but they would raise at least their sons with a sense of a separate Chinese identity. And when continued immigration had extended the influence of Chinese culture, they and their sons would re-sinify to claim the prestige and connections advantageous in a Han-dominated social environment.[128] Rather than pass their fields on to a daughter and future son-in-law, they transmitted them to their own sons (and obligated them to make the requisite Chinese-style ancestral sacrifices). This resulted in a diminishing supply of both land and wives available to aborigine men seeking to marry in the traditional fashion.[129]

Intermarriage with Han (whether uxorilocal or virilocal) was at first exclusively unidirectional: aborigine women married Han men. On a male-dominated frontier, no Chinese women were available to aborigine men to replace the loss of aborigine women to Han men. Chinese officials, worried about the disruptive effects of intermarriage on aborigine communities and the resentment loss of brides caused, advocated a prohibition on intermarriage and tightened immigration policies to remedy the situation.[130] Some evidence indicates plains aborigine men made up part of the deficit by taking wives from their poorer tribal cousins, the mountain aborigines.[131] Plains aborigines could also make up population losses through adoption. Unattached Chinese males could acquire rights in land by assuming the responsibilities of adopted sons in aborigine families.[132] And since Chinese families often gave young daughters away to avoid the expense of raising "other peoples' brides," plains aborigines may have adopted some of these girls. These adopted daughters would have increased the supply of brides available to plains aborigine men.[133] Only when the Chinese population achieved greater sex balance could plains aborigine men begin to find wives among the Han as well. Intermarriage statistics from 1905–8 document a much more balanced exchange of spouses between the two ethnic groups.[134]

Intermarriage was an important channel of acculturation for plains aborigines. Aborigine daughters who married out and Chinese sons-in-law who married in were the most influential transmitters and interpreters of Chinese culture in the aborigine communities. Aborigine village size must have had an important effect on the rate of intermarriage with Han and the timing and significance of its impact. Large villages such as were common among the Siraya could be highly endogamous, and the cultural impact of in-marrying Han would have been diluted in a large population.[135] Large villages were also more likely to be able to withstand the depredations of squatters. Small villages, on the other hand, were more vulnerable in several ways. They were dependent on intervillage networks to recruit spouses, networks that were likely disrupted both by intruding Han settlement and by the availability of single Han males as marriage partners. In small villages in-marrying Han would also have exercised a greater cultural influence.

Internal Stratification and Migration

As plains aborigines adapted to an increasingly Chinese dominated frontier, new kinds of leadership and internal stratification emerged within the tribal villages. The decline of intervillage warfare since the Dutch pacification and the gradual demise of the deer trade meant that heroic warriors and hunters no longer had the skills or prestige considered important to the management of community affairs. Instead, headmen who took the lead in learning the language and ways of the Chinese won increasing prominence. Acting as tribal interpreters, such headmen could mediate between Chinese settlers and officials and the aborigine villagers and, in the process, win control of tribal finances and the lucrative business of managing tax collection, corvée, trade, and the reclamation of tribal lands.[136] These headmen most appreciated the value of an education in a Chinese school for their sons. Thus, within each village there emerged a set of elite families that were also the leaders in sinicization. And these families, in their search for status, adopted Chinese modes of conspicuous consumption (e.g., wearing officials' robes or cultivating orchids) that set them off from their fellows.[137]

The success at sinicization by one set of village families was matched by the comparative failure of others. Within each village, families could be distinguished as more or less sinicized, more or less in command of the Chinese language or religion, more or less educated in Chinese ways of business and government. Some families married daughters to Chinese; others did not. Some families became tolerably good at Chinese-style farming; others remained attached to hunting or the newer occupations of carting, herding, and lumbering. And some families learned to manage their finances in the new cash economy; others fell in debt to unscrupulous traders or interpreters and had to pledge their property.

This emerging differentiation within villages led to a process of fission in which the less sinicized families migrated to the foothills, where remnant deer herds and wild oxen were more numerous, stands of timber could be cut and hauled to the lowlands, in oxcarts, for sale, and new fields could be cleared for gardening and agriculture. The establishment of hill colonies by Hsin-kang *she* and other tribes of the southwest core is reported as early as the 1750's.[138] In the foothill regions plains aborigines could pursue more traditional ways of life.

We have seen in its land policies how the government encouraged or even sponsored this trend. Although in theory aimed at protecting the land rights of the aborigines *in situ*, in actual enforcement the land policies enunciated by the government often drew boundaries limiting Han settlement that paralleled the foothills. It was easier for the government to assign rights to unreclaimed foothill lands rather than attempt to reassign rights to plains lands already occupied by Chinese. We have also seen that from 1746 on, and culminating in the 1790 establishment of the aborigine military colonies, the government sought to use the plains aborigines to build a foothill defense network aimed against the wild aborigines of the mountains. To the extent that these policies were predicated on aborigine skill at farming, they met with only mixed success. But the opportunities for hunting and herding in the foothills attracted some plains aborigines. These advantages, of course, diminished even in the foothills as deforestation and overhunting continued throughout the nineteenth century.

In 1865 William A. Pickering, attached to the customs service in Tainan and intrigued by the history of plains aborigine relations with the Dutch, visited the village of Hsin-kang. He found there Pepo-hoans (Taiwanese for *p'ing p'u fan*, plains aborigines) who dressed like Chinese and had forgotten their own language: "The chief of this village was a Pepo-hoan, who was a small mandarin, having gained some military rank as a reward for his services in China during the Taiping rebellion. He had brought back from the mainland a singular trophy, in the shape of a small-footed Chinese wife, whom he had captured by his sword and bow." Pickering befriended this chief, who told him that the majority of his tribe had migrated into the interior and gave him an introduction to his people in the foothills.[139] Pickering, joined by the medical missionary Dr. James L. Maxwell, soon made the trip to Kong-a-na (Kang-tzu-lin, in modern Tso-chen *hsiang*, T'ai-nan county) in the lower hills, fifteen miles from Hsin-kang:

> We received a most hearty welcome from the T'ong-su [*t'ung shih*, interpreter], the headman of the tribe, responsible to the Chinese Government. We found him a fine specimen of his race, frank and simple, and without the sophisticated notions of his clansman, our friend the chief of Sin-kang, who had unavoidably been to a certain extent corrupted by Chinese influence.
>
> Here in Kong-a-na, the people were proud of calling themselves "Hoans," or "barbarians" and the old people retained a knowledge of the language spoken by their forefathers.[140]

Despite such traditionalism, Pickering found two sons of the Kong-a-na headman established in business in the Chinese market town of Kuan-ti-miao (in modern Kuan-miao *hsiang*, T'ai-nan county). The cultural conservatism of the hill colonies contrasts with the sinicization of the families who remained in the villages on the plains. Pickering noted that whereas the hill colonists subsisted chiefly by agriculture, they were "very fond of hunting," and that those dwelling on the borders of the "savage territory" served as interpreters and middlemen between Chinese and the mountain tribes.[141] Another nineteenth-century visitor, Joseph B. Steere, also found the plains aborigine hill colonists he visited in Feng-shan operating as traders with the mountain tribes. Most could speak Chinese and had a command of ways Chinese. As with Hsin-kang, other hill colonies reportedly maintained relations with their parent villages on the plains, despite their emerging cultural differences.[142]

Western missionaries arrived in Taiwan in the latter half of the nineteenth century, after the European powers had defeated and humiliated the Chinese empire and its officials. The ability of the missionaries to effect cures with modern medicines impressed the local populace, Han and aborigine alike. But whereas their religious overtures failed to attract Chinese, the missionaries found willing converts in the plains aborigine hill colonies. "They received Christianity readily, the Chinese worship of idols and ancestors having but little root among them."[143] Because the aborigines "were not rich enough" to support many Chinese temples or priests who would oppose the new faith, they were more susceptible to the missionaries' efforts and less restrained in their enthusiasm for Western-style cures. Many plains aborigines converted in waves of enthusiasm, convinced that the powerful missionaries would protect them from further Han encroachment.[144]

The Western traders and missionaries who visited the plains aborigines in the latter half of the nineteenth century found many in a demoralized state. Alcoholism seems to have become prevalent. Although the plains tribes had always known ways to ferment alcohol from glutinous rice or millet, this apparently produced a drink much weaker than that obtained by trading with Chinese.[145] As early as 1722, Huang Shu-ching noted that the barbarians had recently been trading deer products for liquor. Alcohol sped the deterioration of the aborigines' economic position. Aborigines might be tricked into signing away land rights while drunk or forced to pledge lands to cover drinking debts at the exorbitant interest rates charged by traders.[146] Impoverishment and exploitation by Chinese explained the aborigines' movement into hill colonies to most nineteenth-century Western observers.[147] However, the one founding of an aborigine hill colony that Westerners actually observed, that by the Hsin-kang-tzu tribe (of the Taokas group in modern Miao-li county) was said to be necessary because their numbers had "increased very much." The population of the parent group was estimated at a thousand.[148]

The impoverishment of the hill colonies was gradual. At first their economic basis in hunting, herding, and lumbering made them relatively prosperous. With overhunting and gradual deforestation and destruction of animal habitats, poverty set in as their economic base shifted to agriculture in small valleys and on stony hillsides.[149]

But only some colonies of plains aborigines were founded because of the attractions of the foothills; in other cases there was much more push than pull. Some of the largest plains aborigine migrations of the nineteenth century grew out of violent confrontations and dissatisfaction with Chinese.[150] And some of these migrations took plains aborigines not to the foothills but to the plains areas of the east coast, where their more advanced agriculture displaced other plains-dwelling but unsinicized groups.

The plains aborigine opening of the P'u-li basin (in modern P'u-li *chen*, Nan-t'ou county) in 1823–31, remarkable for its attempt to exclude Han Chinese, was the largest of these migrations and illustrates a mixture of push and pull factors.[151] In 1814 Han colonists invaded the P'u-li basin and decimated the raw aborigine inhabitants. In 1817 the Ch'ing government expelled the colonists from the basin, which it considered a restricted area, beyond the reach of its administrative capability. The surviving raw aborigines then invited a group of plains aborigines to colonize the basin to forestall further Han penetration. In 1823 representatives of fourteen plains aborigine villages from central Taiwan signed an extraordinary compact setting forth the principles for opening the P'u-li basin. In the compact the plains aborigines gave an account of their own history under the Ch'ing, couched in language intended to evoke government acquiescence in their colonization scheme.

Because the compact encapsulates the history of the plains aborigines and does so in the cultural terms in which much of that history was negotiated, extended treatment of the compact provides a fitting conclusion to the last chapter of this study to focus exclusively on Taiwan. The plains aborigines use Confucian rhetoric to characterize the three leading groups in eighteenth-century Taiwan: the Ch'ing state, the plains aborigines, and Han immigrants. The compact invokes the teachings of the sage-kings of ancient times to remind officials that their primary duty according to Confucian doctrine is to protect, educate, and nourish their subjects. The language flatters the state for extending its benevolence to the lowly aborigines of far-off Taiwan. The aborigines describe themselves in terms that emphasize the state's obligations to them: they have remained loyal since submitting to imperial authority, and they have rendered military service to the state, yet the state has allocated military colony rents inadequate for plains aborigine survival.

The aborigines' description of themselves as "foolish, easily deceived, and easily cheated" and in need of state protection and assistance betrays an emerging sense of cultural inferiority. The aborigines thereby signal their continuing willingness to play the role Confucianism allots to subjects: that of obedient and dependent schoolchildren, in need of and willing to receive instruction from their superiors. There is no sense that a non-Han identity in any way disqualifies the plains aborigines from government protection. To the contrary, the compact describes the Han settlers as taking advantage of aborigine naïveté to encroach on aborigine property and livelihoods. For this reason unscrupulous Han are to be excluded from the colony. The compact reads:

> From ancient times the sage-kings attached great importance to the people and the teaching of the five relationships, giving priority to the provision of nourishment [*chung min wu chiao wei shih wei hsien*]. The aborigines of each tribe living in far-off Taiwan received the imperial benevolence and entered the empire. All open land was put under aborigine control, and it was left to the aborigines to reclaim the land by themselves or to nourish themselves by collecting large-rents from Han settlers called in to tenant the land. In 1788 the aborigines followed the armies and earned merit [in the Lin Shuang-wen campaigns]; [aborigine] military colonies were established by allotting mountain valleys for reclamation and farming by military colonists. Quotas were set for rations and military colonists, but the colony rents were in reality insufficient.
>
> Alas, the aborigine character is foolish, easily deceived, and easily cheated. Han tenants take advantage and seduce us with loans of cash. Now, nearly all the aborigine lands have been purchased by or pledged to Han. The large-rents have also been encroached on and reduced by Han tenants. The border guard provisions and the colony rations exist in name only. The aborigine border guards and colonists serve without salary. Hungry and cold, they roam the four quarters.
>
> We have called together the interpreters and chiefs of every tribe to consult and deliberate. To find a settled existence for the tribes, we must first find a source of nourishment. Thus, we have come together to survey a site that lies within the boundary but behind the mountains . . . that was originally a place where plains aborigines hunted and trapped deer. The land is flat and the soil is fertile; when opened, it will support many and supply ample provisions to make up for shortfalls in colony rents. Thus, we have gathered together and decided that each tribe should select strong men, each providing for his own needs and supplying his own tools, to go there to reclaim, to clear the brambles, and to open the grass lands. When the wilderness has been turned into fields, then it can be surveyed and allotted to the border guards and colonists, and neither the colony rations nor the border guard provisions will be deficient. Thus, there will be food and clothing, and the guards will be provided for and able to fulfill their duties.
>
> However, fearing that the tribes will not be one in purpose, that there will be squabbling, and that what began in earnest will end in apathy, we have collectively established this agreement, and all aborigine kinsmen party to this agreement must be bound by it. When the aborigines of our tribes have done their best to reclaim the land, all reclaimed field and meadow will be surveyed and equally distributed according to each tribe's population. It is prohibited for anyone to enter the mountains and stir up the raw aborigines. It is prohibited for the strong to oppress the weak. It is prohibited to bring in Han Chinese to reclaim this land. It is prohibited to hire Han laborers to manage this land. Any who fail to respect these prohibitions will be publicly chastised and then expelled.[152]

The compact begins by reproaching the Confucian overlords with a passage from the Classic of History (*Shu ching*).[153] The opening passage encapsulates the Mencian theory of government adopted by the Ch'ing, which makes the education and nourishment of the people (regardless of ethnic identity) the responsibility of the cultured elite who hold the reins of state power. The passage reminds the government that its first duty is to guarantee nourishment to the people, so that they will remain obedient and educable subjects. The government's next duty is to teach the five relationships that encapsulate Confucian morality, four of which create hierarchically graded relations between superiors and inferiors. The compact then recites the history of the government's recognition of the aborigines' rights in land and their right to collect rents from Han settlers, the aborigines' loyal service during the Lin Shuang-wen rebellion, and the founding of the military colonies. The aborigines reproach themselves for being so easily taken advantage of by Chinese settlers (and the state for failing to educate and protect them) and for losing much of their inheritance. They resolve to begin again in the new colony, where newly reclaimed farmlands will support the aborigines and enable them to fulfill their duties as military colonists and border guards. To prevent a repetition of past failures, they agree to exclude Han.

The rhetoric of the compact is fully Confucian and Chinese; it appeals for government support of the enterprise in Confucian terms, emphasizing the state's duty to guarantee livelihoods and reminding officials of the loyal services rendered by the aborigines. The compact acknowledges that the government has recognized aborigine land claims, and the aborigines largely blame themselves for the loss of land to Han. There is a strong flavor both of resentment against Han and demoralization over aborigine inability to compete successfully; there is also a sense of helplessness and dependence on government protection. The account of their history ends with the plains aborigine realization that solidarity against Han encroachment is necessary if the new colony is to succeed.

Families from plains aborigine villages in central Taiwan migrated to P'u-li over a period of decades following 1823. Even when motivated by dwindling land reserves and rental incomes, plains aborigine migrations, as we saw above, left populations in the parent plains villages. The uncritically accepted displacement scenario, which assumes Han settlement drove the plains aborigines into the mountains, both ignores the existence of the families and the land rights that remained in the aboriginal plains villages and confuses plains aborigine hill colonies with the distinct ethnic groups of the mountains (whom they partially displaced in the foothills). The complexity of the processes of adaptation and migration and the length of the period over which they took place further belie this simplistic displacement scenario, even while it retains its moral and rhetorical force.

Plains aborigine numbers appear to have remained roughly constant throughout these centuries of geometrically increasing Chinese population. The highest total given by the Dutch censuses for west coast plains groups was about 40,000 (see Table 2.2). The 1905 Japanese census of Taiwan reported 46,000 plains aborigines. (Because the children of Chinese fathers and plains aborigine mothers are enumerated as Chinese, census figures understate the plains aborigine element in the population.) In contrast the Chinese population had reached 660,000 by 1756 and 3 million by 1905 (see Table 6.4).

The dwindling proportion of the population represented by the plains aborigines could hardly pose a threat to government control or be of much value to the government in its divide-and-conquer techniques of rule. Hence, in the nineteenth century no new measures of any significance to protect plains aborigine land rights were adopted, there was much official backsliding in the enforcement of earlier decrees, and corruption in the management of aborigine large-rents increased.[154] The Liu Ming-ch'uan reforms of the large-rent system in the 1880's further diminished the income of plains aborigines from their lands (see Chapters 10 and 12). The Japanese abolition of large-rents after 1895 reduced many plains aborigines to poverty.[155] Nevertheless, the survival to this day of plains aborigine communities in sinicized form owes much to the legacy of their role in the history of Taiwan in the seventeenth and eighteenth centuries.

CHAPTER TWELVE

Conclusion: Frontier Management, Land Tenure, and the Late Imperial State

The Dutch set out in Taiwan to found an entrepôt and fortified trading factory but ended up creating a territorially extensive colony. Within this colony developed a plural society of aborigine villagers, Chinese traders, and immigrant farmers, governed by a Dutch ruling class of company officials, military officers, and missionaries. When the Chengs ousted the Dutch, they transformed a trading colony run as a profit-making enterprise into a military base. They erected a Chinese bureaucratic state to administer and tax Chinese farmers and aborigine villagers, but remained preoccupied with military colonies of soldier-farmers, defense, and their own maritime trading empire. The accession of Ch'ing rule brought peace, the repatriation of armies and civilians, and tax reductions. The Ch'ing installed a substantial military garrison and civil administration to maintain order and collect revenues from an economy dominated by the aborigine trade and a Chinese export agriculture in sugar and rice restricted to the southwest core. Only in the eighteenth century did accelerating Chinese immigration erode the ethnic status quo and present the Ch'ing with new revenue possibilities as well as increasing control costs.

The Ch'ing administration of Taiwan illustrates the large repertoire of policies used by the late imperial state to govern localities, not just directly, but by affecting their social, economic, and cultural development. Restrictions on family migration, rice exports, land reclamation, and settlement, as well as adjustments in land-tax rates, revenues, examination quotas, and the deployment of military and civil bureaucracies, were used to manage the growth of frontier society in Taiwan. The allocation of land rights and land-tax responsibilities, education, ritual performances, recruitment of loyalist militia, and the manipulation of ethnic and communal antagonisms helped the state extend its influence among Han and plains aborigines and achieve its revenue and security goals.

The history of the aborigine large-rent system on Taiwan's western plain reveals an imperial government adopting policies unexpectedly solicitous of the land rights of subordinate indigenes. Understood in historical context, these policies can be seen to result from the late imperial state's shifting assessments of Taiwan's strategic significance, revenue potential, and control costs. On assuming control of Taiwan in 1683, the state's chief concern was to eliminate use of the island as a rebel base, and it adopted quarantine policies aimed at limiting further Han Chinese intrusion that it judged would only disrupt the island's ethnic status quo. In the early Ch'ing view, the additional control costs imposed by expanding Han settlement and reclamation would not be sufficiently offset by growth in land-tax revenues; it was better to minimize costs and maintain control by preserving the status quo, quarantining the island, restricting immigration, and defending the land rights of the plains aborigines. The plains aborigines' status as taxpayers and their utility as military recruits against rebellious Han, other plains tribes, and the head-hunting tribes of the mountains (and the court's fear that the plains aborigines might join them) played a role in sustaining in the government's eyes aborigine claims to rights in reclaimed and unreclaimed land.

When the state discovered itself incapable of controlling the flow of migrants, it reassessed its policies. Under the aggressive Yung-cheng emperor, the quarantine was replaced by pro-colonization measures that lifted restrictions on immigration and reclamation and enrolled new farmlands on the tax registers. The court aimed to create in Taiwan a settled agrarian social order that would finance expanded civil and military control. But to the succeeding Ch'ien-lung administration, the costs of frontier disorder exceeded the benefits of colonization, and it sought ways to slow change on the frontier. The court reimposed restrictions on immigration and reclamation and redrew boundaries between Han and plains aborigine territories, but with only partial success. Han immigrants were already applying a customary-law model of split ownership rights to tenant-reclaimed wasteland. The government then adapted this institutional arrangement to accommodate the competing goals of land-hungry settlers and dislocated deer-hunting plains aborigines and further its own revenue and security interests.

By the late eighteenth century, a large population of Han settlers dominated the frontier and dwarfed the plains aborigine populations. Immigration and settlement had created communities strongly bound by ties of common provenance but only weakly influenced by an emergent Confucian-educated literati. With increasing competition for resources and declining government effectiveness, outbreaks of Han communal strife frequently escalated to destructive proportions before they could be contained. The creation of the aborigine military colonies after the Lin Shuang-wen rebellion institutionalized the role of plain aborigines as a military ally of the dynasty, but communal strife, not plains aborigine welfare, dominated government attention until the 1860's.

The political economy of the Taiwan frontier and assessments of Taiwan's strategic significance changed radically in the late nineteenth century. Foreign aggression forced the Ch'ing to fund expensive military and infrastructural modernization in key regions of the empire. Many of the powers viewed Taiwan as a strategic prize, and the Japanese incursion of 1874 and the French threat of 1884 forced the Ch'ing to give priority to improvement of the island's defenses. The court appointed a vigorous governor and in 1887 raised Taiwan to the status of a province.

To pay for the expenses of modernization and defense, Governor Liu Ming-ch'uan determined to increase Taiwan's land-tax revenues. He conducted a cadastral survey and enrolled large areas of hidden land on the tax registers. Liu also sought to improve the rate of collection and frustrate tax evasion by large-rent holders by assigning the taxpaying responsibility to all small-rent holders; this effectively abolished the tax exemption of land under aborigine large-rents. To compensate the small-rent holders for their new tax burden, Liu reduced the Han and aborigine large-rents. In the case of Han large-rent holders, elimination of their taxpaying responsibility compensated for the reduction in rental income. But aborigine large-rent lands had been tax-exempt, and the reduction in plains aborigine large-rent income was not offset by elimination of taxpaying responsibility.[1] Plains aborigine protests brought no mitigation of this blow to their incomes. Their role in nineteenth-century Taiwanese society was even further weakened by the state's need to maximize its local land-tax revenues (given the uncertainty of subsidies from higher levels of government) to finance Taiwan's new defense and modernization requirements. Thus, the balance between control costs and revenues that had favored protection of plains aborigine land claims and land-tax exemptions in the seventeenth and eighteenth centuries shifted against these interests in the late nineteenth century.

Taiwan was only one of many late imperial frontiers. Both population and the area of agricultural settlement grew tremendously throughout China in the late imperial era. Between 1400 and 1900, China's population quadrupled and cultivated area tripled, despite a dynastic transition in the seventeenth century and catastrophic rebellions in the nineteenth century that caused great population loss in specific regions. Interregional migrations brought agrarian settlers to new frontiers in every corner of China.[2] These large-scale population movements challenged government control and strained finances: How was the state to extend and maintain control along the expanding margins of settlement? And how was the state to finance this control, tax the wealth of the frontier and its newly reclaimed land, and prevent a drain on central government revenues? As Wang Yeh-chien has shown, Ch'ing land-tax administration failed to keep pace with the growth of cultivated area, and the state balanced its budget primarily by limiting expenditures and delaying the search for new tax revenues as long as it could. The growth of the civil and military bureaucracies was accordingly constrained.[3]

But the state's reluctance to expand its land-tax base (sometimes reflecting an assessment that it did not need to, sometimes reflecting a fear of the disruptive effect of cadastral surveys and taxpayer resistance) varied over space and time, as did its civil and military deployments. The state adopted different policies for different frontiers, based on its assessment of strategic significance, revenue potential and control costs. Did that assessment lead to the same cycling between quarantine and pro-colonization policies documented above for Taiwan? What happened to the land rights of indigenous peoples at other margins of expanding Chinese agricultural settlement? Did the late imperial state use the aborigine large-rent solution to accommodate immigrants and indigenes on its other frontiers? Brief comparisons of Taiwan's experience with that of China's southern and northeastern frontiers, and in Appendix F with American colonial experience, will help put the Taiwan case into perspective and show that neither the policy factors considered nor the solutions adopted in Taiwan were unique.

China's Southern Frontiers

Han Chinese settlement had spread to most of South China's river valleys and plains by the fall of the Southern Sung dynasty in the thirteenth century. Indeed, Fukien and Chekiang provinces had become the cultural and demographic center of China under the Southern Sung. In part the gradual infiltration of Han settlers, initially led by frontiersmen and fur traders, expanded the area of agricultural colonization. Some of this colonization was "relatively peaceful" and resulted in an "intersettlement and interfusion" of Han and non-Han peoples and their intermarriage.[4] In other cases, armies of conquest implanted military-agricultural colonies along frontiers to provide border defense and stimulate the expansion of Han settlement,[5] and a history of conflict marks the extension of Han settlement and the displacement of indigenous groups "forced out of their old landholdings."[6]

An early example of Chinese statecraft during a cycle of aggressive frontier expansion is provided by Richard von Glahn's excellent study of the extension of Sung control over the southern Szechwan frontier. When the Sung assumed control of the southern Szechwan borderlands in the tenth century, it inherited a system of nominal overlordship and indirect rule through "haltered and bridled prefectures" (*chi mi chou*). These were tribal districts that acknowledged Sung sovereignty and paid tribute and homage to the Chinese emperor. The Sung left the internal administration and taxation of these districts in the hands of native chiefs, on whom it bestowed official titles. Although the tribes were considered civilized or "cooked" aborigines, both tribal land and population were exempt from direct taxation by the Chinese state.[7] By restricting Han interaction with the native populace, prohibiting Han purchase of tribal lands, erecting barriers between the two groups, regulating their trade, and leaving administration to the native chiefs, the Sung attempted to reduce frontier control costs.[8]

These quarantine policies were undermined by population growth and economic expansion during the eleventh century that increased core area demand for frontier products and caused Han frontiersmen to seek opportunities in the tribal districts. Especially attractive were the haltered and bridled districts of Yü-ching, whose brine wells produced salt in high demand in core areas and provided an important source of state revenue.

To gain access to the salt wells, the government had reached understandings with the native chiefs of Yü-ching. The growing Han presence, however, led to increasing ethnic friction and frequent tribal revolts that jeopardized Sung access to the salt and imposed high control costs on the state. Beginning in the 1070's, when the famous statesman Wang Anshih was in power at court, the Sung sought to impose direct rule over a number of frontier districts, including Yü-ching, to expropriate native lands, and to encourage Han agricultural settlement.[9] Government military forces allied with troops from neighboring raw aborigine tribes to crush resistance to this extension of central power. In the newly conquered areas, the state registered the native population and lands, assessed taxes, and encouraged Han settlement and purchase of native lands.[10] But the high cost of garrisoning the districts soon proved too burdensome. To reduce expenses, the Sung created local militias of Han and cooked aborigines and colonies of soldier-farmers to maintain order. Despite the reduced control costs, revenue shortfalls continued. The Sung soon discovered that native farmers made unreliable taxpayers and that the extent of Han agricultural settlement and tax revenues from land cultivated by Han were inadequate.[11]

The problem of frontier costs outpacing frontier revenues was exacerbated beginning in 1108 when Ts'ai Ching, a disciple of Wang An-shih, initiated an aggressive campaign of frontier expansion without regard for the revenue potential of the territories to be conquered. This drain on the national treasury became intolerable as the dynasty came under increasing pressure from Jurchen attack and internal rebellion. When Ts'ai Ching's policies were reversed in 1121, Sung frontier expansion halted and policies of retrenchment were adopted. Many of the newly created prefectures were abolished, and native subjects were stricken from the tax rolls. Significantly, however, the Yü-ching area retained its garrisons and its status as a prefecture. Yü-ching escaped the retrenchment because salt revenues paid all Yü-ching's administrative costs as well as a substantial subsidy to the regional capital at Chengtu.[12]

What happened to the land rights of the civilized aborigines brought under direct Chinese rule? When land was registered for taxation, the state appears to have confirmed the native ownership of land cultivated by natives. It seems clear, however, that the Sung intended to extinguish tribal title to unreclaimed land and open that land to Han cultivation without obligation to pay tribal fees.[13] Previously, some tribes had required Han settlers to pay indemnities or tribute; there is no indication, however, that such obligations were institutionalized when these areas were brought under direct rule and the land was registered for taxation.[14] Government approvals of Han purchases of native land were conditional on registration of the land for taxation.[15] These cases suggest that the need to maximize local revenue to pay for high control costs caused the Sung state to allocate unreclaimed land to Han settlers and tax such land at the full rate. Thus, the institution of aborigine ground rents on the Sung Szechwan frontier was forestalled by the state's pressing need for local revenues.

Most case studies of Ming and Ch'ing frontier policy and Han-minority relations in south China treat land tenure only cursorily. During the Ming, Chinese settlement in the valleys of Yunnan was spearheaded by conquest and the implantation of military colonies. Sometimes these armies were sent to pacify tribal rebellions; sometimes to establish garrisons along important trade routes. By the fall of the Ming dynasty, the bulk of the non-Han peoples lived in the hills (some of them displaced from the valleys by Han settlers). The Chinese state governed these hill tribes, if at all, indirectly through *t'u ssu* (native chieftains). *T'u ssu* were either tribal chiefs who, by submitting to Chinese rule, gained imperial recognition of their status or the creations of the policy of indirect rule.[16] *T'u ssu* districts paid tribute and even some taxes, usually in trifling amounts, to symbolize their subordination. Native elites handled matters internal to the district, including the allocation of rights in land since no regular land taxes were paid to the central government. The *t'u ssu* system was the institutional descendant of the haltered and bridled prefectures of the T'ang and Sung.[17]

Compared to plains, hills are difficult to control, sparsely populated, and less productive. Thus, few hill districts generated sufficient tax revenues to cover the cost of their administration and defense, and it was economical for the imperial government to rule these areas indirectly, to patrol only the borders, and to leave all domestic matters to the native chiefs. With varying degrees of success, the state prohibited Han from entering the tribal regions and upsetting the ethnic status quo. In some areas, mountain customs stations were set up to regulate the flow of population with a system of passes.[18]

In spite of these quarantine policies, Han traders penetrated many of these districts, and Chinese market towns grew up at central valley locations, serving native villages in the surrounding hills. By extending loans to natives at exorbitant rates of interest, these traders acquired increasing amounts of native land. Native resentment over the loss of tribal land fueled Han-aborigine conflict. As in Taiwan, the government built barriers to divide the two groups and attempted to restrict each group's ownership of land to its respective side.[19] The state also adopted statutes regulating intermarriage and prohibiting Han purchase of *t'u ssu* lands. Sinicization through the education of native children was also encouraged.[20]

The rapid growth of the Chinese population in the eighteenth century made the sparsely populated frontiers of the southwest increasingly attractive to traders in search of products in demand in regional cores and to settlers in search of reclaimable farmland. The Yung-cheng court increasingly abandoned quarantine policies and encouraged Han settlers to reclaim lands in the tribal regions to accommodate a rapidly expanding population immigrating from older settled areas. Native control of the allocation of land rights, however, meant that tribal headmen in *t'u ssu* districts could slow the expansion of Han settlement by refusing to sell or even to rent lands to Chinese; such land also remained outside the state's fiscal reach.[21] The Yung-cheng administration launched campaigns to replace many native chieftains with rotating officials (*kai t'u kuei liu*). Harold Wiens has argued that the government eliminated indirect rule through *t'u ssu* and instituted direct rule by Chinese bureaucrats when (1) *t'u ssu* were disobedient and rebelled, (2) *t'u ssu* were excessively arrogant and oppressive, (3) Han Chinese became so numerous in the tribal districts that the *t'u ssu* tried to expel them, (4) the tribesmen became sufficiently sinicized.[22] In fact, none of these circumstances requires the imposition of direct rule; the first three factors present problems solvable more economically by replacing a troublesome chieftain with a new, more docile one.[23]

Because of its limited fiscal capacity, the Chinese state only found direct rule of frontier territories attractive when a jurisdiction's economic development ensured that local tax revenues would cover the costs of administration or when strategic concerns dictated an administrative presence (that might have to be subsidized by the central government) despite low revenue potential. Except in areas where valuable resources (e.g., copper, salt) or centers of trade were located, only intensive agriculture could yield the tax revenues required to fund direct rule.

When the Yung-cheng government converted large numbers of *t'u ssu* districts to direct administration, it made their lands available to Han farmers. Land surveys and allotments of lands to old and new inhabitants followed immediately, and large areas were enrolled on the land-tax registers. In some areas the government itself organized large-scale reclamation projects.[24] Because the new county governments sold "unworked land" to immigrants, native claims to unimproved land were extinguished and a split-ownership system that might accommodate both native land rights and reclaiming Han settlers failed to develop. Many land surveys were conducted with complete disregard for native land-tenure practices and led to costly revolts.[25] But there are no reports that in response land policies were modified to recognize native claims to unreclaimed land. Of the studies reviewed here, only Ch'en Han-seng's focuses on land-tenure issues, and he found no use of split ownership rights to accommodate natives and Han.[26]

The migration of Chinese settlers into the hills of southwest China was stimulated by newly introduced American food crops. Maize and sweet potatoes made it possible for once-idle hillsides to support large immigrant populations. The encroachment of Chinese farmers on the lands of native hill tribes sparked the Miao rebellions of the late eighteenth century. Similar encroachments underlay the numerous Yao uprisings, although Chinese Triad poaching of Yao cattle and grain was the immediate cause of the large insurrection of 1832. In both cases, local officials were indifferent to native complaints, and the suppression campaigns led to slaughters. In such circumstances, the failure of secondary studies to mention land-tenure policies, other than the implantation of Han military-agricultural colonies following conquest, is not surprising.[27]

Split ownership did structure the land-tenure relations of two South China ethnic groups, the Hakka and Punti of Kwangtung. Hakka migrants moving into the Canton delta in the eighteenth century found not only that the best arable land was already occupied but that local (Punti) landlords also claimed ownership of uncultivated wastelands by virtue of their tax payments. Hakka immigrants seeking to reclaim hillsides, riverbanks, and other idle land had to negotiate with these landlords for rights of permanent tenure.[28] Ordinarily the state considered waste and hill lands that had never been cultivated to be public lands open to reclamation, although the private ownership of hill or other marginal land exploited for wood gathering or occasional cultivation was also recognized.[29] The key to the use of the split-ownership system in this case was the lowland landlords' success in claiming title to unreclaimed land (backed by local governments) in conjunction with both parties' recognition of the benefits derived from reclaiming land and dividing property rights.

Local governments concerned to ensure tax revenues supported the title claims of taxpaying Punti landlords. In contrast, the south China hill tribes (whether within *t'u ssu* districts or not, and unlike Taiwan's plains aborigines) stood outside the regular system of head and land taxes. Thus, any tribal claim to rights in land was fatally weakened in the eyes of local officials responsible for tax collection. Once the balance of power turned against the tribes and the local government could no longer gain political advantage by protecting the integrity of tribal territories, the natives were likely to lose all rights to uncultivated lands to incoming settlers. By contrast, both Punti landlords and Taiwan's plains aborigines enjoyed a government-recognized status as taxpaying subjects before new settlers reached their territories. As a result the government was more willing to ensure their continuing rights in land.

The Hakka-Punti case also reveals the limits of a split-ownership system's ability to accommodate indigenes and immigrants. Serious communal strife between Hakka and Punti broke out in the 1850's and 1860's. The government's solution was to segregate the Hakka in a newly created independent subprefecture, Ch'ih-ch'i. Punti owning land within Ch'ih-ch'i were ordered to exchange it for Hakka lands outside the subprefecture's territory. In this way, the state eliminated friction by segregating both the settlements and the estates of the competing ethnic groups.[30]

Northeast China

In north China under the Ch'ing, in the metropolitan districts around Peking and in Inner Mongolia and Manchuria, Chinese agricultural settlement pressed on the land claims of Mongols and Manchus. The highly productive agriculture of a growing Han population displaced the less labor-intensive modes of exploitation favored by non-Han. The resulting problems of dislocation were addressed in ways that bear a striking resemblance to the solutions adopted in Taiwan.[31]

At the beginning of Ch'ing rule, large areas in the metropolitan districts were confiscated (Chinese tenants and owners were resettled elsewhere) and allotted to the Manchu Banner armies. The new dynasty's goal was to establish ethnically segregated, self-sufficient Banner agricultural colonies to garrison the capital area.[32] But few Bannermen, with their heritage of martial exploits, could work these lands as productively as Chinese farmers. In addition, the end of the dynastic wars idled many Bannermen just as they were acquiring a taste for Chinese luxuries. Banner lands were the main source of wealth Bannermen could tap to finance expensive habits of consumption, and Han farmers stood ready to pay cash to gain access to this valuable farmland. But since the Banner lands were considered a form of public property, the state prohibited outright sales. Bannermen raised cash by pledging away (*tien mai*) their land-use rights to Han farmers in return for cash and rents; a pledge of land also avoided a transfer of title and thereby preserved the land's tax-exempt status.[33]

The governments of K'ang-hsi, Yung-cheng, and Ch'ien-lung were troubled by the growing alienation of Banner garrison lands. When the state outlawed the pledging of Banner lands, the Bannermen and Chinese farmer-creditors invented new ways and new terms to accomplish the same ends. The K'ang-hsi emperor gave government aid to impoverished Bannermen to eliminate the need to pledge Banner lands, but this only made them more dependent and less productive. Even the fiscally conservative and pro-reclamation Yung-cheng emperor was willing to finance the official redemption of lands pledge-sold by Bannermen.[34]

In 1740 the Ch'ien-lung emperor ordered another redemption of pledged Banner land. To avoid disturbances, the court decreed that Chinese farmers should not be evicted from the lands they had acquired by pledge but should remain as tenants. Ma Feng-ch'en describes the nature of the tenure relationship between metropolitan Bannermen and their Chinese tenants:

> A decree of 1740 ordered that changes in the ownership of Banner land should not lead to dismissal of the original tenant farmers if the latter had made all necessary rent payments. . . . Rent increases and eviction of tenants were henceforth forbidden. . . . Many Manchus mortgaged [i.e., pledge-sold] their land to Chinese when in need of money, so that by 1745 half or more of the Banner land was in the hands of Chinese. Some of this land was redeemed by the government, but the tenants still were protected from eviction and rent increases.
>
> For the Chinese tenants the above developments amounted to a trend toward private ownership of land.[35]

A tenant who cannot be evicted and whose rent cannot be increased has a permanent leasehold.[36] The system described by Ma closely resembles the split ownership or two-lords-to-a-field system of south China. Both systems accommodate the claims of state-recognized landowners and the strong bargaining position of cultivators and reclaimers. The land claims of the Bannermen reflected their status not as taxpayers (unlike Punti landlords but like Taiwan plains aborigines, their lands were tax-exempt) but as the military buttress of the dynasty. And as with Taiwan's plains aborigines, their land rights endured much longer than their military effectiveness.[37]

In the northeast border regions, similar permanent leasehold rights evolved when Chinese tenants invested in reclaiming wastelands nominally owned by native Bannermen.[38] For a brief period early in the dynasty, Chinese settlers were encouraged to settle areas of Manchuria (especially Liaotung, in the south, an area long farmed by Chinese) that had been depopulated and abandoned with the conquest of China proper. The state approved this settlement to expand its revenues and help counter Russian Cossack expansion.[39] In 1668, however, the K'ang-hsi emperor decided to close Manchuria north of the Liaotung area (which was circumscribed by the Willow Palisade) to Chinese settlement. This quarantine was designed to ensure a refuge should Manchu rule in China proper collapse, to protect hunting grounds necessary for the preservation of Manchu martial skills and a separate Manchu ethnic identity, and to ensure a monopoly on the lucrative ginseng trade for Manchus. Chinese settlement was also restricted to maintain the segregation of ethnic groups, eliminate points of friction with indigenous tribes, and prevent disruption of the ethnic status quo.[40] The funding of the frontier military government by subsidies from the central government and revenue-rich core provinces and the garrisoning of the area by low-cost military colonies of Bannermen enabled the state to forgo local revenues from taxes on Han-reclaimed land.[41]

Because most Bannermen were indifferent agriculturalists, they relied on immigrant Chinese tenants to do the farming. Chinese migrants entered the restricted regions as seasonal farm laborers and also as artisans, merchants, and doctors. The Manchu court, however, was seeking to prevent permanent Chinese settlement (for the reasons detailed above); it therefore banned the immigration of Chinese women (as it had in Taiwan) and regulated migration by requiring passes from male migrant laborers.[42] Since the Bannermen were happy to get Chinese services, as well as the grain supplies and land rentals produced by Chinese farmers, they helped large numbers of migrants elude these government restrictions. Even the government acquiesced in illicit migration when droughts and famine in North China forced waves of refugees into Manchuria. By 1779 millions of *mou* officially owned by Bannermen were being cultivated by Chinese.[43] Where land was already under cultivation, the Chinese immigrants acquired rights through pledge-sales rather than reclamation. Bannermen pledged their farmlands to Chinese creditors to pay off debts or get cash advances. Again, outright sale to Chinese was barred by statute.[44]

In 1748, after a period of relative indifference to Chinese colonization in areas of Manchuria allotted to Mongol Bannermen, the Ch'ing government began to adopt more restrictive polices. To curb the expansion of Chinese settlement, the government instituted efforts to clarify landownership through exchanges of land to form separate Mongol and Chinese communities (a failure). The court periodically conducted land surveys and prohibited further Chinese colonization. After a few years, Chinese settlement would again be found to have crossed over the survey lines (reminiscent of the Taiwan case). The court also tried ordering the redemption of pledged lands after a set term.[45] This process of debt and official redemption gave rise to tenure relations similar to those described for the metropolitan Banners by Ma Feng-ch'en. Pledge was transformed into a perpetual lease, guaranteeing a rental income to the native owner and giving rise to split ownership rights that accommodated both Bannermen and Han.[46]

In some Mongol areas, leases rather than pledge-sales were used to transfer rights in unreclaimed land to Han farmers. The Manchu government, in an effort to control the process of tribal fission and conquest, had assigned territories to the Mongol tribes and made each tribal prince responsible for the regulation of Chinese colonization within his territory. The princes used long-term or perpetual leases to turn over tracts of tribal land to reclaiming Chinese tenants.[47] In some areas special officials were appointed to collect ground rents from the Chinese colonists; half the proceeds were paid to the ruling prince, and half were divided among the Mongols of the Banner.[48] So in these newly settled areas, a variety of split ownership rights arose to accommodate the interests of Chinese reclaiming tenants and the territorial claims of the natives. The land rights of Mongol tribesmen were protected because of the Mongol alliance to the ruling dynasty, the threat they would pose if alienated, and their role in the court's frontier control strategy.[49]

Two developments in the latter half of the nineteenth century, one fiscal and one strategic, led to the official opening of the Manchurian frontier to Han settlement. As R. H. G. Lee points out, the breakdown in Ch'ing financial administration and the devastation of the revenue-rich provinces caused by the mid-century rebellions cut off the flow of revenues to the deficit provinces of the northeast. Thus, the governments of Kirin and Heilungkiang had to encourage Han colonization and reclamation to generate local revenues from land sales and land taxes.[50]

Moreover, Russian expansion was threatening the Ch'ing court's territorial claims in Manchuria. The Manchus reversed their anti-settlement quarantine policies and began to promote Chinese colonization as a way of forestalling Russian claims.[51] This greatly diminished the role of the Mongol Bannermen in Manchu defense policy. The state opened large amounts of Mongol land to Chinese settlement and extended the system of perpetual leases to compensate the Mongols.[52] In some cases, not long after the land was leased to Chinese, revenue-hungry officials sought to register the land for taxation. Once the former pastureland had lost its tax exemption, it became difficult for Mongols to collect rents from the Han farmers.[53] There was no flood of Chinese immigrants into Manchuria, however, until the early twentieth century when newly constructed railways made it possible to export grain grown in the interior to external markets. Only access to cheap bulk transport could make agricultural settlement of the Manchurian frontier attractive to commercially oriented Chinese immigrants.[54]

The advent of Republican administrations in Manchuria in 1911 introduced some uncertainty in land titles. Many Chinese tenants farming estates owned by Manchus living in Peking succeeded in claiming full ownership of that land. The new government also invalidated land deeds that Mongol princes had issued to Mongol herdsmen settling down to agriculture as a way to forestall Chinese colonization. However, collection of the perpetual rents owed on reclaimed Mongol lands continued because the Chinese officials who collected the rents were able to deduct a percentage for themselves before paying over the rest to the Mongols.[55]

The Mongols' right to collect rents from Chinese immigrants helped them maintain both the consciousness and something of the reality of superiority in their homelands.[56] The slow displacement of the Mongols' pastoral economy and their gradual acculturation contrasts with the harsher fate of another Manchurian group, the Gold. The Gold (also called Fishskin Tartars or Heje) of the lower Sungari faced a sudden and rapid expansion of Chinese settlement beginning in the last decade of the nineteenth century.[57] The Gold were a cognate tribe of the Manchus and were organized into one of the new post-conquest Banners, some as early as 1732, others as late as 1882.[58] Gold livelihoods depended on fishing and hunting by the men and millet farming by the women. The Gold sold furs of sable, deer, and elk and medicinal ingredients such as antlers, elk embryo, and ginseng to Chinese traders and were highly sinicized in their consumption patterns.[59] The expansion of Chinese trade to the Gold also brought with it demoralization through drink and opium. The Gold were easily swindled and often fell into debt to the Chinese traders.[60]

In 1902 the government abandoned its quarantine of the Gold area and opened the territory to Chinese settlement. Strips of the best lands were allotted to the Gold, thanks to the concern for their welfare shown by the Manchus, who saw the Gold as their "own people."[61] At first there was no direct competition for land. The Chinese settlers created fertile fields from extensive marshes along the rivers. A simple plowing was enough to dry them for cultivation. But the expansion of Chinese settlement did drive out the wild game so crucial to Gold livelihoods.[62] Few Gold men were willing or able to learn the Chinese mode of labor-intensive agriculture, and they had little appreciation of the value of their newly allotted fields. By 1930 few Gold owned any land, the bulk of it having apparently been lost through pledge and sale. And the Gold population plummeted as Chinese settlers outbid the pauperized Gold men for Gold wives.[63]

In the Gold case, the allotment of land to individuals seems only to have sped tribal disintegration. The Gold case resembles that of the Kuvalan of I-lan (see Chapter 10) and contrasts with the more gradual changes effected by the expansion of Chinese settlement among the Mongols and Taiwan's plains aborigines, whose land rights were protected through a system of perpetual lease or split ownership.

Strategy, Revenue, and Control Costs in Frontier Administration

In its frontier administration, the Chinese state had two overwhelming concerns: control and revenue. Since the Han dynasty, Confucian statesmen had debated the wisdom of territorial acquisition. Would the expansion of borders add productive regions to the state's fiscal base or would foreign conquests only involve the state in costly campaigns of pacification and burden the populace with heavy taxes?[64] Owen Lattimore captures the dilemma frontiers posed to agrarian empires: "The range of military striking power exceeded the range of ability to conquer and incorporate; the range of uniform civil administration exceeded that of economic integration."[65] And Skinner succinctly observes that for the late imperial state functions of "revenue and defense were inversely related in regional space."[66]

Confucian statecraft was well aware of the pitfalls these dilemmas created for the state. Wang An-shih's aggressive policies of frontier expansion during the Northern Sung mistakenly assumed that the revenue benefit of new territories would exceed the cost of their acquisition and control.[67] Later Confucian historians condemned Wang's policies and blamed their excessive costs for weakening the Sung and contributing to that dynasty's loss of northern China.[68] The founder of the Ming dynasty warned against the temptations of expansion and its costs. He recommended indirect methods for ruling border regions: a tribute system, regulated frontier markets, and the use of barbarians to control barbarians. The licensing and regulation of Chinese merchants, whose sharp practices were often a cause of native unrest on the frontiers, and the segregation of Han farmers within China were key elements of this system.[69]

The limited fiscal capability of the Chinese state meant that the acquisition of a new territory and the extension of direct administration could be justified only if the area were crucial to defense strategy (whether against foreign threats or rebellious Chinese elements) or if its revenue-generating potential was sufficient to defray the administrative costs.[70] In the case of Taiwan, even after paying a high price to defeat the rebel Cheng regime, the court still had to be convinced that the strategic importance of Taiwan justified retaining the revenue-poor island within the empire.

The dramatic rise in population under the Ch'ing accelerated the expansion of Chinese agricultural settlement. For each of its frontiers, the Ch'ing state had to decide whether the intrusion of the Chinese population into tribal areas and disruption of the status quo would increase its revenues or create a drain on its finances by necessitating military pacification and the extension of the civil and military administration. Since the late imperial state expected to raise most of its revenues through taxes on agricultural land, rather than through taxes on commerce or from government monopolies, revenues were primarily increased by adding new fields to the land tax registers.[71]

In both Manchuria and Taiwan, the state was saved the expense of an initial pacification of the natives—in Manchuria because the dynasty originated there, and in Taiwan because it inherited the system of taxation and control created by the Dutch and continued by the Chengs. Thus, it was possible in both cases to install an administration in the absence of a large Han farming population. In the case of Taiwan, the administration incorporated the plains aborigines as taxpayers. So the early Ch'ing court's quarantine of both regions is not surprising. Chinese immigrants were intruders, upsetting what were to the court already satisfactory arrangements in special strategic situations, dynastic for Manchuria and maritime for Taiwan. By preventing Chinese migration and permanent settlement, the state hoped to reduce, in the short term at least, its control costs on strategically important peripheries (although Lan Ting-yüan and others disagreed with this assessment in the case of Taiwan), even though the lands quarantined were fertile plains whose control costs would be low (a little higher perhaps for Taiwan where naval control was crucial) and revenue potential high. But this also meant that a surplus of productive land remained available to settlers. Thus, the land claims of the indigenous peoples could be protected (and land-tax exemptions granted) while accommodating an illegal but unstoppable flow of Chinese immigrants and financing a gradual extension of the civil and military administrations. In Manchuria the status of the native Bannermen as dynastic allies (and potentially dangerous foes, if offended) ensured that the state would stand behind their claims. In Taiwan the state protected the rights of the plains aborigines, who played a similar, if less exalted, martial role in government control and in addition contributed to state revenue. Much of this changed in the late nineteenth century for both Taiwan and Manchuria: a changed political economy and new strategic and revenue needs put pressure on the land rights of the indigenous groups. The tax exemption of aborigine large-rent lands in Taiwan was eliminated, and the quarantine of the Manchurian frontier was replaced by a pro-colonization policy.

In contrast to Taiwan and Manchuria, the tribal populations of China's southwest were concentrated in less productive hilly regions that were both expensive to control and, with a few exceptions, low in revenue potential.[72] The small amounts natives in *t'u ssu* districts paid in the way of taxes went primarily to tribal chieftains rather than to the state. Once expanding Chinese agricultural settlement began to press on these regions, conflicts arose. As military control costs escalated, the state found it necessary to extend direct control. But the only way to ensure that local administration, once established, could be financially self-sufficient in marginally productive areas was to maximize the amount of land reclaimed and enrolled on the tax registers. This required encouraging further Chinese settlement and reclamation and abolishing native claims to uncultivated lands. The natives' exemption from taxation weakened their claims to unreclaimed lands in the eyes of a revenue-hungry state. Cultivated land was both the main productive resource and the premier generator of state revenue in China's agrarian economy.[73] For each frontier region, a cost-benefit calculus of revenue potential, control expenses, and strategic considerations underlay the state's allocation of rights in land and land tax–paying obligations between immigrants and natives.[74]

Appendixes

APPENDIX A

Village Sites of the Plains Aborigines

Chang Yao-ch'i's "Comparative Name List of Plains Aborigine Villages" (1951) correlates aborigine village names from Dutch censuses with village names in Chinese gazetteers (which Abe Akiyoshi's 1938 study of Taiwan place-names identified with modern locales).[1] Based on relative geographical location and sound resemblances (comparing aborigine names as romanized by the Dutch to the Chinese names in Taiwanese pronunciation), Chang identified Chinese equivalents for 57 of 126 Dutch names for villages on the western coastal plain; of these 54 had identifiable locales. The gazetteers listed another 51 villages that could not be matched with Dutch names. Of these 44 were identified with modern sites, making a total of 98 identifiable locales. The list and maps that follow show these 98 plains villages. Chang lists only four Pazeh (An-li) villages; I have followed Abe and given all eleven sites for the fifteen named settlements.[2] I have also added Nei-yu, A-li-shan, and Shui-sha-lien to the maps; they are given in the early Chu-lo gazetteer list and in Huang Shu-ching.[3] Since Chang published his list, Nakamura Takashi and Raleigh Ferrell have proposed a few additional Dutch/Chinese equivalents.[4] A few additional village names not included in Chang's list (which is restricted to eight plains ethnolinguistic groups) appear in the tax lists (Appendix B) and in the military colony lists (Appendix E).

Abe gives two locales each for A-hou and Fang-so (in Feng-shan county).[5] A-hou (also known as Ta-kou) is said to have moved from its earlier location in the west due to the raiding of the pirate Lin Tao-ch'ien in the pre-Dutch era. Fang-so, Abe says, moved east under pressure from the Chengs; this claim conflicts with Dutch sources that already put Pangsoia (Fang-so's Dutch equivalent) in its easterly location.[6] Perhaps some tribe of unknown name did make such a move and joined the Fang-so group. The 1935 census, however, shows plains aborigines living in numerous, less well known villages in the western half of Feng-shan.[7] The Chien-shan-tzu *she* in the Feng-shan area mentioned in Ch'ien-lung records may be a remnant of the original Fang-so group.[8] I have tentatively located Chien-shan-tzu in T'ien-liao *hsiang*, Kao-hsiung county, where the 1935 census reports a plains aborigine population.

Chang's ethnolinguistic identifications are based on Ogawa Naoyoshi's work in historical and comparative linguistics. The proper number of ethnolinguistic groups is a matter of controversy. Subdivision is always possible. Tsuchida Shigeru has distinguished three groups within the Ketagalan of northern Taiwan, adding Kulon and Basai as ethnolinguistic designations.[9] The Hoanya could be divided between Lloa in the north and Arikun in the south. Makatau can be distinguished from Siraya, and Taivoan included within Siraya.[10] Ferrell has proposed that Mao-wu-su be removed from the Favorlang (Babuza) group and classed with Papora[11] and that Ta-wu-lung be listed with Taivoan instead of Siraya (there is some confusion between Ta-wu-lung-t'ou and Ta-wu-lung-p'ai).[12] The proper identification of the constituent villages of the Taivoan is particularly controversial, and there is some divergence between Chang and Abe on the one hand and the T'ai-nan county draft gazetteer on the other.[13]

The list of villages given here follows the ethnic identifications given by Chang Yao-ch'i.[14] In addition to ethnolinguistic affiliation, the list indicates whether a village is identifiable in the Dutch census, served as a tax unit in 1684 and 1737 (see also Appendix B below), as a *t'un* unit in 1790 (see Appendix E below), or as a site of one of the aborigine schools founded in 1734.[15] The list also indicates those villages having a plains aborigine population in excess of 30 persons in or near the *original* village locale in 1935. This population information is drawn from the 1935 census,[16] which identifies plains aborigine population by village, and enables us to determine the modern distribution of the plains aborigine population, which totaled 57,812 in 1935. Ch'en Cheng-hsiang has mapped this distribution.[17] Although the 1935 census is undoubtedly highly reliable, one serious omission has come to my attention. The census fails to list the large population of descendants of the Chu-ch'ien *she*, who are organized in a seven-surname corporation at Hsin-she (near Chu-pei) in Hsin-chu county.[18]

PLAINS ABORIGINE VILLAGES

Key

A: identified in Dutch census
B: tax unit in 1684
b: tax subunit in 1684
C: site of aborigine school founded in 1734
D: tax unit in 1737
d: tax subunit in 1737
E: *t'un* unit in 1790
F: population greater than 30 persons reported near the original village site in the census of 1935

Siraya

1. Fang-so ABCDEF
2. Chia-t'eng ABCDEF
3. Li-li BCDEF
4. Hsia-tan-shui ABCDEF
5. Shang-tan-shui ABCDEF
6. A-hou ABCDEF
7. Ta-lou BCDEF
8. Wu-lou BCDEF
9. Ta-chieh-tien BCDE
10. Cho-hou bCDEF
11. Ta-mu-hsiang bdF
12. Chiao-pa-nien bdF
13. Hsin-kang ABCDEF*
14. Yü-p'ao bdF
15. Ta-wu-lung (t'ou & p'ai) ABCDEF*
16. Mu-chia-liu-wan (Wan-li) ABCDE
17. Hsiao-lung ABCDEF
18. Ma-tou ABCDE

Taivoan

1. Ch'ieh-pa E
2. Mang-tzu-mang EF
3. Hsiao-li EF

Saaroa

1. Nei-yu bdEF

Hoanya

1. To-lo-kuo ABCDEF
2. Chu-lo-shan ABCDE
3. Ta-miao BCDE
4. T'a-li-wu ABCDE
5. Ch'ai-li (Tou-liu-men) ABCDE
6. Mao-erh-kan ABCDEF
7. Nan BCDE
8. Ta-wu-chün ABCDE
9. Ta-t'u BCDE
10. Nan-t'ou AbCdEF
11. Pei-t'ou ABCDE
12. Wan-tou-liu
13. Mao-lo AbCdE

Tsou

1. A-li-shan BDE

Babuza (Favorlang)

1. Hsi-lo BCDE
2. Mei-li bCDE
3. Tung-lo ABCDE
4. Erh-lin ABCDEF
5. Ma-chih-lin BCDEF
6. Pan-hsien ABCDEF
7. Chai-tzu-k'eng bCdE
8. Mao-wu-su ABDEF
9. A-shu ABCDE

Pazeh

1. An-li CDEF
2. Hu-lu-tun dE
3. Hsi-shih-wei dE
4. Weng-tzu dEF
5. Mao-li-lan dE
6. Chih-tzu dEF
7. Ma-shu-chiu dE
8. P'u-tzu-li AdE
9. She-liao
10. Ta-nan
11. Shui-ti-liao
12. Shan-t'ou
13. Ta-ma-lin
14. A-li-shih dE
15. Wu-niu-lan AdE

*Three schools are listed for Hsin-kang in 1734, one each at She-nei, She-k'ou, and Hsi-tzu-k'ou. Two schools are listed for Ta-wu-lung, one at T'ou-she and one at She-tzu.

Thao

1. Shui-sha-lien DE

Papora

1. Ta-tu AbCDEF
2. Shui-li AbdE
3. Sha-lu ABDE
4. Niu-ma AbCDE

Taokas

1. Ta-chia-hsi ABCDE
2. Ta-chia-tung AbCdEF
3. Jih-nan AbdEF
4. Jih-pei bdE
5. Shuang-liao AbdE
6. Fang-li AbdE
7. Miao-yü bdEF
8. Yüan-li bdEF
9. T'un-hsiao bdEF
10. Miao-li bdEF
11. Chia-chih-ko bdEF
12. Hou-lung BCDEF
13. Hsin-kang-tzu bdEF
14. Chung-kang bdEF
15. Chu-ch'ien ABCDE
16. Hsüan-hsüan A

Ketagalan

1. Hsiao-li AbdEF
2. Kuei-lun AbdEF
3. Nan-k'an BCdEF
4. K'eng-tzu bdEF
5. Pai-chieh AbdEF
6. Wu-lao-wan AbdEF
7. Pa-li-fen (Tan-shui) ABCDE
8. Chi-jou-shan
9. Kuei-pei-t'un bdE
10. Hsiao-chi-lung bdE
11. Chin-pao-li AbdE
12. Ta-chi-lung BdE
13. San-tiao AbdEF
14. Ma-ling-k'eng
15. Feng-tzu-chih AbdE
16. Fen F
17. Hsia-lao-pieh F
18. Pei-t'ou (Nei & Wai) AbdE
19. Ch'i-li-an
20. Mao-shao-weng bdE
21. Ta-lang-tun AbdE
22. Kuei-mu-tsu AbdE
23. Sha-ma-ch'u
24. Li-mo
25. Lei-li AbdE
26. Liao-a-pa-li
27. Hsiu-lang
28. Ta-ta-yu bdE
29. Li-tsu AbdE
30. Miao-li-hsi-k'ou AbdE
31. Nan-kang

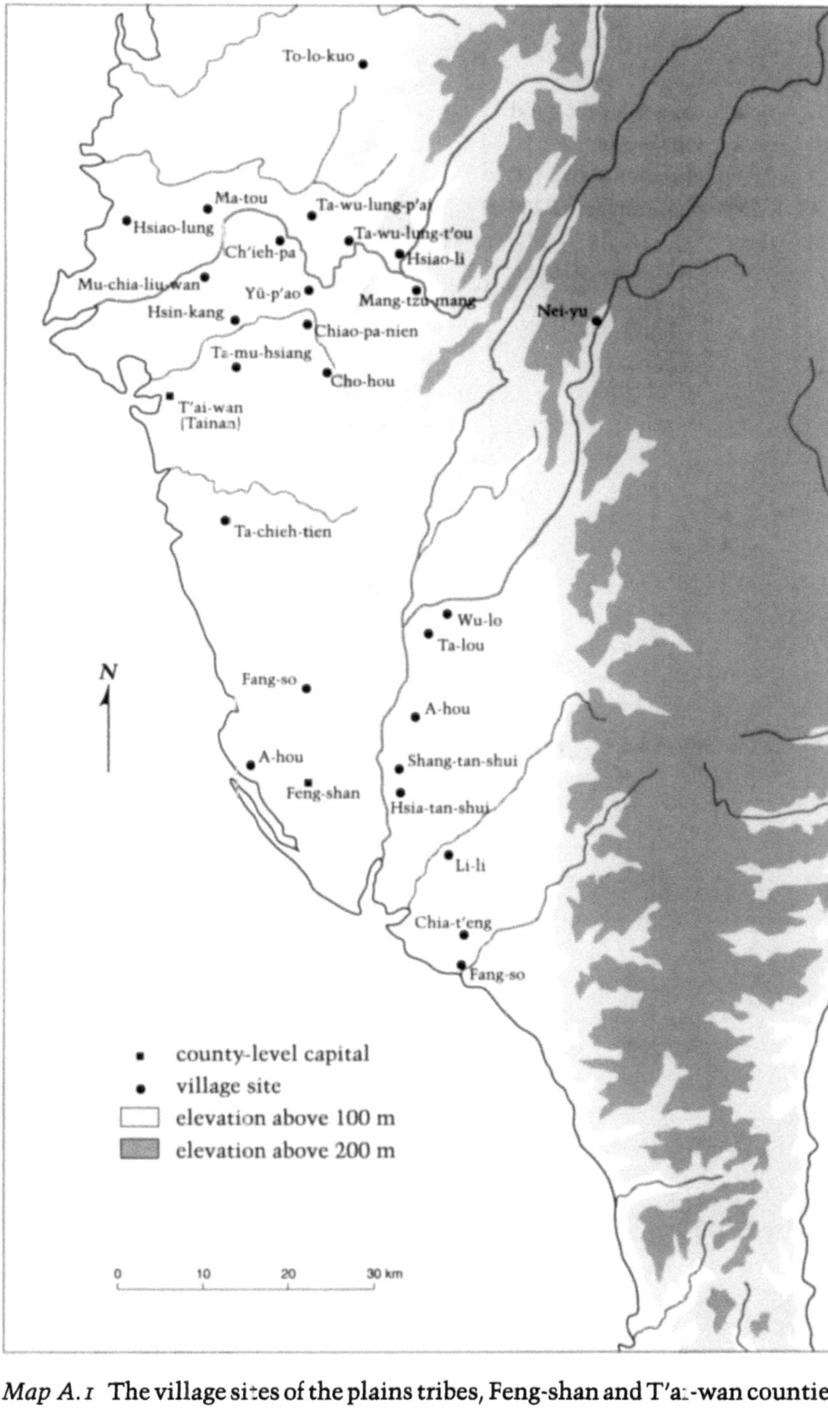

Map A.1 The village sites of the plains tribes, Feng-shan and T'ai-wan counties

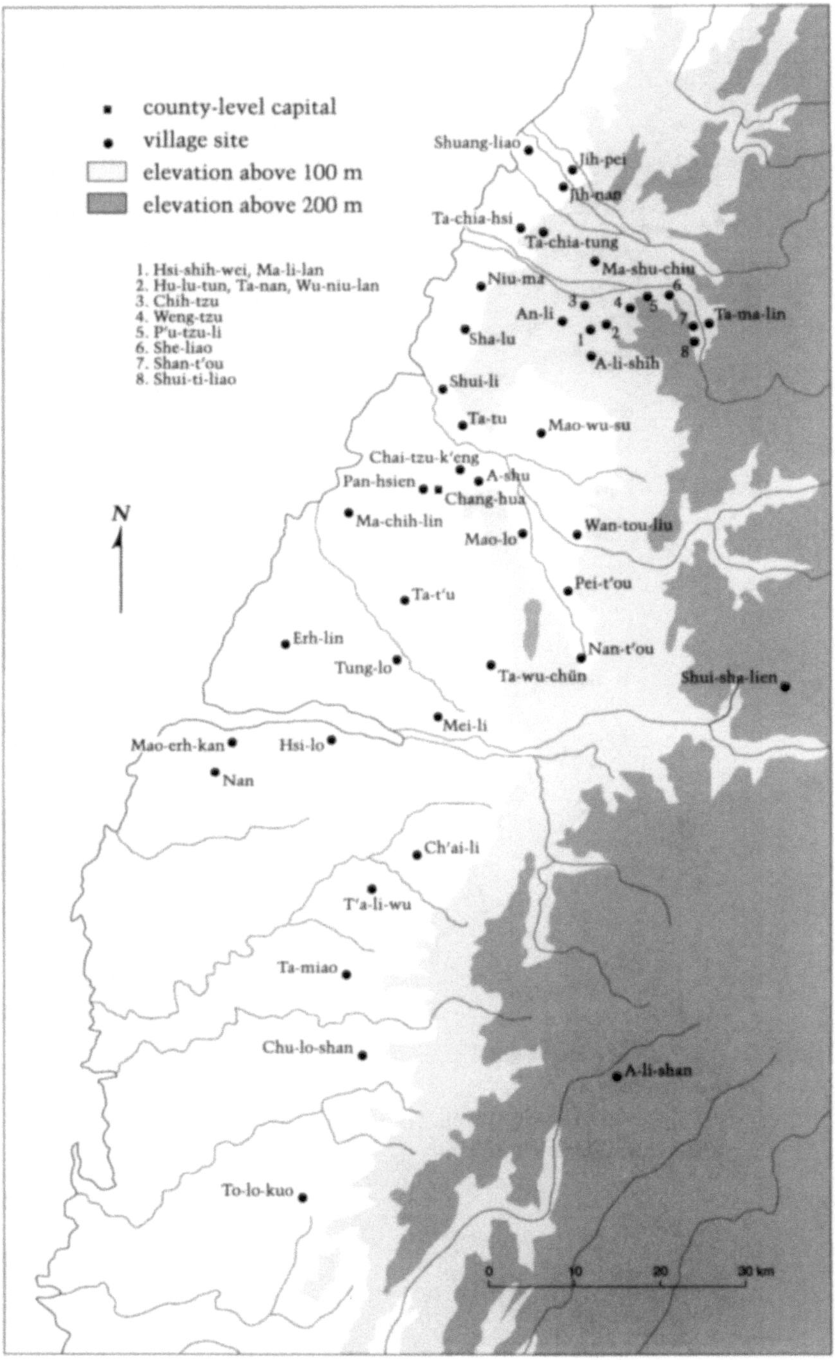

Map A.2 The village sites of the plains tribes, Chu-lo and Chang-hua counties

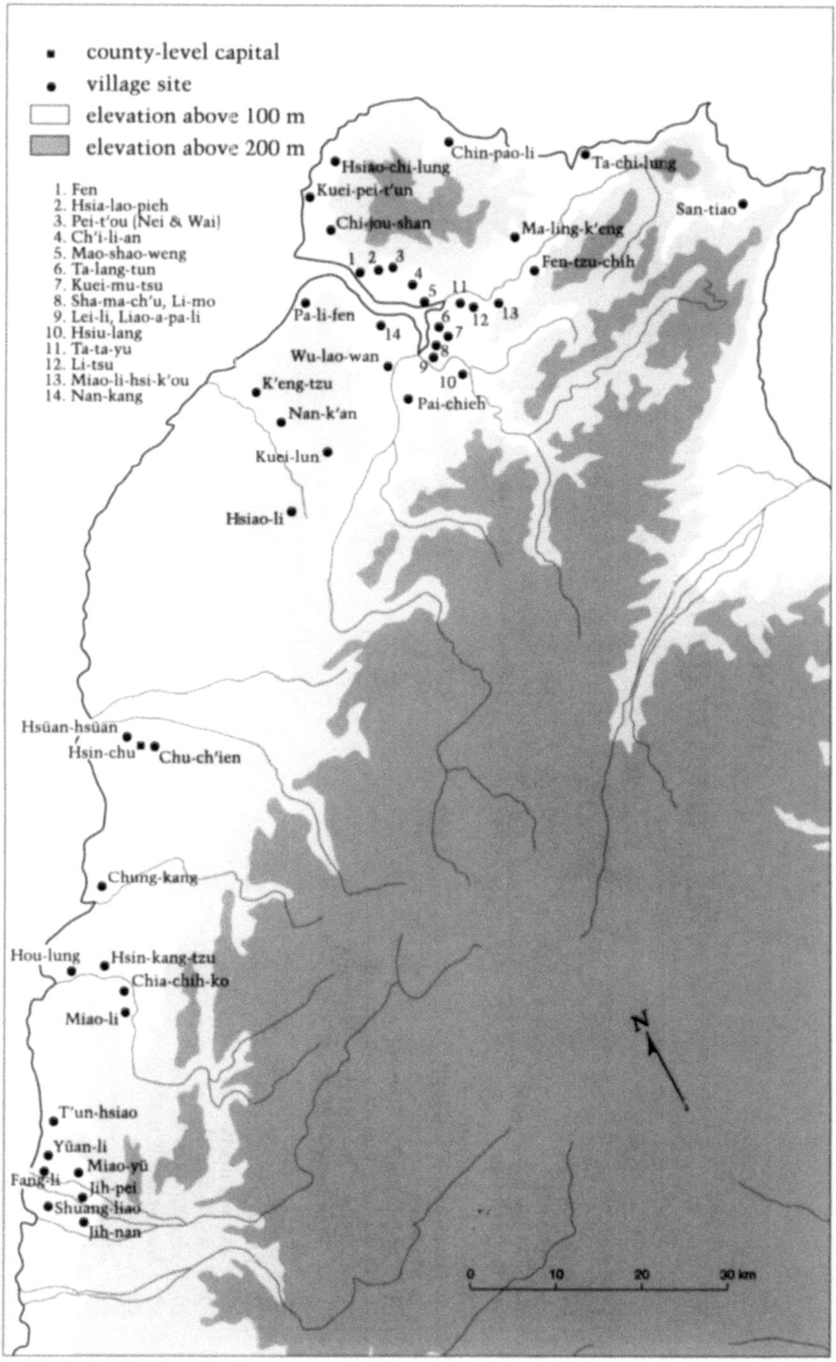

Map A.3 The village sites of the plains tribes, Tan-shui subprefecture

APPENDIX B

Tax Quotas of the Plains Tribes

Tribal name[a]	Cheng quota[b] in deerskins	Cheng quota[b] in *liang*	1684 quota[c] in *liang*	1737 quota[d] in *liang*	1737 quota[d] in *ting*	1790 *t'un* quota[e] in *ting*
T'ai-wan county						
1. Hsin-kang	3,900	936	458.64	35	175	201
2. Cho-hou (Cho-kang)	included in Hsin-kang tax unit			14	70	68
3. Ta-chieh-tien	1,620	388.8	190.512	24	120	31
Chu-lo/Chia-i county						
1. Hsiao-lung (Ou-wang)	3,846	923.04	452.2896	24.6	123	41
2. Ma-tou	1,470	352.8	172.872	23.2	116	50
3. Wan-li (Mu-chia-liu-wan)	963	231.12	113.2488	23.4	117	46
4. Ta-wu-lung-t'ou (as a tax unit also includes Chiao-pa-nien, Mu-kang [Ta-mu-hsiang], Yü-p'ao)	7,779	1,866.96	914.814	38.6	193	16
5. Nei-yu	included in Ta-wu-lung-t'ou tax unit					10
6. Hsiao-li	—	—	—	—	—	20
7. Ch'ieh-pa	—	—	—	—	—	20
8. Mang-tzu-mang	—	—	—	—	—	30
9. Ta-wu-lung-p'ai	—	—	—	—	—	20
10. To-lo-kuo (Tao-ko-kuo)	2,670	640.8	313.992	14	70	20
11. Chu-lo-shan (Chia-i)	555	133.2	65.268	12.4	62	20
12. A-li-shan	1,320	316.8	155.232	34.4	172	47
13. Chi-ling-an	109	26.16	12.9008	included in A-li-shan tax unit		
14. Ta-kuei-fo	152	36.48	17.9828	included in A-li-shan tax unit		
15. Ta-miao	1,158	277.92	136.1808	12.4	62	15
16. T'a-li-wu[f]	432	103.68	50.8032	11.8	59	20
17. Chái-li (Tou-liu-men)	3,000	720	352.8	21.6	108	38

Chang-hua county						
1. Mao-erh-kan	2,100	504	246.96	18.8	94	29
2. Nan (Mao-erh-kan-nan)	6,858	1,645.92	806.5008	40.4	202	12
3. Hsi-lo	1,740	417.6	204.624	20.2	101	56
4. Shui-sha-lien	—	—	98.5[g]	137.6	688	90
5. Tung-lo	3,150	756	370.44	20.4	102	152
6. Mei-li	included in Tung-lo tax unit			19.4	97	50
7. Erh-lin	3,615	867.6	425.124	16.8	84	28
8. Ta-wu-chün	1,407	337.68	165.4632	19.4	97	28
9. Ta-t'u	900	216	105.84	18.2	91	76
10. Ma-chih-lin	1,836	440.64	215.9136	20.8	104	23
11. Pan-hsien	2,820	676.8	331.632	22.8	114	13
12. Chai-tzu-k'eng (Chai-k'eng-tzu)	included in Pan-hsien tax unit					33
13. Ta-tu-pei	included in Pan-hsien tax unit			23.6	118	31
14. Ta-tu-chung	included in Ta-tu-pei tax unit					47
15. Ta-tu-nan	included in Ta-tu-pei tax unit					31
16. Shui-li	included in Pan-hsien tax unit			included in Ta-tu-pei tax unit		26
17. A-shu	603	144.72	70.9128	21.4	107	30
18. Pei-t'ou	4,263	1,023.12	501.3288	34.6	173	128
19. Nan-t'ou	included in Pei-t'ou tax unit					23
20. Mao-lo[h]	included in Pei-t'ou tax unit					45
21. Mao-wu-su	252	60.48	29.6352	9.0	45	10
22. Sha-lu (Ch'ien-shan, Hui-ma)	198	47.52	23.2848	11.0	55	27
23. Niu-ma-nan (Kan-en)	included in Sha-lu tax unit			9.2	46	35
24. Niu-ma-pei	included in Sha-lu tax unit			included in Niu-ma-nan tax unit		14
Tan-shui subprefecture						
1. An-li[i]				12.0	—	112
2. A-li-shih	included in An-li tax unit					119
3. Wu-niu-lan	included in An-li tax unit					32
4. P'u-tzu-li[j]	included in An-li tax unit					144

APPENDIX B
(continued)

Tribal name[a]	Cheng quota[b] in deerskins	Cheng quota[b] in *liang*	1684 quota[c] in *liang*	1737 quota[d] in *liang*	1737 quota[d] in *ting*	1790 *t'un* quota[e] in *ting*
5. Hu-lu-tun		included in An-li tax unit				25
6. Hsi-shih-wei		included in An-li tax unit				23
7. Mao-li-lan		included in An-li tax unit				12
8. Weng-tzu		included in An-li tax unit				25
9. Chih-tzu		included in An-li tax unit				20
10. Ma-shu-chiu		included in An-li tax unit				38
11. Ta-chia-hsi (Peng-shan, Te-hua)	1,143	274.32	143.4168	70.0	350	40
12. Ta-chia-tung		included in Ta-chia-hsi tax unit				72
13. Shuang-liao		included in Ta-chia-hsi tax unit				86
14. Jih-nan		included in Ta-chia-hsi tax unit				74
15. Jih-pei		included in Ta-chia-hsi tax unit				70
16. Fang-li		included in Ta-chia-hsi tax unit				44
17. Yüan-li		included in Ta-chia-hsi tax unit				12
18. Miao-yü (Hsing-lung)		included in Ta-chia-hsi tax unit				8
19. T'un-hsiao		included in Ta-chia-hsi tax unit				25
20. Hou-lung	840	201.6	98.784	61.4	307	39
21. Hsin-kang-tzu		included in Hou-lung tax unit				52
22. Miao-ko (a combination of Miao-li and Chia-chih-ko)		included in Hou-lung tax unit				30
23. Chung-kang		included in Hou-lung tax unit				33
24. Chu-ch'ien[k]	3,750	900	378	17.8	89	95
25. Nan-k'an	840	201.6	98.784	included in Tan-shui tax unit		13
26. K'eng-tzu	included in Nan-k'an tax unit			included in Tan-shui tax unit		26

27. Kuei-lun	included in Nan-k'an tax unit			included in Tan-shui tax unit		14
28. Hsiao-li	included in Nan-k'an tax unit			included in Tan-shui tax unit		20
29. Pa-li-fen[l] (Tan-shui tax unit)	192	46.08	22.5792	115.8	579	5
30. Pei-t'ou (Nei and Wai)		included in Tan-shui tax unit				18
31. Mao-shao-weng		included in Tan-shui tax unit				4
32. Wu-lao-wan		included in Tan-shui tax unit				22
33. Pai-chieh		included in Tan-shui tax unit				13
34. Kuei-tun (a combination of Kuei-mu-tsu and Ta-lang-tun)		included in Tan-shui tax unit				15
35. Kuei-pei-t'un (Ta-t'un)		included in Tan-shui tax unit				11
36. Hsiao-chi-lung		included in Tan-shui tax unit				10
37. Li-tsu		included in Tan-shui tax unit				14
38. Lei-li		included in Tan-shui tax unit				24
39. Miao-li-hsi-k'ou (Hsi-k'ou)		included in Tan-shui tax unit				14
40. Ta-ta-yu		included in Tan-shui tax unit				16
41. Feng-tzu-chih		included in Tan-shui tax unit				20
42. Ta-chi-lung	192	46.08	22.5792	included in Tan-shui tax unit		14
43. Chin-pao-li	included in Ta-chi-lung tax unit			included in Tan-shui tax unit		26
44. San-tiao (San-ch'iao)	included in Ta-chi-lung tax unit			included in Tan-shui tax unit		21
Feng-shan four[m]						
1. Chia-liu-t'ang	420	100.8	49.392	49.392	—	—
2. Lang-ch'iao	435	104.4	51.156	51.156	—	—
3. Liu-ch'iu	84	20.16	9.878	9.80	—	—
4. Pi-nan-mi	585	140.4	68.796	68.796	—	—

APPENDIX B
(continued)

Tribal name[a]	Cheng quota[b]		1684 quota[c]	1737 quota[d]		1790 *t'un* quota[e]
	in deerskins	in *liang*	in *liang*	in *liang*	in *ting*	in *ting*
Feng-shan eight[n,o]						
5. Fang-so (A-chia)	—	640.656	568.728	57.2	286	39
6. Chia-t'eng (She-lien)	—	596.376	532.872	56.0	280	121
7. Li-li	—	342.720	307.728	32.0	160	69
8. Hsia-tan-shui (Ma-li-ma-lun)	—	576.504	519.048	58.4	292	111
9. Shang-tan-shui (Ta-mu-lien)	—	520.416	463.392	47.4	237	84
10. A-hou	—	342.432	306.792	32.2	161	71
11. Ta-lou	—	520.776	463.536	46.8	234	155
12. Wu-lou (Ta-tse-chi)	—	194.976	182.520	19.6	98	50

[a]Alternative tribal names are given in parentheses.
[b]The Cheng quotas are reconstructed from the 1684 quotas as explained in Chapters 4 and 5. Deerskins are valued at 0.24 *liang*.
[c]*CLHC*: 97–100.
[d]1737 quotas are from *TWFC*:Fan: 191–200, levied at 0.2 *liang* per *ting*.
[e]1790 *t'un ting* quotas are from Cheng Hsi-fu 1976.
[f]After T'a-li-wu, the Chu-lo gazetteer lists a Hou-men *she*, with a 1684 tax quota of 49.392 *liang* (Cheng quota of 420 deerskins, 100.8 *liang*) (*CLHC*: 98). Hou-men *she* does not reappear in any other tax list.
[g]A group of six Shui-sha-lien tribes submitted in 1693 and were assigned this tax quota.
[h]Abe (1938) lists Wan-tou-liu near Mao-lo, but Wan-tou-liu does not appear on any tax lists.
[i]When An-li submitted in 1715, it was assigned a tax quota of 12 *liang* or 50 deerskins. The An-li group included five named units, one of which, Sao-su, does not reappear on any tax lists.
[j]Abe (1938) lists five subdivisions of P'u-tzu-li that do not appear on any tax lists: She-liao, Ta-nan, Shui-ti-liao, Shan-t'ou, and Ta-ma-lin.
[k]Huang Shu-ching (1957) and Abe (1938) list a Hsüan-hsüan *she* that does not appear on the tax lists.
[l]The Tan-shui tax unit also includes Chi-jou(-shan) *she*, which is not listed in 1790 (*CLHC*: 99; *TWFC*:Fan: 200). Abe (1938) also lists in the Taipei basin: Fen, Hsia-lao-pieh, Ma-ling-k'eng, Ch'i-li-an, Liao-a-pa-li, Nan-kang, Hsiu-lang, Sha-ma-ch'u, and Li-mo.
[m]As noted in Chapter 5, the Feng-shan four were unaffected by the 1737 tax adjustments.
[n]The Cheng quotas are reconstructed from the 1684 quotas as explained in Chapter 5. Individual tribal quotas understate the total because the 753 old and infirm and 40 women cannot be assigned to individual tribes.
[o]The 1684 tax quota was levied in *shih* of husked rice, converted here at 0.72 *liang* per *shih* (*TWFC*:Yü: 247).

APPENDIX C

Measures of Land and Grain

Cultivated land in Taiwan was measured in *chia,* one of which equals 11.3 *mou.* The *mou* is the usual mainland measure of area. One *chia* equals 2.396 acres or 0.96992 hectares. The *chia* is unique to Taiwan as a measure of land area and was in use under the Dutch. Thus, some scholars have sought to find a Dutch origin for the *chia,* but Nakamura cites evidence that it was a new measure to the Dutch as well. The Dutch governor Caron described the *chia* as 50 fathoms on a side and equal to about one *morgen.*[1] One scholar has argued that the *chia* originated from measuring land with spears (*ko*). A square, 25 *ko* on a side, encloses one *chia.* The origin of the *chia* remains a mystery.[2]

The *shih* is a measure of volume or capacity, although it is sometimes confused with the *tan,* a measure of weight.[3] The *shih* equals about 2.94 bushels or 103.6 liters. Taiwan's tax grain was measured from Cheng times in *kuan tou,* also known as *tao tou,* which equal only 80 percent of a full *tou* (*man tou*).[4] The full *tou* was one-fifth of the standard *ts'ang hu.*[5] In 1790, due to the expense of putting down the Lin Shuang-wen rebellion, tax grain was ordered measured by the *man tou,* thereby effecting a 20 percent increase in taxes.[6]

For tax purposes two volumetric units of unhusked rice were set to equal one unit of milled rice.[7] This compares unfavorably with the present-day ratio of 1.44 units of milled rice. Wang Shih-ch'ing accounts for this discrepancy by the lower quality of grain and poorer winnowing common in the Ch'ing era.[8] Ch'üan and Kraus state, however, that even today milling reduces "volume by 50 per cent and reduces weight by some 15 to 20 per cent, although the commonly accepted figure for oriental rice is 35 to 40 per cent."[9] This is more in line with the Ch'ing ratio. Hand milling may have yielded a slightly bulkier product than steam milling.

One *shih* of milled rice equals approximately 138.75 catties, 82.81 kg, or 182.6 lb.[10] One metric ton of milled rice equals 12.076 *shih* of milled rice; to get 12.076 *shih* of milled rice one needs twice that amount by volume or 24.152 *shih* of unhusked rice (which should weigh approximately 20 percent more than 1 MT).

APPENDIX D

Measures of Governmental Presence in Eighteenth-Century China

To govern its strategic periphery in Taiwan, the Ch'ing deployed a higher density of both civil and military officers compared to China as a whole (see Chapter 7). This appendix presents data that support this generalization. These data suggest that interprovincial variation in civil and military presence in the eighteenth century was substantial and had an important impact on local development that is deserving of greater scholarly attention.

A comparison of the population and area of Taiwan's counties to the average county population and average county area for China as a whole and for mainland Fukien demonstrates that Taiwan's counties were larger in area and smaller in population than those in China and mainland Fukien (see Table D.1).

Table D.2 presents data on both the gross and plains areas of Taiwan's county-level units. (In reading Table D.2, remember that the area assigned to Chu-lo in 1684 was divided between Tan-shui subprefecture, Chang-hua county, and Chu-lo county in 1723.) The Ch'ing attempt to restrict Han settlement to the plains areas in effect reduced the administered region to a territory that fell within the normal range of effectiveness of county magistrates; the plains areas of T'ai-wan and Feng-shan, and Chu-lo after 1723 are below the national average (gross) area, but the plains areas of the northern units of Chang-hua and Tan-shui and Chu-lo before 1723 are larger than average. Since high mountain areas beyond effective Chinese jurisdiction have not been excluded from the gross area figures for China and Fukien in Table D.1, Taiwan's plains area figures do not necessarily make the better comparison.

Table D.2 also reveals the much smaller area of T'ai-wan county, which was less than half the average for China and Fukien and contrasts sharply with the area of the frontier counties. T'ai-wan county contained half of Taiwan's Han population in 1684 (i.e., 40,000, assuming that T'ai-wan county's population reflected the proportion of the island's Han head-tax quota assigned to it), far below the average county population nationwide; its small area must be attributed to the strategic importance of maintaining control over the prefecture's metropolitan county.

Magistrates had to control both territory and population; control declined both at great distances and when population increased in numbers. Other things being equal, a magistrate could exercise greater control over a smaller area and a smaller

TABLE D.1
Average Size of County-Level Units in Eighteenth-Century China, Mainland Fukien, and Taiwan

	ca. 1700		ca. 1735		1764–77	
	km²	pop.	km²	pop.	km²	pop.
China[a]	2,236	99,400	2,481	147,000	2,350	186,000
Mainland Fukien[b]	—	—	—	—	2,037	178,000
Taiwan[c] (gross area)	8,438	62,333	5,063	83,000	5,063	168,000
Taiwan[c] (plains area)	3,569	—	2,141	—	2,141	—

[a]China's population is estimated at 150 million in 1700, 200 million at the end of the Yung-cheng reign in 1735, and 267 million in 1776 (Ho Ping-ti 1959: 264–70, 282; see also Table D.3 below). The number of county-level units—1,509 ca. 1700; 1,360 ca. 1735; 1,436 in 1764—is from Ch'ü 1962: 2. The area figures are from Perkins 1969: 219, which gives the gross areas of the eighteen provinces according to Ch'ing sources for 1790, for a total of 3,374,797 km².

[b]In 1777 mainland Fukien's population was reported to be 10,666,273 (*KCTCL*: 40.818–19) in approximately 60 county-level units (compare Bielenstein 1987 and Wang Yeh-chien 1973: 99). The area of mainland Fukien according to Republican-era data is 122,200 km² and according to the 1790 Ch'ing data 139,048 km² (Perkins 1969: 219). The Ch'ing figure must include Taiwan.

[c]Taiwan's population is estimated at 187,000 ca. 1700, 415,000 in 1735, and 840,000 in 1777 (based on the population and growth rates shown in Table 6.4). The number of county-level units in Taiwan is three in 1700 and five after 1723. The subprefecture created to administer the large expanse of land and water in the Pescadores in 1727 has been excluded from the analysis, although its small population has not been deducted from the population figures. The areas of Taiwan's county-level units are presented as both gross areas (from the western coast to the mountain divide) and, in the next row, as plains areas, excluding mountain and high foothill areas (see Table D.2).

population. The two dimensions of a magistrate's jurisdiction, area and population, had to be balanced to maintain minimal administrative effectiveness. Control could be increased by reducing, to varying degrees, either or both of the dimensions. Figure D.1 represents some possible designs for county jurisdictions, with the area of the enclosed rectangle representing the "size" of the jurisdiction as determined by the combined effect of population and area. A smaller rectangle indicates a higher degree of control and a larger rectangle less control (compare the areas labeled A and B). Because population densities varied, and both dimensions of area and population affected control, jurisdictions of the same combined "size" could have very different dimensions. Jurisdiction C represents a county in a densely populated area, and jurisdiction D a county in a sparsely populated area. Although smaller in area, jurisdiction C is nevertheless comparable in "size" (and control) to jurisdiction D. The size of each jurisdiction therefore reflects a particular trade-off between the two dimensions of area and population.

Based on the population and area figures reported in Table D.3 (see the caveats on these data in the notes to the table), Table D.4 gives provincial averages for the two dimensions of county size, population per magistrate and area per magistrate. Because provinces incorporated territories of widely varying population densities, terrain, and economic development, a variation summarized by Skinner's distinction between cores and peripheries, the provincial averages represent no more than the mean of a normal curve distribution of county areas and populations *within* each province.[1] Counties in densely populated core areas

TABLE D.2
Areas of Taiwan's County-Level Units Through the Eighteenth Century[a]
(km²)

County-level unit	Gross area	Plains area
Chu-lo (1683)	18,499	7,799
Tan-shui[b]	6,755	2,917
Chang-hua[c]	7,900	2,592
Chu-lo (1723)[d]	3,844	2,290
T'ai-wan[e]	1,092	812
Feng-shan[f]	5,722	2,097
TOTAL	25,313	10,708

[a]The area figures are calculated from township areas in *Statistics on Civil Affairs, Taiwan Province,* no. 9 (1980), table 6. Mountain and high foothill townships were identified by reference to topographical maps and excluded from the plains areas. All east coast counties (I-lan, Hua-lien, and T'ai-tung) and all but three townships of Nan-t'ou county were excluded.

[b]The area of Tan-shui subprefecture is the sum of the areas of modern T'ai-pei, T'ao-yüan, Hsin-chu, and Miao-li counties.

[c]The area of Chang-hua county is the sum of the areas of modern T'ai-chung, Chang-hua, Nan-t'ou (three townships only), and Yün-lin (above the old Hu-wei river) counties.

[d]The area of Chu-lo county after 1723 is the sum of the areas of modern Yün-lin (below the old Hu-wei river), Chia-i, and T'ai-nan (above the Tseng-wen river) counties.

[e]The area of T'ai-wan county is that of modern T'ai-nan county below the Tseng-wen river.

[f]The area of Feng-shan county is the sum of the areas of modern Kao-hsiung and P'ing-tung counties.

would be expected to be above the provincial average in population per magistrate but below the provincial average in area per magistrate; the reverse would hold true for counties in the sparsely populated peripheries. Also, secure counties might be larger on the combined dimensions, and strategic counties, where tighter control was desirable, smaller. What is most striking is the very wide range of variation in averages among provinces (for military presence too, see Table D.6); some are twice as large as the national average, and some only half as large.

The greatest density of magistrates per capita (fewer people per county-level unit) was in the sparsely populated frontier provinces of Kwangsi, Yunnan, Kweichow, Szechwan, and Shensi, frontier areas that also had high numbers of soldiers per capita (see below and the summary Table D.9 that orders the provinces by population density). Kansu (also a frontier area with a high number of soldiers per capita) is an interesting exception to this pattern: Kansu had an above average number of people per county-level unit (combined with the largest area per county). Since Kansu's reported population is suspiciously large, determination of the actual extent of this discrepancy must await further research. The frontier provinces of Kwangsi, Yunnan, Kweichow, Szechwan, and Kansu also had the largest areas per county; Shensi diverges from the pattern with a below average area per county. Thus in general, the sparsely populated frontier provinces combined the greatest density of magistrates per capita with the lowest density per area. Within provinces or macroregions, we would expect this pattern to describe counties in the peripheries rather than in the cores. This accords with the argument made in Chapter 7 that because friction of distance limited the territorial range of administrative effectiveness, counties in sparsely populated peripheries tended to have smaller than average populations because they could not effectively encompass the area that would hold the average county population. This was also the pattern found for Taiwan. The dense military presence per capita in these areas meant that frontier government generally had a strongly military cast.

In the most densely populated provinces, population per county rather than friction of distance becomes the limiting factor on county size and the range of a magistrate's effectiveness. Thus, the rich, densely populated provinces of Kiangsu and Chekiang combined county areas significantly below average with populations per county significantly above average; in these areas further consolidation of counties would have created unwieldy populations per county. It is in areas where magistrates had to deal with large county populations that the pattern noted by Skinner in which magistrates enlisted local elites as instruments of control was most important. Thus, the range of a magistrate's effectiveness was limited by a county's "size," when size is understood in both spatial and demographic senses. In sparsely populated areas the spatial component of size was the limiting factor on effectiveness; in densely populated areas the demographic component was the limiting factor.

In areas of middling population density, the demographic and spatial limits on administrative effectiveness had a less one-sided effect on county size, which makes it easier to see how strategic concerns dictated the need for greater or lesser administrative presence. Secure interior areas could get by with low densities of both civil and military presence; thus interior provinces like Anhwei, Kiangsi, Hupei, and Hunan had both above-average county areas *and* above-average county populations. In contrast, the metropolitan province of Chihli (where the security of the capital was at stake) had the highest density of magistrates per area and, after the frontier provinces mentioned above and Shansi, the next greatest density of magistrates per capita. Although the large number of

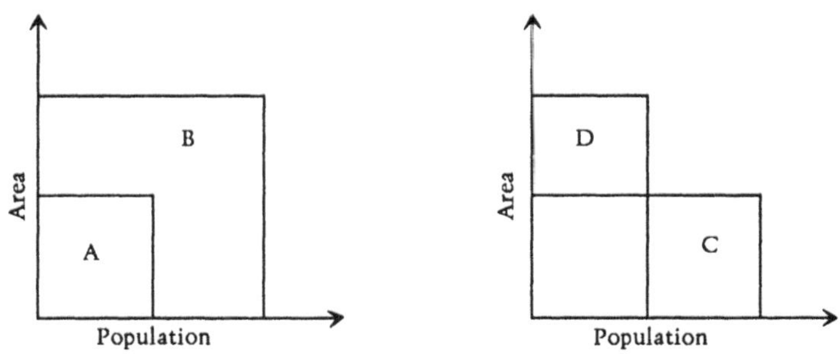

Fig. D.1 Models of county "size"

TABLE D.3

Area and Population of the Eighteen Provinces in the Late Eighteenth Century

Province	Area, 1790 (km²)[a]	Population, 1776[b]	Population density
Kansu	270,659	15,068,473	56
Shensi	129,762	8,193,059	63
Shansi	143,697	12,503,415	87
Chihli	153,267	20,567,175	134
Shantung	169,270	21,497,430	127
Honan	169,270	19,858,053	117
Hupei	179,277	14,815,128	83
Hunan	197,125	14,989,777	76
Kiangsi	187,658	16,848,905	90
Anhwei	139,266	27,566,929	198
Kiangsu	102,433	28,807,628	281
Chekiang	101,790	19,364,620	190
Fukien	139,048	11,219,887	81
Kwangtung	206,586	14,820,732	72
Kwangsi	203,450	5,381,984	26
Yunnan	280,719	3,102,948	11
Kweichow	167,840	5,003,177	30
Szechwan	433,680	7,789,791	18
TOTAL	3,374,797	267,399,111	79

[a]The provincial area figures from the 1790's are those given to Staunton by Ch'ing officials (Perkins 1969: 219; Staunton 1797: 467). These give only aggregate areas for three pairs of provinces, Shensi-Kansu, Anhwei-Kiangsu, and Hupei-Hunan. I have allocated these aggregate areas according to the relative size of the provinces in Republican-period reports (Kuan 1955). The largest discrepancies between the Ch'ing area figures and more modern figures result from the addition of border areas to Yunnan and Shensi-Kansu and the division of Sikang from Szechwan in the Republican figures (Perkins 1969: 219). Chihli (Hopei) under the Ch'ing included considerable areas to the north of the great wall (sparsely populated Ch'eng-te prefecture and K'ou-pei-san *t'ing*) that were not included in Republican or modern Hopei; the Staunton figure, while larger than that for Republican Hopei (Kuan 1955 gives 140,122 km²), is too small to have included these areas. Including these areas greatly increases Chihli's total area and average area per county and reduces its overall population density. Republican Hopei, with 132 counties, had a considerable density of counties. Area figures for the other provinces generally diverge from Kuan's Republican figures by less than 10 percent; the chief exception is the Ch'ing figure for the area of Shantung, which is 16 percent larger than the figure given by Kuan. The inevitable inaccuracies in these area figures are unlikely to have a material effect on the simple comparisons being made in this appendix. Unfortunately I know of no serious published attempt to come up with more accurate area figures for the eighteenth century. The Ch'ing figures presumably have the advantage of reflecting the perspective of the imperial bureaucracy.

[b]Population figures for 1776 are reported in *Ch'ing ch'ao wen hsien t'ung k'ao*, chüan 19 (1936 Commercial Press ed.); see also Perkins 1969: 207. Judging from Skinner's (1987) re-evaluation of the Ch'ing population reporting system, the 1776 figures, which result from the 1775 effort to revive the *pao chia* population reporting system, are likely to be the most reliable of those reported in the late eighteenth century.

counties per area in Chihli and the north China provinces of Shantung, Shansi, and Honan has been attributed to their long history of settlement and the weight of tradition,[2] the high density of Green Standard and Banner soldiers in Chihli suggests that the court also deployed a large number of magistrates per area and per capita to ensure the security of the strategic capital area (and perhaps as a civil check on the dense military presence). In the balance of the north China plain, the relatively high density of magistrates may have compensated for a sparse military presence. Fukien and Kwangtung came closest to having both average areas per county and average county populations.

Thus, I see considerations of control determining the sizes of counties and dictating the pattern in which a relatively fixed number of county-level units was distributed across China, in contrast, for example, to an approach emphasizing the economics of revenue extraction.[3] Magistrates had to control both people and territory, and there were limits to the number of people and the amount of territory a magistrate could effectively control. The need to spread control over both people and territory required a balancing to create a unit of the appropriate combined spatial and demographic dimensions over which a magistrate could achieve some minimal administrative effectiveness. Densely and sparsely populated territories required different balancings of the spatial and demographic dimensions of county size. A third variable, strategy, led to the designation of areas where greater or lesser degrees of control were desirable. Where these considerations led to the creation of revenue-poor (underpopulated) county-level units, subsidies from higher-level units of government made up for the fiscal shortfall. Although these hypotheses have only crudely been illustrated with provincial-level data here, more sophisticated statistical measures and comparison of subprovincial regions, differentiating cores and peripheries, should show the same principles in operation.[4]

TABLE D.4

Civil Presence in Late Eighteenth-Century China by Province

Province	No. of county-level units, 1786[a]	Avg. county area (km^2)	Avg. county pop.
Kansu	58	4,667	259,801
Shensi	83	1,563	98,712
Shansi	103	1,395	121,392
Chihli	147	1,043	139,913
Shantung	107	1,582	200,911
Honan	107	1,582	185,589
Hupei	68	2,636	217,870
Hunan	71	2,776	211,124
Kiangsi	77	2,437	218,817
Anhwei	59	2,360	467,236
Kiangsu	68	1,506	423,642
Chekiang	77	1,322	251,489
Fukien	64	2,173	175,311
Kwangtung	90	2,295	164,675
Kwangsi	65	3,130	82,800
Yunnan	70	4,010	44,328
Kweichow	48	3,497	104,233
Szechwan	131	3,311	59,464
TOTAL	1,493	2,260	179,102

[a]Provincial area and population are based on Table D.3 and the number of counties on Bielenstein 1987: 97–135. County-level units include *hsien*, *t'ing*, and *chou*. Wang Yeh-chien 1973: 99 gives closely comparable numbers of counties for 1753 (Wang's total is 1,501), with three exceptions: 60 (instead of 48) for Kweichow, 95 (instead of 103) for Shansi, and 141 (instead of 147) for Chihli.

TABLE D.5
Military Presence in Eighteenth-Century China, Mainland Fukien, and Taiwan

	ca. 1700		ca. 1735		ca. 1776	
	km²/ soldier	pop./ soldier	km²/ soldier	pop./ soldier	km²/ soldier	pop./ soldier
China[a]	3.97	176	3.97	235	3.97	314
Mainland Fukien[b]	—	—	—	—	2.04	178
Taiwan[c] (gross area)	3.16	23	2.53	42	2.53	84
Taiwan[d] (plains area)	1.34		1.07		1.07	

[a]The total military force remained relatively stable throughout the eighteenth century at approximately 600,000 Green Standard soldiers and 250,000 Bannermen (Powell 1955: 11–12; Smith 1974: 136, 141; Kessler 1976: 108; see also Table D.6). Area and population figures for China are the same as in Table D.1.

[b]Approximately 70,000 Green Standard soldiers and 2,000 Bannermen were stationed in Fukien (Kessler 1976: 105, 109); I have subtracted 12,000 soldiers allotted to Taiwan and the Pescadores in 1776. Area and population figures for mainland Fukien are the same as in Table D.1.

[c]The figures assume a total of 8,000 soldiers in 1684–1733 and 10,000 soldiers after 1733. In both cases naval garrisons in the Pescadores have not been included, and the figure understates the actual density of military presence in Taiwan prefecture. Gross area is 25,313 km²; see Table D.2. Population figures are the same as in Table D.1.

[d]Plains area is 10,708 km²; see Table D.2.

Table D.5 enables us to make a crude comparison of the military presence in Taiwan with that in China and mainland Fukien. The density of soldiers in Taiwan was much greater than in China, whether measured by area or population. Taiwan's soldiers had, on average, smaller areas per man to patrol and defend, even when the high mountain territory is included, and much smaller if only plains areas are considered. But these averages should not lead us to think that all points were evenly defended. The spatial distribution of troops was highly uneven, with large concentrations around strategic centers (see Chapter 7). The difference in the ratio of civilian population to soldiers between China and Taiwan is particularly striking; in 1700 Taiwan had more than seven times the number of soldiers per population; in 1735 the ratio was more than five times, and in 1777, after years of immigration, it was still more than three times. This table also reveals the large military presence in mainland Fukien circa 1776, greater than average for China in terms of both square kilometers and population per soldier. The figure for square kilometers per soldier in Fukien is even less than Taiwan's, when gross area is used.

Table D.6 gives a crude indication of the density of Green Standard and Banner forces by area and population in the eighteen provinces for the late eighteenth century. The wide variation in military presence among the provinces points to the need for studies of how strategic considerations determined the distribution of military forces across the cores and peripheries of China's regions.[5] The large concentration of Green Standard forces in provinces such as Fukien, Kwangtung, Kansu, and Yunnan (and the very small numbers in Honan, Anhwei, and Kiangsi) reveals the inadequacy of the standard characterization of their deployment as "widely dispersed."[6] Better known is the uneven distribution of Banner forces. More than half of all Banner forces were concentrated near the imperial capital in Chihli province, with the next largest concentrations in Manchuria and Turkestan, leaving less than one-quarter distributed among the provinces outside Chihli. Green Standard forces did not garrison territories outside the eighteen provinces.[7]

The same principles that determined the distribution of county units and their size can also be seen to affect the distribution of the military forces. The military also sought to control both territory and population, to balance its presence on both spatial and demographic dimensions, and to heighten control on both dimensions in strategic areas. The provinces combining high density of soldiers per capita and per area were Chihli (where the combined density of military presence was greatest), Fukien and Kwangtung on the southeast coast, and Shensi-Kansu on the northwest corridor. These provinces, which along with Kiangsu and Chekiang had the largest provincial contingents in absolute numbers, guarded strate-

TABLE D.6

Military Presence in Late Eighteenth-Century China by Province[a]

Province	Green Standard 1785[b]	Banner forces 1825[c]	Total	km²/ soldier	Pop./ soldier
Kansu	46,574	12,030	58,604	4.6	257
Shensi	37,922	6,588	44,510	2.9	184
Shansi	25,752	9,284	35,036	4.1	357
Chihli	49,402	165,717	215,119	0.7	96
Shantung	17,504	2,446	19,950	8.5	1,078
Honan	11,874	920	12,794	13.2	1,552
Hupei	17,794	6,628	24,422	7.3	607
Hunan	23,604	—	23,604	8.4	635
Kiangsi	13,929	—	13,929	13.5	1,210
Anhwei	8,428	—	8,428	16.5	3,271
Kiangsu	40,319	6,454	46,773	2.2	616
Chekiang	40,037	3,944	43,981	2.3	440
Fukien	63,119	2,463	65,582	2.1	171
Kwangtung	68,094	5,265	73,359	2.8	202
Kwangsi	23,588	—	23,588	8.5	228
Yunnan	41,353	—	41,353	6.3	75
Kweichow	37,769	—	37,769	4.4	132
Szechwan	32,112	2,672	34,784	12.5	224
[Manchuria	—	44,144	44,144]		
[Turkestan	—	14,208	14,208]		
TOTAL[d]	599,174	282,763	881,937	4.1[d]	325[d]

[a]Provincial area and population are based on Table D.3.

[b]Green Standard troop strengths are given in the *Ch'ing ch'ao wen hsien t'ung k'ao* (1936), chüan 179. For dating, compare Lo Erh-kang 1945: 44. Only aggregate figures are given for two pairs of provinces, Kiangsu-Anhwei and Shensi-Kansu. I have allocated these aggregate figures according to the relative size of provincial contingents reported by Wade for 1849 in the case of Kiangsu and Anhwei (Wade 1851: 255) and by Kessler for 1685 in the case of Shensi and Kansu (Kessler 1976: 109).

[c]Banner troops totaled 282,763 in 1825 (Wade 1851: 254). Of these troops, 165,717 garrisoned the metropolitan province of Chihli, 14,208 Turkestan, and 44,144 Manchuria. The remaining 58,694 Banner troops were spread among the provinces outside Chihli. The largest provincial concentrations were in the northwest provinces of Kansu (12,030), Shansi (9,284), and Shensi (6,588), which together accounted for nearly half of all Banner troops outside Chihli.

[d]Averages exclude the Banner totals for Manchuria and Turkestan and are therefore based on a total troop strength of 823,585 within the eighteen provinces.

gic frontiers. The large contingents in the two densely populated core provinces of Kiangsu and Chekiang created an above-average number of soldiers per unit of area but not per capita, which strengthened the defense of two key revenue-producing provinces. These strategic provinces contrast with secure interior provinces that had the lowest density of soldiers per capita and per unit of area: Honan, Anhwei, and Kiangsi, followed by Hupei, Hunan, and Shantung. An above-average presence per capita in the sparsely populated frontier provinces of Kwangsi, Yunnan, Kweichow, and Szechwan, helped compensate for a below-average number of soldiers per area.

Taiwan, as a frontier area with a high density of soldiers per area and per population, most resembles the strategically important frontier areas Shensi and Kansu and the southeast coastal provinces of Fukien and Kwangtung. Comparison of subprovincial regions, differentiating cores and peripheries (beyond the scope of this study) is needed to refine the picture of strategic areas presented in the table.[8] The strategic significance of many core areas in the southeastern coastal provinces confounds a simple correlation of high economic development or population density with low military presence (see Table D.9 below).

The distribution of the Ch'ing military illustrates a key element of the Ch'ing political economy: it maps both the coercive arm of the state and the spatial pattern of its largest expenditures. Military expenditures accounted for half to two-thirds of the state's budget. Thomas Wade estimated annual military expenditures at 30.9 million taels.[9] This constituted 55 percent of the central government's tax quotas in the late eighteenth century (56.2 million taels) and 42 percent of revenues when surcharges are included (73.8 million taels).[10] The economic impact of the military, both in terms of the burden on local revenue and the level of military expenditures in the local economy, was greatest in the sparsely populated, revenue-poor frontier areas of the southwest and the northwest, which required subsidies from the central government to sustain their military garrisons.

The wide interprovincial variation in the civil and military presence of the state points both to the need for studies of Ch'ing local government sensitive to significant regional variations and to the need for readily accessible nationwide disaggregated data on additional indicators. As further examples of significant differentials in government impact by province, I present two tables, one showing variation in land-tax revenues and the other variation in the number of *chin shih* degree holders.

Table D.7 shows the distribution of land-tax revenue quotas by province. Wang Yeh-chien estimates in 1753 that land taxes accounted for 74 percent of total revenues, followed by the salt tax (12 percent), native customs (7 percent), and miscellaneous taxes (7 percent). Approximately half the salt-tax revenues came from Kiangsu, a further indication of that province's fiscal importance.[11] The eight most densely populated provinces (62.5 percent of total population), which compose the two regions of the lower Yangtze and the north China plain, accounted for 73 percent of total land-tax revenues. The rich lower Yangtze provinces (Kiangsu, Chekiang, Anhwei, and Kiangsi) accounted for 40.4 percent of land revenues, and the four provinces of the north China plain accounted for 32.4 percent. These two regions thus constituted the fiscal core of the empire. Counties in all these provinces collected above average revenue totals (except Chihli where the

TABLE D.7
Land-Tax Revenues in Late Eighteenth-Century China by Province
(in taels)

Province	Revenues (1753)	Avg. revenue/ county	Revenue/ 1,000 pop.
Kansu	1,024,000	17,655	68.0
Shensi	2,413,000	29,072	294.5
Shansi	4,135,000	40,146	330.7
Chihli	3,180,000	21,633	154.6
Shantung	5,301,000	49,542	246.6
Honan	4,885,000	45,654	246.0
Hupei	2,081,000	30,603	140.5
Hunan	2,000,000	28,169	133.4
Kiangsi	3,849,000	49,987	228.4
Anhwei	3,812,000	64,610	138.3
Kiangsu	8,583,000	126,221	297.9
Chekiang	5,627,000	73,078	290.6
Fukien	1,925,000	30,078	171.6
Kwangtung	2,625,000	29,167	177.1
Kwangsi	664,000	10,215	123.4
Yunnan	730,000	10,429	235.3
Kweichow	361,000	7,521	72.2
Szechwan	878,000	6,702	112.7
TOTAL	54,073,000	36,218	202.2

SOURCES: Wang Yeh-chien 1973: 70. Revenue figures include taxes levied in cash and in kind, as well as surcharges. Provincial population data are from Table D.3; the number of counties is from Table D.4.

large number of counties and the large amount of tax-exempt Banner land lowered average county revenues), and the counties of Chekiang and Kiangsu collected from two to more than three times the average revenue per county.

Most surprising is the high per capita tax burden imposed on the relatively poor populations of Shansi and Shensi. Proximity to the capital (increasing the need to fund a significant defense and exposing these provinces to direct extractive power) and responsibility for the logistical support of armies in the northwest, rather than ability to pay, most likely explains this heavy tax burden.[12]

Table D.8 shows the distribution of *chin shih* degree holders by province. Holders of the select *chin shih* degree were qualified to hold government office and constituted the national bureaucratic elite. Society awarded the highest prestige to *chin shih,* and they wielded significant influence in their native localities. Thus *chin shih* degree holders were a key link between state and society in late imperial China (see Chapter 7). The distribution of *chin shih* reflects both the differential academic success of the rich lower Yangtze provinces of Kiangsu and Chekiang and the effect of *provincial* quotas designed to increase the chances of candidates from backward provinces. Note the above-average number of *chin shih* per population in academically undeveloped Yunnan and Kweichow.[13]

Table D.9 summarizes the foregoing tables and discussion. The table orders the data by provincial population density, which is a rough proxy for level of economic development. This table makes it easier to identify provinces where strategic concerns have heightened or lowered government presence (e.g., Chihli

TABLE D.8

Number of Chin Shih in Late Eighteenth-Century China by Province

Province	*Chin shih* (1736–95)[a]	*Chin shih*/ million pop.	*Chin shih*/ county
Kansu-Shensi[b]	228	10	1.6
Shansi	311	25	3.0
Chihli	488	24	3.3
Shantung	259	12	2.4
Honan	282	14	2.6
Hupei	212	14	3.1
Hunan	128	9	1.8
Kiangsi	540	32	7.0
Anhwei	216	8	3.7
Kiangsu	644	22	9.5
Chekiang	697	36	9.1
Fukien	301	27	4.7
Kwangtung	252	17	2.8
Kwangsi	102	19	1.6
Yunnan	129	42	1.8
Kweichow	129	26	2.7
Szechwan	159	20	1.2
TOTAL	5,177	19	3.5

[a]Ho Ping-ti 1962: 228. Excluded from the provincial totals are 179 Bannermen *chin shih* and 29 *chin shih* from Liaoning. Provincial population data are from Table D.3; the number of counties is from Table D.4.

[b]Ho gives only a combined total for the provinces of Shensi and Kansu. For the entire Ch'ing period, Shensi produced 82 percent of the Shensi-Kansu combined total (Ho Ping-ti 1962: 228). Applying that percentage to the Ch'ien-lung reign totals would give Shensi 187 *chin shih*, 23 *chin shih* per million population, and 2.3 per county. Kansu would have 41 *chin shih*, for 3 per million, and 0.7 per county.

vs. Anhwei) or revenue extraction (e.g., Shensi) beyond what we might predict on the basis of population density and economic significance. It also illustrates the discrepancy in frontier areas between high military expenditures and low revenues. In sum, these data provide support for, and enable an assessment of, G. W. Skinner's generalization that for the late imperial state, functions of "revenue and defense were inversely related in regional space."[14]

The use of provincial-level measures may raise questions in some quarters. Students of local history in China need to understand the structure of regions and the extent of regional variation if they are to properly interpret and locate their findings in a larger context. Skinner's work has established the importance of studying regional variation to the social and economic history of China. But to insist that comparison can be done only at the macroregional level (or between economic-functional units) is to impede, at this stage at least, rather than foster regional systems analysis, for two reasons.

First, the sources for local history are organized by province and other administrative units and not by economic-functional region. It is often impossible to disaggregate the information contained in these sources (for example, the 1776 population figures). Macroregional analysis, however sophisticated, can be of little use when data are reported on a different basis. The functional integration of

TABLE D.9

Population Density and Governmental Presence in Late Eighteenth-Century China by Province

Province	Pop./ km^2	km^2/ county	Pop./ county	km^2/ soldier	Pop./ soldier	Taels/ county	Taels/ 10^3 pop.	*Chin shih*/ county	*Chin shih*/ 10^6 pop.
Kiangsu	281	1,506	423,642	2.2	616	126,221	297.9	9.5	22
Anhwei	198	2,360	467,236	16.5	3,271	64,610	138.3	3.7	8
Chekiang	190	1,322	251,489	2.3	440	73,078	290.6	9.1	36
Chihli	134	1,043	139,913	0.7	96	21,633	154.6	3.3	24
Shantung	127	1,582	200,911	8.5	1,078	49,542	246.6	2.4	12
Honan	117	1,582	185,589	13.2	1,552	45,654	246.0	2.6	14
Kiangsi	90	2,437	218,817	13.5	1,210	49,987	228.4	7.0	32
Shansi	87	1,395	121,392	4.1	357	40,146	330.7	3.0	25
Hupei	83	2,636	217,870	7.3	607	30,603	140.5	3.1	14
Fukien	81	2,173	175,311	2.1	171	30,078	171.6	4.7	27
Hunan	76	2,776	211,124	8.4	635	28,169	133.4	1.8	9
Kwangtung	72	2,295	164,675	2.8	202	29,167	177.1	2.8	17
Shensi	63	1,563	98,712	2.9	184	29,072	294.5	{ 1.6	{ 10
Kansu	56	4,667	259,801	4.6	257	17,655	68.0		
Kweichow	30	3,497	104,233	4.4	132	7,521	72.2	2.7	26
Kwangsi	26	3,130	82,800	8.6	228	10,215	123.4	1.6	19
Szechwan	18	3,311	59,464	12.5	224	6,702	112.7	1.2	20
Yunnan	11	4,010	44,328	6.8	75	10,429	235.3	1.8	42
AVERAGE	79	2,260	179,102	4.1	325	36,218	202.2	3.5	19

macroregions and the boundaries that define them are historical products, as work by Paul Smith (1988) and Joseph Esherick (1987) has shown, and should be treated as hypotheses rather than givens. To require that every local study attempt to encompass multi-provincial areas as vast as one of the eight macroregions (and to delineate across provinces regional boundaries as they changed over time) is to impose an unrealistic burden that can end up frustrating rather than stimulating scholarship. It is ironic that macroregional analysis, which initially requires disaggregating provincial data and then aggregates the eighteen provinces into only eight units of comparison, creates measures (e.g., urbanization rates reported by macroregions) that cannot be compared to data available only at the provincial level. However, only three provinces have core areas in more than one macroregion: Kwangtung (Lingnan and Southeast Coast), Chekiang (Southeast Coast and Lower Yangtze), and Anhwei (Lower Yangtze and North China, whose boundaries Skinner is now redrawing). Most macroregions group provinces that have contiguous cores, and crosscut provincial boundaries only along the peripheries. Analyses that make core-periphery distinctions at the provincial level are thus largely compatible with and can contribute to macroregional analysis.

Second, the administrative hierarchy was as much a part of the spatial structure of eighteenth-century China as were physiographic regions. The political and military chain of command was also significant economically, because the state defined important patterns of expenditure and revenue collection. When the subject of interest centers on the political system, the administrative structure of regions should be foregrounded. By no means am I counseling that research ignore regional structures that crosscut administrative units, or core-periphery relations within those units. Skinner's (1977c) brilliant analysis of the articulation of the bureaucracy to regional space demonstrated the importance of these sources of variation to government control strategies. Disaggregation, where possible, is always preferable.

But our sources come from a world where most data were organized and reported by administrative units, and there is often no way of disaggregating that data further. Data on many indicators are frequently available only at relatively high levels of aggregation and are considered reliable only in specific periods. To fail to use that data to uncover and measure spatial variation across administrative units impoverishes the analysis of local systems and deprives local studies of a valuable source of larger-scale comparisons. Thus, Susan Naquin and Evelyn Rawski, in adopting a macroregional framework to analyze regional variation in eighteenth-century Chinese society, apparently ignored indicators of regional variation such as those presented in the tables in this appendix because only provincial-level data were available.[15] Researchers conducting national-level studies should make it a priority to uncover and report indicators, disaggregated at the provincial or lower level, that can contribute to the analysis of regional variation and aid students pursuing local studies. It is unrealistic to expect each local study to invent national indicators.

The simple comparisons of civil and military presence, revenues, and *chin shih* production across the eighteen provinces in this appendix are intended to alert students of eighteenth-century China to important regional variations in the structure of the imperial administration and its impact on local society, as well as the possibility of measuring this variation. I hope it will stimulate the search for better and more numerous indicators of variation that will enable more sophisticated analyses. Skinner (1977c) found a rich source of data in the Register of Officials (*Chin shen ch'üan shu*) and proposed a number of hypotheses about administrative strategies based on his analysis of regional variations for the single year, 1893. Ch'ing historians have yet to test these hypotheses against the *diachronic* data contained in the Registers, which were issued several times yearly from the mid-eighteenth century on (for some analysis of Taiwan along these lines, see Chapter 7). Students pursuing local studies need published works giving indicators reported for disaggregated units on a nationwide basis that enable them to assess the uniqueness of their own localities.[16] Only when that first generation of studies has been completed will it be feasible to move toward finer regionalizations.

APPENDIX E

Territorial Organization of the Aborigine Military Colonies

T'un site		Allotted to[a]		
Locale	Area in *chia*	*T'un* no.	Village	No. of colonists
Feng-shan county				
		1	Fang-so (S)	39
1. P'u-ch'iang-lin	327	1	Chia-t'eng (S)	121
		1	Li-li (S)	69
		1	Hsia-tan-shui (S)	111
2. Hsia-nan-p'ing-ting	273	2	Ta-lou (S)	155
		1	Shang-tan-shui (S)	60
		2	Shang-tan-shui (S)	24
3. Shang-nan-p'ing-ting	219	3	Cho-hou (S)	68
		2	Wu-lou (S)	50
4. Nan-p'ing-ch'i	43			
		2	A-hou (S)	71
5. Nan-lin-k'ou	229	3	Ta-chieh-tien (S)	31
		3	Hsin-kang (S)	201
6. Ta-pei-p'ing	247			
Ch'iang-t'eng-lin	90	rented out		
T'ou-she-shan-chiao	74	rented out		
Chia-i county				
1. Shih-chang-li	11	4	Nei-yu (R)	10
		4	A-li-shan (O)	7
2. Ta-p'u	25	5	A-li-shan (O)	40
3. Ch'ien-chen	28			
Chang-hua county				
1. Yung-p'ing-k'eng	169	4	Hsiao-lung (S)	41
		4	Ma-tou (S)	50
		4	Hsiao-li (V)	20
2. Pa-niang-k'eng	159	4	Wan-li (S)	46
		5	Shui-sha-lien (A)	90
3. Ta-ku-p'o	176	4	Ta-wu-lung-t'ou (S)	16
		4	Ch'ieh-pa (V)	20
		4	Mang-tzu-mang (V)	30
		4	Ta-wu-lung-p'ai (S)	20
		8	Ta-tu-chung (P)	47

APPENDIX E
(continued)

T'un site		Allotted to[a]		
Locale	Area in *chia*	*T'un* no.	Village	No. of colonists
4. Sha-li-pa-lai-chi-chi	320	4	Chia-i (Chu-lo-shan) (H)	20
		4	To-lo-kuo (H)	20
		5	Ta-miao (H)	15
		5	T'a-li-wu (H)	20
		6	Tung-lo (B)	152
		6	Ma-chih-lin (B)	23
		6	Erh-lin (B)	28
5. Nei-mu-chia	187	5	Ch'ai-li (H)	38
		7	Pei-t'ou (H)	128
6. Shui-ti-liao	597	5	Hsi-lo (B)	56
		5	Mao-erh-kan (H)	29
		5	Nan (H)	12
		6	Ta-t'u (H)	76
		6	A-shu (B)	30
		7	Chai-tzu-k'eng (B)	33
		7	Ta-tu-pei (P)	31
		7	Ta-tu-nan (P)	31
		7	Mao-wu-su (B)	10
		8	A-li-shih (Z)	119
		8	Shui-li (P)	26
		8	Niu-ma-nan (P)	35
		8	Niu-ma-pei (P)	14
		8	Wu-niu-lan (Z)	32
		8	Sha-lu (P)	27
7. Chiao-li-lin	50	6	Mei-li (B)	50
8. Wan-tou-liu	87	6	Ta-wu-chün (H)	28
		6	Pan-hsien (B)	13
		7	Mao-lo (H)	45
9. Hu-tzu-k'eng	33	7	Nan-t'ou (H)	23
		9	Ma-shu-chiu (Z)	38
		9	An-li (Z)	112
10. Cho-lan-p'u	316	9	Weng-tzu (Z)	25
11. Chi-yu-p'u	94	9	Hu-lu-tun (Z)	25
12. Tung-shih-chiao	13	9	Chih-tzu (Z)	20
		9	Hsi-shih-wei (Z)	23
		9	P'u-tzu-li (Z)	144
		9	Mao-li-lan (Z)	12
Tan-shui subprefecture				
1. Ma-ling-p'u	196	10	Jih-pei (T)	70
		10	Jih-nan (T)	74
		10	Ta-chia-hsi (T)	40
2. Huang-ni-t'ang	205	10	Shuang-liao (T) (also at Huai-tzu-p u)	44
		10	Ta-chia-tung (T)	72
3. Ssu-fang-lin	61			

APPENDIX E

(continued)

T'un site		Allotted to[a]		
Locale	Area in *chia*	*T'un* no.	Village	No. of colonists
4. Wu-ling-p'u	412	11	Chu-ch'ien (T)	95
		11	Fang-li (T)	44
		11	Yüan-li (T)	12
		11	T'un-hsiao (T)	25
		11	Miao-yü (T)	8
		11	Shuang-liao (T)	42
		11	Hsiao-li (K)	20
5. Hsiung-chiao-wan	73	11	Hou-lung (T)	39
		11	Hsin-kang-tzu (T)	52
6. Nei-wan	22			
(also San-wan	8)			
7. Yen-shui-kang	74	11	Miao-ko (T)	30
		11	Chung-kang (T)	33
		12	Wu-lao-wan (K)	22
		12	Pai-chieh (K)	13
		12	Li-tsu (K)	14
		12	Lei-li (K)	24
8. Shan-k'eng-tzu	74	12	Miao-li-hsi-k'ou (K)	14
9. Huai-tzu-p'u	115	12	Ta-ta-yu (K)	16
10. Chien-shan-chiao	37	12	Feng-tzu-chih (K)	20
		12	Kuei-tun (K)	15
		12	Pa-li-fen (K)	5
		12	Kuei-pei-t'un (K)	11
		12	Pei-t'ou (K)	18
		12	Mao-shao-weng (K)	4
11. Pa-lien-kang	20	12	Ta-chi-lung (K)	14
12. Ch'i-tu	65	12	Chin-pao-li (K)	26
13. T'ien-liao-kang	10	12	San-tiao (K)	21
		12	Hsiao-chi-lung (K)	10
14. San-chiao-yung	65	12	Kuei-lun (K)	14
		12	Nan-k'an (K)	13
		12	K'eng-tzu (K)	26
Ta-ku-k'an	172	rented out		
Yang-mei-p'u	249	rented out		
Chiu-hsiung-lin	35	rented out		

SOURCES: *TWSHF*: 1.381-96; Cheng Hsi-fu 1976.

[a]For the numbers assigned military colonies, see Table 10.2. The letters in parentheses following the village names are ethnic identifications:

A: Thao	B: Babuza	H: Hoanya
K: Ketagalan	O: Tsou	P: Papora
R: Saaroa	S: Siraya	T: Taokas
V: Taivoan	Z: Pazeh	

APPENDIX F

Indians and Settlers in North America

The comparison of different frontiers in Chapter 12 is limited to the not inconsiderable variety confronted by the late imperial Chinese state. Hence it assesses strategy, control costs, and revenue potential from the viewpoint of Confucian statecraft and the institutions and culture of the late empire. The expansion of agricultural settlement and the disposition of indigenes' land rights in China could also be compared to similar processes in recent centuries in many lands, for example, the Japanese colonization of Ainu territories,[1] Hispanic colonization in Latin America, Russian colonization in Central Asia, and so forth. Cross-national comparisons, when the cases diverge on so many variables and the traditions of statecraft are so different, are necessarily crude, but they can also illuminate relationships that would otherwise go unnoticed. Subject to these caveats, I will attempt a modest and brief comparison of the Chinese cases with the case most familiar to me and readers of this study, the interaction of American Indians and English colonists on the eastern seaboard of the United States.

The economies of most woodland Indians were based on male hunting, fishing, and trading and female horticulture. As in Taiwan, the fur trade was a leading factor in the earliest stages of foreign economic penetration. To ensure their own security as well as access to fur supplies, the early colonists manipulated Indian alliances and played on inter-tribal antagonisms. An important point of contrast with Taiwan, however, is the demographic destruction brought to American Indians with the introduction of Eurasian diseases, particularly smallpox and measles. In Taiwan, and in South China generally, new diseases were not suddenly introduced by the expansion of Han settlement, and indeed the prevalence of malaria slowed Han expansion.[2]

How did land-hungry colonial farmers negotiate rights in native lands? In the earliest stages, land was either purchased in exchange for trade goods or simply squatted on, as in the case of sites abandoned by villages depopulated by epidemics. In the wake of settler-Indian wars, land was also claimed by right of conquest.[3] To avoid the threat to peace caused by unscrupulous land dealings, colonial governments required official approval of all transfers of Indian land.[4] This concern to manage and control relations with the Indians accelerated after the French and Indian Wars. In 1754 the British imperial government sought to centralize control of Indian affairs, and with the Proclamation of 1763 it barred settlers from acquiring lands beyond a boundary drawn along the watershed of the Appalachians. Attempts to enforce this proclamation alienated the "borderers," who then became active supporters of the revolutionaries on the coast.[5] After the Revolution, the new government continued the basic framework of British Indian policy: recognition of Indian land titles, a government monopoly on acquisitions of land from the Indians, treatment of the tribes as independent nations under a treaty system, and regulation of the Indian trade with particular concern to control unscrupulous traders and the sale of whiskey.[6]

The encroachment of land-hungry settlers constantly challenged government control of the acquisition of Indian lands. Although the government had the authority to remove squatters from Indian lands, it rarely had sufficient military force to do the job. And because of the settlers' political power in the new democratic nation, the government frequently lacked the political will to enforce its own laws.[7] Its usual solution was to negotiate the purchase of Indian lands already settled by squatters.[8] After the Louisiana Purchase, the government sought to exchange lands west of the Mississippi for lands ceded by the eastern tribes.[9] The government frequently concluded treaties with cooperative subgroups who claimed to represent entire tribes.[10] The Jacksonian era saw many treaties that were in reality forced purchases (in Jackson's terms, an exercise of the government's power of eminent domain).[11] As part of the Jacksonian treaties of removal, acreage allotments were made to individual Indian families. These were most valuable to those with advanced agricultural skills, often half-blood descendants of white traders. Predictably such land meant little to Indian men who knew nothing of agriculture, and much allotted land was quickly sold.[12] The bulk of the Indian population still committed to hunting was encouraged or forced to emigrate to the west.[13]

The extinction of Indian title through treaty purchase and the removal of the Indian population westward was the conscious goal of the land-hungry settlers. To them it was obvious and right, in the words of James Monroe, that "the hunter or savage state requires a greater extent of territory to sustain it, than is compatible with the progress and just claims of civilized life, and must yield to it . . . for the earth was given to mankind to support the greatest number of which it is capable, and no tribe or people have a right to withhold from the wants of others more than is necessary for their own support and comfort."[14] Others argued that removal would safeguard the Indians from destructive influences such as alcohol and give them a longer time to acquire the ways of "white" civilization.[15] The Jacksonians sound rather like Lan Ting-yüan and Tan-shui subprefect Wang P'ing, who advocated aggressive colonization and a similar allotment program (not adopted) in the Yung-cheng reign (although the thrust of the Chinese arguments always centered on whether settlement served state, not private, goals).

Why did Indian title have to be extinguished to allow for the expansion of agricultural settlement? Why wasn't a system of permanent leasehold or split ownership adopted? It was not for the lack of an institutional model. Anglo-American property law did provide for permanent leaseholds. Tenants who reclaimed farms on the manors of the Hudson valley often did so under a "durable lease," by which they acquired ownership of all lands they improved in exchange for paying the manor patentee a perpetual ground rent.[16] As in Taiwan, these ground rents averaged about 10 percent of the farm produce, and many were commuted to fixed cash amounts.[17] But in pre-revolutionary New York and in the other colonies, transactions in Indian land were conducted solely through the government treaty system and resulted in permanent alienations rather than leaseholds.[18] After the Revolution, the perpetual-lease model lost popularity. In the first half of the nineteenth century, the Jacksonians attacked the manorial leasehold tenure system as "feudal" and offensive to the yeoman ideal of fee simple ownership and direct payment of land taxes.[19] The manor owners were eventually forced by delinquencies to sell off their estates.[20]

The treaty framework for federal-Indian relations applied a model of international relations to two very unevenly matched nations. The U.S. government did make use of Indian allies in Indian wars, but it did not need them to put down settler rebellions, and its technological superiority made the balance of power less favorable to the natives than it was in the Chinese cases discussed above. The value of Indians as military allies was thus reduced.[21] The Indians were not taxed and were also denied the privileges of citizens.[22] Under the treaty framework, government jurisdiction ended, for most purposes, at tribal boundaries. This meant that encroaching settlers could not gain secure title to lands in Indian territories until the government effected removal of the tribal nation and extended federal administration. The alternative of long-term leases of land located in foreign jurisdictions, not unknown in international law (witness the Panama Canal), would not have appealed to Jacksonians in search of fee simple ownership.[23] The treaty system made the preservation of Indian "nations" in the midst of expanding agricultural settlement anomalous, accentuated racial differences, and encouraged segregation through removal rather than acculturation.[24] The recognition of separate Indian jurisdictions, like the *t'u ssu* districts of southwest China, created an obstacle to agricultural expansion and administrative control that was ultimately eroded or removed.

As we saw in Chapter 12, absent special strategic consideration, the financially limited Chinese state extended direct administration only when local revenues could help defray the costs. In comparison, the U.S. federal government had a stronger, more diverse fiscal base (its customs revenues were substantial). Thus, it was better able to finance aggressive frontier policies and control costs and was concerned more to please its land-hungry yeoman settlers (who had the vote) than to generate revenue from reclaimed land.[25] In the North American case, the calculus of revenue needs, control expenses, and strategic considerations produced an allocation of rights and duties with respect to frontier land that heavily favored the settlers and disadvantaged the Native American population.

Reference Matter

Notes

For complete author names, titles, and publication data for the works cited here in short form or as acronyms, see the Bibliography, pp. 535–72.

CHAPTER ONE

1. Barclay (1954: 5), Hsieh Chiao-min (1964: 136), Etō (1964: 43–44), and Eberhard (1982: 123) exemplify the displacement argument. On the growth rate of Taiwan's Han population, see Chapter 6.

2. Davidson (1903: 563), Takekoshi (1907: 120, 122), Yen (1965: 10, 11, 17, 19), and Samuel Ho (1978: 12) cite both the displacement scenario and plains aborigine land rights. Meskill's treatment of the plains aborigines is especially contradictory. Despite passages (1979: 35, 46, 48, 345) recognizing the existence of aborigine large-rent rights on land reclaimed by Han settlers, Meskill frequently lapses into displacement rhetoric. In several passages (1979: 42, 50, 252, 254), she claims that the plains tribes resisted the advance of Chinese settlement by force and by 1750 had been displaced from the Western plain.

3. See Ferrell 1969*a*; Treistman 1972; and Stamps 1980.

4. For reflections of the "neglect" hypothesis in the best English-language historical studies of Taiwan (which have concentrated on the nineteenth century), see Meskill 1979:31, 36–37; and Lamley 1981: 291, 316. Chapter 7 of this study shows that the Ch'ing sent especially experienced, not low-caliber, officials to its strategic periphery on Taiwan (contra Meskill 1979: 31). For a study of one region of nineteenth-century Taiwan that documents the substantial presence of government administration, see Allee 1987. Readers of Meskill's excellent study should remember that the Lins of Wu-feng were the greatest of Taiwan's local strongmen and that in many other parts of nineteenth-century Taiwan the local government enjoyed a much stronger hand vis-à-vis local power holders. The neglect hypothesis is a popular theme in histories of Taiwan in part because it is a convenient vehicle for nationalism. Chinese Nationalist historians see in Taiwanese rebellions resentment against Ch'ing neglect and the early expression of anti-Manchu Chinese nationalism. Communist historians see Ch'ing neglect and Taiwanese revolts as the inevitable result of a corrupt feudal system

based on class exploitation. Advocates of Taiwan independence see neglect as the fate of Taiwan under any mainlander-dominated government. Ch'ing neglect and Taiwanese revolts also provided Japanese imperialists a justification for colonial tutelage. For an excellent study of the political uses of Taiwan historiography, see Croizier 1977.

5. See, e.g., Kuhn 1977 and Naquin and Rawski 1987: 130–33.

6. The southeast coast was linked most importantly to Japan, the Spanish Philippines, and Southeast Asia; the Dutch hoped to use Taiwan as a base from which to profit from the commerce generated by the southeastern coastal economy. See Rawski 1972, Viraphol 1977, and Ng 1983. For a conceptualization of regional economic cycles, see Skinner 1977*b*, *c*, 1985. For the relationship between land tenure and regional economic cycles, see Shepherd 1988*a*.

7. Ho Ping-ti 1959; Wang Yeh-chien 1973: 7, 84–92; Shepherd 1988*a*.

8. Skinner 1977*a*, *c*; Elvin 1973: pt. 1. The Chinese empire was governed through a centralized bureaucracy of rotating officials, financed largely by taxes on privately held land, not through a hereditary aristocracy governing fiefs and paying feudal dues; see Creel 1964.

9. Skinner 1977*c*; Appendix D; on Taiwan, see Chapter 7.

10. Lattimore 1962*c*; Elvin 1973: 91–93. The political economy of the late imperial Chinese state, compared with those of contemporary European states and the Chinese state in the nineteenth and twentieth centuries, is significantly characterized by the absence of serious foreign competitors for state power. This international security relieved the Chinese state of the need to develop a financial administration capable of funding large military expenses; see McNeill 1982. The inability to command a larger proportion of the social product crippled the Chinese state's response to the Western military challenge in the nineteenth century.

11. Elvin 1973: 91–93; Wang Yeh-chien 1973: 80; Ray Huang 1974: 313–23, 1988: 152–53, 162, 169–71, 182–86, 193–95; S. Mann 1987: 7, 12–18; Naquin and Rawski 1987: 22, 219. In addition to the inability to conduct cadastral surveys, Ray Huang points to the dependence on lateral transfers, the cumbersome matching of an expenditure to a specific revenue source, lack of a central treasury, the use of fixed quotas, and crude accounting and banking services as major weaknesses in late imperial fiscal administration. After land taxes, the balance of revenues came from the salt tax (12 percent), native customs (7 percent), and miscellaneous taxes (7 percent) (Wang Yeh-chien 1973: 72). Confucian fiscal practice thus relied most heavily on land taxes, the revenue source comparativists believe has the highest cost of collection, especially compared to customs taxes. Skinner (1977*a*) emphasizes, in addition to fiscal considerations, that problems in controlling the field administration of a vast empire limited the size of the state bureaucracy and restricted the state's penetration of local society and its extractive capabilities; see also Zelin 1984: 306. For a further discussion of how these factors operated on the Taiwan frontier, see Chapters 7 and 8.

12. On some frontiers, the state abrogated aboriginal claims to undeveloped land, encouraged Han settlement and reclamation, and registered for taxation as much land as soon as possible after the establishment of county government, but there were also areas where, as in Taiwan, the land rights of indigenous tribes were protected. For examples and an elaboration of this argument, see Chapter 12.

13. Thus, Meskill's account (1979: 33, 43) of the Yung-cheng-era policies that created a new county in Chang-hua and legalized Chinese rental of aborigine lands suggests they were adopted to relieve overcrowding and never hints at their important revenue and expenditure consequences; see Chapter 8.

14. Incredibly, the three standard English-language studies of Ch'ing local government (Hsiao Kung-ch'uan 1960, Ch'ü 1962, Watt 1972) have no chapters on the military and barely mention the existence of military forces available to local government. Similarly, studies of Ch'ing finance have focused on civilian revenue gathering and expenditure and neglected the fact that half to two-thirds of the state's budget was spent on the military (R. J. Smith 1974: 129). Wade (1851: 416) estimates annual military expenditures at 30.9 million taels; this constitutes 55 percent of the government's tax quotas in the late eighteenth century (56.2 million taels) and 42 percent of revenues when surcharges are included (73.8 million taels) (Wang Yeh-chien 1973: 72). Skinner 1979 is the major recent exception to neglect of the military bureaucracy; see also Perdue 1989.

15. Indeed, the documentation for much economic history is limited to records created and preserved by states in their tax-collecting and tax-spending roles. Feuerwerker 1984 provides a broad overview of the Chinese state and economy.

16. See Goody 1971, McNeill 1982, M. Mann 1986, and Tilly 1990 for excellent examples of historical studies of political economy that recognize the importance of the "mode of destruction" (Goody's phrase).

17. See Hsu Wen-hsiung 1980*a* for a review of the few scattered references to Taiwan in the Chinese historical record before the seventeenth century. On early trade, see Hirth and Rockhill 1911, Kerr 1958, and Wang Gungwu 1958; on the occupation of the Pescadores by Chinese fishermen in the seventeenth and eighteenth centuries, see Thompson 1964: 165–70.

18. Campbell 1903: 26; Thompson 1964: 165–70, 1968; Hsu Wen-hsiung 1980*a*: 6.

19. Even Taiwanese deerskins (which were the key trading commodity in the seventeenth century and are mentioned in Wang Ta-yüan's account of 1349 [Thompson 1964: 169]) became valuable only when mainland and other sources of hides dried up or lost their comparative advantage.

20. Outside Taiwan the groups that appear most closely related to the Formosan groups are in the Philippines; Luzon lies directly to the south of Taiwan. See Ogawa 1944. The estimate of 100,000 allows for uncounted mountain villages outside the largest Dutch count of 68,000; see Chapter 2.

21. *She* is variously translated as aborigine tribe, village, or settlement. The word "tribe" is used in this study as nothing more than a synonym for aboriginal village or settlement; its use is not intended to invoke evolutionary theories of stages or levels of sociocultural integration or to suggest multi-village federations based on an ethnolinguistic unity.

22. The term "plains aborigine" (*p'ing p'u fan*) is thus not an ethnic designation; nor, strictly speaking, is it a geographical designation, for there were aboriginal groups on Taiwan's east coast (Kuvalan, Ami, Puyuma) who inhabited plains territories yet remained outside Chinese jurisdiction in the centuries studied here. "Plains aborigine" is therefore a *historical* category that includes the eight ethnolinguistic groupings of villages (Siraya [including Makatau and Taivoan], Hoanya, Favorlang, Pazeh, Papora, Taokas, Kulon, and Ketagalan/Basai) that oc-

cupied the western plains and were compelled to submit to Dutch and Chinese jurisdiction in the seventeenth and eighteenth centuries. The Kuvalan of I-lan submitted and joined the plains aborigine category in the nineteenth century. See Map 2.1 for these ethnolinguistic groupings. The term "civilized aborigine" translates *shu fan* when used in Chinese sources to refer not only to plains aborigine submission to Chinese authority but also to the historical Chinese view that saw the sinicization of the plains aborigines as an acceptance of the superiority of Chinese culture. This usage emphasizes the contrast with the "raw" aborigines of the mountains, whom the Chinese considered uncivilized, wild (*yeh*) and, after head-hunting raids, savage (*hsiung*). The term "aborigine" has traditionally been used in Western ethnography to refer to Taiwan's aboriginal inhabitants in contrast to the immigrant Han Chinese; it is now also the preferred English translation of the self-appellation *yüan chu min* adopted by Taiwan's pan-aborigine movement (see Hsieh Shih-chung 1987: 139–40). The Chinese term *fan* is also translated as "foreigner" or "barbarian," to reflect the sinocentric perspective. Aborigine ethnolinguistic groupings are discussed in greater detail in Chapter 2 and in Appendix A.

23. See Mabuchi 1954.

24. "Chinese" is also a complex term, referring broadly to Confucian civilization and the Chinese empire and all its peoples and more narrowly to the most numerous ethnic group of China, the Han. From 1644 China was ruled by the Manchus, a foreign conquest dynasty; the term "Chinese government" after that date refers to the Manchu dynasty and the Chinese literati in its employ.

25. Some Taiwanese of Fukien descent have recently discovered that their forebears were not Han but She, an acculturated minority group inhabiting villages in many parts of Fukien; see *Jen chien tsa chih* 26:10–12 (Dec. 1987) and Wang Sung-hsing 1988.

26. Lamley (1981: 282–83) makes clear that as a descriptive term "subethnic" points to subcultural variations (based primarily on dialect and provenance) within the Han settlers on Taiwan and gives us a convenient means of marking off intra-Han rivalries from Han-aborigine rivalries. These are important distinctions to keep in mind in discussions of the Taiwan frontier, and they make "subethnic" a useful term. Harrell's (1990: 109) objection, seconded by Crossley (1990*b:* 14–15), to the use of the term "subethnic" should be rejected. It is Harrell (and not Lamley) who reifies ethnicity and mistakenly assumes that "full ethnic divisions" and "ethnic activity" have a special status as sociological phenomena. The objection misrepresents a descriptive term as a claim that conflict between *sub*ethnic groups had distinctive sociological dimensions. For the view that ethnic conflict is not distinguished from other types of community conflict in terms of sociological dynamics, see Chapter 10 and Coleman 1957.

27. Wang Shih-ch'ing 1974: 72–73, 1976: 50.

28. Wang Shih-ch'ing 1976: 52–53; *TPHCK:* 5, ref. 34.

29. Wang Shih-ch'ing 1976: 52; on bounty rent, see Ch'en Ch'i-yen 1953.

30. Copies of the 1778 and 1816 contracts are in the author's possession.

31. *CDI:* 56–58.

32. *TSF:* 1–2, 113–51.

33. Okamatsu 1902: 94. See also Shih T'ien-fu 1990. Work under way by Shih T'ien-fu, Chuang Ying-chang, and their colleagues will produce better estimates of the extent of aborigine large-rent in T'ao-yüan, Hsin-chu and Miao-li counties.

34. See, e.g., the tablets from a nearby Han village studied by Emily Ahern (1973: following p. 130), which list Wu-kung and Hsi-ho, districts in north China, as the place of origin ("hall names") for the surnames in question.

35. The genealogy gives the aboriginal name, Chih-mu-liu, for Hsiao Na-ying. I know of no evidence that he used a Chinese surname during his lifetime. The two characters for Hsiao, one for the surname and one for the tribe, are identical in sound but written differently.

36. A history of Taiwan that ignores the plains aborigines makes no more sense than would a history of Manchuria or Kweichow that ignored the existence of non-Han peoples.

37. Hsiao-li was known to the Dutch as Sausauly (Nakamura 1963–64: 81).

38. The Chu-lo county gazetteer thus notes that the Ch'ing was administering the aborigine villages by means of an institution that had originated under the Dutch. The Ch'ing used a variety of tax-farming institutions to generate revenue from trade elsewhere in its empire (see R. Lee 1970: 87–88; S. Mann 1987).

39. For some migrants, the Taiwan frontier may not have been their first encounter with non-Han aboriginal groups. The Yao were numerous in upland areas of northern Kwangtung, and villages of She were scattered about Fukien (see note 25 above). I have no information, however, on what land-tenure relations evolved in these cases (see Kellogg 1926, 1927).

40. Ch'en Pin, and many Han Chinese officials who followed him, held strongly protectionist views toward aborigine land rights and against Chinese settlement. Their conservative views were informed by Confucian political theories on the importance of preserving the livelihoods of subject peoples and by their assessment of the political economy of frontier control (see Chapter 9). Positing a special sympathy for non-Han peoples on behalf of the Manchus cannot explain Ch'ing policies toward Taiwan: this would not account for Han literati like Ch'en Pin or for the aggressive pro-colonization policies favored by the Yung-cheng emperor.

41. See Chapter 6 for the demographic history of Taiwan. In 1737 marriage of Han males to aborigine women was prohibited to protect the tribes from depopulation and to eliminate a further source of Han-aborigine friction. This prohibition complements other Ch'ien-lung era attempts to tighten restrictions on the activities of Han settlers.

42. The earth-oxen (*t'u niu*) boundaries shown in Map 1.1 for the San-hsia area were dug at various dates in the eighteenth century. See *TKI:* 1. 131, 133–34; Wang Shih-ch'ing 1953: 40–41; and Abe 1938: 144.

43. Lamley 1977*a*.

44. On the decline of government control in nineteenth-century China, see Kuhn 1970.

45. Wolf and Huang 1980.

46. On An-li, see Chang Yao-k'un 1955.

47. Lamley 1981: 302–5; also Hsu Wen-hsiung 1980*b:* 94; Meskill 1979: 87–89; Ownby 1990.

CHAPTER TWO

1. The best seventeenth-century accounts, focusing on the Siraya, are those of Candidius (Campbell 1903: 9–25) and Wright (Shepherd 1986); Shepherd 1990 reconstructs the Siraya system of kinship and marriage. Important Dutch archival material has recently been published for the first time; see the Zeelandia day-registers (Blusse et al. 1986). Most of this material focuses on trade, and although it has long been exploited by scholars of the Dutch period, such as Nakamura Takashi (e.g., 1963–64), new studies using this material promise to enrich our understanding of the colony. The most interesting new ethnographic material from the Dutch archives is the account of the 1623 visit to Hsiao-lung (Blusse and Roessingh 1984: 65). Campbell's 1903 translation of Dutch missionary correspondence, as well as Dutch historical sources, remains the most comprehensive collection treating life among the plains aborigines under Dutch rule.

2. The alternative possibility that Formosan aboriginal languages represent an early isolate of populations marginal to the main path of Austronesian migration cannot be ruled out. In either case, the comparative study of Taiwan's aboriginal languages and cultures is of unique importance to understanding Austronesian prehistory.

3. Cf. Paul Li 1985.

4. Bellwood 1985: 232. Bellwood argues that by 3000 B.C. some of these Austronesians were moving south to Luzon, beginning a journey that would ultimately encompass the entire Pacific. Any reconstruction of Taiwan's prehistory at this point must remain tentative, both because of the many gaps that remain in our knowledge of Taiwan and because our knowledge of the archaeology of adjoining areas is expanding rapidly. Bellwood's reconstruction, which links Austronesian expansion to the spread of rice cultivation from the lower Yangtze area, for instance, requires the presence of rice cultivation in Taiwan at a date earlier than has yet been established by archaeologists (cf. Bellwood 1985: 213, 223). In a cursory overview of this nature, no attempt can be made to indicate the many qualifications necessary when evaluating the competing hypotheses of the archaeologists. See Liu I-ch'ang 1988: 18 for the prehistoric cultural sequence currently accepted for Taiwan.

5. Bellwood 1979: 203–7, 1985: 213–16; Chang Kwang-chih 1972: 441–42, Stamps 1980.

6. Sung Wen-hsün and Lien 1984.

7. Cf. Ferrell 1969*a:* 11. Liu I-ch'ang, pers. comm. 1990.

8. Ferrell 1969*a:* 11, 27, 51–58; see also the comparative studies of mythology by Edward Norbeck (1950) and Ho T'ing-jui (1967). Studies of the nature of the interaction between Taiwan and the Austronesian jar burial cultures of the late neolithic and early metal ages are badly needed. These cultures, which appear to have emerged in the first millennium B.C., ultimately achieved a very wide distribution in the Philippines (Tabon, Kalanay), Borneo (Niah), and even Vietnam (Sa-huynh). In the metal age these cultures are associated with iron and with glass and carnelian trade beads (Bellwood 1979: 212–13, 220, 1985: 246–47, 275–78, 304, 316–17). The jar burial cultures appear to define a northeastern sphere of interaction within Southeast Asia that was relatively isolated from a more active

trade channel linking mainland Southeast Asian centers of trade and metallurgy to Indonesia (Bellwood 1979: 225, 1985: 278–80).

9. Scott 1985: 60.

10. Wolff 1976.

11. Ferrell 1969*a:* 30; Mabuchi 1974*c*.

12. See Ferrell 1969*a* for the most systematic survey; see also Ch'en Chi-lu 1968; Mabuchi 1960.

13. This classification is based on Ferrell 1969*a*, as subsequently revised by Ferrell 1980; Paul Li 1985, n.d.; and Tsuchida 1985. The most important revision links the Atayalic languages to several northwest coastal languages that were included in a largely residual Paiwanic grouping in Ferrell 1969*a*. This classification is based primarily on comparisons of lexical data (the number of items compared is greatly expanded in Paul Li n.d.) that group together languages with high percentages of shared cognates, a method that, when used in isolation, makes it difficult to distinguish similarities due to shared innovations from those due to borrowing or differential rates of retention of cognate forms. Additional work incorporating studies of syntax and phonology is needed to refine our understanding of the genetic relations of these languages. Classifications of this nature necessarily oversimplify, by giving the impression of sharp boundaries and precise distances between languages and by disguising the complexities due to dialectical variations within languages and historical relations between languages due to interaction and borrowing that are not genetic.

14. Ferrell 1969*a:* 23.

15. Ibid.: 35, 46, 51.

16. Ferrell 1969*a:* 27–28, 1969*b:* 165–66.

17. Ferrell 1969*a:* 10, 1969*b:* 165.

18. Campbell 1903: 10; Ferrell 1969*b:* 165. Candidius's comments may also reflect his market mentality, which assumes the desirability of producing surpluses for market, a market that did not, however, exist in aboriginal Taiwan.

19. Campbell 1903: 10, 52, 254; *BD:* 33; Blusse and Roessingh 1984: 69–70.

20. Campbell 1903: 11; Ferrell 1969*b:* 165–66; *BD:* 32.

21. Campbell 1903: 11–12; Thompson 1964: 175. Far from competing with the deer herds for fields, swiddening had the effect of increasing the edge between forest and grassland, and it is in this "ecotone" that species such as deer thrive (Peterson 1977).

22. Campbell 1903: 10–12, 257; Blusse and Roessingh 1984: 75. Intervillage warfare further reduced the contribution of agriculture to subsistence because it destroyed crops and during head-hunting season made work in the fields dangerous.

23. Campbell 1903: 11.

24. Campbell 1903: 16, 139–40, 368; Thompson 1964: 174.

25. Thompson 1964: 173.

26. Ferrell 1969*a*: 10.

27. Curwen and Hatt 1961: 180. Today the Yami of Orchid Island are famous for irrigated terraces of taro.

28. Pelzer 1945: 48; Ch'en Chi-lu 1968: 321. Happart's dictionary of Favorlang gives *baban* for earthen dam (Campbell 1896; see also Thompson 1969: 76).

29. Schlegel 1979: 69. Aborigines adjusted their crop inventory according to

ecology. Taiwan's mountain aborigines find millet easier to grow than rice at higher elevations and grow increasing proportions of yams and taro and less grain toward the subtropics (Segawa 1953: 49; Fogg 1983: 112–13; Bellwood 1985: 216, 234–35).

30. Permanent village sites are compatible with shifting fields (Li I-Yüan et al. 1962: 447–48; Spencer 1966: 145–47).

31. On the case of Taraquang, see Campbell 1903: 122; on the case of Ta-mu-hsiang (Dutch: Tavakan), see ibid.: 111, 134, 159. There is also the possible case of Hsin-kang moving from the site of Sakam.

32. *CHFSHC*: 59; Thompson 1969: 116; Blusse and Roessingh 1984: 72.

33. The Siraya farmsteads included large residences, built on earth and stone platforms a man's height above the ground (*CCKTH*: 12; Campbell 1903: 21; Ferrell 1969*a*: 52, 1969*b*: 167; Blusse and Roessingh 1984: 72).

34. *BD*: 348; Campbell 1903: 125.

35. Campbell 1903: 174–76.

36. Mabuchi 1970: 354, 359, 361–62; Ferrell 1971: 225, 231. There is one mention of a Dutch attempt to restrict a tribe's hunting territory in 1642 (*BD*: 376). Aborigine land tenure is discussed further in Chapter 9.

37. Campbell 1903: 12–13; Thompson 1964: 175; Blusse and Roessingh 1984: 73, 75.

38. Campbell 1903: 10; Ferrell 1969*a*: 41, 1969*b*: 165.

39. *CCKTH*: 12, 16; Campbell 1903: 18, 256; Thompson 1969: 59.

40. Ferrell 1969*a*: 14–15, 30, 41; Mabuchi 1974*c*; Liu I-ch'ang, pers. comm. 1990.

41. Hirth and Rockhill 1911: 165–66.

42. On the identity of P'i-she-ye, see Wada 1929: 130–36; *TWFC*:Liu: 480–81. Scott (1985: 21, 80–81) has reviewed Philippine boat-building and seafaring skills and argues that Visayan seamen could have reached Fukien, but only by way of Taiwan. The Siraya of the seventeenth century had no oceangoing craft, but other groups did, including bamboo sailing rafts (Thompson 1964: 176; Ferrell 1969*a*: 52–53, 58–59).

43. Ferrell 1969*a*: 13–15.

44. *CHTWHC*: 548; *FSHC*: 5, 164; de Mailla, quoted in Campbell 1903: 511–12; Keesing 1962: 13; Goodrich and Fang 1976: 928; Thompson 1969: 104.

45. Quoted in Thompson 1964: 176–77.

46. *BD*: 49, 108; Ts'ao 1954*b*. On the fluidity of the categories "fisherman" and "pirate," see Murray 1987.

47. Blusse and Roessingh 1984: 70, 72, 77; *BD*: 33; see also Campbell 1903: 27. Men's houses were a regular feature of Sirayan matrilineal society; the young and middle-aged men were organized in age-grade ranks and slept in men's dormitories, apart from their wives (Shepherd 1990). Candidius reports that there was a men's house for every twelve to fourteen households (Campbell 1903: 21).

48. Campbell 1903: 12, 21. The natives of Tan-shui and I-lan also had surpluses of rice the Dutch were anxious to get by trade (*BD*: 415).

49. *BD*: 49; Nakamura 1959: 25; Campbell 1903: 21, 115.

50. *BD*: 415; Campbell 1903: 21; Ferrell 1969*b*: 166. Rawski (1972: 66) documents the production of these goods in Chang-chou for trade, and Viraphol (1977: 51–52, 85) documents their role in foreign commerce.

51. Campbell 1903: 12; Álvarez 1930: 2.427; Ch'en Chi-lu 1968: 169, 213, 235. Ch'en Ti offered this perhaps fanciful interpretation: "In the beginning of the Yung-le period [1403–24], the eunuch Cheng [Ho] carried the Imperial Edict across the seas to the various barbarians; the Eastern Barbarians alone hid far away and would not be coerced. Thereupon their families were bequeathed brass [or, copper] bells which they were to hang about their necks—which is to make dogs of them. But they have handed these down to the present as treasures" (Thompson 1964: 176).

52. Campbell 1903: 11; Thompson 1969: 82, 140; Ferrell 1969*b*: 184.

53. Campbell 1903: 18, 21, 256; Thompson 1969: 66, 70; Ch'en Chi-lu 1968: 163–201; Ferrell 1969*b*: 168.

54. Campbell 1903: 16, 23. On harvest taboos, see Ch'en Chi-lu 1968: 26; and Shepherd 1986.

55. Boxer 1963: 180, 1965: 220; Sung Ying-hsing 1966: 60–64; Wills 1972: 5.

56. Campbell 1903: 37, 64, 499; Huber 1990: 295.

57. Campbell 1903: 131; cf. de Beauclair 1970: 388.

58. Quoted in Thompson 1964: 177.

59. Campbell 1903: 256.

60. Quoted in ibid.: 232.

61. Ibid.: 74–75, 256, 541; Ch'en Chi-lu 1968: 357–66; de Beauclair 1970.

62. Blusse and Roessingh 1984: 76; *BD*: 48–49.

63. Campbell 1903: 168–73. There is no evidence of aboriginal tobacco cultivation until the eighteenth century, although Chinese were cultivating a small amount in Taiwan by 1645 (*BD*: 456; cf. Ch'en Chi-lu 1968: 69–70). De Mailla found tobacco growing widely in 1715 (Campbell 1903: 506). The earliest evidence found by Rawski (1972: 73) of tobacco cultivation in Chang-chou dates from 1628, although the 1623 reference to "Chinese tobacco" suggests that the plant was being grown and traded before that time (Blusse and Roessingh 1984: 76).

64. Campbell 1903: 5, 499; *BD*: 11; Ts'ao 1979: 363.

65. Campbell 1903: 254.

66. Nakamura 1959: 29–31; Chou Ming-hung 1963: 106; Putnam 1988: 16–19, 42–47. See also note 21 to this chapter.

67. *CLHC*: 196; *TWFC*:Fan: 473; Kuo Shui-t'an 1959: 32; Chou Ming-hung 1963: 109–12; Sung Ying-hsing 1966: 64; G. V. Smith 1977: 148–49. In Japan, Burakumin leather workers specialized in the production of these goods (Price 1966: 20–21).

68. Nakamura 1959: 24; Keesing 1962: 31; Peterson 1977: 67; G. V. Smith 1977: 78–80, 89; Viraphol 1977: 10, 275.

69. Campbell 1903: 506; Nakamura 1959: 41; Sung Ying-hsing 1966: 67.

70. Campbell 1903: 550; Ch'en Chi-lu 1968: 34.

71. Blair and Robertson 1903–9: 35.148; Campbell 1903: 254; Nakamura 1954: 65, 1959: 26; Ch'en Chi-lu 1968: 45–47.

72. *BD*: 414, 420; Liao Han-ch'en 1959: 4, 16. The Chu-lo gazetteer (*CLHC*: 195) reports the Dutch used the coal in ironworks.

73. Campbell 1903: 231; Nakamura 1951: 94, 110.

74. Nakamura 1936, 1937, 1951.

75. Campbell 1903: 290.

76. Chang Yao-ch'i 1951. Area figures were drawn from *Statistics on Civil Affairs, Taiwan Province* (Taiwan Provincial Government, Department of Civil Affairs), no. 9 (Apr. 1980): 30–39; and *The Statistical Abstract of Taipei Municipality* (Taipei Municipal Government, Bureau of Budget, Accounting and Statistics), 1981: 24–25.

77. Campbell 1903: 134, 202, 254, 256.

78. Ferrell 1969*a*: 27–28, 30.

79. Ch'en Cheng-hsiang 1959–61: 1.56, 97; Hsieh Chiao-min 1964: 44–53. The comparative scarcity and localization of water are commonly used to explain a pattern of nucleated Chinese villages in southern Taiwan; the abundance of water is similarly used to explain dispersed settlement in the north (Ch'en Cheng-hsiang 1959–61: 1.258; Hsieh Chiao-min 1964: 160). Two points eliminate this variable as an explanation here. The way Han agricultural villages (whether nucleated or dispersed) exploit the natural environment differs considerably from the way villages of hunters and horticulturalists (whether large or small) exploit the environment. Second, the spatial distribution of nucleated vs. non-nucleated Han settlement does not correspond to the distribution of large vs. small aborigine villages.

80. Campbell 1903: 111, 130, 134, 159, 180. Some of the inhabitants of this village are reported to have migrated to Hsin-kang in 1658 (Nakamura 1956*b*: 13).

81. Campbell 1903: 205–6, 214, 223.

82. *BD*: 48.

83. Campbell 1903: 117–18, 124, 134.

84. Ibid.: 115, 137; Thompson 1969: 138.

85. Village endogamy is a common solution to this "matrilineal puzzle"; see Schneider 1961: 27; Gough 1961: 553, 559, 561; and Fox 1967: 101–3.

86. Campbell 1903: 20.

87. Mabuchi 1960: 129, 139; Ferrell 1969*a*: 50–51, 56.

88. Mabuchi 1960: 133, 135. In the early twentieth century, Taiwan mountain groups, all of whom practiced a similar kind of agriculture, lived in settlements of various sizes and patterns. This variation as well, according to Mabuchi (1960: 129, 131–32, 136–37; see also Ferrell 1969*a*: 34), can be explained only by variation in the social organization of these groups. The closest parallel to the Siraya is the matrilineal Ami (Mabuchi 1960: 133; Ferrell 1969*a*: 56; Shepherd 1990).

89. Ferrell 1969*a*: 52, 1969*b*: 167, 182.

90. Nakamura 1956*b*: 14; see also Lai Yung-hsiang 1970: 104.

91. High mortality, by breaking apart extended households, could lead to an increased number of household fragments.

CHAPTER THREE

1. For the puzzle of Taiwan's isolation before the sixteenth century, see Chapters 1 and 2. See Hsu Wen-hsiung 1980*a* for the scattered references to Taiwan in the Chinese historical record before the seventeenth century. On the expansion of East Asian trade in the sixteenth century, see Rawski 1972: 67–68; Iwao 1976; and Atwell 1982. On Ming maritime policies and piracy, see Elvin 1973: 217–24; and So Kwan-wai 1975. On the activities of fishermen in Taiwan waters, see Ts'ao

1954*b*, 1956; and Nakamura 1955. On Lin Tao-ch'ien, see Campbell 1903: 511–12; Thompson 1969: 104; and Goodrich and Fang 1976: 928. Another pirate, Lin Feng (Limahong), is reported in Taiwan in 1574; see Goodrich and Fang 1976: 917.

2. Paske-Smith 1930: 6; see also Campbell 1903: 56. On the 1603 campaign, see Thompson 1964: 170–71; and under the entry for Shen Yu-jung in Goodrich and Fang 1976: 1192–94. Li Tan, the Captain China at Hirado, played an important role in the indirect trade through Taiwan; see Goodrich and Fang 1976: 872–73.

3. Chang T'ien-tse 1934: Boxer 1963: Rawski 1972: 67–68; Atwell 1982.

4. Boxer 1965: 26–27. The Dutch had launched a global war on the Portuguese and Spanish seaborne empires. Wallerstein's analysis of the rise of Dutch economic power suggests several developmental parallels with coastal southern Fukien. In both cases the shortage of arable forced the population to farm both land and sea intensively. The fishing industry fostered the growth of seafaring and shipbuilding skills and stimulated participation in long-distance trade. The resulting growth of trade then stimulated the development of local export industries (see Rawski 1972: chap. 4; Wallerstein 1980: 39–46).

5. Campbell 1903: 25–27. Admiral Shen Yu-jung sailed his fleet to the Pescadores in 1604 to convince the Dutch to leave; see Goodrich and Fang 1976: 1193.

6. Campbell 1903: 27.

7. Campbell 1903: 28–34; see also Blusse 1973. Fukien governor Nan Chu-i directed the negotiations from the Chinese side; see Goodrich and Fang 1976: 872–73, 1086–87. The Chinese name "Taiwan" derives from "Tayouan," the aboriginal place-name for the sandy peninsula on the west side of the harbor. The Dutch referred to the main island as Formosa. To maximize continuity with later chapters, when equivalents can be identified, Chinese forms of place-names in Taiwan will be privileged over the Dutch. For Dutch names I have preferred the spellings (which vary greatly in the sources) given in the index to Campbell 1903. See Appendix A for a discussion and sources relating to the identification of Dutch and Chinese equivalents for aborigine village names and for maps locating the villages. To avoid anachronism, two major exceptions to the use of Chinese forms seem appropriate in discussion of the Dutch period. These are the use of Tayouan (Chinese: *Ta-yüan*) for the peninsula on which the Dutch built Zeelandia Castle, a site later known as An-p'ing (the port of Tainan), and Sakam (Chinese: *Ch'ih-k'an*), the site on the mainland across the harbor from Zeelandia where the Dutch built Fort Provintia, which later became the city of Tainan.

8. Campbell 1903: 25–26, 52–54, 74. Goodrich and Fang's (1976: 871) suggestion that European trade rivalries may well have been mirrored by Fukienese-Cantonese rivalries on the Chinese side deserves researching.

9. Campbell 1903: 58–59, 63; Boxer 1965: 108–9.

10. Blusse 1984.

11. The decision to invest in the expansion of the Taiwan colony was probably spurred by the Japanese adoption of the policy of seclusion in 1633, which eliminated competition from Japanese merchantmen and Catholic Europeans. This opened the prospect of large profits in the Japanese trade for the Dutch and increased the importance of Taiwan to them (Iwao 1976: 15).

12. Ch'en Shao-hsing 1964: 96; Wills 1972: 15.

13. Wills 1974: 24.
14. Campbell 1903: 391.
15. *BD*: 31, 49; Murakami 1975: 113–14; Blusse and Roessingh 1984: 66.
16. Campbell 1903: 35; Murakami 1975. Chinese sources, such as the Taiwan prefectural gazetteer of 1694 (*TWFC*:Kao: 3), quoted by de Mailla in his 1715 essay, say the Dutch acquired the Tayouan site by a ruse. According to this legend, the Dutch got the Japanese, their predecessors in the Tayouan trade, to agree to let them have as much land as could be enclosed by an ox skin. The Dutch proceeded to cut the skin into fine strips and enclosed a considerable area (Campbell 1903: 512). The legend mirrors Dido's ruse to obtain land to found Carthage; curiously, no Dutch source known to me confirms this account; cf. *HHTWHC*: 333; Takekoshi 1930: 112.
17. *BD*: 48; Campbell 1903: 37; Murakami 1975: 116–17. Cangans were "multicoloured cotton cloths from Coromandel" (Huber 1990: 295). The Dutch traded widely in the textiles produced in Coromandel, the southeast coast of India, around the city of Madras (Boxer 1965: 220).
18. Campbell 1903: 547. Some sources say the Sinkandians moved from Sakam to Hsin-kang after a skirmish with the Dutch (*TNHCK*: 2.55; Chuang Sung-lin 1959: 5–6).
19. *BD*: 48–49; Blusse 1984: 172. Chang Yao-ch'i (1951) identifies modern sites (all in T'ai-nan county) for these aborigine villages: Hsin-kang (Dutch: Sinkan) = Hsin-shih *chen*; Hsiao-lung (Dutch: Soulang) = Chia-li *chen*; Ma-tou (Dutch: Mattau) = Ma-tou *hsiang*; and Mu-chia-liu-wan (Dutch: Bakloan) = An-ting *hsiang* (some sources give Shan-hua *chen*).
20. Campbell 1903: 96.
21. The Japanese had, on several occasions before the arrival of the Dutch, contemplated colonizing Taiwan; see, e.g., Iwao 1959. The 1628 conflict with the Japanese led to a costly ban on Dutch trading in Japan that lasted until 1632 (Kato 1976: 54).
22. Campbell 1903: 36, 42, 56–57; Blusse 1984: 162.
23. Campbell 1903: 45–46; 93–94; Wills 1972: 7; Blusse 1984: 164–66.
24. Campbell 1903: 78, 93–95. Candidius reports kicking over the sacrifices Sinkandians offered to their gods (ibid.: 25).
25. Ibid.: 96, 98–99.
26. *BD*: 230; Campbell 1903: 109; Blusse 1984: 172–73.
27. Campbell 1903: 116.
28. Ibid.: 100, 116; Blusse 1984: 173–74.
29. Campbell 1903: 100, 102–3; Blusse 1984: 174.
30. Campbell 1903: 106, 111, 117. Wen-kang (Dutch: Wankan) was located on the coast of modern Chia-i county, somewhere between the mouths of the Pa-chang and P'o-tzu rivers (see Lu Chia-hsing 1965: 299; Ts'ao 1979: appendix).
31. Campbell 1903: 106, 116–17, 133.
32. Ibid.: 109, 117–19.
33. Ibid.: 123–24.
34. *BD*: 112–13, 126.
35. Campbell 1903: 121, 123–26.
36. Ibid.: 118, 121–22, 152. Chang Yao-ch'i (1951) locates Ta-wu-lung (Dutch: Tevorang) in modern Ta-nei *hsiang*, T'ai-nan county, and Chu-lo-shan (Dutch: Tirosen) in Chia-i city. No Chinese equivalent has been identified for Favorlang, which referred to the Chang-hua area.

37. Campbell 1903: 129, cf. 119–20. Ma-tou was also required to return the skulls and any relics of the murdered Dutchmen, to pay compensation, and to "bring two pigs to the Castle on the anniversary day of the murder" (ibid.: 119; *BD*: 151). The natives signaled a desire for peaceful relations, if not submission, by sending the Dutch a spear; it was apparently the territorially oriented Dutch who invented the ritual of submitting a betel palm (Campbell 1903: 118–19).

38. Campbell 1903: 130.

39. Ibid.: 130–31.

40. Ibid.: 122, 131, 162; Davidson 1903: 24; Caron and Schouten 1935: 87. De Beauclair (1970: 388) reports a Dutch staff was preserved by a Paiwan chiefly family into the twentieth century. The Dutch staff appears also to have inspired the rattan wand used by the shamanesses of Chi-pei-soa today (Shepherd 1986). For a depiction of a delegates meeting ca. 1650, see Fig. 3.1.

41. Campbell 1903: 131–32.

42. Ibid.: 140.

43. Ibid.: 174, 180, 186–88; *BD*: 193, 212, 243–44. Chang Yao-ch'i (1951) locates Tung-lo (Dutch: Dovale) in P'i-t'ou *hsiang*, Chang-hua county.

44. Campbell 1903: 233–34; *BD*: 347–49, 375.

45. *BD*: 168–69; Campbell 1903: 55; Blair and Robertson 1903–9: 35.147; Liao Han-ch'en 1959: 4–5, 17.

46. Nakamura 1956*a*: 24–25.

47. Boxer 1941: 408–9.

48. Spanish missionaries were active among the tribes of Chin-pao-li and T'a-pa-li, situated on the northern coast near Keelung (Ōkuni 1960: 14–15, 17).

49. Blair and Robertson 1903–9: 22.185–86; Nakamura 1956*a*: 26.

50. Nakamura 1956*a*: 26. Davidson (1903: 20) and Liao Han-ch'en (1952: 43) give July 1629 as the date of the fort's construction.

51. Blair and Robertson 1903–9: 32.173–75.

52. Nakamura 1956*a*: 27. No copy of the *Vocabulary* has yet been discovered in any archive.

53. Álvarez 1930: 2.427. Over 140 years later, Pulauan, known to the Dutch as Pinorouan and to the Chinese as Wu-lao-wan (present-day Hsin-chuang *shih*, T'ai-pei county), would join with three other native groups in signing the San-hsia land grant of 1773.

54. Álvarez 1930: 2.427; Nakamura 1956*a*: 26; Ōkuni 1960: 17.

55. Blair and Robertson 1903–9: 32.224–25; Ōkuni 1960: 18.

56. *BD*: 180; Blair and Robertson 1903–9: 32.249–50; Fernandez 1959: 5; Ōkuni 1960: 20; Wills 1972: 9.

57. Liao Han-ch'en 1952: 44, 1959: 5; Nakamura 1956*a*: 31; Ōkuni 1960: 21. Fernandez (1959: 6) claims that the Spanish retaliated for the murder of Muro and his party and thereafter missionaries were able to travel among the villages without fear of attack; Fernandez also claims that a total of 4,500 natives were converted during Spanish rule. In light of later events, this seems an exaggeration.

58. Blair and Robertson 1903–9: 35.140; Fernandez 1959: 6; Liao Han-ch'en 1959: 2.

59. Liao Han-ch'en 1959: 2–4.

60. Chuang Sung-lin 1959: 14; Wills 1972: 9.

61. The governor's lack of interest in preserving a colony was suspected to reflect the influence of Jesuits jealous of their rival Dominicans in Taiwan (Blair and Robertson 1903–9: 35.162).

62. *BD*: 379–80; Liao Han-ch'en 1959: 6.

63. Chuang Sung-lin 1959: 15.

64. *BD*: 438–49; Campbell 1903: 205, 210–11; Liao Han-ch'en 1959: 6.

65. Campbell 1903: 233; Nakamura 1936, 1937.

66. Coolhaas 1964: 608–9, 649, 704–5. I am greatly indebted to John Wills for an oral summary of the above passages from the Dutch.

67. *BD*: 313, 364, 452, 472–73.

68. Campbell 1903: 196, 386, 403.

69. Ibid.: 212, 232; *BD*: 443–44; Nakamura 1964: 78.

70. Nakamura 1964: 67–71, 82; Iwao 1976.

71. Campbell 1903: 15–16.

72. Ibid.: 93, 96, 103.

73. Ibid.: 110.

74. Ibid.: 6, 115, 130, 254.

75. Coyett 1975: 14.

76. Campbell 1903: 120, 162.

77. Ferrell (1969*a*: 16) seems to exaggerate the extent of the Dutch impact on village leadership systems; cf. de Mailla's description of 1715 (Campbell 1903: 509).

78. Campbell 1903: 221–24; Nakamura 1951: 110.

79. Campbell 1903: 207, 222–24; Nakamura 1951: 110; Wills 1972: 10.

80. Campbell 1903: 164.

81. Ibid.: 115, 228–29.

82. Ibid.: 540. See Boxer 1965: 337–38 for a salary scale for East India Company personnel. Ordained clergymen were among the highest paid employees, with salaries equal to those of senior merchants and army and ship captains.

83. Campbell 1903: 92–93.

84. Ibid.: 100, quoting the minutes of the Formosa Council, Nov. 17, 1629.

85. Campbell 1903: 199. The Dutch also believed that marriages between missionaries and native women would advance the cause of Christianity (ibid.: 92, 99, 101, 179).

86. Quoted in ibid.: 105.

87. Ibid.: 312–13.

88. Ibid.: 78, 86, 105; Kuepers 1978: 14–15.

89. Although he gives no reasons why this should be so, we may point to the increasing presence in those years of Japanese along the coast and Chinese traders in the villages; see Campbell 1903: 23, 89–90, 148, 158.

90. Ibid.: 95–96.

91. Ibid.: 103, 135.

92. Ibid.: 103, 105.

93. Ibid.: 123. At the end of 1628, Candidius reported that 128 Hsin-kang residents had learned prayers and "were able to answer in the most satisfactory manner with regard to the principal articles of our Christian faith"; however, he considered these converts unready for baptism until they had practiced Christianity for a time (ibid.: 25, 95). Baptism came only upon successful examination in doctrine. By September 1636 Junius claimed to have baptized 862 in the Hsin-kang; this undoubtedly reflects increased enthusiasm, on the part of both Junius and the villagers, following the Dutch victories of 1635–36 (ibid.: 143).

94. Ibid.: 139–40.

95. Ibid.: 139.

96. Ibid.: 138, 154, 165. Nowhere are these "idols" described; they were likely fetishes of some symbolic significance, perhaps the skulls taken in head-hunting expeditions or carved wood planks in the Paiwan style. It is unlikely that they were "graven images" (see Shepherd 1986: 35). Chang Yao-ch'i (1951) locates Ta-mu-hsiang (Dutch: Tavakan) in Hsin-hua *chen*, T'ai-nan county.

97. Campbell 1903: 138, 165.

98. Ibid.: 179; see also 182.

99. Ibid.: 186.

100. Ibid.: 219, 288–89, 292; Kuepers 1978: 23.

101. Campbell 1903: 15, 21, 76–77, 96; Blusse and Roessingh 1984: 68, 71.

102. *BD*: 33; Campbell 1903: 19–20, 95; Blusse and Roessingh 1984: 70. For a fuller explanation of these unusual customs, see Shepherd 1990.

103. Campbell 1903: 162, 182–83, 186.

104. Ibid.: 143, 179; Shepherd 1990.

105. Campbell 1903: 162–63, 176–77. Wills (1972: 11) aptly calls them "blunderbuss Christians."

106. Campbell 1903: 240.

107. Ibid.: 165, 214, 224.

108. Ibid.: 140, 147, 225–26.

109. Ibid.: 149, 167–69, 224, 296.

110. Ibid.: 108, 144.

111. Ibid.: 161, 179, 345.

112. Ibid.: 81, 150, 207, 287–88. Kuepers (1978: 10–11) explains that clerks in holy orders were ministers who had not yet finished their theological studies and that catechists, or "visitors of the sick," had no formal theological education and were not allowed to administer sacraments or to preach.

113. Campbell 1903: 156, 239, 241–42, 258, 303–5.

114. Ibid.: 197, 207, 259–60, 301–3.

115. Ibid.: 228, 311–12.

116. Ibid.: 192–93, 202–3, 224–26, 240, 345.

117. Nakamura 1956*b*; Lai Yung-hsiang 1970: 83–111.

118. Campbell 1903: 142–46, 306–9.

119. Terrien de Lacouperie 1887: 417; Murakami 1933.

120. Campbell 1903: 103, 110, 148, 188, 191, 210.

121. Ibid.: 96–97, 100, 121; *BD*: 348.

122. Campbell 1903: 142, 150.

123. Ibid.: 86, 150, 153, 191.

124. Ibid.: 80, 191.

125. Ibid.: 191, 193, 211.

126. Ibid.: 202–4.

127. Ibid.: 202–3, 208–13.

128. Ibid.: 216–17. In 1647 the Reverend Joannes Bavius, holder of the judicial office at Hsiao-lung, died. Governor Pieter Overtwater (1646–50) appointed a factor to take over the judicial post, but was careful to cite precedents from before Caron's time. Moreover, the factor he appointed was also an elder in the church. Nor did Overtwater challenge "the superintendence of the clergymen" already in place in the other villages (ibid.: 220–21).

129. Ibid.: 207–8, 211–13, 215, 216.

130. Ibid.: 237, 243; Kuepers 1978: 28.

131. Campbell 1903: 236–44. Junius had baptized 5,000 and married 1,000 (ibid.: 193).

132. Ibid.: 231–34.

133. Kuepers 1978: 29–33.

134. Campbell 1903: 249, 265, 267, 298.

135. Verburg quickly discovered how entrenched clerical power was in Taiwan—his own company subordinates, the second-in-command, Coyett, and Captain Thomas Pedel—supported Gravius, and Gravius was defiant when Verburg demanded that he "justify himself for having written the libellous letter." Verburg was not the sort of leader who could rise above the fray, especially when he felt his own authority was being challenged. He sought to humiliate Gravius by accusing him of issuing poll-tax papers without authorization, an accusation later judged to be deliberately false (ibid.: 264–69, 272, 282).

136. Verstegen absolved Gravius of any irregularity in the poll-tax case but had him tried for extorting money from a Chinese. He upheld the authority of the governor to approve the assignment of clergy to specific villages (ibid.: 270–74, 282).

137. Despite this partial victory and the subsequent departure of Gravius from the island, Verburg was dissatisfied by Verstegen's compromise report, accused him of bias, and continued to pile up charges against the clergy. He accused Gravius of beating a Hsiao-lung man to death and the Reverend Gilbertus Happart of robbing Chinese leaseholders in Favorlang (ibid.: 276–80, 290). These charges were apparently never pressed.

138. Ibid.: 296.

139. Ibid.: 297. Conflict between church and company was common throughout the Dutch seaborne empire (Boxer 1965: 148–72).

140. Campbell 1903: 252. Verburg's criticism in this and other matters echoes that offered by the Reverend Junius. Verburg criticized the replacement of Junius's simpler catechism in the schools and freed the *inib*s after their conversion as Junius had promised and against Gravius's advice. But Verburg was not motivated by a desire to revenge Junius. Rather, he found Junius's criticisms valuable as ammunition against the clergy he faced. Verburg would surely have butted heads with Junius if their terms had overlapped, for Junius had earlier challenged the authority of Governor Traudenius (ibid.: 191, 237, 288, 293–95).

141. Ibid.: 295.

142. The clergy was unwilling to serve in the south; but a clerk in holy orders and soldier-schoolmasters willing to be posted there had been found (ibid.: 198–99). The clerk, Hans Olhoff, built up a system of schools against heavy odds before he died in 1651. His successor also quickly fell victim to disease (ibid.: 215–16, 276). In 1653 ague and measles took a heavy toll in both south and north. The natives were so affected that there was fear the neglect of the rice fields might lead to hunger. Two of the four clergymen resident in Taiwan, and many more schoolmasters, succumbed. The effects were still being felt in the south in 1654. Matters declined so rapidly there that in 1654 Verburg's successor, Governor Cornelius Caesar, argued with dismay: "It would have been better never to begin the work of conversion in those places rather than allow so many baptized persons to turn again to heathenism. Our purpose could just as well have been served by stationing a judicial officer with some soldiers amongst them, who would have gained their good will and insured their allegiance." Even the clergy, still personally anxious to avoid serving in the south, were at this time resigned to a reduction of effort there (ibid.: 290–91, 298).

143. Ibid.: 203, 220. Not including Candidius and Junius, 27 clergymen served in Taiwan from 1636 to 1662, on tours of duty that averaged four years. The pioneer missionaries Candidius and Junius served terms of eight and fourteen years, respectively; see ibid.: 86.

144. Ibid.: 299. The next year, Reverend Anthonius Hambroek volunteered to serve permanently in the south. This was rejected by the company's council in Batavia, on which ex-governor Verburg was now active, in favor of putting the southern schools under the control of political functionaries (ibid.: 301–2, 304). Over this great distance, Verburg was able to continue his old quarrel with the clergy and his personal enemy, Coyett, who was appointed governor in 1656. The Taiwan clerics objected to the restriction of their role in the south (ibid.: 311).

145. Ibid.: 309, 317.

146. Ibid.: 204, 230–31, 291.

147. Ibid.: 314–16.

148. Ibid.: 317–18.

149. *BD*: 31, 49.

150. Campbell 1903: 36; Wills 1972: 7.

151. *BD*: 213, 244, 328, 363; Campbell 1903: 210–11.

152. Nakamura 1959: 34–35.

153. *BD*: 193; Campbell 1903: 174–75, 186.

154. Campbell 1903: 187.

155. One possible reference is to aborigines who "ill-treat the Chinese provided with our licenses" and "passports," but the licenses mentioned may have been fishing rather than hunting licenses (ibid.: 106, 117).

156. *BD*: 152, 168.

157. Campbell 1903: 149, 160, 167–73, 174–76.

158. Ibid.: 205–6; *BD*: 232–33.

159. Campbell 1903: 119–20.

160. Ibid.: 149; *BD*: 180.

161. Campbell 1903: 149.

162. Ibid.: 103–4.

163. Ibid.: 155; *BD*: 211.

164. *BD*: 363.

165. Campbell 1903: 222, quoting the day-journal of the delegates meeting, Mar. 14, 1647.

166. *BD*: 411–12, 414.

167. *BD*: 247; Campbell 1903: 176, 187.

168. *BD*: 391, 455; Nakamura 1959: 33.

169. *BD*: 423–44; Cator 1936: 16–21; Nakamura 1963–64.

170. *BD*: 440, 455; cf. Campbell 1903: 180 for 1639.

171. Campbell 1903: 274.

172. Ibid.: 290.

173. Ibid.: 134, 187, 267, 282; see notes 135–37 to this chapter.

174. Campbell 1903: 274–75.

175. Ibid.: 296.

176. Nakamura 1963–64: pt. 2.24–25.

177. Wills 1972: 17–18.

178. For the eighteen years for which there are figures, a total of 1,179,454 deerskins were exported from Taiwan to Japan (Nakamura 1959: 34–35). The Dutch exported comparable amounts from Thailand: 1,970,124 deerskins between 1633 and 1663, and 1,453,000 deerskins between 1664 and 1694 (G. V. Smith 1977: 80). Unfortunately, I have discovered no information on how the deerskin trade was organized in Thailand.

179. Nakamura 1963–64: pt. 1.81.
180. Nakamura 1963–64: pt. 2.84, 1964: 66–71.
181. Nakamura 1963–64: pt. 2.24–25.
182. Campbell 1903: 254; see also 10, 257.
183. Ibid.: 10, 11; *BD*: 363.
184. Campbell 1903: 248–49; *BD*: 246–47.
185. Campbell 1903: 230.
186. Ibid.: 202, 214, 224.
187. *BD*: 439; Pelzer 1945: 72.
188. Campbell 1903: 307.
189. Ibid.: 248–49; Nakamura 1954: 66. See Chapter 11 for later developments.
190. *BD*: 439. My reading of this passage conflicts with that of Nakamura 1954: 58 and agrees more with that of Kuo Shui-t'an 1959: 44. The rice tax paid to the company, as distinct from a rent paid to aborigines, was one-tenth of the harvest (not a fixed rate per *chia*) and in 1644 totaled 1,640 reals (Nakamura 1963–64: pt. 2.16).
191. Campbell 1903: 168.
192. Wills 1972: 19; Coolhaas 1964: 758.
193. Campbell 1903: 63.
194. Ibid.: 460.
195. Ibid.: 410.
196. *BD*: 34; Thompson 1964: 176–77; Blusse and Roessingh 1984: 70, 72, 77. The interpreters communicated with the Dutch in Portuguese, the lingua franca of Far Eastern commerce at the time (Boxer 1941: 415).
197. *BD*: 31, 49; Blusse and Roessingh 1984: 66.
198. Campbell 1903: 106, 133.
199. Ibid.: 113, 114, 136. Chang Yao-ch'i (1951) locates Fang-so (Dutch: Pangsoia) in Lin-pien *hsiang*, P'ing-tung county.
200. Campbell 1903: 114–15, 118, 127–29, 136–37. One such village was Lang-ch'iao (Heng-ch'un), at the southern tip of the island, which demonstrates the extent of the Chinese trading network.
201. Ibid.: 134, 187; *BD*: 33.
202. See Campbell 1903: 210–11; *BD*: 244, 412, 417, 422, 432, 438–39.
203. *BD*: 320, 412; Campbell 1903: 211, 224.
204. For Taiwan's fishing industry in this era, see *BD*: 48–49, 108, 193, 312; Campbell 1903: 106, 210–11, 254; Ts'ao 1954*b*, 1956; and Nakamura 1955, 1963–64: pt. 2.8–12.
205. Chiang Shu-shen 1986: 5.
206. Campbell 1903: 201–2.
207. Ibid.: 209, 282.
208. Ibid.: 187.
209. Ibid.: 187; *BD*: 243.
210. It is likely that Chinese merchants rather than village traders themselves made the bids and that the poorer traders worked as agents of the merchants.
211. Campbell 1903: 180, 282, 285–86, 289.
212. Ibid.: 385; Blusse and Roessingh 1984: 77.
213. Campbell 1903: 10; Nakamura 1954: 57.
214. In 1624–25, Li Tan had encouraged Chinese to emigrate to Taiwan. Li Tan's son accused the Dutch-employed interpreter Cheng Chih-lung (Iquan) of extorting "squeeze" from these immigrants (Boxer 1941: 414–15). By 1628 Cheng Chih-lung (the father of Cheng Ch'eng-kung) had seized control of Li Tan's fleet

(Li had died in 1625) and made peace with the Ming government. Chinese sources report a serious drought in Fukien while Hsiung Wen-ts'an was governor there (1628–32). Cheng Chih-lung is said to have proposed to supply farmers with draft oxen and cash subsidies and transport them to Taiwan to relieve the famine. However, the many Chinese versions of this story give conflicting dates (some in the 1640's), and I have found no Dutch corroboration (Nakamura 1954: 56–57; Kuo Shui-t'an 1959: 17–18; Ch'en Shao-hsing 1964: 91–95; Goodrich and Fang 1976: 563; Huber 1990: 265–68).

215. Chiang Shu-shen 1986: 2–3.

216. *BD*: 180, 193; Boxer 1939: 464.

217. *BD*: 69. The Dutch had on occasion enslaved Chinese captives taken in naval battles, but I have not seen references to their use as farm labor in Taiwan (Campbell 1903: 30–31).

218. Kuo Shui-t'an 1959: 17; Chiang Shu-shen 1986: 3.

219. The tax rate was 0.25 reals per month or 3 reals per year (Nakamura 1954: 58–59; Ch'en Shao-hsing 1964: 106; Chiang Shu-shen 1986: 4, 7–8, 12).

220. Ch'en Shao-hsing 1964: 106–11. In 1651 the poll-tax rate was raised to 0.29 reals per month or 3.48 reals per year (Chiang Shu-shen 1986: 13–14).

221. After the Kuo Huai-i rebellion in 1652, the company abolished the exemption of women from the poll tax; the company was confident that Chinese would migrate to Taiwan in any case, given the increasing chaos on the mainland (Huber 1990: 289).

222. Campbell 1903: 391; Nakamura 1954: 59. See Struve 1984: 116, 189, for accounts of these events from the perspective of the Southern Ming resistance and Cheng Ch'eng-kung.

223. Campbell 1903: 63–64; Huber 1990: 273, 275.

224. Campbell 1903: 7–8; Nakamura 1954: 60–61.

225. *BD*: 179–80; Rawski 1972: 48–49. The area required to produce 100,000 catties of sugar is approximately 40 hectares. See Chapter 6.

226. Campbell 1903: 116–17.

227. By 1660, however, there were a few scattered farms at greater distances, as the evacuation ordered by Coyett in 1660 reveals; see Campbell 1903: 394, 466. See Ts'ao 1954*a*: 81 for a map of Chinese-cultivated areas in the Dutch period.

228. *BD*: 417; Campbell 1903: 231, 459.

229. Nakamura 1954: 61; Iwao 1955.

230. *BD*: 246–47; Campbell 1903: 155. By 1647 there were 4,000 head on the island (Chiang Shu-shen 1986: 8).

231. *BD*: 193; Ao et al. 1954: 45, 46; Chiang Shu-shen 1986: 6.

232. Nakamura 1963–64: pt. 2.84. Even after the end of the tax holiday, it is unlikely that the 10 percent tax imposed on rice harvests from the 1640's was applied without distinguishing land reclaimed through company investment from land reclaimed by private capital (unfortunately the sources do not treat these matters). In their usual fashion, the Dutch farmed out the collection of the rice tax (ibid.).

233. Ibid.; Wills 1972: 18. The company followed similar policies exempting sugar from taxes in Batavia (Cator 1936: 11).

234. Campbell 1903: 249, 298, 299, 395; Ao et al. 1954: 46, 52.

235. *TWFC*:Fan: 182; Ao et al. 1954: 46; Nakamura 1963–64: pt. 2.16.

236. Nakamura 1954: 58; Chiang Shu-shen 1986: 6.

237. Campbell 1903: 396; Nakamura 1954: 67–69, 1963–64: pt. 2.20 (overleaf). Why this should be has not been made clear. In the early years sugar may have been favored over rice (Campbell 1903: 155; *BD*: 246). Sugarcane takes eighteen months to mature and thus ties up land area, but its labor requirements are less than those of rice and, though seasonally concentrated, complementary to the rice cycle (Gallin 1966: 53–54, 69; *contra* Rawski 1972: 49). I do not know the extent to which either rice or sugarcane was grown in dry or irrigated fields during the Dutch period, but I suspect dry fields were common for both crops. One 1645 report suggests that sugarcane was given priority over rice in irrigated fields (*BD*: 456). Rice, of course, had an advantage in that it was both a commercial and a subsistence crop. Huber (1990: 277–78) describes an overexpansion in the sugarcane acreage in 1650 that caused a labor shortage at harvesttime; this was followed by a contraction in the sugarcane area in the succeeding year. In Batavia, the long slack periods associated with the sugar industry were seen as having an "unfavorable influence on public order and morals," and similar conditions may well have existed in Taiwan (Cator 1936: 11).

238. *BD*: 472; Nakamura 1954: 62; Iwao 1955: 53–56; Wills 1972: 15, 18; Huber 1990: 275. After Taiwan fell to Cheng Ch'eng-kung in 1661, prices rose in the Dutch colony of Java and its sugar industry expanded (Cator 1936: 11; Iwao 1955: 60).

239. *BD*: 347–48; Kuo Shui-t'an 1959: 26–28, 36–39.

240. *BD*: 243, 312, 424–25; Nakamura 1963–64: pt. 2.24–25.

241. Nakamura 1964: 68–71.

242. *BD*: 428; Campbell 1903: 63, 393, 463; Boxer 1939: 462–63; Wills 1972: 5, 13–14; Huber 1990: 270, 283–84.

243. Campbell 1903: 386, 403, 459. Wills (1972: 16–17) states the Dutch garrison still numbered only a thousand in 1655.

244. Huber 1990: 270–75, 283, 288.

245. Ibid.: 285–86; Campbell 1903: 459; Wills 1972: 17.

246. Campbell 1903: 64, 388, 396.

247. Ibid.: 392–96, 461–66; Fu 1966: 2.1–2.

248. Campbell 1903: 393. This claim, unlike that of the later Boxers, turned out to be true (ibid.: 70, 420). The Cheng troops also made effective use of rattan armor; see note 5 to Chapter 5.

249. Campbell 1903: 393–94, 435.

250. Ibid.: 395, 403, 465–66.

CHAPTER FOUR

1. Hummel 1943–44: 109, 415. For an account of Cheng Ch'eng-kung's role in the Ming resistance, see Struve 1984. See Wong 1983 and Hung Chien-chao 1981 for detailed narrative accounts of the Cheng regime and Croizier 1977 for a superb account of the historiography of Cheng Ch'eng-kung.

2. Campbell 1903: 70–71, 413, 427, 455; Yang Ying 1958: 186–87; Chiang Jih-sheng 1960: 244.

3. Yang Ying 1958: 187; Fu 1966: 1.25–28; cf. Campbell 1903: 84, 318, 421; Wills 1972: 20.

4. Campbell 1903: 318, quoting the Zeelandia day-journal entry for May 17, 1661.

5. Campbell 1903: 322.

6. Ibid.: 63–64; see also 210–11.

7. Ibid.: 126, 324.

8. Ibid.: 323.

9. Ibid., quoting the Zeelandia day-journal entry for Aug. 27, 1661.

10. Yang Ying 1958: 188; Chiang Jih-sheng 1960: 205. By August 1661, the Chinese were forcing natives to drop their Christian and Dutch names (Campbell 1903: 323).

11. Yang Ying 1958: 188–89; Chuang Chin-te 1961: 61.

12. Ts'ao 1954*a*: 73; Yang Ying 1958: 189.

13. Campbell 1903: 323.

14. Yang Ying 1958: 188–90.

15. Ibid.: 189–90; Campbell 1903: 444. See Appendix A for maps locating aborigine villages.

16. Campbell 1903: 322–23; Coyett 1975: 90.

17. Coyett 1975: 92. Modern Ta-tu *hsiang* lies in T'ai-chung county.

18. Yang Ying 1958: 191; Juan Min-hsi 1958: 38; Chiang Jih-sheng 1960: 204, 233; Sheng 1976: 87. The Dutch cited this incident as one reason Cheng executed several hundred Dutch prisoners (Campbell 1903: 84, but cf. 327; Coyett 1975: 93).

19. Campbell 1903: 327, 444; Chiang Jih-sheng 1960: 204.

20. Campbell 1903: 445; Yang Ying 1958: 191–93; Juan Min-hsi 1958: 39–40; Chiang Jih-sheng 1960: 205.

21. Juan Min-hsi 1958: 39; Chiang Jih-sheng 1960: 205. Chang Yao-ch'i (1951) locates T'a-li-wu (Dutch: Dalivo) in Tou-nan *chen*, Yün-lin county.

22. Ts'ao 1954*a*: 84; Juan Min-hsi 1958: 39; Chiang Jih-sheng 1960: 205–7.

23. Abe 1938: 250. A similar situation may have existed at Ta-mu-hsiang (see *TNHCK*: 2.107; *TKI*: 1.75).

24. Yang Ying 1958: 193–94.

25. In 1660, when attack seemed imminent, the Dutch had noticed that "Chinese debtors in Tayouan became far slower in their payments than they formerly had been" (Campbell 1903: 392); see also Wills 1972: 20.

26. Campbell 1903: 455.

27. See *CLHC*: 96, 168; Juan Min-hsi 1958: 40; Ts'ao et al. 1959: 192; Chiang Jih-sheng 1960: 208, 408; Thompson 1969: 112. The Cheng method of taxing fishermen also continued the Dutch practice (*CLHC*: 96, 104; *TWFC*:Fan: 473; *FCTCTWF*: 166; Huang Shu-ching 1957: 164; Yang Ying 1958: 190).

28. Wills 1974: 41, 51–52, 67.

29. Hummel 1943–44: 111, 415; Juan Min-hsi 1958: 40–43; Chiang Jih-sheng 1960: 244.

30. Juan Min-hsi 1958: 44; Chiang Jih-sheng 1960: 234–35, 239.

31. *TWFC*:Liu: 486; Wills 1972: 19, 1974: 144.

32. The Chengs styled their government in Taiwan a regional government (*mu fu*) of the deposed Ming dynasty and not a center of imperial government. The Chengs continued to use Yung-li reign dates, although that heir to the Ming throne had been executed in 1662 (Hung Chien-chao 1981: 125, 177, 252, 284). Cheng Ching headed a Ming government that had only a spiritual emperor: "Cheng Ching never failed to perform the rituals of his paying tribute to the non-

present emperor on the first and fifteenth day of each month. Similar rituals were followed when he had to make important personnel appointments. On such occasions, he would wear his court apparel, face north, make a report to an empty throne with Chu Shu-kuei [a Ming prince] standing on the left side of it, and then burn the report" (ibid.: 296). Burning memorials is a standard Chinese means of communicating with gods.

33. Juan Min-hsi 1958: 44; Chiang Jih-sheng 1960: 237, 239; Sheng 1976: 78.

34. Ch'en Shao-hsing 1964: 117.

35. Chiang Jih-sheng 1960: 244. In 1668 Shih Lang estimated that there were 30-odd brigades in Taiwan, varying in strength from 200 to 600 men, for a maximum of 18,000 troops (ibid.).

36. Ts'ao et al. 1959: 139, 194.

37. Hummel 1943–44: 111; Chiang Jih-sheng 1960: 260, 267, 401.

38. *KHSL*: 135; Ch'en Shao-hsing 1964: 118. Most studies of Taiwan's historical demography fail to take into account these tremendous swings in population under the Chengs; see Chapter 6.

39. Ch'en Shao-hsing 1964: 117.

40. See *HMC*: 104; Ura 1955; Ts'ao et al. 1959: 136; Chuang Chin-te 1961: 59–60; Fu 1966: 1.28; and Kessler 1976: 39–41. Struve (1984: 158–59) gives an excellent account of the strategic considerations behind the Ch'ing policy of evacuation.

41. Hsieh Kuo-ching 1932: 576; Ts'ao 1954*a*: 76; Ch'en Shao-hsing 1964: 115; Fu 1966: 1.39, 43, 46.

42. *HMC*: 104; Hsieh Kuo-ching 1932: 578–79; Ch'en Shao-hsing 1964: 114; Fu 1966: 1.50.

43. Ch'en Shao-hsing 1964: 106; see also Chiang Shu-shen 1986 and Huber 1990: 274, 289.

44. Ts'ao 1954*a*: 76–77; Chiang Jih-sheng 1960: 244, 258. Being married, of course, was no guarantee that a soldier's wife was present in Taiwan; rather than accompany her sojourning husband, a wife properly remained in the household of her in-laws.

45. *TWFC*:Kao: 112; Ts'ao 1954*a*: 76, 79; Chiang Jih-sheng 1960: 291.

46. Since there does not seem to have been a land *tax* (only a harvest tax) under the Dutch, this must refer to a *rental* rate on land reclaimed under Dutch financing (Ao et al. 1954: 51; Azuma 1954: 87; Ts'ao 1954*a*: 75).

47. Ts'ao 1954*a*: 75; Cheng Hsi-fu 1974*a*: 100. See Table 8.5 for the complete Cheng land-tax rate schedule.

48. See *TWFC*:Fan: 182; *FCTCTWF*: 164–66.

49. Cheng Hsi-fu 1974*a*: 101. The Cheng state-owned area is only three-fourths the Dutch figure of 12,252 *morgen* (roughly equivalent to the same number of *chia*) in 1660 (Campbell 1903: 396; Nakamura 1954: 69), which suggests that some farmland reclaimed in the Dutch era was not put under state ownership. If the *morgen* equals only 80 percent of a *chia* as Huber (1990: 275) argues, there is no discrepancy.

50. Chuang Chin-te 1961*a*: 62; see the map in Ch'en Han-kuang 1961: 53 and Map 4.1.

51. Chiang Jih-sheng 1960: 235, 259.

52. Quoted in Ts'ao et al. 1959: 194; see also 139.

53. Chiang Jih-sheng 1960: 244; Ch'en Han-kuang 1961*a*: 46.

54. Ts'ao 1954*a*: 83; Ts'ao et al. 1959: 138, 196–97; Nakamura 1954: 68.

55. Ts'ao 1954*a*: 83–84. These techniques were used in this area until the construction of the Chia-nan irrigation system in the 1920's (Pasternak 1972*a*: 195–97, 1972*b*: 42).

56. For the Cheng maritime empire, see Wong 1983: 142–44, 153–56; and Hung Chien-chao 1981: 187–91. Yamawaki (1976: 113) emphasizes the profits Cheng Ching made by carrying silk goods acquired from Chinese junks at Manila to Japan.

57. Hsieh Kuo-ching 1932: 595; Ts'ao et al. 1959: 101, 136; Viraphol 1977: 44–45.

58. Ts'ao et al. 1959: 78, 163; Chiang Jih-sheng 1960: 267.

59. Ts'ao et al. 1959: 78–79. In 1683 the Manchus would cite this supplying of war matériel to the Chengs as reason for denying trade to Europeans; the prohibition was, however, rescinded the next year (ibid.: 106, 109).

60. Ibid.: 91, 138; Paske-Smith 1930: 85.

61. Ts'ao et al. 1959: 138, 196; Sheng 1976: 86.

62. Nakamura 1963–64: pt. 2.4; Chiang Shu-shen 1986: 13–14.

63. Cheng Hsi-fu 1974*a*: 98, 104. Cheng taxes were levied in *ch'eng ch'ien* at 400 *wen* to the ounce (*liang*) of current silver (*shih yin*), which was equal to 0.7 ounces of pure silver (*wen yin*) or 0.7 taels. Reports from the 1620's mention the real trading at 0.73 taels and 0.8 taels (*BD*: 42; Campbell 1903: 41). In the 1660's, the tael was worth 3.5 florins, and the real was worth 2.5 florins; this puts the real at 0.71 taels (Boxer 1965: 341; Wills 1974: 27). The standard conversion rate put the real at 0.72 taels (Chang Yung-wu 1954: 25; Wang Ching-liang 1963: 12).

64. Cheng Hsi-fu 1974*a*: 98–99.

65. Nakamura 1962: 70. Florins have been converted to reals at the rate of 2.5 to 1.0.

66. Cheng Hsi-fu 1974*a*: fig. 3.2.

67. For this figure, see Chapter 5. The description there of the monopoly merchant system under the Ch'ing applies in large part to the system under the Chengs.

68. *TWFC*:Kao: 129–30; Cheng Hsi-fu 1974*a*: 102.

69. Ts'ao et al. 1959: 162; Chiang Jih-sheng 1960: 267; Thompson 1964: 195.

70. *CLHC*: 291; Thompson 1964: 195, 201, 1969: 98; Sheng 1976: 87.

71. *CLHC*: 188; Chiang Jih-sheng 1960: 235–36; Thompson 1964: 186.

72. Hummel 1943–44: 111, 879; Juan Min-hsi 1958: 45–46.

73. Ts'ao et al. 1959: 98–99, 101; Hung Chien-chao 1981: 264; Wong 1983: 174–75, 182.

74. Liao Han-ch'en 1953: 28; Huang Shu-ching 1957: 133; Chiang Jih-sheng 1960: 375–76, 394, 398.

75. Chiang Jih-sheng 1960: 408; Thompson 1969: 112.

76. *CLHC*: 300; see also Ts'ao et al. 1959: 139.

77. Chiang Jih-sheng 1960: 410.

78. Fu: 1966: 1.56.

79. Campbell 1903: 515; Juan Min-hsi 1958: 60; Chiang Jih-sheng 1960: 409–10.

80. Hummel 1943–44: 653; Ts'ao et al. 1959: 161–64; Fu 1966: 1.59–60.

81. Shih Lang 1958: 51. A ceremony in which the victor conferred official caps and robes on the submitting party was standard Chinese practice. Wills (1974: 67) reports such a ceremony when Cheng defectors submitted to the Ch'ing.

CHAPTER FIVE

1. *TWHC*: 232; *TWFC*:Liu: 423.
2. *TWHC*: 243–44; Paske-Smith 1930: 120 (citing a British East India Company report that refers to Commander Wu as Go Chungea); Huang Huan-yao 1986*a*: 144–45. This use of aborigine braves is the first instance under the Ch'ing of a pattern that will play a prominent role in the fate of the plains aborigines. We shall see below and in Chapter 10 how the Ch'ing used plains aborigine troops to help maintain order, among both Han Chinese and other plains aborigine tribes.
3. Shih Lang 1958: 53–54. Reality appears not to have measured up to the ideals expressed in this proclamation. English merchants resident in Taiwan report that Shih Lang's subordinates, if not Shih Lang himself, were extorting large bribes from people in all walks of life (Paske-Smith 1930: 118).
4. *KHSL*: 128, 135; Ts'ao 1954*a*: 80; Chuang Chin-te 1964: 1.
5. Ho Yu and his "cane-shield brigade" of former Cheng soldiers subsequently won fame in battles against the Russians (Hummel 1943–44: 621; Fu 1966: 1.73; Mancall 1971: 338; Kessler 1976: 102). The Chengs had used rattan shields, effective against muskets, in their struggles with the Dutch (see Chapter 3). Other Cheng soldiers were recruited into Banner forces and formed river patrols in Manchuria (R. Lee 1970: 37).
6. Shih Lang 1958: 67, 69; Chuang Chin-te 1964: 2. The English merchants resident in Taiwan estimated that two-thirds of the Han population left for the mainland and attributed the exodus to misgovernment. In January 1684 they stated that government troops' abuse of the populace after the death of the Ch'ing official Poee "vexed them so sore, that to purchase a peaceable life, not possible to be enjoyed either upon Tywan (or Formosa) among them, they forsook good, faire, and stately houses, and gave away precious household stuff, and departed for China . . . which is the only cause that this countrey now wants two thirds of her Chinese inhabitants" (Paske-Smith 1930: 119).
7. Ch'en Shao-hsing 1964: 117. In the first month of 1684, eight months before he estimated that half the population had left, Shih Lang put Taiwan's population at only 100,000 (*KHSL*: 131). Almost all treatments of Taiwan's seventeenth-century history mistakenly assume that the Han population grew without interruption and fail to take into account the effect the substantial repatriation at the beginning of Ch'ing rule had on development; see Chapter 6 below.
8. For the debate, see *KHSL*: 131; Shih Lang 1958: 59–62; Chuang Chin-te 1964: 1; Fu 1966: 1.60–61; and Wong 1983: 187–91. Despite his seeming commitment to annexation, Shih Lang had covered his bases had the emperor decided not to keep Taiwan. While on Taiwan, Shih had approached a Dutchman who had been a Cheng prisoner to inquire if the Dutch wanted the island back and how much they would pay for it (Wills 1984: 148–49).
9. *KHSL*: 130–34; Hsieh Kuo-ching 1932: 579. For the court the reopening of foreign trade would bring customs revenues that would lighten the tax burden then being borne disproportionately by the interior provinces (Kessler 1976: 96;

Ng 1983: 188). The endless campaigns on the southeast coast had disrupted the local economy and the flow of tax revenues while requiring the state to finance large armies. Earlier in 1680, the court had relaxed the coastal evacuation policy to help relieve these strains (Wong 1983: 166–67). See Zelin (1984: 3–4) for the background of the early Ch'ing concern with the threat excessive expenditure posed to fiscal balance. In December 1683, English merchants resident in Taiwan were given to understand that the customs revenues expected from the opening of foreign commerce were needed to defray the expenses of the army to be garrisoned in Taiwan (Ts'ao et al. 1959: 173–74). Leonard (1984: 71–72) stresses the internal security considerations that led the court to legalize the junk trade as a means of restoring the southeast coast's economy and social order but ignores the fiscal advantages. I thank John Wills for his comments on the Japanese trade.

10. *TWFC*:Kao: 5; Ch'en Cheng-hsiang 1959–61: 1.8. See Chapter 7 for a more extended treatment of government organs in Taiwan.

11. For proposals to create *t'u ssu* jurisdictions in Taiwan, see Chapter 9. Aborigines in the mountains and on the east coast, once included in the Dutch censuses, broke away from Dutch influence by the 1660's and were not resubjected to state power for centuries.

12. *CLHC*: 154–55. A contemporary observer recognized some intermediate categories. There were those who paid only the aborigine head tax but did not give labor service, and those who paid no tax at all yet could not be called wild or untamed (*yeh*) (Yü 1959: 11). The raw and cooked, or "strange" and "familiar," distinction was used throughout China. Other designations for civilized aborigines included *p'ing p'u*, plains in contrast to mountain aborigines (*CHFSHC*: 59), and *pai fan*, white aborigines ("white is to black as cooked is to raw") (Liao Chiung-jan 1948: 6, cf. *TTTCS*: 648–49).

13. The five categories are the Han head tax, the land tax, the *lu hsiang* (land revenues, including the aborigine head tax), the *shui hsiang* (water revenues, which included charges on boats at fishing harbors), and miscellaneous taxes (*CLHC*: 83–96). For the fiscal significance of aborigine taxes, see Chapter 8.

14. *CLHC*: 96; *CHFSHC*: 110.

15. *TWFC*:Kao: 161; *CLHC*: 86, 102.

16. Ho Ping-ti 1959: 24–35, 101–16; Ray Huang (1974: 40) reports cases from the late Ming in which a tribe and the government negotiated tax quotas.

17. *CLHC*: 86; *TWFC*:Chou: 316. The 1711 tax holiday celebrated the fiftieth year of the K'ang-hsi reign.

18. At the beginning of Ch'ing rule, no tribes were included within the boundaries of T'ai-wan county, which were closely drawn around the prefectural city of Tainan.

19. The four Feng-shan units will receive little attention here since few details are given in the gazetteers. Three of them apparently threw off Chinese rule very early and did not resubmit until the early Yung-cheng years, when they were assigned low tax quotas in deerskins commuted to cash (*FSHC*: 72; *CHFSHC*: 60, 114; see also the quote from de Mailla cited below and Appendix B). These four tribes were not located on the major southern plain; that area was occupied by the group of eight discussed separately below.

20. *FCTCTWF*: 166; Cheng Hsi-fu 1974*a*: 106.

21. *CLHC*: 100. Thus, I argue that the Ch'ing kept the nominal rate of 0.24

ounces of silver per skin and did not convert this rate from the Cheng currency, as they did other tax rates (see Chapter 8), and that the Chengs levied fixed quotas on the villages and did not collect separate rates for different kinds of skin (contra Cheng Hsi-fu 1974*a*: 105–6).

22. *CLHC*: 96.

23. *TWFC*:Kao: 161; *CLHC*: 86, 102.

24. This area is covered by Dutch census regions 1, 2, 3, and 4; see Table 2.1 and Nakamura 1936.

25. The eight southern tribes appear to have paid more in the aggregate, however, because of the high proportion of villagers categorized as taxable heads.

26. *CLHC*: 85, 99–100; *KHSL*: 144.

27. *TWFC*:Fan: 478–79; *CHFSHC*: 113.

28. *TWFC*:Kao: 161; *FSHC*: 82; Cheng Hsi-fu 1974*a*: 102.

29. *TWFC*:Yü: 247; *FCTCTWF*: 165.

30. *FSHC*: 78; *YCSL*: 12.

31. The total population in 1650 was 11,451, compared to the Cheng total of 4,345 taxed heads (Nakamura 1936: 5–6).

32. *TWFC*:Chou: 322–23; *CHFSHC*: 44; Huang Shu-ching 1957: 149.

33. *KCTYC*: 7.156–57 (YC 4.12.21). Although assessed in grain, the tax after 1726 was commuted for payment to cash at the standard rate of 0.36 taels per *shih* of unhusked rice (0.72 per *shih* of husked rice).

34. *CHFSHC*: 256–57; *TWFC*:Fan: 360.

35. *CLHC*: 168; *TWFC*:Fan: 473.

36. *CLHC*: 96; *TWFC*:Kao: 161; *TWFC*:Chou: 304–5. The Chu-lo county gazetteer (*CLHC*: 96) states that the initial character *p'u* is not a standard character in the Mandarin dialect and that it is a homonym of another character pronounced *p'u*. In the southern Fukien dialects (including Taiwanese) *p'u* is pronounced *pak*, and means "to hire or rent for a long time; to charter or apprentice; to farm as revenue" (Douglas 1873: 357). *P'u she* thus means to farm a tribe's aboriginal tax. The word *p'u* occurs frequently in the land contracts discussed in later chapters. *P'u*, though an unusual character, appears regularly in the memorials and decrees of the central government that form the basis of this study. Kawada (1928: 94) reports finding compound words using *p'u* in a K'ang-hsi-era encyclopedia. Thompson (1969: 139) has speculated that the term *p'u she* is a transliteration of the contemporary Dutch word *pachter*, which also meant tax farmer.

37. *TWFC*:Kao: 161; Lan 1958*b*: 55; *TWFC*:Fan: 473; *CLHC*: 103.

38. Thompson 1969: 139.

39. Ibid.: 70, 105, 109; *CLHC*: 103, 172; *TWFC*:Liu: 65.

40. Thompson 1964: 195–96.

41. *TWFC*:Kao: 161, 248; Huang Shu-ching 1957: 170; Lan 1958*b*: 56. Observers also noted that interpreters demanded sexual favors of aborigine women (*YTHC*: 22).

42. *TWFC*:Kao: 161.

43. Thompson 1964: 197–98; paragraph breaks added.

44. *TWFC*:Liu: 424; Ch'en Pin 1961: 15. Both Wang Min-cheng and Ch'en Pin also supported policies to protect aborigine land rights; see Chapter 9.

45. The gazetteer (*CLHC*: 168) reports the abolition in the "preceding year," which I take to mean the year before publication.

46. *CLHC*: 168.

47. *CHFSHC*: 112.

48. *CLHC*: 102–3.

49. Liang 1956: 59. The Chinese term is *tzu feng t'ou kuei*, or sealed by the taxpayer himself and inserted into the silver chest (Ch'ü 1962: 134, 289).

50. From south to north these were Hsin-kang, Mu-chia-liu-wan, Hsiao-lung, Ma-tou, To-lo-kuo, and Chu-lo-shan, the major southwest core villages. See Maps A.1 and A.2. Chang Yao-ch'i (1951) locates To-lo-kuo (Dutch: Dorko) in Tung-shan *hsiang*, T'ai-nan county.

51. One source attributes this practice to an order by the intendant Kao Kung-ch'ien, who served 1692–97 (*HHTWHC*: 472); Kao's complaints about the excesses of the monopoly merchants are noted below in the discussion of aborigine corvée.

52. *CLHC*: 103. Chang Yao-ch'i (1951) locates Ta-miao (no Dutch equivalent) in Min-hsiung *hsiang*, Chia-i county; T'a-li-wu (Dutch: Dalivo) in Tou-nan *chen*, Yün-lin county; and Ch'ai-li (Dutch: Takkais) in Tou-liu *shih*, Yün-lin county.

53. Ch'ü 1962: 22–32.

54. *CLHC*: 103.

55. *TWFC*:Fan: 478–79; *CHFSHC*: 113. Twentieth-century textbooks have mythologized a Chinese tribal interpreter, Wu Feng (for naive accounts of the myth, see Inō 1928: 3.507–12; and Miyakawa 1960: 45–46). According to the myth, Wu Feng sacrificed himself in order to shame the A-li-shan tribe into renouncing head-hunting. For an account of the creation of this myth during the Japanese colonial era, see Weng 1986.

56. Lan 1958*b*: 56.

57. In another essay Lan (1958*a*: 25) notes in passing that certain Tan-shui area Chinese, knowledgeable in aborigine languages, were actively contracting for monopoly merchant rights over some tribes in the then remote I-lan plain on the northwest coast. The system of monopoly privileges thus seems to have exceeded even the reach of the official tax system. No civil or military presence was extended to I-lan until the early nineteenth century.

58. *YCCPYC*: 142.

59. *CLSL*: 118.

60. S. Mann 1987: 15–16.

61. Ibid.: chaps. 2–3.

62. Ibid.: 15–16.

63. See Zelin 1984.

64. *YTHC*: 22; Huang Shu-ching 1957: 108.

65. Li Ju-ho 1970: 8; *CLSL*: 1.

66. *TWFC*:Kao: 249.

67. Ch'en Pin 1961: 15–16. Ch'en proposed to pay for aborigine oxcarts at 0.002 *liang* per *li*; by 1743, 33 years later, the rate had increased to 0.005 *liang* of silver per *li* (*CLSL*: 31).

68. Huang Shu-ching 1957: 166. One source attributes the prohibition on using aborigine bearers to Prefect Feng Hsieh-i, who served 1713–15 (*YTHC*: 22). The abusive practices mentioned by Huang were not unique to Taiwan, for they could also be found in the Ch'ing post system in non-frontier areas (see Cheng Ying-wan 1970: 31).

69. Thompson 1969: 54, 63, 67. The aborigine runners' reputation for speed was confirmed in a demonstration put on for Governor-general Gioro Man-pao in 1717 (Chang Wei 1978: 68). Besides the *ma ta*, there were other subordinate

officials in each tribe: the *chia shou*, who was responsible for the administration of the corvée (*TWFC*:Liu: 101; Tai Yen-hui 1976: 349–50), and the *huo chang*, a foreman who was possibly a work-group leader (Huang Shu-ching 1957: 163; Yü 1959: 37; Thompson 1964: 195).

70. Lan 1958*b*: 55.

71. Ibid.: 56.

72. *YCCPYC*: 222; *CLSL*: 31.

73. *NPPW*: 380–82.

74. *CTPT*: 991.

75. Huang Shu-ching (1957: 168) also gives a brief account of these events, but mistakenly dates them to 1689 (KH 28, instead of KH 38) and differs in some small details (Lan 1958*b*: 58 gives the date as 1699). See Appendix A for maps locating aborigine villages.

76. These four tribes were among the six described earlier as living near the county seat and more sophisticated in ways Chinese.

77. *CLHC*: 279.

78. *CLHC*: 280. Another instance of the willingness of the Tan-shui tribes to cooperate with the government occurred in 1721 when the Chin-pao-li tribe turned four shipwrecked Ryukyuan sailors over to the authorities (Yang Liang-kung et al. 1975: 155–61).

79. Huang Shu-ching 1957: 168.

80. *CLHC*: 100; *TKI*: 1.132.

81. Campbell 1903: 509–10. Ch'en Pin, who was intendant 1710–15 and became governor of Fukien in 1715, fits de Mailla's description.

82. *TWFC*:Yü: 522. Unfortunately none of the sources discusses the background of this Lin Wu-li and his "disciples" (the characters given may in fact be the transliteration of an aborigine name). That all gazetteer sources mention him would suggest that he played some special role in the revolt. The failure to investigate his background, however, seems to indicate that his role was not in fact decisive and that he is mentioned by name simply because he was the leader of the first tribe to revolt. The memorials in the *KCTYC* series mention by name the leaders of many other tribes when they surrender, but give no special significance to Lin Wu-li. It is clear, however, that the Ch'ing officials involved in the pacification of the revolt considered Ta-chia-hsi to be the chief instigator, despite the many intervening events, especially those of the fifth month of 1732, discussed below (*KCTYC*: 20.703–4 [YC 10.11.3], 20.721–22 [YC 10.11.4]).

83. See Chapter 7 for a list of the offices created in 1731.

84. See *KCTYC*: 19.307–9 (YC 10.1.14), 19.352 (YC 10.1.24), 20.336–38 (YC 10.7.29); and Ch'en Ch'iu-k'un 1975: 95–96. That the rebels initially attacked only Subprefect Chang and his yamen runners was taken as good evidence by other officials that Chang's mismanagement had caused the outbreak (*KCTYC*: 19.350–51 [YC 10.1.24]).

85. *KCTYC*: 19.286 (YC 9.12.28); *TWFC*:Yü: 663.

86. Hou-lung was located well to the north of the rebel area and had probably not been subject to Subprefect Chang's labor requisitions. The Hou-lung chief, Wu-p'ai, and the An-li chief were active in negotiating with the rebels on behalf of the government a few months later in the third month of 1732 (*KCTYC*: 19.570–71 [YC 10.3.24], 19.603–4 [YC 10.4.6]). Hou-lung and An-li were active again in the ninth month of 1732 in assisting government troops in the pacification of rebel tribes (ibid.: 20.735–41 [YC 10.11.7]).

87. Ibid.: 19.345–45 (YC 10.1.24), 19.490–91 (YC 10.2.25).
88. Ibid.: 19.307–9 (YC 10.1.14); *TWFC*:Yü: 663.
89. *KCTYC*: 19.582–83 (YC 10.3.28), 19.653 (YC 10.4.19).
90. Chang T'an 1970*a*: 25–30. For the Chu I-kuei rebellion, see Chapter 6.
91. *TWFC*:Yü: 662, *YCSL*: 40.
92. *KCTYC*: 19.708–10 (YC 10.5.7), 19.850–51 (YC 10.5*.10), 20.205–6 (YC 10.7.3).
93. Ibid.: 19.900–901 (YC 10.5*.24), 19.914–15 (YC 10.5*.24), 20.64–65 (YC 10.6.11), 20.659–61 (YC 10.10.21).
94. Ibid.: 20.510–11 (YC 10.9.7), 20.735 (YC 10.11.7).
95. Ibid.: 20.64–65 (YC 10.6.11); *TWFC*:Yü: 663.
96. The official reports also blame certain Chinese who had married into the tribes (described as aborigines' sons-in-law, *fan hsü*) for stirring up the aborigines (*KCTYC*: 20.164 [YC 10.6.28]).
97. Ch'en Ch'iu-k'un 1975: 97; *CLSL*: 24, 25.
98. *KCTYC*: 20.308–9 (YC 10.7.26). Wang had recently completed a term as Taiwan brigade general and been appointed commander-in-chief of land forces in Fukien (*YCSL*: 39).
99. *KCTYC*: 20.161–62 (YC 10.6.28), 20.187 (YC 10.7.2).
100. Ibid.: 20.443 (YC 10.8.28), 20.735 (YC 10.11.7); *TTTCS*: 26, 775; Chang Yao-k'un 1955: 13.
101. *KCTYC*: 20.735–41 (YC 10.11.7); *TWFC*:Yü: 663.
102. See *KCTYC*: 21.232–33 (YC 11.3.7), 21.627–28 (YC 11.5.28), 21.760–61 (YC 11.6.27). The burden of keeping as many as 700 prisoners from these three tribes caused one official to recommend that the "aborigine women, who were good farmers," should be helped to reclaim land or given their own land to farm (ibid.: 21.826–27 [YC 11.7.15]).
103. *YCSL*: 42; *TWFC*:Liu: 353, 355, 356.
104. *YCSL*: 50.
105. *CLHC*: 98–100.
106. Chiang Jih-sheng 1960: 204, 233.
107. Huang Shu-ching 1957: 128; Thompson 1969: 98.
108. Huang Shu-ching 1957: 128–29, 134; Thompson 1969: 98, 104. Even under the Dutch it was noted of a leader of the Papora ("Middag") that "he would never suffer any Christians to dwell in his dominions, allowing them only to travel through it" (Campbell 1903: 6).
109. *KCTYC*: 21.158–59 (YC 11.2.20).
110. This land was resurveyed and tribal rights to an aborigine large-rent were reaffirmed by local officials in 1778 (*TTTCS*: 601–3). An important 1772 decree guaranteeing aborigine large-rents was issued in response to a dispute between Ta-chia and its tenants; see Chapter 9.
111. Ibid.: 330–31, 601–3. See also an An-li land contract of 1733 (ibid.: 26–28) that speaks of its "merit in pacifying aborigines."
112. *YCSL*: 43–44; *TWFC*:Liu: 320.
113. Lan 1958*b*: 61–62.
114. *TWFC*:Liu: 333–34; *TWFC*:Fan: 290–91.
115. See also the account of a dispute involving access to land owned by an aborigine woman of the Kan-en *she* (Niu-ma *she*) in 1739 (*TAHLCC*: 135–40).

116. *TWFC*:Liu: 597–98. Bestowing Confucian maxims as names to mark submission to imperial authority and the attainment of civilization was a long-standing practice. For Sung dynasty examples relating to the sinicization of non-Han peoples, see von Glahn 1987: 116–19.

117. *TAHLIC*: 67–68; *CLSL*: 5–9; *TWFC*:Yü: 186. See Chapter 9 for a discussion of related policy reversals with respect to reclamation of aborigine lands.

118. *TWFC*:Fan: 200.

119. *TWFC*:Liu: 33; *TWFC*:Yü: 186, 245. See Appendix B for changes in the tax quotas of each plains village over time.

120. *TWFC*:Fan: 199–201; *TWFC*:Yü: 263. For changes in policy affecting taxation of aborigine lands, see Chapter 9.

121. Despite these reductions, the Chu-lo magistrate found it worthwhile to order the construction of special yamen halls for the collection of aborigine taxes in 1740 and 1741 (*TWFC*:Fan: 63).

122. *TWFC*:Yü: 247, 255.

CHAPTER SIX

1. See Ng 1983 for a detailed account of the recovery of southern Fukien's economy and coastal trade after 1683 (unfortunately Ng fails to assess the extent of destruction caused by the coastal evacuation). See Viraphol 1977; Leonard 1984: 71–73; and Blusse 1986: 115, 121–23 for the recovery of Fukien's trade with Southeast Asia. That Canton's trade with the West eventually eclipsed the trade of the Amoy network (especially with the growth of the tea trade in the late eighteenth century [Naquin and Rawski 1987: 103]) is insufficient reason to characterize the eighteenth century as a "dark age" for the southeast coast (*contra* Skinner 1985: 279).

2. Chuang Chin-te 1964: 2. See Chuang Chin-te 1964 and Ch'en Shao-hsing 1964 for valuable overviews of immigration policies; I rely on these throughout this chapter. Shih Lang's hostility toward Ch'ao-chou and Hui-chou pirates was the source of the third restriction, which was relaxed in 1696, after his death (*TWFC*:Fan: 362). During the Chu I-kuei rebellion of 1721, Hakka settlers (many of whom hailed from Ch'ao-chou, which included Chia-ying in this period, and Hui-chou) allied with the Ch'ing forces to suppress the rebels, who hailed from Fukien. In recognition of their meritorious service, the Ch'ing commander Lan T'ing-chen requested that all restrictions on Hakka immigration be lifted (Ch'en Han-kuang 1954: 65). Unlike immigrants from Fukien, migrants from Kwangtung had to cross a provincial boundary to go to Taiwan; this complicated their enrollment on local population registers and their qualification for examination quotas (see *TAHLPC*: 209–13 and the last section of Chapter 7).

3. A secondary motive for the restriction of rice shipments, mentioned by Huang Shu-ching in 1722, was to reduce the risk that rice would fall into the hands of pirates (Wang Shih-ch'ing 1958*a*: 19).

4. Ch'en Ta 1940: 130–35; Purcell 1965: 26.

5. Ho Ping-ti 1959: 138–39; Huang Pei 1974: 241–45; R. Lee 1970: 78.

6. Lattimore 1934: 80; Serruys 1981: 496; R. Lee 1970: 184. See also Chapter 12.

7. Fu 1966: 1.193; Viraphol 1977: 74, 76. Of course, population pressure alone

does not explain why migrants elected to go to Taiwan. Residents of the southeast coast could also go into trade in Southeast Asia or reclaim land in the hilly interior or along the coast. Unfortunately, we know little about how the emigrant communities evaluated their options or organized their networks. Nor do we know much about the comparative magnitude of the various streams of migration or how specific events affected the timing of movement. It seems likely that in the eighteenth century the stream of migrants going to Taiwan was the largest; it certainly was larger than the number going to Southeast Asia. See, e.g., Viraphol 1977: 333; Freedman 1979: 62; and Blusse 1986: 85.

8. *TWFC*:Chou: 325–26, 349; *CHTTWSL*: 30; *HMC*: 105.

9. Fu 1966: 1.61, 2.494; Mancall 1968: 88; Viraphol 1977: 55–57, 84–85, 287.

10. Fu 1966: 1.122–23; Viraphol 1977: 55–56; Ng 1983: 186–90. Concern for state security was especially high at this time because of the advanced age of the emperor and the succession crisis that was demoralizing the bureaucracy (Wills 1979: 232–33; S. Wu 1979: 185).

11. Chuang Chin-te 1964: 3.

12. Ibid. *KHSL*: 167–68; *HMC*: 106. *HMC*: 106 gives the date as 1719 (KH 58).

13. *TAHLPC*: 236; Wills 1979: 233. This policy paralleled the 1717 maritime ban, which called on Chinese traders living abroad to return immediately to China. The court saw those who stayed abroad too long as a potential source of disturbance and threatened them with punishment if they delayed their return (Fu 1966: 1.157–59, 193, 2.515; Viraphol 1977: 56; Ng 1983: 198).

14. Ho Ping-ti 1959: 152; Purcell 1965: 36; Freedman 1979: 62.

15. Wills 1979: 232–33.

16. This summary account of the Chu I-kuei rebellion is drawn primarily from Lan 1958*b*: 1–8 and secondarily from Huang Shu-ching 1957: 85–93, the revised Feng-shan gazetteer (*CHFSHC*: 272–77), and the Veritable Records (*KHSL*: 174). Lan's account accords with the confessions of Chu and Tu Chün-ying (*TAHLCC*: 2–3, 18–19). I know of no careful modern attempt to reconstruct the course of the rebellion, which would require reconciling several accounts and identifying numerous place-names. Studies of Chu I-kuei have been retarded by Ming restorationist and Heaven and Earth Society fictions (see Croizier 1977: 66–67).

17. Tu Chün-ying was 55 in 1721 and had come to Taiwan in 1707 from Haiyang county in Ch'ao-chou (*TAHLCC*: 18). There appears to have been some prior communication between the two bands through one Yen Tzu-ching, who, though considered by both Tu and Chu to be Tu's confederate (ibid.: 33, 19), had been active in the formation of Chu's band (ibid.: 8, 11).

18. Auxiliaries from these villages were called up in 1684 and 1699 (see Chapter 5).

19. The payment of bounties similarly led to murders and the re-escalation of the Ta-chia-hsi revolt of 1731–32 (see Chapter 5).

20. A separate incident in which plains aborigines from Hsin-kang engaged in looting in Tainan and were massacred by the inhabitants is noted in Huang Shu-ching 1975: 86, *TWFC*:Liu: 489, and *CHFSHC*: 273, but not in Lan 1958*b*. These events suggest a general breakdown of order and the boiling over of plains aborigine resentments.

21. Ironically this benefited the government by denying the rebels any means of spreading the revolt across the strait.

22. Lan (1958*b*: 97) mentions the assistance rendered by the plains aborigines of Pei-t'ou *she* in resisting rebels in Tan-shui.

23. *TWFC*:Fan: 627–29.

24. *KHSL*: 175.

25. Hummel 1943–44: 440.

26. Chuang Chin-te 1964: 3.

27. Lan 1958*b*: 51–52.

28. *YCCPYC*: 142–43.

29. Chuang Chin-te 1964: 4.

30. *KCTYC*: 11.123 (YC 6.8.18).

31. Viraphol 1977: 70–71, 84; Ng 1983: 194–98.

32. Chuang Chin-te 1964: 5; Lan 1958*b*: 68.

33. *HMC*: 106; *CHTTWSL*: 30.

34. Lan 1958*b*: 61–64.

35. Hummel 1943–44: 440.

36. *TAHLIC*: 21; Chuang Chin-te 1964: 6.

37. *TWFC*:Yü: 123, 369; *TWFC*:Fan: 3–4. Despite the influx of population, the unbalanced sex ratio persisted. Two criminal cases involving murder and homosexuality were reported in 1743 (*TAHLCC*: 177–90).

38. *KCTYC*: 21.361–62 (YC 11.4.5); *TAHLPC*: 227.

39. Chuang Chin-te 1964: 9.

40. *CLSL*: 38–39.

41. Chuang Chin-te 1964: 9–11; *CLSL*: 49–50.

42. Chuang Chin-te 1964: 11.

43. Ibid.: 13, 17, 50.

44. In 1754, the emperor had also relaxed the ban on overseas Chinese merchants' returning to Fukien (Fu 1966: 1.193).

45. Chuang Chin-te 1964: 13.

46. Ibid.: 16.

47. *TAHLPC*: 241–44.

48. Chuang Chin-te 1964: 18–19.

49. In 1776, the families of officials were for the first time since the Chu I-kuei rebellion allowed unconditionally to accompany them to Taiwan (Kuo T'ing-i 1954: 100). The court had prohibited this in 1721 (*TWFC*:Fan: 99; *TAHLCC*: 36). The prohibition apparently was adopted because of the role the relatives of the Feng-shan magistrate had played in causing the Chu I-kuei rebellion (*CHTWHC*: 554). After 1734 an exception was made for officials beyond forty years of age who lacked male heirs (*TWFC*:Fan: 100).

50. Chuang Chin-te 1964: 40–42.

51. Ibid.: 44.

52. Ibid.: 46; see also Chapter 10.

53. Chuang Chin-te 1964: 45; *CTPT*: 1011.

54. Chuang Chin-te 1964: 48.

55. Han Tsung was charged with extorting 37,584 *yüan* while serving as magistrate in Tan-shui and in the port of Tainan. Chiao Ch'ang-fa, who had served as Tan-shui magistrate and as the subprefect of aboriginal affairs in the port of Lukang, was charged with extorting 17,334 *yüan* (ibid.: 50).

56. *TAHLPC*: 232.

57. Skinner 1987: 68. Skinner's careful analysis of the Ch'ing population-reporting system, which shows how it could produce exaggerated numbers as well as undercounts, is required reading for all who would use these reports. The following is a summary of my more extensive evaluation of Fukien and Taiwan *pao chia* population reports; see Shepherd 1988*c*.

58. *KCTCL*: 16.102–3.

59. Ho Ping-ti 1959: 38–39.

60. *CHTTWSL*: 38.

61. Wang Yeh-chien 1986: 84–87; on the 1829 figures, see below and Shepherd 1988*c*. Ch'en K'ung-li's (1990: 81–88) estimates match those adopted here.

62. Of this 534,157 hectares, 278,190 hectares (52 percent) were classified as paddy; 150,456 hectares of paddy (28 percent of the total cultivated area) were classified as irrigated and drained (JCRR: 11; S. C. Hsieh and T. H. Lee 1966: 49). Lee Teng-hui (1971: 36–37) gives slightly different estimates of total cultivated, paddy, and irrigated acreage.

63. Perkins 1969: 16–17.

64. Lee Teng-hui (1971: 36) estimates that "200 man days and 100 animal days were required for reclaiming one hectare of land."

65. See also Ng 1983: 103.

66. Note that a lower person/land ratio would require a proportionally greater cultivated area and make the higher population estimates even more implausible.

67. S. C. Hsieh and T. H. Lee 1966: 50; JCRR: 23; Lee Teng-hui 1971: 37; Samuel Ho 1978: 17, 60, 357. Lee Teng-hui (1971: 33) cites estimates of a yield of 1 MT of brown rice per hectare under the Dutch (see Ao et al. 1954: 45–47) and 1.3 MT by 1895.

68. Perkins 1969: 14–17.

69. In 1717 the Chu-lo gazetteer estimated yields of 60–70 *shih* of grain on one *chia* of the highest-grade paddy, and 30–40 *shih* of grain on one *chia* of the lowest-grade paddy (*CLHC*: 87). A yield of 70 *shih* of unhulled grain equals 35 *shih* of milled rice (volume is reduced 50 percent by milling) or 2.898 MT (1 *shih* of milled rice equals 82.81 kg); the yield of 30 *shih* equals 15 *shih* of milled rice or 1.242 MT. The low-grade paddy yield compares well with the yield range (1.0–1.3 MT/hectare) I use in estimating average yield for total cultivated area (paddy and dry land). On measures of land and grain, see Appendix C. An estimate from the late 1780's (setting the rent schedule on military colony land) stated that first-grade paddy would produce 80 *shih* of grain per *chia* (*CTPT*: 1042), or 3.312 MT of milled rice per hectare.

70. Perkins (1969: 14, 17) estimates a 1770 yield of 1.52 MT of unhusked grain per hectare, which (because weight is reduced by "15 to 20%" by milling [Ch'üan and Kraus 1975: 93]) gives a range of 1.22–1.29 MT of rice per hectare. I use Perkins's assumption that two catties equal a kilogram to convert his yield data to MT.

71. Wang Yeh-chien (1986: 88) cites modern studies as well as Ch'ing estimates that put annual rice consumption per person at 2.5 *shih* or 203 kg. Using this per capita consumption figure would expand the cultivated acreage necessary to support a population of one million to an even higher range of 156,154 to 203,000 hectares. Samuel Ho's lower figure of 133.7 kg is for 1910 Taiwan. Ho (1978: 94, 312, 357) estimates for 1910 Taiwan an annual per capita *production* of rice of only 188.6 kg that is consistent with yields of 1.3 MT per hectare but that would make consumption of 203 kg per capita impossible (without imports, and they did not occur). Ch'ing soldiers received a rice allowance of 0.3 *shih* per month or 3.6 *shih* a year. This yields 298 kg a year, well above even Wang Yeh-chien's estimate. Using per capita consumption figures as a proxy for estimating the minimum production needed for domestic consumption should yield conserva-

tive estimates of cultivated acreage. Of course, total production must exceed consumption, since it must fund (the overlapping categories of) seed grain, rental and tax payments, and export sales (see Lee Teng-hui 1971: 72). Rice consumption in Taiwan was supplemented by many other foods, especially sweet potatoes.

72. Wang Yeh-chien 1986: 91; Ng 1983: 117, 131.

73. *TWFC*:Yü: 723.

74. See Ch'üan and Kraus 1975: 98, 212.

75. Ng 1983: 133. One catty equals 0.59682 kg.

76. Lee Teng-hui 1971: 38; JCRR: 47; S. C. Hsieh and T. H. Lee 1966: 55. Varieties of sugarcane vary both in yield of cane per hectare and in percentage of sugar content.

77. The estimated area under sugarcane cultivation is considerably less than the estimated 92,000 *chia* of dry fields under cultivation (at least twice the 46,000 *chia* of dry fields registered for taxation by 1762; see Table 6.5). Ng (1983: 104) erroneously assumes that all land registered for taxation in the "dry" category was devoted to the cultivation of sugar. In fact much dry land was devoted to rice, wheat, barley, and sweet potatoes; even in 1903 at least 30 percent of the rice crop area was not irrigated (*CLHC*: 193; S. C. Hsieh and T. H. Lee 1966: 49; JCRR: 11, 23). If all of Taiwan's dry fields (73 percent of total registered acreage) had been devoted to sugar, there would not have been sufficient rice acreage left to feed the population, let alone supply exports.

78. If annual sugar consumption was 4.5 kg per person as it was in 1911 (Samuel Ho 1978: 98), then a population of a million would consume only 4,500 MT, an amount too small to affect our cultivated acreage estimates.

79. Ibid.: 48, 356. For the importance of sweet potatoes as a supplemental staple in eighteenth-century Fukien and Taiwan, see *CLHC*: 198; Rawski 1972: 51; Ng 1983: 21, 131.

80. Samuel Ho 1978: 312, 357. Although I know of no evidence suggesting that sweet potato yields changed from the eighteenth to the twentieth century, it is likely that sweet potato cultivation was more intensive and sweet potato consumption higher in the more crowded conditions of 1901–10 than in 1750.

81. Ho Ping-ti 1959: 43–45, 47–48, 53; Skinner 1987: 68.

82. From 1773 to 1777, the reported population of Taiwan increased from 765,721 to 839,803, and Fukien's reported population (including Taiwan) increased from 8,158,249 to 11,506,081 (*KCTCL*: 33.411, 40.818–19). The comparison is made for the years 1773 and 1777 because of gaps in the reporting series for the intervening years.

83. For these regulations, see Shepherd 1988*c*.

84. Ho Ping-ti 1959: 56; Bielenstein 1987: 125. Liang Fang-chung (1980: 400) cites yet another figure of 1,748,000 given for the population of Taiwan in the 1812 (Chia-ch'ing 17) Institutes (*hui tien*). This number contradicts the 1811 and 1824 figures (could it be the source of the 1824 figure?), and there is no evidence that it is not also fabricated.

85. The leading students of Taiwan's history (Inō Yoshinori, Lien Heng, Ch'en Shao-hsing) have all accepted the 1811 figure, despite its obvious demographic implausibilities, apparently because it was the only figure available to them between 1684 and 1893 (Inō 1928: 2.238; Lien Heng 1977: 124–26; Ch'en Shao-hsing 1964: 159–60). They did not have access to the figures for the late eigh-

teenth century now available from the Ch'ing archives. However, it is curious that none of them seems to have been aware of or to have evaluated the *Chia-ch'ing i t'ung chih* figure, though it should have been easily accessible to them. The acceptance of the high 1811 figure forced Ch'en Shao-hsing to attribute an implausibly high rate of annual growth during the long period from 1680 to 1811 (2.2 percent) and an implausibly low rate (0.3 percent) and a Malthusian crisis to the balance of the nineteenth century (Ch'en Shao-hsing 1964: 164–66). It also led him to underestimate the contribution continuing migration from Fukien made to Taiwan's population in the nineteenth century, which was particularly marked in the tea-growing areas of northern Taiwan. Also frequently cited in the literature is a figure given by Lien Heng (1977: 124) from the *Fu-chien t'ung chih* of 3.2 million for Taiwan's population in 1887. This figure, in addition to being implausible in light of the 1893 figure and succeeding Japanese censuses, is apparently without any basis. Nor can it be salvaged by accepting exaggerated numbers of refugee emigrants in the wake of Japanese conquest (which probably include fleeing troops briefly garrisoned in Taiwan and never included in census figures; see Lamley 1973: 252); the close agreement of the 1893 and 1896 figures mentioned in the text further indicates the implausibility of a large number of emigrants in 1895 (Ch'en Shao-hsing 1964: 162). Summary accounts of the growth of Taiwan's population by Ho Ping-ti (1959: 164–65), Samuel Ho (1978: 10–11), and J. Meskill (1979: 43) based on the earlier studies accept both the 1811 and the 1887 figures that I reject here.

86. Ch'en Shao-hsing 1964: 160–62.
87. Barclay 1954: 13.
88. Shih Lang 1958: 66–69.
89. Ts'ao 1954*a*: 81.
90. *TWFC*:Kao: 250–51.
91. Yü 1959: 31.
92. Ng 1983: 133.
93. Wang Shih-ch'ing 1958*a*: 18.
94. *TWFC*:Chou: 323–24; *CLHC*: 276–77; Wang Shih-ch'ing 1958*b*: 14.
95. Chang Wei 1978: 65–66.
96. Ch'en Shao-hsing 1964: 130. Spence (1966: 109–16) gives an account of the operation of rice price stabilization measures under K'ang-hsi. Regular reports of rice prices and harvest conditions were submitted to the emperor from every province.
97. Ch'en Shao-hsing 1964: 130; Huang Shu-ching 1957: 51; Wang Shih-ch'ing 1958*a*: 19.
98. *YCSL*: 15; Viraphol 1977: 76.
99. *YCSL*: 28, 32; *TAHLPC*: 173–74; Wang Shih-ch'ing 1958*a*: 27. See Chapter 8.
100. As Ng (1983: 195–96) points out, Kao also criticized the parochial viewpoint of opponents of more liberal rice export policies. The advocates of strict regulation were ignoring the needs of the southeast coast while they focused narrowly on the Taiwan situation. Kao suggested that those responsible for local order and stable rice prices in Taiwan were putting their official careers ahead of the interests of the larger region, a problem the court had met with in overcoming opposition to interprovincial grain trade in other parts of the empire.
101. *YCCPYC*: 103–4; Wang Shih-ch'ing 1958*a*: 19.
102. Ng 1983: 104; Ch'en Ch'i-nan 1987: 69.
103. Ng (1983: 116, 165) argues that rice prices in Taiwan in the 1720's remained both "stable and lower than that of southern Fukien, indicating the

abundance of rice supplies," and that price rises in Taiwan resulted from speculation and increased mainland demand rather than from supply shortages. Wang Yeh-chien (1986: 99, 105) draws similar conclusions from price data for 1746–56.

104. Ch'üan and Kraus 1975: 66–67; Ng 1983: 196.

105. Fu 1966: 1.157–59; Viraphol 1977: 70, 88, 94. In 1727 Fukien's Hsing-Ch'üan circuit intendant was moved to Amoy as part of the plan to reopen trade (banned since 1717); the Taiwan-Amoy intendant's duties were accordingly restricted to Taiwan (*YCSL*: 18; see also Ng 1983: 65–66). Fukien at this time was beginning to receive shipments of low-priced Thai rice (Viraphol 1977: 85, 294).

106. Ng 1983: App. A, 128.

107. Wang Yeh-chien 1986: 94, 99–100, 102. The averages are obtained from the chart on p. 100 (where the set of Taiwan data is mislabeled "Fu-chou" [lower box]) and reduced by the December index on p. 102.

108. Ch'en Shao-hsing 1964: 129.

109. *CLSL*: 23. This led to a disturbance in Ch'ao-chou (*CLSL*: 23–25).

110. *TWFC*:Yü: 722–23; Wang Shih-ch'ing 1958*a*: 20.

111. Chuang Chin-te 1965: 61–63. In the fall of 1745, a bad harvest in Fukien put pressure on Fukien officials to find supplies of rice. The Fukien governor devised a plan to buy a large amount of grain in Taiwan, which the emperor approved. The Fukien governor also memorialized on the corrupt practices of Taiwan local officials in charge of rice purchases. The governor proposed sending commissioners from Fukien to make the purchases. The Taiwan censors then memorialized that such purchases would overburden Taiwan's own supplies. These conflicting reports tried the emperor's patience. In 1747, the new governor of Fukien investigated the situation and confirmed the need to ensure Taiwan's own supplies (ibid.: 63–66).

112. *TWFC*:Yü: 243–44; *CLSL*: 107–8; *TAHLPC*: 174, 176–77; Viraphol 1977: 84–88.

113. Although I doubt there was an absolute decline in grain exports in these years, there may have been a decline in the proportion of the harvest exported. Two explanations seem possible. Per capita productivity may have declined temporarily as virgin land lost some of its fertility and before irrigation works were developed. Or perhaps a growing division of labor within Taiwan meant that processed goods and handicrafts formerly imported were now being produced locally by a work force consuming home-grown rice. Ch'üan and Kraus (1975: 77–78) note a decline in the interregional rice trade after 1730 in Hunan (cf. Skinner 1977*b*: 713*n*30).

114. Wang Yeh-chien (1986: 91) and Ng Chin-keong (1983: 117, 131) cite approvingly the censors' 1742 estimate that Taiwan was exporting at least 800,000 *shih* of unhusked rice per year to the southeast coast (see *TWFC*:Yü: 723).

115. *CLSL*: 30; *CHTTWSL*: 76; Viraphol 1977: 92.

116. *CLSL*: 61; Wang Shih-ch'ing 1958*a*: 21.

117. *TAHLPC*: 171–76.

118. Viraphol 1977: 94. In the early Ch'ien-lung years, several measures benefited foreign trade at Amoy (and Canton). In 1736 and 1738, the customs taxes were reduced (Fu 1966: 1.169, 170). In 1742, the court decided not to prohibit the Java trade, despite the desire of some officials to retaliate for the Dutch massacre of Chinese in Java the year before (Fu 1966: 1.172–74). In 1747 Spaniards were

allowed to trade at Amoy (also in 1755; Fu 1966: 1.182–83, 197). And in 1754, the prohibition on the return of Chinese merchants living in Southeast Asia was lifted (Fu 1966: 1.193). The restriction of the European-American trade to Canton in 1757 did not disrupt Amoy's Southeast Asian junk trade (Ng 1983: 58–59; Leonard 1984: 61, 74).

119. Viraphol 1977: 118, 201; see also Davidson 1903: 445.

120. See Beattie 1979 and Perdue 1987 for the development during the eighteenth century of rice export economies in the middle Yangtze region oriented toward the rice-deficit Lower Yangtze. Immigration and reclamation in these Han-dominated areas were not subject to quarantine restrictions. Bridgman (1838: 418) adds another way in which coastal Fukien was dependent on Taiwan: "Many parts of the opposite shore in Fuhkeen are so barren, that without the aid of the oil-cakes from Formosa, used in manuring the sandy hills, even the sweet potato would not be produced." Oil-cakes were commonly made from pressed seeds of sesame, turnip, and other plants (Sung Ying-hsing 1966: 6).

121. Ng 1983: 217.

122. *TAHLPC*: 74.

123. The high wages ("three times" those of the mainland) noted in the Chu-lo gazetteer of 1717 (*CLHC*: 149), were still high ("double") in the late Yung-cheng years (Ng 1983: 41). Taiwan enjoyed a reputation for a high standard of living in those years (Ng 1983: 105).

124. *TWHC*: 57, 60; Lu 1965. On the spatial distribution of Hakka settlement, see Chapter 10 and Shih T'ien-fu 1987.

125. *TWHC*: 56; *TWFC*:Chou: 323.

126. *YCCPYC*: 43–44; *FCTCTWF*: 156.

127. Ch'en Ch'iu-k'un 1975: 57–59.

128. *CLHC*: 146, 149.

129. On land-saving technologies, see Hayami and Ruttan 1985: 73–75, 124, 310–11; see also Elvin 1973: 211–12.

130. See, e.g., Wang Sung-hsing 1972 on the Pa Pao Chün irrigation system and gazetteer sections listing irrigation works, e.g., *CLHC*: 34–42.

131. See Chapter 8 for a further discussion of land registration.

132. *TWFC*:Chou: 323; Thompson 1964: 187.

133. *CLHC*: 110, 298.

134. See Huang Shu-ching 1957: 128–29, 134; and Chapters 5 and 7.

135. *CLHC*: 110; Shih T'ien-fu 1990.

136. *CLHC*: 118, 287; Yü 1959: 22.

137. *CLHC*: 30–31, 111, 288; *TTTCS*: 2.

138. *CLHC*: 30; *TWFC*:Liu: 79; *TWFC*:Yü: 73. The prefectural gazetteer of 1768 (*TWFC*:Yü: 73) actually lists only 66 villages, but 22 of these are new.

139. *TWFC*:Fan: 69; *TWFC*:Yü: 75. In counting villages, one must remember that one village may be twice the size of another and still count as only one village. Unfortunately, the village lists for the southern counties are not comparable across gazetteers and do not permit us to document in this way the expansion of Han settlement taking place there.

140. *CLHC*: 29–32; *TWFC*:Liu: 78–85; *TWFC*:Yü: 72–90.

141. Some caution is required in using market counts since the county gazetteers used criteria that seem quite idiosyncratic in compiling some of the early

lists. The Chu-lo county gazetteer of 1717 (*CLHC*: 28–32) lists nearly as many markets (23) as it does Han settlements (26), underlining both the loose criteria it used to designate markets (the 1740 gazetteer drops six of these from its list; they reappear in 1768) and the additional role of markets (especially the northern ones in areas where the Han population was sparse) in the aborigine trade (76 aborigine settlements are listed). The late K'ang-hsi gazetteers for T'ai-wan (1720) and Feng-shan (1719) counties give similarly inflated lists of markets (cf. *CLHC*: 32; *TWHC*: 90–92; and *FSHC*: 26–27). The prefectural gazetteer of 1694 (*TWFC*:Kao: 39, 48) lists a single market for all of Chu-lo (at Mu-chia-liu-wan) and 23 Han settlements, ten of which had only one or two decimal security units (*chia*). Markets specializing in aborigine trade are mentioned in early Ch'ien-lung years for mountainous areas near Shui-sha-lien (*TAHLPC*: 295) and for A-li-kang in Feng-shan (near the Wu-lou tribal settlement) (*CHFSHC*: 32). Hsiao-lung and Hsin-kang-tzu markets in Chu-lo county, just north of Tainan, specialized in trade between civilized aborigines and Han (*TWFC*:Yü: 87). On these communities, see also *NPPW*: 144–45, 422–25, 428–29.

142. Skinner 1977c.

143. The 1761–64 population figures are not wholly reliable since they come from a period of yamen fabrication of *pao chia* reports (see above). We might also expect the remote Tan-shui frontier to be comparatively underreported.

144. The number of markets and streets in Tainan grew substantially in the early eighteenth century (Ng 1983: 111). A noncomparability similar to that between markets arises for village totals. Chang-hua in 1768 has twice as many markets for the same number of villages as Tan-shui, but we can be sure that Chang-hua's population was more than twice as large, as a glance at the registered land figures in Table 6.5 confirms. The obvious care that must be taken in interpreting gazetteer market data should serve as a caveat to those using them without benefit of close temporal series that allow checking for consistency.

145. Ch'en Cheng-hsiang 1959–61: 2.536–37; DeGlopper 1980: 161. DeGlopper gives an excellent review of the state of transportation in Ch'ing Taiwan.

146. Crissman (1972: 253–54) emphasizes another factor behind Taiwan's marketing pattern. Frequent civil disturbances and feuding impeded the development of small periodic markets. Instead villages relied on itinerants (who bought safe passage) for small-scale trading and services.

147. DeGlopper 1980: 146–47. This pattern by which grain was hauled by oxcart to streams and rivers where it went by raft and small boat to coastal ports for shipping to Tainan and from there to Amoy is described in memorials discussing the need for grain transport subsidies (*TAHLPC*: 172; *TWFC*:Yü: 243) and by Ng Chin-keong (1983: 105–11).

148. I have been unable to locate three of the market towns listed for Chu-lo in 1740 and six in 1768. I have been unable to locate one of the towns listed for Chang-hua in 1768. In 1768, seven markets were listed for the city of Chu-lo, four for the city of Chang-hua, and two for the port of Pen-kang.

149. Maps of the spread of Han agricultural settlement, most of them based on data compiled by Inō (1928: 3.386–90; see also Ch'en Shao-hsing 1964: 151–54) can be found in Chou Hsien-wen 1957: 15–18, Ch'en Cheng-hsiang 1959–61: 1.31, and Chang Ch'i-yün 1962: B43. They are all somewhat impressionistic.

150. See C. Smith 1976: 36–37, 47–49, for a description of this generic pattern based on the literature in economic geography.

CHAPTER SEVEN

1. Skinner 1977c: 308.

2. For the conversion from the Cheng to the Ch'ing territorial administration, see Chapter 5. For a brief treatment of the educational bureaucracy and the administration of the examination system, see below.

3. Minor adjustments were made in the boundaries of T'ai-wan county in 1731 and 1734 (*CHTWHC*: 28).

4. *Hsün chien* had primarily police duties; *hsien ch'eng* acted as police commissioners in their subdistricts (Ch'ü 1962: 8–9, 12).

5. Watt 1972: 15.

6. See *CHTTWSL*: 13–14; Chang T'an 1970*b*: 22–23. Experienced officials who served in Taiwan were guaranteed promotion if they completed their terms of office without a misstep. Jurisdictions with three of the possible four post designations—frequented (trade center, *ch'ung*, C), troublesome (busy yamen, *fan*, F), wearisome (unremunerative, *p'i*, P), and difficult (insecure locale, *nan*, N)—were rated important (Watt 1972: 46–47, 1977: 358; Skinner 1977c: 314–15). Skinner (1977c: 317–18) discovered that a substantial number of two-character posts, most frequently those designated F *and* N, were also rated important (had an additional "secret" strategic designation) and were therefore assigned to experienced officials instead of Board-appointed novices. The court appears to have assigned this strategic component to Taiwan's counties, for they are unlikely to have warranted the number of post designations required for special appointments. No Register of Officials (*Chin shen ch'üan shu*) is available for the late seventeenth or early eighteenth centuries to test this hypothesis, but it receives support from the post designations for 1773 (see below). Reflecting the influence of the neglect school of Taiwan historiography, Meskill (1979: 31, 36–37) argues that Taiwan was governed by officials of lower than average caliber.

7. Skinner 1977c: 306, 312, 321.

8. Ibid.: 307.

9. Chou Hsien-wen 1957: 58; cf. Ch'ü 1962: 9. Ng (1983: 63–64) asserts that the coastal defense subprefect in Amoy was a subordinate of the Ch'üan-chou prefect rather than the Taiwan-Amoy intendant.

10. Skinner 1977c: 334. In financial and legal matters, the intendant and prefect were also subordinates of the provincial financial commissioner and provincial judge. These two officials reported directly to the Board of Revenue and Board of Punishments, respectively, and thereby "enjoyed an independent position vis-à-vis the governor general and governor," at least before 1850 (Ho Ping-ti 1959: 66).

11. *KHSL*: 136; Li Ju-ho 1970: 13.

12. *TWHC*: 108; *CLHC*: 115; *KHSL*: 138; Shih Lang 1958: 61–62.

13. The Ch'ing army of the Green Standard was recruited from hereditary garrisons planted at strategic points throughout the eighteen provinces. No law of avoidance prevented Ch'ing military officers from serving in their native

locality (see Chapter 10). In the provinces, the Manchu Banner forces were concentrated in seven strategic cities, including Fukien's capital, Foochow. The banners served as a check on the ethnically Chinese Green Standard forces, which, while more numerous, were widely, though not evenly, distributed in small units to provide for local security (Kessler 1976: 105, 107–10; see also Appendix D). For a detailed account of the Ch'ing military in Taiwan, see Hsü Hsüeh-chi 1987. The significant role of the military in the Ch'ing political economy remains the most neglected field of Ch'ing history; see Introduction.

14. Li Ju-ho 1970: 15.

15. *HMC*: 84; Hsü Hsüeh-chi 1987: 4. Wade (1851: 374) suggests he was also subordinate to the Manchu general-in-chief (*chiang chün*) in Foochow.

16. Skinner 1977*a*: 19–21.

17. Skinner's presentation (1977*a*: 18–21) obscures this point because his basis of comparison is different. He points out that counties were created on peripheries at lower than expected rates *if* one expected that per capita administrative services remained constant across dynasties and the total number of counties was allowed to increase. My comparison follows Skinner by accepting that the total number of counties does not increase and then asks how those counties will be distributed with regard to population and administrative area across densely populated cores and sparsely populated peripheries (in accord with Skinner 1977*c*: 312). When Skinner (1977*c*: 345) argues that the strategy was to minimize county areas along peripheries, he is not suggesting that the county areas actually achieved in peripheries were smaller than those in cores. The point is that the areas peripheral counties encompassed were smaller than the areas that would contain the average county population. The confusion stems from collapsing the two independent dimensions of population and territory.

18. Skinner 1977*c*: 312. A comparison of the population and area of Taiwan's counties with the average county population and average county area for China as a whole, and for mainland Fukien, demonstrates that Taiwan's counties were, as predicted, larger in area and smaller in population than those in China and mainland Fukien; see Appendix D.

19. A crude comparison of the military presence in Taiwan shows that the density of soldiers was much greater in Taiwan than in China, whether measured by area or population (see Appendix D). Taiwan's soldiers had, on average, smaller areas per man to patrol and defend, even when the high mountain territory is included, and much smaller if only the plains areas are considered. Not all points, however, were evenly defended. The spatial distribution of troops was highly uneven, with large concentrations around strategic centers (see text). The difference in the ratio of civilian population to soldiers between China and Taiwan is particularly striking: in 1700 Taiwan had 7.6 times the number of soldiers per population; in 1735 the ratio was 5.6, and in 1777 it was 3.8. Appendix D also reveals the large military presence in mainland Fukien, which was greater than average for China, as both square kilometers per soldier and population per soldier indicate. The figure for square kilometers per soldier was even less in Fukien than it was in Taiwan, if the calculation is based on gross area.

20. See Wang Yeh-chien 1973: 18, 101; Wang does not, however, analyze the pattern of military expenditures. The argument here is developed to apply to

sparsely populated strategic peripheries. Coastal Fukien, a strategic periphery and a densely populated regional core, was able to contribute much more to defense expenses (see Skinner 1977*c*: 332).

21. Elvin 1973: 97. Thus, all three of Taiwan's major eighteenth-century revolts, the Chu I-kuei rebellion in 1721, the double revolt of aborigines and Han in 1731–32, and the Lin Shuang-wen rebellion in 1786–88, were suppressed only with troops dispatched from Amoy.

22. The Ch'ing also attempted to exert direct control over settlers by requiring them to register in *pao chia* units, where they were subject to collective guarantees. Periodic attempts to extend the *pao chia* and tighten its enforcement in Taiwan were often made in conjunction with the attempts to tighten restrictions on immigration (see Chapter 6) or to redraw boundaries and conduct land surveys (see Chapter 9).

23. *CLHC*: 110–13.

24. Proposals that cost little or were self-financing were much more likely to win approval from a state that abhorred increasing expenditures that reduced central government revenues. The late imperial state expected its local administrative units to be financially self-sufficient (preferably contributing to the revenue of higher levels of government) and not rely on subsidies from higher levels of government (see Wang Yeh-chien 1973: 18; R. Huang 1974: 175–82; and Zelin 1984: 1–12; see also Chapter 8).

25. The essay goes on to assert that the miasmatic (malarial) and unhealthy conditions of the Taiwan frontier should present no obstacle: "For just as Fukien and eastern Kwangtung have been opened since the Sung and Yüan dynasties in spite of miasma, so will Taiwan be opened. As settlers clear the frontier, insects, snakes, and noxious influences will be eradicated. With sanitation and medicine there need be no anxiety about the environment" (*CLHC*: 113).

26. *CLHC*: 120–21; see also 51.

27. Lan 1958*b*: 30.

28. Ibid.: 54.

29. Ibid.: 31–32, 62, 72. Lan's arguments stress the benefit of colonization to the government rather than to settlers; for Lan fostering government control (and its civilizing influence) also justifies disappropriating aborigines.

30. Ibid.: 56.

31. *CHFSHC*: 361.

32. Huang Shu-ching 1957: 134.

33. Lan 1958*b*: 54.

34. Kuo T'ing-i 1954: 98.

35. Huang Shu-ching 1957: 167.

36. Ibid.: 112; Thompson 1969: 78.

37. Lan 1958*a*: 40.

38. Chuang Chin-te 1966*b*: 6–7.

39. Lan 1958*a*: 40–41. Ten *ch'ien* equal one tael.

40. For the removal of aborigine land from the tax registers in 1722, see Chapter 9.

41. Kuo T'ing-i 1954: 99; Lan 1958*a*: 33; Chuang Chin-te 1966*b*: 6–7.

42. *CHFSHC*: 11; Huang Shu-ching 1957: 167.

43. Mancall 1971: 116. See Waldron's reassessment of the Chinese wall-building tradition and the analogy in Ming policy between maritime closure and the debate over Mongol border policy (1990: 174–78).

44. Ho Ping-ti 1959: 158–59; R. Lee 1970: 6.

45. See below and Appendix D for a discussion of the comparative territorial size of Taiwan's counties and how the boundary policy attempted to limit the territory Taiwan's magistrates were required to administer.

46. By no means do I consider the dynamics of these fluctuating policies to be unique to the Taiwan or even Chinese frontiers. They also typified the American frontier; see Appendix F.

47. On the Manchurian frontier, a military government operating from garrison towns also preceded civil rule (R. Lee 1970: 60, 72–73).

48. *CLHC*: 110; *TWFC*:Kao: 71, 73. *CLHC*: 121–22 says there was a total of 250 men in the coastal patrols.

49. Sheng 1953: 50; *CLHC*: 122, 125.

50. *CLHC*: 173, 280. See Chapter 5 for the 1699 aborigine disturbances.

51. *CLHC*: 115, 122–23.

52. *CLHC*: 110, 115–18, 125; *KHSL*: 158–59; this officer was also known as the Pa-li-fen *ch'ien tsung* (*CLHC*: 118).

53. Sheng 1953: 51; *KHSL*: 160, 161, 169–70.

54. For his successful defense, Tan-shui second captain Ch'en Ts'e was promoted to the office of Taiwan brigade general (*KHSL*: 171, 173; *TWFC*:Fan: 334).

55. Chuang Chin-te 1965: 53; *KHSL*: 175; Li Ju-ho 1970: 1, 15; *TAHLCC*: 3–5. See Chapter 8 for the high cost of the military establishment and the consequent gap between revenues and expenditures for Taiwan. A decision taken shortly after the Chu I-kuei rebellion to relocate the brigade general to the Pescadores (which remained under government control during the rebellion) was soon reversed (*KHSL*: 175, 178). Minor adjustments in the distribution of soldiers within Taiwan were made in 1723 (*YCSL*: 3).

56. Li Ju-ho 1970: 13–15; also *TWFC*:Fan: 304.

57. *KCTYC*: 16.774–75 (YC 8.8.10), 17.94–95 (YC 8.10.21). Another second captain, but no additional soldiers, was added to the Tan-shui battalion in early 1731 before the rebellions (*YCSL*: 37–38).

58. *TWFC*:Yü: 375. Before he got his plan adopted, Hao had first to defeat a plan that would have financed the addition of only 2,000 men to Taiwan's garrisons by reducing Fukien's cavalry by 930 men, which cost the same (*KCTYC*: 21.750 [YC 11.6.27]). As part of the reorganization, the Taiwan brigade general was given a seal (*kua yin*) that endowed him with broader than usual powers. This followed the model of the brigade generals on the frontiers of Shansi and Shensi (*TWFC*:Liu: 317; Hsü Hsüeh-chi 1987: 156). Before Hao's larger plan was approved, the Tan-shui battalion was put under a first captain (*tu ssu*) and another sub-lieutenant was added (*YCSL*: 42–44).

59. Li Ju-ho 1970: 14, 16; see also Chapter 10.

60. *TWFC*:Liu: 316–17, 320.

61. See, e.g., *CLSL*: 78.

62. *CLHC*: 29, 95; Huang Shu-ching 1957: 33; Wang Shih-ch'ing 1958*b*: 11. The Tan-shui granary founded in 1716 may have fallen quickly into disrepair, since the 1746 prefectural gazetteer lists no granaries in Tan-shui (*TWFC*:Fan: 65). By 1768 many granaries are listed in Tan-shui (*TWFC*:Yü: 69).

63. *CLHC*: 110.

64. Chou Hsien-wen 1957: 3.

65. *TWFC*:Kao: 50. The dispatch stations (*p'u*) were probably extended at the

same time the granaries mentioned earlier were founded in 1716. Each station was manned by three couriers (*p'u ping*) (*TWFC*:Liu: 342, *TWFC*:Fan: 93), who carried documents between officials and may have provided transport and travel services (Cheng Ying-wan 1970: 10, 18, 26; Ch'ü 1962: 61, 154). As we saw in Chapter 5, much of the porterage and oxcart services required by traveling officials were provided through the corvée on civilized aborigines (also Li Ju-ho 1970: 8).

66. After the Chu I-kuei rebellion, officials were prohibited from taking their families with them to Taiwan (*TWFC*:Fan: 99; see also note 49 to Chapter 6). The intendant lost his *ping pei* designation (which gave him the power to move troops) after he proved useless against the rebels. The intendant was again endowed with the power to move troops after 1767 and after the Lin Shuang-wen rebellion was given the right to directly memorialize the throne (*TWFC*:Yü: 126; Hsü Hsüeh-chi 1987: 188–89).

67. *KHSL*: 175; *TWFC*:Fan: 97; Chuang Chin-te 1965: 53. The censors were referred to as *hsün T'ai yü shih*. At about the same time, the court instituted a similar policy of dispatching inspecting censors to its Manchurian frontier (R. Lee 1970: 76).

68. *YCSL*: 3–4; *TWFC*:Liu: 80; *TWFC*:Fan: 40; *TWFC*:Yü: 119–20, 262.

69. The population estimate is based on the growth rate data presented in Table 6.4.

70. Ch'ü 1962: 2. Skinner's (1977*a*: 21) theory of core-county consolidation has yet to be tested by an analysis that identifies the locations of the counties consolidated and the new counties created in the Yung-cheng reign. The consolidation of counties took place after Chang-hua and Tan-shui were created; that these two revenue- and population-poor units were not abolished in this consolidation underlines the importance of the factors discussed in the text.

71. See Appendix D for evidence that Taiwan's counties remained larger than average in area and smaller than average in population at least through 1777.

72. For a discussion of these changes in Amoy, see Ng 1983: 61–67. Watt (1977: 359) notes that the Ch'ing government often conditioned the creation of a new post or the elevation of a post's classification on the abolition or demotion of another; the state thereby maintained both bureaucratic control and budgetary equilibrium. We have seen this affect the creation of counties; for another example of this principle at work in the creation of functionally specific posts, see Chapter 9. On the Pescadores, see *YCSL*: 18; *TWFC*:Fan: 98.

73. Chou Hsien-wen 1957: 3.

74. Skinner (1977*c*: 304–6, 321) has pointed to the strategic significance of the spatial distribution of subprefectures (*t'ing*) in the Ch'ing territorial administration (Skinner pays most attention to independent subprefectures, which were apparently not invented until the early nineteenth century [Ch'ü 1962: 2], but his analysis retains validity for earlier periods). *T'ing* were typically situated in the peripheral areas of peripheral prefectures (Skinner 1977*c*: 309), and Tan-shui fits that description. Skinner found that a narrower span of control, allowing greater access to channels of communication and closer supervision, and the use of more experienced magistrates characterized subprefectures placed on sparsely populated but strategically important frontiers. This does not, however, invalidate Brunnert and Hagelstrom's observation (1912: 426; *contra* Skinner 1977*c*: 322)

that subprefectures on the borders of the empire were likely to be transformed into ordinary prefectures. This was especially true for regions experiencing dramatic increases in Han population. Thus, in 1875 Tan-shui *t'ing* was raised to the status of a prefecture (T'ai-pei *fu*) and subdivided into three *hsien* and a *t'ing* (Wang Shih-ch'ing 1953: 11; Ch'en Cheng-hsiang 1959–61: 1.13). R. Lee (1970: 132, 136, 162) gives numerous similar examples for Manchuria. Skinner's analysis eliminated the dynamic frontiers of Manchuria and Taiwan from consideration and treated only static frontiers. Skinner's analysis also does not treat functionally specific subprefectural offices (e.g., aborigine affairs, *li fan t'ing*, and coastal defense, *hai fang t'ing*) whose jurisdictions overlapped those of the regular territorial administrative units. In this regard, see also Ng Chin-keong's (1983: 61–67) discussion of the administrative status of Amoy.

75. *CHTTWSL*: 10; *YCSL*: 36. As noted above, *hsün chien* had primarily police duties within their districts (Ch'ü 1962: 8). The posting of *hsün chien* to Mao-wu-su and the area north of Hou-lung was recommended as early as 1728 (YC 6.5.6) by the censors Hsia and Ho (*KCTYC*: 10.395–97).

76. Sheng 1953: 56; Lan 1958*b*: 61–62. Lan was angered that the subprefect had built offices at Sha-lu, in northern Chang-hua county, instead of at Chu-ch'ien.

77. *TWFC*:Yü: 60, 67; *TSTC*: 51. More yamen construction was going on in 1751 (*TAHLPC*: 153–54). In 1759 four gates and cannon towers were constructed, making Chu-ch'ien into a more proper administrative center (Sheng 1953: 56–57; Lamley 1977*b*: 158, 161).

78. *TWFC*:Fan: 57–58; Lan 1958*a*: 27–30, 1958*b*: 53; Lamley 1977*b*: 182–83; Chiang Tao-chang 1980: 135. Huang Shu-ching (1957: 87) noted that Tainan's accessibility to the sea (and the lack of walls) made it easy for government naval forces to retake it.

79. *YCSL*: 45–46; *TWFC*:Fan: 57–59; *KCTYC*: 23.259 (YC 12.6.28). Troops from Fukien suppressed both the Chu I-kuei rebellion in 1721 and the double revolt of 1731–32.

80. In 1747, after receiving a memorial reporting that the censors were abusing their authority and that their tours of inspection (which were the occasion of tremendous squeeze) were a cause of disruption in Taiwan, the Ch'ien-lung emperor considered eliminating the office. But in the end, it was decided their services were still needed because Taiwan was a "turbulent frontier across the seas" (Chuang Chin-te 1965: 67–69). When the censors failed to investigate and report on a serious Han-aborigine conflict in 1751 (see Chapter 9), the emperor decided that dispatching censors to Taiwan only once every three years would be sufficient (Chuang Chin-te 1965: 70–71). In 1765 another incident convinced the emperor that dispatching the censors rarely served any purpose, and he decided they should be dispatched only on special imperial order (Chuang Chin-te 1965: 72). In 1781 and 1782, the censors gave inadequate and contradictory reports on corruption in Taiwan and on the measures taken to apprehend the bandit Hung Lung (Chuang Chin-te 1965: 74; *CLSL*: 253–54).

81. Chuang Chin-te 1965: 53–54, 75. The tours of inspection of the censors sent to the frontier region of Manchuria were also reduced in frequency during the Ch'ien-lung reign, primarily because these tours were also occasions of great extortion (R. Lee 1970: 76).

82. *TWFC*:Yü: 66–67.

83. Watt 1972: 15.

84. The Registers of Officials (*Chin shen ch'üan shu*) for 1773, 1777, and 1785 give the following rankings and classifications (see note 6 to this chapter for the classification scheme):

a. Taiwan military intendant: preferment appointment (*t'i*), most important

b. Taiwan prefect: preferment appointment, important, CFN

c. T'ai-wan magistrate: transfer appointment (*tiao*), important, CFN, one assistant magistrate

d. Feng-shan magistrate: transfer appointment, important, FN (strategic component), one assistant magistrate, one subdistrict magistrate

e. Chu-lo magistrate: transfer appointment, important, FN, one assistant magistrate, two subdistrict magistrates

f. Chang-hua magistrate: transfer appointment, important, FN, one assistant magistrate, two subdistrict magistrates

g. Tan-shui subprefect: medium, two subdistrict magistrates

h. North route aborigine affairs subprefect: important

i. Coastal defense and south route aborigine affairs subprefect: important

j. P'eng-hu second-class subprefect: medium

Preferment and transfer appointments to "important" posts were nominated by governors from officials having at least five and three years experience, respectively (Watt 1972: 46). All posts in Taiwan are ranked important, with the exception of the subprefects of Tan-shui and P'eng-hu. Subprefectural posts were required to be filled only by previously experienced officials (ibid.: 47; Skinner 1977*c*: 321). The CFN post designation for T'ai-wan county recognizes Tainan's importance as a commercial center and revenue source as well as its strategic importance; the other counties are designated only FN, pointing to their security problems, and raised to "importance" by the addition of a "secret" strategic component, as predicted by Skinner (1977*c*: 315–17).

85. *CHHC*: 38.

86. *CTPT*: 958–59, 1011; *TSTC*: 51–52.

87. See Chapter 10.

88. For surveys of these institutions, see Ch'ü 1962 and Hsiao Kung-ch'uan 1960.

89. Skinner 1977*a*: 20–23, 1977*c*: 336–41. See also Shepherd 1989.

90. For these Ch'ing cultural policies, see Watt 1977 and Feuchtwang 1977.

91. On the prominence of Fukienese degree holders, see Ho Ping-ti 1962: 234–39, 249–51.

92. Elvin 1973: 92.

93. Kracke 1957; Ho Ping-ti 1962: 185–87.

94. Sun 1961: 209–10; Ch'ü 1962: 162; Ho Ping-ti 1962: 27–28, 35.

95. Ho Ping-ti 1962: 184–85.

96. Ibid.: 187–88.

97. *TWFC*:Yü: 340–42; *FCTCTWF*: 240, 249.

98. Ho Ping-ti 1962: 179, 183.

99. Chang Shih-ch'u 1954: 27–28.

100. *TWFC*:Yü: 340.

101. Compare *TWFC*:Kao: 324 (1694) and *TWFC*:Yü: 354–65 (1768).

102. *TWFC*:Yü: 457; Chang Shih-ch'u 1954: 29–30. In 1739 a petition to create a special Taiwanese quota for the *chin shih* degree was rejected; the petitioner was told to resubmit when the number of Taiwanese at the metropolitan exam reached ten (*TWFC*:Yü: 457). By the end of the eighteenth century, Taiwan had produced only three *chin shih*.

103. Compare Esherick 1987: 45–47. This discussion of military careers must unfortunately be brief; the gazetteers give no information about quotas or other details of the less prestigious military examination track.

CHAPTER EIGHT

1. Shih Lang 1958: 54–55.
2. *KHSL*: 126; *TWFC*:Fan: 612.
3. Shih Lang 1958: 61–62.
4. Ibid.: 66–69.
5. *CLHC*: 85; Cheng Hsi-fu 1974*a*: 104.
6. *TWFC*:Yü: 278–82; *CLHC*: 102.
7. *TWFC*:Yü: 267; *CLHC*: 100–101. The water-revenue taxes were collected by a harbor tax farmer (*p'u kang*) (*CLHC*: 96). In later years, miscellaneous taxes of all kinds proliferated, and corruption in their collection grew worse. In 1877 they were largely abolished (Chou Hsien-wen 1957: 106).
8. *CLHC*: 86–87; for land-tax rates, see Table 8.5.
9. Both the Chu-lo gazetteer of 1717 (*CLHC*: 87) and Huang Shu-ching in 1722 (*TWFC*:Yü: 241) cite 0.3 taels per *shih* of unhusked rice as the lowest price.
10. *TWFC*:Yü: 241.
11. Ibid.: 242. The gazetteer exaggerates the differences between Taiwan's land-tax system and that in the mainland. Taxes in kind and taxes on dry land were collected in other provinces (Ch'ü 1962: 140; Wang Yeh-chien 1973: 32). Calculating the tax in unhusked rice may have been unique, but the collection of the tax in unhusked rice was not. Much of the large amounts of unhusked rice stored in government granaries (Ch'üan and Kraus 1975: 33–35) came from tax collection rather than purchase. Paying taxes in unhusked rice saved peasants the expense of milling but added to the expense of transport and storage (Wang Yeh-chien 1973: 32).
12. Statutory revenues and expenses reflect only a fraction of the income and expenses of a yamen. Wang Yeh-chien (1973: 56–57) gives examples of two yamen whose actual expenses were six and ten times their statutory expenses. Income from customary fees for services and squeeze undoubtedly kept up with the growth in Taiwan's population and economy better than did its statutory revenues.
13. See Hsü Hsüeh-chi (1987: 72–76, 337–42) for measures taken to provide from Fukien sources the cash salaries of troops rotated to Taiwan. These salaries were the largest source of Taiwan's fiscal imbalance. We may be sure that in preparing his annual accounts the Fukien provincial treasurer was made well aware that Taiwan, far from being a revenue producer, was a revenue consumer. Compare R. Lee (1970: 75) who cites revenue and expense reports for Kirin and Heilungkiang that document large deficits and the need for interprovincial subsidies for those frontier governments.
14. See *KHSL*: 171; Huang Shu-ching 1957: 85. When the court forgave Taiwan's taxes in 1721 (after a typhoon added to the devastation of the Chu I-kuei

rebellion), it cited figures in cash and grain that accord with those given in Table 8.4 (*TAHLCC:* 1, 39).

15. Ch'ü 1962: 132. The Chu-lo gazetteer (*CLHC:* 85) notes that this decree was implemented in Taiwan.

16. *TWFC:*Yü: 245.

17. Ibid.: 246; *CLSL:* 57; Chou Hsien-wen 1957: 104–5. This reform, which created a joint land and labor-service tax, had taken place in most mainland provinces between 1716 and 1729 (Ch'ü 1962: 132).

18. *TWFC:*Yü: 262, 264.

19. S. Mann 1987: 15–16, 40–41.

20. *YCCPYC:* 50; *TWFC:*Liu: 242; Hui 1959: 109; Zelin 1984: 163.

21. By 1742 the government purchase price of 0.36 tael per *shih* of unhusked rice was already oppressive, since the market value had risen to 0.7 tael per *shih* (*TWFC:*Yü: 723–24). This accords with the price data analyzed by Wang Yeh-chien (1986: 94, 99–100, 102) discussed in Chapter 6. Another source gives the government price at 0.4–.45 taels per *shih* ca. 1744 (*TWFC:*Yü: 244).

22. Zelin 1984: 163–65. Only 4,025 taels of the total *yang lien* amount of 11,840 taels is attributed to tax surcharges (*hao hsien*) collected in Taiwan; this reflects Taiwan's low aggregate revenues. The remainder was apparently allocated from the income derived from official estates (*TWFC:*Yü: 304–6; Zelin 1984: 163). Taiwan's tax surcharge rates were 0.09 tael per tael of head tax and 0.1 *shih* or 0.05 tael per *shih* of grain (*TWFC:*Yü: 242, 247).

23. Hsü Hsüeh-chi 1987: 338.

24. *CHTTWSL:* 62; *TAHLPC:* 173; *HMC:* 185–92.

25. In 1741 yearly relief-grain purchases, which had reached 120,000 *shih*, were reduced to 70,000 *shih*. A 1742 plan to purchase a reserve of 400,000 *shih* of relief grain to be used as required in Fukien is discussed at *CHTTWSL:* 51 and *TWFC:*Yü: 722–24. Relief-grain purchases ended in Taiwan in 1755; amounts allocated had been insufficient to cover transport costs (*TAHLPC:* 171–76; *TWFC:*Yü: 241–44; see also Chapter 6).

26. Ho Ping-ti 1959: 210–11.

27. On budget surpluses, see Naquin and Rawski 1987: 219 and Chang Te-ch'ang 1972: 256–57. By the late eighteenth century, inflation was causing a decline in the value of tax revenues collected in cash. Officials made up this decline and funded new expenses required to serve an expanding population by collecting additional surcharges and fees (Wang Yeh-chien 1973: 57–61).

28. Wang Yeh-chien 1973: 27–30, 52–54, 131. Ho Ping-ti's (1959: 118–19) review of Ch'ing fiscal policy also stresses the late imperial fiscal ethic that tax quotas should remain fixed and the government should live within fixed revenues.

29. No foreign threat forced China to increase its defense expenditures in the eighteenth century (or to borrow or create innovative technologies), in contrast to the interstate competition and arms races pushing European states to increase their fiscal take (McNeill 1982). The empire was thus left totally unprepared, fiscally and otherwise, for the challenge of the nineteenth century.

30. Wang Yeh-chien (1973: 89–90, 96) documents how areas experiencing high rates of reclamation and immigration ("developing" areas) during the eighteenth and nineteenth centuries substantially increased their contribution to land-tax revenues while (because reclamation outpaced registration for taxation) the pro-

portion of cultivated land registered for taxation in these areas fell. These conditions also characterized Taiwan. Between 1750 and 1908, although revenues from the land tax nationwide declined as a proportion of the total budget, they nearly doubled in absolute amount (ibid.: 70–75, 80).

31. The 8 million tael expense of crushing the Lin Shuang-wen rebellion in the 1780's dwarfed Taiwan's total revenues as well as the entire land-tax revenue of the province of Fukien of 1.9 million taels (ibid.: 70; Naquin 1976: 360). According to Wang Yeh-chien (1973: 18, 101), Fukien fell into the small category of self-sufficient provinces. It collected revenues sufficient only to cover its own expenses and made no contribution to the central government or other provinces. Most frontier provinces were deficit provinces receiving subsidies from higher levels of government. Zelin (1984: 163–65) reports that Fukien's military expenses were so burdensome that the Yung-cheng court allocated interprovincial subsidies to Fukien. Thus Fukien's fiscal self-sufficiency appears to postdate the Yung-cheng reign (1723–35). It is likely that the general prosperity of the succeeding Ch'ien-lung reign made filling tax quotas easier, making the paying of subsidies to defend Taiwan less burdensome for Fukien and the central government, and easing the pressure on Taiwan to produce more revenue.

32. *CLHC:* 86; *CHHC:* 162. I speculate that much of the colony land was under shifting cultivation and was abandoned with the depopulation in the early years of Ch'ing rule. In one documented case such land was left unplanted and given out to a private reclaimer as early as 1685 (*TTTCS:* 1).

33. *CLHC:* 86; Hui 1959: 109.

34. The Feng-shan gazetteer (*FSHC:* 24, 64; see also *TWHC:* 229) says these managers were in charge of local granaries as well as of taxes and corvée. There is some mystery about the institution of *kuan shih,* since a tax farmer chosen by his village would not have title to all its land and thus does not properly belong in a list of "masters of the land." Moreover, the *kuan shih*'s own exemption from taxation would last only as long as his service to the government, which, when ended, would return his land to the ordinary status of property owner (cf. Tai Yen-hui 1962: 66). An alternative interpretation is that the *kuan shih* was a tax collector (hired by a tax farmer?), who, when he discovered unreported land in cultivation, extorted a fee from the delinquent farmer. This fee then became a rent and the right of the tax collector a property right (Hui 1959: 127; see also Murakami 1933: 141).

35. An important addition to the list of "masters of the land" is the estate of Marquis Shih (Ching-hai Hou). After his victory over the Chengs, Shih Lang was ennobled as a marquis and given title to large areas in Feng-shan and southern Chu-lo (Chia-yi). To reclaim these lands, he called in settlers from whom he collected a rent, out of which he paid the land tax. Although much of these lands was sold in the nineteenth century, the large-rent right (*ta tsu*) on thousands of *chia* was still owned by the Shih family in 1895 when the Japanese took control of Taiwan. The uniqueness of these estates is the "feudal" origin of the land title; in tax terms they bore the same obligations as other property owners (*yeh hu*), although the tax rate may have been lighter than most. Hui (1959: 126) says the rental rate was 2–3 *shih* per *chia* on paddy land and that the tax was paid out of the rent. Since taxes on paddy before 1729 ranged from 5.5 to 8.8 *shih* per *chia,* this only makes sense if the Shihs' tax was especially light (or large areas re-

mained unregistered), unless the 2–3 *shih* per *chia* rate represents the after-tax income of the Shihs', which seems unlikely.

36. Jamieson 1921: 79–81; Hui 1959: 91–92; Huang P'ei 1974: 240–45.

37. Hui 1959: 92–93.

38. Ibid.: 94; *TKI:* 1.127.

39. For examples of reclamation agreements, see *TTTCS:* 59–73; Okamatsu 1902: ref. 16. See Shepherd 1988*a:* 421–24 for a discussion of how different processes led to the creation of split ownership in many regions of China.

40. *CLHC:* 87. See Chapter 6 for a discussion of these yield data.

41. *CLHC:* 95–96.

42. Land-tax rolls were organized by households rather than as land registers or cadastres (see Kuhn 1979: 106–8).

43. *CLHC:* 121.

44. *CLHC:* 136, 148; *FSHC:* 13; *TAHLPC:* 173. In the early years this reduced the state's cost of collecting tax grain since the landlords paid taxes into the granaries in the prefectural capital; in later years with both landlords and cultivated land located far from the capital, the expense of transporting tax grain grew substantially (*TAHLPC:* 173–74).

45. For examples, see *TTTCS:* 61–63.

46. *TAHLPC:* 323; *TAHLCC:* 131; see also Chapter 10.

47. *FCTCTWF:* 165–66.

48. Lan 1958*b:* 54.

49. Here Lan is articulating the consensus that kept the Ch'ing (whose revenues until the Taiping rebellion were generally sufficient) from ever conducting a nationwide cadastral survey (Wang Yeh-chien 1973: 27; see also Ho Ping-ti 1959: 116–21).

50. *KCTYC:* 7.162. See Zelin 1984: chap. 1 for an assessment of the fiscal problems confronting the Yung-cheng emperor.

51. *YCCPYC:* 43. This suggests that less than half the reclaimed area was registered. My estimates of the reclaimed area necessary to support the population and export production ca. 1750 suggest an even larger proportion of land area remained unregistered (see Table 6.3).

52. *TWFC:*Chou: 321, 327. Note in Table 8.3 that registered area grew faster than tax grain; this reflects the fact that new land was registered primarily in lower tax grades. Table 6.5 shows a declining proportion of paddy fields.

53. *YCCPYC:* 43–44.

54. *KCTYC:* 15.835.

55. *TWFC:*Liu: 135, 159. See Table 6.5 for land registrations by county. The figures for the earliest settled counties in the later years show little increase and take on the character of quotas that reflect less and less the reality of reclaimed acreage. The revenue-hungry frontier districts of Chang-hua and Tan-shui, however, continued to record sizable increases throughout the eighteenth century. Note also that the percentage of registered land that was irrigated and subject to higher tax rates declined over time in all but Tan-shui (and latter-day Chang-hua). This reflects both the slower pace at which irrigated land was created and the lack of success in getting taxpayers to register land in high tax-rate categories. For another reference to a land survey in 1729 in Chang-hua, see *TAHLPC:* 17.

56. *YCCPYC:* 44.

57. A similar proposal to limit large-scale reclaimers was made in the later Yung-cheng years by acting Taiwan prefect Shen Ch'i-yüan (*CSWP:* 9–10).

58. Ch'en Ch'iu-k'un 1975: 49–50.

59. Lan-Chang-hsing and Mao-wu-su were located near the modern city of Taichung.

60. *YCCPYC:* 59–60.

61. Chang Kuo was *ts'an chiang* of the north-route battalion between 1705 and 1709 (*CLHC:* 128).

62. *YCCPYC:* 113–14.

63. It is interesting that Yung-cheng, who had a reputation for strictness in fiscal policy and a desire for increased revenue, is so willing to compromise those values in this case in favor of minimizing administrative effort and cost. Earlier, in his response to Governor Mao Wen-ch'üan's memorial of 1725 (YC 3.11.19) relating to the Lan-Chang-hsing incident, he had criticized Lan's shortsightedness (*YCCPYC:* 4), but a year later the emperor preferred not to offend his naval commander. There may well be some bureaucratic rivalries underlying these memorials. Ng Chin-keong (1983: 76–77) reports a 1729 incident in which Yung-cheng once again avoided offending Lan when Kao reported a conflict between the "parochial" Lan and the Amoy intendant. A variant account of the origin of Lan-Chang-hsing village is given in the 1725 memorial (YC 3.10.16) by the censors Ching K'ao-hsiang and Shan-chi-pu, which is the earliest account of the incident I have seen (*KCTYC:* 5.279–80). The censors say Chang registered the land with Chu-lo county in 1710, but that after nine tenants were killed by raw aborigines in 1719 Governor-general Gioro Man-pao had the village disbanded and the land struck from the registers. In 1722, when the local magistrate set up Man-pao's raw aborigine boundary (see Chapter 7), he placed the area in the restricted zone. But when in 1724 Commander Lan opened the area, the lowly magistrate was powerless to prevent it. The censors concluded that as a result of illegal opening of land, another incident of headtaking had occurred. For additional information on the Lan-Chang-hsing arrangements with the Mao-wu-su tribe, see Chapter 9.

64. This affair, by revealing his cousin Lan T'ing-chen's private investments in Taiwan; raises questions about the motivations behind Lan Ting-yüan's pro-colonization writings. We cannot assume that Lan himself had any interests in Taiwan or that any conflict of interest would have been perceived in advocating aggressive colonization and profiting from it, if he had. However, this affair gives us a more concrete sense of the milieu in which Lan Ting-yüan's interest in Taiwan policy took shape. Part of this milieu included relatives anxious to profit from reclamation on the frontier. Lan's background becomes even more intriguing with the recent discovery that his family was not Han but She (Wang Sung-hsing 1988). Lan's descendants in Fukien (motivated in part to take advantage of the exemption from the one-child policy accorded to minorities) recently reclaimed their She ethnic status. This raises many question about Lan's personal psychology. As a highly educated and acculturated literatus, did Lan suffer from status anxiety over his minority background? Did he advocate aggressive colonization to compensate for his minority ethnicity, to prove himself more Han than Han? Did his own success at assimilation cause him to despise minorities who demonstrated less ability and motivation, minorities that reminded him of his own degraded background?

65. Ch'en Shao-hsing 1964: 138.

66. *TZ:* 1.53.

67. The distinction between the 1731 and 1744 changes is confused in the prefectural gazetteers of 1746 (*TWFC:*Fan: 167) and 1768 (*TWFC:*Yü: 242). The 1740 prefectural gazetteer of Liu Liang-pi (*TWFC:*Liu: 129) does record that the post-1729 rate was to be set at the low-grade tidal-land tax rates of T'ung-an county without regard to subgrades. The Tan-shui subprefecture gazetteer of 1870 (*TSTC:* 94) confuses the distinction by giving 1731 as the date of change and then reporting the tax rates by land subgrades (as only the 1744 decree required).

68. *CLSL:* 37.

CHAPTER NINE

1. The chief sources for this chapter are the Ch'ing Veritable Records, the Ch'ing Code and Institutes, early Japanese legal studies (*TWSH, TKI, TTTCS*), local court decisions, land patents, and tenancy contracts. The gazetteers and the Veritable Records provide a basic chronology of events; occasionally they contain detailed accounts of disputes and rebellions. These have been supplemented by the firsthand accounts and essays of important scholars and officials who sojourned in Taiwan. Students of Taiwan's land-tenure system are especially fortunate in having rich collections of primary materials. Patents and land contracts dating from this period, some of them incorporating court decisions resolving land disputes, have been used throughout this chapter both to supplement and to act as a check on the generalizations of memorialists, essayists, and gazetteer editors that most students of history are limited to.

2. Jamieson 1921: 80, 83, 91, 103. The Ch'ing also recognized rights over uncultivated grazing lands, such as those held by Mongols; see Chapter 12 and Serruys 1968: 298–99.

3. Okamatsu 1902: 94; Shih T'ien-fu 1990: 74.

4. Li I-yüan et al. 1962; Mabuchi 1970, 1974*b*.

5. See Huang Huan-yao 1986*b:* 292 on an example from Hsi-k'ou *she* in the Taipei basin. See also Shepherd 1988*b*.

6. Compare the impact of the beaver fur export trade on the Iroquois in North America; see Hauptmann and Knapp 1977 and Jacobs 1972.

7. See *TNHCK:* 2.102, 105.

8. *Taiso ken shobun shimatsu;* Wu Hsin-jung 1978: 46, 49, 251. For disputes over land belonging to Ma-tou in the eighteenth century, see *NPPW:* 406–10; for contracts relating to land owned by the four tribes in the eighteenth century, see Murakami 1933.

9. The Taiwan private law study (*TWSH*) claims that from the beginning of Ch'ing rule in Taiwan, Chinese were not, in theory at least, allowed to cultivate aborigine lands on any terms. However, the wording of the undated Board of Revenue regulation cited in support of this theory is identical to that of the regulation adopted in 1746 and is not to be found in any document recorded before that time (cf. Hui 1959: 96; *TWSH:* 1.342–43; *CLSL:* 51).

10. Inō 1904: 76; Kuo T'ing-i 1954: 103; Wen Chi 1957: 68.

11. Azuma 1954: 88. Ch'en had already gained experience in Taiwan as T'ai-

wan county magistrate, 1702–4 (*TWFC:*Yü: 126, 139). As noted in Chapter 5, both Wang Min-cheng and Ch'en Pin were also concerned about the exploitation of plains aborigines by tribal merchants and interpreters.

12. Ch'en Pin 1961: 16.

13. Ibid.

14. See *TKI:* 1.124, 2.120.

15. *TTTCS:* 767–68.

16. S. Wu 1970: 129; Ch'en Pin 1964: 80. Unfortunately, the decrees of the governor of Fukien mentioned by Ch'en seem not to be extant.

17. Watt 1972: 91; S. Mann 1987: 20.

18. S. Wu 1970: 127.

19. *TWFC:*Chou: 316.

20. Huang Shu-ching 1957: 166; *TWFC:*Fan: 479.

21. *CLHC:* 86.

22. Lan 1958*b:* 54.

23. Huang Shu-ching 1957: 167; Thompson 1969: 98, 108.

24. *CLHC:* 110.

25. Quoted in Huang Shu-ching 1957: 165.

26. *TTTCS:* 328, 650, 698, 700–701; Thompson 1969: 98.

27. The Ch'ing code prohibited the sale of land in *t'u ssu* (aborigine chieftain) jurisdictions. But this provision was only adopted in 1777, many years too late for our purposes, and would have applied to Taiwan, which lacked *t'u ssu,* only by analogy (Jamieson 1921: 85, *TLTI:* 278).

28. *TKI:* 1.125.

29. *TWFC:*Kao: 161; *CLHC:* 123; Lan 1958*b:* 54–55.

30. *YCCPYC:* 113.

31. *TTTCS:* 2; also *TWSHF:* 1.186.

32. See the patents dated 1708 (KH 47.4), *TTTCS:* 1–2; 1718 (KH 57.12), *CDN:* 60; 1724 (YC 2.11), *TTTCS:* 3; 1724 (YC 2.12), *TTTCS:* 3–4; and 1727 (YC 5.2), *TTTCS:* 5, amended 1730 (YC 8.9), *TTTCS:* 7–8. One of the earliest contracts for the Hsin-chu area, dated 1733, also follows the model of paying the tribal tax in exchange for land; see Shih T'ien-fu 1990: 80–81.

33. *TTTCS:* 1–2.

34. Ch'en-Lai-Chang was a corporate name for a partnership of land developers that very probably included the Taipei interpreter Lai K'o; see Yin 1982: 177–84, 243. Lai K'o was also involved in the reclamation of the Shu-lin area near San-hsia, discussed in Chapter 1.

35. Inō 1904: 76.

36. *TKI:* 1.7, 125, 127.

37. Because other contemporaneous contracts are not extant, I cannot identify the tribal officers named in the 1709 patent as members of any one tribe, or as officers of the collective tax-unit, Tan-shui *she,* which included all the Taipei basin tribes (*CLHC:* 99).

38. *TKI:* 1.125.

39. *CLHC:* 99.

40. *TTTCS:* 18–19; *CLHC:* 98.

41. Compare *TKI:* 2.120. For example, in the 1733 contract for the territory of Mao-erh-ting in Hsin-chu, the Han reclaimer agreed to pay only 20 taels, but the

Chu-ch'ien *she*'s tax obligation was 378 taels (Appendix B; Shih T'ien-fu 1990: 81).

42. The agreements include a 1730 (YC 8.9) contract that pairs up with a patent of 1727 (YC 5.2), as amended in 1730 (YC 8.9), between a reclaimer and the Wu-lao-wan *she* (*TTTCS:* 5–8); a 1774 (CL 39.8) contract with the Nan *she* that refers back to a 1730 (YC 8) agreement (ibid.: 18–19); and a court decision dated 1711 (KH 50) (ibid.: 22–23).

43. Ibid.: 325. Chang Yao-ch'i (1951) locates Ta-wu-chün (Dutch: Tavokol) in She-t'ou *hsiang*, Chang-hua county.

44. Ibid.: 334–35.

45. *TWFC*:Fan: 51–52, 694–95.

46. *TTTCS*: 328, 650.

47. See *TAHLCC*: 216.

48. *TTTCS*: 18.

49. *CLHC*: 113.

50. Murakami 1933: 140–41.

51. Abe 1938: 265.

52. *TWFC*:Liu: 367.

53. Murakami 1933: 142. The land was at Fen-chi-hu, on the 1722 raw aborigine boundary (Huang Shu-ching 1957: 167), in present-day Hsin-pei *hsiang*, P'ing-tung county.

54. For examples, see *TTTCS*: 59–63.

55. See the examples for lands of An-li *she* in *TTTCS*; cf. pp. 76 and 283 and pp. 26 and 63.

56. *TAHLPC*: 17; *YCCPYC*: 113.

57. For examples, see *TTTCS*: 335–79, 538; for two possible examples of earlier date, see ibid.: 601–3.

58. Lan 1958*b*: 54.

59. Hui 1959: 97.

60. *Yung-cheng hui tien* 1733 (YC 11) 27.25a–b.

61. *YCSL*: 12.

62. Later editions of the Institutes, however, eliminate all reference to the taxation of tribal lands from this provision, revising it to conform with regulations adopted in the Ch'ien-lung reign that exempted aborigine lands from taxation (see below; *Ch'ien-lung hui tien tse li* 1763 [CL 28] 35.41b; and *CHTTWSL*: 43 [Kuang-hsü ed.]).

63. *YCCPYC*: 44. For portions of this memorial dealing with problems of reclamation and concealing land from taxation, see Chapter 8.

64. *TWFC*:Yü: 132; *YCCPYC*: 38. The Shui-sha-lien tribes had first submitted to Chinese authority in 1693 when they were assigned a cash tax quota (*CLHC*: 99–100). According to Huang Shu-ching, they had taken advantage of the Chu I-kuei rebellion "to kill their interpreters and revolt." Huang, however, reports that by a combination of threats and inducements at least some of them had surrendered again to the Chinese by the first month of 1723 (Thompson 1969: 92). Apparently not all of them remained submissive, for Kao Ch'i-cho reports in 1727 that "ever since the Chu I-kuei rebellion the Shui-sha-lien savages [*hsiung fan*] have not paid their aborigine head tax and moreover have been involved in many cases of burning and killing and ought to be punished." The headman A-lung, whom Huang reports as surrendering in late 1722, Kao reports as surrendering again in 1724 (*YCCPYC*: 124). As a result of the successful 1724 campaign, "countless skulls" were recovered from the headhunters, and the surrendering tribes agreed to resume payment of their taxes (*YCCPYC*: 124). Subprefect Wang's

role in the campaign had been to lead a combined force of civilized aborigines and Han militiamen in an attack from the rear on one of the rebels' mountain hideouts (*YCCPYC*: 37–39; *TWFC*:Liu: 477).

65. *YCCPYC*: 44. In the nineteenth century a similar plan was adopted for the I-lan area on the east coast (Hui 1959: 97); see Chapter 10. Okamatsu's *Provisional Report* (1902: 48, 53) mistakenly reports that Wang's scheme was adopted, and Meskill (1979: 33) repeats the error. The completed private law studies do not claim Wang's plan was implemented.

66. *CSWP*: 2–4, 9–10; Yin 1982: 152.

67. *CSWP*: 7–9.

68. *KCTYC*: 15.835–36.

69. All the land was in Chang-hua county (*TWFC*:Liu: 137, 159, 168).

70. *CHFSHC*: 11; Huang Shu-ching 1957: 167; Thompson 1969: 139.

71. *YCCPYC*: 141–42.

72. Ibid.

73. Huang Shu-ching 1957: 167.

74. *KCTYC*: 10.121.

75. Ibid.: 5.279–80; *YCCPYC*: 59–60, 113–14.

76. Huang Shu-ching 1957: 168.

77. Kao, while previously serving as Yunnan-Kweichow governor-general, had sought to impose Chinese landownership patterns on aborigines (K. Smith 1970: 229).

78. *TAHLPC*: 17–18.

79. Farming land near raw aborigine tribes might seem equally dangerous to civilized aborigines and Han, yet the statute only barred the latter. The government apparently had some faith in the ability of the civilized tribes to avoid the kind of trouble with the raw aborigines that would require it to intervene. After all, the civilized tribes had centuries of experience dealing with their mountain cousins.

80. See *YCCPYC*: 3–4.

81. *KCTYC*: 12.669–71 (YC 7.3.10).

82. *CHTTWSL*: 148; Hui 1959: 97.

83. In 1734 Governor-general Hao Yü-lin reported that 175 *chia* of illegally reclaimed land had been enrolled on the tax registers in accordance with provisions allowing reclaimers of land opened without licenses to escape punishment if they voluntarily reported it for taxation (*TKI*: 1.127). Although border lands were apparently not involved, this is another reflection of the government's reluctance to disturb settlers already in place.

84. *CHTTWSL*: 168; *TLTI*: 513.

85. *TTTCS*: 600–601.

86. Yin 1982: 221–22.

87. *KCTYC*: 21.158–59 (YC 11.2.20).

88. *TTTCS*: 601–3.

89. Ibid.: 330–31.

90. Ibid.: 767–68.

91. For biographical details on Chang Ta-ching, who first won the confidence of An-li by helping cure an epidemic, then married the daughter of the An-li chief, and later amassed a sizable fortune through land development schemes involving An-li, including much land concealed from taxation, see Yin 1982: 123, 204–14.

92. *TTTCS*: 23–28. The Chu-lo gazetteer of 1717 (*CLHC*: 36, 41, 261) men-

tions several earlier examples of cooperation between Han and aborigines in the construction of irrigation works, but we lack contracts that would shed light on the nature of the agreements involved.

93. *CLSL*: 9; *TLTI*: 314, 470; *TWFC*:Yü: 583; *CHTTWSL*: 27, 166.

94. *TWFC*:Yü: 186; see also Chapter 5. Plains aborigines continued to pay this head tax separately after the Han land and labor-service taxes were united in 1747. The 1747 decree explains that this is because the aborigines do not pay tax on the land they cultivate, thereby confirming its tax-exempt status (*CHTTWSL*: 37). Pai and Yen may have thought lower taxes would reduce internal pressure on tribes to lease land to Han, a practice that they considered to be disturbing to frontier social order and that Pai's 1737 memorial (discussed below) seeks to restrict.

95. *CHTTWSL*: 24, 169; *TLTI*: 505.

96. *CHTTWSL*: 167; *TLTI*: 477.

97. *CLSL*: 9. A different version of this memorial states that a line should be drawn according to the boundaries of aborigine fields leased for reclamation (*p'u k'en fan t'ien*) and that any land beyond, if encroached on (*yüeh k'en*) or occupied by force, should be returned to the aborigines (*TKI*: 1.128).

98. *TWFC*:Fan: 483; also *TWSH*: 1.347; Hui 1959: 97.

99. Squatting on land is described as *ssu chan*, illicitly occupying, by Pai, and as encroaching or forcible occupation "beyond the contractually specified boundaries" by Hao.

100. Pai's use of the term *ch'i mai*, purchase by contract, to describe this category of land introduces some ambiguity. Hao used *p'u* and *p'u mai*. Outright purchase of aborigine lands had never been given explicit government sanction. In 1724 an imperial decree had approved Han rental (*tsu*) of aborigine land. In approving "purchases by contract" was Pai seeking to give retroactive sanction to purchases? Probably not. The words *mai* (purchase) and *mai* (sell) rarely occur alone in Ch'ing property law. When either *mai* occurs in a document, two questions have to be answered to determine the meaning. What subset of the bundle of rights that make up complete ownership is being transferred? Is the transfer revocable or irrevocable? Usually these words occur in combinations that mean that only certain rights have been transferred to the purchaser and other rights remain in the hands of the seller, for example, *chao mai*, recruiting-a-tenant-sale (see *TTTCS*: 650–51 and note 103 below); *tien mai*, pledge-sale; *p'u mai*, lease-purchase; and *huo mai*, revocable sale (see van der Valk 1949: 79). Buyer and seller in these transactions remain obligated by rights and duties after the exchange is consummated. When the transfer of rights is total and absolute and all relations between buyer and seller are cut (what I call an absolute or irrevocable sale), the character for sale is used, as in the phrases *tu mai chin ken*, *mai tuan*, and *chüeh mai yung pu hui shu* (see *TLTI*: 283; Okamatsu 1902: 31, 38, 79; Jamieson 1921: 88). Because Pai did not use one of these phrases, I conclude that he was using the already vague term *mai* (sell) in a loose way and that he gave approval to a range of transactions that encompassed past leases but not absolute sales. This interpretation eliminates differences between Pai's meaning and Hao's.

101. Again, Pai's word choice introduces some ambiguity in interpreting the decree. Pai says illicit purchases (*ssu mai*) are to be forbidden (in Chinese there is no implication that therefore "licensed purchases" might be approved, as there is

in the English translation). But Hao says lease-purchases (*p'u mai*) are to be forbidden. Is there a discrepancy? Again the ambiguity of *mai* (purchase) could lead us to misunderstand Pai's words to mean that only absolute sales of aborigine lands were prohibited, leaving settlers free to lease land from tribes. The 1746 decree discussed below prescribes punishments for *ssu p'u*, illicit leases, of aborigine land. I argue that Pai means to forbid the same range of lease transactions as Hao. Hao's language forbids all lease-purchases, *p'u mai* (acquisitions of tenant rights). Does Hao's forbidding only leases mean that he intended to approve future absolute sales, which his language does not explicitly forbid? No. Again, we must recall that absolute sales had never before been given official sanction. Nor from a policy point of view would it make sense for Hao to forbid the alienation of some aborigine land rights through leases while approving the complete alienation of land in absolute sales. What range of transactions is included in "lease-purchase" (*p'u mai*)? We have already analyzed a *p'u mai* lease transaction. In the 1735 dispute over the 1709 Taipei patent, the agreement that obligated the reclaimers Ch'en, Lai, and Chang to pay the aborigine tax on the tribe's behalf was labeled a *p'u mai* (*TKI*: 1.125). Ordinarily a *p'u mai* gave rise to a right of permanent tenancy under the large-rent model.

102. Although the language is not identical, I argue that no discrepancy is intended between what Hao forbade (*p'u mai*) and what the 1724 decree allowed (*tsu*). Usually *tsu* denotes the relation between a landlord and an ordinary, nonpermanent tenant, and *p'u mai* establishes a right of permanent tenancy. Thus technically, if these vague terms were being used with precision, Hao's forbidding future *p'u mai* would leave Han settlers free to arrange for short-term renting of tribal land. I think both the policy rationale of the decree and later developments show that Hao intended to forbid all kinds of Han farming in tribal regions. For a further twist on these relations, see below for Governor-general Fu-k'ang-an's 1788 attempt to distinguish tenancies created by *tien mai* in order to frustrate the tax-avoidance schemes of Han settlers.

103. This is a good example of the use of *mai* (sell) in a contract, in the compound *chao mai*, which means not an absolute sale but a lease transaction calling for annual rents. The 1727 contract describes the same 1725 transaction as a lease to reclaim, *p'u k'en* (*TTTCS*: 699). Okamatsu (1902: 39) notes the use of *chao* in *chao keng* and *chao p'u* to denote leases.

104. *TTTCS*: 650–51; the 1727 contract is at 699–700.

105. Ibid.: 325–36; two others are at 326–27. The original 1725 contract was most likely a reclamation contract similar in terms to the contract dated 1723 for what is apparently a different parcel but concluded between the same parties, Ting and the Ta-wu-chün tribe, and concerning the same irrigation construction.

106. Ibid.: 699–700.

107. The decree argued that "although these officials have not taken land claimed by others to reclaim, their families and tenants abuse their authority to browbeat others and stir up trouble. Moreover, when immigrants encroaching onto aborigine land [*fan ti*] meet resistance, they seek to commend [*t'ou hsien*] land to military officers. . . . Thus, suits between Han and aborigines occur without end. To forbid this without a thorough investigation will not pacify Han-aborigine relations. Send officials to investigate. All land formerly belonging to military officers found not to occupy aborigine land and over which there are no

suits between Han and aborigines, and whether it is now owned by the original owner himself, his descendants, or a purchaser, should be left to be managed as before. If the land encroaches on the aborigine-settler boundary [*min fan ti chieh*], investigate. Return Han land to Han and aborigine land to aborigines, and do not allow confusion and strife. Henceforth, reclamation by military officials is forbidden. In the future if military officials reclaim land under another's name, the case of the officer in question should be turned over for strict handling and the land is to be confiscated" (*CLSL*: 34–35; *CHTTWSL*: 43–44, 149). This decree is strongly reminiscent of Governor-general Kao's 1726 memorial making the same general complaint concerning reclamation by military officials, especially in the case of Lan T'ing-chen and Lan-Chang-hsing village.

108. Civil officials, but apparently not military ones, had always been explicitly barred from acquiring land in their official jurisdictions (*TLTI*: 279; Staunton 1810: 100).

109. *CLSL*: 38–39.

110. Twenty years later, in 1766, a functionally specific jurisdiction for the management of aborigine affairs was created, but it was a subprefecture staffed by a rotating civil official, not a native chieftain; see below.

111. *CLSL*: 45–46. Kao Shan had visited Taiwan in 1730 and 1744; see Chapter 6.

112. *CLSL*: 46.

113. For early Ch'ien-lung examples following the large-rent model, see *TTTCS*: 446–47, 538–41.

114. *CLSL*: 50–51.

115. Ibid.

116. *CLSL*: 51.

117. *CLSL*: 53.

118. *CLSL*: 59–60.

119. Ibid.

120. *CLSL*: 64. The order to create grain reserves was repeated in 1756 (*TAHLPC*: 81). The prefectural gazetteer lists the granaries established (*TWFC*:Yü: 68–70). For the stone inscription of a related decree of 1759, see *CPPW*: 68.

121. In 1744 a settler in Feng-shan county, who had crossed the boundary to build an embankment and canals to irrigate his land, was attacked by raw aborigines. The raw aborigine boundary had been established to protect settlers from such attacks by preventing the crossing of the line in either direction. The report on the incident found the farmer at fault for not observing the boundary. But interpreters and chiefs were also ordered to observe the law and arrest savage aborigines, who were "not to be allowed to act blindly and cause trouble" (*CLSL*: 39).

122. *CLSL*: 65–66.

123. Two months later another decree revealed the more timid side of Ch'ing policy. This order approved the continued purchase of Ryukyuan sulfur (used in making gunpowder). Formerly, sulfur had been acquired from the Tan-shui–Keelung area. But Tan-shui was an area where "aborigines and Han live interspersed. . . . As soon as sulfur works are opened there, bandits will cause trouble." Thus, the continued purchase of Ryukyuan sulfur was recommended. Here the fear of disorder involving bandits and aborigines prevented the Ch'ing court from developing its own sources of a strategic item, whose value Shih Lang had once cited as reason for the retention of Taiwan (*CLSL*: 67; *CHTTWSL*: 184).

124. *CLSL*: 79–80.
125. Abe 1938: 103.
126. Wang Shih-ch'ing 1953: 43–44.
127. *CHTWHC*: 404; *HHTWHC*: 1; Abe 1938: 253–54.
128. *TWSHF*: 1.232.
129. *TAHLCC*: 215–23; *CLSL*: 88–94.

130. A contract of 1772 reveals that Pei-t'ou *she* was involved in another dispute at this time (*TTTCS*: 205). In 1743 the tribe had hired Han laborers to construct an irrigation canal. A dispute erupted over payment of their wages. The case went before magistrate Lu Kuang-lin (Chang-hua magistrate, 1744–45; *CHHC*: 76). To resolve the dispute, Lu ordered the tribe to rent 200 *chia* of land to tenant farmers and then use the rent deposits collected to pay the wages. The 1738 restrictions on renting aborigine land to Han seem to have been no obstacle to the adoption of this remedy.

131. As a child, San-chia had been adopted by Ko-mai-i, a prominent member of the Pei-t'ou *she*.

132. *TWFC*:Liu: 201; Huang Shu-ching 1957: 123. Fu-ku and very likely all its neighbors were Atayal tribes (Ch'en Shao-hsing 1950: 2).

133. A hundred soldiers had been posted at Liu-shu-nan since 1738 (*CLSL*: 12; the location is in present-day Wu-feng *hsiang*, T'ai-chung county).

134. *CLSL*: 88.
135. *CLSL*: 89, 94.
136. *CLSL*: 104; *TAHLCC*: 215–23.
137. *TAHLCC*: 222.
138. Ibid.: 221–22; see *TLTI*: 275; Jamieson 1921: 82.

139. One case shows in an unexpected way how troublesome interpreters could be. In the fourth month of 1753, the Tan-shui subprefect reported the raising of a red banner in Ta-lang-tun port (just north of the Ta-chia-la land granted in the 1709 patent) as a sign of rebellion. On the banner was written: "Kuo is the successor to the Chou" (the ancient dynasty, 1122–255 B.C.) and "Lead the aborigines of the eight Tan-shui tribes and the Chinese villagers to exterminate avaricious officials." One Liu Ho-lin, who was trying to wrest the position of tribal interpreter away from a Mr. Kuo, was discovered to have raised the banner in an attempt to implicate Kuo in a rebellion (and thereby get him removed from his office). Liu, however, was arrested before he caused any further disturbance to the locality (*CLSL*: 95, 100). Liu, we know independently, was a landholder in the Wu-ku *hsiang* area of the Taipei basin. This land was on the west bank of the Tan-shui river, across from Tan-shui town (*TPHCK*: 5.ref. 37). Some of the land Liu had reclaimed was declared to be aborigine land and returned to aborigine control in the late 1770's (see below). On this incident and the role of interpreters in the negotiation of the reclamation of tribal lands generally, see Yin 1982: 239 and *passim*.

140. Liu Ho-lin's raising a banner of revolt, though a failure in his case, seems to have set off a rash of similar occurrences, all involving Han only (see *CLSL*: 96–97, 100, 101). For instances of raising a flag of rebellion to frame an enemy in 1752 and 1760, see *TAHLPC*: 163–65, 235–38.

141. The Shui-sha-lien tribes had been repacified in campaigns of the early Yung-cheng years (see above).

142. *CLSL*: 83–84; *TAHLPC*: 309–11, 314–16.
143. *CLSL*: 111.

144. *CLSL*: 76; *TTTCS*: 978–79. The Tan-shui gazetteer notes land-tax payments began in 1757 (*TSTC*: 95; *TWFC*:Yü: 309–10; Okamatsu 1902: 68–69, 91). For a 1760 report that raw aborigine raids had caused the Ch'üan-t'ou-mu-shan tenants to flee, see below.

145. In 1757 the Tan-shui subprefect decreed that land on the north route that was formerly wasteland, that was neither civilized nor raw aborigine ancestral land, and that lay *beyond* the raw aborigine boundary should be considered ownerless and thus open to Han reclamation (*TKI*: 1.124). The full decree (which I have not located) must have qualified this statement, for otherwise the boundary policy would have been seriously modified, which other sources do not indicate happened at this time. Once again the definition of ancestral tribal territorial claims beyond the boundary is left vague (see the 1760 decree and note 158 to this chapter).

146. *TWFC*:Yü: 813; *CTPT*: 145; *CPPW*: 66–68.

147. *TWFC*:Yü: 583.

148. *CLSL*: 118.

149. In 1757, 1,360 *chia* in Chang-hua and 814 *chia* in Tan-shui were entered on the tax rolls. In 1759, another 2,584 *chia* were added in Chang-hua. In Tan-shui, 530 *chia* were added, and 282 *chia* "beyond the boundary" were subtracted from the area added in 1757; in 1762 another 1,123 *chia* were added (*TWFC*:Yü: 218–20).

150. *CLSL*: 118.

151. *TWFC*:Yü: 220, 239, 262, 310; see also *TWFFIT*: 75.

152. *CLSL*: 118. A number of sites are known to have been "earth-oxen" ditches, including one of uncertain date that stretches from Ying-ko to Pa-te and puts San-hsia and Ta-ch'i (in the southwest corner of the Taipei basin) in a restricted area within the territories of the Hsiao-li and Kuei-lun plains tribes (Wang Shih-ch'ing 1953: 40–42; *TKI*: 1.131, 133–34, see fig. 1.1). See also Shih T'ien-fu 1989*b*: 34.

153. *TKI*: 1.128. I have not located this decree in the central government sources; it may have been a local court decision.

154. *TPHCK*: 5.ref. 13.

155. *CLSL*: 126.

156. This may be a reference to the confiscations ordered at Shui-sha-lien in 1751 (see above).

157. *CLSL*: 126–27.

158. This strengthens the interpretation of the decree of 1757 (see note 145 to this chapter), which opened to Han cultivation land *beyond* the boundary not part of ancestral plains aborigine claims, as referring to a very narrow category of land.

159. In contrast, the 1759 decree protecting aborigine rights to rental income does not confine its application to any subset of tribal lands or impose any obligations on the tribes.

160. *CPPW*: 68; Abe 1938: 173–74.

161. *TTTCS*: 350.

162. *TAHLPC*: 241–44.

163. *CLSL*: 145–46.

164. *CLSL*: 150.

165. Su asserted (*CLSL*: 148) that "houses of bamboo and grass are very easy to move and rebuild" (contrary to the opinions of Lan Ting-yüan; see Chapter 7).

166. One of these villages is Chia-chih-ko, described as an "empty civilized aborigine village" (*CLSL*: 148). Chia-chih-ko had revolted and was pacified in 1737 (*CLSL*: 5, 7, 8–9). I have no other information as to why the site should have been abandoned. The 1790 aborigine military colony roster indicates that Chia-chih-ko had combined with the neighboring tribe of Miao-li.

167. *CLSL*: 147–48.

168. *CLSL*: 148–49; *TKI*: 1.128 (which dates this memorial 1767 instead of 1766).

169. *TPHCK*: 5.ref. 26.

170. *TTTCS*: 648–49.

171. Okamatsu 1902: ref. 18.

172. *TTTCS*: 203–5.

173. *CLSL*: 150; *CHHC*: 393–95.

174. The office Su cited as precedent, the Subprefecture for Yao Affairs in Kwangtung province, was created in 1703 by the same process of eliminating another subprefectural office (a *hai fang t'ung chih*) and using its budget for the new one (Liao Chiung-jan 1948: 17, 28, 35). This Ch'ing practice of conditioning the creation of a new office on the abolition of an old one is noted in Chapter 7; see Watt 1977: 359.

175. *CHHC*: 393–95. Recall that a proposal to establish an aborigine jurisdiction on the model of the native chieftains (*t'u ssu*) of China's southwest had been rejected in 1745; see above.

176. Tai Yen-hui 1976: 335.

177. *CLSL*: 300; *CHHC*: 38, 67–68; Chuang Chin-te 1964: 40–42.

178. Chang Yao-ch'i 1951: app. 2.3–7; Ch'en Shao-hsing 1964: 142–48.

179. *CLSL*: 14.

180. *TLTI*: 271–72.

181. *CHTTWSL*: 37.

182. *CLHC*: 86.

183. *TWSHF*: 1.320–21; *TTTCS*: 542–43.

184. *TKI*: 2.125.

185. *TWSHF*: 1.293–94; *TKI*: 2.143–44; *TTTCS*: 322–23.

186. Tai Yen-hui 1953: 22, 37–39.

187. *CTPT*: 1043; *TACC*: 11, 33; *TKI*: 2.126–27.

188. For an example, see *TTTCS*: 768–69.

189. See ibid.: 445, 707.

190. Okamatsu 1902: 23, 79.

191. Tai Yen-hui 1976: 366; see also Chapters 10 and 12.

192. Li Pen-nan, the second subprefect of aborigine affairs, served from 1770 to 1773 (*CHHC*: 56).

193. Chiang Yün-hsün served as intendant 1769–71 (Liu Chih-wan 1957: 68).

194. Tuan Chieh served as Tan-shui subprefect 1766–67 (*TSTC*: 208).

195. *TWSHF*: 1.338–39; *TTTCS*: 648–49.

196. It is curious that the 1772 decision does not mention whether the land was registered for taxation. If the Han tenants in this case had been relieved of a taxpaying obligation when aborigine land let to Han (and returned to aborigine management) was declared tax-exempt by the decree of 1768, requiring them to pay a higher aborigine rent would not have increased their overall burden. Since the logic of both the 1767 and the 1768 decree was to avoid a double rent and tax burden for tenants of aborigine land, the subprefect's failure to apply this rationale suggests that it did not apply to the facts of the case. This would be the case if the land had never been registered for taxation, and since the 1768 decree

now gave sanction to nonpayment of taxes on aborigine land let to Han, there may have been no such double burden. But if the land was registered, it is possible that the 1768 tax exemption was not given retroactive effect to all aborigine land, and that the court in 1772 was simply not concerned about avoiding the double burden. The government had given no retroactive effect to earlier changes in the land tax rate.

197. Note also that the clear contractual language submitted as evidence was carefully reviewed but was not binding and was overridden by considerations of policy.

198. Recall the similar situation from the 1721 Hsia-tan-shui contract, cited above, in which aborigines also successfully petitioned for a rent increase over the contracted amount by appealing to the magistrate.

199. I thank Shih Chin, who helped me puzzle out the language of the decision, for this insight.

200. *TTTCS*: 343; Okamatsu 1902: ref. 23.

201. No mention is made of paying taxes in the contract (*TPHCK*: 5.ref. 26; for the same terms in a contract of 1771, see *TTTCS*: 547–48).

202. *TPHCK*: 5.ref. 13.

203. *TTTCS*: 553.

204. For a contract calling for the same split in capital contribution, dated 1772, see Okamatsu 1902: ref. 17.

205. *CDI*: 56–58.

206. See Hui 1959: 103. A reclamation contract (*p'u k'en*) of 1742 by the Lei-li *she* of the Taipei basin (*TKI*: 3.19) contains a similar clause: the tribe will register the land for taxation, if necessary, and it is to be of no concern to the tenants. Although in 1742 we would expect the Han tenants to be responsible for paying land taxes on aborigine land let to Han, it still made sense for a tribe seeking to protect its land rights to guard against the possibility that someone else's registering the land would compromise the aborigine claim. Compare the statement of H. B. Morse (1913: 86): "So much is the payment of land tax an incident of possession, especially in the case of farm lands, that holding land-tax receipts for three successive years is, in the absence of deeds, accepted as *prima facie* proof of ownership."

207. Okamatsu 1902: refs. 18, 19. The Lius were descendants of the Liu Ho-lin who raised a banner to wrest away the position of interpreter in the 1753 incident mentioned in note 139 to this chapter.

208. Also mentioned in a contract of 1765; see *TPHCK*: 5.ref. 20; *TSTC*: 75.

209. Chou served 1767–72 (Liu Chih-wan 1957: 67).

210. Chi served 1771–74 (ibid.: 70).

211. Sung served 1771–74 (*TSTC*: 209).

212. *TSTC*: 209; *CHHC*: 72.

213. These lists are a part of the 1780 contract; see Okamatsu 1902: ref. 19.

214. The Wu-lao-wan tribe was engaged in a separate, though probably related, dispute over irrigation rights during these same years. See the contracts of 1765, 1769, and 1774 in *TPHCK*: 5.refs. 20, 23, and 27. During the land dispute with the Lius, the Han settler Chao Meng-chiang assisted the Wu-lao-wan tribe. To express their gratitude, the tribe offered to give the large-rent rights on 2 *chia* of land to Chao, but he refused to accept. The tribe then gave the rents to the local earth

god temple to endow purchases of incense and lamp oil (*TTTCS*: 653; the contract is dated 1774).

215. *NPPW*: 406–7; see also 409–10.

216. *NPPW*: 410–12; see also Wu Hsin-jung 1978: 167.

217. For some other examples from these years of contracts noting official intervention to protect aborigine land rights, see *TTTCS*: 203–5 (Pei-t'ou *she*, 1772 and 1776), 362 (Miao-li-hsi-k'ou *she*, 1773), 601–3 (Kan-en or Niu-ma *she*, 1778; also *CPPW*: 75–77).

218. *CLSL*: 252; *TAHLIC*: 165.

219. *TAHLCC*: 283–85, 294, 308.

220. Ibid.: 307.

221. Ibid.: 294, 301, 307; *TACC*: 1–2; *CTPT*: 989.

222. See also the 1785 aborigine reclamation contract on land newly declared to be "within the boundary" (*TTTCS*: 378–79).

223. Hui 1959: 95. A patent issued to a Mr. Yang in 1727 for land in the Taipei basin near Wu-lao-wan (modern Hsin-chuang) that refers to the land as a "government resource" (*kuo yung chih yüan*) cannot be taken as a denial of any obligation to aborigine tribes, for, although the patent itself makes no reference to it, we know there were separate agreements to pay aborigine rents on this land (*TWSHF*: 1.231–32; *TKI*: 1.7, 2.123). This patent thus conforms to the same model as the 1709 Taipei patent (see above) and similarly denies any obstruction of aborigine lands (*yü fan min wu ai*), which the regulations required if a patent were to be issued. Apparently the reference to "government resource" is meant only to point to its taxpaying potential, newly emphasized for aborigine land let to Han by the decree of 1724.

224. Nineteenth-century materials distinguish the rental income of corporately owned tribal property (*kung k'ou liang tsu*) from that of privately held tribal property (*ssu k'ou liang tsu*) (Okamatsu 1902: 54–55).

225. See, e.g., *TTTCS*: 452, 701 (privately held), 334–35 (corporately held). Note that the injunction against the sale of aborigine land applied only to sales to Han; aborigines could sell outright their (privately) held land to other aborigines; in such cases no tribal rent was required of the purchaser (Hui 1959: 100).

226. One Japanese study asserts that the government's policy of conferring on tribes rights in land beyond the raw aborigine boundary was an expression of ultimate government ownership and not a recognition of tribal land rights per se (*TKI*: 1.123). This agrees with the emphasis here on the role of the government's control strategies in frontier land policy.

227. On these themes, see Watt 1972: 83, 91; and S. Mann 1987: 20. See also Metzger 1970 and Zelin 1984: 9.

228. *CSWP*: 4.

229. It is hoped that future research, using Japanese-era cadastres, will test the hypothesis that the government most strictly enforced aborigine land claims along the raw aborigine border. But there are several striking exceptions to this generalization, including the site of the market town of Tung-lo, under aborigine large-rents (*CPPW*: 16–18), and the disputes over coastal land in which aborigines were involved, two just north of Tainan (*NPPW*: 386–87, 428–29) and one near Lu-kang (*CPPW*: 98–100).

CHAPTER TEN

1. Analyses of these late eighteenth-century developments have usually served only to provide background for the Liu Ming-ch'uan reforms of the aborigine large-rent system in the late nineteenth century.

2. From the Hsin-chu area comes an additional example of plains aborigine strife with raw aborigines (*KCTYC*: 8.557–58), and an example of an appreciation of the usefulness of plains aborigines in defense against raw aborigines in 1721 (Chang Wei 1978: 73).

3. *TAHLCC*: 3; *TWFC*:Liu: 489; *KHSL*: 174; on the Chu I-kuei rebellion, see Chapter 6. The Dutch also had trouble maintaining discipline over aborigine troops in the 1641 campaign against Tung-lo and Favorlang (see Chapter 3).

4. *TWFC*:Fan: 627–28.

5. Huang Huan-yao 1986*a*: 144, 192–93.

6. Ibid.: 139–40.

7. Elvin 1973: 107. Cavalry, which was restricted to government troops, was of limited significance in military campaigns in Taiwan. Seen from the perspective of the reigning military technology, the famed imperial hunts were much more than acts of nostalgia for a Manchu tribal past (Kessler 1976: 106).

8. R. Smith 1974: 140, 144; Huang Huan-yao 1986*a*: 135–36.

9. *HHTWHC*: 372; *CLSL*: 155, 157, 161; Davidson 1903: 77; Huang Huan-yao 1986*a*: 146–47.

10. *CLSL*: 164, 167.

11. *TAHLCC*: 67, 85, 91, 99.

12. *CLSL*: 156; *TAHLPC*: 57, 92.

13. *CLSL*: 172, 187; Inō 1904: 113.

14. *CLSL*: 161, 163, 196, 200.

15. *CLSL*: 198–99, 205.

16. Skinner (1976: 335) usefully contrasts urban-oriented sojourning with emigration for colonization, but I prefer to emphasize how emigration evolved out of a sojourning strategy, even for agriculturalists. For examples and notices of chain migration to Taiwan, see Pasternak 1969: 558; Meskill 1979: 57; Lamley 1981: 297; and Chuang Ying-chang 1989. On Hakka seasonal laborers, see *CLHC*: 136–37, 148; Lamley 1981: 300; Shih T'ien-fu 1987: 64, 156–78; and Chuang Ying-chang 1989: 176.

17. On the unbalanced sex ratio, see *CLHC*: 137, 148; Barclay 1954; Ch'en Shao-hsing 1964; Meskill 1979: 32; Hsu Wen-hsiung 1980*b*: 88; Lamley 1981: 297; Shepherd 1991.

18. Meskill 1979: 45–47; Lamley 1981: 298; Ng 1983: 135–37, 163–67.

19. See Meskill 1979: 52–53 and Lamley 1981: 299–300 for notices of this pattern and citations of the conventional literature.

20. *TPHCK*: 5.4–6; Hsü Chia-ming 1973; Wang Shih-ch'ing 1974: 73, 81; Lamley 1981: 300. Shih T'ien-fu (1987: 4) points out that if Ch'üan-chou migrants came to dominate coastal areas because they arrived first, they were foolish to choose to settle in the windswept, sandy coastlands instead of the fertile inland plains.

21. Shih T'ien-fu 1987: 117–18, 127.

22. Ibid.: 64, 175–76, 179–80.

23. Shih's analysis of frontier colonization thus neatly complements Skinner's 1976 analysis of the export of specialized talent in urban sojourning. What re-

mains to be established is the temporal sequencing of the various streams of migration to Taiwan. When did the flow run fastest and from where? For each stream, was the pace of the flow determined by population pressure and distress on the southeast coast or the pull of frontier opportunity on Taiwan? What alternative destinations in China's cities, the interior, or in Southeast Asia were open to the emigrants?

24. Shih T'ien-fu 1987: 86–87, 180. For other maps showing the local concentrations of the different subethnic groups in Taiwan, see Hsieh Chiao-min 1964: 150 and Ch'en Cheng-hsiang 1959–61: 1.229. Ch'en Han-kuang (1972) reprints the 1926 survey of Han provenance of the inhabitants of each of Taiwan's townships.

25. *CLHC*: 145, 147; Pasternak 1969: 554–56; Wang Shih-ch'ing 1974: 86; Meskill 1979: 57; Hsu Wen-hsiung 1980*b*: 88–91; Chuang Ying-chang 1989: 179.

26. In an important article, Pasternak (1969) refutes Freedman's (1966: 162–65; cf. 1979: 344) hypothesis linking lineages to frontier conditions by showing that migration to the frontier inhibited rather than stimulated lineage growth and fostered voluntary associations on non-agnatic bases of shared experience and provenance. A more relevant comparison to Taiwan comes from Freedman's work on immigrant associations in Singapore (1979: 61–83). See also *CLHC*: 142; Meskill 1979: 52–53; Sangren 1984; Chuang Ying-chang 1989: 185. Harrell (1981) neatly illustrates the varied patchwork of forms of village social organization within a small area of northern Taiwan.

27. Early Ch'ien-lung gazetteers report the construction of a large number of temples by immigrant subethnic groups to honor patron deities; this activity apparently reflects both growing community resources and heightened subethnic consciousness (*TWFC*:Yü: 332, 647–49).

28. On suspicion between groups, see *TWHC*: 63. For examples of early intermixing, see Wang Shih-ch'ing 1974: 73 and Lamley 1981: 302–3.

29. On violence on the coast generally, see Lamley 1977*a* and Freedman 1958: 105–13; on P'ing-ho county in Chang-chou, see Meskill 1979: 53, 56–57; on the Hakka, see Shih T'ien-fu 1987: 171.

30. *CLHC*: 137, 147; Lamley 1972, 1977*a*; Hsu Wen-hsiung 1980*b*: 90–92; Ownby 1990.

31. Lamley 1981: 303–4; see also Hsu Wen-hsiung 1980*b*: 94. This also fits Meskill's (1979: 87–89, 258–62) "strongman era."

32. Kuhn 1970.

33. On the sociological dynamics of how specific disputes escalate into general hostility and how social networks polarize (regardless of whether the disputes have anything to do with "ethnicity"), see James S. Coleman's 1957 classic, *Community Conflict*.

34. Lamley 1977*a*; Hsu Wen-hsiung 1980*b*.

35. *TAHLCC*: 2.

36. Ibid.: 42.

37. *CHFSHC*: 255–60, 267, 343–46, 352–53; *KHSL*: 173; *YCSL*: 2; *CLSL*: 5, 24.

38. *NPPW*: 420–22; *CPPW*: 78–79. The loyalty of Hakka to the Ch'ing in Taiwan contrasts starkly with their anti-Manchu reputation during the Taiping rebellion and underlines the importance of contextually specific factors, not "ethnic identity," in social alignments.

39. *CLSL*: 209–10; *CHTTWSL*: 14.
40. *CLSL*: 409, 499
41. *TAHLCC*: 211–15; *TWFC*:Yü: 391.
42. *CLSL*: 217; *CHTTWSL*: 15.
43. *CLSL*: 248–49.
44. *CLSL*: 250–52.
45. *CLSL*: 253–54; Chuang Chin-te 1965: 74.
46. *CLSL*: 261.
47. *CLSL*: 265.
48. Hummel 1943–44: 100.
49. *CLSL*: 248, 254, 258; *TAHLCC*: 243.
50. *NPPW*: 412–17.
51. *CLSL*: 259; Campbell 1903: 516–18.
52. *CLSL*: 261, 263, 267. See Ownby (1990) for an excellent blow-by-blow account of the 1782 strife; see also the map in Lin Wei-sheng 1938: 32.
53. *CLSL*: 269.
54. *CHHC*: 363; *TAHLCC*: 248–50, 278; Davidson 1903: 78–79.
55. *TAHLCC*: 268, 273; *CLSL*: 272–73, 284.
56. *YLH*: 33; *CLSL*: 271; *CHHC*: 363; *TAHLCC*: 264, 269; *TFT*: 200.
57. *TAHLCC*: 262, 308–12; *TWFC*:Yü: 96, 468.
58. Huang Shih-chien was a native of P'ing-ho county, Chang-chou, and in 1730 succeeded to the title Duke of Hai-ch'eng (*YCSL*: 34; *TAHLCC*: 259). The K'ang-hsi emperor originally conferred this title on Huang's senior clansman, Huang Wu, the infamous general who advocated the removal of the coastal population in the campaigns against the Chengs (Hummel 1943–44: 339, 355; Oxnam 1975: 128–36).
59. *CLSL*: 267–68.
60. *CLSL*: 278.
61. *CLSL*: 281, 285.
62. *CLSL*: 286–88; *TAHLCC*: 283–85, 294, 308.
63. *CLSL*: 291; *TAHLCC*: 270. Ta-li-i Lin participation in rebel activity began earlier and was substantially greater than Meskill (1979: 63) realized.
64. *TAHLCC*: 290–94.
65. For related stone inscriptions of 1783 and 1784 concerned with control of local criminal activities, see *NPPW*: 418–20.
66. See also *TAHLCC*: 308–12; *CTPT*: 1041.
67. See Jamieson 1921: 105–6.
68. Abstracted from *TAHLCC*: 290–94; see also *TAHLPC*: 321–26.
69. *TAHLCC*: 301, 307.
70. *CLSL*: 288. The terms of county magistrates were similarly lengthened in 1788 after the Lin rebellion (*CTPT*: 959).
71. *CLSL*: 289.
72. *CCH*: 896–99, 922–32; Hummel 1943–44: 680–82.
73. Nivison 1959: 209; see also Hummel 1943–44: 289–90.
74. *CCH*: 818; *CTPT*: 891, 981–82; *CLSL*: 318.
75. *CTPT*: 970–75.
76. *TSTC*: 258–59.
77. *CLSL*: 300–301; *TAHLPC*: 327–29; *CLSL*: 303.

78. *CTPT*: 927, cf. 132; *CHHC*: 363. The society itself had reportedly been founded twenty years earlier in Chang-p'u county, Chang-chou (Tai Hsüan-chih 1977: 418). There is an enormous literature debating the history of the Heaven and Earth Society. Treating these debates is beyond the scope of this study; see Tai Hsüan-chih 1977 for a well-reasoned account.

79. *CTPT*: 397, 978, 1041; *CHHC*: 364.

80. *CLSL*: 310.

81. Lei Kung is the god of thunder, who strikes down evildoers (Mathews 1960: 601).

82. *TAHLCC*: 317–24; *CLSL*: 334; Chuang Chi-fa 1982: 216–17.

83. *CTPT*: 859; *CHHC*: 364; *CLSL*: 310–11. I attempt to describe only a "consensus" view of these events. The exact role played by the secret societies (Were they social clubs, mercenary bands, or revolutionary cells?) and the connection between the Yang family dispute and Lin Shuang-wen in Ta-li-i is a matter of scholarly controversy. For discussion of discrepancies between sources and more detailed studies of these events, see Jung 1979; Chuang Chi-fa 1982; Lai Fu-shun 1984; and forthcoming work by Ownby.

84. *CLSL*: 313, 319, 804; *CHHC*: 366.

85. This chronology is drawn from Lai Fu-shun 1984: 39–41 and Chuang Chi-fa 1982: 183–267.

86. Ch'en K'ung-li (1990: 155–58, 163, 167) puts the total troop strength (including the local garrisons) at 20,000 under Huang Shih-chien, 30,000 under Ch'ang Ch'ing, and 60,000 under Fu-k'ang-an. The 8 million tael amount (Naquin 1976: 360) dwarfs Taiwan's total revenues (see Chapter 8) as well as Fukien's total annual land-tax revenue of 1.9 million taels (Wang Yeh-chien 1973: 70).

87. *CTPT*: 145.

88. *CTPT*: 171.

89. *CTPT*: 205, 208.

90. *CTPT*: 187. See Jung (1979: 361–62) for details of high-level policy debates over the costs and benefits of sending troops into the raw aborigine territory.

91. *CTPT*: 201, 221.

92. *CTPT*: 315, 791, 1029.

93. *CTPT*: 482.

94. Ibid.

95. *CTPT*: 861.

96. *CLSL*: 146.

97. *CTPT*: 1029–30; *CLSL*: 649, 671, 676. One interesting sidelight revealed yet another role played by raw aborigines in the rebellion. The rebels seemed to have plentiful supplies of gunpowder—more than could be explained by the supplies they captured in battle. Reports came in that the rebels were manufacturing it at their stronghold at Ta-li-i and were not dependent on an external supply. A check of the Taiwan prefectural gazetteer revealed that northern Taiwan had large sulfur deposits and that Feng-shan had a river named the "sulfur stream." Soldiers were dispatched to stop any smuggling of sulfur at either site (*CTPT*: 379). Illegal mining was discovered at Tan-shui, but links to the rebels were not directly established; later investigators discovered that the sulfur mined there was only traded for smuggled salt (*CTPT*: 476–77, 1035). After his capture Lin Shuang-wen revealed the secret in his confession. The rebels obtained sulfur from the inner mountains by trading with the raw aborigines. They converted lime into saltpeter and then combined that with the sulfur to make gunpowder (*CTPT*: 966).

98. *CHHC*: 365, 367.
99. *CTPT*: 102.
100. *CTPT*: 732.
101. *CTPT*: 168, 408.
102. *CTPT*: 408, 415. One fascinating case of cooperation with the rebels involved a female plains aborigine diviner and curer in Chuang Ta-t'ien's entourage. She had married a Han settler but was a widow when she was swept up in the rebellion. Her chants before battle brought divine protection to rebel warriors. See Liu Ju-chung and Miao Hsüeh-meng 1984: 272–73; Chuang Chi-fa 1982: 232; and *CTPT*: 339–40. I thank David Ownby for the Liu reference.
103. *CTPT*: 201.
104. *CTPT*: 201, 442.
105. *CTPT*: 415, 733.
106. *CTPT*: 168, 733.
107. *TWFC*:Fan: 290–91; see also Chapter 5.
108. *CTPT*: 377, 495.
109. *CTPT*: 498; unfortunately individual villages and the number of their recruits are not listed.
110. *CTPT*: 821.
111. *CTPT*: 720, 793; *TWFC*:Fan: 71.
112. *CTPT*: 950, 1029; *TWFC*:Fan: 69, 70.
113. *CLSL*: 323.
114. *CTPT*: 371.
115. *CTPT*: 379.
116. *CTPT*: 532–33.
117. *CTPT*: 624–25.
118. *CTPT*: 542.
119. *CTPT*: 733.
120. *CTPT*: 625, 805, 965.
121. *CTPT*: 275–76.
122. *CTPT*: 462; *TSTC*: 275–76.
123. *CTPT*: 651, 482, 821; *CHHC*: 368. T'ung-an settlers continued to play a swing role in the feuds of the nineteenth century (see below; Huang Ch'i-mu 1953; and Lamley 1972).
124. *CTPT*: 341.
125. *CTPT*: 337–38. Ch'ien-lung had been anxious to know early in the campaign whether the boundary had served as an effective barrier against rebel penetration of raw aborigine territory. On Yang Ching-su's policies, see Chapter 9.
126. *CCH*: 818, 851–54.
127. *CTPT*: 644–45.
128. *CTPT*: 806.
129. *CTPT*: 1009.
130. *CLSL*: 655, 669, 707, 727.
131. *CTPT*: 638–39.
132. Policies favoring the spatial segregation of ethnic groups were a standard element of Ch'ing statecraft, closely related in theory to the boundary policies reviewed in Chapter 7 (see also Chapter 12 below). In the seventeenth century, the dynasty sought to reduce conflict between Manchu Bannermen and Han by relocating Han and creating exclusive Manchu areas, both in Peking and in surrounding villages (Wakeman 1985: 477–79). The nineteenth-century communal conflict between Hakka and Punti in Kwangtung was ended by resettling Hakka in a separate subprefecture and exchanging lands between Hakka and Punti areas (Lo Wan 1965).
133. *CTPT*: 805; cf 810.
134. *CTPT*: 916, 992.
135. *CTPT*: 805–6, 912.
136. *CTPT*: 892.
137. Hummel 1943–44: 7–8, 254.
138. *Ssu-ch'uan t'ung chih* 1816: 87.12–25.
139. The *Ssu-ch'uan t'ung chih* of 1816 (87.15) calls this *kai t'u wei t'un*, replacing chiefs with military colonies, in contrast to *kai t'u wei liu*, replacing chiefs with rotating civil magistrates (see also Wiens 1954: 192–94, 232–33).

140. Hummel 1943–44: 254.
141. *CTPT*: 366, 432, 466, 623.
142. *CTPT*: 778, 877–78.
143. Wakeman 1966: 65; Kuhn 1970: 21, 29–30.
144. *CTPT*: 912.
145. See Chapters 5 and 7 and *CHHC*: 189.
146. *CTPT*: 949–50.
147. *CTPT*: 887, 949.
148. Lamley 1972: 19. Lamley (30–32) also notes various attempts in the nineteenth century to follow or cut across provenance in the organization of local militia.
149. *CTPT*: 965.
150. *CTPT*: 887, 1018.
151. *CTPT*: 950–51; cf. *TACC*: 28.
152. *CTPT*: 987–90, dated CL 53.6.3; the Veritable Records (*CLSL*: 611) date it a few days earlier, 53.5.29.
153. *CTPT*: 987–88.
154. *CTPT*: 991. Commoners were prohibited from keeping weapons; at the end of the rebellion, loyalist braves were ordered to hand in all weapons to be recast into agricultural implements (*CTPT*: 845).
155. *CTPT*: 991.
156. *TACC*: 1.35 says 1760.
157. *CTPT*: 989.
158. Cf. *CTPT*: 1043 and *TACC*: 11. Conceivably, Fu could be distinguishing two categories of land here rather than one. The confusion stems from his use of ambiguous terminology. *Mai tuan* would ordinarily mean unconditional sale, free of any obligation to the former owner. And although *tien mai* is a form of pledge, redemptions of aborigine land were rare. As discussed above, *tien mai* of aborigine land carried with it the unusual obligation to pay an aborigine rent. If Fu had wanted to distinguish these two, he should have specified a separate tax rate for *tien mai* land. That only one category of land is being discussed here is supported by Prefect Yang T'ing-li. Yang, who was among those charged with carrying out the surveys that would lead to the implementation of Fu-k'ang-an's plan, states specifically that sold land (*mai tuan*) is to be taxed at the low T'ung-an sand-land rate in order to guarantee an income to both Han and aborigines (*TACC*: 33). In part the inability to use unambiguous terminology reflects the flexibility and variety of arrangements negotiated with respect to land within general legal categories; nevertheless, failure to be more explicit did result in confusion with respect to the tax treatment land received. Governor-general Wu-la-na's memorial of 1790 included a brief report on the status of the 11,204 *chia* found reclaimed beyond the boundary at the time of the 1784 survey. Of this total, 1,961 *chia* were found to be "aborigine owned and cultivated" and therefore tax-exempt. Unfortunately, Wu-la-na's failure to mention specifically lands Han had rented (*tsu p'u*) from the tribes that, like aborigine-cultivated land, were also (on Fu-k'ang-an's order) to be tax-exempt makes me suspect that the 1,961 *chia* includes both categories of tax-exempt land. Allowing for adjustments from the resurvey and the subtraction of rebel land, an area of 8,780 *chia* (of the original 11,204) remained. That which Han had bought (*mai tuan*) from aborigines was to

be registered for taxation. Wu-la-na then adds that areas that have been illicitly reclaimed (*ssu k'en*) should be distinguished according to land quality and either taxed or not (*TACC*: 9). Once again the failure to use explicit terminology confuses the meaning. What does *ssu k'en* mean in this context? It probably refers to land that Han reclaimed without the usual agreement (either *tsu p'u* or *mai tuan*) with civilized aborigine tribes. In the early Ch'ien-lung decrees, in contrast, the terms *ssu p'u* and *ssu mai* were used for agreements that lacked official sanction (*TACC*: 8). If the *ssu k'en* land is to be taxed, it is interesting that the settlers are not also ordered to compensate the aborigines by paying rents and thus to conform to the *mai tuan* model set by Fu-k'ang-an. The failure to mention *tsu p'u* lands, coupled with contradictory references to *ssu k'en* land and tax-exempt land, makes Wu-la-na's report on this topic curiously incomplete. A few of the locales where aborigine land was sold (*mai tuan*) to Han are listed, but unfortunately area figures are not given. A few areas were granted tax-exempt status because of their very low productivity (*TACC*: 8–9).

159. In fact, the four places Fu-k'ang-an lists figured in the last days of the rebellion, and both the settlers and raw aborigines there aided the government in its search for rebel remnants (see *CTPT*: 863).

160. *TACC*: 33.

161. *CTPT*: 989–91. The central government had already called for strengthening the earth-oxen boundary (*CTPT*: 840).

162. *CTPT*: 1044, also 993, 1008–9, 1029, 1033.

163. *CTPT*: 1044. Hsü fails to mention at this point that the 5,000 *chia* to be allotted to the colonists had yet to be converted to paddy fields. Elsewhere Hsü estimated yields on reclaimed land (first-grade paddy) at 80 *shih* per *chia* (*CTPT*: 1042). What, then, does the 30–40 *shih* per *chia* estimate represent? The yield from farming dry land? Or the expected rental (50 percent) on the land once it was reclaimed, irrigated, and rented out (this alternative is less likely since he seems to rule out renting)?

164. *CTPT*: 158, 495, 861.

165. *CTPT*: 862, 934, 1036; *TACC*: 27.

166. *CTPT*: 790; *CHHC*: 72–73.

167. *TACC*: 1–15, 35.

168. Chuang Chin-te 1960: 47.

169. Ibid.: 102.

170. Ibid.: 102–3.

171. The areas cited in the letter differ considerably from those finally decided on; in Feng-shan especially a much larger area was later made available (cf. *TACC*: 48–49).

172. Chuang Chin-te 1960: 103.

173. Curiously Wu-la-na mistakenly attributed the 1784 survey to Fu Kang, governor of Fukien in 1781 and acting governor-general at that time (*CLSL*: 249), rather than to Furgun (Fu-le-yün, the characters for the two Fu's are identical), who was governor-general in 1784 and was named as having ordered the survey by Fu-k'ang-an (*CTPT*: 989). The mistake is repeated in *HHTWHC*: 93.

174. *TACC*: 2.

175. This is repeated in various phrasings, three times; see *TACC*: 2, 7, 10.

176. Ibid.

177. *TACC*: 7, 8; *CTPT*: 1042.

178. *TACC*: 11.

179. *TWSHF*: 1.398; *TACC*: 10–11.

180. *TACC*: 7, 14.

181. A small discrepancy exists in the salary figures for Chang-hua, where four collectors are listed as receiving 60 *yüan* each, but the total is given as only 210 *yüan* (*TWSHF*: 1.40); and for Tan-shui, where it is stated that there are five collectors but only four are named and given salaries (ibid.: 398).

182. *TACC*: 11–12. Unfortunately, the colony rent income is given only in cash figures at the county level, and there is no way to estimate the land areas of the few tracts listed (there is no comprehensive list).

183. *TWSHF*: 1.397–402; *TACC*: 12–13.

184. *TACC*: 9–10; on deeds, see Okamatsu 1902: 58.

185. *TACC*: 2–3; cf. *CTPT*: 987.

186. *TACC*: 5; *CTPT*: 1044.

187. *TACC*: 5–6.

188. *CTPT*: 988.

189. Chuang Chin-te 1960: 103.

190. *TACC*: 37–38.

191. I draw my information on linguistic identity from Chang Yao-ch'i 1965. For the plains aborigine villages and their ethnolinguistic affiliations (including subgroupings not distinguished by Chang), see Appendix A.

192. *CTPT*: 987–88.

193. *TACC*: 3.

194. *TWSHF*: 1.385–86.

195. See, e.g., the contract of 1773 of coastal Pei-kang village (*TTTCS*: 360–61). Pei-kang, "having no tenanted land to rely on," complains that an unnamed neighboring tribe had encroached on its territory to let out land to Han. An official intervened to ensure Pei-kang's rights to a rent from forested land cleared by Han tenants.

196. *CTPT*: 950, 987.

197. Unfortunately, I have been unable to pinpoint the bulk of the colony sites, and I am unable to demonstrate the validity of these criticisms for the spatial allotment in general.

198. *CTPT*: 989.

199. *TACC*: 6.

200. *CTPT*: 988. The *Ssu-ch'uan t'ung chih* of 1816 (87.12) reports widely varying ratios among the *t'un lien* colonies, but all less than 100 braves per sergeant.

201. *CTPT*: 962–63.

202. *CTPT*: 1029; *CLSL*: 649, 671, 676.

203. See, e.g., Cheng Hsi-fu 1976: 112, 124.

204. Tai Yen-hui 1953: 2.

205. *TACC*: 14.

206. This practice then spread to other counties; see Cheng Hsi-fu 1976: 126.

207. Ibid.: 124, 126; Chuang Chin-te 1960: 89.

208. *CHHC*: 78.

209. Tai Yen-hui 1953: 17–19. San-hsia's Shih-san-t'ien is an example of colony land rented out in the Chia-ch'ing period by a contract that cites these reasons; see Chapter 1.

210. *TTTCS*: 779–80.

211. Cheng Hsi-fu 1976: 125, 126.

212. Ibid.: 124–30.

213. *CTPT*: 905–6.

214. *CTPT*: 958–59.

215. *CLSL*: 664.

216. *CLSL*: 601–2 (the memorial is dated 1786); Jung 1979: 376; Register of

Officials for 1794. See Watt 1972: 71 on imperial appointment to important prefectural posts.

217. Chuang Chin-te 1965: 75.

218. *CTPT*: 977–82.

219. *CTPT*: 970–74, 842–43.

220. *CTPT*: 912, 960, 1005.

221. *CTPT*: 960–63 and *CLSL*: 605–6 give slightly different versions.

222. This area had earlier been suggested as appropriate for aborigine military colonies (*CTPT*: 956).

223. *CTPT*: 960–63; *CLSL*: 605–6.

224. *CTPT*: 134–35; Lamley 1977*b*: 183.

225. *CTPT*: 840, 945–48.

226. *CTPT*: 789, 1044–45; *TAHLPC*: 159.

227. *CTPT*: 947, 976. These limits were originally adopted in part to prevent supplies falling into the hands of pirates. Given the resurgence of piracy in the following years, lifting the restriction may have backfired (see Leung 1977: chap. 8).

228. *CTPT*: 963–64, 1011; *CLSL*: 929–30.

229. Hummel 1943–44: 23–24, 254–55, 289–90; Jung 1979: 367–68. Imperial Commissioner Fu-k'ang-an became governor-general of Fukien and Chekiang in late 1788 (*CLSL*: 642).

230. *CLSL*: 678, 680–82.

231. *CLSL*: 687–90. *CTPT*: 119 gives the subethnic identity.

232. *CLSL*: 685, 694–95, 698.

233. *CLSL*: 700–702, 704–5.

234. *CLSL*: 708–10, 712.

235. *CHHC*: 377; *CLSL*: 714–15; Yao 1957: 117.

236. *CTPT*: 861; *CLSL*: 716; Yao 1957: 123.

237. *CLSL*: 719. The growth of piracy in Fukien in these years followed the upsurge of piracy in Kwangtung that was linked to the Tayson rebellion in Vietnam (see Leonard 1984: 80 and Murray 1987).

238. *CLSL*: 716–17, 719; *CCSL*: 3.

239. *CLSL*: 724–25.

240. *CCSL*: 5–6; Hummel 1943–44: 774.

241. *CTPT*: 638–39.

242. Lamley 1977*b*, 1981; see also Chapter 7.

243. Huang Huan-yao 1986*a*: 194–96.

244. Inō 1928: 3.884–85; cf. Cheng Hsi-fu 1976: 126.

245. Chang Yao-ch'i 1951: app. 2.3–7; Liu Chih-wan 1958; Hsieh Jih-chang 1979*a*. For a discussion of the P'u-li migration, see Chapter 11.

246. Cf. Ferrell 1969*a*; Treistman 1972; and Mabuchi 1974*a*: vol. 2 *passim*.

247. Hsu Cho-yun 1972: 56.

248. Lamley 1977*b*: 192–93.

249. *KMLCL*: 141–42; see also the statute of 1826 in *CHTTWSL*: 40. This resembles the solution proposed by Tan-shui prefect Wang P'ing in 1727 but not adopted (see Chapter 9). As noted above, Yang T'ing-li had previously been involved in the survey of lands for the aborigine military colonies and was familiar with the policy rationale underlying Taiwan precedents relating to plains aborigines.

250. *KMLCL*: 122–24.

251. Negishi 1964: 13–14.

252. Lamley 1977*b*, 1981: 305; Meskill 1979; see Chapter 7 on the increasing numbers of degree-holders.

253. Huang Huan-yao 1986*a*: 194–96.

254. Yen 1965; Rawlinson 1967; Kuo T'ing-i 1973: 184; Lien Chan 1973; Meskill 1979: 182.

255. Chou Hsien-wen 1957: 5–6; Speidel 1976: 447; Shih T'ien-fu 1989*a*: 16. In 1869 the government had cut in half the number of troops stationed in Taiwan. In 1881 troops were reduced again, a situation that lasted until Liu Ming-ch'uan rebuilt Taiwan's military (Speidel 1976: 449–51).

256. Davidson 1903; Speidel 1976.

257. Liu Ming-ch'uan 1958: 222; Meskill 1979: 186–89.

258. As Lan Ting-yüan would have predicted, the cadastral survey led to a revolt in central Taiwan (Speidel 1976: 454).

259. Tai Yen-hui 1953: 37–40, 1976: 366.

260. Myers 1974: 456; Speidel 1976: 453.

261. Speidel 1976: 447, 452.

262. See Table 8.4.

263. Takekoshi 1907: 130; Hummel 1943–44: 527–28; Speidel 1976. By 1905 the Japanese colonial cadastral survey had doubled the area of land registered under Liu Ming-ch'uan (Myers 1974: 456).

CHAPTER ELEVEN

1. Although I do not see cultures as collections of easily separable and discrete traits, neither do I assume the perfect integration of consensus sociology. I favor the view of cultures as "shreds and patches" rather than "seamless webs."

2. The tendency to reify ethnicity and to find ethnic consciousness operating in all times and places is encouraged by systems of entitlement and representation (common in modern nation-states), which require individuals to identify with an ethnic or nationality group (see Anderson 1983). Another way in which ethnic studies exaggerate the sociological significance of ethnicity is the emphasis on ethnic *identity*. These studies commonly observe that in different situations an individual may seek to identify with different ethnic groups and describe these individuals as having multiple ethnic "identities." Sociologically it would be more appropriate to see ethnicity operating in such situations as a status characteristic, rather than as the integrated aspect of personality implied by the term "identity." For an argument that ethnicity has no independent theoretical status in sociology and a discussion of status characteristics and expectation states and their relational and situational quality, see Berger et al. 1977.

3. For example, plains Indian eagle feather headdress and powwows have been adopted by Native Americans throughout North America. On inventing traditions and reifying ethnicity, see Hobsbawm and Ranger 1983; for Chinese cases, see Croizier 1977 and Waldron 1990: chap. 11. Crossley's recent work on the Manchus (1990*a*) provides a nice example; the speed and degree of acculturation by the Manchus so alarmed the Ch'ien-lung emperor that he instituted programs aimed at maintaining a separate Manchu identity.

4. See Banton's exposition of the rational choice theory of ethnicity (1983:

chaps. 6–8) for an explanation of how the structure of group competition affects boundary maintenance and ethnic consciousness (see also Barth 1969).

5. My insistence on a thoroughgoing historical circumstantialism and skepticism about attempts to read the concept of ethnicity into Chinese social history is shared by at least two contributors to a recent issue of *Late Imperial China* (Crossley 1990*b*; Ownby 1990). But I reject Crossley's attempt (1990*b*: 2–5) to reify the descriptive term "sinicization," which she overloads with preconceptions about assimilation, conquest dynasties, and the charisma of Chinese culture. Instead, I use "sinicization" to refer simply to a process of acculturation in which a non-Chinese group adopts elements of the Chinese culture with which it is in contact. Why the group adopts Chinese cultural elements, which elements it adopts and which it rejects, and whether the adoption has any effect on ethnic identity and consciousness are topics best left to separate analyses; they should not be loaded onto a single concept. Crossley (1990*a*, *b*) falls victim to the ethnicity literature (and its obsession with ethnic consciousness) when she fails to distinguish acculturation from assimilation and ethnic identity in her discussions of the Manchus. The Manchus provide an interesting case precisely because of the tension between their rapid sinicization and the Manchu elite's desire to preserve a separate group identity. Apparently assuming that acculturation is unproblematic, Crossley documents that the Manchus adopted many elements of Chinese culture and discarded in the process many of their own traditions and language, but she leaves the reasons for Manchu acculturation/sinicization unanalyzed in order to focus primarily on the policies attempting to heighten/reinvent Manchu identity. Students of acculturation have long been aware that adoption of foreign cultural elements is not just borrowing; it involves complex decisions regarding the prestige ranking, selection, reinterpretation, replacement, and incorporation of cultural elements (cf. Herskovits 1948: 523–60).

6. For discussions of some of these issues, see Shepherd 1986, 1988*b*.

7. Several studies of plains aborigine groups are under way or contemplated by members of the Taiwan History Field Research Office of the Academia Sinica. I am currently at work on a historical ethnography of the Siraya and have written a number of papers (see the Bibliography).

8. Thompson 1964: 193, 195.

9. Thompson 1969: 52, 92, 105, 138–39.

10. See Chapters 5, 6, and 7 for the late timing of agricultural expansion in the north.

11. Thompson 1969: 105. De Mailla also reported seeing herds of deer and smoked venison in the markets in 1715 (Campbell 1903: 506).

12. *CHFSHC*: 72, 77; Thompson 1969: 102–3, 126, 138. For a critique of romantic notions that the cultures of hunting groups make them natural conservationists, uniquely in tune with nature, see Krech 1981. On the aborigine tax burden and the excesses of interpreters, see Chapter 5.

13. *TWFC*:Liu: 496; *CHTWHC*: 432–33.

14. *CLHC*: 297; *CHFSHC*: 403. On the progressive expansion of settlement, see Chapter 6.

15. Aborigine exports were not limited to deer products; laver and water creepers are mentioned above (see also Thompson 1969: 109). The Chu-lo county gazetteer (*CLHC*: 162) records that some aborigines wove rattan baskets that they

sold to Han, who lacquered them and added brass locks, for resale. Some aborigine groups grew a fragrant rice coveted by Han (*CLHC*: 191), and others a special tea (*CLHC*: 295). But these small specialty items were insufficient to replace the deer industry.

16. Thompson 1969: 55, 76, 102, 122.

17. Ibid.: 80–81, 100, 108, 111.

18. Ibid.: 105; Thompson 1964: 175; and see Chapters 2 and 3.

19. Thompson 1964: 181.

20. See Chapter 3; *CHTWHC*: 409; and Thompson 1969: 96. On male plowing, see Boserup 1965.

21. *FSHC*: 92; *CLHC*: 191.

22. Thompson 1969: 116.

23. Shih T'ien-fu 1990. Shih argues that excessive demands for corvée labor by abusive Chinese officials disrupted both aborigine farming and deer hunting. In my view, Shih's argument underestimates the role of overhunting in the decline of the deer trade and exaggerates both the ease with which male aborigine hunters could become farmers and their desire to do so.

24. *TWFC*:Chou: 316; *CHTWHC*: 405.

25. Campbell 1903: 248–49; Ch'en Han-kuang 1960: 16–17; Thompson 1964: 175.

26. *CLHC*: 146, 149; Ch'en Han-kuang 1960: 21–22; Thompson 1964: 185.

27. *YTHC*: 221; *TWFC*:Kao: 248; Huang Shu-ching 1957: 108.

28. Thompson 1969: 93, 101, 110; Gallin 1966: 62.

29. Campbell 1903: 2, 16, 17; Thompson 1969: 76, 84, 102; Coyett 1975: 6.

30. *CLHC*: 149; Ch'en Han-kuang 1960: 16.

31. *TWFC*:Liu: 491. Ingold (1980: 242) notes that the rapid propagation of a species introduced by man into an environment where it has no natural enemies (and sometimes depopulated of a competing species like deer or buffalo by overhunting) is a familiar ecological phenomenon. He cites cattle in Brazil and the American west as examples.

32. Chang Yao-ch'i 1951: app. 2.6; Ch'en Han-kuang 1960: 16. Ch'en Cheng-hsiang's (1959–61: 2.534) map of cattle density per cultivated area shows the highest densities in the mountain foothills. Wang Shih-ch'ing's (1969) study of cattle markets does not discuss the role of areas producing for export. Both water buffalo and cattle were raised in Taiwan. Water buffalo were bred primarily for drawing plows, and draft cattle were bred for pulling carts (Ho Yhi-min 1966: 53–55).

33. Yü 1959: 22; Thompson 1969: 85.

34. Thompson 1969: 73.

35. *CLHC*: 164; *CHTWHC*: 405.

36. *TWFC*:Yü: 93–94, 97–98; *CHFSHC*: 41.

37. *CLSL*: 64; *TAHLPC*: 81.

38. *CLHC*: 36, 41, 261; *TSTC*: 73–74, 77.

39. Schwartz 1968: 278–79.

40. R. Smith 1983: 6, 107.

41. See below for a discussion of prestige processes. On prestige as a means of social control, see Goode 1978 and Shepherd 1989.

42. Bol 1987: 483–86; von Glahn 1987: 250–51.

43. Ruey 1972: 637; Wang Gungwu 1984. These issues are discussed more thoroughly in Shepherd 1989.

44. There can thus be no confusing of Confucian "culturalism" with a democratic pluralism that celebrates ethnic diversity. On the Confucian model of didactic leadership, see Silin 1976.

45. Watt 1972: 83, 91.

46. Lattimore (in his introduction to Schram 1954: 17) notes that the imperial state desired that pastoral nomads on its Central Asian frontier, even after submitting and pledging loyalty, retain their skills as cavalrymen who could serve the state militarily. See also Serruys 1968: 304–5 on the Mongols in China during the Ming.

47. *CSWP*: 5.

48. See Chapter 12 for Wang An-shih's similar views. Shen also recognized the need to protect aborigine livelihoods (see Chapter 9).

49. Wang Gungwu 1984: 5, 9.

50. Inō 1904: chap. 5; Rawski 1979.

51. Inō 1904: 550–53; Thompson 1969: 73, 85; Rawski 1979: 136–37; Kelleher 1989. Inō 1904: 523–27 reprints a nineteenth-century set of five-character couplets that explain imperial government and Confucian morality to aborigines and criticize aborigine customs that violate these norms.

52. Inō 1904: 533–34, 544–45; Hsiao Kung-ch'uan 1960: 186–88; R. Smith 1983: 109–11; Kelleher 1989.

53. Hsiao Kung-ch'uan 1960: 250–52.

54. *TWFC*:Kao: 33. These may have continued schools that Yü Yung-ho suggests existed under the Chengs (Thompson 1964: 186). The Ming refugee scholar Shen Kuang-wen is also reported to have taught in the aborigine village of Mu-chia-liu-wan during the Cheng period (*TWFC*:Fan: 393–94).

55. *TWFC*:Chou: 65–66; *TWFC*:Fan: 137; Inō 1904: 510.

56. *YTHC*: 22–23; *TWFC*:Fan: 102; Ch'en Pin 1961: 16, 1964: 63.

57. Ch'en Pin 1964: 71.

58. *CLHC*: 134.

59. *CLHC*: 79–80; *TWHC*: 85; *FSHC*: 23.

60. Huang Shu-ching 1957: 109, 117, 149.

61. Ibid.: 171; *TWFC*:Fan: 103, 140.

62. *TWHC*: 82; *CLHC*: 79; Inō 1904: 511–12, 517; see also Brunnert and Hagelstrom 1912: 128, 215; and Hucker 1985: 269.

63. *TWFC*:Yü: 342–49; *TWFC*:Kao: 173–78; also Feuchtwang 1977.

64. By 1768 a few adjustments had been made in the list of schools through mergers, additions, and deletions (*TWFC*:Liu: 332–33).

65. Liu-shih-ch'i et al. 1961: 1; Inō 1904: 515.

66. *TWFC*:Yü: 360–61. The county gazetteers compiled 1717–20 reported a larger number of community schools among Han, founded primarily in response to a 1709 order of Fukien governor Chang Po-hsing (a famous scholar); the gazetteers list eight schools in Chu-lo, eighteen in Taiwan, but only two in Feng-shan (*CLHC*: 79; *TWHC*: 85; *FSHC*: 23). Later prefectural gazetteers, however, fail to confirm the continued existence of many of these village schools.

67. Ho Ping-ti 1962: 29, 36.

68. *CTPT*: 168, 733.

69. Kracke 1957; Ho Ping-ti 1962: 185.

70. Inō 1904: 516–17.

71. I argue elsewhere (Shepherd 1989) that prestige processes can explain why Watson (1988) finds in Chinese culture a unity of standardized rituals (where *appearances* count) rather than a unity of beliefs. For a discussion of prestige as a social control system, see Goode 1978.

72. Lattimore offers a nice example showing how direct contact can impede acculturation when groups see themselves competing against each other and how prestige dynamics can facilitate acculturation (which Lattimore calls assimilation) even though contact is indirect. Lattimore contrasts two Mongol groups: "Among the easternmost Gorlos Mongols, who were in contact with the Manchus of Kirin, there was a tendency for these agricultural communities to lose their language and become completely Chinese in character. This was because the Mongols tended to model themselves on the Manchus, and as the Manchus became assimilated [i.e., acculturated] to the Chinese, so did the Mongols. Farther south, among the Khorchins, there was less Manchu influence and the Mongols were in direct contact with the Chinese of the Chinese Pale. Here the traditional antagonism between Mongols and Chinese was more effective, and Mongol farming villages, even though surrounded by Chinese communities, retained their language and national character with really extraordinary tenacity. It is thus possible to find, within eighty or a hundred miles of Mukden, even at the present day, Mongol villages where the people have lived for generations in the Chinese manner, and yet still preserve the Mongol language—although of course most of them, the men especially, speak Chinese as well" (1934: 85–86). Where Mongols emulated the high-prestige ruling Manchus, they inadvertently became highly sinicized, despite the lack of direct contact with Chinese. But where direct contact fueled competition with Chinese farmers, Mongols tenaciously held on to their language and separate identity, despite acculturation to many other Chinese ways. Lattimore notes that all Mongols took pride in their martial history and their "class-consciousness of being the superior race, lords of the land, entitled to tribal subsidies in the form of rentals from the Chinese" (1934: 87; see also Chapter 12).

73. Relevant to studies of acculturation is Merton's (1968: 319–20) concept of "anticipatory socialization," whereby an individual or group adopts the values of a prestigious reference group to which it aspires but does not belong. Anderson's (1983: 55, 58, 85–88) analysis of the rise of nationalisms within colonial empires also relies heavily on blocked (vs. open) channels of social mobility, an analytic point somewhat obscured by his use of the term "pilgrimage." See Skinner (1973) for an elegant example of the importance of avenues of mobility for the acculturation of Chinese in Southeast Asia.

74. See Hsieh Shih-chung 1987 for the stigmatized identity of contemporary aborigine groups in Taiwan.

75. Thompson 1964: 188, 1969: 96 (cf. 109). See Wang Gungwu (1984: 8–12) for comments on the significance of clothing.

76. *YTHC*: 22; Thompson 1964: 174, 180, 191. See Inō 1904: 534–36 for a late nineteenth-century list of customs aborigines were expected to learn in order to become civilized.

77. De Mailla's description of 1715 matches Yü's of 1697, but he may be draw-

ing on gazetteer accounts at this point rather than direct observation (Campbell 1903: 509). For Chinese drawings of the plains aborigines, see *CLHC*;*CCKTH*; Liu-shih-ch'i et al. 1961; Chang Yao-ch'i 1965: 528. Let me take this opportunity to express my admiration of Laurence Thompson's superb translations (1964, 1969) of Yü Yung-ho's and Huang Shu-ching's accounts, on which I have relied extensively in this section.

78. Thompson 1964: 186.

79. Ibid.: 189; Thompson 1969: 49–50. No "color bar" between Han and aborigines restricted interaction or intermarriage.

80. We may attribute the persistence of Dutch motifs to lagging emulation or, more romantically, to a counterculture of resistance to Chinese domination. However, if Dutch styles expressed a symbolic protest against increasing Chinese dominance in the eighteenth century, they should have gained in prominence, rather than disappeared, as Chinese dominance increased. When Western missionaries arrived in the late nineteenth century, plains aborigines attempted to revive their Dutch connections (see Shepherd 1988*b*).

81. *CLHC*: 156, 167; Thompson 1969: 53, 65.

82. *TWFC*:Kao: 187; *YTHC*: 20; Thompson 1964: 180.

83. Murakami 1933; Thompson 1964: 183, 1969: 53. De Mailla in 1715 reported meeting several aborigines who could still speak Dutch and write in the Dutch alphabet (Campbell 1903: 510).

84. *CLHC*: 163; *TWFC*:Kao: 189; *TWFC*:Liu: 106.

85. Thompson 1969: 52, 57, 60.

86. Ibid.: 101; Chang Yao-ch'i 1965: 558. For the portrait, see Inō 1904: 520.

87. *TWFC*:Fan: 474–75; *CHTWHC*: 404; *TWFC*:Yü: 583, 813; Thompson 1969: 118.

88. Thompson 1969: 55, 62, 121.

89. Ibid.: 69; *CLHC*: 167, 293; *YTHC*: 21. On the importance to Chinese of coffin burial and ancestor worship at graves, *contra* Watson (1988: 12), see Shepherd 1989.

90. Huang Shu-ching 1957: 149; Thompson 1969: 57, 107.

91. Thompson 1964: 193.

92. Ibid.: 186, 195, 196.

93. *CLHC*: 188; *TWFC*:Liu: 498; Thompson 1964: 181, 191.

94. *IGS*: 17; a similar case is reported for I-lan (Hsu Cho-yun 1972: 53).

95. Shepherd 1988*b*.

96. *CLHC*: 286; *RCSS*: 2, 43–44.

97. *NPPW*: 402–3, 406–7; *CPPW*: 167.

98. MacKay 1895: 238; Pickering 1898: 66; McGough 1976: 15; Shepherd 1988*b*.

99. Hung Hsiu-kuei 1973: 508–9.

100. Shepherd 1986.

101. Tai Yen-hui 1941–42: pt. 4.17.

102. Thompson 1969: 78–79; Seaman 1978: 16, 114.

103. Thompson 1964: 196–97, 1969: 49–50.

104. Thompson 1964: 196.

105. Of course, traditional Chinese theory assumed that sinicization/Confucianization was the result of a recognition by lesser peoples of the intrinsic

superiority of Chinese culture. On contemptuous Chinese attitudes toward aboriginal cultures, see Hsieh Shih-chung 1987: chap. 5.

106. For these movements among five separate ethnolinguistic groups of plains aborigines, see Shepherd 1988*b*; see also below.

107. In my fieldwork, I discovered that a common way to invent a Han ancestry is to claim the aborigine ancestor who first adopted a Han surname was instead a Han immigrant who married into an aborigine village. In this way non-Han, aboriginal customs can be explained as a legacy of aboriginal ancestresses, without compromising a claim to Han identity through the male line, all-important in the Han system. In cases of highly unusual surnames, these attempts at reinterpretation of group history are less plausible and sometimes require "tracing" the ancestor to a remote area of China where library research has revealed the presence of the surname. Even in cases of common surnames, however, some plains aborigines have misidentified native places on the mainland (Ch'en Ch'un-mu 1982: 81).

108. Thompson 1964: 180, 1969: 101. De Mailla in 1715 also described aborigine marriages as uxorilocal (Campbell 1903: 509).

109. Inō 1904: 535–36, 556–62.

110. *TNHCK*: 2.53, 63; Wen 1957: 563–65; Li Chi-hua 1989*a*: 13.

111. Tai Yen-hui 1941–42: pt. 5.12–13; Wu Hsin-jung 1978: 168, 273.

112. Thompson 1964: 191–92, 1969: 54.

113. *TWFC*:Fan: 440.

114. *TWFC*:Liu: 105; also *CHFSHC*: 69.

115. Thompson 1969: 54, 61, 76, 84, 95, 102. On widows in Ch'ing society, see S. Mann 1985.

116. *TWFC*:Liu: 457.

117. Ch'en Ch'un-mu 1982.

118. Inō 1904: 524–25, 534–35, 544. For an excellent discussion of Chinese stereotypes of non-Han women reflecting these Confucian norms, see Diamond 1988.

119. The 1905 census reports only 0.5 percent of plains aborigine women with bound feet, compared to 1.5 percent of Hakka women and 68 percent of Hokkien women. Plains aborigines in contact primarily with Hakka rather than Hokkien were exposed to a different set of expectations with respect to female footbinding and related roles.

120. Shepherd 1988*b*. It remains unclear what constellation of factors resulted in the retention of traditional female dress and ornamentation. Did it reflect an aborigine feminism determined to reject Han definitions of female gender (high rates of intermarriage to Han husbands suggests this is unlikely to be the only explanation)? Did aborigine women believe the traditional costume was more attractive to both Han and aborigine men? Or did aborigine elders demand the wearing of traditional dress as a means of asserting control over wives and daughters and announcing a claim against Han suitors, perhaps to circumscribe a separate marriage market and impress on aborigine women a distinct ethnic loyalty?

121. Hatao 1903: 326–27; Wen 1957: 146–48.

122. Steere 1874: 304; Hsieh Jih-chang 1979*a*: 6.

123. Tai Yen-hui 1941–42: pt. 5; Ch'en Han-kuang 1963: 133; Hsieh Jih-chang 1979*a*; Wei 1981.

124. *TWFC*:Fan: 694.

125. *CHFSHC*: 112. Thompson 1964: 196; Chapter 5. Yü Yung-ho also reports that some tribesmen felt honored if a Chinese visitor was attracted to the village women (Thompson 1964: 192–93).

126. For notices of intermarriage, see Thompson 1969: 120, 137; Juan Ch'ang-jui 1971: 61. On gender differences in acculturation generally, see Spindler and Spindler 1958.

127. This is also the interpretation several writers have given to an obscure passage by Huang Shu-ching describing a sworn brother system; see Thompson 1969: 84 and Chang Yao-ch'i 1965: 626. On its face the passage implies wife-sharing.

128. For parallel processes on the Tibetan frontier, see Ekvall 1939: 39, 43–47. Juan Ch'ang-jui (1971) describes a different result of continuing acculturation (and desinification) that occurred when in-marrying Han males became isolated in an Ami community on Taiwan's east coast and the second wave of Han immigration never materialized to stimulate re-sinification. Juan found the most enduring legacy transmitted by these Han men to their largely Ami descendants was the Chinese ancestor cult. The wealthier members of this highly acculturated group of families identified themselves as Han but were considered by the local Han to be aborigine and by the local Ami to be "mixed" (1971: 58). Pursuing Chinese-style agriculture under conditions of abundant unreclaimed land and a labor shortage reduced the desire to exclude daughters from inheritance and put a premium on the labor that Ami sons-in-law could contribute. So these families of Han patriarchs pursued an expansionary pattern and recruited in-marrying spouses for *both* sons and daughters. On another highly acculturated Chinese group, the Baba (Malay-speaking Chinese) of Malacca, see Tan Chee Beng 1988: 144, 230.

129. Wen 1957: 570; Hsieh Jih-chang 1979*a*: 42–43.

130. *CHFSHC*: 85, 112; see also Chapters 6 and 9 and note 96 to Chapter 5.

131. Steere 1874: 314; Li Chi-hua 1989*b*.

132. Li Chi-hua 1989*b*: 84–86.

133. The frequency of adoption of Chinese girls by plains aborigines has yet to be documented, but for the parallels among mountain aborigines, see Matsuzawa 1989: 94–95, and among Malays, see Swift 1965: 111.

134. The annual volumes on vital statistics from the Japanese period (*Taiwan jinkō dōtai tōkei*) report ethnic intermarriages. Of 1,864 marriages contracted by plains aborigine women from 1905 to 1908, 72 percent were with plains aborigine men, 27 percent with Han men (19 percent Hokkien and 8 percent Hakka), and 1 percent with mountain aborigine men. Of 1,672 marriages contracted by plains aborigine men during this period, 80 percent were with plains aborigine women, 18 percent with Han women (14 percent Hokkien and 4 percent Hakka), and 2 percent with mountain aborigine women. Although most plains aborigines married plains aborigines, there was a substantial amount of intermarriage with Han, 27 percent for the women and a sizable 18 percent for the men. The disparity reflects a continuing loss of plains aborigine women to the Han, only partially compensated by the in-marriage of Han women. We do not know what form these marriages took. It is possible that many plains aborigine men were marrying Han women uxorilocally. The continuing disadvantage in the marriage market of the

plains aborigine men is also suggested by the lower number of marriages they contracted.

135. See Chapter 2 for the contrast in average village size between the Siraya and other plains groups.

136. Tai Yen-hui 1976: 336, 362. Tai discusses the corruption of plains aborigine large-rent collection in the nineteenth century, which in some cases came under the control of Han managers.

137. Chang Yao-ch'i 1965: 558; Thompson 1969: 101; Meskill 1979: 35.

138. Steere 1874: 312–14; Hatao 1903.

139. Pickering 1898: 115–16.

140. Ibid.: 117.

141. Ibid.: 65, 66, 142.

142. Steere 1874: 312–14; Hung Hsiu-kuei 1973: 448; Wu Hsin-jung 1978: 46, 49, 261.

143. Steere 1874: 304.

144. Pickering 1898: 79, 116; Carrington 1977: 255, 266; Shepherd 1988*b*.

145. Pickering 1898: 66; Thompson 1964: 193, 1969: 51–52, 93.

146. Thompson 1969: 117; Tai Yen-hui 1976: 363, 365.

147. Steere 1874: 304, 310; Pickering 1898: 65–66; Campbell 1915: 249.

148. See Bax 1875: 117–34 and MacKay 1895: 240. The 1935 census also reports a plains aborigine population of over 1,000 at Hsin-kang-tzu; see *KCK*: table 4.

149. Steere 1874: 312–13.

150. On the 1804 migration to I-lan and the migration to P'u-li beginning in 1823, see Chang Yao-ch'i 1951: app. 2; Inō 1928: 3.884–85; Mabuchi 1954. See also Chapter 10.

151. Hsieh Jih-chang 1979*a*: chap. 2, 1979*b*: 55. Hsieh recounts the dramatic story of P'u-li in full detail. P'u-li corresponds to the Shui-sha-lien region, mentioned frequently in Chapter 10.

152. For the full text of the compact, see Liu Chih-wan 1958: 39–40.

153. Legge 1960: 316, The Book of Chou, Book III, Paragraph 10. Legge includes commentary on the passage and the meaning of "five relationships." The compact lifts the quoted passage, *chung min wu chiao wei shih*, slightly out of context to give it the intended meaning. The drafting of the compact must have been done by a plains aborigine degree holder, if not a Han scribe. See Watt (1972) for the Ch'ing theory of good government and the importance of nourishment and education in Mencian thought. I thank Liu Chi-lun for his assistance in identifying the quoted passage.

154. Cheng Hsi-fu 1976: pt. 2; Tai Yen-hui 1976.

155. Tai Yen-hui 1953: 37–41, 1976: 366; Speidel 1976: 453.

CHAPTER TWELVE

1. Tai Yen-hui 1953: 37–41, 1976: 366; Speidel 1976: 453. See Chapter 10 for Liu's aggressive policies toward mountain aborigines and other aspects of Taiwan's changed political economy in the nineteenth century.

2. Ho Ping-ti 1959; Perkins 1969: 16; Wang Yeh-chien 1973: 87. For an argument that most social historians have failed to appreciate the social implications

of the tremendous expansion of cultivated area that accompanied China's population growth, see Shepherd 1988*a*.

3. Wang Yeh-chien 1973: chap. 5; Skinner 1977*a*.

4. Wiens 1954: 182; J. Lee 1978: 20, 39.

5. Wiens 1954: 144–45, 194; Wang Gungwu 1958: 116–17; J. Lee 1978: 21–22.

6. Wiens 1954: 187.

7. Ibid.: 208–14; von Glahn 1987: 16, 37, 40, 124.

8. Von Glahn 1987: 95–96, 183–84.

9. Ibid.: 71–72, 83–84, 86–89.

10. Ibid.: 95–98, 103–4, 109, 138.

11. Ibid.: 116–18, 124, 137–38.

12. Ibid.: 87, 118, 122–24, 124, 242.

13. Tribesmen obligated to pay fees to the native chiefs paid the Sung a lower tax rate on their land. Land cultivated by Han was taxed at the full rate because they owed no tribal fees (ibid.: 109, 137–38).

14. Ibid.: 186–87.

15. Ibid.: 95–96. Von Glahn (ibid.: 95–96, 138) makes several references to the use of pledge and redeemable sale (*tien, tien mai*) in Sung discussions of frontier land transactions, but mistranslates *tien* as mortgage (see McAleavy 1958). Although von Glahn does not discuss in detail why the parties used *tien* to structure their transactions, I speculate that Han found redeemable sale attractive because they could acquire land at less than its market value confident that the natives would be unable to redeem the land. In addition, I suspect Han settlers used *tien* to acquire native land to evade prohibitions on absolute sale and to avoid transfer taxes and the taxes assessed against Han-owned land. See note 33 to this chapter and the accompanying discussion below.

16. Cushman 1970: 74, 206; J. Lee 1982*b*: 287–89.

17. Wiens 1954: 214, 224–25, 227–28, 238, 340–41.

18. *TLTI*: 711; Cushman 1970: 142–44; Huang P'ei 1974: 281, 296–97.

19. Clarke 1911: 143, 148; Stevenson 1932: 601, 604; Lombard-Salmon 1972: 174–76. Such usury was prohibited in 1781; see *TLTI*: 400. Forcible encroachment on Miao lands in Kweichow was specifically prohibited in 1833; see *TLTI*: 279.

20. *TLTI*: 278, 314; Jamieson 1921: 43, 85; Lombard-Salmon 1972: 224–26, 292; Huang P'ei 1974: 297.

21. Wiens 1954: 340; K. Smith 1970: 71; Huang P'ei 1974: 241, 288–89.

22. Wiens 1954: 222–23.

23. This was often done by manipulating succession struggles (ibid.: 222, 232).

24. Wiens 1954: 224–25, 238; K. Smith 1970: 153; Huang P'ei 1974: 242, 244, 293.

25. Ch'en Han-seng 1949: 9; Wiens 1954: 341; K. Smith 1970: 229.

26. Ch'en Han-seng 1949: 62.

27. Wiens 1954: 190–91; Ho Ping-ti 1959: 146; Cushman 1970: 220, 223; Kuhn 1970: 47. Contrast this with the preservation of the Ta-chia tribes' land rights following suppression of their revolt in 1732 (see Chapter 5).

28. Ch'en Han-seng 1936: 52; Lo Wan 1965: 93; Cohen 1968: 254–56. See Leong 1983 for the relation between Hakka migrations and regional economic cycles and Palmer 1987 for a careful study of split ownership in Hong Kong.

29. Jamieson 1921: 80, 83, 85, 91, 103–4; see also Chapter 8.

30. Lo Wan 1965: 109; Cohen 1968: 278. The spatial segregation of subethnic settlements was also discussed as a possible solution to communal strife in Taiwan in the wake of the Lin Shuang-wen rebellion (see Chapter 10).

31. This review focuses on China's northeastern frontiers and slights the northwest. The northeastern frontiers experienced the greatest expansion of agricultural settlement and produced the case studies that pose the land-tenure issues of concern here. Ch'ing expansion into the northwest in this period seems to have been primarily a matter of strategic calculation (mixed with the Ch'ien-lung emperor's search for military glory), and agrarian settlement was spearheaded by military colonization rather than an expanding Han population. Of course, the cost of governing the northwest posed many fiscal issues for the Ch'ing. Recent work on the northwest has been done by Joanna Waley-Cohen (1991) and Peter Perdue (1989).

32. Ma 1956: 336; Kessler 1976: 15, 105. Much of the confiscated area had been imperial or princely estates of the former Ming ruling house.

33. Liu Chia-chü 1964: 131. A pledge of land (*tien* is frequently mistranslated "mortgage") served the same tax-avoidance function on Banner lands as it served on Taiwan's tribal lands (both categories of land were tax-exempt). Absolute purchase of Banner land was not only illegal but undesirable, since a transfer of title (which pledge-sales avoid) would jeopardize the tax exemption (Tai Yen-hui 1953: 37–39). Ma Feng-ch'en (1956: 350) notes of Chinese farmers on Banner lands: "In mortgage [i.e., pledge-sale] cases not only did they acquire a de facto right of ownership, but also incidentally became exempt from taxation (because the land was nominally Banner land)." Pledge-sales preserved the tax exemption by avoiding a transfer of title. The tax exemption on Banner land made commoners willing to pay higher prices for rights to cultivate it (Liu Chia-chü 1964: 147).

34. Liu Chia-chü 1964: 147. The Yung-cheng emperor also experimented with relocating Bannermen on military colonies reclaiming land in Jehol and revitalizing the metropolitan garrisons by implementing a well-field system (Huang P'ei 1974: 177–79; R. Lee 1970: 123).

35. Ma 1956: 350, translating Ma 1936: 387–88; see also Liu Chia-chü 1964: 170. *Tien* transactions involve the pledging of land (the Bannermen gave up their use rights in return for cash and rents) not its mortgage (where the owner typically retains use rights and pays interest on the loan).

36. In Taiwan, too, the *tien mai* of tribal land commonly required the payment of rent to the tribes and made the land irredeemable; see Tai Yen-hui 1953: 22.

37. Ma 1956: 350; Liu Chia-chü 1964: 147. It would be a mistake to think Taiwan was following a Banner model. The dates of the important decrees (Taiwan's are earlier) point rather to the opposite conclusion. The better view sees both solutions as evolving from a set of pre-existing property institutions.

38. Riasanovsky 1938: 233; Hsiao I-shan 1958: 5.

39. Liu Chia-chü 1964: 187; R. Lee 1970: 78–79; Oxnam 1975: 164.

40. Ho Ping-ti 1959: 158–59; R. Lee 1970: 21, 184; Kessler 1976: 105.

41. Lattimore 1932: 178–80; R. Lee 1970: 75–76.

42. Lattimore 1932: 65, 1934: 19, 80–85; Serruys 1981: 496–97.

43. Lattimore 1934: 80; Ho Ping-ti 1959: 159–60; Rossabi 1975: 193–94.

44. Lattimore 1934: 79–81; R. Lee 1970: 102, 124; Rossabi 1975: 195.

45. Lattimore 1934: 80–82, 86, 240.

46. Unfortunately none of the secondary studies offers sufficient detail on the tenurial terms, and this must remain a tentative conclusion.

47. Lattimore 1934: 76–78, 83.

48. Ibid.: 199, 202–3. R. Lee (1970: 20, 136–37, 203–4) states that the proceeds of land sales and taxes were split between the government and the Banners.

49. See Oxnam 1975: 162.

50. R. Lee 1970: 126.

51. Ibid.: 117, 127–28, 149; Ho Ping-ti 1959: 160. This parallels the way the foreign threat to Taiwan brought pressure to increase revenues through the land tax; see above.

52. Lattimore 1932: 128–29, 1934: 94–98; Ho Ping-ti 1959: 160; R. Lee 1970: chaps. 6 and 7.

53. Serruys 1979: 471–73.

54. Lattimore 1934: 99–100.

55. Lattimore 1932: 65, 105.

56. Ibid.: 86.

57. This expansion was led by opium cultivation (ibid.: 192–93). The contrast of Mongols to Gold resembles the contrast of plains aborigines to the Kuvalan of I-lan (see Chapter 10). On the vicissitudes of Mongol acculturation, see Chapter 11.

58. R. Lee 1970: 34, 121; Lattimore 1962*b*: 346, 349.

59. Lattimore 1962*b*: 355, 366–69.

60. Lattimore 1932: 122–23; R. Lee 1970: 110.

61. Lattimore 1962*b*: 352; R. Lee 1970: 121.

62. Lattimore 1962*b*: 343, 352, 361.

63. Ibid.: 352, 353, 360; R. Lee 1970: 121.

64. Loewe 1974: 96–98, citing the *Discourses on Salt and Iron*.

65. Lattimore 1962*c*: 487. Lattimore's "economic integration" is too general; from the point of view of state goals, the key dimension of "economic integration" and development is revenue potential. Only economically advanced regions could reliably provide revenue surpluses to the state. Note also that Lattimore's set of relationships points to the importance of assessing the impact of new arms technologies on the state's military range, a point neglected by most of us who study China (see McNeill 1982 for the beginning of a correction). Lattimore's (1962*c*: 476–77) brilliant essay also points to important ecological differences between northern and southern frontiers; the similarities noted here in the Ch'ing state's approach to Taiwan and Manchuria, however, caution against exaggerating these differences. I argue that ecological differences became significant only as they affected the calculus of strategy, revenue, and control costs that determined the political economy of the Ch'ing state's approach to all its frontiers.

66. Skinner 1977*c*: 308. See the data in Appendix D that corroborate Skinner's generalization.

67. J. T. C. Liu 1959: 48–51, 56–57; von Glahn 1987: 98, 101, 207–8. Von Glahn (1987: 206, 212, 250–51) seems to exaggerate the significance of Wang Anshih's professed faith in the ability of native tribes to sinicize. Wang's pronouncements on this topic strike me more as rhetoric intended to discount the costs of imposing control in order to win support for his policies of frontier expansion. When natives became obstacles to the realization of his policies, Wang and his followers did not hesitate to support coercive measures, including forced removal (von Glahn 1987: 108, 128).

68. J. T. C. Liu 1959: 12; von Glahn 1987: 123–24, 268–69.

69. Rossabi 1975: 149–50, 153, 167, 171; Fletcher 1978: 37; Wu Chi-hua 1981. Kracke (1957) notes that the late imperial Chinese state also awarded generous examination quotas to border peoples as a means both of co-opting the preexisting elite and of creating a loyal Confucian elite (see also Chapters 7 and 11 on education).

70. Lo Jung-pang 1968: 52; R. Huang 1974: chap. 8. The central government resisted allocating subsidies to frontier provinces at the expense of neighboring provinces and its own share of tax revenues. For the Chinese state's attempts to limit administrative expenses and bureaucratic proliferation by consolidating and reallocating county-level units, see Chapter 7 and Skinner 1977*a*. See Wang Yeh-chien 1973 for the priority the state gave to a fixed budget and limiting expenditure growth.

71. Wang Yeh-chien 1973; S. Mann 1987.

72. Some areas did produce significant local revenue, e.g., the salt areas discussed by von Glahn (1987) during the Sung and the copper mines of Yunnan during the Ch'ing (K. Smith 1970; Wang Yeh-chien 1973: 88–89; J. Lee 1982*a*: 742–43).

73. In 1753, 74 percent of total revenues were from the land tax (Wang Yehchien 1973: 80).

74. Compare Solinger's (1977) analysis of PRC policies in the southwest.

APPENDIX A

1. Abe 1938: 22–36. Not treated here are Kuvalan villages in I-lan on the east coast that Chang Yao-ch'i (1951) also lists.

2. Abe 1938: 27–28.

3. *CLHC*; Huang Shu-ching 1957.

4. Nakamura 1963–64; Ferrell 1969*b*.

5. Abe 1938: 244–45, 259, 276.

6. Nakamura 1954: 59; Ferrell 1971: 233.

7. *KCK*: table 4.

8. *NPPW*: 376–77; *TAHLCC*: 141–49.

9. Tsuchida 1985.

10. See Mabuchi 1953; Ferrell 1969*a*, 1971.

11. Ferrell 1969*b*.

12. Ferrell 1971.

13. *TNHCK*: 2.60–61.

14. Chang Yao-ch'i 1951.

15. *TWFC*:Yü: 333–34. Note that several villages listed in the gazetteers consulted by Chang Yao-ch'i (1951) never had additional status as tax units, *t'un*, or school sites.

16. *KCK*: table 4.

17. Ch'en Cheng-hsiang 1959–61: 1.247.

18. See *HCHTFT*: 99, 234–35; Li Chi-hua 1989*a*.

APPENDIX C

1. Chiang Shu-shen 1986: 6. Huber (1990: 275) estimates the *morgen* was only 0.8 hectares.

2. Nakamura 1954: 62–63. Chiang Jih-sheng (1960: 206) gives 30 *ko* to a side; see also Lu 1956.

3. Ch'üan and Kraus 1975: 79, 92.

4. *CHHC*: 162; *TWFC*:Yü: 241; Chou Hsien-wen 1957: 98.

5. Ch'üan and Kraus 1975: 79, 84–92; *TSTC*: 94.

6. Chou Hsien-wen 1957: 98. It was common in the Ch'ien-lung era to collect tribute grain on a "discount basis," counting full units as equal to only 80 percent. Taiwan, though not responsible for tribute grain, thus seems only to be catching up to mainland practices at this point in time (Ch'ü 1962: 141, 294). Azuma (1955: 69) gives the date for conversion to *man tou* as 1788.

7. *TWFC*:Yü: 222, 242.

8. Wang Shih-ch'ing 1958*b*: 15.

9. Ch'üan and Kraus 1975: 93.

10. Ibid.: 98; Ng 1983: xiv.

APPENDIX D

1. See Whitney (1970: 147) for an indication of the range of intraprovincial variation in county areas.

2. Ibid.: 145.

3. Ibid.: chap. 4; Skinner 1977*a*: 18.

4. See Whitney 1970: 64, 150 for examples of possible statistical methods of comparison.

5. Cf. Skinner 1979. For some comparable measures of military presence for Europe, see Tilly 1990: 79.

6. See, e.g., Kuhn 1970: 10, 23.

7. Wade 1851: 254, 335.

8. Cf. Skinner 1979.

9. Wade 1851: 416; R. Smith 1974: 129.

10. Wang Yeh-chien 1973: 72. Immanuel Hsu (1983: 6) estimates military expenditures at 22.4 million taels or 63 percent of total expenditures of 35.3 million taels.

11. Wang Yeh-chien 1973: 72; see also Staunton 1797: 468 and Edkins 1903: 26.

12. Cf. Morse 1921: 104. Forthcoming work by Peter Purdue on the northwest campaigns should shed light on these issues (see Perdue 1989).

13. Cf. Ho Ping-ti 1962: 185–88, chap. 6.

14. Skinner 1977*c*: 308.

15. Naquin and Rawski 1987: 138–39.

16. Skinner (1977*b*, *c*) and Whitney (1970) frequently report computations, but not the data on which the computations are based that might be of value to other studies. Perkins (1969) and Wang Yeh-chien (1973) are exemplary in supplying disaggregated data.

APPENDIX F

1. Peng and Geiser 1977; Takakura 1960.

2. Wiens 1954: 335

3. Collier 1947: 114–15.

4. Prucha 1962: 6.

5. Collier 1947: 116–17; Prucha 1962: 13.

6. Prucha 1962: 2–3.
7. Ibid.: 142–47.
8. Ibid.: 155.
9. Ibid.: 171–74.
10. Ibid.: 37; Young 1961: 33.
11. Prucha 1962: 234.
12. Young 1961: 11, 75.
13. Ibid.: 9, 39; Prucha 1962: 226.
14. Prucha 1962: 226–27; see also 240–41.
15. Ibid.: 225; Young 1961: 50.
16. Kim 1978: 173–74, 179, 187.
17. Ibid.: 194, 200–201, 211–13. Some colonies practiced other forms of land tenure, e.g., headright or township systems (ibid.: 18–19, 129–30).
18. Ibid.: 134–35.
19. In Taiwan (and China generally), an attractive feature of split ownership rights was the insulation from oppressive and corrupt tax collectors it provided to commoner permanent tenants because the influential large-rent holders remained responsible for taxpaying (Shepherd 1988*a*: 422); American tax collectors apparently did not instill sufficient fear in Jacksonians to make them more amenable to a split-ownership solution.
20. Ellis 1967: 158–61; Kim 1978: 162–63.
21. Young 1961: 89–90; Wiens 1954: 333–34.
22. Young 1961: 16. Nineteenth-century American agricultural expansion was spurred by markets created by industrial capitalism, whereas Han Chinese expansion in eighteenth-century Taiwan was spurred by pre-industrial markets for rice and sugar; this difference, however, is of no analytic significance in the explanation of the different outcomes for tribal land rights on the two frontiers. The differences in military technology and state finance, on the other hand, are important.
23. In the twentieth century, long-term leases of Indian lands have become common (Schlesinger 1967).
24. Cf. Young 1961: 5.
25. See Prucha 1962: 32–33.

Bibliography

Works cited by acronym here or in the Notes are listed under the acronym.

Abe Akiyoshi 安培明義
1938 *Taiwan chimei kenkyū* 台灣地名研究 (Researches in Taiwan place-names). Taipei: Bango kenkyūkai.

Ahern, Emily Martin
1973 *The Cult of the Dead in a Chinese Village*. Stanford: Stanford University Press.

Allee, Mark
1987 "Law and Local Society in Late Imperial China: Tan-shui Subprefecture and Hsin-chu County, Taiwan, 1840–1895." Ph.D. dissertation, University of Pennsylvania.

Álvarez, José María
1930 *Formosa, geográfica e históricamente considerata*. 2 vols. Barcelona: Librería Católica Internacional.

Anderson, Benedict
1983 *Imagined Communities: Reflections on the Origin and Spread of Nationalism*. London: Verso.

Ao T'ien-huo 奥田彧 et al.
1954 "Ho ling shih tai chih T'ai-wan nung yeh" 荷領時代之台灣農業 (Taiwan's agriculture in the Dutch period). *TY* 25: 38–53.

Atwell, William S.
1982 "International Bullion Flows and the Chinese Economy Circa 1530–1650." *Past and Present* 95: 68–90.

Azuma Yoshio 東嘉生
1954 "Ch'ing tai T'ai-wan chih t'u ti so yu hsing t'ai" 清代台灣之土地所有形態 (Patterns of landownership in Ch'ing Taiwan). *TY* 25: 86–102.
1955 "Ch'ing tai T'ai-wan chih ti tsu kuan hsi" 清代台灣之地租關係 (Tenancy relationships in Ch'ing Taiwan). *TY* 32: 61–73.

Banton, Michael
1983 *Racial and Ethnic Competition*. Cambridge, Eng.: Cambridge University Press.

Barclay, George W.
1954 *Colonial Development and Population in Taiwan*. Princeton: Princeton University Press.

Barth, Fredrik, ed.
1969 *Ethnic Groups and Boundaries*. Boston: Little, Brown & Company.

Bax, Bonham W.
1875 *The Eastern Seas: Being a Narrative of the Voyage of H.M.S. "Dwarf" in China, Japan and Formosa*. London: J. Murray.

BD *Pa-ta-wei-ya ch'eng jih chi* 巴達維亞城日記 (Batavia diary). Murakami Naojirō 村上直次郎, ed.; Kuo Hui 郭輝, trans. 2 vols. Taipei: T'ai-wan sheng wen hsien wei yüan hui. 1970. Chinese translation of Vols. 1 and 2 of Murakami's 1937 Japanese edition of *Dagh register gehouden int Casteel Batavia, 1624–1645*.

Beattie, Hilary
1979 *Land and Lineage in China: A Study of T'ung-ch'eng county, Anhwei, in the Ming and Ch'ing Dynasties*. Cambridge, Eng.: Cambridge University Press.

Bellwood, Peter
1979 *Man's Conquest of the Pacific*. New York: Oxford University Press.
1985 *Prehistory of the Indo-Malaysian Archipelago*. New York: Academic Press.

Berger, Joseph, M. Hamit Fisek, Robert Z. Norman, and Morris Zelditch, Jr.
1977 *Status Characteristics and Social Interaction: An Expectation States Approach*. New York: Elsevier.

Bielenstein, Hans
1987 "Chinese Historical Demography, A.D. 2–1982." *Bulletin of the Museum of Far Eastern Antiquities*, no. 59 [entire issue].

Blair, E. H., and J. A. Robertson, eds.
1903–9 *The Philippine Islands, 1493–1803*. 55 vols. Cleveland: A. H. Clark.

Blussé, Leonard
1973 "The Dutch Occupation of the Pescadores (1622–1624)." *Transactions of the International Conference of Orientalists in Japan*, 18: 28–44.
1984 "Dutch Protestant Missionaries as Protagonists of the Territorial Expansion of the VOC on Formosa." In *Conversion, Competition and Conflict*, Dick Kooiman, Otto van den Muijzenberg, and Peter van der Veer, eds., pp. 155–84. Amsterdam: Free University Press.
1986 *Strange Company: Chinese Settlers, Mestizo Women and the Dutch in VOC Batavia*. Verhandelingen, 122. Leiden: Koninklijk Instituut voor Taal-, Land- en Volkenkunde.

Blussé, Leonard, and Marius P. H. Roessingh
1984 "A Visit to the Past: Soulang, a Formosan Village Anno 1623." *Archipel* 27: 63–80.

Blussé, Leonard, M. E. van Opstall, and Ts'ao Yung-ho
1986 *De Dagregisters van het Kasteel Zeelandia, Taiwan, 1629–1662*, vol. 1, *1629–1641*. The Hague: Martinus Nijhoff.
Blust, Robert
1982 "The Linguistic Value of the Wallace Line." *Bijdragen Tot de Taal-, Land- en Volkenkunde* 138: 231–50.
Bol, Peter K.
1987 "Seeking Common Ground: Han Literati Under Jurchen Rule." *Harvard Journal of Asiatic Studies* 47.2: 461–538.
Boserup, Ester
1965 *The Conditions of Agricultural Growth: The Economics of Agrarian Change Under Population Pressure*. Chicago: Aldine.
Boxer, C. R.
1939 "Chinese Abroad in the Late Ming and Early Manchu Periods." *T'ien hsia Monthly* 9.5: 447–68.
1941 "The Rise and Fall of Nicholas Iquan." *T'ien hsia Monthly* 11.5: 401–39.
1963 *The Great Ship from Amacon: Annals of Macao and the Old Japan Trade, 1555–1640*. Lisbon: Centro de estudos históricos ultramarinos.
1965 *The Dutch Seaborne Empire, 1600–1800*. London: Penguin Books.
Bridgman, E. C.
1838 "Remarks on Formosa." *Chinese Repository* 6: 418–27.
Brunnert, H. S., and V. V. Hagelstrom
1912 *Present Day Political Organization of China*. Shanghai: Kelly & Walsh.
Buck, J. L.
1937 *Land Utilization in China*. Shanghai: Commercial Press.
Campbell, William
1888 *The Gospel of St. Matthew in Sinkan Formosan, with Corresponding Versions in Dutch and English*. London: Trubner & Co.
1896 *The Articles of Christian Instruction in Favorlang-Formosan, Dutch, and English, from Vertrecht's MS. of 1650; with Psalmanazar's Dialogue Between a Japanese and a Formosan, and Happart's Favorlang Vocabulary*. London: Kegan Paul.
1903 *Formosa Under the Dutch, Described from Contemporary Records*. London: Kegan Paul.
1915 *Sketches from Formosa*. London: Marshall.
Caron, François, and Joost Schouten
1935 *A True Description of the Mighty Kingdoms of Japan and Siam*. 1663. Introduction by C. R. Boxer. London: Argonaut Press.
Carrington, George W.
1977 *Foreigners in Formosa, 1841–1874*. San Francisco: Chinese Materials Center.
Cator, W. J.
1936 *The Economic Position of the Chinese in the Netherlands Indies*. Chicago: University of Chicago Press.

CCH *Ch'ing ch'i hsien lei cheng hsüan pien* 清耆獻類徵選編 (Classified biographies of famous men of the Ch'ing). Li Huan 李桓, comp. 1884–90. *TW* 230.

CCKTH *Ch'ing chih kung t'u hsüan* 清職貢圖選 (Selected drawings of Ch'ing tribute bearers). 1751. *TW* 180.

CCSL *Ch'ing Jen-tsung shih lu hsüan chi* 清仁宗實錄選輯 (Selections from the Veritable Records of the Chia-ch'ing reign). *TW* 187.

CDI *Chōsa dai ikkai hōkokusho furoku sankōsho* 調查第一回報告書附錄參考書 (Supplementary reference source for the first report on the investigations of the first department). Kyoto: Rinji Taiwan kyūkan chōsakai, dai ichibu. 1903.

CDN *Chōsa dai nikkai hōkokusho dai ikkan furoku sankōsho* 調查第二回報告書第一卷附錄參考書 (Supplementary reference source for the second report on the investigations of the first department). Kobe: Rinji Taiwan kyūkan chōsakai, dai ichibu. 1906.

Chang Ch'i-yün 張其昀

1962 *Chung-hua min kuo ti t'u chi* 中華民國地圖集 (National atlas of China). Taipei: Kuo fang yen chiu yüan.

Chang Kwang-chih

1963 "Introduction." *Asian Perspectives* (Special Taiwan Section) 7: 195–202.

1972 "Neolithic Cultures in the Coastal Areas of Southeast China." In *Early Chinese Art and Its Possible Influence in the Pacific Basin*, vol. 2, *Asia*, Noel Barnard, ed., pp. 431–57. New York: Intercultural Arts Press.

Chang Shih-ch'u 張是初

1954 "Ch'ing tai T'ai-wan chih k'ao shih chih tu" 清代台灣之考試制度 (The examination system in Taiwan during the Ch'ing period). *Wen hsien chuan k'an* 5.1–2: 27–32.

Chang T'an 張菼

1970*a* *Ch'ing tai T'ai-wan min pien shih yen chiu* 清代台灣民變史研究 (Researches on the history of popular disturbances in Ch'ing Taiwan). *TY* 104.

1970*b* "Ch'ing tai ch'u ch'i chih T'ai cheng ts'e ti chien t'ao" 清代初期治台政策的檢討 (A discussion of early Ch'ing policies on the governance of Taiwan). *T'ai-wan wen hsien* 21.1: 19–44.

Chang Te-ch'ang

1972 "The Economic Role of the Imperial Household in the Ch'ing Dynasty." *Journal of Asian Studies* 31.2: 243–74.

Chang T'ien-tse

1934 *Sino-Portuguese Trade from 1514 to 1644*. Leiden: E. J. Brill.

Chang Wei 張葳

1978 "Chi p'ien yu kuan T'ai-wan ti K'ang-hsi ch'ao Man wen tsou che" 幾篇有關台灣的康熙朝滿文奏摺 (Some Manchu memorials concerning Taiwan from the K'ang-hsi reign). *T'ai-wan jen wen* 2: 65–73.

Chang Yao-ch'i 張耀錡

1951 "P'ing p'u tsu she ming tui chao piao" 平埔族社名對照表 (A com-

parative name list of plains aborigine villages). *Wen hsien chuan k'an* 2.1–2 [entire issue].
1965 *T'ung chou chih* 同冑志 (Assimilation). *T'ai-wan sheng t'ung chih kao*, vol. 8, part 3. Taipei: T'ai-wan sheng wen hsien wei yüan hui.

Chang Yao-k'un 張耀焜
1955 "An-li ta she yü T'ai-chung p'ing yeh chih k'ai fa" 岸裡大社與台中平野之開發 (The An-li tribe and the opening of the T'ai-chung plain). *Chung hsien wen hsien* 1: 4–28.

Chang Yung-wu 張庸吾
1954 "Ch'ing chi T'ai-wan chih huo pi liu t'ung k'ao" 清季台灣之貨幣流通考 (An investigation of the circulation of currency in Ch'ing Taiwan). *TY* 25: 16–30.

Chao Ch'uan-ch'eng
1956 "A Ship's Voyage from Luzon to China in the Eighteenth Century." In *Chinese Social History: Translations of Selected Studies*, E-tu Zen Sun and John DeFrancis, eds., pp. 352–60. Washington, D.C.: American Council of Learned Societies.

Chao Kang
1986 *Man and Land in Chinese History: An Economic Analysis*. Stanford: Stanford University Press.

Ch'en Cheng-hsiang 陳正祥
1959–61 *T'ai-wan ti chih* 台灣地志 (A geography of Taiwan). 3 vols. Taipei: Fu-ming ch'an yeh ti li yen chiu so.
1961 *T'ai-wan ti ming tz'u tien* 台灣地名辭典 (A dictionary of Taiwan place-names). Taipei: Fu-ming ch'an yeh ti li yen chiu so.

Ch'en Chi-lu
1968 *The Material Culture of the Formosan Aborigines*. Taipei: Taiwan Museum.

Ch'en Ch'i-nan 陳其南
1987 *T'ai-wan ti ch'uan t'ung Chung-kuo she hui* 台灣的傳統中國社會 (The traditional Chinese society of Taiwan). Taipei: Yün ch'en wen hua shih yeh.

Ch'en Ch'i-yen 陳棋炎
1953 "Ch'ing tai T'ai-wan lung en tsu chih jo kan fa lü wen t'i" 清代台灣隆恩租之若干法律問題 (Various legal problems concerning *lung en* rents in Ch'ing Taiwan). *She hui k'o hsüeh lun ts'ung* 4: 1–31.

Ch'en Ch'iu-k'un 陳秋坤
1975 "Shih pa shih chi shang pan yeh T'ai-wan ti ch'ü ti k'ai fa" 十八時紀上半葉台灣地區的開發 (The settlement of Taiwan in the early eighteenth century). M.A. thesis, National Taiwan University.

Ch'en Ch'un-mu 陳春木
1982 "Chien chieh Ch'ing tai i p'ing p'u tsu ku mu" 簡介清代一平埔族古墓 (Introducing an old plains aborigine grave from the Ch'ing dynasty). *Nan ying wen hsien* 27: 67–96.

Ch'en Han-kuang 陳漢光
1954 "T'ai-wan i min shih lüeh" 台灣移民史略 (Brief history of migration to Taiwan). In *T'ai-wan wen hua lun chi* 台灣文化論集 (Collected essays on Taiwanese culture), Lin Hsiung-hsiang 林熊祥, ed., pp. 47–74. Taipei: Chung-hua wen hua ch'u pan shih yeh wei yüan hui.
1960 "T'ai-wan pan lun niu ch'e chih chin hsi" 台灣板輪牛車之今昔 (The plank-wheeled oxcart of Taiwan, past and present). *T'ai-wan wen hsien* 11.4: 14–32.
1961*a* "Cheng shih fu T'ai yü ch'i k'ai k'en" 鄭氏復台與其開墾 (The Cheng recovery of Taiwan and its opening). *T'ai-wan wen hsien* 12.1: 39–54.
1961*b* "T'ai-nan hsien Liu-chung-ch'i chih Wu-t'ai-tsu ch'ung pai" 台南縣六重溪之五太祖崇拜 (The worship of Wu-t'ai-tsu at Liu-chung-ch'i, Tainan). *T'ai-wan wen hsien* 12.4: 146–55.
1963 "Kao-hsiung hsien P'ao-tzu-liao p'ing p'u tsu chia tsu kou ch'eng" 高雄縣匏仔寮平埔族家族構成 (Family organization of the plains aborigines of P'ao-tzu-liao, Kao-hsiung county). *T'ai-wan wen hsien* 14.3: 129–33.
1968 "T'ai-wan nan pei lu ko ying chih kuan piao" 台灣南北路各營職官表 (A list of official positions in the garrison forces on the south and north routes of Taiwan). *T'ai-wan wen hsien* 19.4: 106–44.
1972 "Jih chü shih ch'i T'ai-wan Han tsu tsu chi tiao ch'a" 日據時期台灣漢族祖籍調查 (The investigation of ancestral place of registration of Han Taiwanese in the Japanese period). *T'ai-wan wen hsien* 23.1: 85–104.

Ch'en Han-kuang 陳漢光 and Lai Yung-hsiang 賴永祥, eds.
1957 *T'ai-pei ku yü t'u chi* 台北古輿圖記 (Historical maps of the Taipei area). Taipei: T'ai-pei shih wen hsien wei yüan hui.

Ch'en Han-seng
1933 *The Present Agrarian Problem in China*. Shanghai: China Institute of Pacific Relations.
1936 *Agrarian Problems in Southernmost China*. Shanghai: Kelly & Walsh.
1945 *The Chinese Peasant*. Oxford Pamphlets on Indian Affairs, 33. Bombay: Oxford University Press.
1949 *Frontier Land Systems in Southernmost China: A Comparative Study of Agrarian Problems and Social Organization Among the Pai Yi People of Yunnan and the Kamba People of Sikang*. New York: Institute of Pacific Relations.

Ch'en K'ung-li 陳孔立
1990 *Ch'ing tai T'ai-wan i min she hui yen chiu* 清代台灣移民社會研究 (Researches on Ch'ing period Taiwan's immigrant society). Amoy: Hsia-men ta hsüeh ch'u pan she.

Ch'en Pin 陳璸
1961 *Ch'en Ch'ing-tuan kung wen hsüan* 陳清端公文選 (Selected writings of Ch'en Pin). *TW* 116.

1964 *Ch'en Ch'ing-tuan kung nien p'u* 陳清端公年譜 (Chronological biography of Ch'en Pin). Ting Tsung-lo 丁宗洛, ed. *TW* 207.

Ch'en Shao-hsing 陳紹馨

1950 *Jui-yen min tsu hsüeh ch'u pu tiao ch'a pao kao* 瑞岩民族學初步調查報告 (Preliminary reports of anthropological researches in Pinsebukan). Wen hsien chuan k'an 1, 2. Taipei: T'ai-wan wen hsien wei yüan hui.

1964 *Jen k'ou p'ien* 人口篇 (Population). *T'ai-wan sheng t'ung chih kao*, vol. 2, part 1, *Jen min chih*. Taipei: T'ai-wan sheng wen hsien wei yüan hui.

Ch'en Shih-chi

1982 "Student Teams Excavate 3000-Year-Old Tombs." *Free China Review* 32.11: 35–37.

Ch'en Ta

1940 *Emigrant Communities in South China*. New York: Institute of Pacific Relations.

Ch'en Ti 陳第

1959 "Tung fan chi" 東番記 (An account of the eastern barbarians). In *Min hai tseng yen* 閩海贈言 (Words of praise from the Fukien sea), Shen Yu-jung 沈有容, ed., pp. 24–27. 1617. *TW* 56.

Cheng Hsi-fu 鄭喜夫

1974*a* "Ming Cheng wan ch'i T'ai-wan chih tsu shui" 明鄭晚期台灣之租稅 (Taxes in late Cheng Taiwan). *TY* 113: 97–115.

1974*b* "Ch'ing tai P'eng-hu chih tsu shui" 清代澎湖之租稅 (Taxes in the Pescadores during the Ch'ing). *TY* 113: 116–32.

1976 "Ch'ing tai T'ai-wan 'fan t'un' k'ao" 清代台灣「番屯」考 (A study of aborigine military colonies in Ch'ing Taiwan). 2 parts. *T'ai-wan wen hsien* 27.2: 111–30; 27.3: 58–89.

Cheng Ying-wan

1970 *Postal Communication in China and Its Modernization, 1860–1896*. Cambridge, Mass.: Harvard University, East Asian Research Center.

CHFSHC *Ch'ung hsiu Feng-shan hsien chih* 重修鳳山縣志 (Feng-shan county gazetteer, revised). Wang Ying-tseng 王瑛曾, ed. 1764. *TW* 146.

CHHC *Chang-hua hsien chih* 彰化縣志 (Chang-hua county gazetteer). Chou Hsi 周璽, ed. 1830. *TW* 156.

Chi Ch'ao-ting

1936 *Key Economic Areas in Chinese History*. London: Allen & Unwin.

Chiang Jih-sheng 江日昇

1960 *T'ai-wan wai chi* 台灣外記 (Unofficial record of Taiwan). 1704. *TW* 60.

Chiang Shu-shen

1986 "The Chinese Population in Formosa, 1623–1661." Paper presented to the Conference on the History of Fukien and East-West Relations in the Seventeenth and Eighteenth Centuries, Sinologisch Institut, Leiden University.

Chiang Tao-chang
1980 "Walled Cities and Towns in Taiwan." In *China's Island Frontier*, Ronald G. Knapp, ed., pp. 117–41. Honolulu: University Press of Hawaii.

Ch'ien-lung hui tien tse li 乾隆會典則例 (Regulations, [Ch'ing] Institutes, Ch'ien-lung edition). 1763.

Chin shen ch'üan shu 搢紳全書 (Register of officials). Peking: quarterly.

Ch'ing ch'ao wen hsien t'ung k'ao 清潮文獻通考 (Compilation of important documents of the Ch'ing dynasty). 1936. N.p.: Commercial Press.

Chou Hsien-wen 周憲文
1957 *Ch'ing tai T'ai-wan ching chi shih* 清代台灣經濟史 (Economic history of Ch'ing Taiwan). *TY* 45.

Chou Ming-hung 周鳴鴻
1963 "Lu tsai T'ai-wan" 鹿在台灣 (Deer in Taiwan). *TY* 76: 104–16.

CHTTWSL *Ch'ing hui tien T'ai-wan shih li* 清會典台灣事例 (Taiwan precedents from the Ch'ing Institutes). *TW* 226.

CHTWHC *Ch'ung hsiu T'ai-wan hsien chih* 重修台灣縣志 (Taiwan county gazetteer, revised). Wang Pi-ch'ang 王必昌, ed. 1752. *TW* 113.

Ch'ü T'ung-tsu
1962 *Local Government in China Under the Ch'ing*. Cambridge, Mass.: Harvard University Press.

Ch'üan Han-sheng and Richard A. Kraus
1975 *Mid-Ch'ing Rice Markets and Trade: An Essay in Price History*. Cambridge, Mass.: Harvard University, East Asian Research Center.

Chuang Chi-fa 莊吉發
1982 *Ch'ing Kao-tsung shih ch'üan wu kung yen chiu* 清高宗十全武功研究 (Researches on the ten great military campaigns of the Ch'ien-lung emperor). Taipei: National Palace Museum.

Chuang Chin-te 莊金德
1960 "T'ai-wan t'un cheng chih hsing fei" 台灣屯政之興廢 (History of the institution of military colonies in Taiwan). *T'ai-wan wen hsien* 11.4: 33–107.
1961 "Cheng shih chün liang wen t'i ti yen t'ao" 鄭氏軍糧問題的研討 (A discussion of the Chengs' problem in provisioning their army). *T'ai-wan wen hsien* 12.1: 55–66.
1964 "Ch'ing ch'u yen chin yen hai jen min t'ou tu lai T'ai shih mo" 清初嚴禁沿海人民偷渡來台始末 (A history of early Ch'ing prohibitions on crossing to Taiwan). Parts 1 and 2. *T'ai-wan wen hsien* 15.3: 1–20; 15.4: 40–62.
1965 "Hsün T'ai yü shih ti she li yü fei chih" 巡台御史的設立與廢止 (The establishment and abolition of the censors overseeing the Taiwan circuit). *T'ai-wan wen hsien* 16.1: 53–77.
1966*a* "Ch'ing t'ing tui T'ai-wan shih shih chin hai cheng ts'e ti ching wei" 清廷對台灣實施禁海政策的經緯 (The Ch'ing policy of prohibiting travel to Taiwan). In *T'ai-wan wen wu lun chi* 台灣文物論集 (Collected essays on Taiwanese culture), pp. 95–120. Taipei: T'ai-wan sheng wen hsien wei yüan hui.

1966b "Lan Ting-yüan ti chih T'ai tang lun" 藍鼎元的治台讜論 (The remonstrances of Lan Ting-yüan on the governance of Taiwan). *T'ai-wan wen hsien* 17.2: 1–27.

Chuang Sung-lin 莊松林

1959 "Ho-lan chih T'ai-wan t'ung chih" 荷蘭之台灣統治 (The Dutch government of Taiwan). *T'ai-wan wen hsien* 10.3: 1–26.

Chuang Ying-chang

1989 "Settlement Patterns of the Hakka Migration to Taiwan." *Bulletin of the Institute of Ethnology, Academia Sinica* 66: 169–93.

CITCTWF *Ch'ing i t'ung chih: T'ai-wan fu* 清一統志台灣府 (The section on Taiwan prefecture of the *Ch'ing i t'ung chih*, Chia-ch'ing ed.). 1842. *TW* 68.

Clarke, Samuel R.

1911 *Among the Tribes in South-west China*. London: China Inland Mission.

CLHC *Chu-lo hsien chih* 諸羅縣志 (Chu-lo county gazetteer). Ch'en Meng-lin 陳夢林 and Chou Chung-hsüan 周鍾瑄, eds. 1717. *TW* 141.

CLSL *Ch'ing Kao-tsung shih lu hsüan chi* 清高宗實錄選輯 (Selections from the Veritable Records of the Ch'ien-lung reign). *TW* 186.

Cohen, Myron

1968 "The Hakka or 'Guest People': Dialect as a Socio-cultural Variable in Southeastern China." *Ethnohistory* 15.3: 237–92.

Coleman, James S.

1957 *Community Conflict*. New York: Free Press.

Collier, John

1947 *Indians of the Americas*. New York: New American Library.

Coolhaas, W. P.

1964 *Generale Missiven, 1639–1655*, vol. 2. The Hague: Martinus Nijhoff.

Coyett, Frederick

1975 *Neglected Formosa: A Translation from the Dutch of Frederic Coyette's "'t Verwaerloosde Formosa."* Inez de Beauclair, ed. San Francisco: Chinese Materials Center.

CPPW *T'ai-wan chung pu pei wen chi ch'eng* 台灣中部碑文集成 (Collected stone inscriptions from central Taiwan). *TW* 151.

Creel, H. G.

1964 "The Beginnings of Bureaucracy in China." *Journal of Asian Studies* 23.2: 155–84.

Cressey, George B.

1955 *Land of the 500 Million*. New York: McGraw-Hill.

Crissman, Lawrence

1972 "Marketing on the Changhua Plain, Taiwan." In *Economic Organization in Chinese Society*, W. E. Willmott, ed., pp. 215–59. Stanford: Stanford University Press.

Croizier, Ralph C.

1977 *Koxinga and Chinese Nationalism: History, Myth, and the Hero*. Cambridge, Mass.: Harvard University, East Asian Research Center.

Crossley, Pamela
1990*a* *Orphan Warriors: Three Manchu Generations and the End of the Qing World*. Princeton: Princeton University Press.
1990*b* "Thinking About Ethnicity in Early Modern China." *Late Imperial China* 11.1: 1–35.
CSWP *Ch'ing ching shih wen pien hsüan lu* 清經世文編選錄 (Selected writings on Ch'ing statecraft). 1827. *TW* 229.
CTPT *Ch'in ting p'ing ting T'ai-wan chi lüeh* 欽定平定台灣紀略 (Imperially commissioned history of the pacification of Taiwan). *TW* 102.
Curwen, E. Cecil, and Gudmund Hatt
1961 *Plough and Pasture: The Early History of Farming*. New York: Collier.
Cushman, Richard D.
1970 "Rebel Haunts and Lotus Huts: Problems in the Ethnohistory of the Yao." Ph.D. dissertation, Cornell University.
Davidson, James W.
1903 *The Island of Formosa: Historical View from 1430 to 1900*. New York: Macmillan.
de Beauclair, Inez
1970 "Dutch Beads in Formosa?" *Bulletin of the Institute of Ethnology, Academia Sinica* 29: 385–93.
DeGlopper, Donald
1980 "Lu-kang: A city and Its Trading System." In *China's Island Frontier*, Ronald G. Knapp, ed., pp. 143–65. Honolulu: University Press of Hawaii.
Dernberger, Robert F., and R. M. Hartwell
1983 *The Coterminal Characteristics of Political Units and Economic Regions in China*. Ann Arbor: University of Michigan, Center for Chinese Studies.
Diamond, Norma
1988 "The Miao and Poison: Interactions on China's Southwest Frontier." *Ethnology* 27.1: 1–25.
Douglas, Carstairs
1873 *Chinese-English Dictionary of the Vernacular or Spoken Language of Amoy*. London: Trubner & Co.
Eberhard, Wolfram
1982 *China's Minorities: Yesterday and Today*. Belmont, Calif.: Wadsworth.
Edkins, J.
1903 *The Revenue and Taxation of the Chinese Empire*. Shanghai: Presbyterian Mission Press.
Ekvall, Robert B.
1939 *Cultural Relations on the Kansu-Tibetan Border*. Chicago: University of Chicago Press.
Ellis, David M., et al.
1967 *A History of New York State*. Rev. ed. Ithaca: Cornell University Press.

Elvin, Mark

1970 "The Last Thousand Years of Chinese History: Changing Patterns in Land Tenure." *Modern Asian Studies* 4.2: 97–114.

1973 *The Pattern of the Chinese Past*. Stanford: Stanford University Press.

Esherick, Joseph W.

1987 *The Origins of the Boxer Uprising*. Berkeley: University of California Press.

Etō Shinkichi

1964 "An Outline of Formosan History." In *Formosa Today*, Mark Mancall, ed., pp. 43–58. New York: Praeger.

FCTCTWF *Fu-chien t'ung chih T'ai-wan fu* 福建通志台灣府 (Materials on Taiwan prefecture from the Fukien gazetteer). 1871. *TW* 84.

Fei Hsiao-t'ung

1946 *Peasant Life in China*. New York: Oxford University Press.

Fernandez, Pablo

1959 *One Hundred Years of Dominican Apostolate in Formosa: Extracts from the Sino-Annamite Letters, Dominican Missions and Ultramar*. Felix Bautista, trans. Quezon City.

Ferrell, Raleigh

1969*a* *Taiwan Aboriginal Groups: Problems in Cultural and Linguistic Classification*. Monograph no. 17. Nankang: Academia Sinica, Institute of Ethnology.

1969*b* "Paiwanic Ethnolinguistic Groups of the West-Central Taiwan 'Black Pottery' Culture Area." *Bulletin of the Institute of Ethnology, Academia Sinica* 28: 159–96.

1971 "Aboriginal Peoples of the Southwestern Taiwan Plain." *Bulletin of the Institute of Ethnology, Academia Sinica* 32: 217–35.

1980 "Phonological Subgroupings of Formosan Languages." In *Austronesian Studies*, Paz B. Naylor, ed., pp. 241–54. Michigan Papers on South and Southeast Asia, no. 15. Ann Arbor: University of Michigan, Center for South and Southeast Asian Studies.

Feuchtwang, Stephan

1977 "School-temple and City God." In *The City in Late Imperial China*, G. W. Skinner, ed., pp. 581–608. Stanford: Stanford University Press.

Feuerwerker, Albert

1984 "The State and the Economy in Late Imperial China." *Theory and Society* 13: 297–326.

Fletcher, Joseph

1978 "Ch'ing Inner Asia Circa 1800." In *The Cambridge History of China*, vol. 10, *Late Ch'ing, 1800–1911*, Part 1, John K. Fairbank, ed., pp. 35–106. Cambridge, Eng.: Cambridge University Press.

Fogg, Wayne H.

1983 "Swidden Cultivation of Foxtail Millet by Taiwan Aborigines." In *The Origins of Chinese Civilization*, David Keightley, ed., pp. 95–115. Berkeley: University of California Press.

Fox, Robin
1967 *Kinship and Marriage: An Anthropological Perspective*. Harmondsworth, Eng.: Penguin Books.

Freedman, Maurice
1958 *Lineage Organization in Southeastern China*. London: Athlone Press.
1966 *Chinese Lineage and Society: Fukien and Kwangtung*. London: Athlone Press.
1979 *The Study of Chinese Society*. G. W. Skinner, ed. Stanford: Stanford University Press.

FSHC *Feng-shan hsien chih* 鳳山縣志 (Feng-shan county gazetteer). Ch'en Wen-ta 陳文達, ed. 1719. *TW* 124.

Fu Lo-shu
1966 *A Documentary Chronicle of Sino-western Relations*. 2 vols. Tucson: University of Arizona Press.

Gallin, Bernard
1966 *Hsin Hsing, Taiwan: A Chinese Village in Change*. Berkeley: University of California Press.

Gamble, Sidney G.
1963 *North China Villages: Social, Political, and Economic Activities Before 1933*. Berkeley: University of California Press.

Geertz, Clifford
1963 *Agricultural Involution: The Processes of Ecological Change in Indonesia*. Berkeley: University of California Press.

Goode, William J.
1978 *The Celebration of Heroes: Prestige as a Social Control System*. Berkeley: University of California Press.

Goodrich, L. Carrington, and Fang Chao-ying, eds.
1976 *Dictionary of Ming Biography, 1368–1644*. 2 vols. New York: Columbia University Press.

Goody, Jack
1971 *Technology, Tradition, and the State in Africa*. London: Oxford University Press.

Gough, Kathleen
1961 "Variation in Residence." In *Matrilineal Kinship*, D. M. Schneider and K. Gough, eds., pp. 545–76. Berkeley: University of California Press.

Harrell, Stevan
1981 "Social Organization in Hai-shan." In *The Anthropology of Taiwanese Society*, E. M. Ahern and H. Gates, eds., pp. 125–47. Stanford: Stanford University Press.
1990 "From Xiedou to Yijun, the Decline of Ethnicity in Northern Taiwan, 1885–1895." *Late Imperial China* 11.1: 99–127.

Hatao Yamato 旗尾山人
1903 "Banshoryō kannai Shinkō, Takukō oyobi Daiketsuten sha jukuban no iju oyobi enkaku" 蕃薯藔管内新港, 卓猴及び大傑巓社熟蕃の移住及び沿革(The migration of Fan-shu-liao's Hsin-kang, Cho-hou, and Ta-chieh-tien). 2 parts. *Taiwan kanshū kiji* 3.3: 231–40; 3.4: 323–34.

Hauptmann, Laurence, and Ronald G. Knapp
1977 "Dutch-Aboriginal Interaction in New Netherland and Formosa." *Proceedings of the American Philosophical Society* 121.2: 166–82.
Hayami, Yujiro, and Vernon P. Ruttan
1985 *Agricultural Development: An International Perspective*. Rev., exp. ed. Baltimore: Johns Hopkins University Press.
HCHTFT *Hsin-chu hsien ts'ai fang ts'e* 新竹縣采訪冊 (Guide to Hsin-chu county). *TW* 145.
Herskovits, Melville J.
1948 *Man and His Works: The Science of Cultural Anthropology*. New York: Alfred A. Knopf.
HHTWHC *Hsü hsiu T'ai-wan hsien chih* 續修台灣縣志 (Taiwan county gazetteer, revised). Hsieh Chin-luan 謝金鑾, ed. 1807. *TW* 140.
Hirth, Friedrich, and W. W. Rockhill, trans.
1911 *Chau Ju-kua: His Work on the Chinese and Arab Trade in the Twelfth and Thirteenth Centuries*. St. Petersburg: Imperial Academy of Sciences, Printing Office.
HMC *Hsia-men chih* 廈門志 (Gazetteer of Amoy). Chou K'ai 周凱, ed. 1832. *TW* 95.
Ho Ping-ti
1959 *Studies on the Population of China, 1368–1953*. Cambridge, Mass.: Harvard University Press.
1962 *The Ladder of Success in Imperial China*. New York: Columbia University Press.
Ho, Samuel P. S.
1978 *Economic Development of Taiwan, 1860–1970*. New Haven: Yale University Press.
Ho T'ing-jui
1967 *A Comparative Study of Myths and Legends of Formosan Aborigines*. Asian Folklore and Social Life Monographs, no. 18. Taipei: Orient Cultural Service.
Ho Yhi-min
1966 *Agricultural Development of Taiwan, 1903–1960*. Nashville: Vanderbilt University Press.
Hoang, Peter
1922–23 "Law of Land Tenure in China: A Practical Treatise on Legal Ownership." 2 parts. *China Law Review* 1.2: 90–96; 1.5: 232–44.
Hobsbawm, Eric, and Terence Ranger, eds.
1983 *The Invention of Tradition*. Cambridge, Eng.: Cambridge University Press.
Hsiao I-shan 蕭一山
1958 "Ch'ing tai tung pei chih t'un k'en yü i min" 清代東北之屯墾與移民 (Military colonization and immigration in Manchuria during the Ch'ing period). *Hsüeh shu chi k'an* 6.3: 1–45.
Hsiao Kung-ch'uan
1960 *Rural China: Imperial Control in the Nineteenth Century*. Seattle: University of Washington Press.

Hsieh Chiao-min
1964 *Taiwan, Ilha Formosa: A Geography in Perspective*. London: Butterworth.

Hsieh Jih-chang, Chester 謝繼昌
1979*a* *Structure and History of a Chinese Community in Taiwan*. Monograph no. 25. Nankang: Academia Sinica, Institute of Ethnology.
1979*b* "P'ing p'u tsu chih Han hua" 平埔族之漢化 (Sinicization of the plains aborigines). *Bulletin of the Institute of Ethnology, Academia Sinica* 47: 49–72.

Hsieh Kuo-ching
1932 "Removal of Coastal Population in Early Tsing period." *Chinese Social and Political Science Review* 4: 559–96.

Hsieh, S. C., and T. H. Lee
1966 *Agricultural Development and Its Contributions to Economic Growth in Taiwan*. Economic Digest Series, no. 17. Taipei: Chinese-American Joint Commission on Rural Reconstruction.

Hsieh Shih-chung 謝世忠
1987 *Jen t'ung ti wu ming: T'ai-wan yüan chu min ti tsu ch'ün pien ch'ien* 認同的汚名:台灣原住民的族羣變遷 (Stigmatized identity: ethnic change among Taiwan aborigines). Taipei: Tzu li wan pao she.

Hsü Chia-ming 許嘉明
1973 "Chang-hua p'ing yüan Fu-lao-k'o ti ti yü tsu chih" 彰化平原福佬客的地域組織 (Territorial organization of the Hoklorized Hakka in the Chang-hua plain). *Bulletin of the Institute of Ethnology, Academia Sinica* 36: 165–90.

Hsu Cho-yun
1972 "I-lan in the First Half of the Nineteenth Century." *Bulletin of the Institute of Ethnology, Academia Sinica* 33: 51–70.

Hsü Hsüeh-chi 許雪姬
1987 *Ch'ing tai T'ai-wan ti Lü ying* 清代台灣的綠營 (The Green Standard Army in Taiwan during the Ch'ing dynasty). Nankang: Academia Sinica, Institute of Modern History.

Hsu, Immanuel
1983 *The Rise of Modern China*. Oxford: Oxford University Press.

Hsu Wen-hsiung
1980*a* "From Aboriginal Island to Chinese Frontier: The Development of Taiwan Before 1683." In *China's Island Frontier*, Ronald G. Knapp, ed., pp. 3–28. Honolulu: University Press of Hawaii.
1980*b* "Frontier Social Organization and Social Disorder in Ch'ing Taiwan." In *China's Island Frontier*, Ronald G. Knapp, ed., pp. 87–105. Honolulu: University Press of Hawaii.

Huang Ch'i-mu 黃啓木
1953 "Fen lei hsieh tou yü Meng-chia 分類械鬭與艋舺 (Communal strife in Meng-chia). *T'ai-pei wen wu* 2.1: 55–58.

Huang Huan-yao 黃煥堯
1986*a* "Ch'ing chi T'ai-wan fan jen tui ti fang chih an ti kung hsien: I

fan chi ch'i kung neng ti t'an t'ao" 清季台灣番人對地方治安的貢獻—義番及其功能的探討 (The contribution of aborigines to the maintenance of local order in Ch'ing period Taiwan: a discussion of loyalist aborigines and their function). *T'ai-pei wen hsien* 75:131–97.

1986*b* "Ch'ing chi T'ai-wan fan huan ch'eng yin chih t'an t'ao" 清季台灣番患成因之探討 (A discussion of the causes of aborigine disturbances in Ch'ing Taiwan). *T'ai-pei wen hsien* 77: 283–318.

Huang P'ei

1974 *Autocracy at Work: A Study of the Yung-cheng Period, 1723–1735*. Bloomington: Indiana University Press.

Huang, Ray

1974 *Taxation and Governmental Finance in Sixteenth Century Ming China*. Cambridge, Eng.: Cambridge University Press.

1988 *China: A Macro History*. Armonk, N.Y.: M. E. Sharpe.

Huang Shu-ching 黄叔璥

1957 *T'ai hai shih ch'a lu* 台海使槎錄 (A tour of duty in the Taiwan sea). 1736. *TW* 4.

Huber, Johannes

1990 "Chinese Settlers Against the Dutch East India Company: The Rebellion Led by Kuo Huai-i on Taiwan in 1652." In *Development and Decline of Fukien Province in the 17th and 18th Centuries*, E. B. Vermeer, ed., pp. 265–96. Leiden: E. J. Brill.

Hucker, Charles

1985 *A Dictionary of Official Titles in Imperial China*. Stanford: Stanford University Press.

Hui Ts'un 惠邨

1959 "Ch'ing tai T'ai-wan ti tsu fu" 清代台灣的租賦 (Land taxes in Taiwan during the Ch'ing period). *T'ai-wan wen hsien* 10.2: 91–147. Abridged translation of *TWSH*, vol. 1: 246–74, 342–80, 387–469.

Hummel, Arthur W., ed.

1943–44 *Eminent Chinese of the Ch'ing period (1644–1912)*. 2 vols. Washington, D.C.: U.S. Government Printing Office.

Hung Chien-chao

1981 "Taiwan Under the Cheng Family, 1662–1683: Sinicization After Dutch Rule." Ph.D. dissertation, Georgetown University.

Hung Hsiu-kuei 洪秀桂

1973 "Nan-t'ou Pa-tsai-hai jen ti tsung chiao hsin yang" 南投巴宰海人的宗教信仰 (Religious beliefs of the Pazeh of Nan-t'ou). *Wen shih che hsüeh pao* 22: 445–509.

IGS *Itabashi gai shi* 板橋街志. (Gazetteer of Pan-ch'iao). 1933.

Ingold, Tim

1980 *Hunters, Pastoralists, and Ranchers*. Cambridge, Eng.: Cambridge University Press.

Inō Yoshinori 伊能嘉矩

1904 *Taiwan bansei shi* 台灣蕃政志 (History of aborigine policy in Taiwan). Taipei: Taiwan sōtokufu.

1928 *Taiwan bunkashi* 台灣文化志 (A cultural history of Taiwan). 3 vols. Tokyo: Tōkōshoin.

Iwao Seiichi 岩生成一

1955 "Ho Cheng shih tai T'ai-wan yü Po-ssu chien chih t'ang ch'a mao i" 荷鄭時代台灣與波斯間之糖茶貿易 (The trade in tea and sugar between Taiwan and Persia during the Dutch and Cheng periods). *TY* 32: 53–60.

1959 "Shih ch'i shih chi Jih-pen jen chih T'ai-wan ch'in lüeh hsing tung" 十七世紀日本人之台灣侵略行動 (Aggressive activities toward Taiwan by Japanese during the seventeenth century). *TY* 71: 1–23.

1976 "Japanese Foreign Trade in the 16th and 17th Centuries." *Acta Asiatica* 30: 1–18.

Jacobs, Wilbur R.

1972 *Dispossessing the American Indian*. New York: Scribner.

Jamieson, George

1921 *Chinese Family and Commercial Law*. Shanghai: Kelly & Walsh.

JCRR *Taiwan Agricultural Statistics, 1901–1965*. Economic Digest Series, no. 18. Taipei: Chinese-American Joint Commission on Rural Reconstruction. 1966.

Johnston, William R.

1940 "Emphyteusis: A Roman 'Perpetual' Tenure." *University of Toronto Law Journal* 3.2: 323–47.

Juan Ch'ang-jui 阮昌銳

1971 "Ta-kang-k'ou Han jen ti A-mei-hua" 大港口漢人的阿美化 (The acculturation of the Ta-kang-k'ou Han to the Ami). *Bulletin of the Institute of Ethnology, Academia Sinica* 31: 47–64.

Juan Min-hsi 阮旻錫

1958 *Hai shang chien wen lu* 海上見聞錄 (A record of what was seen and heard on the sea). *TW* 24.

Jung, Richard Lee Kuan

1979 "The Ch'ien-lung Emperor's Suppression of Rebellion: The White Lotus and the Triads, 1774–1788." Ph.D. dissertation, Harvard University.

Kato Eiichi

1976 "The Japanese-Dutch Trade in the Formative Period of the Seclusion Policy." *Acta Asiatica* 30: 34–63.

Kawada Shiro

1928 "The Tenant System of Formosa." *Kyoto University Economic Review* 3.2: 86–146.

KCK *Shōwa jūnen kokusei chōsa: kekkahyō* 昭和十年國勢調查:結果表 (Results of 1935 national census: statistical tables). Taipei: Sōtoku kambō rinji kokusei chōsabu, 1937. Table 4: Shuzoku keitō betsu jinkō 種族系統別人口 (Population by ethnic group).

KCTCL *Kung chung tang Ch'ien-lung ch'ao tsou che* 宮中檔乾隆朝奏摺 (Palace memorials of the Ch'ien-lung reign). 75 vols. Taipei: National Palace Museum, 1982–88.

KCTYC *Kung chung tang Yung-cheng ch'ao tsou che* 宮中檔雍正朝奏摺 (Palace memorials of the Yung-cheng reign). 32 vols. Taipei: National Palace Museum, 1977–80.

Keesing, Felix
1962 *The Ethnohistory of Northern Luzon*. Stanford: Stanford University Press.

Kelleher, M. Theresa
1989 "Back to Basics: Chu Hsi's Elementary Learning (*Hsiao-hsüeh*)." In *Neo-Confucian Education: The Formative Stage*, W. T. de Bary and John Chaffee, eds., pp. 219–51. Berkeley: University of California Press.

Kellogg, C. R.
1926 "The San Tak of Fukien Province." *China Journal of Science and Arts* 4.5: 238–42.
1927 "Further Notes on the Aborigines of Fukien." *China Journal of Science and Arts* 6.2: 94–100.

Kerr, George W.
1958 *Okinawa: The History of an Island People*. Tokyo: Charles E. Tuttle.

Kessler, Lawrence D.
1976 *K'ang-hsi and the Consolidation of Ch'ing Rule, 1661–1684*. Chicago: University of Chicago Press.

KHSL *Ch'ing Sheng-tsu shih lu hsüan chi* 清聖祖實錄選輯 (Selections from the Veritable Records of the K'ang-hsi reign). *TW* 165.

Kim, Sung-bok
1978 *Landlord and Tenant in Colonial New York: Manorial Society, 1664–1775*. Chapel Hill: University of North Carolina Press.

KMLCL *Ko-ma-lan chih lüeh* 噶瑪蘭志略 (Gazetteer of Ko-ma-lan). *TW* 92.

Knapp, Ronald G.
1976 "Chinese Frontier Settlement in Taiwan." *Annals of the Association of American Geographers* 66: 43–59.

Kracke, E. A.
1957 "Region, Family, and Individual in the Examination System." In *Chinese Thought and Institutions*, J. K. Fairbank, ed., pp. 251–68. Chicago: University of Chicago Press.

Krech, Shepard
1981 *Indians, Animals and the Fur Trade: A Critique of Keepers of the Game*. Athens: University of Georgia Press.

Kuan Wei-lan 官蔚藍
1955 *Chung-hua min kuo hsing cheng ch'ü hua chi t'u ti jen k'ou t'ung chi piao* 中華民國行政區劃及土地人口統計表 (Statistical tables on administrative arrangements, land, and population in the Republic of China). Taipei.

Kuepers, J. J. A. M.
1978 *The Dutch Reformed Church in Formosa, 1627–1662: Mission in a Colonial Context*. Switzerland: Nouvelle Revue de Science Missionaire.

Kuhn, Philip A.
1970 *Rebellion and Its Enemies in Late Imperial China: Militarization and Social Structure, 1796–1864*. Cambridge, Mass.: Harvard University Press.
1977 "Origins of the Taiping Vision: Cross-cultural Dimensions of a Chinese Rebellion." *Comparative Studies in Society and History* 19.3: 350–66.
1979 "Local Taxation and Finance in Republican China." In *Political Leadership and Social Change at the Local Level in China from 1850 to the Present*, S. Mann Jones, ed., pp. 100–136. Select Papers, no. 3. Chicago: University of Chicago, Center for Far Eastern Studies.

Kuo Shui-t'an 郭水潭
1959 "Ho jen chü T'ai shih ch'i chih Chung-kuo i min" 荷人據台時期之中國移民 (Chinese immigrants in Dutch-ruled Taiwan). *T'ai-wan wen hsien* 10.4: 11–45.

Kuo T'ing-i 郭廷以
1954 *T'ai-wan shih shih kai shuo* 台灣史事概說 (A historical outline of Taiwan). Taipei: Cheng chung shu chü.
1973 "The Internal Development and Modernization of Taiwan, 1683–1891." In *Taiwan in Modern Times*, Paul K. T. Sih, ed., pp. 171–240. New York: St. John's University Press.

Lai Fu-shun 賴福順
1984 *Ch'ien-lung chung yao chan cheng chih chün hsü yen chiu* 乾隆重要戰爭之軍需研究 (Research on the logistics of Ch'ien-lung's important campaigns). Taipei: National Palace Museum.

Lai Yung-hsiang 賴永祥
1970 *T'ai-wan shih yen chiu ch'u chi* 台灣史研究初集 (First collection of researches in Taiwan history). Taipei: San min shu chü.

Lamley, Harry J.
1972 "Private Conflict: The Hsieh-tou Phenomenon in Taiwan and South China." Paper prepared for the Conference on Taiwan History, Asilomar, Calif.
1973 "A Short-lived Republic and War, 1895: Taiwan's Resistance Against Japan." In *Taiwan in Modern Times*, Paul K. T. Sih, ed., pp. 241–316. New York: St. John's University Press.
1977*a* "Hsieh-tou: The Pathology of Violence in Southeastern China." *Ch'ing-shih wen-t'i* 3.7: 1–39.
1977*b* "The Formation of Cities: Initiative and Motivation in Building Three Walled Cities in Taiwan." In *The City in Late Imperial China*, G. W. Skinner, ed., pp. 155–209. Stanford: Stanford University Press.
1981 "Subethnic Rivalry in the Ch'ing Period." In *The Anthropology of Taiwanese Society*, E. M. Ahern and H. Gates, eds., pp. 282–318. Stanford: Stanford University Press.

Lan Ting-yüan 藍鼎元
1958*a* *Tung cheng chi* 東征集 (Record of the eastern campaign). 1732. *TW* 12.

1958b *P'ing T'ai chi lüeh* 平台紀略 (History of the pacification of Taiwan). 1732. *TW* 14.

Lattimore, Owen
1932 *Manchuria: Cradle of Conflict.* New York: Macmillan.
1934 *The Mongols of Manchuria.* New York: John Day Co.
1962a *Studies in Frontier History: Collected Papers, 1928–1958.* London: Oxford University Press.
1962b "The Gold Tribe, 'Fishskin Tatars' of the Lower Sungari." In Lattimore 1962*a*: 339–402.
1962c "The Frontier in History." In Lattimore 1962*a*: 469–91.

Lee, James
1978 "Migration and Expansion in Chinese History." In *Human Migration: Patterns and Policies*, William H. McNeill and Ruth S. Adams, eds., pp. 20–47. Bloomington: Indiana University Press.
1982a "Food Supply and Population Growth in Southwest China, 1250–1850." *Journal of Asian Studies* 41.4: 711–46.
1982b "The Legacy of Immigration in Southwest China, 1250–1850." *Annales de demographie historique*, 1982: 279–304.

Lee, Robert H. G.
1970 *The Manchurian Frontier in Ch'ing History.* Cambridge, Mass.: Harvard University Press.

Lee Teng-hui
1971 *Intersectoral Capital Flows in the Economic Development of Taiwan, 1895–1960.* Ithaca: Cornell University Press.

Legge, James
1960 *The Chinese Classics*, vol. 3, *The Shoo King, or the Book of Historical Documents.* Hong Kong: Hong Kong University Press.

Leonard, Jane Kate
1984 *Wei Yüan and China's Rediscovery of the Maritime World.* Cambridge, Mass: Harvard University, Council on East Asian Studies.

Leong, S. T.
1983 "The Hakka Chinese: Ethnicity and Migrations in Late Imperial China." Unpublished ms.

Leung Man-kam
1977 "Juan Yüan (1764–1849): The Life, Works and Career of a Chinese Scholar-Bureaucrat." Ph.D. dissertation, University of Hawaii.

Li Chi-hua 李季樺
1989a "Chu-ch'ien she ti 'San' hsing" 竹塹社的"三"姓 (The Sans of Chu-ch'ien). *T'ai-wan shih t'ien yeh yen chiu t'ung hsün* 10: 11–14.
1989b "Ch'ing tai 'Fan erh chih lao erh wu ch'i' yüan yin ch'u t'an" 清代"番兒至老而無妻"原因初探 (A preliminary inquiry into the reasons for the failure of aborigines to marry in the Ch'ing period). In *T'ai-wan shih yen chiu hsüeh shu yen t'ao hui lun wen chi* 台灣史研究學術研討會論集 (Collected essays from the seminar on Taiwan historical research), Ch'en Ch'i-chen 陳溪珍, ed., pp. 73–106. Taipei: T'ai-wan shih chi yen chiu chung hsin.

Li I-yüan 李亦園 et al.
1962 *Ma-t'ai-an A-mei tsu ti wu chih wen hua* 馬太安阿美族的物

質文化 (Material culture of the Vataan Ami). Monograph no. 2. Nankang: Academia Sinica, Institute of Ethnology.

Li Ju-ho 李汝和

1970 "Ching tai T'ai-wan pan ping chih tu yü t'un t'ien mu ping chih i" 清代台灣班兵制度與屯田募兵之議 (The system of rotating soldiers and proposals for military colonies and local recruitment in Ch'ing Taiwan). *T'ai-wan wen hsien* 21.2: 1–21.

Li, Paul Jen-kuei

1985 "The Position of Atayal in the Austronesian Family." In *Austronesian Linguistics at the 15th Pacific Science Congress*, Andrew Pauley and L. Carrington, eds., pp. 257–80. Pacific Linguistics Series C, no. 88. Potts Point, NSW: Australian National University.

n.d. "Classification of Formosan Languages: Lexical Evidence." *Bulletin of the Institute of History and Philology, Academia Sinica*, forthcoming.

Liang Fang-chung 梁方仲

1956 *The Single-whip Method of Taxation in China.* Cambridge, Mass.: Harvard University, Chinese Economic and Political Studies.

1980 *Chung-kuo li tai hu k'ou, t'ien ti, t'ien fu t'ung chi* 中國歷代户口，田地，田賦統計 (Statistics on population, land, and land taxes for successive Chinese dynasties). Shanghai: Jen min ch'u pan she.

Liao Chiung-jan 廖炯然

1948 *Yao min kai k'uang* 傜民概況 (The condition of the Yao). Shanghai: Chung hua shu chü.

Liao Han-ch'en 廖漢臣

1952 "Hsi-pan-ya jen chü T'ai k'ao" 西班牙人據台考 (The Spanish occupation of Taiwan). *T'ai-pei wen wu* 1.1: 41–46.

1953 "T'ai-pei hsien ti k'ai fa" 台北縣的開發 (The opening of T'ai-pei county). *T'ai-pei hsien wen hsien ts'ung chi* 1: 27–32.

1959 "Ho jen ching lüeh pei pu T'ai-wan" 荷人經略北部台灣 (The Dutch policy of control of northern Taiwan). *T'ai-pei wen wu* 8.3: 1–17.

Lien Chan

1973 "Taiwan in China's External Relations, 1683–1874." In *Taiwan in Modern Times*, Paul K. T. Sih, ed., pp. 87–170. New York: St. John's University Press.

Lien Heng 連橫

1977 *T'ai-wan t'ung shih* 台灣通史 (A comprehensive history of Taiwan). Taipei: Yu shih wen hua shih yeh kung ssu.

Lieu, D. K.

1928 "Land Tenure Systems in China." *Chinese Economic Journal* 2.6: 457–74.

Lin Wei-sheng 林偉盛

1988 "Fen lei hsieh tou man yen ch'üan T'ai ti fen hsi" 分類械鬪蔓延全台的分析 (An analysis of the spread of communal strife throughout Taiwan). *T'ai-wan feng wu* 38.3: 27–51.

Liu Chia-chü 劉家駒
1964 *Ch'ing ch'ao ch'u ch'i ti pa ch'i ch'üan ti* 清朝初期的八旗圈地 (The policy of land allotments for the Eight Banners in the early Ch'ing). Wen shih ts'ung k'an 1. Taipei: Kuo li T'ai-wan ta hsüeh.
Liu Chih-wan 劉枝萬
1955 "T'ai-chung hsien k'ai fa shih." 台中縣開發史 (History of the opening of T'ai-chung county). *Chung hsien wen hsien* 1: 29–41.
1957 "Ch'ing tai T'ai-wan fang chih chih kuan nien piao." 清代台灣方志職官年表 (Chronological table of officials serving in Ch'ing Taiwan according to local gazetteers). *T'ai-wan wen hsien* 8.3–4 [entire issue].
1958 *Nan-t'ou hsien yen ko chih k'ai fa p'ien kao* 南投縣沿革志開發篇稿 (Draft history of the settlement of Nan-t'ou county). Nan-t'ou wen hsien ts'ung chi, vol. 6. Nan-t'ou: Nan-t'ou hsien wen hsien wei yüan hui.
Liu I-ch'ang 劉益昌
1988 "Shih ch'ien shih tai T'ai-wan yü Hua nan kuan hsi ch'u t'an" 史前時代台灣與華南關係初探 (A preliminary inquiry into the relations between prehistoric Taiwan and South China). In *Chung-kuo hai yang fa chan shih lun wen chi* 中國海洋發展史論文集 (Collected essays on the history of China's maritime development), vol. 3, Chang Yen-hsien 張炎憲, ed., pp. 1–27. Publication no. 24. Nankang: Academia Sinica, Institute of the Three People's Principles
Liu, James T. C.
1959 *Reform in Sung China: Wang An-shih (1021–1086) and His New Policies.* Cambridge, Mass.: Harvard University Press.
Liu Ju-chung 劉如仲 and Miao Hsüeh-meng 苗學孟
1984 *T'ai-wan Lin Shuang-wen ch'i i tzu liao hsüan pien* 台灣林爽文起義資料選編 (Selected materials on the rebellion of Lin Shuang-wen in Taiwan). Fu-chien jen min ch'u pan she.
Liu Ming-ch'uan 劉銘傳
1958 *Liu Chuang-su kung tsou i* 劉壯肅公奏議 (Memorials of Liu Ming-ch'uan). *TW* 27.
Liu-shih-ch'i 六十七 et al.
1961 *Fan she ts'ai feng t'u k'ao* 番社采風圖考 (Customs of the barbarian villages illustrated). *TW* 90.
Lo Erh-kang 羅爾綱
1945 *Lü ying ping chih* 綠營兵志 (A treatise on the Army of the Green Standard). Chungking: Shang wu yin shu kuan.
Lo Jung-pang
1968 "Policy Formation and Decision-making on Issues Respecting Peace and War." In *Chinese Government in Ming Times*, C. O. Hucker, ed., pp. 41–72. New York: Columbia University Press.
Lo Wan
1965 "Communal Strife in Mid-nineteenth Century Kwangtung: The Establishment of Ch'ih ch'i." *Harvard Papers on China* 19: 85–119.

Loewe, Michael
1974 *Crisis and Conflict in Han China*. London: Rowman.

Lombard-Salmon, Claudine
1972 *Un exemple d'acculturation chinoise: La province du Gui Zhou au XVIIIe siècle*. Paris: Ecole Française d'Extrême Orient.

Lu Chia-hsing 盧嘉興
1956 "T'ai-wan ti chi 'chia' chih yen pien k'ao." 台灣地積「甲」之演變考 (A study of change in the *chia* as a land measure in Taiwan). *T'ai-wan wen hsien* 7.1–2: 51–58.
1965 *Lu-erh-men ti li yen pien k'ao.* 鹿耳門地理演變考 (A study of the changing geography of Lu-erh-men). Taipei: T'ai-wan shang wu yin shu kuan.

Ma Feng-ch'en 馬奉琛
1936 "Ch'ing ch'u Man Han she hui ching chi ch'ung t'u chih i pan" 清初滿漢社會經濟衝突之一般 (Social and economic conflicts between Manchus and Han in the early Ch'ing). Part 3. *Shih huo* 4.9: 384–402.
1956 "Manchu-Chinese Social and Economic Conflicts in Early Ch'ing." In *Chinese Social History: Translations of Selected Studies,* E-tu Zen Sun and John DeFrancis, eds., pp. 333–51. Washington, D.C.: American Council of Learned Societies.

Mabuchi Tōichi 馬淵東一
1953 "Takasago zoku no bunrui" 高砂族の分類 (Retrospect on the classifications of the Formosan aborigines). *Minzokugaku kenkyū* 18.1–2: 1–11.
1954 "Takasago zoku no idō oyobi bunpu, dainibu" 高砂族の移動および分布第二部 (Migration and distribution of the Formosan aborigines, part 2). *Minzokugaku kenkyū* 18.4: 319–68.
1960 "The Aboriginal Peoples of Formosa." In *Social Structure in Southeast Asia,* George P. Murdock, ed., pp. 127–40. Chicago: Quadrangle Books.
1963 "Land Tenure System Among the Central Tribes of Formosa." In *Proceedings of the Ninth Pacific Science Congress of 1957,* vol. 3, p. 146. Bangkok.
1970 "Magico-religious Land Ownership in Central Formosa and Southeast Asia." *Bulletin of the Institute of Ethnology, Academia Sinica* 29: 349–83.
1974*a* *Mabuchi Tōichi chosakushū* 馬淵東一著作集 (Collected essays of Mabuchi Toichi). 3 vols. Tokyo: Shakai shisōsha.
1974*b* *Ethnology of the Southwestern Pacific.* Asian Folklore and Social Life Monographs, 59. Taipei: Orient Cultural Service.
1974*c* "Forge of the Malayan Type in Aboriginal Formosa." *T'ai-wan yin hang chi k'an* 25.2: 259–70.

MacKay, George L.
1895 *From Far Formosa.* J. A. MacDonald, ed. New York: Revell.

Mancall, Mark
1968 "The Ch'ing Tribute System: An Interpretive Essay." In *The Chinese World Order,* J. K. Fairbank, ed., pp. 63–89. Cambridge, Mass.: Harvard University Press.

1971 *Russia and China: Their Diplomatic Relations to 1728.* Cambridge, Mass.: Harvard University Press.

Mann, Michael

1986 *The Sources of Social Power,* vol. 1, *A History of Power from the Beginning to A.D. 1760.* Cambridge, Eng.: Cambridge University Press.

Mann, Susan

1985 "Widows in the Kinship, Class and Community Structures of Qing Dynasty China." *Journal of Asian Studies* 46: 37–56.

1987 *Local Merchants and the Chinese Bureaucracy, 1750–1950.* Stanford: Stanford University Press.

Mathews, R. H.

1960 *Chinese-English Dictionary.* Cambridge, Mass.: Harvard University Press.

Matsuzawa Kazuko

1989 "The Social and Ritual Supremacy of the First-born: Paiwan Kinship and Chieftainship." Ph.D. dissertation, Syracuse University.

McAleavy, Henry

1958 "Dien in China and Vietnam." *Journal of Asian Studies* 17: 403–15.

McGough, James P.

1976 "The Role of the Sinicized Aborigines in the Development of Taiwan." Paper presented to the American Anthropological Association Meeting.

McNeill, William H.

1982 *The Pursuit of Power: Technology, Armed Force and Society Since A.D. 1000.* Chicago: University of Chicago Press.

Meiji sanchū hachi nen rinji kokō chōsa: Kekkahyō. 明治38年臨時戶口調查:結果表 (First provisional household census: general volume of statistical tables). Tokyo. 1908.

Merton, Robert K.

1968 *Social Theory and Social Structure.* Enl. ed. New York: Free Press.

Meskill, Johanna M.

1979 *A Chinese Pioneer Family: The Lins of Wu-feng, Taiwan, 1729–1895.* Princeton: Princeton University Press.

Metzger, Thomas

1970 "The State and Commerce in Imperial China." *Journal of Asian and African Studies* 6: 23–46.

Miyakawa Hisayuki

1960 "The Confucianization of South China." In *The Confucian Persuasion,* A. F. Wright, ed., pp. 21–46. Stanford: Stanford University Press.

Morse, H. B.

1921 *The Trade and Administration of the Chinese Empire.* 3d rev. ed. New York: Russell & Russell.

Murakami Naojirō 村上直次郎

1933 *Sinkan Manuscripts.* Taipei.

1975 "Je-lan-che ch'eng chu ch'eng shih mo" 熱蘭遮城築城始末 (The construction of Zeelandia Castle). Shih Wan-shou, trans. *T'ai-wan wen hsien* 26.3: 112–25.

Murray, Dian

1987 *Pirates of the South China Coast, 1790–1810.* Stanford: Stanford University Press.

Myers, Ramon

1971 "The Research of the Commission for the Investigation of Traditional Customs in Taiwan." *Ch'ing-shih wen-t'i* 2.6: 24–54.

1972 "Taiwan Under Ch'ing Imperial Rule, 1684–1895: The Traditional Economy." *Journal of the Institute of Chinese Studies of the Chinese University of Hong Kong* 5.2: 373–409.

1974 "Taiwan's Agrarian Economy Under Japanese Rule." *Journal of the Institute of Chinese Studies of the Chinese University of Hong Kong* 7.2: 451–74.

Nakamura Takashi 中村孝志

1936 "Ranjin jidai no bansha kokō hyō" 蘭人時代の蕃社户口表 (The Dutch period aborigine census, 1650). *Nanpō dozoku* 4.1: 42–59.

1937 "Ranjin jidai no bansha kokō hyō (2)" 蘭人時代の蕃社户口表（二）(The Dutch period aborigine census, part 2, 1655). *Nanpō dozoku* 4.3: 182–96.

1951 "Sen roppyaku yonjū shichi nen no Taiwan bansha kokō hyō" 1647年の台灣蕃社户口表 (The 1647 census of Taiwan aborigines). *Yamato bunka* 31: 92–110.

1954 "Ho ling shih tai chih T'ai-wan nung yeh chi ch'i chiang li" 荷領時代之台灣農業及其獎勵 (Agriculture and its encouragement in Taiwan under the Dutch). *TY* 25: 54–69.

1955 "Ho ling shih tai T'ai-wan nan pu chih tzu yü yü yeh" 荷領時代台灣南部之鯔魚漁業 (Mullet fishing in southern Taiwan under the Dutch). *TY* 32: 43–52.

1956*a* "Shih ch'i shih chi Hsi-pan-ya jen tsai T'ai-wan ti pu chiao" 十七世紀西班牙人在台灣的佈教 (Spanish missionaries in Taiwan in the seventeenth century). Lai Yung-hsiang, trans. *T'ai-pei hsien wen hsien ts'ung chi* 2: 21–36.

1956*b* "Ho-lan jen tui T'ai-wan yüan chu min ti chiao hua: i 1659 nien chung nan pu shih ch'a pao kao wei chung hsin erh shu" 荷蘭人對台灣原住民的教化：以一六五九年中南部視察報告爲中心而述 (Dutch proselytization of Taiwan aborigines: an account based on the 1659 report of the inspection of south and central Taiwan). Lai Yung-hsiang and Wang Shui-cheng, trans. *Nan ying wen hsien* 3.3–4: 1–20.

1957 "Shih ch'i shih chi Ho-lan jen tsai T'ai-wan ti t'an chin shih yeh" 十七世紀荷蘭人在台灣的探金事業 (Dutch gold-hunting in Taiwan in the seventeenth century). *TY* 44: 101–23.

1959 "Shih ch'i shih chi T'ai-wan lu p'i chih ch'u ch'an chi ch'i tui Jih mao i" 十七世紀台灣鹿皮之出產及其對日貿易 (The production of deerskins in seventeenth-century Taiwan and their trade to Japan). *TY* 71: 24–42.

1963–64 "Oranda chika Taiwan ni okeru chiba no shozei ni tsuite" オランダ治下台湾における地場の諸税について (On the various taxes in the territory of Formosa under Dutch colonization). 2 parts. *Yamato bunka* 41: 62–84; 42: 1–27, 84.

1964 "Oranda no Taiwan keiei" オランダの台湾経営 (The Dutch administration of Formosa). *Tenri daigaku gakuhō* 43: 66–83.

Naquin, Susan

1976 *Millenarian Rebellion in China.* New Haven: Yale University Press.

Naquin, Susan, and Evelyn Rawski

1987 *Chinese Society in the Eighteenth Century.* New Haven: Yale University Press.

Negishi Benji 根岸勉治

1964 "Ko-ma-lan shu fan i tung yü Han tsu chih chih min" 噶瑪蘭熟番移動與漢族之殖民 (The migration of the civilized aborigines of I-lan and Han settlers). *T'ai-wan feng wu* 14.4: 7–15.

Ng Chin-keong

1983 *Trade and Society: The Amoy Network on the China Coast, 1683–1735.* Singapore: Singapore University Press.

Nivison, David S.

1959 "Ho-shen and His Accusers: Ideology and Political Behavior in the Eighteenth Century." In *Confucianism in Action,* D. S. Nivison and A. F. Wright, eds., pp. 209–43. Stanford: Stanford University Press.

Norbeck, Edward

1950 *Folklore of the Atayal of Formosa and the Mountain Tribes of Luzon.* University of Michigan, Museum of Anthropology, Anthropological Papers no. 5. Ann Arbor: University of Michigan Press.

NPPW *T'ai-wan nan pu pei wen chi ch'eng* 台灣南部碑文集成 (Collected stone inscriptions from southern Taiwan). *TW* 218.

Ogawa Naoyoshi 小川尚義

1944 "Indonesia-go ni okeru Taiwan takasago-go no ichi" インドネシア語に於ける台灣高砂語の位置 (The place of the Taiwan aborigine languages among the Indonesian languages). *Taiheiyō ken* 1: 451–502.

Okamatsu Santarō

1902 *Provisional Report on Investigations of Laws and Customs in the Island of Formosa.* Kobe: Kobe Herald.

Ōkuni Toko [Suke] 大國督

1960 *T'ien chu chiao lai T'ai ch'uan chiao i pai nien chien shih* 天主教來台傳教壹百年簡史 (History of one hundred years of Catholicism in Taiwan). Translation of *Taiwan Katoritsuku shoshi,* Taipei, 1941. Ch'en Chia-lu, trans. Kaohsiung: T'ien chu chiao tao ming hui.

Ownby, David

1990 "The 'Ethnic Feud' in Qing Taiwan: What Is This Violence Business Anyway? An Interpretation of the 1782 Zhang-Quan Xiedou." *Late Imperial China* 11.1: 75–98.

Oxnam, Robert B.
1975 *Ruling from Horseback: Manchu Politics in the Oboi Regency, 1661–1669.* Chicago: University of Chicago Press.
Palmer, Michael
1987 "The Surface-Subsoil Form of Divided Ownership in Late Imperial China: Some Examples from the New Territories of Hong Kong." *Modern Asian Studies* 21.1: 1–119.
Paske-Smith, Montague
1930 *Western Barbarians in Japan and Formosa in Tokugawa Days, 1603–1868.* Kobe: J. L. Thompson.
Pasternak, Burton
1969 "The Role of the Frontier in Chinese Lineage Development." *Journal of Asian Studies* 28: 551–61.
1972*a* "The Sociology of Irrigation: Two Taiwanese Villages." In *Economic Organization in Chinese Society,* W. E. Willmott, ed., pp. 193–213. Stanford: Stanford University Press.
1972*b* *Kinship and Community in Two Chinese Villages.* Stanford: Stanford University Press.
Pelzer, Karl
1945 *Pioneer Settlement in the Asiatic Tropics.* New York: American Geographical Society.
Peng, Fred C. C., and Peter Geiser
1977 *The Ainu: The Past in the Present.* Hiroshima: Bunka Hyōron.
Perdue, Peter
1987 *Exhausting the Earth: State and Peasant in Hunan, 1500–1850.* Cambridge, Mass.: Harvard University, Council on East Asian Studies.
1989 "The West Route Army and the Silk Road: Grain Supply and Qianlong's Military Campaigns in Northwest China (1755–1760)." Unpublished ms.
Perkins, Dwight
1969 *Agricultural Development in China, 1368–1968.* Chicago: Aldine.
Peterson, Jean T.
1977 "The Merits of Margins." In *Cultural-Ecological Perspectives on Southeast Asia,* William Wood, ed., pp. 63–73. Southeast Asia Series, no. 41. Athens: Ohio University.
Pickering, W. A.
1898 *Pioneering in Formosa: Recollections of Adventures Among Mandarins, Wreckers, and Head-hunting Savages.* London: Hurst & Blackett.
Potter, Jack
1970 "Land and Lineage in Traditional China." In *Family and Kinship in Chinese Society,* Maurice Freedman, ed., pp. 121–38. Stanford: Stanford University Press.
Powell, Ralph L.
1955 *The Rise of Chinese Military Power, 1895–1912.* Princeton: Princeton University Press.

Price, John
1966 "A History of the Outcaste." In *Japan's Invisible Race*, George De Vos and Hiroshi Wagatsuma, eds., pp. 6–30. Berkeley: University of California Press.
Prucha, Francis Paul
1962 *American Indian Policy in the Formative Years.* Cambridge, Mass.: Harvard University Press.
Purcell, Victor W.
1965 *The Chinese in Southeast Asia.* 2d ed. London: Oxford University Press.
Putnam, Rory
1988 *The Natural History of Deer.* Ithaca, N.Y.: Comstock Publishing Associates.
Rawlinson, John L.
1967 *China's Struggle for Naval Development, 1839–1895.* Cambridge, Eng.: Cambridge University Press.
Rawski, Evelyn
1972 *Agricultural Change and the Peasant Economy of South China.* Cambridge, Mass.: Harvard University Press.
1979 *Education and Popular Literacy in Ch'ing China.* Ann Arbor: University of Michigan Press.
RCSS *Rochiku shō shi* 蘆竹莊史 (Local history of Lu-chu *chuang*). Taipei. 1933.
Report on the Control of Aborigines in Formosa. Taipei: Taiwan Sōtokufu, Bureau of Aboriginal Affairs. 1911.
Riasanovsky, V. A.
1938 *Chinese Civil Law.* Tientsin.
Rossabi, Morris
1975 *China and Inner Asia from 1368 to the Present Day.* London: Thames & Hudson.
Ruey Yih-fu
1972 "The Concept of *Chiao* in the Chungyung as a Counterpart of Culture." In idem, *China: The Nation and Some Aspects of Its Culture*, vol. 2, pp. 637–54. Taipei: Yee Wen Publishing.
Sangren, P. Steven
1984 "Traditional Chinese Corporations: Beyond Kinship." *Journal of Asian Studies* 43.3: 391–415.
Schafer, Edward H.
1967 *The Vermilion Bird: T'ang Images of the South.* Berkeley: University of California Press.
Schlegel, Stuart A.
1979 *Tiruray Subsistence.* Quezon City: Ateneo de Manila University Press.
Schlesinger, Robert A.
1967 *The California Indian Lease.* Berkeley: California Continuing Education of the Bar.
Schmalkalden, Caspar
1983 *Die wundersamen Reisen des Caspar Schmalkalden nach West- und Ostindien, 1642–1652.* Weinheim: Acta Humaniora.

Schneider, David M.
1961 "The Distinctive Features of Matrilineal Descent." In *Matrilineal Kinship*, D. M. Schneider and K. Gough, eds., pp. 1–32. Berkeley: University of California Press.

Schram, Louis M. J.
1954 *The Monguors of the Kansu-Tibetan Frontier.* Transactions of the American Philosophical Society, new series 44, Part 1. Philadelphia: American Philosophical Society.

Schurmann, H. F.
1956 "Traditional Property Concepts in China." *Far Eastern Quarterly* 15.3: 507–16.

Schwartz, Benjamin
1968 "The Chinese Perception of World Order, Past and Present." In *The Chinese World Order: Traditional China's Foreign Relations*, John K. Fairbank, ed., pp. 276–88. Cambridge, Mass.: Harvard University Press.

Scott, William H.
1985 *Cracks in the Parchment Curtain and Other Essays in Philippine History.* Quezon City: New Day Publishers.

Seaman, Gary
1978 *Temple Organization in a Chinese Village.* Asian Folklore and Social Life Monographs, no. 101. Taipei: Orient Cultural Service.

Segawa Kōkichi 瀬川孝吉
1953 "Takasago zoku no seigyō" 高砂族の生業 (The means of subsistence among the aborigines of Taiwan). *Minzokugaku kenkyū* 18.1–2: 49–66.

Serruys, Henry
1968 "The Mongols in China, 1400–1450." *Monumenta Serica* 27: 233–305.
1979 "Two Complaints from Wang Banner, Ordos, Regarding Banner Administration and Chinese Colonization (1905)." *Monumenta Serica* 34: 471–511.
1981 "A Study of Chinese Penetration into Caqar Territory in the Eighteenth Century." *Monumenta Serica* 35: 485–544.

Sheng Ch'ing-i 盛清沂
1953 "I wei i shang T'ai-pei shih shih ts'ung k'ao" 乙未以上台北史事叢考 (A historical study of Taipei before 1895). *T'ai-pei wen hsien ts'ung chi* 1: 41–86.
1956 "T'ai-pei hsien chiang yü yen ko chih lüeh" 台北縣疆域沿革誌略 (A history of boundaries of T'ai-pei county). *T'ai-pei hsien wen hsien ts'ung chi* 2: 37–81.
1976 "Ming Cheng nei cheng k'ao lüeh" 明鄭內政考略 (A study of the domestic politics of the Chengs). *T'ai-wan wen hsien* 27.2: 76–94.

Shepherd, John R.
1986 "Sinicized Siraya Worship of A-li-tsu." *Bulletin of the Institute of Ethnology, Academia Sinica* 58: 1–81.
1988*a* "Rethinking Tenancy: Explaining Spatial and Temporal Variation in Late Imperial and Republican China." *Comparative Studies in Society and History* 30.3: 403–31.

1988*b* "Plains Aborigines and Missionaries in Ch'ing Taiwan, 1859–1895." Unpublished ms.
1988*c* "Notes on the Population of Fukien and Taiwan in the Eighteenth and Nineteenth Centuries." Unpublished ms.
1989 "Chineseness and the Politics of Cultural Prestige." Unpublished ms.
1990 "Marriage and Mandatory Abortion Among the Seventeenth Century Siraya." Unpublished ms.
1991 "Marriage Mode and Marriage Market: Spatial, Temporal and Class Variation in Taiwan." Unpublished ms.

Shih Lang 施琅
1958 *Ching hai chi shih* 靖海紀事 (Record of pacifying the seas). 1685. *TW* 13.

Shih T'ien-fu 施添福
1987 *Ch'ing tai tsai T'ai Han jen ti tsu chi fen pu ho yüan hsiang sheng huo fang shih* 清代在台漢人的祖籍分布和原鄉生活方式 (Modes of livelihood in localities of ancestral registration and the distribution by provenance of the Han in Ch'ing Taiwan). Taipei: National Taiwan Normal University, Department of Geography.
1989*a* "Ch'ing tai Ta'i-wan shih chieh ti fen hua yü ch'eng chang" 清代台灣市街的分化與成長 (The spread and growth of cities in Ch'ing Taiwan). *T'ai-wan feng wu* 39.2: 1–41.
1989*b* "Ch'ing tai Chu-ch'ien ti ch'ü ti 'k'en ch'ü chuang'" 清代竹塹地區的「墾區莊」 (Land developer villages in Ch'ing period Chu-ch'ien [Hsin-chu]). *T'ai-wan feng wu* 39.4: 33–70.
1990 "Ch'ing tai T'ai-wan 'fan li pu an keng tso' ti yüan yu" 清代台灣「番黎不諳耕作」的緣由 (The causes of the lack of agricultural skills among aborigines in Ch'ing Taiwan). *Bulletin of the Institute of Ethnology, Academia Sinica* 69: 67–92.

Silin, Robert H.
1976 *Leadership and Values*. Cambridge, Mass.: Harvard University, East Asian Research Center.

Skinner, G. W.
1973 "Change and Persistence in Chinese Culture Overseas: A Comparison of Thailand and Java." In *Southeast Asia: The Politics of National Integration*, John T. McAlister, Jr., ed., pp. 399–415. New York: Random House.
1976 "Mobility Strategies in Late Imperial China: A Regional Systems Analysis." In *Regional Analysis*, vol. 1, *Economic Systems*, Carol Smith, ed., pp. 327–64. New York: Academic Press.
1977*a* "Introduction: Urban Development in Imperial China." In *The City in Late Imperial China*, G. W. Skinner, ed., pp. 3–31. Stanford: Stanford University Press.
1977*b* "Regional Urbanization in Nineteenth Century China." In *The City in Late Imperial China*, G. W. Skinner, ed., pp. 211–49. Stanford: Stanford University Press.
1977*c* "Cities and the Hierarchy of Local Systems." In *The City in Late Imperial China*, G. W. Skinner, ed., pp. 275–351. Stanford: Stanford University Press.

1979 "Social Ecology and Forces of Repression in North China: A Regional-systems Framework for Analysis." Unpublished ms.
1985 "The Structure of Chinese History." *Journal of Asian Studies* 44.2: 271–92.
1987 "Sichuan's Population in the Nineteenth Century: Lessons from Disaggregated Data." *Late Imperial China* 8.1: 1–79.

Smith, Carol
1976 "Regional Economic Systems: Linking Geographical Models and Socioeconomic Problems." In *Regional Analysis*, vol. 1, *Economic Systems*, Carol Smith, ed., pp. 3–63. New York: Academic Press.

Smith, George Vinal
1977 *The Dutch in Seventeenth-Century Thailand.* Northern Illinois University Center for Southeast Asian Studies Special Report no. 16. Detroit: Cellar Book Shop.

Smith, Kent
1970 "Ch'ing Policy and the Development of the Southwest." Ph.D. dissertation, Yale University.

Smith, Paul J.
1988 "Commerce, Agriculture, and Core Formation in the Upper Yangzi, 2 A.D. to 1948." *Late Imperial China* 9.1: 1–78.

Smith, Richard J.
1974 "Chinese Military Institutions in the Mid-nineteenth Century, 1850–1860." *Journal of Asian History* 8.2: 122–61.
1983 *China's Cultural Heritage: The Ch'ing Dynasty, 1644–1912.* Boulder: Westview Press.

So Kwan-wai
1975 *Japanese Piracy in Ming China During the 16th Century.* Lansing: Michigan State University Press.

Solinger, Dorothy
1977 "Minority Nationalities in China's Yunnan Province: Assimilation, Power, and Policy in a Socialist State." *World Politics* 30.1: 1–23.

Speidel, W. M.
1976 "The Administrative and Fiscal Reforms of Liu Ming-ch'uan in Taiwan, 1884–1891: Foundation for Self-strengthening." *Journal of Asian Studies* 35: 441–59.

Spence, Jonathan D.
1966 *Ts'ao Yin and the K'ang-hsi Emperor: Bondservant and Master.* New Haven: Yale University Press.

Spencer, J. E.
1966 *Shifting Cultivation in Southeastern Asia.* Berkeley: University of California Press.

Spindler, Louise, and George Spindler
1958 "Male and Female Adaptations in Culture Change." *American Anthropologist* 60.2: 217–33.

Ssu-ch'uan t'ung chih 四川通志 (General gazetteer of Szechwan). 1816.

Stamps, Richard B.
1980 "New Light on Taiwan's Prehistory." *Asian Perspectives* 20.2: 183–90.
Staunton, George Thomas
1797 *An Authentic Account of an Embassy from the King of Great Britain to the Emperor of China*, vol. 3. London: G. Nicol.
1810 *Ta Tsing Leu Lee: Being the Fundamental Laws, and a Selection from the Supplementary Statutes of the Penal Code of China.* London: T. Cadell & W. Davies.
Steere, Joseph B.
1874 "Formosa." *Journal of the American Geographical Society of New York* 6: 302–34.
Stevenson, Paul Huston
1932 "Notes on the Human Geography of the Chinese-Tibetan Borderland." *Geographical Review* 22.4: 599–616.
Struve, Lynn A.
1984 *The Southern Ming, 1644–1662.* New Haven: Yale University Press.
Sun, E-tu Zen
1961 *Ch'ing Administrative Terms.* Cambridge, Mass.: Harvard University Press.
Sung Wen-hsün 宋文薰 and Lien Chao-mei 連照美
1984 "T'ai-wan shih ch'ien shih tai jen shou hsing yü chüeh erh shih" 台灣史前時代人獸形玉玦耳飾 (Zoomorphic jade earrings of prehistoric Taiwan). *Bulletin of the Department of Archaeology and Anthropology, National Taiwan University* 44: 148–71.
Sung Ying-hsing
1966 *T'ien kung k'ai wu: Chinese Technology in the Seventeenth Century.* E-tu Zen Sun and Shiou-chuan Sun, trans. University Park: Pennsylvania State University Press.
Swift, M. G.
1965 *Malay Peasant Society in Jelebu.* London: Athlone Press.
TACC *T'ai an hui lu chia chi* 台案彙錄甲集 (Taiwan archives, first collection). *TW* 31.
TAHLCC *T'ai an hui lu chi chi* 台案彙錄己集 (Taiwan archives, sixth collection). *TW* 191.
TAHLIC *T'ai an hui lu i chi* 台案彙錄乙集 (Taiwan archives, second collection). *TW* 173.
TAHLPC *T'ai an hui lu ping chi* 台案彙錄丙集 (Taiwan archives, third collection). *TW* 176.
Tai Hsüan-chih
1977 "Origin of the Heaven and Earth Society." Ronald Suleski, trans. *Modern Asian Studies* 11.3: 405–25.
Tai Yen-hui 戴炎輝
1941–42 "Sekizan chihō no heiho zoku" 赤山地方的平埔族 (The plains aborigines of Ch'ih-shan). Parts 1–7. *Minzoku Taiwan* 1.1: 14–16; 1.2: 8–10; 1.3: 10–13; 1.4: 14–17; 1.5: 10–13; 2.2: 14–17; 2.3: 36–37.

1953 "Ch'ing tai T'ai-wan ti t'un chih, yang shan ti, chi t'un t'ien" 清代台灣的屯制養贍地及屯田 (The peasant-soldier system, welfare lands, and military colonies in Ch'ing Taiwan). *She hui k'o hsüeh lun ts'ung* 4: 1–42.

1959 "Ch'ing tai T'ai-wan chih ai chih chi ai tsu" 清代台灣之隘制及隘租 (The systems of *ai* defense and *ai* rents in Ch'ing Taiwan). *TY* 68: 1–36.

1962 "Ch'ing tai T'ai-wan hsiang chuang chih chien li chi ch'i tsu chih" 清代台灣鄉莊之建立及其組織 (The establishment and organization of villages in Ch'ing Taiwan). *TY* 76: 56–85.

1963*a* "Ch'ing tai T'ai-wan chih ta hsiao tsu yeh" 清代台灣之大小租業 (The large-rent and small-rent system in Ch'ing Taiwan). *T'ai-pei wen hsien* 4: 1–45.

1963*b* "T'ai-wan ta hsiao tsu yeh chi k'en t'ien chih kuan hsi" 台灣大小租業及墾田之關係 (The relation between the large- and small-rent system and land reclamation in Taiwan). *T'ai-wan wen hsien* 14.2: 164–65.

1976 "Ch'ing tai T'ai-wan fan she ti tsu chih chi yün yung" 清代台灣番社的組織及運用 (The organization and operation of aborigine villages in Ch'ing Taiwan). *T'ai-wan wen hsien* 26.4/27.1: 329–75.

1979 *Ch'ing tai T'ai-wan chih hsiang chih* 清代台灣之鄉治 (Local government in Ch'ing Taiwan). Taipei: Lien-ching.

Taiso ken shobun shimatsu 大租權處分始末 (History of the disposal of large-rent rights). Manuscript ca. 1900; copy in author's possession. Taipei.

Taiwan jinkō dōtai tōkei 台灣人口動態統計 (Taiwan, vital statistics of the population). Annual publication, 1905–42. Taipei: Sōtokufu, Bureau of Official Statistics.

T'ai-wan sheng t'ung chih kao, chüan ch'i, jen wu chih, ti san ts'e 台灣省通志稿, 卷七, 人物志, 第三册 (Draft Taiwan provincial gazetteer, vol. 7, personages, book 3). 1962. Taipei: T'ai-wan sheng wen hsien wei yüan hui.

Takakura, Shin'ichiro

1960 "The Ainu of Northern Japan." J. A. Harrison, trans. *Transactions of the American Philosophical Society* 50.4 [entire issue].

Takekoshi Yosaburo

1907 *Japanese Rule in Formosa.* New York: Longmans, Green, & Co.

1930 *The Economic Aspects of the History of the Civilization of Japan.* 3 vols. New York: Macmillan.

Tan Chee Beng

1988 *The Baba of Melaka.* Selangor, Malaysia: Pelanduk Publications.

Terrien de Lacouperie, Albert

1887 "Formosa: Notes on mss., Languages and Races, Including a Note on Nine Formosa mss. by E. Colborne Baber." *Journal of the Royal Asiatic Society* 19: 413–94.

TFT *T'ai-wan ts'ai fang ts'e* 台灣采訪册 (A guidebook for Taiwan). 1830. *TW* 55.

Thompson, Laurence
1964 "The Earliest Chinese Eyewitness Accounts of the Formosan Aborigines." *Monumenta Serica* 23: 163–204.
1968 "The Junk Passage Across the Taiwan Strait: Two Early Chinese Accounts." *Harvard Journal of Asiatic Studies* 28: 170–94.
1969 "Formosan Aborigines in the Early Eighteenth Century: Huang Shu-ching's *Fan su liu k'ao*." *Monumenta Serica* 28: 41–147.

Tilly, Charles
1990 *Coercion, Capital, and European States, AD 990–1990*. Oxford: Basil Blackwell.

TKI *Taiwan tochi kankō ippan* 台灣土地慣行一斑 (Overview of land practices in Taiwan). 3 vols. Taipei: Rinji tochi chōsakyoku. 1905.

TLTI *Tu li ts'un i* 讀例存疑 (Concentration on doubtful matters while perusing the Substatutes). Hsüeh Yün-sheng 薛允升, comp. 1905. Huang Ching-chia 黃靜嘉, ed. Taipei: Chinese Materials and Research Aids Center. 1970.

TNHCK *T'ai-nan hsien chih kao* 台南縣志稿 (Draft gazetteer of T'ai-nan county), 2, *Jen min chih* 人民志 (Population history). Tainan: T'ai-nan hsien wen hsien wei yüan hui. 1957.

TPHCK *T'ai-pei hsien chih kao* 台北縣志稿 (Draft gazetteer of T'ai-pei county), 5, *K'ai p'i chih* 開闢志 (Settlement history). Taipei: T'ai-pei hsien wen hsien wei yüan hui. 1959.

Treistman, Judith
1972 "Prehistory of the Formosan Uplands." *Science* 175 (4017): 74–76.

Ts'ao Yung-ho 曹永和
1954*a* "Cheng shih shih tai chih T'ai-wan k'en chih" 鄭氏時代之台灣墾殖 (Land development in Taiwan under the Cheng family). *TY* 25: 70–85.
1954*b* "Ming tai T'ai-wan yü yeh chih lüeh" 明代台灣漁業誌略 (The fishing industry in Ming Taiwan). *TY* 25: 31–37.
1956 "Ming tai T'ai-wan yü yeh chih lüeh pu shuo" 明代台灣漁業誌略補說 (More on fishing in Ming Taiwan). *TY* 40: 16–47.
1979 *T'ai-wan tsao ch'i li shih yen chiu* 台灣早期歷史研究 (Researches on Taiwan's early history). Taipei: Lien-ching.

Ts'ao Yung-ho 曹永和, Lai Yung-hsiang 賴永祥, and Chou Hsüeh-p'u 周學普, comps.
1959 *Shih ch'i shih chi T'ai-wan Ying-kuo mao i shih liao* 十七世紀台灣英國貿易史料 (Historical materials on trade with England in seventeenth-century Taiwan). *TY* 57.

TSF *Tan Hsin Feng san hsien chien ming tsung k'uo t'u ts'e* 淡新鳳三縣簡明總括圖册 (Map collection of Tan-shui, Hsin-chu, and Feng-shan counties). *TW* 197.

TSTC *Tan-shui t'ing chih* 淡水廳志 (Gazetteer of Tan-shui subprefecture). Ch'en P'ei-kuei 陳培桂, ed. 1870. *TW* 172.

Tsuchida Shigeru
1985 "Kulon: Yet Another Austronesian Language in Taiwan?" *Bulletin of the Institute of Ethnology, Academia Sinica* 60: 1–59.

TTTCS *Ch'ing tai T'ai-wan ta tsu tiao ch'a shu* 清代台灣大租調查書 (Investigations of large-rents in Ch'ing Taiwan). *TW* 152.

TW T'ai-wan wen hsien ts'ung k'an 台灣文獻叢刊 (Literary collectanea on Taiwan). 309 titles. T'ai-wan yin hang ching chi yen chiu shih 台灣銀行經濟研究室, ed. Taipei: T'ai-wan yin hang, 1957–72.

TWFC: Chou *Ch'ung hsiu T'ai-wan fu chih* 重修台灣府志 (Gazetteer of Taiwan prefecture revised). Chou Yüan-wen 周元文, ed. 1710. *TW* 66.

TWFC: Fan *Ch'ung hsiu Tai-wan fu chih* 重修台灣府志 (Gazetteer of Taiwan prefecture revised). Fan Hsien 范咸, ed. 1746. *TW* 105.

TWFC: Kao *T'ai-wan fu chih* 台灣府志 (Gazetteer of Taiwan prefecture). Kao Kung-ch'ien 高拱乾, ed. 1694. *TW* 65.

TWFC: Liu *Ch'ung hsiu Fu-chien T'ai-wan fu chih* 重修福建台灣府志 (Gazetteer of Taiwan prefecture, Fukien, revised). Liu Liang-pi 劉良璧, ed. 1740. *TW* 74.

TWFC: Yü *Hsü hsiu T'ai-wan fu chih* 續修台灣府志 (Gazetteer of Taiwan prefecture revised). Yü Wen-i 余文儀, ed. 1768. *TW* 121.

TWFFIT *T'ai-wan fu fu i ts'e* 台灣府賦役冊 (Record of land and corvée taxes of Taiwan prefecture). *TW* 139.

TWHC *T'ai-wan hsien chih* 台灣縣志 (Taiwan county gazetteer). Ch'en Wen-ta 陳文達, ed. 1720. *TW* 103.

TWSH *Taiwan shihō, dai ikkan, fudōsan* 台灣私法, 第一卷, 不動產 (Taiwan private law, part one, real estate). 2 vols. Kobe: Rinji Taiwan kyūkan chōsakai. 1910.

TWSHF *Taiwan shihō furoku sankōsho, dai ikkan* 台灣私法附錄參考書, 第一卷 (Supplementary reference source for Taiwan private law, part one). 3 vols. Kobe: Rinji Taiwan kyūkan chōsakai. 1910.

TY *T'ai-wan yen chiu ts'ung k'an* 台灣研究叢刊 (Collectanea of researches on Taiwan). 116 vols. T'ai-wan yin hang ching chi yen chiu shih 台灣銀行經濟研究室, ed. Taipei: T'ai-wan yin hang, 1950–78.

TZ *Taiwan zeimushi* 台灣稅務史 (History of taxation in Taiwan). 2 vols. Taipei: Sōtokufu. 1919.

Ura Ren'ichi 浦廉一
1955 "Ch'ing ch'u ch'ien chieh ling k'ao" 清初遷界令考 (A study of the early Ch'ing order to shift the frontier). Lai Yung-hsiang 賴永祥, trans. *T'ai-wan wen hsien* 6.4: 109–22.

van der Valk, M. H.
1949 *Interpretations of the Supreme Court at Peking, Years 1915 and 1916.* Batavia: University of Indonesia, Sinological Insitute.

Viraphol, Sarasin
1977 *Tribute and Profit: Sino-Siamese Trade, 1652–1853.* Cambridge, Mass.: Harvard University, Council on East Asian Studies.

von Glahn, Richard
1987 *The Country of Streams and Grottoes: Expansion, Settlement, and the Civilizing of the Sichuan Frontier in Song Times.* Cambridge, Mass.: Harvard University, Council on East Asian Studies.

Wada Sei
1929 "The Philippine Islands as Known to the Chinese Before the Ming Dynasty." *Memoirs of the Research Department of the Tōyō Bunkō* 4: 121–66.

Wade, T. F.
1851 "The Army of the Chinese Empire." 3 parts. *Chinese Repository* 20.5: 250–80; 20.6: 300–340; 20.7: 362–422.
Wakeman, Frederic, Jr.
1966 *Strangers at the Gate: Social Disorder in South China, 1839–1861*. Berkeley: University of California Press.
1975 *The Fall of Imperial China*. New York: Free Press.
1985 *The Great Enterprise: The Manchu Reconstruction of Imperial Order in Seventeenth-Century China*. Berkeley: University of California Press.
Waldron, Arthur
1990 *The Great Wall of China: From History to Myth*. Cambridge, Eng.: Cambridge University Press.
Waley-Cohen, Joanna
1991 *Exile in Mid-Qing China: Banishment to Xinjiang, 1758–1820*. New Haven: Yale University Press.
Wallerstein, Immanuel
1980 *The Modern World-system, II: Mercantilism and the Consolidation of the European World-economy, 1600–1750*. New York: Academic Press.
Wang Ching-liang 王京良
1963 "Cheng shih shih tai T'ai-wan huo pi liu t'ung chih t'an t'ao chi k'ao cheng" 鄭氏時代台灣貨幣流通之探討及考正 (An examination and inquiry into currency circulation in Cheng-era Taiwan). *TY* 76: 11–15.
Wang Gungwu
1958 "The Nanhai Trade." *Journal of the Malayan Branch, Royal Asiatic Society* 31.2: 1–135.
1984 "The Chinese Urge to Civilize: Reflections on Change." *Journal of Asian History* 18.1: 1–34.
Wang Shih-ch'ing 王世慶
1953 *Ti ming yen ko* 地名沿革 (Successive changes in Taiwan placenames). *T'ai-wan sheng t'ung chih kao*, vol. 1, part 2. Taipei: T'ai-wan sheng wen hsien wei yüan hui.
1956 "T'ai-wan ai chih k'ao" 台灣隘制考 (A study of the *ai* defense system in Taiwan). *T'ai-wan wen hsien* 7.3–4: 7–25.
1958*a* "Ch'ing tai T'ai-wan ti mi ch'an yü wai hsiao" 清代台灣的米產與外銷 (Rice production and export in Ch'ing Taiwan). *T'ai-wan wen hsien* 9.1: 15–32.
1958*b* "Ch'ing tai T'ai-wan ti mi chia" 清代台灣的米價 (Rice prices in Ch'ing Taiwan). *T'ai-wan wen hsien* 9.4: 11–20.
1969 "Ch'ing chi chi Jih chü ch'u ch'i nan pu T'ai-wan chih niu hsü" 清季及日據初期南部台灣之牛墟 (Cattle markets in southern Taiwan during the Ch'ing and the early period of Japanese occupation). *T'ai-wan wen hsien* 20.4: 34–52.
1974 "Religious Organization in the History of a Chinese Town." In *Religion and Ritual in Chinese Society*, A. P. Wolf, ed., pp. 71–92. Stanford: Stanford University Press.

1976 "Hai-shan shih hua" 海山史話 (A history of Hai-shan). *T'ai-pei wen hsien* 37: 49–131.

Wang Sung-hsing 王崧興

1972 "Pa Pao Chün: An Eighteenth Century Irrigation System in Central Taiwan." *Bulletin of the Institute of Ethnology, Academia Sinica* 33: 165–76.

1988 "Fang Chang-p'u hsien Lan T'ing-chen, Lan Ting-yüan chia hsiang: Hu-hsi, Ch'ih-ling She tsu hsiang" 訪漳浦縣藍廷珍,藍鼎元家鄉:湖西,赤嶺畲族鄉 (A visit to the hometown of Lan T'ing-chen and Lan Ting-yüan in Chang-p'u county: The She villages of Hu-hsi and Ch'ih-ling). *T'ai-wan feng wu* 38.1: 89–94.

Wang Ta-yüan 汪大淵

1961 *Tao i chih lüeh* 島夷志略 (Brief accounts of the island barbarians). 1349. Appendix to *Chu fan chih* 諸蕃志 (Accounts of the barbarians), by Chao Ju-kua 趙汝适, pp. 63–78. *TW* 119.

Wang Yeh-chien

1965 "The Impact of the Taiping Rebellion on Population in the Southern Part of Kiangsu." *Harvard Papers on China* 19: 120–58.

1973 *Land Taxation in Imperial China, 1750–1911*. Cambridge, Mass.: Harvard University Press.

1986 "Food Supply in Eighteenth-Century Fukien." *Late Imperial China* 7.2: 80–117.

Washburn, Wilcombe E.

1975 *The Indian in America*. New York: Harper & Row.

Watson, James L.

1975 *Immigration and the Chinese Lineage*. Berkeley: University of California Press.

1988 "The Structure of Chinese Funerary Rites." In *Death Ritual in Late Imperial and Modern China*, James L. Watson and E. Rawski, eds., pp. 3–19. Berkeley: University of California Press.

Watt, John R.

1972 *The District Magistrate in Late Imperial China*. New York: Columbia University Press.

1977 "The Yamen and Urban Administration." In *The City in Late Imperial China*, G. W. Skinner, ed., pp. 353–90. Stanford: Stanford University Press.

Wei Hui-lin 衛惠林

1981 *P'u-li Pa-tsai ch'i she chih* 埔里巴宰七社志 (An ethnography of the seven villages of the Pazeh on the P'u-li plain). Monograph no. 27. Nankang: Academia Sinica, Institute of Ethnology.

Wen Chi 溫吉, trans.

1957 *T'ai-wan fan cheng chih* 台灣番政志 (History of aborigine policy in Taiwan). Taipei: T'ai-wan sheng wen hsien wei yüan hui. (Translation of Inō 1904.)

Weng Chia-yin 翁佳音

1986 "Wu Feng ch'uan shuo yen ko k'ao" 吳鳳傳說沿革考 (A study of successive changes in the myth of Wu Feng). *T'ai-wan feng wu* 36.1: 39–56.

Whitney, Joseph B. R.
1970 *China: Area, Administration, and Nation Building.* Research Paper no. 123. Chicago: University of Chicago, Department of Geography.

Wiens, Harold J.
1954 *China's March Toward the Tropics.* Hamden, Conn.: Shoe String Press.

Wigmore, John H.
1887 "The Pledge Idea: A Study in Comparative Legal Ideas." 3 parts. *Harvard Law Review* 10.6: 321–50; 10.7: 389–417; 11.1: 18–39.

Wills, John E., Jr.
1972 "The Dutch Period in Taiwan History: A Preliminary Survey." Unpublished ms.
1974 *Pepper, Guns and Parleys: The Dutch East India Company and China, 1622–1681.* Cambridge, Mass.: Harvard University Press.
1979 "Maritime China from Wang Chih to Shih Lang: Themes in Peripheral History." In *From Ming to Ch'ing*, Jonathan Spence and John Wills, eds., 203–38. New Haven: Yale University Press.
1984 *Embassies and Illusions: Dutch and Portuguese Envoys to K'ang-hsi, 1666–1687.* Cambridge, Mass.: Harvard University, Council on East Asian Studies.

Wolf, Arthur P., and Huang Chieh-shan
1980 *Marriage and Adoption in China, 1845–1945.* Stanford: Stanford University Press.

Wolff, John U.
1976 "Malay Borrowings in Tagalog." In *Southeast Asian History and Historiography*, C. D. Cowan and O. W. Wolters, eds., pp. 345–67. Ithaca: Cornell University Press.

Wong Young-tsu
1983 "Security and Warfare on the China Coast: The Taiwan Question in the Seventeenth Century." *Monumenta Serica* 35: 111–96.

Woodside, Alexander
1983 "Some Mid-Qing Theorists of Popular Schools." *Modern China* 9.1: 3–35.

Worsley, Peter
1984 *The Three Worlds.* London: Weidenfeld & Nicolson.

Wu Chi-hua
1981 "Basic Foreign Policy Attitudes of the Early Ming Dynasty." *Ming Studies* 12: 65–80.

Wu Hsin-jung 吳新榮
1978 *Nan T'ai-wan feng t'u chih* 南台灣風土志 (Local customs of Southern Taiwan). Chang-hua: n.p.

Wu, Silas
1970 *Communication and Imperial Control in China: Evolution of the Palace Memorial System, 1693–1735.* Cambridge, Mass.: Harvard University Press.
1979 *Passage to Power: K'ang-hsi and His Heir Apparent, 1661–1722.* Cambridge, Mass.: Harvard University Press.

Yamawaki Teijiro
1976 "The Great Trading Merchants: Cocksinja and His Son." *Acta Asiatica* 30: 106–16.

Yang Liang-kung 楊亮功 et al., eds.
1975 *Liu-ch'iu "Li tai pao an" hsüan lu* 琉球歷代寶案選錄 (Selections from the *Rekidai hōan* of Okinawa). Taipei: T'ai-wan k'ai-ming shu-tien.

Yang Lien-sheng
1952 *Money and Credit in China.* Cambridge, Mass.: Harvard University Press.

Yang Ying 楊英
1958 *Ts'ung cheng shih lu* 從征實錄 (Veritable record of the punitive expedition). *TW* 32.

Yao Ying 姚瑩
1957 *Tung ch'a chi lüeh* 東槎紀略 (Sketch of my assignment to Taiwan). 1832. *TW* 7.

YCCPYC *Yung-cheng chu p'i tsou che hsüan chi* 雍正硃批奏摺選輯 (Selections from the vermilion rescripts of Yung-cheng). *TW* 300.

YCSL *Ch'ing Shih-tsung shih lu hsüan chi* 清世宗實錄選輯 (Selections from the Veritable Records of the Yung-cheng reign). *TW* 167.

Yen, Sophia Su-fei
1965 *Taiwan in China's Foreign Relations, 1836–1874.* Hamden, Conn.: Shoe String Press.

Yin Chang-i 尹章義
1982 "T'ai-wan pei pu t'o k'en ch'u ch'i 't'ung shih' so pan yen chih chiao ssu chi ch'i kung neng" 台灣北部拓墾初期"通事"所扮演之角色及其功能 (The role and function of the interpreter in the early stages of the reclamation of northern Taiwan). *T'ai-pei wen hsien* 59–60: 97–252.

YLH *Yün-lin hsien ts'ai fang ts'e* 雲林縣采訪冊 (Guidebook for Yün-lin county). Ni Tsan-yüan 倪贊元, ed. 1894. *TW* 37.

Young, Mary Elizabeth
1961 *Redskins, Ruffleshirts, and Rednecks.* Norman: University of Oklahoma Press.

YTHC *T'ai-wan yü ti hui ch'ao* 台灣輿地彙鈔 (Geographical collection on Taiwan). *TW* 216.

Yü Yung-ho 郁永河
1959 *P'i hai chi yu* 裨海紀遊 (Records of travels on a small sea). 1697. *TW* 44.

Yung-cheng hui tien 雍正會典 ([Ch'ing] Institutes, Yung-cheng edition). 1733.

Zelin, Madeleine
1984 *The Magistrate's Tael: Rationalizing Fiscal Reform in Eighteenth-Century Ch'ing China.* Berkeley: University of California Press.

Character List

Personal and place-names are not listed.

ai 隘
ai k'ou 隘口
ai ting 隘丁
an fu ssu 安撫司
chai po 債剝
chai p'u 債贌
chao keng 招耕
chao mai 招賣
chao p'u 招贌
chen piao 鎮標
ch'eng ch'ien 秤錢
ch'eng shou ying 城守營
chi mi chou 羈縻州
ch'i mai 契買
ch'i wai 契外
ch'i yin 欺隱
chia 甲
chia shou 甲首
chiang chün 將軍
ch'iang chan 強佔
chiao hua 教化
chiao ts'e 教册
ch'ien 錢
ch'ien tsung 千總
chih chao 執照
chih li t'ing 直隸廳
chin 斤
chin shih 進士
ch'in 侵
ch'in chan 侵佔
ch'in ju fan chieh 侵入番界
ching t'ien 井田
chiu ch'eng 舊城
ch'iung fan 窮番
chou 州
chü jen 舉人
ch'u ts'ao 出草
chuang 莊
chuang li 莊例
chüeh mai yung pu hui shu
絶賣永不回贖
chün 軍
chung min wu chiao wei shih wei
hsien 重民五教惟食爲先
ch'ung 衝
fan (aborigine) 番
fan (troublesome) 繁
fan hsiang 番餉
fan hsü 番婿
fan she 番社
fan she ti chieh 番社地界
fan ta tsu 番大租
fan ti 番地
fan ting k'ou liang 番丁口糧
fan tsu 番租
fan t'un 番屯
fan yeh 番業
fen fang ch'ien tsung 分防千總
fu chiang 副將
hai fang t'ing 海防廳
hai fang t'ung chih 海防同知
han hua 漢化

han tsu 旱租
hao hsien 耗羨
hsiang 餉
Hsiao (surname) 蕭
Hsiao-li she 霄裡社
hsiao tsu 小租
hsieh piao 協標
hsien 縣
hsien ch'eng 縣丞
hsiung fan 兇番
hsün 巡
hsün chien 巡檢
hsün T'ai yü shih 巡台御史
hua shu fan wei han jen
化熟番爲漢人
huang ti 荒地
hui tien 會典
huo chang 夥長
huo mai 活買
i chih chang tan 易知丈單
i sheng 佾生
i t'ien liang chu 一田兩主
i t'ien san chu 一田三主
i to pao shao 以多報少
jen hsiang pao k'en 認餉包墾
kai t'u kuei liu 改土歸流
kai t'u wei liu 改土爲流
kai t'u wei t'un 改土爲屯
k'ai shan fu fan 開山撫番
k'en tan 墾單
ko 戈
k'o 科
k'o t'ien 課田
kou tien 購典
ku 穀
kua yin 掛印
kuan chuang 官莊
kuan shih 管事
kuan t'ien 官田
kuan tou 官斗
kuei fan t'ien 歸番田
kung k'ou liang tsu 公口糧租
kung sheng 貢生
kuo chi 國計
kuo lu tzu 啯嚕子
kuo yung chih yüan 國用之源
lan k'en 濫墾
li (Chinese mile) 里
li (ritual) 禮
li chia 里甲
li fan t'ing 理番廳
li fan t'ung chih 理番同知
li i chih pang 禮義之邦
li t'ou yin 犁頭銀
liang 兩
lin sheng 廩生
liu min 流民
liu yü 流寓
lo han chiao 羅漢脚
lu hsiang (deer tax) 鹿餉
lu hsiang (land revenues)
陸餉
lung en 隆恩
ma t'a 麻踏
mai (purchase) 買
mai (sell) 賣
mai tuan 賣斷
man tou 滿斗
mei ch'üeh 美缺
mi 米
min fan ti chieh 民番地界
min sheng 民生
mou 畝
mu fu 幕府
mu i hsiang hua 慕義向化
nan 難
pa tsung 把總
pai fan 白番
P'an (surname) 潘
pao chia 保甲
pao k'en 報墾
pao she 包社
p'i 疲
ping pei 兵備
ping pei tao 兵備道
ping wu fang ai min fan ti chieh
並無妨碍民番地界
p'ing p'u fan 平埔番
p'ing t'iao 平糶
p'u (dispatch station) 舖
p'u (lease; Hokkien pak) 贌
p'u fan ti t'ieh hsiang yin
贌番地貼餉銀
p'u kang 贌港

p'u kei 贌給
p'u k'en 贌墾
p'u k'en fan t'ien 贌墾番田
p'u mai (lease-purchase) 贌買
p'u mai (lease-sale) 贌賣
p'u ping 舖兵
p'u she 贌社
p'u te 贌得
p'u ti yin 贌地銀
san kang 三綱
san she 散社
shang wen 尚文
shao 哨
She (minority group) 畲
she (tribe) 社
she fan 社番
she fan hsiang yin 社番餉銀
she hsiang 社餉
she kun 社棍
she shang 社商
she t'ien 社田
sheng fan 生番
sheng k'o 陞科
sheng yüan 生員
shih 石
shih yin 時銀
shou pei 守備
shu fan 熟番
shu fan ti chieh 熟番地界
shui hsiang 水餉
shui shih fu chiang 水師副將
shui shih hsieh ying 水師協營
shui shih t'i tu 水師提督
ssu chan 私佔
ssu k'en 私墾
ssu k'ou liang tsu 私口糧租
ssu mai (illicit purchase) 私買
ssu mai (illicit sale) 私賣
ssu p'u 私贌
ssu t'ien 私田
ta tsu 大租
ta yüan 大元
tai fan na hsiang 代番納餉
tai fan shu hsiang 代番輸餉
tai na hsiang k'o 代納餉課
tai shu she hsiang 代輸社餉
T'ai yün 台運
tan 担
t'ang 唐
tao keng 盗耕
tao piao 道標
tao t'ai 道台
tao tou 道斗
t'i 題
t'i tu 提督
tiao 調
t'ieh fan na hsiang 貼番納餉
t'ieh na fan tsu 貼納番租
tien 典
tien mai 典賣
tien p'u 典贌
t'ien 田
T'ien ti (Heaven/Earth) 天地
t'ien ti (increase younger brothers) 添弟
t'ien ti (land bottom) 田底
ting 丁
ting yin 丁銀
t'ing 廳
tou 斗
t'ou chia 頭家
t'ou chung 偷種
t'ou hsien 投獻
ts'an chiang 參將
ts'ang hu 倉斛
tsu 租
tsu p'u 租贌
ts'un liu 存留
tsung ping 總兵
tu mai 杜賣
tu mai chin ken 杜賣盡根
tu ssu 都司
t'u chu 土著
t'u fan she hsüeh 土番社學
t'u niu 土牛
t'u ssu 土司
t'u t'un 土屯
t'un 屯
t'un lien 屯練
t'un t'ien 屯田
t'un ting 屯丁
t'ung chih 同知
t'ung p'an 通判
t'ung shih 通事

t'ung ts'ao 通草
tzu feng t'ou kuei 自封投櫃
wakō (wo k'ou) 倭寇
wan na k'o yin 完納課銀
wang hua 王化
wang t'ien 王田
wen 文
wen chih chiao hua 文治教化
wen wu kuan t'ien 文武官田
wen yin 紋銀
wu wei 無爲
yang lien 養廉
yeh 野
yeh hu 業户
ying 營
ying p'an 營盤
ying p'an t'ien 營盤田
yu chi 遊擊
yü fan min wu ai 與番民無碍
yüan (dollar) 圓
yüan (dry field) 園
yüan chu min 原住民
yüan tsu 園租
yüeh k'en 越墾

Index

In this index an "f" after a number indicates a separate reference on the next page, and an "ff" indicates separate references on the next two pages. A continuous discussion over two or more pages is indicated by a span of page numbers, e.g., "57–59." *Passim* is used for a cluster of references in close but not consecutive sequence. Individual note numbers are not given where there are multiple references on a page in the Notes section. Chinese personal names are alphabetized under the surname; all other Chinese entries are alphabetized letter by letter, ignoring hyphens, aspiration marks, and syllable and word breaks.

Library of Congress Cataloging-in-Publication Data

Shepherd, John Robert.
Statecraft and political economy on the Taiwan frontier, 1600–1800 / John Robert Shepherd.
p. cm.
Includes bibliographical references (p.) and index.
ISBN 0-8047-2066-5 (acid-free paper)
1. Taiwan—Economic conditions—To 1945. 2. Indigenous peoples—Taiwan—History. 3. Land tenure—Taiwan—History. I. Title.
HC430.5.S38 1993
951.24'903—dc20
91-46158
CIP
REV.

∞ This book is printed on acid-free paper. It has been typeset in 10/12 Trump Mediaeval by Keystone Typesetting, Inc.

The authorized representative in the EU for product safety and compliance is:
Mare Nostrum Group
B.V Doelen 72
4831 GR Breda
The Netherlands

www.ingramcontent.com/pod-product-compliance
Ingram Content Group UK Ltd.
Pitfield, Milton Keynes, MK11 3LW, UK
UKHW012146120726
472909UK00010B/86/J

* 9 7 8 0 8 0 4 7 2 0 6 6 3 *